Special Edition

USING
ISDN
SECOND EDITION

Special Edition

USING
ISDN
SECOND EDITION

Written by James Y. Bryce

Special Edition Using ISDN, Second Edition

Credits

PRESIDENT
Roland Elgey

PUBLISHER
Joseph B. Wikert

PUBLISHING MANAGER
Jim Minatel

ACQUISITIONS MANAGER
Cheryl D. Willoughby

EDITORIAL SERVICES DIRECTOR
Elizabeth Keaffaber

MANAGING EDITOR
Sandy Doell

DIRECTOR OF MARKETING
Lynn E. Zingraf

PRODUCT DIRECTOR
Steven M. Schafer

PRODUCTION EDITOR
Jeff Riley

EDITORS
Elizabeth Barrettt
Thomas Cirtin
Sherri Fugit
Katherine Givens
Hetty Gray
Susan Moore
Nicholas Zafran

ASSISTANT PRODUCT MARKETING MANAGER
Kim Margolius

TECHNICAL EDITOR
J. David Shinn, CNE
Synergetic Resource Corp.

TECHNICAL SPECIALIST
Nadeem Muhammad

ACQUISITIONS COORDINATOR
Jane Brownlow

OPERATIONS COORDINATOR
Patricia J. Brooks

EDITORIAL ASSISTANT
Andrea Duvall

BOOK DESIGNER
Ruth Harvey

COVER DESIGNER
Dan Armstrong

PRODUCTION TEAM
Stephen Adams
Debra Bolhuis
Marcia Brizendine
Jenny Earhart
Erin M. Danielson
Trey Frank
Jason Hand
Daniel Harris
Daryl Kessler
Clint Lahnen
Steph Mineart
Ryan Oldfather
Laura Robbins

INDEXER
Brad Harriman
Tim Tate

Composed in *Century Old Style* and *ITC Franklin Gothic* by Que Corporation.

This book is dedicated to my sons, Russell John Bryce and James Young Bryce IV—representatives of a future that will use the tools we now make to shape a world better even than our highest hopes.

Confucius said, "He who learns but does not think is lost; he who thinks but does not learn is in danger." (Analects 2.15)

About the Author

James Y. Bryce is a writer, speaker, and consultant on communications systems and future technologies. Having learned electronics hands-on in amateur radio, Jim worked with the early phases of integrated circuits. He has a B.A. in philosophy and mathematics and a J.D. in law. He practiced law for 10 years prior to studying computer science and installing the first commercial Ethernet using IBM PCs. He has worked with many of the major network operating systems from their inception. Jim uses this experience to design and improve networks to optimally fulfill an organization's needs. He travels extensively, consulting and presenting issues of high technology to executive and user audiences. Currently he is speaking, writing, and consulting on the convergence of computer and telephone technology as illustrated by the explosive growth of the Internet and ISDN. He resides in Austin, Texas.

From the Author

I really would like to hear from you. Advise me of anything you feel should be corrected, changed, added, or removed in future editions. Of course, I'd love to hear glowing reviews and reports of problems fixed and systems flying as a result of my help with this book.

- **HOME PAGE:** My home page is **http://www.bryce.com/~bryce**, where you'll find a form to register your book. This form gives me an idea of how you like the book and what I can add to future editions of this—or other—books. You may advise me of suggestions, corrections, and additions for the book. My Web page has information to keep you informed of relevant ISDN issues and other emerging technology issues.
- **E-MAIL:** My e-mail address for this book is **ISDN2@bryce.com**. I look forward to receiving any additional observations you may have in addition the Web form.
- **SEMINARS:** I'm very experienced in presenting seminars on subjects of communications and future technologies. Please contact me at **SEMINARS@bryce.com** regarding your interests in this area. My Web site also contains information on seminars, consulting, and other services I provide. I look forward to hearing from you.

Thanks for asking me to help you learn about ISDN. I hope you find some, and maybe all, of the answers you're looking for as you read through this book.

–Jim Bryce

Acknowledgments

Many people helped in gathering, explaining, and checking the information in this book. A few deserve very special mention:

■ James Johnson of Industrial Cyberspace Designs. JJ knows TCP/IP, routers, and Internet backwards and forwards. He spent countless hours guiding me through such stuff and setting up and testing hardware and software. He stayed up many nights checking and re-checking my understanding as reflected in drafts of text.

 T I P JJ has a Web page about such things: **http://www.incyb.com/~incyb**; his e-mail address is **jjhnsn@incyb.com**.

■ The ISDN Goddess. Her most immediate subjects know who she is, but she, modestly, prefers anonymity. She and her court are responsible for bringing ISDN to town (Austin) and have led the way for other areas served by Southwestern Bell. Without her help, I could never have grasped how ISDN really works for the local exchange carrier.

■ Al Mikula and Bruce Kravitz of Vtel who worked with me on the video portions of this book. Al spent the better part of a whole night of his personal time setting up, testing, and assisting in screen captures.

■ Herb Martin of Microsoft devoted much of his personal and weekend time to stepping me through Windows NT and helping me gather information on Windows 95.

■ The Texas ISDN Users Group. TIUG members and meetings tested the products, services, and wills of many vendors while teaching everyone the ins and outs of this new ISDN technology in the process.

■ Chris Bryce, my wife, reader of every draft, drawer of every illustration, and supporter beyond belief when it seemed things never would work, no one would ever call back or answer e-mail, and I would not survive the ordeal of producing such a big tome so quickly.

■ Jamey Bryce, our young son, who made it all worthwhile, and his big brother Russell, who helped in ways he doesn't even know.

For as I passed along, and observed the objects of your worship, I found also an altar with this inscription, 'To an unknown god.' (Acts 17:23)

The Greeks were afraid of offending even an unknown god so they set up an altar just to be sure. My problem is much the same as theirs.

There are so many people to acknowledge for helping with this book it's hard to begin. The real problem is knowing many people helped and also knowing I've misplaced their names, never had them, or, worse, overlooked them. So, please, all you folks that helped and somehow I missed—here's my altar—thanks and a tip of the hat.

For the rest of you, I'll do the best I can to get your names spelled right and thank you for the countless gyrations many of you went through to provide answers, equipment or software, and maybe all three, so I could put the material together for this book. There is no particular order to this list, but it should be longer.

Keith Sklower of the Internet Engineering Task Force took time out during a meeting in Stockholm to review and comment on my brief remarks about PPP and Multilink PPP. Bob Larribeau, head of the California ISDN Users Group, explained the CIUG's interoperability testing to me. Dan Kegel, whom I finally met at NetWorld+Interop in Las Vegas during the Spring of 1996 spends countless hours maintaining the best little ISDN Web site in the universe; his efforts have made a profound difference in this book and ISDN. Rhonda Cooperstein of Bellcore hits the road weekly preaching the way to organize ordering ISDN and took time to explain it to me. John R. Behrman of Tetra Engineering shared countless ideas about ISDN and did yeoman duty in technical editing the first edition. Gene Chesser, President of the Texas ISDN Users Group, created an important organization and aided me in the real world of ISDN testing.

A number of people with hardware and software firms helped provide the products that are so important to use and understanding of ISDN; many others gave the benefits of their experience and education. Among those persons and firms are: Elizabeth A. Cardinale, Bob Jones, Jeniffer Wade, Robyn Aber, Julia Kisch, and Keith Hedley of 3Com; Leslie Conway, Stacy Thomas, and Amy Porten of Adtran; Sid Sung and Nancy Keen of Alpha Telecom; David Mays of Ascend Communications; Ham Mathews and Jerry Nichols of Digi International; Bruce Laird of Combinet (now Cisco); Tony Asaro of Gandalf; Sean Dalton and Bob Olshansky of GTE; Jeff Milloy and Ginny Walker of ISDN Systems Corporation (now US Robotics); Donna Loughlin of NetManage; Troy Trenchard, Bobby Clay, Craig Iwata, Ed Alcoff, Randy Sutherland, and Mike Hakkert of Cisco; Jamey Fleck of Intel; Barry Schofield of Lion Communication Industries; Jim Webster and Lisa J. Volmar of Motorola; Susan Wolbrueck and Ed West of ISDN*tek; Shirral Davis of IBM; Deanna Leung of Spry; Joe Licari and Ann Thorne of Symantec; Ann Krauss of Frontier Technologies; Mary Campbell of Vivo; David Huebel of JRL Systems; Jeremy W. Porter and KevinTX of Freeside Communications; Art Daddona and John Darden of Signet Partners; Robert W. Brown of RWB Telecommunications Consultants; Terry Nathan of Floppy Joe's; Nicole Lee and David Goodtree of Forrester Research; Lauri M. Lentz and Sanders Wilson of U.S. Robotics; Mike Thompson of Connectix; Charles Nieman of Trancell; Mary Bell Lopez Howard of Shiva; Amal Abed of Farallon; Dale Rensing of Proteon.

And the staff of Que including Cheryl Willoughby, Jim Minatel, Andrea Duvall, Stephanie McComb, Steve Schafer, Jeff Riley, Christy Miller, and Doshia Stewart, among many others with whom I didn't have direct contact but who are listed on the credits page or worked beyond such printed recognition. Special thanks to Jeff Taylor, Macmillan's tireless western sales manager, who endured my strange habits while we shared a room during Fall COMDEX in 1995; his generosity kept me off the late-night streets of Las Vegas. And thanks to the Macmillan road show crew.

Despite everyone's help, reality and experience assure me some errors may have crept in; all programs have bugs; all books have errors. I take full responsibility for any errors whether glaring or subtle and ask your indulgence and gentle notes to assist me in making corrections and posting the same on my Web page.

Thanks, JB

We'd Like to Hear from You!

As part of our continuing effort to produce books of the highest possible quality, Que would like to hear your comments. To stay competitive, we *really* want you, as a computer book reader and user, to let us know what you like or dislike most about this book or other Que products.

You can mail comments, ideas, or suggestions for improving future editions to the address below, or send us a fax at (317) 581-4663. For the online inclined, Macmillan Computer Publishing has a forum on CompuServe (type **GO QUEBOOKS** at any prompt) through which our staff and authors are available for questions and comments. The address of our Internet site is **http://www.mcp.com** (World Wide Web).

In addition to exploring our forum, please feel free to contact me personally to discuss your opinions of this book: I'm **sschafer@que.mcp.com** on the Internet and ID **71034,3406** on CompuServe.

Thanks in advance—your comments will help us to continue publishing the best books available on computer topics in today's market.

Steve Schafer
Title Manager
Que Corporation
201 W. 103rd Street
Indianapolis, Indiana 46290
USA

Contents at a Glance

VI | **Appendixes**

Contents

III | ISDN Computer Hardware

IV | Software & Applications

Introduction

Right away I'd like to say "Thank you," to the many people who bought the first edition and gave it such an enthusiastic reception I had to start on this second edition before my keyboard cooled. If you've read the first edition, you'll find many things the same and many things changed. Let's first take a look at what's the same. ■

TIP Please visit my web site **http://www.bryce.com/~bryce** to register your book and give me your observations.

This book is written for the computer user seeking to use ISDN. I'll assume you're familiar with basic computer terms. Perhaps you've tried to understand what ISDN is and how to use it by perusing books in your local library or bookstore; I did the same. Unfortunately, virtually all books written on ISDN are aimed at very technical audiences and the telephone industry. As a computer user, you don't speak telephone; because telephone writers don't speak computer, you've found yourself in a quagmire of seemingly new concepts and languages.

As I was cleaning the quicksand from my shoes, I wondered why I couldn't find something written for me? I mean, I've worked with computers for years; I've given hundreds of seminars about, written about, and supported local area networks. I should be able to understand this ISDN stuff from a single book. I wanted to get connected to the Internet, communicate with associates' offices, and support clients' sites using ISDN for its high data rate—at least in comparison to an analog modem—and its quick connect/disconnect features. But no matter how much I looked, I couldn't find a suitable book.

At first, I was convinced that entry into the telephone world was the technological equivalent of the descent into Hell that Dante so well described by the inscription over its entrance: "Abandon hope all ye who enter here." As I dug deeper, I decided telephones, like computers, were less a Divine Comedy and all too often "Much Ado About Nothing." The push and shove of the marketplace, the conflict of standards, the undercurrent of regulations, and the increasing roar from the developing horizon of open competition differ only in tempo and key between computers and telephones. It'll take some time to convert the dissonance now raging as sound and fury into a symphony of well-orchestrated melody, or, at least, a decent tune.

What's the Purpose of This Book?

This book is designed to meet your need for information on the telephone technology known as *Integrated Services Digital Network* (*ISDN*). ISDN has been developing for the last 20 years, but has not been widely available or reasonably tariffed in the United States or Canada until recently. Its growth has been retarded by conflicts among implementations making ISDN offerings of one company incompatible with those of another. Now uniform standards called National ISDN 1 and National ISDN 2 (NI-1, NI-2, ...) are emerging, driving compatibility and development. Future standards will bear the number of the years adopted, NI97.

Fundamentally, ISDN gives digital telephone service to any site reached by ordinary copper wire twisted pair. ISDN increases the data rate delivered to you over the existing telephone system. It provides end-to-end digital connection from your house or office to any other ISDN equipped site in the world. Virtually all of the telephone system, except the final link between you and the telephone central office, is digital and has been for several years. But this final link (the "local loop" in telespeak) has been analog and therefore subject to noise and data rate restraints that seriously limit development and use of modern computer, video, and other technologies.

ISDN removes these restraints. The time is ripe for its use. The hardware and software are in place. ISDN provides the backbone for:

- Telecommuting from homes and remote locations
- High speed connection to the Internet and use of "killer apps" like Netscape with the World Wide Web
- Video that really functions and is cost effective
- Cooperative applications such as "white boards"
- Corporate network wide area interconnection

Widespread adoption of ISDN will hit us more quickly than any previous enabling high technology. After implementation of a reliable base, mainframes took perhaps 30 years to integrate fully into our economy, minis perhaps 15, micros 10, and local area networks maybe five.

In the year prior to the first edition, 1994, the Internet moved from a somewhat obscure playground for academics, defense contractors, and a few scientific companies who could afford the time to deal with arcane hardware and software to a vibrant, glitzy necessity for doing business. Then there were perhaps a dozen or so Internet books in general trade publication. Now, a trip to any bookstore with a significant computer section shows hundreds of Internet-related titles. In my opinion ISDN—as an enabling technology for Internet and many other applications—will have a similar growth.

The events between the first and second editions have borne out my predictions for ISDN growth. In the section entitled "How this Book is Organized," I explain what's been changed and added.

Following the suggestions several of you made in response to my web site, I've brought the Apple Macintosh in at appropriate places throughout the book. It's important to recognize that ISDN is platform independent. While circuit board technologies are specific to a machine, connections through the serial or local area network ports are not. This means the serial port equipment described in Chapter 9, *Selecting an External Terminal Adapter,* can be used with a Mac. I've included a description of setting up the Motorola BitSURFR with the Mac; similar options are available for the 3Com Impact. In Chapter 11, *Establishing ISDN for LANs,* I present the Farallon Netopia that even has a connection for LocalTalk. Please remember, any of the routers I mention can be used with a Mac that's configured for TCP/IP; in fact they can be with any machine running TCP/IP connected to a LAN.

Who Should Use This Book?

Anyone wanting to find out about the most exciting way to do wide area networking, including the Internet, will find this book interesting and helpful. I don't expect you to be some sort of data comm or telephone guru.

I'll provide the information needed to acquire service, select hardware and software, and make ISDN work so you can reach the Internet and other sites with a vastly improved performance than that available through analog telephony. ISDN is the enabling technology for all the other exciting communications developments coming down the pike at the end of this century and carrying us into the next millennium.

Everyone, from a hobbyist to a complex business user, will benefit from this book. Super experts in the area of ISDN may even glean a few pithy observations to add to their arsenal.

Or maybe you're in a very important area vital to ISDN: you're a regulator or legislator concerned with understanding the technology so the laws and rules you make will best serve your constituents into the next century of computers and telephony. We all appreciate your taking the time to learn.

What Do You Need To Know To Read This Book?

You need some conceptual grasp of computer technology. I expect you're conversant with day-to-day use of personal computers and telephone modems. Conversant means "have used"; it does not mean "know how to program or wire up." No heavy duty technical knowledge is presumed.

What Have You Learned When You've Read This Book?

You'll be able to discuss the concepts of ISDN and enumerate the features, functions, costs, and benefits expected from ISDN implementations in business, education, government, and charitable and personal settings. You'll be able to select, purchase, connect, and configure the software and hardware necessary to establish useful ISDN service. You'll understand how to order ISDN service from a telephone company.

You'll have vicariously lived through the experiences of pioneers, thereby avoiding mirages, poisoned waterholes, and arrows in the back. You'll even have been introduced to the regulatory morass that is said to control telephony in the United States, affording you an opportunity to wail at city hall, the public utility commission, the FCC, or Congress with some semblance of knowledge.

What Hardware or Software Do You Need To Use This Book?

You need no special software to read and understand this book. The various ISDN hardware products may have associated software for their use bundled with the products. Communications applications may need appropriate drivers to recognize the hardware.

NOTE The hardware and software I describe in this book is almost entirely IBM PC and Microsoft Windows/DOS based. ISDN is usable in any environment—UNIX, Macintosh, minicomputers, etc. I've chosen the PC/Windows platform because I expect you are familiar with it, regardless of any others you're also using. A great deal of the information is totally platform independent or clearly transportable to other arenas.

You also don't need any special hardware for this book. Of course, to use ISDN, you'll need ISDN hardware to access the telephone system ISDN services. The hardware may be a card, separate "ISDN modem," or router.

In a number of chapters I'll discuss the hardware and software requirements for ISDN, present installation and configuration examples, and help you choose gear for your particular needs.

How Is This Book Organized?

This book is divided into five parts that include 20 chapters. Each represents a different area for exploring and understanding ISDN:

- Part I, "What Is ISDN?" lays the groundwork and context of ISDN.

  Chapter 1, "Exploring ISDN History," explains the origins and fundamentals of telephony and computers, together with current effects of emerging technologies such as the Internet.

  Chapter 2, "Understanding Standards and Regulations," digs into this very necessary part of ISDN which is, after all, a part of telephony, one of the most regulated industries in the world. Standards give us a taste of the tremendous effort thousands of people have expended to make things using ISDN talk to one another. The second edition covers the effect of the new U.S. Telecommunications Act. This revision of the 1934 act was long overdue and has major implications for you—including emergence of serious competition in the local loop, where ISDN Basic Rate Interface technology lives.

- Part II, "Theory and Terminology," dives into the real nitty gritty of ISDN. Don't worry; I've been too often exposed to explanations that end up being constant recitations of protocols, bits, bytes, and other details. I'm offering some of this to you, but I try to make it digestible and meaningful.

  Chapter 3, "Defining Narrowband ISDN," hits the meat of why you're here. It explains the types of services offered currently and how they work in conceptual detail.

  Chapter 4, "Choosing Services," straightens out perhaps the most confusing aspect of ISDN that many people run into right off the bat—the overwhelming variety of options available. This chapter lays the groundwork for Chapter 7, which explains how to order these services.

Chapter 5, "Signaling with ISDN," translates the sophisticated means used by your equipment to explain what it wants as your telephone company's switch and how that switch talks with other switches.

Chapter 6, "Unscrambling APIs," takes on the application program interfaces used to talk with ISDN equipment and presents the major ones currently in the market.

■ Part III, "ISDN Computer Hardware," lays out the selections you must make, starting with ordering service from the telephone company and picking out the devices to hook up to your computer.

Chapter 7, "Ordering ISDN Services," applies the concepts and terms developed in Chapter 4 on choosing services, working you through the potential maze at your telco. Much of the first edition was concerned with explaining how to order ISDN, a complex and frustrating exercise. With the second edition I'm able to present new ways of ordering that substantially simplify your task. Chapter 7 has an extensive new section entitled "The Web-Based Answer to ISDN Order Simplification" that illustrates Microsoft's streamlined method of ordering ISDN. This began in support of ISDN ordering in the United States and Canada and is slated to cover the world in an effort to make your ISDN ordering life easier.

Chapter 8, "Wiring and Powering Your ISDN System," explains the constraints governing the telephone company's wiring to your location and then your needs for wiring up your home or business.

Chapter 9, "Selecting an External Terminal Adapter," takes up the case for what is sometimes called an "ISDN modem" (an oxymoron, as a modem modulates and demodulates from analog to digital and back, while ISDN is digital on both sides of the device). We'll look at three widely used external ISDN terminal adapters and go through their installation, configuration, and use. In this chapter, as in the others on equipment and software, the good, the bad, and the ugly are revealed.

Chapter 10, "Putting an Adapter Inside Your Computer," covers the alternative of a circuit board that plugs into your computer's bus and connects to ISDN. We'll look at some simple ones and some very complex ones. In the second edition, Chapter 10 is extensively revised by adding new products and information on Microsoft's software support for a number of cards.

Chapter 11, "Establishing ISDN for LANs," looks at LANs, of course, but is not restricted to LANs. The devices here are routers or, perhaps, bridges. Some of the advantages of LAN type connection can be realized by a single machine with a LAN card connected to an ISDN router (or bridge) device. In the second edition changes to Chapter 11 are the most exciting of all. Within one year routers have gone from boxes that cost $1,000 or more and took a team of obsessed computer nerds to set up, to near appliances costing less than $500 that are set up through a graphical user interface, often a web browser. Here are my fearless observations/predictions on routers for ISDN:

Routers will become the preferred way to use ISDN with your computer.

Routers will be easier to set up than VCRs, far easier.

Routers will cost the same as the prevailing general purpose top speed modem. Today an external 28.8 kbps modem goes for about $200. By this time next year the fast general purpose modem may be 33 kbps for $200. Expect routers for ISDN to sell for the same price!

1996 will become known as "The Year of the ISDN Router." You heard it here first.

As you read Chapter 11, you'll see how the router makers have moved full speed ahead to accomplish this. Most now have a graphical user interface; you'll see how this works for many of the popular routers. There have not been a large number of companies entering the external terminal adapter or internal card market. There has been little truly new product development or differentiation within such devices. Conversely, I found it nearly impossible to keep up with the new entries building routers. Product development and differentiation for routers is exploding. The result? More features and functions at a far lower cost.

■ Part IV, "Software and Applications." There are several issues with software use on ISDN. Some applications are made just for ISDN.

Chapter 12, "Opening Windows 95 and NT to ISDN," provides the latest information on Windows 95 and Windows NT use with ISDN. The two are closely related in communications design. For the second edition, Chapter 12 updates you about Microsoft's emphasis on ISDN. It's clear that Bill and his gang think ISDN is the way to go, and they're making sure you get the idea in all their software products.

Chapter 13, "Tying It Together: Two B or Not Two B," shows how two or more B channels (the fundamental information carriers for ISDN) can be joined to increase data rates. We'll talk about issues of BONDING, Multilink PPP, and compression. In the second edition the work of the IETF continues with the Motorola compression conflict resolved, Multilink PPP just about finished and the details of compression still being ironed out.

Chapter 14, "Pictures and Video with ISDN," hits the exciting frontier ISDN opens up for graphics and video over telephone circuits. Sharing graphical information in applications simultaneously is a part of this. The second edition adds some details to the existing cast of characters. But the big news is crashing the price barrier to below $200 for video teleconferencing; that's right, $200!

Chapter 15, "Changing Telephones to ISDN," broaches the question of totally changing the kind of phone you use. With the second edition you'll find more on the equipment to use, especially in the SOHO (small office/home) world.

Chapter 16, "Putting ISDN to Work," gets down to what you can actually do with ISDN not only at work, but also in your personal life. Telecommuting is a large part of this.

Chapter 17, "ISDN Access for Internet Providers and Corporations," looks at the flip side of the connection most of you are probably considering. Providers have vastly greater loads to carry. ISDN can be a big benefit. The second edition adds new equipment and methods.

- Part V, "The Future," tastes some of the possibilities coming soon.

   Chapter 18, "Anticipating Broadband ISDN," launches into rather heavy technologies for shipping many millions of bits each second. We unmask those buzz works like frame relay, ATM, and SONET. You may be using some of these right from your business soon.

   Chapter 19, "Forecasting Changes Due to ISDN," steps out on a limb giving you some ideas of how ISDN will change the future.

   Chapter 20, "Alternatives to ISDN," is new with the second edition. It heats things up with the debate about ISDN being a transitional technology on the way to one or a combination of the others in the title. You'll find out what the others are and how everything, including ISDN, fits together.

- Appendixes and Bibliography.

   Appendix A, "World Wide Web References for Standards and Organizations," gives World Wide Web references for standards and organizations. It would have been impossible to write this book without the Web and other resources of the Internet. I expect more and more research will rest on Internet techniques. This appendix will give you a good start.

   Appendix B, "ISDN Products: What To Ask and Who To Ask," provides a list of companies that make ISDN products. I've included suggestions on questions to ask while shopping. I've also included Internet addresses and Web sites for many of the companies.

   Appendix C, "Internet Service Providers Offering ISDN," was originally designed to be a list of Internet service providers using ISDN. Such lists go out of date so quickly I decided to point you to Internet lists that are maintained on the subject.

   The Bibliography is designed to be easy to use. I've described the entries and how I found them helpful. You'll find both books and periodicals listed. In the last part I've listed trade shows because I think these shows are among the best sources for current information on particular products.

Conventions Used in This Book

This book uses various conventions designed to make it easier to use. That way, you can quickly and easily learn about ISDN and related hardware and software.

You can manipulate through many of the programs, installations, and configurations described in this book using the familiar Windows interface. If you get stuck, try holding down Alt and choosing a hot key, such as F for File, to get out and start over. In some circumstances you'll be working in terminal emulation mode and entering rather obtuse commands in UNIX, DOS, or specialized router syntax. Most of this is in Chapter 11 during configurations of routers. I wish I could avoid this detail, but since you can't understand the current router products, please bear with me. As I show at the end of Chapter 11, help is on the way.

The following table contains typeface conventions used to indicate special text.

Typeface	Meaning
Italic	Italic is used to indicate variables in commands or addresses, and terms used for the first time.
Bold	Bold is used for text you type and to indicate actual addresses for Internet sites, newsgroups, mailing lists, WWW pages, and more.
`Computer type`	This special type is used for commands (such as the DOS `COPY` or UNIX `cp` command).

N O T E Notes provide additional information that may help you avoid problems or offer advice or general information related to the topic at hand. ▪

 T I P Tips suggest easier or alternative methods of executing a procedure.

CAUTION
Cautions warn you of hazardous procedures and situations that can lead to unexpected or unpredictable results, including data loss or system damage.

 TROUBLESHOOTING

Troubleshooting sections anticipate common problems... and then provide you with practical suggestions for solving those problems.

▶ **See** "Ordering ISDN Services," **p. 141**

Cross-references direct you to related information in other parts of the book.

What Is ISDN?

Exploring ISDN History

We're about to spend several hundred pages on a telephone technology called *Integrated Services Digital Network,* ISDN for short. Why should you, a computer user, be interested in this seemingly obscure telephone technology? Because you want:

- A faster data rate when you connect your computer to other systems over the phone system.

- Faster setup and teardown when you place a data call. This means it's frequently only a second or so from the time you place a call until it's connected; likewise it only takes a second or less to finish and disconnect a call. Contrast this with a modem call that takes 30 or more seconds to set up and several seconds to close out.

- More information about a call in progress. ISDN provides information on the calling and called parties' directory numbers, the type of call, data or voice, for example, and several other aspects of the call.

In the past, ISDN seemed relegated to the back pages of technical journals; but during 1995, more and more ISDN stories appeared in the general press. Something happened – ISDN became a viable option for business and personal use. While it's true there still is quite a bit of variation in telephone company charges for ISDN, these variations are now the subject of widespread news coverage. All this interest has accelerated in the United States with the passage of the Communications Act of 1996, a total rewrite of the Communications Act of 1934 that governed telecommunications in the U.S. for more than a half century.

With so much happening, it's time to see what ISDN is all about by learning some of the terminology and concepts right away. This chapter covers the sources of telephone and computer technology and examines why the two are flowing together today. ■

Quick Introduction to ISDN

You must be interested in ISDN because you're reading this book. So let's find out what ISDN really is. For openers, where did the acronym ISDN come from? If you answered *Integrated Services Digital Network*, and I'm sure you did, does that really answer the question? Let's go a little deeper.

- **Integrated** implies that all the parts are designed so they work well together and make things easy; that is, so they are *more* working together rather than *less* working together. For ISDN it means at least that voice and data transmission is integrated over one system. You can make up your mind on this after you've finished the book and tried your hand at really making ISDN function. In the beginning the I in ISDN mainly referred to using the same system to carry telephone and computer information. The phone companies expected to sell the idea to businesses for computer communications within their offices. The costs of alternative technology in the form of local area networks kept their plan from becoming a reality.

- **Services** implies the network does something for us; it's going to serve us. Services available through ISDN include bearer services, supplementary services, teleservices, and signaling services. These buzzwords are explained later so I won't spend your time here other than to suggest you can do everything using ISDN that you now do with "POTS" (Plain Old Telephone Service) plus a whole lot more.

- **Digital** is the heart of the matter. The *raison d'être* of ISDN. Digital technology breaks information into a simple string of ones and zeros; these turn out to be cheaper to transmit and more flexible to use than the other form of information, analog. We'll plunge into digital and contrast it with analog, along with a little history just below.

- **Network** lets us get through pretty quickly. A network ties a bunch of equipment together so the entire collection of stuff can *more or less* work together and exchange information.

Raison d'être

The sidebars you'll find scattered throughout this book are as much for your amusement as for your enlightenment. *Raison d'être* is the way a French speaker would say *reason for being* and is tossed in by a writer to try to convince the reader that the author is sophisticated.

The Advantages of ISDN

▶ **See** the section entitled "Basic Rate Interface (BRI)," **p. 75**

▶ **See** the section entitled "Bearer Services," **p. 144**

Initially, ISDN's primary attraction is the data rate it delivers over most existing twisted pair wire (the standard type of wiring used for telephones) going into your house or office. ISDN's basic rate interface (BRI), the type that interests most people, gives two B channels, each with a data rate of 64 kilobits per second (kbps). The B channels, "bearer channels," are used for user information. In addition, a third channel, the D channel, is used primarily for call control running at 16 kbps. Figure 1.1 shows what a BRI is conceptually; don't be misled by this diagram into thinking ISDN is carried on some special kind of cable. The BRI is actually carried on only one twisted pair from your local telephone exchange to your house or business.

FIG. 1.1
ISDN Basic Rate
Interface.

Basic Rate Interface (BRI)

2 B Channels (64 kbps each)

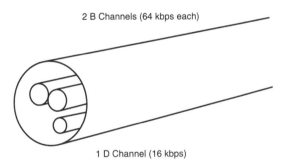

1 D Channel (16 kbps)

When Is 1000 Really 1024?

Throughout this book and in the literature of ISDN you will see references to kilobits per second (kbps) or megabits per second (mbps). In the computer world when talking about information storage in bytes, the term "kilobyte" means 1024 bytes. The number is an even power of two. So when you are counting kilo or megabytes, you use powers of two. In the world we are entering now, telephone communications, we are speaking of bits per second, where kilo is an even 1000, and mega is an even 1,000,000. If you don't believe it, wait for Chapter 3 and count the bits in a second's transmission on a B channel; you'll get 64,000 exactly.

Another type, primary rate interface (PRI), offers 23 B channels at 64 kbps and a 64 kbps D channel in its North American version. Figure 1.2 shows the idea.

N O T E   In Europe, a PRI has 30 B channels and one D channel. To make things even more
interesting, once you have a PRI line into your location, the D channel on the first line may
handle the signaling for other PRIs. Consequently, your additional PRIs have 24 (North America) or 31
(Europe) B channels and no D channels. ■

FIG. 1.2   Primary Rate Interface (PRI)
ISDN Primary Rate
Interface in North
America.

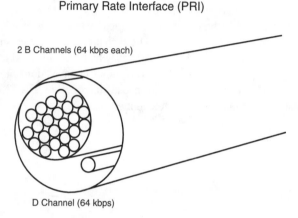

So we have two forms of ISDN generally available. BRI gives us two B channels and PRI gives
us 23 channels. For the individual or small business, BRI is usually the most important.

Comparing ISDN Speeds with POTS

How does this compare with the analog telephone modem world? Take a look at Figure 1.3 and
you'll see BRI offers several times the data rate over what ISDN aficionados derisively call
POTS (Plain Old Telephone Service). Remember to compare oranges to oranges. Most modem
vendors tout their data rates with compression. So a modem that works at 14.4 kbps with 4 to 1
compression delivers 56.6 kbps. It looks almost as good as an ISDN B channel. Don't be misled. Compression only works on compressible data. Little other than the simplest text compresses as much as 4 to 1. But, far more important compression techniques can be used on
ISDN. Now take the 64 kbps B channel and consider 4 to 1 compression; you have 256 kbps
Wow! Couple this with the possibility of using two B channels together and, if you believe in
the compression argument, you are at 512 kbps. Not bad. Of course the point is that compression should not enter into your measurements because it varies with the data form itself. Instead, consider the raw line speed.

▶ **See** the discussion of compression in Chapter 13, "Tying It Together: Two B or Not Two B,"
p. 419

ISDN also has the added advantage of inherently lower noise. Consequently, your chances of
realizing the design data rate of 64 kbps on a B channel are far greater than achieving 28.8
kbps on an analog line, as most analog lines are subject to noise degradation.

FIG. 1.3

Data Rate Comparison (More Is Better).

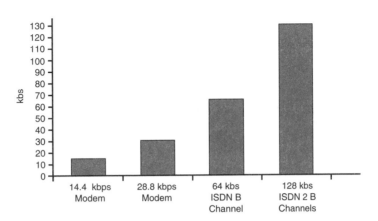

Now you've probably heard all about data transmission speed on ISDN. But chances are no one told you about ISDN's *call setup* or *teardown* advantages. Setup is the process of establishing a call from the moment you finish dialing until the other equipment answers. Teardown is the reverse process of disconnection. ISDN, in conjunction with your ISDN hardware, can do either in one or two seconds (often half a second). Compare that to modems that may take 30 seconds or a minute to figure out how to hook to each other. You've been through the cat fight sounds from your modem as it painfully tries to synch with another. When you place an ISDN call, you're freed from auditory assault. Okay, so you turn off the sounds on your modem (and risk not knowing when something doesn't work); you still have to wait enough time to grab a snack from the next room before you're connected.

If you use ISDN with software that can rapidly time out and then reestablish connection, you can save a bundle on telephone, online service, and Internet access costs based on connect time. All you do is set a short time out. Now while you read that long Web page, time runs out, the connection drops, and your charges drop, too. You click on a hyperlink. The line comes up, grabs the new page and goes back down. It's so fast you don't even know it happened. Take a look at Figure 1.4 and notice the one or two second time for establishing (setting up) an ISDN call in contrast to the 30 seconds or more in the usual analog modem call. The seconds along the vertical axis measure the time from the end of your dialing until establishment of a connection and negotiation of protocols with the machine you're calling.

N O T E So, now you're at the mercy of the negotiation for security and protocols between you and the called equipment. Although this can be very fast, a second or so; remember that D channel— it's always up. Even when the B channels disconnect, the D channel keeps the security and protocol authentication alive enabling the next call in a sequence to avoid that delay. Today this technique is not in general use, but that is anticipated shortly. ▪

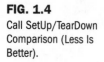

FIG. 1.4
Call SetUp/TearDown
Comparison (Less Is
Better).

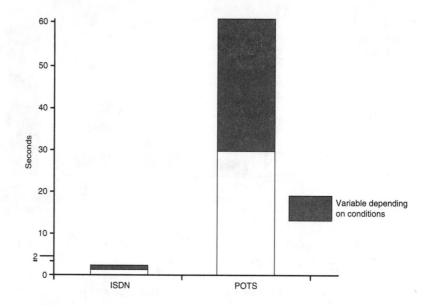

Variable depending
on conditions

Other ISDN Advantages

Just for icing on the cake, you can get information about a call in progress without interrupting the call. Plain old telephone service uses *in-band* signaling to advise you of control events such as a call waiting. You're interrupted on the phone by a click or special sound. "ISDN uses *out-of-band* signaling, called *common channel signaling*. Remember the D channel? Out-of-band signaling provides the information about the call in progress, plus much more: telephone numbers, the identity of the types of equipment in use at your location, and the identity of the types of equipment at the location of the called party. Out-of-band signaling provides this information in a way that does not interfere with your applications using the B channel(s).

Here's another way the D channel can help. While scanning through some files on a file transfer protocol (ftp) server, you find a 10 megabyte jewel. On POTS you start the download and go to lunch. On ISDN you start the download on a single 64 kbps B channel. You have set up your system with your Internet access provider so that most of the time you're connected on only one B channel, but you made a special deal—when you want a second B channel, you get it, for an added cost, only on demand. When the server starts the file transfer, your equipment and that of the provider determine the single B channel is running at capacity for several seconds, then they cut in the second B channel. You get double the data rate, and pay for it only when you need it. This magic works through D channel control.

Telephone History

Living in the late 20th century has its benefits. Diseases and inconveniences experienced by our great grandparents often no longer exist. Polio and smallpox are virtually eradicated. Tomorrow you can be anywhere. Now, this instant, you can talk to almost anyone anywhere in the world. We are told the pace of knowledge growth is exponential and that we must embark upon the *information highway* connecting all those in the post industrial age through one vast network. We are told that should we fail to heed this advice, we are threatened with professional, cultural, and personal collapse.

But ask a proponent of this change about its source. Ask the direction such progress progresses. Ask and you will most often be met with a rush of words about returning government to the people, delivering movies on demand, speeding business transactions so the velocity of money through the economy increases the multiplier effect and with it total planetary wealth. Ask specifically about origins of electronic communications, and you may be given a glimmer of the stories of Samuel F. B. Morse and Alexander Graham Bell.

▶ **See** the section entitled "Digital and Analog," **p. 70**

The stories aren't new to us. The original inventions of each man are quaint by today's standards, but Morse's telegraph and Bell's telephone probably shaped our contemporary world more than any other inventions. And now the irony. We are revisiting the telegraph of Morse when we use that most modern of communication techniques, digital. We are casting out the whole of Bell's basic invention and returning to a clicking key, albeit a rapidly clicking and electronic key. Let's find out how Morse has pulled ahead of Bell and why we should care in a book on ISDN.

How Telegraphy Relates to Digital Communications

When Bell spilled the acid and yelled over that first rudimentary phone, "Dr. Watson. Come here. I need you," we were already well into communicating by electricity. Morse had first demonstrated his genius conveying a more profound thought, "What hath God wrought," between Baltimore and Washington. Telegraphy, patented by Morse in 1844, had played a major role in the United States during the Civil War and the opening of the west. Telegraphy was first (Bell won his first telephone patent in 1876) and telegraphy is a digital technique.

At this point in writing I originally launched into a somewhat technical tirade on digital and analog theory. Let's hold that for Chapter 3, "Defining Narrowband ISDN," and just talk about telegraphy for a minute to get the idea.

When a telegraph key is closed, electric current flows. When the key is opened, current does not flow. That's really all there is to it: two states, on and off, one and zero. Does this sound familiar? Figure 1.5 shows the basic circuit. The plot of amplitude versus time shows the variation in electrical voltage. In the case of telegraphy, information really has five components:

- A long space between words
- A shorter space between letters
- An even shorter space between the elements of letters, dots and dashes
- Dots
- Dashes

When we start talking about digital technique, we find we need only the two states, on and off; and we usually interpret them as one and zero, respectively. All information can be encoded in this form.

FIG. 1.5
Telegraph Circuit.

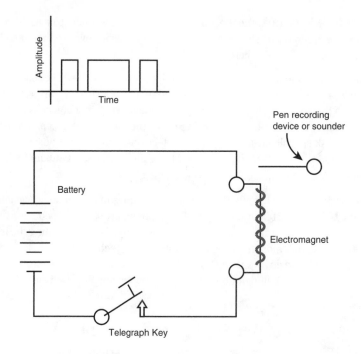

In Morse's first version, opening and closing the key caused marks to be made on a moving paper, then the marks were read by an operator. Soon telegraphers found they could follow the dots and dashes simply from the sounds made by the marking device, and the inscription machine was discarded for a sounder. This communication by either the existence, *mark,* or lack of existence, *space,* of an electrical signal over time gave us our first digital signaling system. See Chapters 3, 5, and 18 for more details on digital protocols for ISDN.

To use this system, we had to agree on how we would encode information. For example, in the International Morse Code, the letter "A" is sent as one short sound followed by one long sound, dit dah, or dot dash. The time space between sounds making up a letter is shorter than the space between letters in a word; the space between letters is shorter than the space between words. Telegraphy code established a *protocol* for communication and set the *standard* for the future. Need for such a protocol to render the information into an understandable form is basic to digital communication.

> **CAUTION**
>
> Strictly speaking, a protocol defines rules of timing and data format. Usually you speak of protocols at low levels, bit-oriented, byte-oriented or character-oriented protocols. A device called a *protocol analyzer* shows data in such forms. Protocols are just a part of the standards that must be followed. For some reason, I and many others find it hard to keep from mixing up protocols and standards as terms in discussion.

dit dit, dit dit dit, dah dit dit, dah dit

The International Morse Code is the telegraphy language used throughout the world. The title of this sidebar spells out ISDN in International Morse Code.

The American Morse Code is also known as Railroad Morse, since its use was limited almost exclusively to dispatching and other interstation communications on US and Canadian railroads and in wire services they provided to such third parties as Western Union. This form no longer has any active use in the world.

Bell's Improvement Over the Telegraph

Years later Bell came along and found a way to make electricity vary in amplitude and frequency with sounds. His method took the direct current electricity Morse simply switched on and off and fashioned it into a stream of continuously changing levels of voltage varying over time. These variations precisely mimicked in electrical changes the continuous variations in air pressure our ears detect as sound. Bell transmitted this to a device that turned the electrical variations back into variations in air pressure we sense as sound. Bell, just as Morse, depended on time to supply the final component, frequency, to convey not only the pressure of the air, but the rapidity with which the pressure grew and then fell, giving the sound a higher or lower pitch. This continuous variation of a signal mimicking in one form (here electricity) something in another form (here sound) is *analog transmission*.

Figure 1.6 shows the basic telephone circuit. The graph shows amplitude on the vertical axis and time on the horizontal axis, just as in the earlier illustration of telegraphy (refer to Fig. 1.5). The key is that analog techniques must follow exactly the variations in one phenomenon by using variations in another phenomenon. There is no way to determine if a random change in the received signal is important or unimportant. With digital techniques, we know the signal can only be on or off; we encode to transmit the information and decode at the other end. If there are problems in a digital signal that distort the on and off (one and zero) stream, we can detect the errors and make statistically based decisions on how much distortion has been created.

Probably neither Morse nor Bell would have considered it feasible to switch things on and off fast enough to encode sounds, much less pictures; probably neither entertained the idea, but this is exactly what we do when we encode sound and video and all other information into digital form. Our digital logic is based on millions of switches acting just like tiny telegraph keys sending a stream of on and off states that reduce to ones and zeros. Through agreements on protocols and standards, these ones and zeros are translated into sounds, pictures, text, and dollars.

 TIP "Location, location, and location." That's the response of a successful tycoon who was asked the three most essential elements in real estate. Look at history and answer the three most essential elements in successful technology: "Standards, standards, and standards."

FIG. 1.6
Telephone circuit.

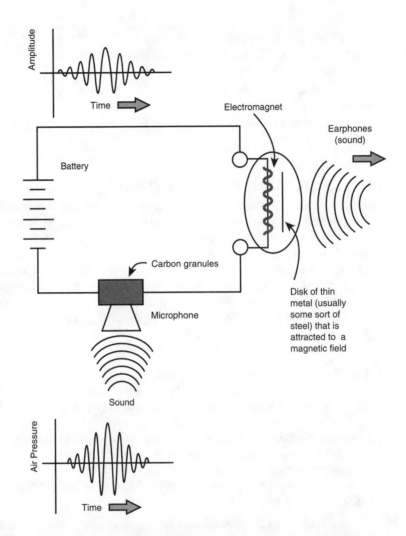

A protocol of dots and dashes defined Morse Code and helped give rise to worldwide communication using electricity. Modern communications protocols are simply the logical extension of telegraphy's initial idea. ISDN is shorthand for agreements providing standards embodied in technology converting the telephone system from Bell's analog design to Morse's digital model. The more things change, the more they stay the same. We're going back to the on and off of telegraphy.

Major Components of Telephone Systems

Over the history of telephone developments, it has become apparent that telephone systems are composed of two major parts:

- Transmission
- Switching

Each is essential to telephone communication and each plays a big role in the current importance of ISDN to you.

Transmission

Transmission gets a signal from point A to point B. In particular, transmission is concerned with issues surrounding transmission media. There are four types of media used in with telephone technology. By the way, I'll use the term *telephony* from here on as a sort of shorthand for telephone technology:

- Twisted pair cable
- Coaxial (coax) cable
- Fiber optic cable
- Radio

Due to noise and attenuation characteristics we'll look at more in Chapter 3, fiber optic cables carry the most information the greatest distance and twisted pair copper cables carry the least information the shortest distance. Coaxial cable falls somewhere in between. Radio is frequently restricted due to the need to share spectrum space with others.

Prior to wide use of fiber, long distance carriers relied on coaxial cable supplemented with microwave radio. The two were using fundamentally analog radio technology to carry signals. However, in more recent technology both have been used for digital transmission. Fiber with digital technology has proven more economic and capable of carrying vastly more information; microwave and coax are being phased out.

Today essentially all of the telephone system is based on fiber optic cables carrying digital signals. Cities are connected by interexchange carriers using fiber. Central offices within cities are connected to each other using fiber optics. The only place you'll find much copper twisted pair running analog signals today is the *local loop,* the cable from the central office to your office or house. And guess what? It's the local loop that is the determining factor in the data rate, noise, and errors associated with your use of the telephone system. The local loop is the weak link.

Long ago the local exchange carriers and the interchange carriers decided it was in their best interests to use fiber optics for telephone exchange to telephone exchange communication; this decision saved them a lot of money. It also saved them a lot of money to be sure the signals going down those cables were digital signals since our whole electronic technology has concentrated on perfecting digital transmission for nearly 40 years.

But you're faced with a twisted pair to the telco switch. And that twisted pair places a severe limit on the data rate that can be delivered to you. ISDN helps get the last gasp of use out of that twisted pair because it delivers a digital, rather than analog signal. Soon we'll have to go to fiber, coax or wireless methods. Now, twisted pair is the best most of us have, so let's get the most out of it. We can anticipate development of a competitive market for improvement in media. Where telephone companies once amortized their plant and equipment costs over a 20- to 40-year period, the life span of emerging technologies cuts that time frame to an average of five years…and demands more bang from each buck spent.

Adam Smith

Adam Smith penned *An Inquiry Into the Nature and Causes of the Wealth of Nations* (1776). A basic premise in this classic work of capitalist economics is that the self-interested pursuit of gain by a number of businesses in an open, competitive market will determine the price and quality of goods or services as though an *invisible hand* had control. Look what has happened with the price and performance of computers in a competitive market. Look what has not happened with the price and performance of telephone services in a *regulated monopoly* market.

Switching

When I was a boy growing up in rural Texas, our phone number was 1417-J; the J indicated a *party line*. For those of you who don't know what that is, it means that someone else had a phone on the same line at his house and you could hear him talking.

We also had a different way of making a call. When you picked up the receiver, it was separate from the transmitter (microphone). You were not greeted with a dial tone; there was no dial. A pleasant, female voice asked "Number please?" to which you said 1397-W or whatever. Now, down at the local phone company, the woman asking was frantically plugging and unplugging one line into another on a big switchboard. I remember well that day when *the phone company* told us we could use the new dial on our phones and for the first time Waxahachie, Texas entered the world of automated exchanges all in one leap from "Number please?" to direct distance dialing. Wow!

The first automated exchanges were collections of magnetically operated rotary switches that stepped through each pulse sent from the dial. A connection was made to another such switch that stepped to the next digit and so on. Hence the name of the equipment *step by step*. Following this design, a more elaborate and flexible, but still electromechanical design called a *crossbar switch* began to take over.

As we moved into the 1960s, the initial electronic switches were used. They were based on analog technology, as the telephone still was analog. The 1970s saw the development of the first digital switches concurrently with the flow of digital information on the transmission side of the equation. Now there was every economic reason to keep information in digital form throughout the system. Conversion back and forth through switches was expensive. So, with rare exception, it became to the operating companies' advantage to use both digital switches and digital transmission lines. Look at Figure 1.7 for an idea of how the telephone system is tied together and the locations of digital and analog information.

FIG. 1.7
Telephone network.

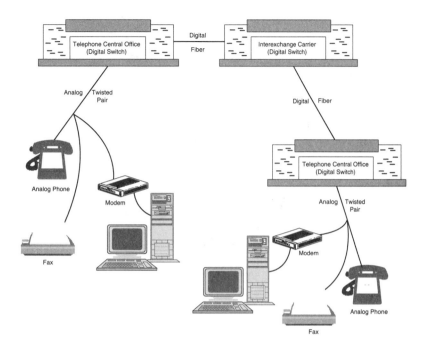

But at the very end this wonderful digital information system was converted to analog for that last mile or two down the twisted pair copper loop. This conversion was not cheap. It needed *codec devices,* electronic gear to convert digital to analog and back. Basically "codec" is telespeak for "modem." Use of this conversion was deemed cheaper than rewiring the loop or going to a digital technique and placing new digital equipment at the subscriber's location. It was also cheaper than making the digital-to-analog conversion there.

Today ISDN finishes the job. It delivers digital information to the subscriber. The subscriber decides whether or not the equipment he connects is digital or analog and supplies the connection devices to make it work.

N O T E   Although it looks like just about anything can be connected to an ISDN system, be aware it takes special electronics to use ISDN. If you attempt to call an analog modem with your ISDN equipment, it won't connect. If someone with an analog modem attempts to call your ISDN equipment, nothing happens. Although there are some ISDN devices that embed analog modems for such instances and some that go so far as to be able to detect the difference and automatically switch, some equipment is not so agile. In short, moving to ISDN provides no backward compatibility with POTS; so don't throw your modems out yet. Figure 1.8 assumes use of ISDN electronics that enables connection of analog gear to use one or more B channels. We'll cover this in more detail in Chapters 3, 8, and 9. ▪

FIG. 1.8
ISDN invades the
network.

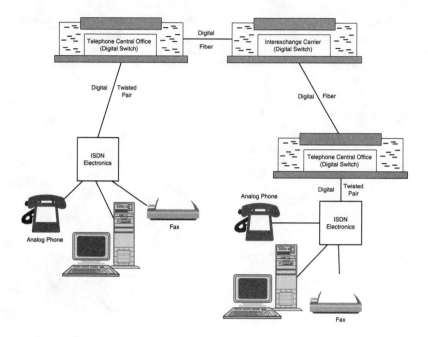

Factors Affecting ISDN Availability

Here are the factors that play into our efforts to make ISDN work for you.

- You must have a local telephone company (the telespeak is *local exchange carrier, LEC*) making ISDN available to your area.

- The carrier may have a digital switch, but surprise; that switch may not be ISDN-compliant, or it may not be compliant with the new National ISDN standards you need for the equipment you buy.

- The local exchange carrier may be able to get ISDN to a switch for you but still be unable to supply a cable adequate to carry the digital information from the switch to you.

- Everything above may be technically possible, but there may not be a tariff filed with the appropriate government regulatory authority allowing the carrier to connect ISDN to you.

- And, finally, the switch may be right, the wires may work, the tariff may be available, but the price to you may be horrendous.

  ▶ **See** Chapter 2, "Understanding Standards and Regulations," which provides suggestions for handling regulatory issues such as tariffs and mandated availability of service, **p. 37**

Computer History

Computer communications constantly shifts back and forth between analog and digital forms. When the signal is put on the ordinary voice-grade type of telephone line that runs as the local loop from the telephone central office to your business or house, it must be converted to analog. The telephone company supplies a codec to convert digital to analog and make this happen.

If the signal will be used in your local area network stand-alone computer, it must be digital. You buy a *modem* to convert analog to digital and make this happen. Isn't this absurd? You just bought a device to convert the signal back to what it was a few miles away. The phone company bought a device to do the reverse!

With ISDN we move away from the analog system that has tethered us to our local telephone exchange. With ISDN we originate our communication within our computers and other devices in digital form and it stays in digital form. Along the way it may become subject to many protocols arising from standards that seek to package it as digital information for carriage through the worldwide network. ISDN has emerged as that standard that makes this work; it assures us of the greatest possibility of being understood anywhere in the world of telephony.

The evolution of computing has actually followed a path similar to that of telephony. But the telling difference has been the role of regulation. Telephone systems have been considered *natural monopolies* and computer companies simply become *unnatural monopolies*. As we move into the 21st century, we may dispense with monopolies altogether; time will tell.

The Age of Mainframes

As computers became commercially feasible during the 1950s, they were viewed with awe as very expensive, special-purpose machines. Some prognosticators forecast there would never be need for more than a handful of computers throughout the world. Tremendous increases in speed and reductions in cost brought by integrated circuits put those forecasts to rest.

All of these early machines were built on *batch processing*. A machine was programmed to solve a given problem, usually an arithmetic problem. The unique information, the data, making up a specific instance of the problem was fed into the machine, and, if the program was properly constructed, the correct answer came out in the form of printed material. Then the next problem was presented in the form of different data. When all problems of the same type were solved, the next program was loaded, and the process began again.

As the power of machines increased, researchers discovered most of the time and effort of the computer was spent not in solving the problem at hand, but rather in reading the information in and spewing it out. It was found these tasks could be assigned to smaller, subsidiary computers. Those communicating with the outside world became known as *front end processors*. Those that helped the computer work with its more internal devices, such as tapes and disks, were known as *back end processors*.

Released from front and back end processing, the main machines had vast amounts of time and computing power that were not being used, yet cost huge amounts of money. The problem: "How to use this leftover computing power?"

Designers looked at the developing front and back end processors and found a technology that would combine quite well with changes in design of the main computer. Now the main computer was designed to work on more than one problem at once, *multitasking,* by suspending work on a problem awaiting results from, for example, some disk drive in the back end system. While operation was suspended on that problem, another could be undertaken. As the back end made better use of the main computer's resources, a similar expansion in the use of the front end allowed several users access to the main computer at the same time. *Multiuser* technology was born.

At first cards and tapes fed these more complex systems. Then the video display terminal gave humans a much closer look at what was going on and large collections of terminals were connected to a host computer through a front end processor—the advent of terminal-to-host or slave/master computer networks. Figure 1.9 shows the basic terminal-to-host network.

FIG. 1.9
Terminal-to-Host
Network.

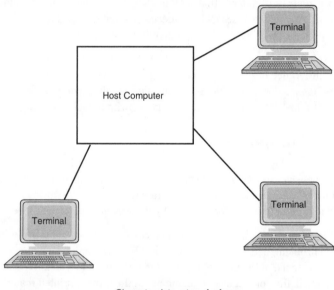

Character data rates of a few
kilobits per second

During the 1960s, terminal-to-host networks grew rapidly. Mainframe computers became giant devices often doing small tasks. Statistical research in several installations showed that machines capable of solving the most difficult calculations of science in seconds were primarily being used for rudimentary word processing. The power of machines increased as size and cost decreased. The minicomputer appeared already designed for multitasking and multiuser applications. But the concept of one master device connected to tens or hundreds of slaves persisted. The logic of the central machine was shared among all the terminals that could do nothing without the host.

The Birth of Microcomputers

The mid-1970s saw growth of a new technology; one that was not forecast by many seers and actively shunned by most major computer companies. The microcomputer began, in the view of many, as a toy assembled from parts by electronic hobbyists. Clearly it had no practical business use and would go the way of the hula hoop or CB radio—just a fad.

But some companies took the microcomputer seriously, spending large amounts of research and development money on its future. Xerox was one of those most farsighted. At its Palo Alto Research Center, Xerox built very advanced microcomputers. Careful study implied that the costs of many peripheral devices, such as disk drives, and printers would be much greater than could be justified for a single microcomputer. This research found the primary advantage to computers in their capability to process large quantities of information and make it available to other computers.

Xerox Sees the Future, Then Overlooks It

It is one of the major ironies of the computer industry that Xerox created a great deal of the fundamental technology for distributed microcomputer networks, yet Xerox failed to profit or become a market leader in the field. Xerox developed the *Ethernet,* the first well-defined, effective, and widely accepted local area network. Xerox developed the graphical user interface generally known as the *desktop* and the mouse pointing tool for it. Xerox developed the *clearinghouse,* a naming and database convention that keeps track of everything in a complex network. Xerox did much of the initial research on microcomputers. Each of these developments was adopted by major segments of the industry and led to substantial profits for other companies. But Xerox never became a major player in the revolution. Scientific and engineering foresight does not ensure business and marketing success.

Distributed Computing and Networks

Linking the new microprocessors together in a communications system, a network, solves both the need to share expensive equipment and to share information. The micros can share physical devices and share information at the same time. Since the machines were stand-alone devices capable of doing substantial computing, the logic of the network was distributed among the several microcomputers. Computer networks of this sort distribute logic among several different devices, rather than confining it to one central host; they drive the revolution in wedding telephones to computers. A distributed logic computer network has a number of important characteristics:

■ **Intelligence:** Nodes on the network each have sufficient intelligence to operate independently of the network if furnished with locally attached peripherals such as disk drives and printers. Thus, each device is a computer in its own right. Because each communication point—node—is a computer; this relationship frequently is called *peer-to-peer,* in contrast to *terminal-to-host,* where the devices are not computers. In *terminal-to-host,* the devices simply are able to send and receive information to and from some connected computer.

■ **Cohesiveness:** The entire network system is cohesive so that its function is to provide capabilities that are more than the sum of the individual parts. There is an element covered by the German word *gestalt* in a network; gestalt means what I just said: the whole is greater than the sum of its parts. In the most advanced networks, unused computing power available on any processor in the system may be used to help any other machine on a complex problem.

- **Transparency:** Resources are available to any machine on the network with a high degree of transparency. Individual machines look at the network as a collection of devices, such as disk drives and printers, already familiar in stand-alone machine operation. The network extends the abilities of the individual without submerging it in a mesh of complexity. Ideally, network resources should be available by a simple name with no need to indicate location, scheduling, or other details; this simplifies network management and growth.

- **Redundancy:** Because the network consists of a large number of machines, probably of similar type, reliability should increase. Alternative sources of computing power are available over the network in the event any one should fail.

  ▶ **See** the section entitled "ISO OSI Model," **p. 41**

These characteristics imply a great deal of intelligence contained in the network structure itself, and this is the course chosen through the standard model for computer communication developed by the International Standards Organization (ISO). We'll discuss some of these standards in chapter 2.

Networks of the kind now being built are most concerned with peer-to-peer communication that requires each device be a computer in its own right. The work of Alan Turing and others on the *theory of computability* demonstrated that any discrete state machine (a fancy way of saying a digital computer, or a device that uses a method that can be reduced to conditions of true and false, one and zero) is equivalent to any other such machine. Therefore the simplest PC is equivalent to the most expensive supercomputer; all we buy in spending more for the supercomputer is the speed of its otherwise equivalent calculations. As the machines are computational equivalents, they may be engaged in *peer-to-peer* communications. Since the logic is spread around these peer-to-peer networks, it is said to be *distributed*. Figure 1.10 diagrams the basic idea, showing a network cable joining several computers exchanging various forms of information.

There are instances in such networks where communications do not utilize peer-to-peer relations. Perhaps the most frequently cited example is that of a large machine acting as a host with personal computers in a network connected physically to the host through a communications server with each PC running a terminal emulation program. Current networks often furnish this *virtual terminal* service as one of many ways machines may relate across a network.

In the past, networks were established to share the expensive central processor that would have otherwise been seriously underutilized. In distributed networks, the initial impetus was strangely similar—since there are a number of individual processors, emphasis was on sharing peripheral devices.

With large machines, the primary cost was the machine itself. With micros, the computers are often less expensive than peripherals such as high-capacity disk drives, complex laser printers, and plotters. So the economic push for networking first came from a need to share expensive physical peripherals.

FIG. 1.10

Distributed logic peer-to-peer network.

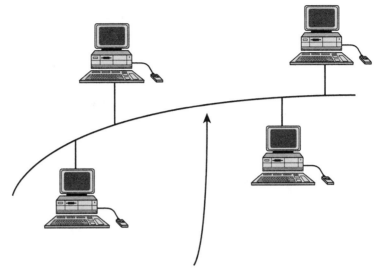

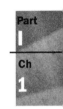

Characters, graphics, audio, video at tens,
hundreds, or thousands of kilobits per second

The cost of many peripherals has dropped substantially with each passing year, though high quality and capacity devices are often still difficult to justify on a single microcomputer basis in many applications. But the speed and convenience of information exchange over a network more than justify the cost of most networks, regardless of the economics of device sharing.

Information that otherwise would be effectively locked up in the storage units of a single machine may now be made available to every user on the system. Primary examples of such information include programs that may be used by several users at the same time and by shared databases. There are concerns about inadvertent destruction of the data in a network, but these concerns can be handled with appropriate software.

Electronic mail in a network offers a major advance in the means of doing business. Because mail messages are created at the convenience of the sender and reviewed and answered at the convenience of the receiver, substantial savings in time for all parties are realized. Users may use the mail system to prevent interruptions and schedule their work on tasks. Distribution lists allow easy notification to several users at once.

Redundancy in hardware and software as suggested in the characteristics listed above offers a degree of reliability far beyond that of a terminal-to-host system that is totally dependent on the host for all activity.

Because each machine is a computer, the power of the network may be increased or decreased in a modular fashion by adding or removing machines. There is no need to remove a machine that has become too small due to the demands on its time by more terminals. Instead, each machine can be retained and moved to appropriate positions throughout the network.

Networks are driving the future of computing. Networks that have been local in nature, or restricted to a single building or campus of buildings, must be connected over greater distances to other divisions of the organization in other cities or other countries to realize fully all the advantages of networking.

Each organization, government, school and, most importantly, each individual, now is realizing the need to connect, not just with related organizations or persons, but to any and all, anywhere at anytime. Computers are no longer simply isolated boxes of information for one entity. All computers can and will be connected to exchange information.

The resource that can connect all these computers and all these networks together is the telephone system. The telephone technology that can do this best is ISDN.

The Origins of ISDN

The first word in ISDN is *integrated* for integrated voice and data. When ISDN became available the emphasis was primarily on its use to provide Centrex-type service. Centrex is a sort of *private branch exchange* (PBX) in the telephone company's central office. A business that wants to have a flexible telephone system with a lot of telephone lines and selections on its phones has historically had three choices:

- If it is a smaller business, it could install a key set system with buttons on each telephone instrument to select lines. Originally, these keys connected to a relay device (a *key service unit,* or KSU) that made the line connections.
- If the business is large enough, it could install a private branch exchange (PBX) to handle the same function.
- Or it could choose Centrex, a system local exchange carriers sell that uses a portion of the central office switching equipment to function as a PBX even though the equipment is really at the central office location.

With the breakup of the Bell System in the mid-1980s, the attractiveness of Centrex began to fade in light of third-party PBX solutions. ISDN was in large measure designed to recapture this market for the local exchange carrier. The extension of digital signals to the business site would allow very flexible telephone functions—flexibility on a par with or better than competitive systems supplied by PBX vendors. So the 1980s saw development of ISDN telephones and central office switches with this target market of businesses that needed PBX service in mind.

The designers integrated computer communications. But phone companies and most large organizations almost always have followed what some call the military style of strategic planning. That is, planning for the last war and then losing the next by overlooking technological and social changes entirely.

The same thing happened to the initial thrust of ISDN. It failed to deliver voice service at a price that was competitive with PBX vendors who outflanked the entire design with more economical designs. ISDN, as a computer network within a business, was aimed at terminal-to-host computing that needed maybe 19.2 kbps communications. In that light, the 64 kbps of ISDN looked fantastic. But the days of hosts delivering characters to terminals were already over. Businesses needed a way to get whole files and graphics among computers communi-cating as peers. The local area network solved that problem economically at millions of bits per second around a building or campus. ISDN as a local area network was expensive, slow, and ineffective.

The original ISDN offerings had another fatal flaw: the systems were proprietary. Since the idea was to sell voice and data service within a business, there was not much need to make sure a particular company's ISDN would work with all the remaining ISDN in the world or with hardware the seller didn't manufacture or sell.

By the late 1980s, telephone operating companies were crying that there was no market for ISDN, or at best it was a niche market, so there was no need to supply it, and if it were supplied it must be at a high tariff as a special premium service. When asked why they didn't offer ISDN, they responded, "Nobody wants it." Then, of course, nobody did want it.

- It was not available;
- It was overpriced if available;
- The standards didn't fit together;
- Nobody's hardware talked with anyone else's.

The Internet and the Rebirth of ISDN

ISDN developed somewhat in countries with telephone organizations that saw benefits from its use; these were predominantly PTTs (government Postal, Telephone, and Telegraph agencies). In the United States, it took the efforts of farsighted people in organizations such as the National Institute of Standards and Technology (NIST), industry, and creative users to see a way out. These groups formed the North American ISDN Users' Forum in 1988, and in early 1992 established a standard known as National ISDN-1 (NI-1). This was quickly followed by NI-2. NI-3 is near completion. Each is a closer step to ISDN as a complete and open system with the possibility of connecting the products of any manufacturer and the signals of any carrier to those of any other using ISDN. The field has become ripe for rebirth of ISDN.

Now salespeople from hardware vendors and telephone companies roll out their newly standardized offerings. They have new phones and new computer equipment. But they are still saddled with the ideas of the past. They still think of ISDN as primarily an enabling technology for communications among a given firm's sites and with a central office for Centrex-like voice service. And now—really about mid-1994—they are hit over the head by a several-million-user gorilla: the Internet.

The explosion of the Internet upon our society and economy that only became visible to the commercial sector in 1994 is proving to be the undercurrent *killer app* churning for a decade. By 1995, it was fair to say: "If you aren't on the Internet, you aren't in business."

The Internet began more than 20 years ago as an experiment called *ARPAnet*. The United States Department of Defense wanted to find out if it was possible to build a communications system among computers that would be robust enough to harness the computing power of widely separated computers and resilient enough to survive major failures in several of its computers and links. It was assumed the network itself would be unreliable, so protections to route around failures were built in. All the computers on the network were considered peers and all the computers were given the responsibility to pass communications. See Figure 1.11, where a single small office LAN is connected to a stand-alone computer, and both are connected to a large site, with multiple LANs all using the Internet represented by the cloud. I don't know when a cloud became the symbol for a large, interconnecting network, but it is.

FIG. 1.11
The Internet.

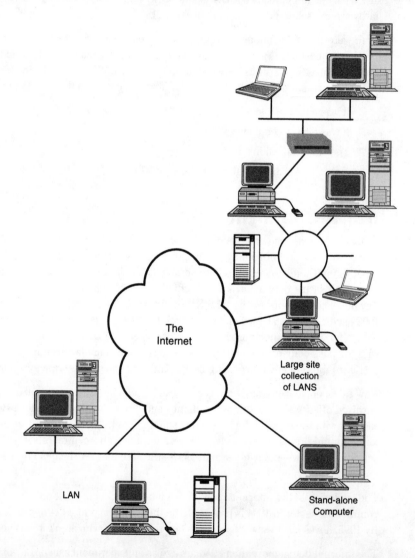

The
Internet

Large site
collection
of LANS

LAN

Stand-alone
Computer

As time went on, defense contractors and academic institutions began to attach to the Internet. With the lifting of restrictions on commercial use formerly applied to a major segment of the Internet (that portion known as NSFnet) in 1994, thousands of commercial organizations began to transact business, market, and advertise over the Internet, placing its growth on the steep slope of a hockey stick curve (see Fig. 1.12).

FIG. 1.12

Growth of the Internet.

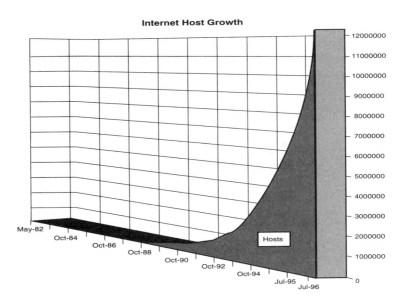

The Internet is often defined as a network of networks. It joins local area networks and individual computers into one worldwide information infrastructure. There is no central authority directing the Internet. However, there are rules governing the protocols that tie it together. Users of the Internet follow these rules, protocols, and standards for their own, enlightened self-interest. There is no governmentally enforced law that the rules be followed. But everyone knows failure to use the proper protocols in the proper way will quickly result in chaos and a useless system. Anytime someone violates a rule considered fundamental, many, perhaps thousands, of the users police the violator by devices such as *flames* (electronic mail messages pointing out the transgression). Internet service providers that establish connectivity usually terminate the connection of troublesome users to ensure continued viability of the Internet.

Why include this discussion on the Internet in a book about ISDN? What connects all of these computers together? Remember there is only one worldwide communication system that joins virtually every person to every other person—the telephone system. There is only one technology currently capable of delivering a standard, digital signal to those persons—ISDN. The irony of all this is the complete failure of ISDN designers, standards promulgators, book writers, and telephone companies to realize the demand flowing from the Internet.

All of a sudden, access to the Internet, considered in some telco planning as maybe the 20th most important source of ISDN connections, rockets to a solid number one. Plans for equipment and transmission lines go out the window in the face of multiples of anticipated demands. Tariffs demanding high prices and based on a few users are highway robbery in the face of thousands of users ready to share the cost. Remote communities whose telcos have remained in the dark ages with 40-year-old, step-by-step, mechanical switches demand immediate ISDN at the same price available in the biggest cities. In a nut shell, ISDN demand now stems from:

- The killer app of the Internet, World Wide Web with a graphical browser like Mosaic, plus multimedia elements such as sound and video, that demand the capacity of ISDN's basic rate interface (BRI) at 64 to 128 kbps making ISDN connection a virtual necessity for effective Internet usage.
- Telecommuting with all features, including video and shared applications.
- Mass defection of dedicated line and switched 56 kbps users.

This is an exciting time to be alive and participate in a technological revolution that will change the face of society, the economy, and the world so much that my youngest son, born toward the end of 1994, will see things in ways we never dreamed of only a few years ago.

From Here...

ISDN provides you with two B channels delivering 64 kbps of true digital information over the twisted pair copper wire now installed to your business or residence and connected to your local telephone company. Digital signaling provides higher data rates over these copper wires because it solves problems of noise and attenuation inherent in analog circuits. Computers are digital devices, so it is more efficient to connect to a digital telephone link than to convert to analog through a modem for the connection. Besides, most of the telephone system is already digital, with the exception of the local link to residences and businesses; ISDN makes this last few miles digital too. Using Internet with the killer app World Wide Web demands the speed of ISDN to realize the full power of network-delivered graphical interfaces and multimedia elements such as sound, pictures, and video. Telecommuting requires similar applications and the power of ISDN. See the following to find out how this all fits together:

- Chapter 2, "Understanding Standards and Regulations," explains standards and regulations that are related to ISDN. Keep an eye on this while you plan.
- Part II, "Theory and Terminology," dives into some of the technical details you'll need for a more thorough understanding of ISDN. Read it now, if you like, or skim through and jump to the next part.
- Part III, "ISDN Computer Hardware," gets to the nuts and bolts issues of ordering ISDN service, wiring it in, and selecting ISDN hardware.
- Part IV, "Software and Applications," looks at software issues, expanding your data rate by joining B channels, using video over ISDN, and issues surrounding BBS and Internet service providers.
- Part V, "The Future," jumps off into the great unknown. Things will never be the same; how will they affect you?

Understanding Standards & Regulations

As strange as it may sound, standards and regulations make both computers and telephones the really useful devices and systems they are. Think about it. If there were no standards, the computers or phones of one manufacturer probably couldn't talk with those of another. Of course, it is more complicated. When two parts of a computer are involved in communication with other computers and one part has standardization and the other doesn't, the computers usually can't communicate; it's the same with phones.

Setting standards really involves a nearly overwhelming collection of possible ways of connecting this to that in endless combination. Before we can have standards, at least effective standards that can be economically implemented for everyone, we have to have a way to talk about what is talking to what. If you're confused at this point, so was everyone a decade or so ago when there was no *metastandard* to follow in actually promulgating widely accepted ways of doing things. We'll see how this was worked out in something called the *ISO OSI Reference Model*.

The types of standards available in the marketplace and their effect on ISDN in particular

You'll learn what standards are all about and where they come from.

Standards-setting organizations such as the International Standards Organization and the International Telecommunications Union

Many of the organizations themselves are parts of other organizations; you'll learn how they all fit together.

The ISO OSI Standard Reference Model that is often called the *seven layer model of communications*

When you master this "Seven Layer Model," you'll have the key to understanding and talking about data communications.

Standards affecting ISDN, especially the standards from the International Telecommunications Union

Since ISDN is a telephone technology, all the telephone companies in the world have agreed on its form; you'll see the results of this agreement.

But standards are only part of the equation of agreements that make things work. Regulations provide another shared basis. We must consider legislation, rules, and court decisions to find out what is going on. This won't be a legal treatise, but you'd better understand that the law is deeply involved in telephony *and* whether or not you can use it *and* at what price.

An understanding of the legal context of standards and regulations is especially vital now, at least in the United States. The Telecommunications Act of 1934 has governed U.S. telecommunications for more than half a century. All the players understand it. True, many players were thrown off guard by the breakup of the Bell System in the mid-1980s, but, overall, the industry has adapted. Now, a new act is hitting—starting in 1996. This is a total rewrite of the 1934 Act, seeking, at least in its broad goals, to bring about widespread telephone competition. With this type of competition, the restraints on the Bell System imposed a decade earlier are broken; and the regional Bell operating companies (RBOCs) are beginning to rejoin one another. Will this result in real competition, or will the United States end up with a giant, unregulated monolith calling all the shots in telecommunications? Place your bets; you can't escape playing in this one.

Let's get our feet back on the ground and look at how standards are worked out today. While doing this we'll compare how the computer industry looks at networks in contrast with the telephone industry's way of seeing things. The two technologies will be growing together in the next few years through a process we're starting to call *computer telephony integration*; it's a good idea to go with the flow. ■

Types of Standards

At the dawn of computer communications, no standards existed. All networks were the products of private companies that jealously guarded their turf. It was in the best interest of each company to make sure its communication system did not connect to and interact with those of other computer companies and to keep most of the internal workings of the system secret. This strategy assured each company its customers would have to buy the company's future products on pain of being unable to exchange information with some new, different vendor's device. You could say there was a tendency to make users *true blue*.

As Bob Dylan sang, "The times they are a changin'," information about how computers worked and how they might communicate began to be of academic and business interest. Schools of computer science sprang up within the educational system. Courses in business schools began to include computer theory and practice. Business users began to ask questions their computer company representatives didn't want to answer. Questions like: "Why can't your 30 series machine talk to your 360 series machine?" and "Why can't any of your machines talk to the other guy's 660 machine?" Pressure began to build for standards that would allow connection of systems and sharing of information. This pressure gained expression through various organizations that establish standards.

There are lots of ways to look at standards, and we'll use several methods. Right now let's give names to standards based on where they come from:

- Voluntary standards
- Regulatory standards
- Voluntary standards imposed by regulation
- De facto standards
- Proprietary standards

Voluntary standards are the product of organizations that have been established to create standards. The primary examples for our topics are the International Telegraph and Telephone Consultative Committee (CCITT) and the International Organization for Standardization (ISO). ISO has a totally voluntary membership composed of designated bodies from participating nations and nonvoting observer organizations. The United States is represented by the American National Standards Institute (ANSI). CCITT is a committee of the International Telecommunication Union (ITU), a United Nations organization; its members are governments. Under a 1993 reorganization, the CCITT has been replaced by the International Telecommunication Union-Telecommunication sector (ITU-T).

N O T E The acronyms from the ITU-T often don't seem to fit because they come from the formal French names of the organizations. France led the world in establishing standards with the metric system and acted as the geographic location for physical standards until replication through atomic processes rendered meter sticks and mechanical clocks obsolete.

Regulatory standards are standards established by government departments or agencies. They are usually the product of formal rule-making procedures and carry the force of law for those subject to them. For example, the United States Department of Defense has adopted a collection of computer communication protocols (TCP/IP) that must be met by providers under military contracts.

Voluntary standards imposed by regulation are standards created by voluntary organizations and subsequently adopted by an affected or interested government department, agency or legislative body.

De facto standards are almost always the result of some company's major force in the marketplace. This force causes other organizations to accept a standard set by the dominant company. The emergence of the PC based on IBM's original designs is one of the best examples of a de facto standard. Right now MS DOS and Windows, both from Microsoft, have set the overwhelming de facto standard for personal computers; there's even the prospect of Windows NT being ported to larger machines.

Proprietary standards might look like de facto standards at first blush. But the distinguishing feature of a proprietary standard is its lack of availability to competitors of the company that created it. A de facto standard is either usable at no charge or at a cost that is nominal compared to the standard's market value. The Ethernet, though patented by Xerox, was licensed for a nominal fee and became first a de facto standard and then, with technical modifications, a voluntary standard, ISO 8802-3 or IEEE 802.3. The Macintosh computer remained a proprietary standard for over a decade until Apple decided to license its design to third parties, thereby, maybe, establishing a de facto standard.

The standards-setting organizations that impact most on computers and communications include:

- National Institute of Standards and Technology (NIST). This is a branch of the U.S. Commerce Department formerly known as the National Bureau of Standards. NIST now is leading the way in much of high technology communications. **http://www.nist.gov**

- International Telecommunications Union—Telecommunications sector (ITU-T), previously known as the Consultive Committee on International Telegraphy and Telephony (CCITT). **http://www.itu.ch**

- American National Standards Institute (ANSI) **http://www.ansi.org**

- International Standards Organization (ISO) **http://www.iso.ch**

- North American ISDN Users Forum (NIUF) **http://www.niuf.nist.gov/misc/niuf.html**

- The National ISDN Council is an organization of telephone companies and public switched network switch vendors. They have worked in conjunction with the North American ISDN Users Forum to provide standardization of ISDN.

- Federal Telecommunications Standards Committee (FTSC)

- Electronic Industries Association (EIA) **http://www.eia.com**

- Defense Communications Agency (DCA)

- Institute of Electrical and Electronics Engineers (IEEE) **http://www.ieee.org**

- European Computer Manufacturers Association (ECMA) **http://www.ecma.ch**

- Corporation for Open Systems (COS). The COS is composed of a number of computer and telephone equipment vendors. It supports the Open Systems Interconnection Model as a vehicle for creation of communications systems that are open for connection to everyone. We'll be discussing this model in just a bit. During 1994, COS sponsored the ISDN Solutions '94 project that brought together efforts at ISDN standardization.

TIP   As with many things, there is a life cycle. So it is with organizations. It's currently unclear whether or not COS continues to be a viable organization.

- Internet Engineering Task Force (IETF) establishes standards for the Internet. The fundamental protocols of the Internet are collectively referred to by two of their important members: transmission control protocol and Internet protocol "TCP/IP." The entire suite of protocols designed for the Internet has proven so versatile it has become the de facto standard for most computer communication among different types of machines and operating systems. This wide use of the TCP/IP protocol suite is true, whether or not

Internet connection is involved. As we'll see in Chapter 13, the point to point protocol PPP and its related PPP Multipoint protocol (MP) are vital to ISDN usage, especially the use of multiple B channels through a standard. **http://www.ietf.org**

- The ISDN Forum was created in early 1996. Forum members include Ascend, 3Com, Bay Networks, Intel, Motorola, US Robotics, Lucent Technologies, and Cisco. The ISDN Forum's goal is to accelerate ISDN deployment so that manufacturers can profit from equipment sales. The Forum's initial standardization thrust focused on two tasks: automating ISDN equipment installation through detection of the type of central office switch used by the telephone company, and determining the service profile identifier (SPID). Take a look at the press announcement (**http://www.att.com/press/0196/ 960123.nsa.html**) for general information.

- The Vendors' ISDN Association (VIA) was created in mid 1996. This organization seems to have grown out of concern over the original thrust of the ISDN Forum, which may be metamorphosing into VIA. VIA's initial goal is much the same: rationalization of SPIDs. However, its membership excludes any companies that could be members of the National ISDN Council, that is telephone companies and switch makers; it seems the idea is to foster standards that may in some instances be contrary to those of such companies. Time will tell what organizations are actually effective.

- Telecommunications Information Networking Architecture Consortium (TINAC) is a group of some of the largest communications and computer organizations in the world. TINAC is laying the groundwork for software to merge telecommunications, computing and entertainment. **http://www.tinac.com**

  ▶ **See** Chapter 5, "Signaling with ISDN," focusing on "Of SPIDs and Buses," for an explanation of the SPID, **p. 110**

Generally, standards work to the advantage of the user because equipment and software must be built in a manner that is open and understood. Comparisons among vendors' products may be made fairly and the possibilities of intercommunications among vendors' products are high.

The primary disadvantage of standards is the time, usually measured in years, it takes to have them approved. Sometimes the technology has become obsolete by the time it is standardized. Another problem centers on the political aspects of standards development and approval. Vendors seek to protect their interests by actively serving on or lobbying standards committees. Often a vendor delays the process to gain market advantage. Sometimes options are introduced into a standard that have the effect of destroying its utility while protecting a vendor's ground. All this said, recognize that the standards being established now for our communications are turning out to be a great help.

ISO OSI Model

Let's take a closer look at the standard model that furnishes the basis for everything else we'll do in telephone and computer networks. Please meet the Reference Model of Open Systems Interconnection.

Part

I

Ch

2

This model is the product of years of work by many organizations. The results have all been compiled by the International Standards Organization and are often known, for those of you with a crying need for yet another acronym, as the ISO OSI model.

This standard is called a *reference model*. It is a form to be followed in the design of actual systems that will be implemented. It specifies the functions that are to be fulfilled at each level in communication between telephone systems, computers, or telephone systems and computers. After years of carefully analyzing processes involved in communications, the standards-setters arrived at seven layers that are thought to be adequate to encompass all communications functions. See Figure 2.1.

FIG. 2.1

ISO OSI standard reference model.

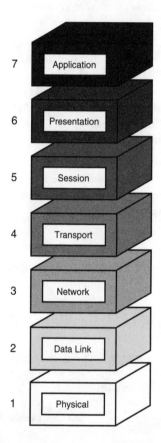

7   Application

6   Presentation

5   Session

4   Transport

3   Network

2   Data Link

1   Physical

The whole idea of the model is to provide a common ground for design of standard implementations, enabling the interconnection of many systems. The model also gives a way of looking at existing standards that aids in fitting them into the overall scheme of open systems.

The hooker in all this is that while the model suggests a conceptual way of designing a communication technology, it does not govern or mandate a particular implementation of the model. So a company may design a telephone or computer system that performs the functions outlined and places the functions in neat little layers. But this is not enough to make the implementation open. Others must agree to design in accord with the implementation. The OSI ISO model makes it easier to interoperate; it does not guarantee interoperation.

Layering is the trick that makes it all work. Think of each of the numbered and named layers as black boxes. You don't know what goes on inside the boxes (unless you have to make the box). But you do know what the box is supposed to do, its functions, and what goes in and comes out (its interfaces).

Part

I

Ch

2

If you're a programmer, each layer in the model is like a program specification with the functions of a module and its input/output parameters given. The programmer's job is to make the box meet the specs; no one else should be concerned with how. The basic rules for the layers are:

- Each layer represents a different level of abstraction; the lowest layers are more concrete, the higher more abstract.
- Each layer contains well-defined functions that are closely related.
- Interfaces, boundaries, between the layers are clear and offer a place to collect and define the information that must flow between adjacent layers.

Figure 2.1 is a sketch of what the model is all about. Consider the interior of each box to be unknown. When communication is initiated by an application running on a device, the information starts flowing from the top down through each layer and comes out the bottom. This application could be a word processing program on a computer or a voice spoken into a telephone.

Visualize a cable connecting the bottom of one model to the bottom of another. The information created flows from the original device through the cable and enters the second device, starting at the bottom, and works its way up to the top. Figure 2.2 shows two devices connected and communicating.

The whole trick to this is realizing the real power of the model in releasing us from any need to think about what goes on in any one of the boxes (unless it is our job to design the inside of that box). All we really care about is whether or not the boundaries (buzzword, *interfaces)* between the layers are known and properly defined. If they are, then different persons and organizations may design different layers using totally different technologies and still be sure they will fit together and pass information correctly.

FIG. 2.2

Two devices communicating over the ISO OSI model.

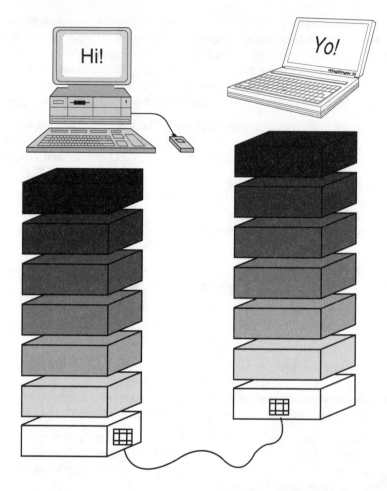

Figure 2.3 shows little plugs and sockets drawn between the layers to furnish an analogy of this process. When the plugs and sockets fit together, information passes; when they do not, it does not. With that in mind, let's take a look at what the model requires *functionally* at each layer.

■ **Layer 1:** The *physical layer* is concerned with transmitting raw bits, electrical impulses, light, and radio signals over a communications medium—for example, a cable. The primary concern of a designer for this layer is mechanical and electrical, or optical, matters. Specifications for wave shapes, signaling rates (so many bits per second), cables and connectors are involved in this layer.

■ **Layer 2:** The *data link layer* takes the bits passed by the physical layer, and creates and recognizes *frame* boundaries; by this technique it transfers units of information to the other end of the physical link. Frame is not the term used by ISO. Its terminology is "physical-layer-service-data-unit; frame will do quite well for us, thank you. This layer is sandwiched between layer three "network" above and layer one "physical" below. Several additional functions may be included, depending on the network. Layer two also contains the rules governing access to the network cable, *media access control*. These are the rules that are followed to move information into and out of the medium.

▶ **See** "ISDN Physical Layer," **p. 84**

▶ **See** "ISDN Data Link Layer," **p. 86**

FIG. 2.3

Interfaces among ISO OSI model layers.

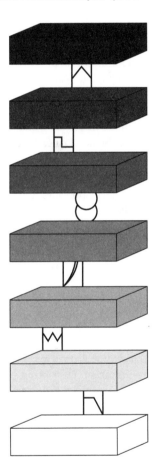

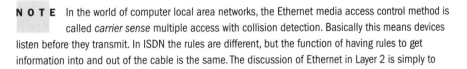

N O T E In the world of computer local area networks, the Ethernet media access control method is called *carrier sense* multiple access with collision detection. Basically this means devices listen before they transmit. In ISDN the rules are different, but the function of having rules to get information into and out of the cable is the same. The discussion of Ethernet in Layer 2 is simply to

continues

continued

relate a commonly known computer network standard to similar issues in the ISDN world. The explanation is certainly not intended to be complete; that would take considerably more space than justified for our subject. ■

■ **Layer 3:** *The network layer* controls operation of subnetworks that might intervene between the two communicating devices. This layer routes information among different networks. Now our model is becoming more complex. Here we're not involved with a single network; rather, we are connecting one network to another using an intervening network. In a stand-alone personal computer network, this layer would not be used. Connection to outside networks would bring it into play. Connection of two distinct networks through the public telephone system is an illustration of communication involving an intervening network. *Internetwork* is the proper term, where layer 3 functions would be invoked. Figure 2.4 shows this. Notice that the telephone network only involves layers one through three. As a general rule, the core of ISDN that carries our information only involves these first three layers. However, special functions, such as telephone features, may involve higher layers.

■ **Layer 4:** The *transport layer* splits up information into appropriate sizes (segments information) so it will fit into packets of the right size for the networks being used. In many cases it ensures all the packets arrive at the other end without errors, and are assembled in order and without duplication. Therefore, it provides end-to-end data integrity and quality of service.

▶ **See** "ISDN Network Layer," **p. 86**

▶ **See** "Packet Switching," **p. 86**

N O T E Oops. I've thrown around the terms *packet* and *frame* a bit now and not explained them. If you don't know the words, just consider them as ways of saying the information is stuffed into an electrical envelope of certain dimensions. It can only be so big. If your message is too large, it has to be cut up (segmented) to fit in a stream of several packets. The transport layer's job is to break up and number the packets at the transmitting end and reassemble them in message order at the receiving end. Strictly speaking, the *frame* involves all seven layers and encloses the packet. The *packet* contains only layers three through seven. The terms packet and frame are frequently misused. To determine exactly what you're talking about requires analysis of the contents, layer by layer. I hope you're beginning to see the value of understanding the layered concepts in the ISO OSI model. ■

■ **Layer 5:** The *session layer* controls the establishment and continuation of a particular communication between devices. It coordinates interaction between end-application processes, keeping the two devices talking to each other and maintaining a connection. Most of the telephone usage we are talking about here uses such connection-oriented operation. In some cases, communication proceeds without a connection. X.25 packet communication is such a technique that is supported within ISDN. We'll look at X.25 a bit in Chapter 3, "Defining Narrowband ISDN."

FIG. 2.4
Internetworking.

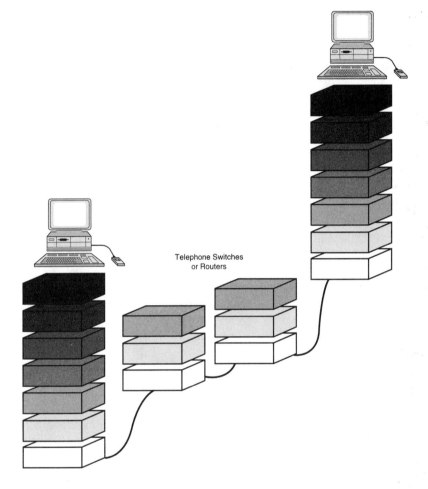

Telephone Switches
or Routers

■ **Layer 6:** The *presentation layer* performs conversions on information. These include conversion of code sets, encryption, text compression, and protocol conversion for virtual terminal communication. File formats that differ between devices may also be translated by this layer. If you have an IBM PC, it thinks in the codeset ASCII where the letter A is 100001. When it communicates with an IBM mainframe, there's a problem because the mainframe thinks in EBCDIC where A is a different binary sequence. The presentation layer works this out. For our telephone issues, this layer is involved in *compression*; a method of getting much higher effective data rates for text and other simple data by squeezing out spaces and analyzing redundant string forms.

■ **Layer 7:** The *application layer* contains the final particulars required for programs to communicate. This layer establishes means for making the network appear transparent to user devices, joining the communications stream to the individual device. At the very top of this seventh layer, the actual applications processes are running. These could be programs doing the desired work or persons having a conversation on the phone.

If you have the feeling you understood what was going on when you dug in at layer 1, but were totally lost by layer 7, don't feel alone. The level of abstraction increases exponentially as you go up.

TIP Use the ISO OSI model as a tool every time you look at anything in communications. Ask yourself where in the model the hardware or software in question functions. In particular, ask vendors where their products fit; a surprising number of reps don't really know, but will tie the issue down for you through their technical staffs. Often you'll save yourself a lot of time you would have spent chasing after products that really don't solve your problems. After a while, thinking in terms of the layers will become second nature to you and will be your first question.

Standards Affecting ISDN

At this point, we could really dig deeply into a collection of hundreds, no thousands, of standards numbers and letters. It is important to be at least inoculated against the main ones because you'll run into them again and again as you use ISDN. But the majority of ISDN standards proper, while interesting, are not subject to much discretionary action on your part. (That's a politician's way of saying "you can't change 'em and you have no choice, so why bother?") So you really only need to dig into the details of a few standards; in most cases you'll have to make a decision or two on those few, and we'll be looking at them with those prospective decisions in mind.

ISDN Standards Proper

Let's start off by looking at the ISDN standards created by folks in the telephone world. These are the ones you have little control over, but need at least a smattering of exposure to so you can avoid total confusion.

CCITT (now the ITU-T) work on standards for a digital telephone system begun in the 1960s. As time went on, a number of committees and working groups developed the idea. As the 1980s began, enough had been defined for manufacturers to actually design and build equipment. Unfortunately, the standards still were not complete or consistent, so interoperability and other major issues were not solved. ISDN made its first, and false, start as an answer to PBX vendors. Remember the history covered in the first chapter? ISDN didn't sell.

In the years that followed, the core standards of ISDN gradually were completed. The name of the organization changed from CCITT to ITU-T in 1993; for our purposes, it's all the same. The I-Series recommendations embody that core. The standards break down into six sets:

- **I.100 General Concepts:** Explains what ISDN is about.
- **I.200 Service Capabilities:** Describes the services actually provided to users. These services are telegraphy, telephony, data, teletext, facsimile, videotext, and message handling.
- **I.300 Network Aspects:** Outlines the way the network provides the services to the user.

■ **I.400 User-Network Interfaces:** Specifies the physical configuration for ISDN equipment, transmission rates, and protocols.

■ **I.500 Internetwork Interfaces:** Explains how an ISDN system connects to a system using an earlier technology.

■ **I.600 Maintenance Principles:** Provides for service and network testing.

A detailed listing of titles of these recommendations would go on for several pages, and I promised not to drown you in standards you won't be making any decisions on. So let's just take a short look at the general description of ISDN in I.120.

▶ **See** Appendix A, "World Wide Web References for Standards and Organizations," **p. 573**, for a reference to these standards.

Part
I
Ch
2

N O T E   *In Recommendation I.120 the ITU-T explains the broad outlines of ISDN:*

1 Principles of ISDN

1.1 The main feature of the ISDN concept is the support of a wide range of voice and non-voice applications in the same network. A key element of service integration for an ISDN is the provision of a range of services using a limited set of connection types and multi-purpose user-network interface arrangements.

1.2 ISDNs support a variety of applications, including both switched and non-switched connections. Switched connections in an ISDN include both circuit-switched and packet-switched connections and their concatenations.

1.3 As far as practicable, new services introduced into an ISDN should be arranged to be compatible with 64 kbps switched digital connections.

1.4 An ISDN will contain intelligence for the purpose of providing service features, maintenance, and network management function. Their intelligence may not be sufficient for some new services and may have to be supplemented by either additional intelligence within the network or possibly compatible intelligence in the user terminals.

1.5 A layered protocol structure should be used for the specification of the access to an ISDN. Access from a user to ISDN resources may vary, depending upon the service required and upon the status of implementation of national ISDNs.

1.6 It is recognized that ISDNs may be implemented in a variety of configurations according to specific national situations.

2 Evolution of ISDNs

2.1 ISDNs will be based on the concepts developed for telephone IDNs [integrated digital networks] ISDNs may evolve by progressively incorporating additional functions and network features, including those of any other dedicated networks. Among these network features are circuit switching and packet switching for data, providing for both existing and new services.

2.2 The transition from an existing network to a comprehensive ISDN may require a period of time extending over one or more decades. During this period, arrangements must be developed for the interworking of services on ISDNs and services on other networks.

continues

continued

2.3 In the evolution toward an ISDN, digital end-to-end connectivity will be obtained via plant and equipment used in existing networks, such as digital transmission, time-division multiplex switching, and/or space-division multiplex switching. Existing relevant recommendations for these constituent elements of an ISDN are contained in the appropriate series of Recommendations of CCITT or CCIR.

2.4 In the early stages of the evolution of ISDNs, some interim user-network arrangements may need to be adopted in certain countries to facilitate early penetration of digital services capabilities. Arrangements corresponding to national variants may comply partly or wholly with I-Series Recommendations. However, the intention is that they are not specifically included in the I-series.

2.5 An evolving ISDN may also include switched connections at bit rates higher and lower than 64 kbps. ■

I think the writers did a good job of spelling out the elements of ISDN. Let's touch on a few issues and define some concepts at the same time.

▶ **See** "Switching," **p. 24**

1.2 talks about *switching*. This is pretty clear. When you call someone on the phone the telephone equipment takes your telephone line and switches it so it connects to the phone of the person you're calling. But what is a *non-switched* connection? In this case, the phone company makes a permanent tie between your phone and another; the line, in telco jargon, is *nailed up*. This creates a *dedicated connection* between the two.

There are two ways to do switching:

■ Circuit switching
■ Packet switching

When *circuit switching* is used, a communications channel is set up when the calling session begins and stays connected during the entire time of the call. When the call is completed, the channel is released for others to use in different switching arrangements; but, during the call, the full capacity of the circuit is devoted to your call, whether or not you or the other party are actually saying anything. Using a circuit switching method, the system must establish the circuit, transfer the signal during the call, and break the connection by disconnecting at the end of use. This is the traditional voice telephone method.

Packet switching—the movement and routing of information packets—works in a totally different way. The easiest way to understand how it works is to use the postal system as a model.

When posting a letter, first you gather the information to be sent (data) and put it in a form that the other person can read, characters printed on a sheet of paper. Then you put the letter in an envelope and write your return address (sender's address) and the destination address (recipient's address) on the outside of the envelope. You place the proper amount of postage on the envelope and may request special services such as certified mail. Then you drop the envelope into a post box, where it is mixed up with a number of other envelopes going to many different places. It next finds itself in a truck bound for some central sorting area. There it's scrambled with thousands of other envelopes, shot down seeming miles of conveyor systems, pitched into canvas carts, dumped into a cargo container that's loaded in an aircraft hold, flown across the country…until the process reverses at the destination post office and the friendly postperson shoves it into your mail box.

Picture the packet as the envelope and its contents. Within the communications system, the packet can travel among all the intervening telephone exchanges. The packet independently advises each exchange of the destination sought as the exchange equipment reads the address information. When the equipment determines the destination from the address, it routes the packet to the next exchange until it arrives at the exchange directly connected to the destination. There the exchange places the packet on the cable leading to the destination.

Figure 2.5 shows an idealized form of such a packet. In fact, this is a frame as I mentioned in the previous note. See how the packet is enclosed. The flags at each end say, "Here's a frame," and "There goes a frame." Addresses of both sender and recipient are in the address field. The control field carries some overhead specific to the network protocol being used. The real information is within the information field. The frame check sequence is a number created by the sending equipment doing some complex arithmetic on the frame contents. At the receiving end, the equipment runs the same arithmetic on the received contents. If the results agree, the packet most probably got through unscathed; if they don't agree, something has been scrunched and a retransmission will be requested.

N O T E Now it's time to discuss the packet versus frame issue. Strictly speaking, the frame encapsulates the packet. The packet is information carried within the frame. The frame is concerned with ISO OSI layers one and two, the physical and data link layers. These include the addresses of the transmitting and receiving devices. All information higher, starting with layer three, the network layer, and beyond constitutes the packet proper.

The real trick in packets is the fact that each one carries the addressing. There is no need to depend on the system providing a physical, end-to-end circuit independent of other traffic. A large part of the reason we use circuit switched systems is to isolate the communicating parties from one another. If all were put on a single circuit, they would interfere because circuit traffic does not contain any way to distinguish among the different conversations going on simultaneously. Packets, because they contain addressing, do this automatically. We can have a number of different conversations among several unrelated parties and none interfere with any other. Equipment is designed to select only those packets for a particular destination specific to each party.

Oh, there's one more major trick. We make the packets of a limited size, a few tens to a few thousands of bytes in length. That way the amount of time a packet takes going by a point in a system operating at many thousands or millions of bits a second is very small. And that means the packets of a large number of users can be interleaved within a given physical transmission link, like a cable, and everyone thinks they have their own dedicated circuit. The fact is the reverse. The packets are switched by the action of the packet addressing system sensed by the electronics at the telephone exchanges. No circuit from one user to another is ever physically established. This results in a much more efficient use of transmission cable resources because we can have a lot of users wedging their communications together.

FIG. 2.5

Idealized packet
encapsulated in a
frame.

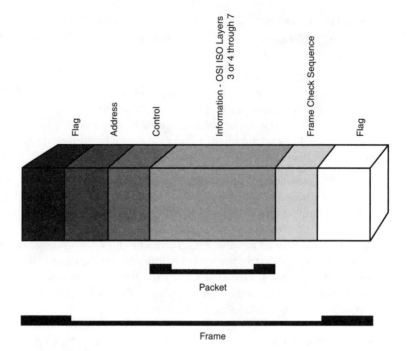

Packet

Frame

When all the math and experiments are run, it turns out that voice communication, because it requires a fixed bit rate to transmit the voice and usually proceeds rather continuously during a conversation, is best handled by circuit switching. On the other hand, computer information is almost always bursty in nature; computers grab a lot of information from the network and then chew on it for a while. Here packet switching is most efficient because other users can take advantage of the quiet times in any given session. The protocols established for a packet system take care of letting others share the time. Protocols are the rules of the road, the laws of packet exchange. Protocols are sort of like a standard language. Since we're speaking English, we follow the rules of the English language to be sure we can understand one another.

Figure 2.6 shows packets traveling across interconnected networks. The full seven layer model at each end represents the devices and software that are communicating. The application process on the machine at the left inserts information it wants to send (let's say it's a word-processing document). As this information goes down from layer seven, each layer adds more information to assist in the communication. Finally, the whole packet is encapsulated in a frame at layer two and converted to a series of electrical or optical pulses at layer one.

This travels to the next stack of three layers. This device is a part of the intervening networks. Computer people would consider it a router because it is concerned with the first three layers of the model. In the telephone world, it is a switch. It accepts the packet, examines it up through layer three and determines where to send (route) it next. This continues until the packet arrives at the other communicating device, where it proceeds up through the seven layers with information stripped off at each layer. Finally, the document appears at layer seven and is passed to the word processing program.

FIG. 2.6
Packets crossing a
series of interconnected
networks.

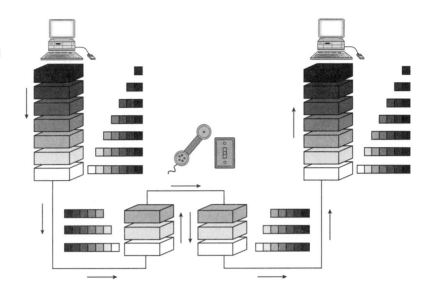

Look at how each layer is mirrored in the packet and each layer in both end devices strips the packet "fields" with information for it. Each pair of layers on the end devices is in communication with its twin at the other end. When you grasp this diagram, you grasp the entire communications technology, including the basis for understanding the next steps in speed, frame relay, and asynchronous transfer mode (ATM).

▶ **See** "Frame Relay," **p. 522**

▶ **See** "Asynchronous Transfer Mode (ATM)," **p. 529**

Frame relay and ATM are neither fully circuit switching nor fully packet switching. These new modes that have developed along with ISDN offer more efficient means of handling both voice and data traffic. For that reason, they are a part of the future as data rates and we move into broadband ISDN. Their place is covered in Chapter 18, "Anticipating Broadband ISDN."

Just to be complete, here are a few other important Q series standards that affect use and control of ISDN for the user. You'll see these mentioned frequently.

Your Tax Money at Work?

The detailed standards, and all of the ITU specifications, are available from **http://www.itu.ch.** But, despite the fact that ITU is a part of the United Nations and that the tax dollars of all member nations support the UN and ITU; there is a fee (measured in thousands of US dollars) to use this resource. I suggest you exercise whatever influence you can to remove such absurdly high fees whenever any governmental, or quasi-governmental, entity attempts to levy such fees. The governments of many countries are now placing their laws, regulations, court decisions, etc. on the Internet. In many cases, citizen pressure overcomes attempts to extract high fees. In the meantime, other sources, such as the books mentioned in the bibliography, especially those by William Stallings, contain detailed information on the most important standards.

continues

continued

You may also order the standards in paper form from the ITU for a fee. It appears the ITU fears a loss of revenue from paper sales and attempts to make up any possible lost revenue with Internet access fees. In addition, various commercial firms reprint and sell the standards, all too frequently, at rather high prices.

- **Q.920:** ISDN User—Network Interface Data Link Layer—General Aspects. This defines the second layer protocols used for communication with you.
- **Q.921:** ISDN User—Network Interface Data Link Layer Specification. More of the same.
- **Q.930:** ISDN User—Network Interface Layer 3—General Aspects. This talks about the network layer issues of communication over ISDN.
- **Q.931:** ISDN User—Network Interface Layer 3 Specification for Basic Call control. You'll hear this one cited frequently. The question is almost always how much can a given piece of hardware or software communicate with ISDN to make things happen using Q.931.
- **Q.932:** Generic Procedures for the Control of ISDN Supplementary Services. Again more control; we'll see what a lot of these services are in Chapter 4, "Choosing Services."

Non-ISDN Standards That Make a Difference

It would be interesting to go on and on about ISDN standards, but for the most part your decisions on them center on ordering ISDN services, the subject of Chapter 7. So we'll move on to other standards that are important and that can seriously affect your use of ISDN. Many of these are covered in context in the coming chapters. This section just pulls them together so you can get a feeling for how the big picture looks.

API Family   TAPI, TSAPI, CAPI, WinISDN are all application program interfaces (API) that concern how an application running on your computer can talk to the telephone system and make things happen. Some of the hardware and software you may be considering may support one or more of these. Often, support for appropriate APIs will be important for your decision. Chapter 6, "Unscrambling APIs," deals with these issues. In the ISO OSI model, these APIs fit in at layer seven, the application layer, and talk all the way down to layers two and three, where most of ISDN resides.

Network Drivers   In many instances, a computer card designed to plug into ISDN will communicate with the computer by using standards developed for local area network cards. The most widely developed standards are *Open Data-link Interface* (ODI) developed by Novell and *Network Driver Interface Specification* (NDIS) developed by Microsoft and 3Com. Because these drivers are so well understood, it makes it simple for software authors to use the cards. In this case, the driver fits between layer three (network) and layer two (data link) of the ISO OSI Model.

Rate Adaption V.110 and V.120 are standards of the ITU-T that govern what a system should do when the data rates offered by ISDN can't be matched by the device. To make this happen, bits must be added to the transmission to make, say, a 19.2 kbps data stream from your computer's serial port fit into a 64 kbps B channel.

TIP Is it "Adaption" or "Adaptation?" The original work was done in Europe, where advanced engineering and efficiency favor "adaption." In the United States, laid-back Southern influence has added an additional syllable, you all.

V.110 is most widely used in Europe. It carries asynchronous data rates from 2.4 to 19.2 bps and synchronous rates of 48, 56 or 64 kbps. V.110 does not support any error correction. So any corrections must be handled by higher, therefore slower layer protocols. V.110 has not become popular in North America.

V.120 is a more robust protocol. It is based on Link Access Procedure for the D channel (LAPD or sometimes LAP-D), a protocol that is also at the basis of ISDN D channel signaling. This design allows V.120 to multiplex B channels on ISDN; multiplexing provides a means of tying several channels together to send a common communication. V.120 is becoming popular in North America as the method of adapting the rate of an asynchronous serial port on a computer to ISDN.

N O T E We could now spend a considerable time discussing synchronous versus asynchronous. Let's cut to the chase. Asynchronous communication consists of a short series of bits, usually seven or eight, surrounded by "stop bits" that tell the receiving computer when to start and stop counting bits and therefore when it has received a byte. Therefore, asynchronous communications embeds its timing within every few bits. Synchronous communication sends perhaps thousands of bits with no internal information telling how to break those bits up into meaningful information, bytes. It relies on some form of external clocking, synchronizing, or signal to keep the transmitting and receiving machines in lock step. ▓

TCP/IP It's a fair bet you've heard of TCP/IP. This is shorthand for Transmission Control Protocol/Internet Protocol. TCP/IP is a large collection of standards developed over the last 20 years through the joint efforts of the United States government, government contractors, the military, and the academic community. TCP/IP is the foundation of the Internet; as a result, it is available to run on every computer that has any economic presence today. TCP/IP was developed prior to the ISO OSI model, so it does not fit perfectly into the layers. As a rough rule, TCP is a layer four, transport protocol, and IP is a layer three, network protocol.

▶ **See** "The Internet and the Rebirth of ISDN," **p. 33**

When you say TCP/IP, you don't really mean just those two protocols. You include a whole suite of others that operate up through and including layer seven, application. For example, there is File Transport Protocol (FTP), Simple Mail Transport Protocol (SMTP), and on and on. Standards regarding TCP/IP are developed by the Internet Engineering Task Force (IETF) and distributed as a part of the Requests for Comment (RFC).

So far as ISDN is concerned, TCP/IP is important for two reasons:

- Internet access. The whole of Internet uses TCP/IP. When you connect to the Internet from a remote site using ISDN, you will probably be using Point-to-Point Protocol (PPP), a member of the TCP/IP family.

- Tying together two (or more) B channels may be effected using the Multilink Point-to-Point Protocol (MPPP or MP. The acronyms seem to vary even within the IETF committee itself). This tying channels together goes hand-in-hand with the PPP Compression Control Protocol (CCP) specification for compression over PPP. These standards are among the most important of the TCP/IP standards, so far as use of ISDN is concerned. These standards provide a widely accepted method of joining multiple B channels with ISDN. In the past, you had to use proprietary methods. The industry has now come to an agreement on channel aggregation and compression. This issue is covered in more detail in Chapter 13, "Tying It Together: Two B or Not Two B." (I know it's a bad pun; forgive me, Bill Shakespeare, or whoever wrote all those plays and poems.)

X.25   X.25 is the most widely used packet switching standard. It is important to you because in North America you can use X.25 on B or D channels for ISDN. In some cases, such as credit card verification, use of the D channel for X.25 gives you more communications capacity without disturbing the channels you usually use for communication, the B channels. As long as your X.25 traffic is quick, small, and infrequent, this may be a good choice. But some tariffs are designed to charge outrageously for such activity. Check it out carefully.

H.320   H.320 covers a collection of standards from the ITU-T that governs video conference systems. Most companies providing theater, room, or desktop video conference equipment have adopted H.320 as the means of communication with different vendors' systems. We'll talk more about this in Chapter 14, "Pictures and Video with ISDN."

Okay, that's enough on standards for now. I hope this has given you sufficient perspective to at least catch the buzzwords when they come up. In many cases we'll return to some of these standards in the context of use; consider yourself vaccinated.

Regulations Affecting ISDN

All the technical standards in the world won't make a telephone system work in today's legal world. So now we'll talk about telephone regulation.

Brief

Have you ever wondered what lawyers carry in their briefcases? Briefs of course. (I'll ignore another obvious pun.) If you've ever seen a legal brief, you'll understand the meaning of "oxymoron."

Historically, telephones were considered monopoly businesses. As a result, governments reacted by:

- Taking over the systems and running them as a government agency. I'll leave it to your politics to determine how that works out; unless of course you've traveled in a country that has such a Postal Telegraph and Telephone (PTT) agency—about 95 percent of the world's countries. Then you don't need politics, you just need a phone.
- Creating a complex antitrust structure regulating monopoly to prevent the telephone companies from taking over the country. Again, I'll leave it to your politics on how this has worked out. You probably can get a phone, but for how much?

The regulated monopoly scheme is used in Canada and the United States. Alexander Graham Bell jumped back and forth between the two countries after he left Scotland. Telephone development leaped forward in both when he beat his nearest competitor to the patent office by only a few hours. Both countries have generally followed the "private" sector route. In the United States, AT&T, as the historic parent of the Bell System, has always been a private sector organization.

In any case, regulation of telephone companies comes from several sources:

- Statutes passed by legislative bodies, such as the U.S. Congress and the Parliament of Canada
- Statutes passed by the legislatures of the states and provinces
- Rules and regulations made by administrative organizations created by legislative bodies
- Ordinances of local governments
- Administrative hearings and court cases

Laws and court cases that do not even specifically address communications may have a profound effect on establishment of communications industry standards and development of markets. Antitrust laws are the best example; consumer protection laws are another.

Since we need to start somewhere, and this chapter is already longer than planned, I'll jump from Mr. Bell and his invention to the 1960s; nothing much happened between. "The Phone Company" tried to take over the country. The U.S. Department of Justice said no. The Communications Act of 1934 established the Federal Communications Commission, and the Age of Aquarius dawned.

Carterfone   1968: *Carterfone Device in Message Toll Telephone Services,* 13 F.C.C.2d 420, *recon. denied,* 14 F.C.C.2d 571 (1968) is the landmark case breaking through the wall erected by Bell to prevent attachment of what we now call customer premises equipment (CPE). This created a whole new industry making devices that could be used with and connected to the telephone system. Prior to *Carterfone,* only telephone company-supplied equipment could be connected. With competition, technological development provided far more function at less cost than would have otherwise occurred. Let's bring it down to your computer. Without Carterphone, you'd only be able to get your modem from the phone company; I leave the data rate and price of that modem to your imagination.

Actually, there were cases before *Carterfone. Hush-A-Phone,* 20 F.C.C. 391, *reversed, 238 F2d 266 (D.C. Cir. 1956), on remand,* 22 F.C.C. 112 (1957), concerned a little plastic ring that went around the mike on a telephone handset. The purpose was to cut down noise in a crowded area. Bell argued that even this violated their absolute right *and duty* to protect the telephone network from possible damage. The FCC bought it; the appeals court didn't and reversed the FCC.

Carterfone was far more threatening to Bell because it provided a way for the handset to be placed in a cradle so the mike and earphone were next to similar devices connected to a radio transceiver. Using voice control, the caller could communicate with mobiles, thereby avoiding Bell's monopoly on radio phones. The court based its rule on the fact the means of connection did not threaten to harm the network. It was then only a short hop to hardwired connection to the twisted pair, and now we have modems and ISDN devices.

Phone Patch

The Carterfone case is especially amusing to radio amateurs who have been physically connecting the telephone twisted pair to their equipment since the early 1940s. This well-known technique was, and still is, used to provide communications to military and other persons far away from home. As a ham in the 1950s, I probably ran hundreds of "illegal" phone patches.

MCI   While *Carterfone* was going on, the application by Microwave Communications, Inc. that had been pending since 1963 finally came to a head. You probably know the company by its acronym, MCI. MCI, 18 F.C.C.2d 953 (1969), *recon. denied,* 21 F.C.C.2d 190 (1970) granted MCI the authority to operate long distance services over microwave links. The rest is history. If you don't believe it, dig out some long distance bills from 1965 and compare them with those of 1995. Thirty years later, there is several hundred percent inflation, and costs of calls dropped faster than inflation rose. It's not just technology; it's competition.

Divestiture   On November 20, 1974 the Justice Department filed its third antitrust case against the Bell System. The case was initially assigned to Judge Joseph C. Waddy, who became terminally ill prior to significant progress. By that quirk of history, Judge Harold H. Greene took over the case on his first day on the federal bench, June 22, 1978. Telephones have never been the same. Judge Greene pushed the case forward, appointed special masters and concluded the first phase of the case with an agreed judgment in 1982, *United States v. AT&T,* 552 F.Supp. 131 (D.D.C. 1982). This created the Baby Bells (or RBOCs, the Regional Bell Operating Companies), Bellcore, and AT&T as separate entities. Judge Greene has continued supervision of the case ever since. So, it seems the divestiture resulted in a career for Judge Greene and for many communications lawyers; membership in the communications bar has more than doubled since then.

Implementation of the breakup began at the first second of 1984, midnight January 1. It caused more changes in telephone communications technology than all the brilliant laboratory work and standards efforts that went before, and in a far shorter period of time. Now, the former components of the Bell System are in competition with each other, not only for directory advertising, but for other services consistent with the judgment. Over time, this competition is expected to become complete as restrictions are removed, or the former Bell System components will join together again, claiming competition from others "made us do it."

Federal Telecommunications Act of 1996   As an example of what's happening, notice that both the United States Congress and the President signed the Telecommunications Act of 1996 early in that year. This has shaken the entire structure of the telecom environment. In effect, it freed the local exchange carriers to compete in the long distance market, just as soon as each carrier provides a competitive local exchange environment for third-party entry. The local exchange carriers must cooperate with competitors, giving them access to the local loops and enabling their central offices to offer local service.

TIP   Ring up http://www.bell.com/legislation/s652final.html for the full text of the federal law. Be warned; this site belongs to the advocates of only one side of the controversy. The names they use are cloaked in transparently self-serving public relations rubric.

However, the devil is in the details. While the LEC's advertising claims that they are very open to competition, they're all down at the various regulatory bodies, including the Federal Communications Commission, inserting stalling tactics in every nook and cranny they can find.

Some LECs, for example in Texas, set all this up prior to passage of the federal law, through well-planned lobbying efforts. The new Texas telecom act, mentioned in additional detail below, specifically forbids very large interexchange carriers (telespeak for long distance carriers, and here designating AT&T, MCI and Sprint) from entering the local market through simple resale of a LEC's local loops. The Texas law requires the big long distance companies to build out a large percentage of local loops on their own.

Another "but" surfaces: but the Federal Communications Commission, and those arguing the side of the long distance companies, believe federal law pre-empts all these restrictions in state statutes.

Totally Biased Opinion

If these guys would spend their time and resources on product development and honest marketing, rather than playing "gotcha" in the legal system, we'd have 100 Megabits/second to every house and business in the U.S. at a cost of $US10/month. That great a measure of progress is essentially what's happened in the computer world over the last couple of decades. Let's get rid of the morass of special-interest regulation and use the antitrust laws to control the ones using their sheer size to bully and dominate the market.

All this said, the federal law is no panacea for the working classes (that's you and me). A lot of regulation is designed to ensure the continued use of high-grade mahogany in phone company executive suites. With competition, portions of the law balance possible loss of income to existing phone companies. Other portions speak to fair dealing in negotiations between the LECs and their prospective competitors. That should be interesting to watch!

But let's stick with just two areas: how the law affects ISDN's potential and where a ton of money might be hijacked.

Universal Service   Section 254 concerns *universal service,* that is, providing tele-communications services everywhere, and to everyone throughout the United States, regardless of location or financial means. Whew, that's a tall order. First off, it doesn't mean everyone gets free telephone service, it means:

"QUALITY AND RATES—Quality services should be available at just, reasonable, and afford-able rates." [Sect. 254(b)(1)]

This is a very important issue. It will, of course, be the basis of many arguments regarding ISDN pricing. But, in my view, the most important section follows:

"ACCESS IN RURAL AND HIGH COST AREAS—Consumers in all regions of the Nation, including low-income consumers and those in rural, insular, and high cost areas, should have access to telecommunications and *information services,* including interexchange services and *advanced telecommunications and information services,* that are reasonably comparable to those services provided in urban areas and that are available at rates that are reasonably comparable to rates charged for similar services in urban areas." [Sect. 254(b)(3) emphasis supplied]

Rural access has been a bone of contention for ISDN in every jurisdiction that has a rural popu-lation; that's most of the United States. This provision is that basis for finding a way of bringing "advanced services," among those being ISDN, to rural areas. Of course, the argument that ISDN, at least narrowband ISDN, should no longer be considered an "advanced" service, but as a basic service, should also be put forward.

Eminent Danger of Hijacking   In Chapter 16, "Putting ISDN to Work," I discuss ISDN in the schools, and I sound a caution on complex and expensive telecommunications and video solutions. A few months prior to passage of the federal law, Texas passed a telecommunications act that established the Telecommunications Infrastructure Fund and a board to distribute the $US1.5 billion (in the U.S. a billion is one thousand million, 10 to the 9th power), estimated to be available over a 10-year period. The sharks began gathering during legislative consideration. Whoever could sell gold-plated technology, including expensive telecommunications hook-ups, would make a killing.

Check out my Web site at **http://www.fc.net:80/~bryce/bangbuck.htm** to see the slides and text of my "Bang for the Buck" presentation made to the Texas TIF Board regarding these issues. The complete PowerPoint file is available by an FTP hyperlink on my site. Be sure and give me credit!

While industry representatives sold the fund as a *quid pro quo* in exchange for rate caps on "basic services," the reality is that financing of the fund is being passed through to consumers with add-on fees and threats to levy fees on, among others, Internet service providers. Beware of those in $1000 suits bearing gifts; there is no free lunch; and, by the way, what good are "rate caps" in high-technology industries where, when these rate caps are subjected to competition, the prices always go down dramatically?

"OK. OK," you say, "That's all fine for Texas, but I live in a more enlightened state (province, county, parish, riding or whatever) where that could never happen." Oops, check out that U.S. Telecommunications Act of 1996 again. Section 706 speaks to providing "advanced telecommunications incentives." This section is followed by Section 707, establishing the "Telecommunications Development Fund" (along with a board in Section 714), and then by Section 708, establishing "The National Education Technology Funding Corporation."

Do you begin to see a pattern here? Through an effort, planned for years, the telephone industry lobbied for legislation creating huge telecommunications funds and boards for their administration in each and every jurisdiction they could penetrate. These funds are, ostensibly, to aid education, libraries and medicine in design and development of telecommunications uses. But, as soon as the funds and boards are created, legions of telco marketers, to say nothing of salivating equipment-makers, are on the attack with the most expensive and often proprietary "solutions" to spend that money.

Your duty, since it's your tax money and those guys are fooling around with your kids, is to inform yourself on the most efficient way to spend that money. Only you can do that. The politicians have no idea what technology they voted for, or what the technology is. Most of the educators and medical folks don't either. Fortunately, the librarians—yes, the librarians—have been led down the path before and they are fairly well-informed. Team up with the librarians to make sure we all get the most Bang for the Buck (title of my presentation in the preceding tip); those executives really don't need to overlay rosewood on the mahogany they already have.

Your Role   The last bastion of the regulated telephone monopoly is about to fall, the local loop. ISDN will play a major part here. On the horizon loom alternative technologies that even threaten the phone companies' hold on switching and effectively do away with the bulk of need for switching. With that development, and wireless distribution, the *natural monopoly* doctrine that grounded telecommunications law will be obliterated.

N O T E   A *natural monopoly* is a monopoly that exists because it is either impossible or prohibitively expensive for competitors to enter the same marketplace. As telephones originally developed, it became apparent that a dozen companies all stringing wire everywhere could neither survive economically nor be tolerated by the citizens whose cities were becoming buried in cable. For a hundred years this logic has applied. Now, with broadband transmission, alternative rights of way already in the hands of power, cable and pipeline companies and wireless techniques just around the corner, technology has destroyed this argument. ▪

You are an important part of this change. Right now, legislatures in many states are considering major changes in their telecommunications laws. The U.S. Congress is rewriting the Communications Act of 1934 and your city council, town board, or county government may be considering issues of a local telephone or cable franchise. Every one of these legal actions will affect your ability to get, use, and pay for ISDN.

For example, in Texas House Bill 2128, a total remake of existing Texas law and the involvement of the Public Utilities Commission in telephone regulation was signed into law toward the end of 1995. ISDN is placed in the "Basket Two" (the bill's own words) of telecommunications services, making ISDN a premium, discretionary service. There are three baskets created: Basket One is for basic services, those that must be provided at most favorable rates; Basket Two is for premium and discretionary services, not mandated as universally available and provided at higher rates than calculated in basket one; Basket Three is for services in a competitive market not requiring extensive regulation.

I mention the Texas situation only to show how something like this can affect you, regardless of where you live or work. For so long as delivery of telephone service on the local loop is a monopoly, that monopoly must be regulated to assure delivery of quality services to everyone at reasonable rates. This means the rates are to be based on the company recovering its costs plus a reasonable rate of return.

But removal of a service from the basic designation under the scheme I just described, or some similar plan, places it into an area where the seller, the phone company, can charge not what the service costs plus a reasonable rate of return. Rather, it can charge based on what the company believes the service may be worth to the buyer; this is the standard of a competitive marketplace. Notice that this is highly desirable to the phone company because the vast majority of such services do not really have any, or any significant, incremental cost for addition to the customer's access. It is usually a matter of programming a computer (switch) to provide the service; it's already there. So since there is no real additional cost, anything charged is gravy. Then, if there is no competition to control the price, the telephone company has the best of all possible worlds. It's a regulated monopoly, so no one can compete with it. These "premium, discretionary" services (that often don't cost the phone company much, if anything, more than basic services) are free from regulatory control on prices.

Should ISDN be such a service? Remember, the telephone system is digital except for that last mile or two, the local loop. How does it get to be analog? Through the addition of codexs to convert analog to digital and the reverse. So it really costs more, certainly in the longer run, to supply analog. Yet the cheaper—in underlying cost—digital ISDN almost always is priced higher. Granted, the telephone company has labor and hardware expenses to install ISDN for you. I could argue they would not had they begun planning 10 years ago. But even a cursory look at installation costs and monthly service charges will show huge variations among the Baby Bells. It seems the charges are more a function of the company's vision of what would happen if they pushed (or did not push) ISDN than a realistic assessment of costs. The more optimistic a company is about acceptance and growth of ISDN, the lower installation and monthly charges. The less optimistic, the higher.

N O T E   Check out the March 25, 1996 issue of the "New York Times," in the business section. Magazine research showed a low of about $US17 for unlimited time ISDN BRI service from an Arkansas telephone company. This research also found an identical service priced at thousands of US dollars from other telephone companies. Go figure?! You don't have a copy of the "New York Times" for that day? See **http://www.nytimes.com**. ■

What's wrong with this picture? How did it get this way? Most people aren't familiar with the technology and don't know how to talk with their legislature, Congress, Parliament, public utilities commission, city council. So the only words those bodies hear come from the phone companies, who have every right to be heard. But so do you. Now you know. Now is the time to speak.

From Here...

We've covered a lot of ground. You've seen that there are several kinds of standards: voluntary, regulatory, voluntary imposed by regulation, de facto, and proprietary. We've talked about some of the standards-setting organizations, most notably the ITU-T (formerly CCITT), ISO, and especially for us, the NIUF. The ISO OSI Standard Reference Model gives us seven layers for communications; always try to plug your discussions, equipment, and software into the appropriate layer(s). Standards affecting ISDN include those specifically defining ISDN, and others, like the APIs, that are not a part of the ISDN specifications proper. Finally, we've seen that the regulatory environment affects everything we can do with ISDN, and I hope you'll take some time to learn more and follow regulatory developments as they change and affect you.

In the next part, we'll cover ISDN theory and terminology:

- Chapter 3, "Defining Narrowband ISDN," explains the details of narrowband ISDN with charts and diagrams of basic rate interface (BRI) and primary rate interface (PRI) ISDN.
- Chapter 4, "Choosing Services," tells you about the services that make up ISDN. ISDN has so much more to offer than POTS, it will take a little to sort it all out.
- Chapter 5, "Signaling with ISDN," explains how that special D channel and all these services are controlled and what happens when you ask for things from the network.
- Chapter 6, "Unscrambling APIs," gives you the scoop on TAPI, TSAPI, CAPI, WinISDN, and so on. Now you'll find out what those are and why you should care.

Theory & Terminology

Defining Narrowband ISDN

Wait a minute. What's this "narrowband" stuff? Isn't ISDN the wave of the future? Isn't the future lots and lots of bits per second? Isn't the future "broadband?" The answer is "yes and no." The future will continue to increase bandwidth. Now what's bandwidth? In a few words, bandwidth refers to the carrying capacity of a transmission system. You will hear it expressed in one or more of four units: cycles per second, Hertz, baud, or bits per second.

ISDN gives us quite a selection of bandwidths and provides control over all that capacity through the D channel. In this chapter, we'll look at how this fits together. ■

What bandwidth is and how it's measured

You'll learn it's the single most important measure of what you can do with a communications channel.

The distinction between analog and digital information and how this affects communication

You'll see why digital transmission is more economic and effective than analog.

What the ISDN Basic Rate Interface (BRI) is

You'll find out BRI is what most people mean when they are talking about ISDN and why it's the foundation of the technology.

The use of the D Channel and how it controls calling

Most people overlook the D channel when discussing how to use ISDN with computers. You'll see that the D channel really defines ISDN.

What the ISDN interfaces are

All along the way from you computers to the telephone central office you'll find places where the ISDN signal changes as it moves from one part of the system to another. Learn what these interfaces are.

Bandwidth

Cycles per second (cps) and Hertz (Hz) are two different names for the same thing. Each describes the *frequency* of the signal. Frequency speaks to the number of times a wave is repeated each second. So a single tone sound might have a frequency of 400 cycles per second or 400 Hertz. Notice the concept of "per second" is incorporated in the term "Hertz." This means the strength (amplitude) of a signal rises and falls 400 times each second; a perfect single frequency tone looks like the sine function, if you remember your trigonometry, and is called a *sine wave.* You really don't have to remember trig, just take a look at Figure 3.1.

FIG. 3.1
A single sine wave cycle.

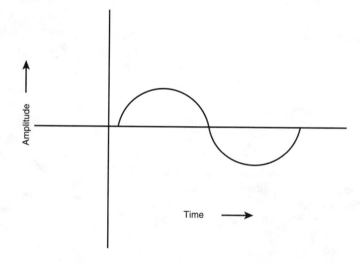

Mathematicians have demonstrated that all other "complex" waves, such as the square waves associated with digital pulses, may be analyzed into collections of sine waves (see Fig. 3.2). Thus, we specify and test our equipment and transmission lines for their capability to carry a range of sine waves from lowest to highest frequency. If this range of frequencies, bandwidth, is adequate to carry all the sine waves that make up the more complex waves needed for our communication system, it is adequate to work at the specified data rate.

FIG. 3.2
A square wave.

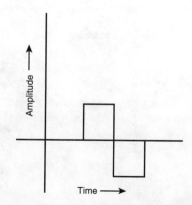

In the air, a rapid change of amplitude (pressure) vibrates air molecules and is sensed by our ears as sound. Radio and light waves vary in the same manner and are detected by electronic equipment or our eyes. For years scientists thought there was a medium that, like air for sound, carried electromagnetic waves. Near the end of the nineteenth century, experiments seemed to demonstrate that such a medium did not exist, but that waves propagate through empty space on their own. The work of Albert Einstein and others played this out and resulted in modern physics that provides a theoretical basis describing waves as traveling without an "ether" medium. To say the least, the ramifications of these theories have changed our world. Fortunately, you don't need to understand these theories to understand ISDN.

Heinrich Hertz (1857-94) was a scientist whose research demonstrated the progressive propagation of electromagnetic waves, their length, velocity, and transverse nature. Hertz showed light, heat, and radio waves to be the same phenomena differing only in frequency. Thirty or forty years ago, his name was adopted as the official replacement for the more descriptive term "cycles per second." Either "Hertz" or "cycles per second" is generally understood, but Hertz is considered the more modern term.

The baud is named after an early designer of telegraph systems. Emile Baudot (1845-1903) developed a method of encoding information on an electrical signal that led to teletype. His system of Baudot Code uses 5 bits giving 32 possible combinations; 2 to the fifth power is 32. It also incorporated a shift between letters and figures essentially doubling the total number possible. Since the shifts themselves (and several of the punctuation marks) are duplicated, the total number of characters in the Baudot code is limited to 52. Use of Baudot code has declined rapidly and computer standards, notably ASCII, have taken its place.

Development of teletype led to a need to measure the amount of information flowing in the system and the term "baud," honoring Baudot, was coined. According to Bell Labs, the electrical encoding used in such systems could only create, at most, twice as many baud as the frequency of the electrical wave. Here the problems began. A channel with an analog "carrier wave" of 3000 Hertz would have 3000 cycles per second available to carry information. Using a method of imposing two units of information on each wave, a method of "modulating" the wave, one could be said to be transmitting at 6000 baud. But modern modulation techniques are not bound by the "twice the frequency rule" and can transmit vastly more information over a typical 2400 baud voice telephone circuit using special coding methods.

 TIP A modem operating at 28,800 bits per second is in fact running at only 2400 baud! Now, you ask, why do so many people, books, and programs refer to "28,800 baud" modems, ports et al. The misuse is so common it just continues to carry forward; I know of no other reason. I suggest you eliminate "baud" from your vocabulary and use only "bits per second."

Which brings us to our final term "bits per second." This simply says that 'x' number of bits are transmitted in one second's time. That's what we want to know and that's what it measures.

▶ **See** "Broadband ISDN," **p. 526**

Now, given an understanding of bandwidth, what's the difference between "narrowband" and "broadband"? The answer really depends on the year you ask the question. A decade or so ago narrowband was an ordinary voice channel capable of carrying, at best, a few thousand bits of information per second; and broadband was capable of carrying a megabit or so per second. Now, in the current context of ISDN, narrowband includes two subscriber services: basic rate interface (BRI) offering about 128 kilobits per second of data transmission; and primary rate interface (PRI) offering about 1.5 megabits per second in North America and about 2 megabits per second in Europe. Broadband ISDN, a service not currently available in the general market, is projected to involve several tens or hundreds of megabits per second in the future. From now on, I'll usually fall into alphabet soup with kbps and mbps; and, just to keep things inconsistent, I include kbs, mbs, and other "reasonable" variations thereon.

Digital and Analog

Understanding the difference between *digital* and *analog* is fundamental to an understanding of just what is going on in most of computing and telecommunication.

Is the World Bits and Pieces or Slithery Slime?

Basically, the difference between digital and analog continues the old discussion of discrete versus continuous. The distinction centers around whether or not a given thing, activity, or whatever may forever be cut up into smaller and smaller units so that a final smallest component is reached. Such arguments speak not only of material items but also of more abstract concepts such as distance and time. Throughout history, numerous thinkers have puzzled over the concepts; see for example: Aristotle: *Physics*, Book IV, Chapter 11; Galileo: *Dialogues Concerning the Two New Sciences*, "III. Second New Science, Treating of Motion. Third Day—Naturally Accelerated Motion"; Immanuel Kant: *The Critique of Pure Reason*, "Transcendental Aesthetic, Section II." A recent exposition of the classic question was offered by Tolstoy:

> "Absolute continuity of motion is not comprehensible to the human mind. Laws of motion of any kind become comprehensible to man only when he examines arbitrarily selected elements of that motion; but at the same time, a large proportion of human error comes from the arbitrary division of continuous motion into discontinuous elements. There is a well-known, so-called sophism of the ancients consisting in this, that Achilles could never catch up with a tortoise he was following, in spite of the fact that he traveled ten times as fast as the tortoise. By the time Achilles has covered the distance that separated him from the tortoise, the tortoise has covered one tenth of the distance ahead of him: when Achilles has covered that tenth, the tortoise has covered another one hundredth, and so on forever. This problem seemed to the ancients insoluble. The absurd answer (that Achilles could never overtake the tortoise) resulted from this: that motion was arbitrarily divided into discontinuous elements, whereas the motion both of Achilles and of the tortoise was continuous." [Leo Tolstoy, *War and Peace*, "Book Eleven: 1812," Chapter I].

It would seem the new science and technology we have now is new only to the extent we have overlooked, forgotten, or never known what had been known long before:

> "What was will be again; what has been done will be done again; and there is nothing new under the sun." [The Bible, Ecclesiastes 1:9 (Jerusalem translation)].

An analog signal is created and handled in electronic circuits as if its one or more characteristics, for example strength (amplitude) or pitch (frequency), can be increased or decreased in amounts that are as large or as small as we want. There is *no quantum of quantity in the quality* we are describing as analog. Okay, that's a little too much alliteration. I'll try again. There is no smallest unit that we can divide our information into. So, a recording of music would, until very recently, use equipment designed to convert sounds received acoustically into variations in electrical frequency, phase and amplitude. These variations track the parallel and continuous variations in the air our ears perceive as sound.

If we had sensory organs that could detect the electrical variations, we could read those variations directly. We wouldn't need any code, protocol conventions or higher math to turn the received electrical impulses into what our nervous systems perceive as sound. These electrical signals would assume an unlimited number of amplitude levels, phase relationships, and frequencies. An analog transducer, such as a microphone, creates an analog stream of information in the new medium (electricity) and conveys a continuous replica of the information in electronic form.

A digital signal presumes there is a *quantum of quantity in the quality* we are describing as digital. Translation: there is a smallest unit we can divide our information into. In its most frequent use with computers, "digital logic," it implies that only two states of electrical signals are recognized: one and zero. Regardless of some variations in the electrical signals in a computer or digital transmission line due to faulty components, noise, or whatever, all are resolved into ones and zeros. This makes a digital system less prone to malfunction in many instances. As strange as it seems, it is possible to create all of mathematics from this simple "two-valued logic"; however, there is some question about how far this may go.

One, Two, Many

Alfred North Whitehead and Bertrand Russell, *Principia Mathematica* (London: Cambridge University, 1st ed. 1910; 2nd ed. 1927). This work demonstrated the derivation of numbers and mathematics within a two-valued logic using five axioms; subsequent researchers demonstrated that one axiom was not required.

Kurt Godel demonstrated that no formal system, such as that of Whitehead and Russell, could be both consistent and complete. Any system must therefore be either inconsistent or incomplete. Godel's paper is available in English: *Kurt Godel, On Formally Undecidable Propositions* (New York: Basic Books, 1962). The most readable book on these kinds of questions is by Douglas R. Hofstadter, titled *Godel, Escher, Bach: An Eternal Golden Braid* (New York: Vintage Books (Random House)—1980.

In any case, it's possible to encode sounds, pictures, and other information into a stream of ones and zeros; the whole trick of encoding otherwise analog material such as sound is the fineness of the sampling of that material. Let's say we want to encode analog sounds into digital information. We build a device that looks at the analog signal and samples it at various times. The more samples we take, the more nearly our digital pulses approximate the analog signal.

Now this seems like a lot of effort to, in effect, actually lose information. The only way we are going to get an exact replica of the analog signal is to sample it an unlimited number of times, and this would probably cost us an unlimited amount of money. Why not just stick with the analog form in the first place? Why do all of this? We prefer to use the digital form because it solves two very troublesome problems: noise and attenuation.

▶ **See** "Major Components of Telephone Systems," **p. 22**

In broad perspective, a telephone system consists of two functions: *transmission* and *switching*. Transmission involves the cables, microwave, and so on that are used to get information from one point to another. Switching involves the equipment the transmission elements are hooked to that direct signals among desired sources and destinations. The larger an analog system becomes, the more expensive and complex its transmission and switching problems. Digital techniques approach transmission and switching differently, and result in considerably less cost and complexity for telephone systems of the size we need—global. Let's look at the major problem areas in an analog system and see how they can be resolved efficiently and economically through a digital approach.

Noise

Noise is anything that does not make up the desired communication; the desired communication is called *signal*. An analog system is by its nature noisy. The first telephone systems were simple analog designs. These systems couldn't transmit sounds very far because of the *noise*. The noise floor is the very least noise that exists in our system after we've removed everything else. Our signal must be above this floor or we lose it in the noise. As the wires of those systems grew longer, more and more noise began to be heard. This noise could come from a number of sources:

- Random motion of the molecules making up the wire (heat)
- Electrical disturbances such as lightning
- Other signals flowing in parallel wires being induced onto our wires (crosstalk)
- Electrical power from adjacent equipment

On a short run, a mile or so, these items tended to stay in the background, unnoticed by, or at least not of concern to, telephone users. But, as the wires became longer, the noise level began to approach that of the signal and could no longer be ignored.

N O T E Communications engineers use the measurement of the ratio of the strength of the signal compared to the strength of the noise, the "signal to noise ratio," as a way of determining how easy or difficult it is to extract the signal from the noise. ▪

A number of techniques were adopted in efforts to overcome various types of noise. These included the use of loading coils, noise canceling circuits that reversed the phase of the noise, shielded and twisted cables, and coaxial cables. Through it all, noise gradually increased and avoidance and cancellation of noise became the bulk of the cost in long distance transmission. Worse, as the noise became stronger, the signal became weaker, attenuated, while going through the system.

Attenuation

As electrical energy travels through a conductor, it encounters resistance to its flow determined by the physical properties of the conductor. This resistance turns some of the electrical energy into heat, random molecular motion, and therefore adds to the noise. Silver has the least resistance of any generally available conductor; copper has a higher resistance, but is much cheaper and is the usual choice for cables.

The attenuation that results from the resistance affects different parts of the signal in different ways. The low frequency components are diminished a little, but the high frequency components are severely reduced. This "frequency selective attenuation" ultimately results in voices that lack most of their high notes. The high ranges contain a good deal of the information needed to understand speech. As transmission lines become longer and longer, you might hear someone's now overly bass voice at the distant end but be unable to understand the words spoken.

The remedy for a weak, selectively attenuated signal in an analog circuit is the addition of an amplifier that takes the received signal and increases its amplitude. In fact, the amplifier must increase the amplitude of the received high frequencies much more than that of the low frequencies to make the voice intelligible; *slope equalization* is the buzzword for this. But, guess what?, at the same time our amplifier is increasing the amplitude of the signal, it is increasing the amplitude of the noise. Enter ever more elaborate and expensive techniques to cancel noise and restore naturalness to the signal. Long distance and international carriers worked diligently perfecting ways to make an analog signal go great distances with low distortion and favorable signal to noise ratio. But their efforts always resulted in very expensive and complicated equipment. It was time to apply William of Ockham's razor.

Part
II

Ch
3

Bill's Razor

William of Ockham was a medieval philosopher who looked over the complicated array of convoluted explanations of how the universe worked and suggested that rather than continue with more and more complex encrustation's upon the historic explanations, one should simply apply a razor to cut off all complexity not needed and continue with the simplest theory even though it was in contradiction to tradition. Sometimes this is called the law of parsimony.

Sample our voice signal several times each second. Then for each sample assign a number representing the characteristics of the analog signal at that instant. The more times we sample, the more numbers we get per second and the closer our approximation of the original, analog, signal. Then, express these numbers in binary form and transmit these binary numbers over our transmission system. It's a miracle. Most of our transmission problems disappear. Why?

N O T E The general rule is that the sampling must be at a rate twice that of the highest frequency sought to be transmitted. For ordinary speech, the highest frequency needed for comfortable intelligibility and fidelity is often considered to be 4 kHz. So, the sampling rate is 8000 times a second. ■

Let's start with noise. Now that we know there are only two possible elements making up our digital signal, ones and zeros, we can design electronic circuits that look for only the unique electrical waveform that represents a one or a zero. This can become quite complicated, but it is at least limited to isolating only two. Contrast this with the analog environment which must consider everything received as signal unless it has other information to the contrary from complex circuits such as noise cancellers.

The same rules regarding attenuation and distortion apply to the digital signal, but we can tolerate a lot of distortion when we're looking for only two states. Since we know how to recognize a perfect one under our system's standard protocols, and we also know the thing we received, although distorted, still falls within the parameters for a one, we can create a perfect one and send it on its way down the next leg of the transmission system. So, rather than amplifying what we received, that is, increasing its strength and thereby retaining and increasing the distortion, we regenerate it; usually the device we use for this is called a *repeater.* Since we know what a perfect one is specified to be under the standard protocols in our system, and we know this thing we received, though distorted, still falls within the parameters for a one, we can create a perfect one and send it on its way down the next leg of the transmission system. *Presto,* all the distortion is gone from the signal. *Chango,* the noise disappears, because it never gave rise to either a one or a zero in our regeneration device.

Amplifier, Repeater, Regenerator

Amplifier, repeater, regenerator: Often these terms are mixed in text or conversation. An amplifier is an analog device that increases the amplitude of a received signal and to a greater or lesser extent, depending on the sophistication of its design, sends it on, noise, distortion, and all. A regenerator is a digital device that determines when a digital one or zero is received, creates a new one or zero, retimes the bit stream and sends it on its way. Unfortunately, usage in the industry is not consistent.. Sometimes a manual or company will call a box that is a digital regenerator an amplifier. Most of the time the term "repeater" refers to a regenerator; in fact repeater is the prevalent term. But sometimes repeater is used to describe what is actually an analog amplifier. When in doubt, figure out what the box is actually doing and don't rely on the often arbitrary nomenclature.

A digital signal seeks to render information to be conveyed by analysis of the information into a collection of discrete electrical signals, each either a one or a zero. Even if we had sense organs that could detect variations of electrical signals, we would not be able to perceive the message being sent because the digital signal is, by definition, not an analog of the original phenomenon. All we could determine is that a series of changes was going on through time: a string of marks and spaces, ones and zeros, frequency x and frequency y, phase 90 degrees and phase 270 degrees.

But, in and of itself, this stream would make no sense. We must have an agreed upon means of taking the ones and zeros and transforming them into something meaningful to us. We must have a protocol that tells us 1000001 is to be interpreted as "A" (in the code set ASCII, our protocol). And we must be more sophisticated. We must know when to start counting ones and zeros and when to stop, and what constitutes a package of information. Timing, synchronization, packets and frames enter the picture. All of this is a part of the standards that make up our communications system. Now let's look at the use of these concepts to improve your computer and telephone connections with ISDN.

▶ **See** "The Advantages of ISDN," **p. 15**

▶ **See** "Bearer Services," **p. 144**

Basic Rate Interface (BRI)

ISDN uses the basic rate interface (BRI) to deliver two channels of 64 kilobits/second each. These *B channels* are designed to carry the information the subscriber wants to transmit across the network. There is a third channel running at 16 kilobits/second. This *D channel* is used primarily to control the flow of information through the network. It provides call setup and teardown, network monitoring, and other overhead functions. As the D channel is separate from the B channels, the signaling is called *common channel*. This is a form of out of band signaling as it is, by definition, not in the same band as the data bearer channels.

The D channel is common to the B channels controlled. In other services, such as your plain old telephone service (POTS), information for telephone network control is carried within the same channel as that of the subscriber using a technique called *in band signaling*. You'll see below how this influences your actual use of the circuit.

Once a call is set up, the D channel is not fully utilized and may be made available for user packet traffic. Call control always takes priority over user packets, but the capacity of the D channel is ideal for such things as credit card identification and simple terminal to host sessions.

Basic rate interface ISDN delivers three separate channels for your use; 2B+D; 64 kbps, 64 kbps, 16 kbps. This is over the same pair of wires that carried only one channel of comparatively small capacity analog information with POTS.

Basic Rate Interface D Channel

Let's start with the D channel. It's the most radical departure from the analog world. In a way, the two most important things ISDN brings to the table are its inherent digital nature and the D channel. In fact, some pundits maintain that ISDN "is" the D channel. Without the D channel, you're left with the bearer (B) channels and signaling techniques that rob bits from those channels.

The Analog World   In the analog world, a telephone call is controlled in band. When you pick up the phone an *off hook signal* is sent to the central office switch which detects the condition and connects you to a dial tone indicating you may proceed to use the system. You enter various tones using the *dual tone multiple frequency* (DTMF) in band signaling available from the buttons on the phone. If you have a rotary phone, you make and break the line rapidly creating pulses that are counted at the exchange switch. In the earlier mechanical switches, the pulses actuated stepper relays that selected each successive number. In modern electronic switches, the pulses are counted and converted to DTMF signals. In fact, there is a whole mini-industry that manufactures devices to convert the pulses to tones since a great deal of the world is still tied to the rotary dial.

Makes you wonder; it takes more equipment to translate the dial pulses than to directly accept the DTMF tones, but many local exchange carriers continue to charge extra for DTMF service. Sort of like the question of why ISDN often costs more than POTS when it is the POTS analog signal that must be converted to digital for carriage through the otherwise digital switch and telephone network. No one ever said telephone system pricing made sense outside the never never world of rate regulation, antiquated telephone accounting methods, and the monopoly marketplace.

Anyway, one way or another, the pulses or tones set up a path to the phone you are calling. Then a ringing current is placed on the line of the called phone. Now this is really a strange beast. All of a sudden we go from a low voltage direct current line to 90 volts of alternating current to ring the bell. If you happen to be holding on to the bare copper wires of the line when it's rung, you'll be rung too. Take note. This could be dangerous.

CAUTION

When working on your telephone wiring, be sure it is disconnected from the line coming into your house or office. Ringer current is not as dangerous as the electric power running through your building, but under the wrong conditions, especially your particular physical condition, it could seriously harm or even kill you. The picture of a movie star taking a bath while using a phone is an invitation to tragedy. Perhaps wireless phones are safe in such circumstances, wired phones never are. Even without ringer current, as is the case with ISDN, transient electrical spikes of hundreds or even thousands of volts may appear on the line from accidental contact with power wiring or lightning strokes. Play it safe.

When the ringer current appears at the called phone, circuitry in the phone directs it to the bell or other attention-getting device and the phone rings. Now at your end (the calling party end) you hear the buzz, buzz you have learned to associate with a ringing phone. There is no direct correlation between the "ringing" you hear in the handset and the actual ringing of the bell on the called phone. This is why you frequently encounter a phone being answered "before it has rung." The physical phone rang at the called party end, but the buzz you as the calling party associate with ringing had not been initiated by the central office switch on your end. Now you know the secret; it's all smoke and mirrors. Since the system is really digital and you're using analog devices at both ends, the digital switches fake what we've come to associate with analog calls. When the called party answers his phone goes "off hook" signaling his central office switch the call has been answered and turning off the ringing current. Your call can now proceed.

You both talk for a while when suddenly you hear a tone in the earpiece of your phone. At the called party's end there is a momentary click, click and loss of a syllable or two you were speaking at the time. You explain you must take another call and depress the switchhook; this sends a momentary off condition to your central office switch which has been programmed to interpret this as a signal to place your original called party on hold and transfer you to the new "call waiting" party. You may now switch back and forth between the two by using the switch hook to signal the central office switch.

We have just outlined the current technology of analog in band signaling. Any time you want to make a change in the call setup, you must interrupt your ongoing call to advise the central office switch of your desires. The same is true for the switch; to advise you, it must signal in band interrupting your call in progress. Your actions in dialing with a rotary dial, DTMF tones or switchhook manipulation create analog signals that must be interpreted into digital instructions for the switch. These are complex, expensive, roundabout ways of adapting the analog local loop to an otherwise digital telephone system.

The ISDN Solution   ISDN does away with this. The D channel becomes the vehicle for signaling. This signaling is called "common channel" as a separate channel for signaling is used, in common, by two or more "bearer" channels that bear the actual information traffic. Your calls are never interrupted because the signal that a call is waiting, for example, is sent over the D channel. When such a signal arrives at your ISDN phone you have determined what will happen. Perhaps a screen on the phone blinks with the number or name of the calling party. Perhaps your computer monitor detects the call and switches you to a data base entry associated with the calling party. In any case, there is no need for signaling in the same channel as you are using to talk. In fact, there is no way for signaling to take place in the B channel. All signaling takes place in the D channel:

Part

II

Ch

3

- When you pick up the handset of an ISDN phone the phone sends a "setup" message on the D channel to the central office switch.
- The switch acknowledges receipt of the message on the D channel and turns on the dial tone for the selected B channel.
- When you dial the phone, it sends each digit to the switch on the D channel.
- After the first digit is dialed, the switch turns off the dial tone on the B channel.
- When the switch has received enough digits to complete the call, it sends a "call proceeding" message to your phone on the D channel.
- The switch then sends a "setup" message to the phone you are calling on that phone's D channel.
- The called phone sends an acknowledgment to the switch.
- When the called phone handset is removed, that phone sends a "setup" message to the switch on the D channel.
- It is expected that the phone will be a multibutton type so the answering party will now select the button for your call; this sends a "connect" message to the switch on the D channel.
- Now the switch sends a "connect" message to your phone on the D channel and connects your selected B channel with that of the called party.
- Now you talk.

During the call, you notice a flash on your phone's viewing panel and hear a beep from the phone; you look at your computer monitor and find it showing an incoming call and offering to retrieve the party's records from your database. Neither you nor the party to whom you are currently speaking are interrupted by tones or clicks; all the signaling for the call waiting is done over the separate D channel while your call proceeds on a B channel. You may select to place your current party on hold by pressing buttons on your phone or making selections on your connected computer. You never use the switchhook. You may leap back and forth between the parties or several other call waiting parties or engage selected ones in conference calling. All this is possible due to the flexibility of D channel signaling.

Notice mention of the connected computer. Although much of the D channel signaling may take place with a fancy ISDN phone, a simple phone, even an old POTS phone, with an appropriate terminal adapter and a PC, used in conjunction with ISDN can give even more flexibility. This is the beauty of ISDN. In the past, all of the tricks of telephones were contained in the switch or your PBX. Now with ISDN and D channel signaling, a great deal of processing may take place in the equipment on your desk as it is working in what is essentially a peer relationship with the switch.

With ISDN, the telephone industry is making the same sort of transition as the computer industry did in moving from terminal to host networks to peer-to-peer and client/server local area networks. More intelligence is being placed nearer the user with the user in control. We may expect this evolution to continue. With network packet protocols taking on more functions that replace historic switch functions expect to see simpler central office switches, more complex network protocols and richer user equipment and choices. All of this results from the move to digital information in the local loop and D channel common channel signaling; these are all elements of ISDN.

Between the switches, Signaling System 7 (SS7) makes all this happen. The ITU-T (then known as the CCITT) first issued SS7 in 1980. Without SS7, most of the power we now have on the D channel would not exist. This is the interplay of standards development, and its importance to you.

With the 128 kbps for two B channels and 16 kbps for the D channel, you find you have access to 144 kbps of line capacity for a basic rate interface. In reality, 160 kbps is used for a single BRI. There is another 16 kbps associated with BRI that is not often mentioned. This 16 kbps is used for performance monitoring and maintenance. Perhaps the most important function of this additional 16 kbps is exchange of checksum information. Besides all this there's another 32 kbps taken for overhead; the ISDN system electrically carries a data rate of 192 kbps.

When a packet of information is transmitted, the originating device inserts a number that is the result of a calculation based on numeric values assigned to the contents of the packet. At the receiving device, the same calculation is performed on the information as received. If the results are different, there has been an error and the receiving device requests a retransmission by sending a *far end bit error* (FEBE) bit back to the transmitting device. This signaling takes place over the additional 16 kbps channel. In addition, the telephone company may perform system tests using this channel; hence another ISDN advantage—a great deal of testing and fault diagnosis may be undertaken at the telephone company central office switch without dispatching field crews.

Okay, so now aren't we ready for the B channels, the real carriers of your information? Not so fast. Remember the D channel is used for signaling and most of that signaling takes place during call setup and teardown. Are we going to waste a 16,000 bps channel during the remainder of the time? Not at all. You may use the unused capacity of the D channel to transmit packet-switched information. In this case, your packet traffic shares the D channel with what the telephone industry calls *Q.931 user-network messaging signals*; this is yet another ITU derived standard. Q.931 is the user side of the equation; SS7 is the telephone company switch side. Telephone switches communicate among themselves using SS7. Since you may also use the B channels for packet traffic, we'll defer a fuller discussion of packet usage until we've covered the essentials of the B channels.

▶ **See** Chapter 5 discussions on DSS1 and SS7, **p. 104, 111**

Theft, Pure Theft

If you live in an area where SS#7 has not been implemented, you may find your ISDN is limited to two B channels, each with only 56 kbps capacity. In this case the remaining 8 kbps of each channel have been "robbed" to do signaling duty normally handled by the Q.931 and SS#7 combination. This limitation applied to a substantial amount of Pacific Bell's California ISDN system when first implemented; over time, the PacBell system will be fully compliant and all its B channels will be 64 kbps. This limitation may also appear when you make a long distance call, if any link in the call is unable to carry a "clear channel 64" signal. Your LEC, local exchange carrier ("the phone company"), and your IXC, interexchange carrier ("the long distance company"), should be able to tell you if and when this limitation applies.

Part
II

Ch
3

Interfaces

Notice the interplay between the elements that make up the telephone system. First you are concerned with the equipment at your location, the *customer premises equipment* (CPE) where ISDN is placing more power in your hands than ever possible in the analog world. Next, your *local exchange carrier* (LEC) has issues related to the switch connected to you. Finally, your local exchange carrier must connect to its other switches or to switches of *interexchange carriers* (IXC). All of this is defined within the International Telecommunications Union standards related to ISDN.

In sum, the standard boils down to *functions* connected by *interfaces*. What? Standards-speak is a world unto itself. The basic idea standards creators pursue is definition of something in such a general way that they do not bind an implementor to a particular manner of doing things. Their only concern is that whatever the implementor does do gives results everyone else can use. It is the "black box" way of looking at things.

The standards folks tell implementors to make black boxes that perform certain functions. To call something a "black box" is to say it is a device that no one but the implementor can see inside. All everyone else knows is the rules for putting things into the box and taking them out, the *interfaces*, and what the boxes are supposed to do to those things, the *functions*. How the box does what it does is of no concern to the outside world. Standards define those interfaces and the functions the box is to perform. If you're familiar with software development, the interfaces are the input/output specifications and the functions are the tasks the program modules are to perform. This sounds just like our earlier discussion of the ISO OSI model; it is.

Let's take the simple example in Figure 3.3. We'll call this the *Whole Number Addition Specification*. The interface on the left top is A, that on the left bottom is B and that on the right is C. I specify that the information form for each interface be a spoken word that is a positive, whole number. The black box is a function I specify for you to perform. The function is to add A to B and present the result at C. Now when I give you two numbers, 3 and 4, you add them using any method you want. You can count them up on your fingers. You may rearrange beads on an abacus. You may use an adding machine, calculator or laptop computer. You might call someone up in Paris and ask them to perform the task. I don't care, so long as the function is performed and the results appear at C. In our example of 3 and 4, C should be 7; if it is not, we know the function was not properly done. I have only specified a function to be performed, not how it is to be performed.

FIG. 3.3

A black box.

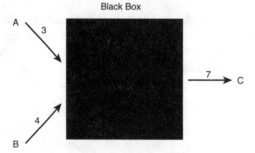

We'll consider ISDN interfaces starting from the middle between you and the telephone company and working back through your system; we'll also look at the equipment you might have. Then we'll take a quick look at the interfaces used by the phone company.

  The wire run from your place to the central office is called the "local loop" in phone-speak.

Figure 3.4 shows the middle, your house or office joined to the central office switch. This is the *U interface*. Electrical signals meeting the specification of the U interface flow over the cable between the central office switch and your house or office. In North America, you are responsible for supplying all the equipment from the U interface forward throughout your system. In this discussion I'll be mentioning terms like NT-1 and TA. In the standards these represent defined sets of functions. In the current real world we usually think of them as physical devices, but there is nothing to keep several of these functions from being incorporated into a single device.

FIG. 3.4

The U interface.

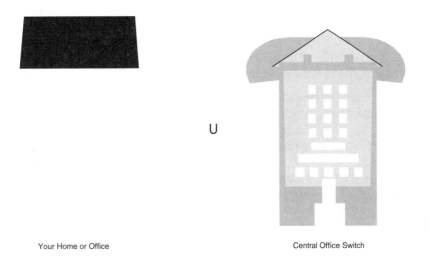

Your Home or Office

U

Central Office Switch

Figure 3.5 illustrates use of the network termination function, NT-1; often this is a separate device. This function creates the S/T interface that actually connects to your equipment. Were you to carefully examine a device incorporating the NT-1 function, you would find the U interface with a single pair copper wire connection back to the phone company's switch and the S/T interface with a two pair connection to your equipment.

FIG. 3.5

The S/T interface.

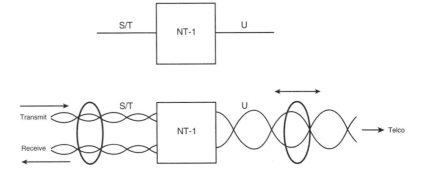

Something happens in the NT-1 device converting a one pair signal from the telephone company into two pair for distribution to your equipment. It is more economical for the telco to use only one pair rather than two. But from your viewpoint, there is a major disadvantage. On the one pair U side you may only connect one NT-1 device. So if you have half a dozen devices to tie onto your ISDN line, you don't want them to require a U interface; you want an S/T interface because the S/T side allows you to connect a number of additional devices.

Basically the U interface side carries full duplex information on the single pair. This means information travels in both directions simultaneously. Engineering constraints prevent such an arrangement from allowing multidrop connections of the sort you probably want for several devices. Consequently, conversion to the S/T interface breaks the signal into two paths, one transmit, one receive. Which is which depends on whether your are looking from the point of view of the NT-1 or a piece of terminal equipment; what is transmission for one is reception for the other. Each signal is now carried on a separate pair, and you are allowed to connect multiple devices. The rules of connection for ISDN are quite different from a POTS installation, but flexibility in the long run is much greater.

A third or even a fourth pair may also be connected to the NT-1; each of these additional pair is used for powering other equipment in your system. In many cases, especially those involving computers, this powering feature in not needed. We'll cover your options in more detail in Chapter 8, "Wiring and Powering Your ISDN System."

N O T E This powering feature appears on the S/T interface. This is a totally separate issue from power on the U interface. In North America, the phone company supplies the U interface to your location, and there are no provisions for power to the NT 1. If you're in North America, this means you must be sure to provide back up battery power, in the event your electrical mains supply fails. In Europe, the telephone company provides such power independent of the regular electrical main power. ▪

One thing becomes clear from the U versus S/T design: equipment that incorporates the NT-1 functions internally with no S/T interface connection limits your use of an ISDN line. You'll see this arrangement in computer boards that connect directly to the BRI U interface. Often this arrangement reduces costs; however, flexibility for use of other equipment on your ISDN line is sacrificed. We'll explore a number of practical options later in the chapters about actually using ISDN.

Figure 3.6 shows the final details at your end. It turns out the S/T interface can be broken in two. If you have a PBX designed for ISDN the NT-1 connects to it using the T interface and the PBX connects to your other equipment using the S interface. In terms of the standard your PBX is performing the NT-2 functions. Electrically, the S and the T are exactly the same; that's why we call them the S/T interface. In my opinion, this design anticipates replacement of the traditional office PBX switch with a software package and a few hardware cards running on a server in your local area network doing double duty as the PBX. That's coming, but for now look at the things you can connect to the S/T interface.

FIG. 3.6
ISDN interfaces at your location.

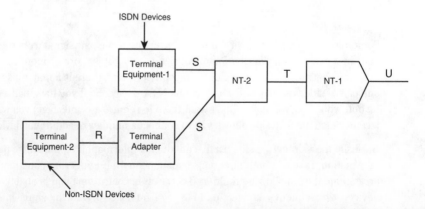

There are so many buzz letters on Figure 3.6, it'll probably help to have a guide:

- Terminal Equipment 1 (TE1) defines the functions performed by terminal devices that are designed for ISDN. They connect directly to the S/T interface and might include an ISDN telephone or computer terminal.

- Terminal Equipment 2 (TE2) simply includes all other terminal devices that are not designed for ISDN. In order to use this equipment on ISDN you must have a terminal adapter.

- A Terminal Adapter (TA) performs the functions needed to connect non-ISDN equipment (TE2) to ISDN. And here we arrive at the final interface on your side of the equation. Terminal adapters create the *R interface*.

N O T E Frequently you will find ISDN terminal adapters marked with an R interface; usually this is understood to be for connection to analog telephone equipment, phones, modem, faxes. You can see the advantage of this; with such a connection you can use your existing analog equipment on the ISDN line. But the R interface is not limited to the analog telephone specification. It could be a connection to totally different equipment so long as that equipment is not ISDN compliant. For example, if you have an existing digital PBX system with phones that are not ISDN, an R interface could be designed to use those phones.

Figure 3.7 shows all the functions and interfaces we have mentioned so far plus the ones on the telephone company side. Ironically, the phone company side is much simpler. This is a harbinger: complexity will be yours; simplicity will be theirs; costs will plummet if there is an open, competitive marketplace.

FIG. 3.7
All ISDN Interfaces.

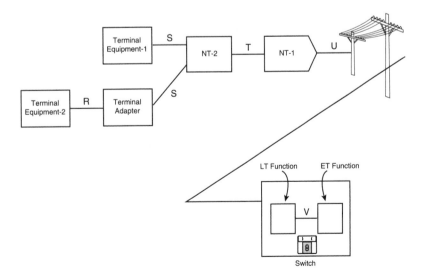

The phone company has only two functions in this model.

- Line termination (LT) is the function of terminating the local loop line in the central office.

- Exchange termination (ET) is the switching exchange termination function also located in the central office. This connects a particular office to other exchanges.
- The V interface is between the line termination and the exchange termination functions. It is probably inside the telephone company switch.

Basic Rate Interface B Channels

Now that we've covered the D channel and the interfaces, we'll look at the B channels, the ones that will do most of your work. A BRI provides two B channels of 64 kbps each. This is like having two independent telephone lines. Each has a different telephone number. The proper term here is *directory number* (DN). In fact, you may have several directory numbers for each B channel. This would allow you to have several devices on the S/T multidrop side of your NT-1 with each device having a different directory number. For example, you could have a FAX machine, a telephone, and a computer all using one B channel, but each with a different directory number. This works through the D channel signaling with each device. Of course these must be TE-1, ISDN terminal, type devices that can communicate with the D channel and make it happen.

Watch that SPID

Watch out. We are now entering the world of ISDN numbers. There are two kinds you must remember. I've already mentioned the directory number (DN). Since you're familiar with that from the POTS world, the only thing new to remember is the capability to have different directory numbers for each device using a B channel. But there is more to it. Your equipment is identified with a *terminal endpoint identifier* (TEI). This, in turn, is wrapped up with the *service profile identifier* (SPID). It is here that things get sticky. How the TEI and SPID numbers are assigned and what they mean can vary from telco to telco and switch to switch. You will need to enter the DN and SPID when you configure your equipment. It is very important to get this information from the telephone company so your configuration goes smoothly. We'll show some of these configurations in Part III, "ISDN Computer Hardware."

Now , the good news. A number of equipment makers provide automatic switch type and SPID detection to simplify your tasks of configuration. There is also a move underway to eventually eliminate the SPID. This move seems to be a product of North American ISDN development, and it is unknown in Europe.

ISDN Physical Layer   We're not going too deeply into this, but let's see some of what is really going on with that ISDN signal. Remember the seven layer model? I really did have a reason for presenting it. We'll look at some of the details of BRI by using the model starting with layer 1, the physical layer.

▶ **See** "ISO OSI Model," **p. 41**

I mentioned ISDN is full duplex communications; full duplex means both transmit and receive are carried on the cable at the same time. How does this work? Much of the magic comes from structure of the ISDN frame at layer one. I'll only talk of how it looks on the S/T interface. It is a different animal on the U interface. In fact, there is a slight difference in its appearance depending on whether you are looking at signal travel from terminal equipment (TE)to network terminator (NT) or the reverse direction. To illustrate, here I'll use travel from NT to TE.

Figure 3.8 shows a frame traveling from a network terminator to a piece of terminal equipment. Let's make this concrete. The network terminator you'll probably have is called an NT-1 and is a little box maybe the size of a small paperback book. Let's say the terminal equipment you have is made to take the ISDN signal and pass it to the serial port of your computer sort of like a modem, in fact chances are it looks a lot like a modem. We'll talk more about such devices in Chapter 9. Anyway, Figure 3.8 an ISDN frame traveling from your NT-1 to your "ISDN modem." Since it's traveling into your modem, the frame is providing your computer information and is flowing in the receive channel.

FIG. 3.8
ISDN frame at S/T interface.

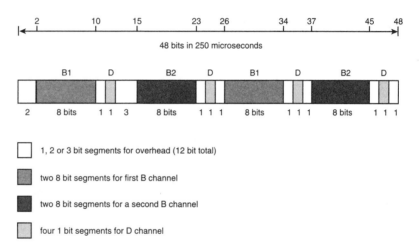

Technical detail is omitted from this diagram so the idea is clearer. Each frame carries 48 bits. Sixteen bits for each B channel and four bits for the D channel. This is a total of 36 bits. The remaining 12 bits are framing and other overhead information. It takes the frame 250 microseconds (250 millionths of a second) to pass. When all this is worked out, the effective data rates are the ones you already know, 64 kbps for each B channel and 16 kbps for the D channel. The overall data rate is 192 kbps, taking into account overhead.

When you examine Figure 3.8, it's apparent what's happening.

- Eight bits are sent for B channel 1,
- Then a bit for the D channel,
- Then eight bits for B channel 2,
- Then a bit for the D channel,
- Then the final eight bits for B channel 1,
- Then a bit for the D channel,
- Then the final eight bits for B channel 2, and
- Then the final bit for the D channel.

After a little overhead, it all starts up again. This happens on both the transmit and the receive pair making the circuit full duplex.

ISDN Data Link Layer   Let's step up to layer two and take a look inside the more complex frames created at that level. Figure 3.9 provides a simplified view of the frame format used for the protocols involved:

- **LAPD:** the protocol used for the D channel called link access procedure for the D channel;
- **LAPB:** the protocol used for the B channel using packet switching mode;
- **I.465/V.120:** rate adaptation in circuit switched mode;
- **LAPF:** link access procedure for frame-mode bearer services also for circuit switched mode.

Details within the frame will differ among these protocols, but the overall frame format is the same (except for LAPF, which combines the address and control fields into one field of 16 to 32 bits).

FIG. 3.9
Frame format of ISDN at layer two, the data link layer.

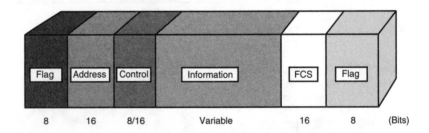

Flag	Address	Control	Information	FCS	Flag	
8	16	8/16	Variable	16	8	(Bits)

At layer one we only saw bits. Here we see something actually being carried in the frame. When we dig deeper, we can find details. For example, the TEI, terminal endpoint identifier I mentioned in the tip above, is one of the elements of the address field. There is considerably more detail in layer two. Addressing involving the TEI and SPID is all you'll typically need to concern yourself with when you use ISDN.

ISDN Network Layer   Network layer control is carried within the information field of layer two. The primary duty of this information is to control the call through the D channel. Q.930 and Q.931 are the standards implementing this control. There are three broad types of messages involved when using circuit mode connection:

- Call establishment
- Call information phase
- Call clearing

Supplementary services are controlled by the Q.932 standard. This allows such things as call holding and waiting. We'll cover more of this control in Chapter 5, "Signaling with ISDN."

Packet Switching   Both the B channels and the D channel can carry packet-switched traffic. The actual switching may be performed by either a packet-switched public data network or an

ISDN switch. The X.25 packet switching protocol is used in either case. Standards groups are working on more efficient packet switching protocols for the future.

Only B channel packet switching is supported in the packet-switched public data network model. The call is set up to the public switch through D channel signaling just as any other call. The B channel then carries the packet traffic. Using a public switch has the advantage of assuring connection to anyone with access to that switch regardless of whether or not their access is through ISDN.

The other way of doing packet switching uses the ISDN switch itself as the packet switch. In this case, either the B channel or D channel can carry packet traffic. Traffic can only go to other ISDN users unless access to packet-switched public data networks is provided through the ISDN switch.

Primary Rate Interface (PRI)

The primary rate interface is in a way more of the same. In North America, it provides 23 B channels and a single D channel, but this D channel has a 64 kbps capacity. In Europe, a PRI has 30 B channels and a 64 kbps D channel. The difference is of course history. In North America a T1 carrier line is defined as having 24 voice channels for a total data rate of 1.544 megabits/second. In Europe, the corresponding system has 30 voice channels using 2.048 megabits/second. When ISDN developed, the difference between the 1.544 Mbs T1 and the 2.048 Mbs "E1" carried forward; the North American PRI is 1.544 Mbs, the European is 2.048 Mbs.

PRI gives another channel type, "H." H channels are currently available in different data rates:

- H0 384 kbps
- H10 1472 kbps (All the US B channels without D)
- H11 1536 kbps (All the US channels in a PRI)
- H12 1912 kbps (All the European B channels)

H11 is an interesting case since it uses all twenty-four 64 kbps channels in a PRI. This means another PRI with a D channel must be used for control.

Since the number of B channels and size of D channel in PRI differs from that of BRI, some of the framing and other standards discussed above differ in detail but not in concept.

Save Your Money

If you have an installation that demands the capacity of PRI, don't order it without first checking the tariffs for ISDN service in your area. It is often less expensive to buy a dozen BRI, than to buy one PRI even though the phone company can deliver a PRI on two twisted pair while the BRIs require a dozen single twisted pair. Tariff disparity is commonplace. This is the reason you'll see rather large routers with an option for a PRI or multiple BRIs, and why sales of ISDN multiplexers and inverse multiplexers for ISDN are booming.

From Here...

We've gotten to know what narrowband ISDN is about by discovering the meaning of bandwidth and the value of digital techniques. The basic rate interface (BRI) furnishes two B channels with 64 kbps capacity each and one D channel with a 16 kbps capacity (2B+D). The distinguishing marks of ISDN are its use of digital information and the common channel signaling control of the D channel. At your location, you'll connect to either the U interface, or to an external NT1 device that creates an S/T interface. The S/T interface has the advantage of allowing multiple devices; the U interface allows only one. A single primary rate interface (PRI) delivers 23 B channels and one 64 kbps D channel in North America and 30 B channels with a D channel in Europe.

Now it's time to see what ISDN can do:

■ Chapter 4 talks about choosing services. Before your ISDN line is installed, you'll need to know what you can do with it.

■ In Chapter 7, we cover actually ordering the services. That is an art in itself.

■ We talked about SS#7. In Chapter 5, "Signaling with ISDN," we'll cover more detail about controlling ISDN between your location and the telco switch and then among switches themselves.

■ When you finish Chapter 6 on APIs, you'll be equipped to tackle actually using ISDN in Part III.

Choosing Services

You probably think of the telephone system as providing some wires and switches to connect you to someone else. So, for you the phone system is a bunch of hardware. Maybe, if you're a computer type, you'll include software as something else that makes up the system. Would it surprise you to know the people in the phone company think differently? From their perspective, the company is a service business. You receive telephone "service."

Regulators and legislators think the same way. As a result, the whole regulatory structure is based on analysis of services and setting rates by comparing the costs involved in their delivery. Regulators believe services that are considered *basic* should be available to everyone at low cost while services that are considered *premium* or *discretionary* can demand much higher prices. Some services that are a part of the standard telephone offerings in some countries cannot even be provided by the telephone company in other countries. The more you learn about this telephone stuff, the stranger it gets.

It helps to look at these services in the seven layer ISO OSI model (see Figure 4.1).

FIG. 4.1
ISDN Services and the
ISO OSI Model.

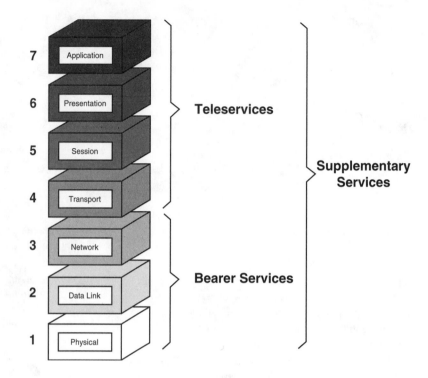

In this chapter, you'll learn what services make up ISDN. You may not be able to buy all of these in your area. Some that may become important are under development or in process of standardization; since they are not yet included in final standards, our discussion may not cover them. Here I'll highlight many of the services that you may find interesting or important—you may even wonder where anyone got the idea some were worth having. ■

Bearer Services

Bearer services are the backbone, the beasts of burden that we usually associate with what we want a telephone system to do—carry information traffic. Many of the services are the same as those found in analog, POTS, service. Bearer services carry the information. They do not change the information content or offer new information itself. Although bearer services may change the very low level nature of bit transmission, the higher level content is delivered intact. So bearer services are concerned exclusively with ISO OSI layers one (physical) through three (network).

Circuit-Mode versus Packet-Mode

We may select either circuit-mode or packet-mode services. Whoa, these terms are thrown around quite a bit. This is a good place to become a lot more specific about their meaning.

N O T E Circuit switching or circuit-mode, packet switching or packet-mode? Switching has been the term for the technologies I am talking about, but now the terms are changing. The ITU-T uses the term "mode."

Visualize circuit-mode as the way signals flow through a typical analog telephone system with a manual switchboard. When you give the operator a number, the operator physically connects the wire from your phone to the wire connected to the phone of the party you are calling. Then, until you hang up, telephone company wiring between your phone and the phone you're calling is dedicated to that call. Even though there may be long periods of silence, the circuit, once established, continues to use substantial telephone network resources. When you finish the call, the operator removes the plugs that tie you to the called party and the equipment is available for other calls.

Expand this to a more complex situation with intervening switchboards that tie you to your friend a thousand miles away and you can see how circuit-mode claims resources that could be put to more efficient use. Replace the operators with automatic exchange switches and you still have the same resource intensive effect. The basic idea of circuit-mode is that you have exclusive use of the total circuit length of the connection for so long as you maintain the call.

N O T E This idea of circuit-mode is important to bear in mind when considering use of ISDN. In some markets ISDN is available for local calls with no time charge. I certainly favor this "flat rate" tariff. However, some users may effectively establish "dedicated ISDN" by leaving an ISDN call connected to the same point, for example an ISP, forever. But ISDN is fundamentally a circuit-mode service. So this "dedicated ISDN" may be an abuse of resources. I'll take this discussion up in more detail in Chapter 17 concerning Internet Service Providers.

Packet-mode is the flip side. Usually we think of packet-mode as exclusively a data carriage method, but, we shall see that is an historic bias, not a technological necessity. Now you don't have exclusive use of the resources. Instead, the telephone company takes your information, breaks it up into collections of limited length, say a thousand bits, attaches your address and the address (phone numbers) of the party you're calling and some other overhead and makes a *packet*.

A packet is a discrete collection of information. It probably doesn't have all of what you want to transmit within it. Your information is broken up into several, maybe hundreds or thousands of packets. Each is numbered in sequence. Each is addressed. Each has some complex arithmetic called a *checksum* to protect against errors. Each packet of your information is transmitted as a distinct entity, but travels in the company of packets from other users communicating over a given path.

Now the transmission resource is much more fully used than was the case with circuit-mode. Now when you have nothing being sent, others still use the same wires to send their packets. When the data rates are high enough, all users still get all the information they want when they want it; yet all effectively share the actual physical circuit connecting points of exchange. The carrier doesn't need to invest so much in switching equipment as the packets themselves, with

Part

II

Ch

4

their embedded addresses, switch themselves. Packet protocols replace costly hardware switching. Costs go down. Effective resource capacity goes up.

As I write this book in mid-1995 there are ten circuit-mode and three packet-mode bearer services defined by the ITU-T.

Circuit-Mode Bearer Services

The ten circuit-mode services are the ones that usually hold the most interest to ISDN users. They behave a lot like the telephone you're already used to. Information is transmitted on B channels. Call control is exercised on the D channel. These services are discussed in the next several sections.

Circuit-Mode 64 kbps Unrestricted, 8 kHz Structured Bearer Service Category   Sometimes called "clear channel" or "transparent" service, this is the most general bearer service and can transmit anything. There is no change in the bit structure of the information transmitted. The 8 kHz refers to timing information contained in the service. This breaks the data into octets, 8 bit units. As a result, the service itself provides synchronization and there is no need for the user's application to add timing.

N O T E   Terminology again. B channel comes from the term bearer, bearer channel. The telephone industry has a standard that is 64 kbps wide, DS-0, predating ISDN. When ISDN began to be specified, 64 kbps was the logical choice. ▪

Circuit-Mode 64 kbps, 8 kHz Structured Bearer Service Category Usable for Speech Information Transfer   This service is specifically designed for speech. Therefore it may apply speech processing and transmit the signal through systems designed to carry speech but destructive of raw data. This has major implications for you. If you're using this service to carry data, it may be altered in transmission. The path may go through analog systems with loading, echo canceling or other technologies that will distort or destroy its character for data carriage.

▶ **See** Chapter 7, "Ordering ISDN services," **p. 141**

Be Sure You're Served with the Right Service

Be careful when you use a service. It's possible for you to have a clear channel 64 kbps connection to your local exchange carrier and then find you're unable to make a satisfactory call through an interexchange carrier (interexchange is telespeak for long distance). I learned this under rather trying circumstances. I arranged the first ISDN video connection for the Texas Public Utilities Commission. The hearing concerned the State's first proposed rule on ISDN. The plan was to have a very knowledgeable corporate officer on the west coast appear as a witness before the Commission. Around midnight, with only ten hours until the hearing, we had all the equipment on our end up and operating. Things worked perfectly when the west coast transmission site called us for an end-to-end test. We then called the west coast for a reverse end-to-end test. Nothing worked. We went through the process several times, checking all of our equipment and connections as we went. Finally, I suggested we change interexchange carriers. Our first call connected and worked perfectly.

Conclusion: The first carrier was providing a speech circuit; the second had clear channel. The PUC ruled in favor of the new ISDN rule. All of this was done on a single BRI.

Circuit-Mode 64 kbps, 8 kHz Structured Bearer Service Category Usable for 3.1 kHz Audio Information Transfer   This is similar to the above method, minus the special forms of speech processing allowed in that service. However, it still uses techniques that will destroy digital data and should be avoided for anything but speech traffic.

Circuit-Mode 64 kbps, 8 kHz Structured Multiuse Bearer Service Category   This service provides the same unrestricted, clear channel transmission as the first service. Then it adds the trick of control through ISDN setting up the correct bearer service for a number of other services and terminals.

Circuit-Mode 2 x 64 kbps, Unrestricted, 8 kHz Structured Bearer Service Category   This service is suitable for data, and provides a way of combining two 64 kbps channels to solve problems associated with independent B channel routing. On a call from Chicago to Moscow, for example, one channel might go through an undersea fiber cable while the other goes by satellite. Serious timing problems can occur when you try to combine the two because there's at least a half-second delay between the transmission and reception of signals relayed by satellite. The service limits the difference in this timing.

Circuit-Mode H Channels   I mentioned the H channels earlier in Chapter 3. They are forms of unrestricted, 8 kHz structured services available at higher data rates over a primary rate interface (PRI). You'll recall:

- H0 384 kbps
- H10 1472 kbps
- H11 1536 kbps
- H12 1912 kbps

Circuit-Mode Multirate Unrestricted, 8 kHz Structured Bearer Service Category   This is the third way to use more than one B channel. On demand, requests made over the D channel can aggregate B channels up to the maximum available in a PRI. The service must be supported at both ends.

Circuit-Mode 56 kbps Bit Robbing Bearer Service—Not ITU-T

This service is an implementation used in some regions of the United States that do not yet have full ISDN with SS#7. In these areas, it is necessary to make adjustments and adapt to T1 carrier systems that take the low order bit from every sixth byte in the user's data stream. The result is a 56 kbps data rate. Protocols such as V.110 and V.120 that provide rate adaptation and mask out the robbed bit are available to bridge the gap pending full 64 kbps service.

▶   **See** "Basic Rate Interface D Channel," **p. 75**

Part

II

Ch

4

N O T E   The 56 kbps bit robbing bearer service is *not* an ITU-T standard. It is simply a work-around
pending upgrades to full 64 kbps service. ▪

Packet-Mode Bearer Services

Circuit-mode uses B channels to convey user's information and the D channel to control the
call. Packet-mode can use both the B and the D channels to send user information.

Public Data Network Virtual Circuit Service, Case A   The original work of the ITU-T standards group considered the alternative of using a public data network for packet-mode traffic
as "case A" with ISDN. You call up a packet switch using 64 kbps unrestricted circuit-mode
service and send the packets over a B or H channel. You'll be using X.25. Once you're connected, you can establish a number of virtual calls over the one connection as in any X.25 call.
This will handle large packet sizes such as 4000 bytes.

What Is X.25?

X.25 is the widely accepted protocol for packet transmission over the worldwide telephone system.
X.25 provides a virtual circuit that delivers packets in a connection oriented service.

A virtual circuit is established when the packet switch begins sending packets to a destination packet
switch; it first establishes a connection with that switch, thus the exchange is connection-oriented;
then it sends the packets in sequence establishing controls to maintain that order at the receiving
location.

This technique is in contrast to a connectionless or datagram service. Now there is never a connection established. Packets are sent to the destination address with the expectation that they may
arrive out of order or never arrive at all. Datagram service remedies this uncertainty by providing
sequencing protocols that reorder the packets at the receiver. If any packets are missing, the receiver
requests retransmission. Most of the use of packet traffic in ISDN is virtual-circuit and connection
oriented.

If this all sounds complex; it is. In fact, how you characterize a communication as connection-
oriented or connectionless, virtual-circuit or datagram, often depends on the level of abstraction you
are using in the discussion.

ISDN Virtual Circuit Service, Case B   Here the ISDN switch becomes the packet switch; thus
ISDN provides the service and your packet traffic can travel on the D channel. This is not
possible in Case A, where your traffic attaches to an external, non-ISDN switch that has no idea
what a D channel, let alone ISDN, is.

The immediate advantage of this service is D channel use. The disadvantage is limited capacity.
The data rata available is about 9600 bps on a BRI; contrast this with the 64 kbps available with
B channel traffic. Still, for many small, time-sensitive applications like credit card verification,
the D channel gives you another communication path. PRI D channel packet is more complex
because of the number of B channels the 64 kbps D channel must control.

▶   **See** "Teleservices," **p. 100**

CAUTION

While D channel packet looks like you're getting something for nothing, watch out. You may be in for a costly surprise! Even though you're taking up 16 kbps of data space with the D channel whether or not anything is going down that pipe, and the addition of packet traffic doesn't make a penny's worth of difference in costs to the telco, there may be an exorbitant tariff attached to D channel packet usage. These tariffs are based on the antiquated idea that data traffic is something special, costly, and needed only by deep-pocketed customers who can spread the cost around. So, the telcos break out and separately charge for various service capabilities already inherent in a technology, even though it costs them nothing more to provide those capabilities. The companies' premium or discretionary tariffs are based on the argument that their rate of return should not be tied to direct costs because the service is not basic to telephony. Look before you leap.

User Signaling Bearer Service   This is an interesting service. It supports D channel messaging among ISDN users. Messages are limited to 128 octets when sent with a control message. If they are sent alone, however, they can be 256 octets long. This is not much information in the usual data communications context, but its adequate for network management or PBX control.

Connectionless Service   This service is still under study. As I said above, most packet service is expected to be connection oriented. But, connectionless service may be a useful and economical way to gather instrumentation data such as meter reading and alarms.

Part
II

Ch
4

Supplementary Services

You can't have supplementary services without bearer services. So once you've determined what bearer services best fit your needs, you must decide what supplementary services you want to add. You may not find all of the following services available in your area. On the other hand, you may find some that aren't listed here; those will probably be unique to a particular brand of switch and not a part of National ISDN. Just remember that these are services and, you guessed it, they may carry added cost.

▶   For more discussion on National ISDN (NIx), **see** "Why Is Ordering Such a Big Problem, and What Is Provisioning?" **p. 142**

One more thing. As you read through the list, you'll notice that most of the supplemental ISDN services are associated with voice telephone service and features you think of with PBXs. Remember that ISDN originally was heralded as a technology to get back business the PBX vendors had taken from the local exchange carriers. It's good to have an idea about all this voice stuff, but, if all you're going to do with ISDN is connect your computer to the Internet, you'll probably not have to get too deeply involved with these issues.

What's in a Name

If you find a service here or elsewhere that you're interested in, but can't find it in your phone company's list of available services, don't despair. Don't be discouraged if, in fact, you can't find ISDN itself. Telcos have marketing and advertising departments that have to justify their existence by dreaming up new names for services that are already perfectly well understood by the telephone community. I once asked the audience at a meeting how many of them would be interested in "Digiline" service. No one raised a hand. I asked how many would be interested in "Smarttrunk" service. Again, no response. Then I asked for a show of hands for ISDN service; about 75 percent shot up. You guessed it. "Digiline" is Southwestern Bell's name for BRI service; "Smarttrunk" is its name for PRI.

Number Identification

▶ **See** "Basic Rate Interface B Channels" **p. 84**

There's a plethora of things you can do with telephone numbers. The buzzword for a telephone number is *directory number* (DN). Don't forget; when you set up your ISDN equipment, you'll need not only the directory number but also the SPID. Caught you. You skipped over that tip in the last chapter. The service profile identifier (SPID) is something tying your particular equipment on the ISDN line to the ISDN switch. The phone company can give you the details for the particular installation they have. Be sure you get it. Let's see what tricks are possible with number identification and ISDN.

- **Direct Dialing In:** This is basically a PBX service. You're assigned a group of numbers so anyone calling in can ring a particular phone. You see this anytime someone with a big company hands you a card with the main company number on it. Then they say, "That number's the switchboard; you can get me directly at xxx-xxxx."

- **Multiple Subscriber Number:** This is very slick. You've probably seen or perhaps have one of those neat little boxes that lets you use a single POTS line for voice data and fax calls. With multiple subscriber number, you can do a lot better. A different directory number is assigned to each device. When a call comes in for, say the fax, the fax answers, and so on. This is far beyond selective ringing where different numbers call the same POTS line but ring differently. ISDN sends information keyed to the physical devices themselves.

- **Calling Line Identification Presentation:** This is the ISDN version of "caller ID" that is available for incoming calls on many POTS systems. If you think about it, the digital form of ISDN information and the packet protocol must contain the calling address. Extracting this is built into ISDN.

- **Calling Line Identification Restriction:** But you're also aware of the controversy over caller ID. So ISDN provides a service restricting release of the caller's number. It may be possible to have this by default or to turn it on and off at will. But think again. The packets contain the information so that 911 and other authorities will always have access. In fact, should you have a protocol analyzer for ISDN, you'd be able to read it from any packet. Reminds me of the gasps I heard from classes of local area network students when I'd fire up a LAN protocol analyzer and read their passwords. Don't worry, most of the network operating systems now provide password encryption, at least as an option. Can calling number encryption be far behind? Then how would the system work?

■ **Connected Line Identification Presentation:** If you're like me, you can't remember who you've just called. This service provides you with the number of the party you just called. That solves the problem. It also could key a database to retrieve information. I know a lot of people may think this is a strange service, but in the context of some of the call centers rapidly calling back on long lists of people, I expect it will be useful to those overworked people.

■ **Connected Line Identification Presentation Restriction:** Now I think I have this right. This service prevents the called party's number from being presented to the person who just called. It took me a while to understand why this would be helpful. After all, the calling party should know the number just called. But ISDN reports back not just the directory number (DN), but also the service point identification (SPID). Preventing a specific identification of the process or device through the SPID may be quite important in building a firewall against intruders that are attempting to damage your system.

■ **Malicious Calls Identification:** This is also a service in the POTS world. A called party can have the telephone company log calls.

■ **Subaddressing:** The really neat thing here is the way this can work into your LAN or other networks. The subaddress can be up to twenty octets long. This allows it to address not only devices on your network but also service access points, processes, on those devices. Since this is offered as a supplementary service, you would expect the telephone company to charge for it. If that's the case, I'll bet you'll find a way within your network protocols to accomplish the same task with no added charges.

Call Offering

These services involve how the call is moved around to different locations or numbers, the places where the call is "offered."

■ **Call Transfer:** When you're in the midst of a call and want to send it elsewhere, you need call transfer. This can be handy if someone calls you to discuss a project and then you decide the person needs to talk to someone else; you can connect them without their having to call back into your system.

■ **Call Forwarding Unconditional:** This allows you to have all your calls sent to another number.

■ **Call Forwarding Busy:** A forwarding variation that only comes into play when your phone is busy. It can be used to route a call to someone else, or to your voice mail.

■ **Call Forwarding No Reply:** A second variation on forwarding, used to route incoming calls to another number if your phone isn't answered after a predetermined number of rings.

■ **Call Deflection:** This is a third variation on forwarding. A call comes in. Prior to answering it, you ask that it be sent, or deflected, to another number. It seems to me, I'd use this in conjunction with a calling line identification presentation.

■ **Line Hunting:** This could be handy. It provides a way for incoming calls to your number to hunt through your equipment for an available slot. We used to call this a "rotary;" it rotated among a user's lines until it found a clear one.

Call Completion

Call completion services cover things like call waiting and call holding. The nice thing about ISDN is it is much more flexible and potentially less intrusive than POTS. For example, call waiting doesn't break into your conversation because the signaling is out of band and on the D channel.

■ **Call Waiting:** You know how this works on POTS. With ISDN, when a call comes in, you aren't notified by an interruption in your conversation because signaling is on the D channel, the common channel. So calls don't destroy your data connections either. The nice thing about ISDN here is that you can keep your call waiting on and not worry about blowing a data transfer.

■ **Call Hold:** I already spend too much time on hold. ISDN does nothing to alleviate that. In fact, ISDN compounds the situation. It is possible to place several calls on hold at once. You say you can do that with a POTS phone. Not exactly. Each of your POTS calls takes up a connection, a line to your facility. With ISDN you may only be connected with one B channel, but have the ability to juggle, say five, call IDs.

■ **Completion of Calls to Busy Subscribers:** I think we used to call this "camp on" in the old days. You call Mary up. Her line is busy. Your phone rings when her line is free, and you can complete the call.

■ **Completion of Calls on No Reply:** Here's a good one. You call Mario. He doesn't answer. Your phone watches his phone. When it detects activity, it calls you back so you can complete the call.

Multiparty Services

The unique element in ISDN multiparty services is the power of the invoker of the service, the controller. That's a fancy way of saying the person who initiates the call has control and can set everything up. It also means that person pays the bill for the special services.

■ **Conference Calling:** The controller can establish a call among parties who can simultaneously communicate. The controller can also establish private conversations with individual parties in the group. And the controller maintains control until deciding to disconnect, which terminates the conference.

■ **Three-Party Service:** Generally known as "three-way calling in the POTS world, this ISDN option gives you the option of conferencing two other parties in one conversation or switching back and forth between the two others in private conversations.

N O T E   Ordinarily, connection among the multiple parties in conference and three-party calls depends on the initiator of the call ("controller" in the conference call) continuing to be connected. A variation on multiparty services allows connections among the parties to continue even when the partyinitiating the call leaves. This "call transfer disconnect" often sparks fear into the hearts of telephone companies. The telephone companies can see some toll-avoiding schemes that would join metropolitan calling areas. Thankfully, these quivering giants are calmed when they are shown how their switches (telespeak for computers) are alerted to any such abuse. Sometimes, you just have to help out those who are less fortunate than you and explain how things may be made to work out. ■

Community of Interest

These services are generally useful to well defined organizations that have security and convenience needs they provide.

- **Closed User Group:** This is a security service. You may specify a closed user group. Then when you make a call the call will not go through unless it is to a member of that group. In a computer environment, this provides an added measure of security assuring you that calls will not be made outside the group. The called party may also specify that a call may only be received from the group.

- **Private Numbering Plan:** This service allows you to assign special numbers to your phones. In this way, a large company or a small organization with widely separated offices can establish what amounts to a private telephone network. Locations in the network are reached by dialing the special numbers, not by using the traditional telephone system numbers. So, at the Humongous Sand and Penguin Company, I can call any phone at any of our three thousand divisions throughout the world by entering a three digit number followed by four other digits. I don't have to fool with country or area codes at all.

- **Multiline Business Group or Citywide Centrex:** I suggested earlier that ISDN is the modern answer to Centrex. You'll recall that Centrex uses a portion of the local exchange carrier's central office switch as a PBX. Although the ITU-T has not defined this service, it is implemented by many local exchange carriers in North America.

- **Multiline Key Telephone Service:** This is another service that is not in the ITU-T standards but is very important in North America. It defines how key telephones are to work and be used. Key telephone are the ones with all the extra buttons, keys, besides those for dialing.

- **Multilevel Precedence and Preemption:** This provides for prioritizing phone traffic. Four levels of precedence are provided. These are based on the original U.S. military design. *Priority, Interrupt, Flash,* and *Flash Override.* Priority is lowest, Flash Override is highest. If you are making a call on Flash and I have authority to use Flash Override and a phone that can enable it, I can seize the line you are using or break through to you in the midst of your call.

- **Priority Service:** This service gives precedence in routing to calls from or to defined numbers. Such a selection would be expected to speed connection or provide more secure paths for the signal.

- **Outgoing Call Barring:** The most typical use of this service is prevention of toll calls from within an organization's phone system. Other restrictions may be programmed in.

Part
II
Ch
4

Charging Services

How are you going to pay for that call?

- **Credit Card Call:** This is not yet defined in the standards, but a number of interim methods for credit card use are being implemented.

■ **Advice of Charges:** It's the end of the month and the phone bill(s) come in. How could you have spent so much on long distance? How can you bill your client for those calls to Lower Blocksteincerech whose PTT has some scheme that inflated your 10-minute call charge to $345.56? The answer is advice of charge when you make the call. The information can be supplied when you set up the call, while you're in the midst of the call, or at the end. Again the magic of the D channel.

■ **Reverse Charging:** This is the fancy name for a collect call.

Additional Information Transfer

■ **User to User Signaling:** This our old friend mentioned in the packet discussion above. You can send additional messages to others in your "PBX" over the D channel.

■ **Incall Modification:** Here's something you cannot do on a POTS line. This feature lets you change the class or category of bearer service you're using in the midst of a call without breaking the connection. For example, you can switch from speech to "clear channel" 64 kbps for data transmission and never hang up the line.

Teleservices

We now enter the gray area of teleservices. Many of these are designed for the European market and are not available from local exchange carriers in the United States due to legal restrictions. As the competitive marketplace develops, these restrictions will be lifted and the LECs will enter a well populated marketplace. As shown in Figure 4.1, teleservices live in the top four layers of the ISO OSI model, while bearer services occupy the lower three layers.

Telephony

Telephony is another never never land of technology and regulation. In Europe, telephony is considered a teleservice. In the United States, regulation currently prevents local exchange carriers (at least those with roots in the Bell System) from providing teleservices. So how can they provide telephony? It would seem, *sub rosa,* (a fancy way of saying: "without every really saying it") the U.S. legal system has transmuted telephony into a bearer service the companies can supply. Therefore, although U.S. law says the telco can't supply services above layer three, the telco can supply telephony, a layer four through seven technology. Interesting?

Emerson on Telephone Regulation

"A foolish consistency is the hobgoblin of little minds, adored by little statesmen and philosophers and divines. With consistency a great soul has simply nothing to do."—Ralph Waldo Emerson (1803-1882) iv. *Spiritual Laws.*

Videotext

This is computer service. Perhaps the most well known is the French Minitel system that has provided millions of terminals for telephone users thereby eliminating telephone books, creating a nationwide electronic mail system, and plunging the French PTT into debates over

Minitel delivered porn services. At this point in technology, we might be on the verge of shoe-horning access to Internet into this bracket.

Telex

This is the telex technology we have used for years. Oops! What telex technology? The teletype machines—you know, the electric typewriters hooked to "phone line" that used to sit in every broker's office and fill the back rooms with noise at newspapers, TV and radio stations. Somehow the glow of a cathode ray tubes with words flowing silently by removed the excitement from all these businesses.

Teletex

This is an updated version of telex with faster data rates. With the advent of electronic mail and expansion of the Internet I question whether this really has any place in future markets.

Telefax

The basis of telefax is Group 4 Fax. This uses digital information at 64 kbps taking full advantage of a B channel. A fax that would take a minute on your regular "Group 3" equipment flashes out in a few seconds. Of course the parties at both ends have to have Group 4 fax machines.

Part
II

Ch
4

Teleconference

Teleconference provides conferencing support for multiple locations. Voice and other information can be exchanged. This is another instance of services offered by telcos that are also available through selection of your own equipment.

Videotelephony

Just what it says—television over ISDN, albeit, television that's not near the quality you've come to expect from your home set. This a rapidly developing technology. Not from the viewpoint of telcos as suppliers as envisioned by this ISDN service, but from use of your own equipment over standard ISDN.

7 kHz Audio

Standard telephony used a 3.1 kHz bandwidth. This service more than doubles that for much higher quality audio. It's still not the quality of a CD, but it beats 3.1 kHz by a mile.

Message Handling

Electronic mail and related services. In the U.S. some telcos are starting to offer voice mail and other services that border on this.

What It All Means

In a nutshell, teleservices exist on the fringe of telephone system business and technology. With the exception of telephony itself, all of the services have non-telco providers, at least in the United States. There is no reason these services need to be married to the ISDN switch. In fact there is no technical reason for even telephony to be offered by the telcos. One way of looking at it is for the telcos to provide up through ISO OSI layer three, and then anyone can provide the higher, teleservices. We're moving in that direction.

The same may be said of many of the supplementary services. While some may be technologically inherent in the first three layers, many can probably be implemented higher up. Non-telco suppliers should offer real selection here too.

From Here...

You've had a chance to see the three areas of ISDN services: bearer, supplementary, and teleservices. This has prepared you to deal with issues surrounding actually ordering and installing ISDN. In future chapters, we'll use the knowledge you've gained.

- Chapter 7, "Ordering ISDN Services," takes the services we've just discussed, puts them in a standardized ordering form, and steps you through dealing with your local exchange carrier.

- Chapter 8, "Wiring and Powering Your ISDN System," looks at the physical layer issues of really hooking up you ISDN equipment and getting those bearer services to work for you.

- Before you get to those issues you can learn about how ISDN signals between your equipment and the central office and between central offices. Chapter 5, "Signaling with ISDN," talks about DSS1 and SS#7.

- You're ready to buy that ISDN terminal adapter. Wait. Look through Chapter 6, "Unscrambling APIs," to understand how your ISDN hardware is going to speak with your computer and applications.

- After all this, you'll be ready to get the ISDN hardware. Chapters 9, 10, and 11 provide a close look at the three broad options you'll need to consider and at some of the popular hardware in the marketplace.

Signaling with ISDN

■ **Signaling between your equipment and the switch takes place using *Digital Subscriber Signaling System Number 1* (DSS1)**

We'll review what this means and how it works.

■ **Once DSS1 talks to the telco switch, your instructions are converted to *Signaling System 7 (SS7)* form. SS7 is used throughout the telephone network until at the last central office switch, your signaling reverts to DSS1 for the final leg of its journey**

Let's find out how Signaling System 7 works for you.

The essential elements of ISDN are its digital nature and its separate control and signaling channel. The potential for computer and telephony development using this signaling will multiply far beyond what the originators of ISDN ever conceived. In a way, signaling is more important than the digital part; of course, it's difficult in this day and age to think of significant and economic signaling that doesn't make use of digital techniques.

Signaling furnishes the basis for redesigning the entire telephone system. Today that system is based on dumb telephones and smart telephone exchanges. With the advent of signaling through ISDN, intelligence can and will move out of the central exchange and be distributed throughout the network. I'd bet that within a matter of years, no more than 15 at best, most of the intelligence in the network will reside at the subscribers' locations and not at the telcos'.

The telcos will devote most of their investment to high capacity transmission lines, capable of handling more than the traditional types and categories of phone company products and services. The companies will move from expensive, multifunctional switches to less expensive, limited function switches with simple architectures composed of millions of repeated modules. These modules will use the asynchronous transfer mode (ATM) technology to zip digital data wherever and however your intelligent equipment wants. Chapter 18, "Anticipating Broadband ISDN," covers ATM technology in detail.

▶ **See** the Chapter 19 section entitled "Moving Control from the Telephone Company," **p. 540**, for a discussion of this change in location of intelligence.

Your mission in this chapter, should you choose to undertake it, is to go where few have gone before. To plunge into a conceptual understanding of the innards of telephone system signaling, emerging unscathed and ready for the task of harnessing ISDN to your system, thereby bringing the fall of the almighty centrally controlled telephone network.

Your reward for this effort will be a more complete understanding of the concepts of ISDN control and signaling. This will pay off when you begin using ISDN and wrestle with what happens there while troubleshooting and designing.

ISDN telepioneers of the world unite. You have nothing to lose but your bondage to the intelligence of the central switch. ∎

 The first reader to determine the identity of the document from which I so crassly paraphrased the foregoing and e-mail the correct answer to me, will be rewarded with an allexpensepaid sandwich of his or her own choosing, collectible when I autograph such winner's book.

Digital Subscriber Signaling System 1 (DSS1)

Digital Subscriber Signaling System 1 (DSS1) is designed so your equipment can ask for services across the network. It is a collection of signaling protocols that are directed at the local exchange carrier's switch. DSS1 is a creature of ISDN only. Analog systems do not and cannot use DSS1 because they cannot send digital signals.

 We're about to talk about Digital Subscriber Signaling System 1 (DSS1). The *ISDN User Part* (ISUP) is not the same thing. Why do I insert this tip prior even to explaining anything? Because the terminology is so intertwined and confusing. If you get this tip now, things are much easier later.

Once DSS1 requests arrive at the switch, the switch interprets them and forwards any requests it does not fulfill across the interexchange network to other switches. This information is carried by Signaling System 7 (SS7). SS7 is much more complex than DSS1. SS7 handles both ISDN and analog calls. We'll get into the details of SS7 later, in the section entitled "Signaling System 7 (SS7)."

Q.931

A great deal of what goes into DSS1 comes from ITU-T standard Q.931. In fact, most literature and talk about this part of signaling often throws everything into Q.931 even though many other standards in the same series are actually involved. In fact, Q.931 deals with basic call control such as bearer services. Supplementary services, such as hold, call waiting, et al, are the subject of Q.932. Enough of the magic numbers for now. How's it work and fit together?

In order to understand what all this is really about, you have to understand the difference between:

- Stimulus signaling
- Functional signaling

In the beginning there was stimulus signaling. Remember my old party-line phone in Waxahachie? When I picked up the receiver the phone went "off hook." This caused a light to flash at the central office telling the operator to plug into the jack near the light and say "Number please." My phone didn't store information or understand what was going on. It could only communicate in very simple ways. The same is true of both a rotary dial and DTMF (tone) phone. They send simple signals to a complex switch that interprets those signals. Even a multibutton phone fits into this scheme of simple devices. In telephone parlance, these are all *stimulus signaling* examples. In computer language, we have the classic dumb terminal (like a POTS phone) to smart host (telco switch) situation (see Fig. 5.1).

FIG. 5.1

Stimulus Signaling. The POTS phone has no intelligence, much like a dumb computer terminal. Both depend on a smart host or switch to do all their thinking. So the POTS phone and dumb terminal communicate only through stimulus signaling.

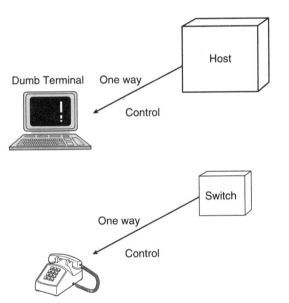

An ISDN phone, on the other hand, has internal intelligence. This means it is some form of a computer. It is capable of understanding complex digital signals from the switch and acting accordingly. In buzzwords, an ISDN phone is a *state machine* that creates different states of operation based on signaling received and sent. Given this capability at the user end, it's just a short step to connecting a full scale computer and really wringing the most out of DSS1. Intelligent devices are engaged in functional *signaling*. Computer people would call this *peer to peer* or *distributed intelligence* communication (see Fig. 5.2).

FIG. 5.2

Functional Signaling. The telephone system on the bottom is much like the computer network on top. Both have intelligent devices at both ends of all connections. As a result every device can engage in functional signaling.

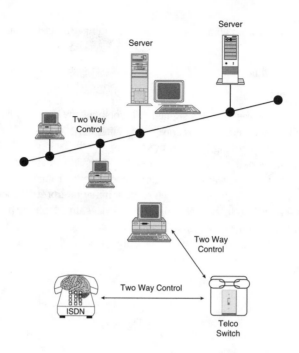

Computing has abandoned the terminal to host model in favor of the peer to peer model. The same is happening in telephony. You may expect the results to be at least as profound in upsetting telephony technology and economics as the computer shift was.

That portion of DSS1 that concerns bearer services, Q.931, fits into the ISO OSI model at layer three, the network layer. Supplementary services fit somewhat into that layer and into the higher layers (see Fig. 5.3).

Information is sent through DSS1 in a structure pictured conceptually in Figure 5.4. Of course, if you cut open a wire while DSS1 is flying by, you won't see anything like Figure 5.4; all the drawing does is show the various fields that make up the protocol in a picture form that reflects their relationships. In reality, everything pictured is made up of strings of ones and zeros, or, more concretely, of variations in electrical states that we interpret as ones and zeros. The protocol defines the meanings we attach to certain groupings of those bits and the drawing helps put everything in perspective. The top part, *protocol discriminator,* is an octet that tells the equipment what protocol this is, DSS1. This octet makes it possible to use protocols other than DSS1 since the discriminator identifies each protocol. The protocol discriminator for Q.931 is always 8.

FIG. 5.3

Digital Subscriber Signaling System 1 and the ISO OSI Model. The Q.931 portion corresponds to layer 3. Q.932, supplementary services, takes in layers 4 through 7 with some involvement with layer 3.

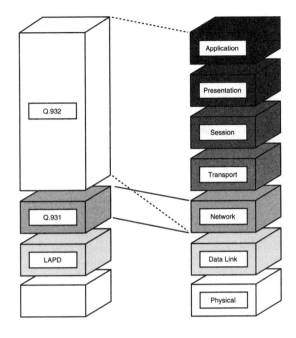

FIG. 5.4

DSS1 Message Structure.

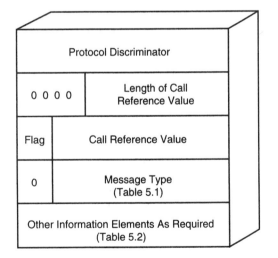

The balance of the structure consists of:

- Length of the reference value
- A flag
- Call reference value itself that tells what call the message concerns

■ Message type that gives the specific control to be undertaken as shown in Table 5.1.

■ Other information elements that concern additional details as shown in Table 5.2. There are no column headings because this is simply a list of possible information elements.

Table 5.1   Message Types in DSS1

Establishment	Information	Clearing	Miscellaneous
Alerting	User Information	Disconnect	Segment
Call Proceeding	Suspend Reject	Restart	Facility
Progress	Resume Reject	Release	Register
Setup	Hold	Restart Acknowledge	Notify
Connect	Suspend	Release Complete	Status Inquiry
Setup Acknowledge	Resume		Congestion Control
Connect Acknowledge	Hold Acknowledge Suspend Acknowledge Resume Acknowledge Hold Reject Retrieve Retrieve Acknowledge Retrieve Reject		Information Status

Table 5.2   Information Elements in DSS1

Reserved	Shift	More Data	Sending Complete
Congestion Level	Repeat Indicator	Segmented Message	Bearer Capacity
Cause	Call Identify	Call State	Channel Identification
Facility	Progress Indicator	Network-Specific Facilities	Notification Indicator
Display	Date/Time	Keypad Facility	Signal
Switchhook	Feature Activation	Feature Indication	Information Rate
End-to-End Transit Delay	Transit Delay Selection and Indication	Packet Layer Binary Parameters	Packet Layer Window Size
Packet Size	Calling Party Number	Calling Party Subaddress	Called Party Number

Called Party Subaddress	Redirecting Number	Transit Network Selection	Restart Indicator
Low Layer Compatibility	High Layer Compatibility	User-User	Escape for Extension

In Table 5.1, all the messages can go in either direction, from the user to the switch or the switch to the user, with the exception of those involving resume and suspend. In the cases of "resume" and "suspend" the messages are always from the user to the switch. In the cases of either acknowledging or rejecting a resume or suspend, the messages flow from the switch to the user.

A detailed description of all the messages in the tables would take us far afield. Most are self-explanatory. The others are covered well in more technical materials suggested in the bibliography. Our goal here is to grasp the concepts of what's going on without becoming too enmeshed in details. Take a look at a call using DSS1 in the following mini-table. The left column shows the common analog language; the right column shows the major DSS1 messages sent by the caller's side. Similar messages would flow back from the called party:

Common Analog Language	Major DSS1 Messages Sent by Caller Side
Phone off hook	Setup
Dial	Call Proceeding
Ringing	Alerting
Answered	Connect
Talking	(None)
Hang up	Disconnect/Release

The example I've just drawn uses Q.931 messages to set up and tear down a call. When you jump into the supplementary services using Q.932, a lot more can happen than you might expect from analog experience. I'll give you a taste.

▶ **See** the section later in this chapter entitled "ISDN User Part (ISUP)," **p. 114**

Remember that POTS uses in-band signaling and ISDN uses out-of-band, common channel signaling. This has some interesting ramifications for features you're used to. Take call waiting. On POTS when you receive a call during the progress of another, you hear a beep and the party you're speaking with hears—nothing—a gap in what your were saying (I'm told that in some technology blighted parts of the States the other party is subjected to various sounds from a beep to a deafening click). This happens because your telco switch grabs the line momentarily to inject the signal that you are receiving another call.

With ISDN, the existence of the additional call is carried over the DSS1/SS7 signaling system. There is no interruption in your current call. Rather, at your prior option, your phone display flashes, your computer screen pops up a notice or a sound comes from the phone itself. The party you're speaking with does not experience a blank space in sound or some strange noises.

Part

II

Ch

5

Now you may have many options. You can switch to the new calling party. You might have things programmed so that the new call goes to a voice mail area. It might be held in a queue. "A queue? What do you mean a queue? A queue of one?" you ask.

This is where things get bizarre from our POTS experience. You might have several calls queued up while you finish the one you're on. You may have a system that will direct the calls to a holding pattern in order of receipt, calling number identification, you name it.

This may sound unwieldy. It is, right now. Your job is to figure out how you can really use such control. You still have only one B channel, let's say. Maybe you want to conference some of the parties together. You can do that with ISDN.

Let's make it more interesting. We've talked about ordinary voice calls. What about data calls and faxes? You no longer lose sleep over being sure you disable call waiting when you make or receive a data call. The waiting state will not damage the data transmission. Let's use this for a purely data instance. You design software or have someone do it for you so the software uses the signaling to queue up a number of data calls. You're not charged by the telco for a call that is not completed even though it ends up in the queue. So you can queue up a number of data calls, analyze them, and complete them in the order in which your software is designed to establish. This can make for very efficient use of circuits. The parts are all there. It's up to you to make it happen. Of course, if you don't want to make it happen, you'll get a chance to pay someone else that designs the program, boxes it up, and sells a million copies at the local drive in software stores. Once you start thinking about this, you'll realize why signaling is where ISDN will make the biggest inroads and lead to a revolution in how we use telecommunications.

Of SPIDs and Buses

One more detail of DSS1 may be of immediate interest and use to you. You'll find most configurations for your equipment will require a *SPID* (Service Profile Identifier). This is a part of DSS1 that makes the *passive bus* work.

Passive bus? SPID? The cable coming out of your NT-1, the S/T interface side that connects to your equipment, can be connected to several pieces of equipment simultaneously. Now that sounds like nothing new. But, remember ISDN can and often has to be configured; telcospeak is "provisioned" to fit the equipment you're using. Remember Chapter 4, "Choosing Services," and look out for Chapter 7, "Ordering ISDN Services."

This means you may have several devices each of a different type on one wire. The SPID works with the telco switch to make this happen and to prevent contention on the bus in the event of multiple calls while one device is tying up a given B channel. The SPID is associated with a logical process using the device. The *terminal identifier* (TEI) also assists and defines the equipment itself. A single TEI might have a number of SPIDs associated with it. This has become so complex that some telcos have opted not to support bus contention. You can usually tell when that is the case because you'll only be able to use one SPID per B channel.

Signaling System 7 (SS7)

Signaling System 7 is designed to handle all types of telephone communications among local (digital) exchange and interexchange switches. This includes both ISDN and POTS (analog), while DSS1 deals only with ISDN.

SS7 is responsible for signaling and control of the entire telephone system except for the local loops. As a result, the reliability of SS7 is a paramount design consideration. SS7 is to have no more than ten minutes of downtime on a link during a year! SS7 is to provide dynamic rerouting over redundant links. Think about it. If this measure of reliability were not included, major portions of the system could be down for hours. Designers and builders have worked long and hard to prevent such failures.

N O T E   Please understand that SS7 is not fully implemented throughout the telephone system in the United States. But the industry is working toward that goal. ▪

As we've already seen, much of the use you'll make sending traffic through the network relies on circuit mode methods. But control of the network through SS7 is packet mode. In fact, when you make a call, the control path through SS7 may be the same as the bearer path. In other cases, the path may be different.

SS7 is so robust it might establish different paths for different B channels. This possibility can lead to timing differences in propagation of originally simultaneous blocks of information. In time-critical applications such as video and in aggregation of B channels this can be a major problem. The solution is the option to specify an allowed variation in B channel propagation times. This is illustrated by the service denominated "circuit-mode 2×64 kbps unrestricted, 8 kHz structured bearer service" described among the bearer services in Chapter 4.

Does this sound complex? Sure. But SS7 is charged with making the complexity transparent to you and your applications.

Part

II

Ch

5

Lasciate Ogni Speranza voi ch'entrate!

"Through me is the way into the woeful city; through me is the way into the eternal woe; through me is the way among the lost people. Justice moved my lofty maker: the divine Power, the supreme Wisdom and the primal Love made me. Before me were no things created, save eternal, and I eternal last. Abandon all hope, ye who enter!"

For those of you who have not personally seen it, this is the inscription over the gate of Hell. We have this on the authority of Dante Alighieri, author of the *Divine Comedy* (Canto III, 1-9).

What Dante withheld from his readers may now be revealed. Just on the other side of the gate, in a nook reserved for technotypes, rests the detailed specification of Signaling System 7 with its twisting paths connecting *signaling points* to *signal transfer points* over *signaling links* and establishing *control planes* to set up *information planes*.

continues

continued

The balance of Dante's depiction of Hell is quite adequate to scare you into salvation without undertaking SS7 theology. But, we'll give it a shot. If you feel compelled to leap over the labyrinthian bowels of such obtuse terminology and emerge safely(?) in the Purgatory of current telephony as we know it, by all means go for it.

The essential element of SS7 of interest to most ISDN users is call management or control establishing the path that will carry your information (*setup*), passing the information (*maintenance*), and tearing down the path when you're finished (*termination*).

SS7 defines three functions that must be invoked to make this "control plane" work:

- **Signaling points:** Places that can handle SS7 messages.
- **Signal transfer points:** Signaling points with the capability to route control messages.
- **Signaling links:** Connections between these points.

Call management sets up a path for your information by traversing signaling points and determining routes through signal transfer points. Signaling links tie it all together. Once the path is established, your equipment transmits information over that path—the "information plane" in SS7 operation.

In order to establish the level of operational reliability that's required of SS7, connections among the signaling points, and especially among the signal transfer points, should have many possible paths. In the event of failure, a signal transfer point (*router* to you computer nerds) can choose an alternative path.

The goal is to have a large, complex, *mesh topology*. This is a fancy way of saying a lot of alternative routes. The most vital signal transfer points ideally should all be connected directly to all other most vital signal transfer points and thus have a fully meshed topology. This could be quite expensive or impossible for more than a handful of such nodes, so network design is hierarchical with these few, vital, nodes on top.

I haven't spared you the protocol diagrams in other areas; why start now? Here's the fundamental one for SS7: Figure 5.5.

The next several sections explain the various parts of this protocol diagram.

Message Transfer Part (MTP)

This consists of the first two layers of the ISO OSI model and part of the third. It's the boxcar that carries everything else along.

The signaling network part of the message transfer part (yes, you got that right, "parts of parts") is really interesting. This is where much of the routing goes on. Look at the procedures for protection in cases of failure or degradation in the links available in Table 5.3.

FIG. 5.5

Signaling System 7
Protocol Diagram.

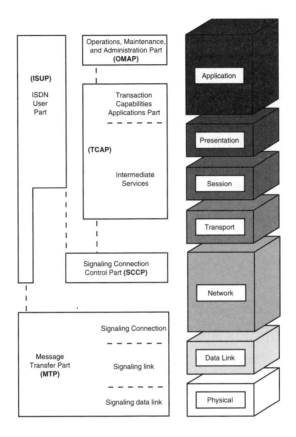

Table 5.3   Signaling Network Management Procedures

Traffic	Link	Route
Changeover	Signaling link activation, restoration, deactivation	Transfer-controlled procedure
Changeback	Link set activation	Transfer-prohibited procedure
Forced rerouting	Automatic allocation of signaling terminals and signaling data links	Transfer-allowed procedure
Controlled rerouting		Transfer-restricted procedure
Signaling point restart		Signaling-route-set-test procedure
Management inhibiting		Signaling-route-set congestion test procedure
Signaling traffic flow control		

I don't want to try to bury you in the detail of traffic control. Just look at the terms that are reasonably self-explanatory and notice the control exercised over routing through SS7.

Message handling functions are involved in figuring out where a message is in its trip through the network and getting it on the next place. The functions have to decide if the message is at its destination or should continue to be relayed, where it should be relayed and where in the complex structure it should be delivered.

Signaling Connection Control Part (SCCP)

This does just what it says; SCCP provides control of connections. Basically SCCP provides additions to the abilities within the message transfer services. It has greater addressing ability for example. SCCP also provides added message transfer services. There are four major functions that it provides:

- Connection-oriented control
- Connectionless control
- Management
- Routing control

Transaction Capabilities Application Part (TCAP)

This is a catchall for functions that don't seem properly to tie into other modules. It is particularly concerned with specialized transactions such as dealing with cellular or mobile equipment roaming, and mapping 800 numbers to underlying directory numbers.

Operations, Maintenance, and Administration Part (OMAP)

This is designed to maintain SS7 itself. Because the entire telephone network is critical to the economy, safety, and security of our populations, this part monitors and, hopefully, avoids, major problems that would result in failures.

ISDN User Part (ISUP)

The real guts are where you and your information come in. This is called the *ISDN User Part*. Remember my admonition in a tip at the first of this chapter: The ISDN User Part is *not* communications between your equipment and your local exchange carrier's switch; that is handled by DSS1 using Q.931 and Q.932 among other protocols.

The ISDN User Part is that part of Signaling System 7 that works with DSS1 and makes what you want happen in the much more complex environment of SS7. You use DSS1 to communicate with your local exchange carrier's switch. That switch uses SS7 to communicate with other switches throughout the network. The ISDN User Part carries the signaling needed to make your information flow through the network. Take our frequent example of a typical call setup, use, and teardown in the context of SS7:

- DSS1 through Q.931 sends a *setup* message on the D channel to the switch. All of the information needed to establish the call, telephone numbers, type of service, etc., is within this message.

- SS7 makes routing decisions passing through a series of switches until the destination switch connected to your called party is reached.

- SS7 at the called party's switch takes the information and converts it back into DSS1 information and transmits that to the called party's equipment on the D channel.

- DSS1 initiates an *alert* message ringing the bell, flashing the screen or whatever at the called party's location.

- The called party answers and a *connect* message is sent back using DSS1 to the switch. The connect message is converted to SS7, sent to your switch, re-converted to DSS1 and sent to your equipment.

When the call is completed:

- The equipment of the party initiating the end of the call sends a *disconnect* message over DSS1 and the switch begins to release the switched path.

- This release is propagated through succeeding switches with timers set to be sure the release is applied in an order that does not leave a link hanging.

- At the opposite party's switch a *disconnect* is sent through DSS1 to that party's equipment.

- As each release finishes a *release complete* message is sent to the preceding switch.

From Here...

We've taken a rapid look at the makeup of ISDN signaling. The subject is much more technical than our brief overview could possibly present. But DSS1 and SS7 are the very backbone of ISDN. Without their cooperation we would have no ISDN and development of the future broadband ISDN network would be impossible. In coming chapters, I'll assemble what we've learned in these theoretical overviews. Understanding the way it fits together will make it much easier for you to use ISDN effectively.

Part
II

Ch
5

- Chapter 6, "Unscrambling APIs," delves into the last great standards mystery area you need to grasp before you can really choose ISDN products and make them work.

- Succeeding chapters in Part III, "ISDN Computer Hardware," get you into the meat. You learn to apply this theoretical knowledge to make ISDN work for you.

Unscrambling APIs

We're headed into it now. Having come through Chapter 4, "Choosing Services," and Chapter 5, "Signaling with ISDN," you're about to run headlong into *application program interfaces* (API). An API provides the connection between your applications and some other hardware or software. The richer an API in features and functions, the easier it is to use the other software or hardware and the less you have to write code or use esoteric commands.

Right away you're probably asking, "What do I need to know about APIs for? Isn't that something programmers do?" Unless of course you're a programmer, then you'll say, "Well, it's about time we got to the really important stuff."

Even if you're not a programmer, you need to know about APIs because they determine what, if anything, you can do with various combinations of hardware and software. When a new area is developing, as ISDN is, the lack of APIs impedes development and use of the technology. In the same way the need to select from a conflicting set of APIs hampers growth. For example, we'll see the CAPI (an API) is widely-accepted in Europe, but hardly known in North America. Were you to buy European products for use in North America, you would probably have to account for this difference and either find some way to support CAPI or write an API that fit North American needs.

WinISDN: designed specifically for ISDN and Windows

You'll find WinISDN makes using an ISDN card easy.

CAPI: designed for general use with ISDN and a number of operating systems

As we look at this, remember CAPI is essential in Europe, but it hasn't caught on in North America.

TAPI: designed for general use with telephony and Windows

You'll learn that Microsoft has designed TAPI to provide a way for you to control telephone use.

TSAPI: designed for LANs and telephone switches using Novell NetWare and AT&T switch designs or emulation's

You'll see that Novell aims to have TSAPI provide a foundation for computer telephony.

TIP   If you're a programmer, you'll want to read this chapter closely. If you're a regular human, feel free to scan the chapter avoiding the dangerous areas—code and commands—but still grabbing the main ideas.

The rubber hits the road for ISDN and APIs at two places:

- Connection between software on your system and the hardware you use to hook up to ISDN
- Connection between the applications you're running and other applications over the telephone network

Developers have come up with a number of solutions. Some use old methods, some use new methods, some are simple, some are complex.

The cheap and dirty way to communicate with a new technology like ISDN is to use an existing way of talking to well-developed earlier technologies. So you'll find:

- APIs for some ISDN products designed around the Hayes AT modem command set
- Using Novell's Open Data-link Interface (ODI) originally designed for talking with network interface cards
- Using the Microsoft/3Com Network Driver Interface Specification (NDIS) also designed for network cards

These methods are all great and get you started. But they were designed for modem or network interface card communication. ISDN is not the same. While modem AT commands know about dialing a phone, they don't know anything about all the complexity of bearer and supplementary services in ISDN. While ODI and NDIS are great for talking to network cards, they have not a clue about dialing a phone.

Which brings us to the second class of APIs, those specifically designed to work with the telephone system. Some are aimed only at ISDN; others are more general. Some work with only one computer operating system, others handle a number of operating systems. We'll look specifically at four APIs that are certain to come up in most discussions of ISDN:

N O T E   There are certainly other APIs that concern ISDN. Intel, for example, is working on *Protocol Independent Interface* (PII) that is based on the Windows Sockets specification (WinSock) though it is not to be a part of the official WinSock spec. PII is designed to allow the WinSock API to be used over multiple network transport providers including ISDN. It conforms to Microsoft's Windows Open Systems Architecture (WOSA). ■

WinISDN

Let's start with WinISDN. It's the simplest being designed only for Windows and only to fill in the gaps needed to do basic telephone functions. This will get our feet wet in issues and methods that surround telephony APIs. And, since I suspect most of you will be using Windows, it may be all you need.

 TIP WinISDN is probably for you if you only use Windows (or DOS inside Windows or Win-OS/2), your hardware supports it, you're using TCP/IP, and you don't need elaborate supplementary services or third-party call control. (See the later sidebar "Is This the Party to Whom I Am Speaking" for a definition of first and third-party call control.)

What Is WinISDN?

WinISDN is the new kid on the block. The WinISDN specification was final in January of 1995. ISDN*tek, an ISDN hardware card maker, NetManage, a maker of TCP/IP software for Internet communication and PSI, a national Internet service provider, teamed up in its design. WinISDN is being incorporated into products from NetManage, Spry, FTP, Frontier, Wollongong, ISDN*tek, IBM, ISDN Systems Corp, 3Com/AccessWorks, Shiva, and Motorola. Other firms are expected to adopt WinISDN.

N O T E There's a TCP/IP stack in Windows 95; this does not offer WinISDN at this time. But you may choose to use some other TCP/IP stack that does contain WinISDN with Windows 95, for instance NetManage Internet Chameleon. I'll defer the specific API additions for Windows 95 to Chapter 12, "Opening Windows 95 and NT to ISDN." ▦

 TIP Read all about it! WinISDN, that is, at **ftp://ftp.netmanage.com/pub/win_standards/winisdn/ winisdn.doc**. You'll find the specs for WinISDN.

Just what do you need to do to use a phone with your PC? This sounds basic, and it is. In a nutshell, you want to perform five tasks as shown in Figure 6.1:

■ Open a telephone line
■ Connect to another device over the telephone line

- Read and write from and through the connection to the other device
- Disconnect
- Close the telephone line

FIG. 6.1

The Phone and the
Computer.

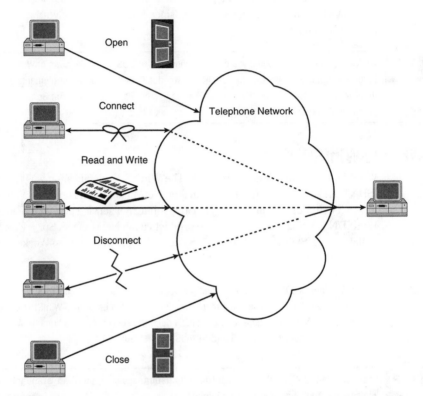

WinISDN performs the five basic tasks we've just defined by slipping in-between the TCP/IP protocol stack on your computer and the ISDN hardware (see Fig. 6.2). To make WinISDN work on your computer, you install the WinISDN.DLL software. It processes the commands and passes them on to your ISDN hardware. At this time, the only products being offered with WinISDN are TCP/IP protocol stacks. If market demand appears significant for other protocols, WinISDN might be adapted to them. Some private developers have used WinISDN for other protocols for internal use.

FIG. 6.2
WinISDN in the ISO OSI
Model.

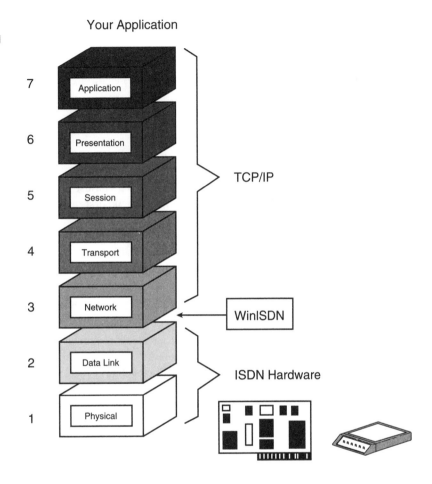

Your Application

7 Application

6 Presentation

5 Session

4 Transport

3 Network

2 Data Link

1 Physical

TCP/IP

WinISDN

ISDN Hardware

Programming with WinISDN

Part
II

Ch
6

CAUTION

We are now entering the obtuse world of programming APIs. The code I am about to present is for your conceptual edification only. If you really want to write code for WinISDN or any of the other APIs in this chapter, get a *Software Developer's Kit* (SDK). These kits are usually reasonably priced and provide utilities and documentation you'll need.

TIP Pack up your old kit bag and head for **http://www.isdntek.com** to find out more about the WinISDN SDK.

WinISDN can place and manage a basic telephone call through these functions:

```
ISDNOpen()
ISDNConnect()
ISDNRead()
ISDNWrite()
ISDNDisConnect()
ISDNClose()
```

The parentheses contain the specifics and parameters for use of the function. If you were to write a program in WinISDN to place a call, you would first reset the ISDN board and then use the function calls with appropriate entries for parameters.

```
ISDNSetRequest(ISDN_REQ_RESET_BOARD;
            ISDNOpen();
                        ISDNConnect();
                                    ISDNRead();
                                    ISDNWrite();
                                    ISDNDisconnect();
            ISDNClose();
```

Most of the parameters are kind of boring and would require a lot of explanation. The ISDNConnect() function has some parameters that are reasonably self-explanatory and will give the idea of the range of flexibility an API must have to deal with ISDN. These are not all the parameters for ISDNConnect(); these concern only the call type. I'll insert some of the descriptions from Chapter 4 where we covered bearer services in the section entitled "Circuit-Mode Bearer Services:

- ISDN_H_CHANNEL
- ISDN_D_CHANNEL
- ISDN_B_VOICE
- ISDN_B_56K: Remember that 56 kbps is not recognized in the ITU-T standard but is used in the United States for bit-robbing bearer service when a telephone system is not able to carry the full 64 kbps and must rob a bit for signaling. This usually means the system lacks SS7.
- ISDN_B_64K
- ISDN_B_112K
- ISDN_B_128K
- ISDN_B_64K_OS: Here's our circuit-mode 64 kbps unrestricted, 8 kHz structured bearer service. The OS refers to "octet synchronous" and simply means the data is broken into octets providing internal synchronization.
- ISDN_B_128K: Octet Synchronous
- ISDN_B_DOV: Data Over Voice
- ISDN_B_VS: Voice Stream Data Pump

- ISDN_B_DS_56K: Data Stream Data Pump
- ISDN_B_DS_64K: Data Stream Data Pump
- ISDN_Intercom: Data Stream Intercom

ISDNConnect( ) also has parameters for passing a *directory number* to dial and a number of other, more technical, parameters. So when WinISDN connects with the telephone switch, it tells the switch the directory number you want and the type of call you're placing. It can establish a different call type for each B channel you have available. So you might have B channel 1 using voice and B channel 2 using 64 kbps structured data (octet synchronous). See Figure 6.3.

FIG. 6.3
Voice and Data Using
Two B Channels.

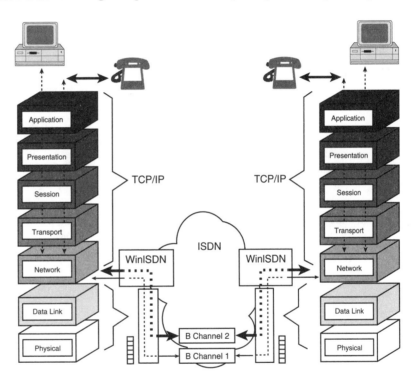

One of the interesting features in WinISDN is its capability to use an "intercom" function to record and play back audio information locally. You might use this with a voice mailbox or answering system.

All of the functions I've described so far fit into the category of "basic" functions of WinISDN:

- ISDNOpen( )
- ISDNClose( )
- ISDNConnect( )
- ISDNDisconnect( )
- ISDNListenForConnection( )

Part
II

Ch
6

- ISDNAccept()
- ISDNReject()
- ISDNRead()
- ISDNWrite()
- ISDNGetEventMask()
- ISDNSetEventMask()

But there's a collection of "advanced" functions that work with ISDN Supplementary Services such as hold and conference along with other Q.932 functions.

Is This the Party to Whom I Am Speaking?

These advanced functions also allow what the telephone industry calls *third-party call control.* When you receive a call and communicate with the calling person, that's *first-party call control.* When you transfer a call to someone else and lose control of the call, it's still first-party call control. But if you have an elaborate PBX or an *automatic call distributor* (ACD), third-party call control may be involved. In this case, control is maintained over the call even after it's sent elsewhere. In ACD systems, the whole point is recognition of an incoming call, direction of that call to a preselected point, and continued control over the call so it may be rerouted as needed. (Before you ask, there is no second-party call control.)

In the context of APIs, WinISDN supports both TAPI and CAPI (we'll be taking them up later in this chapter) to provide for more complex systems that might use the richer APIs or third-party call control. The advanced functions within WinISDN are:

- ISDNGetStatus()
- ISDNFlush()
- ISDNSetRequest()
- ISDNGetIndication()
- ISDNReadCallControl()
- ISDNWriteCallControl()
- ISDNGetConfiguration()
- ISDNSetConfiguration()
- ISDNGetBoardEventMask()
- ISDNSetBoardEventMask()
- ISDNReadInfoElement()

CAPI

Common-ISDN-API (CAPI)was developed in Europe. Germany led the way and now has the most ISDN usage in the world. CAPI's most recent form is version 2.0. CAPI has a much more powerful collection of functions than WinISDN. While WinISDN is designed only for computers using the Microsoft Windows operating system, CAPI supports many more operating systems:

- Microsoft DOS
- Microsoft Windows
- IBM OS/2
- UNIX
- Novell NetWare

 T I P Cap off your research on CAPI with a visit to **http://www.alumni.caltech.edu/~dank/isdn/capi/ capi20.zip** for the specs. Be sure to crawl up to the isdn level and see all the references in Dan Kegel's super ISDN Page.

If you buy European hardware, especially German hardware, for ISDN, expect to receive CAPI support as the first and most heavily developed API. CAPI is designed to handle various permutations of applications and controllers. So you may use:

- A single application and single driver and controller
- One application using multiple drivers and controllers
- Many applications using one driver and controller
- Many applications sharing many drivers and controllers (see Fig. 6.4).

FIG. 6.4
Multiple Applications and Controllers with CAPIIV.

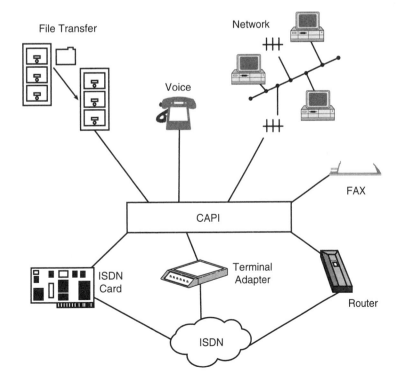

Part
II

Ch
6

CAPI Messages

The interface for CAPI is between layers three and four of the ISO OSI model. In CAPI, communication is through *messages* that are either a *request* from an application followed by a *confirmation* from CAPI or an *indication* from CAPI followed by a *response* from the application (see Fig. 6.5).

FIG. 6.5

CAPI Request/
Confirmation and
Indication/Response.

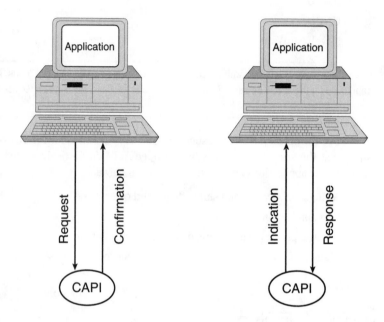

The messages have a fixed length header followed by a variable number of parameters. The header contains details of the CAPI command. Figure 6.6 is a diagram of a CAPI message with an expansion diagram showing header detail. The detail reflects all the contents in the message header. Table 6.1 explains the header contents.

Table 6.1 Message Header Contents

Message	Type	Contents
Total length	word	Total length of the message including the complete message header
ApplID	word	Identification of the application. The application number is assigned to the application by CAPI in the CAPI_REGISTER operation.
Command	byte	Command
Subcommand	byte	Command extension
Message number	word	Message number as described above

FIG. 6.6

CAPI Message Diagram.

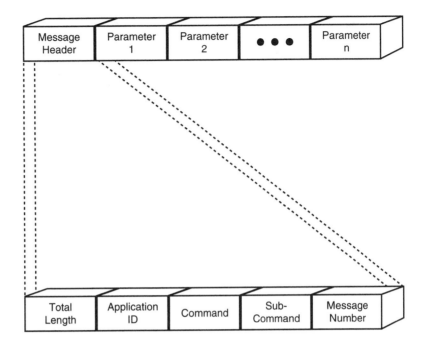

What's This Guy Throwing at Us?

The whole programming language? Why? The answers are yes and no, and because. This isn't the whole CAPI language, but it's all the verbs. I've spared you the parameters and full details; those take 200 pages in the specification. Just look at how tight and detailed the designers made this stuff. Recognize that CAPI is the most complete, most tested, most used ISDN API currently available.

 Program your Web browser for `http://www.avm-usa.com/ capi.htm` to find the system developer's kit for CAPI.

Part II

Ch 6

All of CAPI messages fall into three groups each regarding:

- Signaling protocols for the D channel (see Table 6.2)
- Logical connections for B or D channel communications (see Table 6.3)
- Administrative and other messages (see Table 6.4)

As you examine these tables, notice how everything falls into the categories *request, confirmation, indication* or *response*. Review Figure 6.5 to see how the flow of information supports this.

Table 6.2   Messages Regarding Signaling Protocols

Message	Description
CONNECT_REQ	Initiates an outgoing physical connection
CONNECT_CONF	Local confirmation of request
CONNECT_IND	Indicates an incoming physical connection
CONNECT_RESP	Response to indication
CONNECT_ACTIVE_IND	Indicates the activation of a physical connection
CONNECT_ACTIVE_RESP	Response to indication
DISCONNECT_REQ	Initiates clearing of a physical connection
DISCONNECT_CONF	Local confirmation of request
DISCONNECT_IND	Indicates the clearing of a physical connection
DISCONECT_RESP	Response to indication
ALERT_REQ	Initiates sending of ALERT, i.e. compatibility to call
ALERT_CONF	Local confirmation of request
INFO_REQ	Initiates sending of signaling information
INFO_CONF	Local confirmation of request
INFO_IND	Indicates selected signaling information
INFO_RESP	Response to indication

Table 6.3   Messages Regarding Logical Connections

Message	Description
DISCONNECT_B3_IND	Indicates the clearing of a logical connect
DISCONNECT_B3_CONF	Local confirmation of request
DISCONNECT_B3_RESP	Response to indication
DATA_B3_REQ	Initiates sending of data on a logical connection
DATA_B3_CONF	Local confirmation of request
DATA_B3_IND	Indicates incoming data on a logical connection
DATA_B3_RESP	Response to indication
RESET_B3_REQ	Initiates the reset of a logical connection
RESET_B3_CONF	Local confirmation of request
RESET_B3_IND	Indicates the reset of a logical connection

Message	Description
RESET_B3_RESP	Response to indication
CONNECT_B3_REQ	Initiates an outgoing connection
CONNECT_B3_CONF	Local confirmation of request
CONNECT_B3_IND	Indicates an incoming logical connection
CONNECT_B3_RESP	Response to indication
CONNECT_B3_ACTIVE_IND	Indicates the activation of logical connection
CONNECT_B3_ACTIVE_RESP	Response to indication
CONNECT_B3_T90_ACTIVE_IND	Indicates switching from T.70NL to T90NL
CONNECT_B3_T90_ACTIVE_RESP	Response to indication
DISCONNECT_B3_REQ	Initiates clearing of a logical connection

Table 6.4 Messages Regarding Administration and Other Matters

Message	Description
LISTEN_REQ	Activates call indications
LISTEN_CONF	Local confirmation of request
FACILITY_REQ	Requests additional facilities, e.g. external equipment
FACILITY_CONF	Local confirmation of request
FACILITY_IND	Indicates additional facilities, e.g. external equipment
FACILITY_RESP	Response to indication
SELECT_B_PROTOCOL_REQ	Selects current protocol stack of a logical connection
SELECT_B_PROTOCOL_CONF	Local confirmation of request
MANUFACTURER_REQ	Manufacturer specific operation
MANUFACTURER_CONF	Manufacturer specific operation
MANUFACTURER_IND	Manufacturer specific operation
MANUFACTURER_RESP	Manufacturer specific operation

Part
II

Ch
6

CAPI Message Queues

Communication between an application program and CAPI is through message queues. There is one and only one message queue directed into each registered program. All communication from CAPI to that program must go through the queue. Messages go in a first in first out (FIFO) order.

There is one and only one message queue for messages into CAPI. All communications from all programs going into CAPI must go through that queue in FIFO order (see Fig. 6.7).

FIG. 6.7

Message Queues.

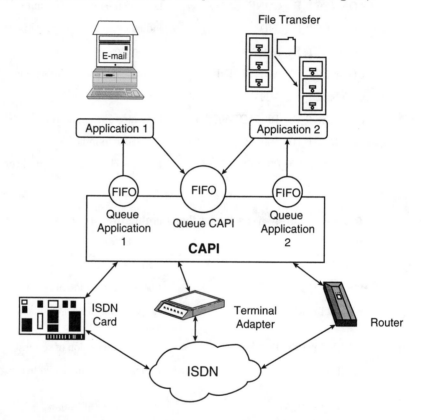

There are only four major operations on CAPI queues. An application must be registered to participate; it's given a unique application number (ApplID) at registration and a queue is established for the application. After that the application may *put* information into the queue to CAPI and *get* information from the application's own queue. When the session is over, the application is *released*; this releases the application's message queue. So it boils down to four operations: register, get, put, release (plus some housekeeping) as shown in Table 6.5.

Table 6.5   CAPI Operations

Operation	Description
CAPI_REGISTER	Register an application
CAPI_RELEASE	Release an application
CAPI_PUT_MESSAGE	Transfer message to CAPI

Operation	Description
CAPI_GET_MESSAGE	Get message from CAPI
CAPI_SET_SIGNAL	Register call-back function
CAPI_GET_MANUFACTURER	Get manufacturer identification
CAPI_GET_VERSION	Get CAPI version number
CAPI_GET_SERIAL_NUMBER	Get serial number
CAPI_GET_PROFILE	Get capabilities of CAPI implementation
CAPI_MANUFACTURER	Manufacturer specific function

CAPI sure looks complete. It's done a great job in Europe and could in the United States. But, at this time who knows what will really happen. Why? The market battle in the United States is pitting Microsoft/Intel against Novell/AT&T with the APIs that follow.

TAPI

Windows Telephony API (TAPI) is a creature of Microsoft and Intel. It's designed specifically for Windows and is included in Windows 95. It's to be included with Windows NT. In short, TAPI is fundamental to the plans of Microsoft and Intel.

Words, Words, Words

A *word* is a defined size of the smallest "chunk" of information that a computer processes. Our Intel 386 and later processors work with a word size of 32 bits. Computer software may with that or smaller word sizes can be made to work on such processors. However, software that uses 16 bit words will be less efficient, and slower, than software designed to use a 32-bit word. WinISDN was originally designed for 16-bit words. It is now being designed to handle 32-bit words. TAPI uses 32 bit words.

TAPI has both a front end API that works with Windows telephony features and a backend service provider interface (SPI) that gives Windows access to telephony hardware and services.

It looks like *deja vu* because TAPI provides services similar to the ones we've seen in WinISDN and CAPI. TAPI can establish, answer, and terminate telephone calls. TAPI can invoke supplementary services such as hold, conference, and transfer. TAPI is extensible to future telephony features.

TAPI is a part of Microsoft's Windows Open Services Architecture (WOSA) designed for large organizations with far-flung operations that need to communicate; the short hand for this is "enterprise computing." Microsoft is doing something similar here to its original work with Windows and printers. Think back to pre-Windows days (if you can). Remember all the complexities of making printers work with each program you installed. Every program had its own

Part
II

Ch
6

drivers for each printer. When you bought a program, a major consideration was whether or not the program had full support for your printer. If it did not, you might end up with use of only a few of your printer's features because you'd have to emulate the lowest common denominator printer between your equipment and the program.

Windows solved all that. Printer makers wrote software drivers to Windows. Application writers wrote programs for Windows. And Windows took care of providing identical, and fully functional, printer support to both. It became a win-win situation and one of the reasons Windows became so popular. TAPI and WOSA seek to capitalize on that basis for the success of Windows.

Application developers write to TAPI. Makers of telephone equipment write to the SPI provided by Microsoft. So each group only has to make one collection of code; that is, if they are satisfied with staying only in Microsoft's camp of Windows clients and Windows NT servers. Looks like Bill Gates might have a plan here?

Competitive Advantage

If CAPI were to become the dominate API in the United States, the several operating systems it supports would be equally advantageous to users in so far as telephony applications for ISDN are concerned. So, users might choose MS-DOS, UNIX, OS/2, Windows, or NetWare and even mix and match operating systems in their telephony environment. But if virtually all applications and hardware makers in the U.S. support only TAPI, all of a sudden we're down to the operating systems of only one software firm. I leave it as a test question for you to figure out the name of that firm. Buzzz, time's up; if you did not answer "Microsoft" take three baby steps back and reread the section "TAPI" from the beginning.

N O T E　Contact managers provide an excellent example of how TAPI integration works. Symantec Corporation's "ACT!" version 2.04 contact manager is TAPI enabled. When a call is received ACT! displays a box where all TAPI call functions are shown. Caller identification can screen pop the caller's ACT! record. Calls can be placed from within ACT!. The TAPI call dialog box provides call transfer, forward and conference call set up. Logging of date, time, and duration of calls is automatic. Evidently, Symantec considers TAPI additions an important selling point; they may be downloaded at no cost. I expect you'll see similar integration and favorable costs in a number of other products. ▪

TAPI is an object-oriented environment. There are three objects that it manipulates:

- Phones
- Lines
- Calls

TAPI includes elements to handle ISDN; so it satisfies our primary need. Currently, TAPI focuses on the desktop, a single PC, and telephone. It is at this point that Novell with TSAPI appears to have an advantage as TSAPI is directed toward the network and call center operation. Microsoft claims that TAPI will be expanded to include these in the future. At any rate the list of companies supporting TAPI is probably in the hundreds at this point. Since it is to be included in Windows 95 and therefore does not cost the end-user anything extra, most developers are betting TAPI will become dominant in a large part of the market.

To make TAPI work, the user simply installs the TAPI.DLL on the machine. Microsoft supplies a software development kit for programmers. The kit has been available free from Microsoft's Internet FTP site and CompuServe.

 T I P Take your ftp software to TAPI at **ftp://ftp.microsoft.com/developr/TAPI/** where you'll find the SDK and lots more.

TAPI supports three telephony services:

- Basic services that correspond to POTS (plain old telephone service) and include ISDN bearer services
- Supplementary services that fit PBX and ISDN supplemental service profiles
- Extended services that allow for development of other services by service providers

Rather than subject you to more tables and diagrams for TAPI, I'm going to do something entirely different. Besides, the coding for TAPI doesn't strike me as to be as pretty as that of CAPI. But, as you'll see, we ISDNers may just have the best of both worlds.

Remember that TAPI is not ISDN specific; TAPI is Windows specific. So what about all that ISDN power developed for using CAPI? Microsoft has promised to provide a CAPI subsystem that uses TAPI within Windows 95. This makes it possible for CAPI supported hardware to work with Windows 95/TAPI out of the box. Microsoft is also preparing WinSock 2 to provide data transport for ISDN among several other protocols. WinSock 2 has been developed by Microsoft in conjunction with the WinSock Forum. When you have WinSock 2 and you write to it, you open up data transmission through not only ISDN, but also through LANs, ATM, and others.

▶ **See** "WinSock," **p. 382**

N O T E WinSock is a standard we'll look at carefully in Chapter 12. Trumpet WinSock is a widely used implementation of that standard. There are many implementations of WinSock in addition to Trumpet WinSock. ■

TAPI is also able to take advantage of Novell's TSAPI; I'll discuss TSAPI in the next section of this chapter. Northern Telecom has made a software product called "Tmap" that maps TAPI calls into the TSAPI environment created by Novell; so your Windows 95 applications with TAPI.DLL enabled and Tmap can call up TSAPI through a NetWare network.

Part

II

Ch

6

> **N O T E**   It's really important to remember that once we stepped into Microsoft's TAPI and Novell's
> TSAPI, we moved from questions of simply supporting ISDN to broader issues of computer-
> telephony integration. This is the reason I started with WinISDN; it's targeted at the most narrow issues
> of making ISDN work with Windows. CAPI encompasses more operating systems, but still focuses only
> on ISDN. By the time we get to TAPI and TASPI, we find ourselves involved in the strategic battles of the
> two industries, computers and telephony trying to merge. In the midst of this Novell and Microsoft are
> battling for turf. ISDN begins to fade into the background as the smoke of battle rises. ■

TSAPI

And, again, now for something completely different. All of the APIs we've seen so far are
"workstation-centric." They operate on your PC and provide little if anything for a telephone
switch or server in the way of new software.

What Party Is This, Speaking?

All of the APIs, up to this point, deal with "first-party call control," as discussed in the sidebar earlier
in this chapter titled "Is This the Party to Whom I Am Speaking?" Novell's TSAPI provides "third-party
call control." The API provides the basis for maintaining control over a call as the call switches about
all over your business, no matter where the parties are.

Novell's approach with Telephony Services API (TSAPI) is "server/PBX-centric." TSAPI supports:

- Microsoft Windows clients
- Novell NetWare clients
- Novell NetWare servers
- AT&T Switches and emulation's thereof

AT&T and Novell are jointly developing and promoting TSAPI as the way to bring together the
user's desktop equipment through a local area network and the telephone switch. TSAPI is
based on the European Computer Manufactures Association standard, Computer-Supported
Telecommunications Application (CSTA).

You'll note that this is the first time the PBX has been brought into our discussion. Novell's
idea is the switch must play a major part in any effective combination of telephony and computing. Figure 6.8 ties it all together. You already have a LAN running NetWare. You add a card
that connects to your PBX. Then you run NetWare Loadable Modules (NLM) for TSAPI. Configure the whole thing, and you're off and running with *computer telephony integration* (CTI).
The software is so sophisticated it can take over a lot of the *operations, administration and
maintenance* (OA&M) functions for the switch.

T I P   To check out the novel view of Novell see **http://netwire.novell.com/SalesMkt/**.

FIG. 6.8
TSAPI Architecture.

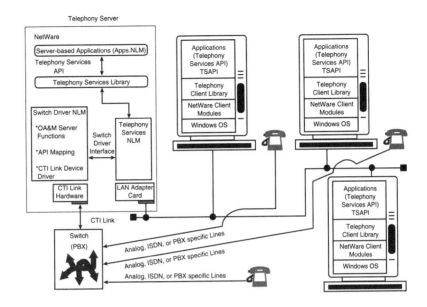

Telephone Switches and LAN Servers

Novell doesn't make telephone switches. Telephone switches are made by companies used to designing and selling into a high dollar, high margin market with long term depreciation and tariffs or government-assured cash flow. Novell, on the other hand, is used to selling into a fiercely competitive computer market with low dollars and low margins involving equipment that depreciates effectively to zero in a few years.

The only difference between a telephone switch and a computer is the name of the box and the maker. Punch out and wire up a few circuit cards, write some software, and your PC becomes a telephone switch. Novell is aiming to undercut the switch makers with LAN servers offering not just "telephony services" but soon "telephony switching services" as NetWare Loadable Modules (NLM) in servers.

I suggest you sell short any stock in a switch maker unless it can prove a capacity and willingness to totally convert to the computer industry way of doing things. Look at the dollar curves of the big computer firms one and two decades ago. Move those curves forward to now. Change the names to switch makers and consider yourself to have found a crystal ball. Try the same with local exchange carriers.

Novell supplies the software that makes this work. The primary elements are:

■ **Switch Driver:** This consists of NetWare Loadable Modules (NLM) designed for the switch you have. It links to the switch, maps protocols in the switch to TSAPI, takes over joint administration and maintenance of the driver for the switch, and supports the driver for the computer telephony integration hardware, some sort of card. This is switch-dependent as are the CTI Link and CTI Link hardware.

Part
II

Ch
6

- **Switch Driver Interface:** This software passes information and control between the switch driver and the Telephony Services NLM. This is switch-independent.

- **Telephony Services NLM:** This provides communication between telephony-enabled applications and the switch driver. Security is administered here. This is switch-independent.

- **TSAPI:** The services, data types and event messages used by telephony-enabled applications to access telephony services. This is switch-independent.

- **Telephony Server Library:** Server-based applications access TSAPI functions through this library. This is switch-independent.

- **Telephony Client Library:** Client-based applications access TSAPI functions through this library. This is switch-independent.

With the three earlier APIs, WinISDN, CAPI, and TAPI, you can execute typical telephone operations such as placing a call. With TSAPI, you can't do that. TSAPI has no way to place a call or perform a number of other such telephone operations. It expects the switch to do that. So, right away, you know that TSAPI is not going to do the simple things you need done to use ISDN.

So Just Where Does TSAPI Fit In?

TSAPI is designed for the larger business that has a PBX and wants extensive telephone and computer integration based on a centralized model. A potential problem with TSAPI is cost. Original information regarding server software costs is pointed in the direction of several thousands of dollars and to an added cost for each client software package. As the competitive feud between Novell and Microsoft heats up, it appears these costs are dropping rapidly.

If you need the computer telephony integration that comes with TSAPI, costs may not be a problem. Besides, you can use the Northern Telecom Tmap software to translate from your TAPI clients (remember TAPI comes with Windows 95) to TSAPI. This reduces costs for you and for application developers. I suspect that, as a result, developers will write to TAPI but not to TSAPI.

For your small office or home, I'll bet TAPI will take over totally with such ISDN help as might be needed from WinISDN and CAPI. TSAPI will probably be totally ignored here, as there would be no need for third-party call features.

However, in existing Novell NetWare small office environments, you might want to consider TSAPI; it'll come down to dollars, and the Tmap option helps a lot. Your alternative is going with TAPI and setting up your LAN based on Windows NT with TAPI for your computer telephony integration.

This is clearly one of Microsoft's best shots at prying you loose from NetWare, and the reason Microsoft is effectively giving TAPI away. Novell reconsidered what were originally high prices on TSAPI.

From Here...

We've dug pretty deeply into the APIs associated with ISDN and telephones. WinISDN provides a simple and effective way of controlling ISDN from Windows. CAPI gives elaborate and elegant ISDN support for MS DOS, Windows, OS/2, UNIX and NetWare. TAPI is built into Windows 95 and provides extensive telephone support including support for ISDN. TSAPI is designed for computer telephony integration using a NetWare server and a telephone switch; it depends on the switch for any ISDN support. You make the choice of the combination that's best for you.

We're now through the gates of theory and ready to cruise the road full speed and put together a practical ISDN solution in Parts III and IV.

- Chapter 7, "Ordering ISDN Services," tells you how to deal with the phone company and lead them through getting ISDN to you.
- Chapter 8, "Wiring and Powering Your ISDN System," shows the path through the rat's nest that might be your current telephone wiring.
- Chapters 9, 10, and 11 help you select the right ISDN hardware for your needs.
- Part IV, "Software and Applications," delves into interesting issues like configuration, multiple B channels, video practical uses, BBS/Internet providers and, surprise, telephones themselves.

Part

II

Ch

6

ISDN Computer Hardware

Ordering ISDN Services

Why a chapter on ordering telephone service? If you asked this question, the chances are you've not yet attempted to order ISDN, or when you ordered it you were very lucky. It's not as simple as POTS. It's not simple at all. Very strange things have been reported by those attempting this task. Upon reaching one telephone company, a caller was told he couldn't have ISDN. He asked why; the response was, "It's illegal." Be prepared for anything.

Having said that, I must point out that things have become much better over time. This chapter goes over the various plans for "order simplification," promulgated by the NIUF and Bellcore. Next, it addresses the fact that both individual telephone companies and makers of ISDN products are introducing additional methods to make it "almost" as easy to order an ISDN line as it is to order a POTS line. I suggest that, very soon, these applications for ISDN will be as easy as POTS:

- Internet access
- Remote office connection
- Video teleconferencing
- Routine voice telephony

What did I leave out? The same things that are complex for POTS:

- Specialized data connections
- Complex voice telephony

Why is ordering such a big problem, and what is provisioning?

You'll learn the problems that come up when you order ISDN.

What are possible approaches to a solution?

Several different methods have been tried to simplify ISDN ordering; you'll examine each.

How does the massive matrix solution work?

If you like big, detailed spreadsheets, you'll like the massive matrix of features and functions available with ISDN.

What about limiting your options?

Perhaps the best way to simplify ISDN ordering is to give only a few options that cover the large majority of cases. You may get a few things you don't need, but the simplicity is worth it.

What is Microsoft's "Get ISDN Now?"

See how Microsoft has waded into the ISDN ordering morass by creating a Web answer to ordering. This could be the answer you're looking for.

Working these last two out with the phone company (ies) has always been the domain of experts and will continue to be. For the rest of us, getting the first four as easy as POTS is nearer than you may think, or have been led to believe.

First, we'll look at how the NIUF and Bellcore have approached the problem with classic large-organization, big standards-setting approaches covering all the options. Next, we'll see the issues, and the routes to their solutions. Then, we jump to how some of the telcos are really ordering, and how the guys at the ISDN box-makers want to help you, resulting in you buying more of their stuff. Now, your choices depend, to some extent, on your telephone company's way of dealing with this. For example, if your telco leads the pack, you probably can leap to "limiting your options," thereby simplifying your ordering. In contrast, if your telco still applies the classic "big time" approach, you must take a minute to understand the NIUF/Bellcore method. Here are the questions we hope to answer:

- Why is ordering such a big problem, and what is provisioning?
- What are possible approaches to a solution?
- How does the massive matrix solution work?
- What are ordering codes?
- What about limiting your options?
- Does your interexchange carrier care about ISDN? ■

Why Is Ordering Such a Big Problem, and What Is Provisioning?

Ordering is a word we all understand. If you want something, you order it. So, if you want ISDN, you order it. But what is *provisioning*? Provisioning is the telephone company's side. A telephone switch must be "provisioned" to supply services. In the case of ISDN, the switch must be designed for ISDN and then must be provisioned to provide such ISDN services as the company wants to supply and has tariff approval to supply. Of course, the switch hardware and software must be able to provide those services. We've come a long way from the "number please" manual switchboard described in the first chapter. There are so many options and possibilities inherent in ISDN generally, and vastly more when combinations are assembled, that making it all work and explaining what it is and how to use it becomes overwhelming.

When you call up for ISDN service, the order person may fill your order promptly and efficiently; the installer may connect you perfectly and test the line to insure it talks to the switch; your equipment supplier may provide excellent software and hardware, but you may find nothing works. Why? The order was accepted based upon what your telephone company considered "generic" ISDN, but you needed some features or capabilities that are not in that generic package. Now comes the hard part: what do you need that you did not get, and what did you get?

N O T E   The way things are changing, it may not be clear who to call for ISDN. Unless you have a competitive supplier of your local phone service, you'll have only one "phone company" to call—the local exchange carrier. If the word "Bell" is or used to be in that company's name (before the breakup of AT&T) that company is generically called an RBOC for regional Bell operating company; sometimes you'll hear it called a "Baby Bell." To be more specific, when you pay your regular phone bill to PacBel, Ameritech, Southwestern Bell, Southern Bell, NYNEX, et al, you're paying your local exchange carrier. If your carrier is GTE (General Telephone and Equipment), that's your local exchange carrier even though it did not come from AT&T.

No matter who it is, the local exchange carrier is the only entity from whom you can order ISDN connection to your residence or business. In certain unusual or very large instances, you may have another choice. A giant business may be able to deal with other entities at certain sites. Alternative carriers may be available in some densely built business areas or in large apartment complexes. As competition grows, more and more of us will have at least two and perhaps more alternatives for a local exchange carrier that offers ISDN.

This involves us in a litany of standards. In the beginning, it was in the interest of switch manufacturers to provide features and capabilities unique to their switch and unavailable or inaccessible to their competitors' switches. This was fine as long as all your ISDN went through only that manufacturer's switch and needed nothing that manufacturer lacked. This placed the onus of making a particular piece of customer-provided equipment work on your back and the back of the customer-provided equipment (CPE) maker. It also made it hard to call other ISDN installations if they didn't have the same configuration and equipment as your local exchange carrier. This led to a period of ISDN stagnation that persisted until 1988, when the North American ISDN Users' Group, the National Institute of Standards and Technology, and Bellcore decided to team up and develop the National ISDN series of specifications, starting with National ISDN 1 (NI-1), finalized in 1991. This was followed by NI-2 that was released in 1994; NI-3 is expected in late 1996. After 1996, the standards will be known as NIx, where x represents the last two digits of the year. Get ready for NI98, NI00, etc.

Each NI-x provides specific descriptions of what a telephone switch is to provide within its provisioning to meet the given specification. Now makers of customer premises equipment and you can be assured that the hardware and software you have will work with any switch meeting a given NI-x standard if the elements of that standard contain everything needed for your particular applications.

Look at what this really says. It brings the switch makers to the table with various sets of least common denominator features and functions. It says if that collection of features and functions includes all you need, it is technically possible for your equipment to work with the switch. It doesn't, however, answer the following questions:

- Given that the switch technically can be provisioned to supply what I need, how do I ask for the particular collection of features and functions that make my device work?

Part
III

Ch

7

- What if the switch supports NI-x, but I need something that is not in NI-x?
- Even if I know how to order the right stuff, and the switch can be provisioned for it, what if there is no tariff for it?

Let's take as a given that the switch your local exchange carrier uses is compliant with the current NI-x specifications. The major ISDN switch makers are AT&T, Nortel (we used to call 'em Northern Telecom—changing company names is a growth industry), and Siemens/ Stromberg Carlson. Each of these companies presently claims to comply with the specifications through NI-2. Of course, your local exchange carrier must purchase the necessary software (and perhaps hardware) to meet the specifications. In some cases, the costs may seem exorbitant; then we return to the magic of telephone accounting and distribution of costs among members of the ratebase (another story). You still have to order the right combination for your installation.

In one sentence, ordering is such a big problem because ISDN offers such a big collection of elements to choose among. For openers, here are the three broad areas of selection:

- Bearer services
- Supplementary services
- Teleservices

Bearer Services

We're first going to figure out what we need in the fundamental BRI bearer services. These are the services that actually carry the information across the telephone network. They are the beasts of burden that do the work we want done.

Number and Type   Right away we discover that we have to select the number and types of channels we need. The combinations break down easily:

- No B channels and one D channel.
- One B channel and one D channel.
- Two B channels and one D channel.

What about some B channels and no D channel? This is a trick question. Think back to our initial discussion of what ISDN is. The D channel is a primary element; it provides the out-of-band signaling on a common channel; it provides all the range of flexibility and control we want from ISDN. With no D channel, there is no ISDN at all. But we may have an application for a D channel with no B channels when we use the D channel packet option. So, first we figure out just which among the selections of Bs and a D we want.

Mode Second, we move on to the question of what mode we want. We may select either circuit mode or packet mode. This lengthens our list quite a bit:

- No B channels and one D channel, using packet mode on the D channel
- One B channel and one D channel, using circuit mode on the B channel and signaling only on the D channel
- One B channel and one D channel, using circuit mode on the B channel and signaling plus packet mode on the D channel
- Two B channels and one D channel, using circuit mode on the B channels and signaling only on the D channel
- Two B channels and one D channel, using circuit mode on the B channels and signaling plus packet mode on the D channel
- Two B channels and one D channel, using circuit mode on one B channel and packet mode on the other B channel, with signaling only on the D channel
- Two B channels and one D channel, with circuit mode on one B channel and packet mode on the other B channel, with signaling plus packet mode on the D channel
- Two B channels and one D channel, with packet mode on both B channels and signaling on the D channel
- Two B channels and one D channel, with packet mode on both B channels and signaling plus packet mode on the D channel

Voice or Data Now throw in the B channel selection of voice or data and mix up a lot more selections.

Whew. It's starting to look complex. Remember Chapter 4, "Choosing Services?" We had not only B channels and D channels, not only circuit mode and packet mode, not only voice and data, we had to contend with unrestricted or speech or 3.1 kHz audio or 7 kHz audio or 2×64 kbit/s and a number of other possibilities.

Supplementary Services

And then we considered the various forms of supplementary services such as calling line identification presentation or subaddressing or call forwarding busy or call waiting or completion of calls to busy subscribers ....and on and on, it seems, forever.

Teleservices

If you're someplace that has teleservice offerings, you could throw in videotext or teletext or teleconference or a number of other options.

Part
III

Ch
7

Possible Approaches to a Solution

Well, you get the idea. The possible combinations of choices are more than you can hold in mind at one time. We need a way of pulling this all together so service can be ordered. So far as I can tell, there are three approaches to dealing with all these choices:

- Avoid them and hope they'll go away.
- Create a massive multidimensional matrix of all "useful" possibilities.
- Look at what is really relevant and provide strictly limited options.

Avoidance

Let's try the avoidance tactic. If you elect this one and try to stick with it, you're heading down the road of denial. You'll become a victim of technology left to writhe on the side of the information highway until your pain is so deep you admit you're powerless over ISDN and seek help from fellow recovering digital drunkards in techno-twelve step programs. Maybe you'll recover. Maybe you won't. I advise against taking that first turn down this path to sure ruin.

Leap into ISDN

Before you go absolutely "bonkers" trying to follow all this for the next several pages, check out two URLs now:

`http://www.alumni.caltech.edu/~dank/isdn/isdn_ai.html#TELCO`

`http://www.microsoft.com/windows/getisdn/home.htm`

The first is Dan Kagel's listing of ISDN dialtone providers for both local exchange and interexchange carriers (local and long distance). This list includes information for the United States, Canada, Europe, Middle East, Australia, Japan, and Russia. By the time you read this, I'm sure Dan will have expanded the list even more. Thanks, Dan.

The second URL is Microsoft's "Get ISDN" homepage. I go into extensive detail with screen shots from this page toward the end of this chapter. If your telco is set up with "Get ISDN," you can order and specify service right on the Web. How's that for order simplification?

Massive Matrix

How about the second way, a massive matrix? Faced with an overwhelming collection of choices, opt for creating a structure to analyze virtually all possible combinations. This is the course taken by NIUF and Bellcore.

In all its efforts regarding order simplification, the National ISDN Users' Forum (NIUF) kept paramount the needs of the small business and residential user. Think about it. These are the users that need the help. Large organizations can fend for themselves with staffs specially trained in telephone terminology. The rest of us are at the mercy of the telephone companies that are just as inexperienced in ISDN as we. So words of thanks to the volunteers working on these standards—thanks very, very much for those long days of boring meetings and those nights away from home you spent to help the rest of us.

Two approaches to order simplification have been devised by NIUF.

- Building Block Approach
- ISDN Ordering Codes Approach

These become somewhat involved, but are well worth understanding should you have anything other than a simple installation. In sum, the building block approach takes a collection of ISDN elements called *feature sets* and *line sets,* selects among them, and builds a working ISDN system for you (see Fig. 7.1).

The ISDN ordering codes approach takes predefined collections of the building blocks that have been shown to satisfy given application environments, mixes these into collections identified by letter, and gives you the final solution (see Fig. 7.2).

FIG. 7.1

Building Block Approach.

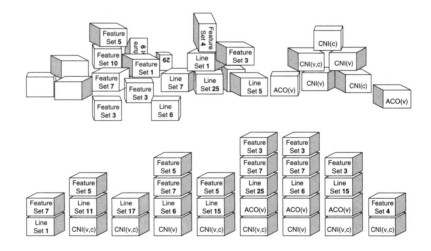

Some of the Many Possible Combinations of Building Blocks Tailored to Individual Needs

Part

III

Ch

7

FIG. 7.2
ISDN Ordering Codes
Approach.

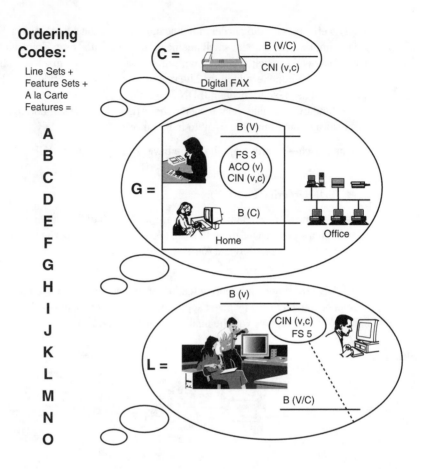

Ordering Codes:

Line Sets +
Feature Sets +
A la Carte
Features =

A
B
C
D
E
F
G
H
I
J
K
L
M
N
O

Building Block Approach   Line sets and feature sets constitute the elements of the building block approach to ordering ISDN. They allow you to build ISDN to fit your needs from a collection of pre-established provisioning options. Over the course of three or four years, the nomenclature used to describe these elements has changed. I'll attempt to show the different forms and meanings to help you talk with your telephone company or understand the NIUF and Bellcore source documents.

Humpty Dumpty on Meaning

"I don't know what you mean by 'glory,'" Alice said.

Humpty Dumpty smiled contemptuously. "Of course you don't—til I tell you. I meant 'there's a nice knock-down argument for you!'"

"But 'glory' doesn't mean 'a nice knock-down argument,'" Alice objected.

"When *I* use a word," Humpty Dumpty said, in rather a scornful tone, "it means just what I choose it to mean—neither more nor less."

"The question is," said Alice, "whether you *can* make words mean so many different things."

"The question is," said Humpty Dumpty, "which is to be master—that's all."

Lewis Carroll, *Through the Looking Glass*

If you feel like you just fell down a rabbit hole and things are not what they seem and words don't mean what they mean, you're on the path to understanding the ordering and provisioning of ISDN.

Line Sets, Also Known as NIIGs   Over the course of three or four years, the nomenclature used to describe this type of building block has changed. Originally the line set was called *NIUF ISDN Interface Groups* (NIIGs). Then someone, in a moment of wisdom, realized the creation of yet another acronym containing acronyms was compounding confusion and decided to make a move back to English. The term is now *line sets*.

I like the use of something that at least has the appearance of being from the mouth of a human being, rather than some plug on a machine. Line sets gives a hint of what it is about. In a basic rate interface (BRI), a line set is concerned with the following:

- Number of B channels
- Call types: voice, circuit-mode data, packet-mode data and the channels on which they are used

When you drop all of this into a pot and stir carefully, you end up with the 29 combinations shown in Table 7.1.

Table 7.1   Line Sets—Call Type and Interface Configuration

Line Set	Information	B	B	D
1	0B+D	x	x	P
2	1B	V	x	S
3	1B	C	x	S
4	1B	V/C	x	S
5	1B	SBP	x	S
6	1B+D	V	x	P
7	1B+D	C	x	P
8	1B+D	V/C	x	P
9	1B+D	SBP	x	P
10	2B	V	V	S
11	2B	V	C	S
12	2B	V	V/C	S
13	2B	V	SBP	S
14	2B	C	C	S

Part

III

Ch

7

continues

Table 7.1   Continued

Line Set	Information	B	B	D
15	2B	C	V/C	S
16	2B	C	SBP	S
17	2B	V/C	V/C	S
18	2B	V/C	SBP	S
19	2B	SBP	SBP	S
20	2B+D	V	V	P
21	2B+D	V	C	P
22	2B+D	V	V/C	P
23	2B+D	V	SBP	P
24	2B+D	C	C	P
25	2B+D	C	V/C	P
26	2B+D	C	SBP	P
27	2B+D	V/C	V/C	P
28	2B+D	V/C	SBP	P
29	2B+D	SBP	SBP	P

V: Circuit-Mode Voice (Speech or 3.1 kHz audio)
C: Circuit-Mode Data (Unrestricted 64 kbps/adapted 56 kbps)
V/C: Alternate Circuit-Mode Voice and Data
SBP: Semi-Permanent B Channel Packet Connection
P: Packet-Mode Data
x: Not Applicable
S: Signaling Only
Not every line set is available from each telco. Line sets apply to both NI-1 and NI-2, with the exception of on-demand B channel packet data.
Table courtesy of NIUF and Bellcore.

Feature Sets, Also Known as NIPGs   A feature set is a collection of ISDN subscription parameters and their settings; the original term for feature sets was *NIUF ISDN Parameter Groups* (NIPGs). There are 10 feature sets. Five concern voice issues involving both electronic key telephone service (EKTS) and other voice selections. The remaining five concern data matters such as circuit-mode data, D channel packet-mode data, and B channel packet-mode data.

When ordering ISDN service, a user selects the appropriate:

- Line set
- Feature set
- Additional ISDN and non-ISDN features *a la carte*

Number of channels is determined by the size and traffic of the business. Then call types break down into three categories that dictate clusters of features in the feature sets defined:

- **Circuit-mode voice (Feature Sets 1.0-5.0):** Features included are common for circuit-mode voice calls. Such functions include call management and control, along with electronic key features.
- **Circuit-mode data (Feature Set 6.0):** Functions needed for circuit-mode data calls.
- **Packet-mode data (Feature Sets 7.0-10.0):** basic and advanced packet functionality.

OK. Let's stop before we get totally buried in techno-speco-stando-speak. What are they saying? At this point in writing, I had to stop and get a good, stiff drink. All of the text and charts from our sincere, dedicated simplifiers began to fade into a morass of jumbled letters and numbers. One more sip of the "table wine of the South" (Dolly Parton, *Steel Magnolias*; table wine of the South = iced tea) and realization began to hit me.

These feature sets take the stuff we talked about in Chapter 4, "Choosing Services"—you remember the different kinds of bearer services, supplementary services, and teleservices—mix them up into what folks who use them all the time have found to be useful, and pour it all out into 10 bowls of goulash with different vegetables in each bowl. Each one satisfies a different need: tomato and broccoli for Bill, ham with carrots and celery for Sue, and chili with hot peppers for James. Let's have a look inside the bowls. Courtesy the NIUF, which did all the work:

A Tip for Ordering ISDN Services for Data

Skim all this detail for the next few pages looking for those portions that might be relevant to you. I expect you're reading this book to use ISDN for data. If this is the case, you can leap over the first five and go straight to NIPG (or Feature Set) 6.0 that concerns circuit-mode data. If you don't plan to use packet-mode features, 6.0 is the only one relevant, and it's only relevant if you want call forwarding. With respect to packet-mode, notice the differences in numbers of logical channels and data rates among the remaining feature sets 7.0 through 10.0.

Feature Set 1.0 Call Forwarding Feature for Voice

One Directory Number Appearance

Call Forwarding Variable

Reminder Notification Sent Base Directory Number

Establish Courtesy Call:

For NI-1: No Answer Required (if supported by switch); otherwise Answer Required

For NI-2: No Answer Required

Part
III

Ch
7

Feature Set 2.0 Advanced Call Forwarding Features for Voice

Feature Set 2.0 contains everything in Feature Set 1.0, PLUS additional Call Forwarding and Message Indicator features

> One Directory Number Appearance
>
> Call Forwarding Variable
>
>> Reminder Notification Sent to Base Directory Number
>>
>> Establish Courtesy Call:
>>
>>> For NI-1: No Answer Required (if supported by Switch); otherwise Answer Required
>>>
>>> For NI-2: No Answer Required
>
> Call Forwarding Interface Busy
>
>> Do Not Establish Courtesy Call
>
> Call Forwarding Don't Answer
>
>> Do Not Establish Courtesy Call
>
> Message Waiting Indicator

Feature Set 3.0 Flexible Calling Features for Voice

> Three Directory Number Appearances
>
> Flexible Calling
>
>> Hold/Retrieve (for individual call or conference)
>>
>> Three-Way Conference Calling
>>
>> Add On:
>>
>>> For NI-1:
>>>
>>>> Add Previously Held Conference Call
>>>>
>>>> Add Previously Held Call to Conference (if supported by switch)
>>>
>>> For NI-2:
>>>
>>>> Add Previously Held Conference to Call
>>>>
>>>> Add Previously Held Call to Conference
>>
>> Drop Last Call
>>
>> Transfer
>>
>>> For NI-1: Explicit (if supported by switch); otherwise Implicit
>>>
>>> For NI-2: Explicit
>>>
>>> Consultation Hold

Feature Set 4.0 Basic Electronic Key Telephone Set (EKTS) Features for Voice

    Basic EKTS

    Multiple Directory Number/Terminal

    User Bridging

    Manual Privacy (Manual Bridged Call Exclusion)

    Hold/Retrieve; Directory Number Bridging; Call Transfer

        Hold/Retrieve (for individual call or conference)

        Directory Number Bridging (Three-Way conference Calling)

        Add On:

            For NI-1:

                Add Previously Held Conference to Call

                Add Previously Held Call to Conference (if supported by switch)

            For NI-2:

                Add Previously Held Conference to Call

                Add Previously Held Call to Conference

        Drop Last Call

        Transfer

            For NI-1: Explicit (if supported by switch)

            For NI-2: Explicit

        Consultation Hold

Feature Set 5.0 Advanced EKTS Features for Voice

    Feature Set 5.0 is based on the Call Appearance Calling Handling EKTS service

        Call Appearance Call handling (CACH) EKTS

        Multiple Virtual Lines (Multiple Directory Number Appearances

        Multiple Directory Number/Terminal

        User Bridging

        Manual Privacy (Manual Bridged Call Exclusion)

        Hold/retrieve; Directory Number; Call Transfer

            Hold/Retrieve (for individual call or conference)

            Directory Number Bridging (Three-way Conference Calling)

            Add On:

                For NI-1:

                    Add Previously Held Conference to Call

> Add Previously Held Call to Conference
> (if supported by switch)

For NI-2:

> Add Previously Held Conference to Call
>
> Add Previously Held Call to Conference

Drop Last Call

Transfer

> For NI-1: Explicit (if supported by switch);
> otherwise Implicit
>
> For NI-2: Explicit
>
> Consultation Hold

Feature Set 6.0 Advanced Call Forwarding Features for Circuit-Mode Data

 This feature set is the only one of the group that might be of interest to those primarily interested in B channel data; that includes most of you considering ISDN for Internet access. If packet data is of interest, Sets 7 through 10 concern cover it.

> One Directory Number Appearance
>
> Call Forwarding Variable
>
> > Do Not Establish Courtesy Call
>
> Call Forwarding Interface Busy
>
> > Do Not Establish Courtesy Call
>
> Call Forwarding Don't Answer
>
> > Do Not Establish Courtesy Call

Feature Set 7.0 Basic D Channel Packet Features

> Switched Virtual Call Service
>
> 1 logical channel (can be User-Specified up to 15)
>
> Packet window size: 2
>
> > D-Bit Modification: No
>
> Throughput class: 9.6 kbps
>
> Maximum user data field: 128 octets
>
> Reverse charge: Yes
>
> Reverse charge acceptance: No
>
> Fast select: Yes
>
> Fast select acceptance: Yes

Negotiation services

    Flow Control Parameter Negotiation (Window Size and
Packet Size: No

    Throughput Class Negotiation: No

RPOA selection: Yes

Feature Set 8.0 Advanced D Channel Packet Features

Switched Virtual Call Service

1 logical channel (can be User-Specified up to 15)

Packet window size: 2

    D Bit Modification: No

Throughput class: 9.6 kbps

Maximum user data field: 256 octets

Reverse charge: Yes

Reverse charge acceptance: Yes

Fast select: Yes

Fast select acceptance: Yes

Negotiation services

    Flow Control Parameter Negotiation (Window Size and
Packet Size): Yes

    Throughput Class Negotiation: Yes

RPOA selection: Yes

Feature Set 9.0 Basic B Channel Packet Features

Switched Virtual Call Service

8 logical channels (can be User-Specified from 1-127)

Packet window size: 2

    D Bit Modification: No

Throughput class: 9.6 kbps

Maximum user data field: 256 octets

Reverse charge: Yes

Reverse charge acceptance: Yes

Fast select: Yes

Fast select acceptance: Yes

Part
III

Ch

7

Negotiation services

Flow Control Parameter Negotiation (Window Size and
Packet Size): Yes

Throughput Class Negotiation: Yes

RPOA selection: Yes

Feature Set 10.0 Advanced B Channel Packet Features

Switched Virtual Call Service

8 logical channels (can be User-Specified from 1-127)

Packet window size: 2

D Bit Modification: No

Throughput class: 19.2 kbps

Maximum user data field: 256 octets

Reverse charge acceptance: Yes

Fast select: Yes

Fast select acceptance: Yes

Negotiation services

Flow Control Parameter Negotiation (Window Size and
packet Size: Yes

Throughput Class Negotiation: Yes

RPOA selection: Yes

ISDN Ordering Codes (IOC), Also Known as Capability Packages Those seeking to simplify
ISDN ordering originally designed "solution sets" as an alternative to the building blocks approach. The emphasis with solution sets was selection of capability packages to solve your
needs in light of certain broadly defined applications. Solution sets allowed you to order ISDN
simply by specifying the applications environment you plan to use. Examples of the applications included work at home and telemedicine.

However, this approach quickly led to a large number of selections, many of which varied only
a very little or not at all. Solution sets themselves needed a solution to their rapidly multiplying
complexity.

ISDN ordering codes (IOC) provide that solution. An ISDN ordering code is a collection of:

- Line sets
- Interfaces
- Feature sets
- A la carte features

Each code is constructed from the experiences of people in the field observing how and what
is ordered for the practical use of ISDN. When all is said and done, 17 capability packages

resulted. These packages are designated from A through Q. Table 7.2 shows the contents of these codes.

Table 7.2 ISDN Ordering Codes (IOC)

(Capability Packages)

A	1	-	-	P	7	-
B	3	C	-	-	-	CNI(c)
C	4	V/C	-	-	-	CNI(v,c)
D	6	V	-	P	7	-
E	6	V	-	P	3, 7	ACO(v), CNI(V)
F	6	V	-	P	5, 7	CNI(v)
G	11	V	C	-	3	ACO(v), CNI(V,C)
H	11	V	C	-	5	CNI(v,c)
I	14	C	C	-	-	CNI(c)
J	15	C	V/C	-	-	CNI(v,c)
K	15	C	V/C	-	3	ACO(v), CNI(V,C)
L	15	C	V/C	-	5	CNI(v,c)
M	17	V/C	V/C	-	-	CNI(v,c)
N	25	C	V/C	P	3, 7	ACO(v), CNI(V,C)
O	25	C	V/C	P	5, 7	CNI(v,c)
P	27	V/C	V/C	P	3, 7	ACO(v), CNI(V,C)
Q	27	V/C	V/C	P	5, 7	CNI(v,c)

V: Circuit-Mode Voice
C: Circuit-Mode Data
V/C: Alternate Voice and Data
P: Packet-Mode Data
ACO: Additional Call Offering
CNI: Calling Number Identification
Numbers represent feature sets
Table courtesy NIUF and Bellcore.

You're really lucky. If you think reading these tables is a chore, you ought to try typing them. I spared you the tables showing how all this relates to each of the switches; this material is essential for telco's provisioning the switches. By the way, at this time two more, R and S, are being considered, but have not yet been adopted; they concern directory number and key (button) assignment.

Part
III

Ch
7

Matching Ordering Codes to Real World Examples   Now relate these codes to the practical world by using the original solution set descriptions. Well, let's not go overboard. I thought I'd hit you with another table. But who needs it? Right! So here are just a few examples of how the ISDN Ordering Codes relate to practical (solution set) things you have to do.

Telecommuting   If you want to work at home and telecommute, the chances are you'll want voice on one B channel with circuit-mode data on the other. It'll be handy to have flexible calling, additional call offering and calling number identification for both voice and data. With this kind of a setup you can use the Internet, log in to the office LAN, and make a lot of voice calls. You want ISDN Ordering Code G.

Credit Card Verification   Your business needs to verify credit cards at point of sale. You need D channel packet and no voice services. You want ISDN Ordering Code A.

Multimedia Collaboration   You want to collaborate with others using multimedia. You'll use data on a B channel, voice or data on another B channel, LAN access, Internet, packet, and such telephony features as calling number identification and additional call offering. You want ISDN Ordering Code N.

Group 3 or Group 4 Fax   You want to use a single group 3 or group 4 (digital) fax, and that's all. Get ISDN Ordering Code C.

Relating Solution Sets to Ordering Codes   All right, all right. Here's Table 7.3 relating the "solution sets" to the ISDN Ordering Codes. But we just can't copy all the details of the various original solution sets. Basically as a practical situation, work at home, for example, goes for more features. Its number and letter get higher. You'll see. And along the way, look at how seemingly unrelated activities (distance learning and telemedicine, for example) end up using the same ISDN Ordering Code. This is the convergence of what is really needed from ISDN that I suggested earlier.

Table 7.3   Relations Between Solutions and ISDN Ordering Codes

Solution Set	IOC
Work at Home 1, Transaction Services 1, Telemetry 1, Distance Learning	A
Video Conferencing 1, Telemetry 2, LAN to LAN 1	B
Fax 1	C
Transaction Services 2	D
Work at Home 2a, Transaction Services 3a, Desktop Collaboration 1a, Distance Learning 2a	E
Work at Home 2b, Transaction Services 3b, Desktop Collaboration 1b, Distance Learning 2b	F
Work at Home 3a, Distance Learning 3a, Telemedicine 1a	G
Work at Home 3b, Distance Learning 3b, Telemedicine 1b	H

Solution Set	IOC
Video Conferencing 2, Telemetry 3, Distance Learning 4, LAN to LAN 2	I
Video Conferencing 3	J
Work at Home 4a, Video Conferencing 4a, Desktop Collaboration 2a, Telemedicine 2a	K
Work at Home 4b, Video Conferencing 4b, Desktop Collaboration 2b, Telemedicine 2b	L
Fax 2	M
Work at Home 5a, Desktop Collaboration 3a, Telemedicine 3a	N
Work at Home 5b, Desktop Collaboration 3b, Telemedicine 3b	O

The numbers and letters associated with the solution sets such as work at home refer to more specifics. In general, the higher the number and associated letter, the more complex the system.

Table courtesy NIUF and Bellcore.

Just to finish up on this topic, we have one more grouping. These are special ordering codes that are keyed to specific vendors' products. The old rules said any vendor that wanted and qualified its products would be issued a specific code. So Fujitsu has a code called "Fujitsu 400 Pkg I." Now the secret to this is really "I" from the ISDN ordering codes, with one or two twists for the Fujitsu product involved. The new rules require at least two vendors to have the same requirements for a code. So we have "Generic Data M" for ADTRAN, Controlware and Digiboard. The idea is to force vendors into the generic codes, if at all possible. I think this is a good direction. The more generic your ISDN is, the easier and more flexible your uses and future planning possibilities. Currently there are 29 such codes. You'll find reference to such codes in the documentation of some manufacturers. It seems to me these special codes will fade out as the generic scheme becomes stable.

 TIP Waffle on over to **http://www.bellcore.com/ISDN/index.html** and look around under ISDN for more on these codes.

Limited Options

If you've made it this far—few may have such raw courage—maybe we can find another way. This is not to say the building block and ISDN ordering codes techniques are not useful. But for some people, for some companies, there may be other ways. It's time to pull out Ocham's razor and cut away the underbrush.

Some local exchange carriers simply look at the mass of variations and possible combinations and decide to limit options. This has the advantage of making selection easier. But it may increase your costs.

You might have to take a switch provisioning you don't ever use. Just about everything you have is that way. Quick, how many of the functions of your word processor do you really use?

Part
III

Ch
7

How many do you know how to use? How many do you know even exist? Yet you paid for all of them. Would the price really be less if you could pick and choose from the huge collections of combinations that would result if all the features were broken out?

In the same way, would your telco really be able to deliver a complex collection of choices for ISDN services more cheaply? Remember all the tariffs each has to have; remember all the training for order and technical staff? In fact, knowing, as you do, that the real cost of providing most of the selections is negligible once you get by the raw line issues of how many and what kind of B channels and D channels, you have to ask the final question. Why not boil it all down to a few selections and go on?

This is the alternative you may find when you call in for ISDN. And here are your selections from one of the big local exchange carriers:

- 0B+D (packet and signaling on D)
- 1B+D (only signaling on D)
- 1B+D (packet and signaling on D)
- 2B+D (only signaling on D)
- 2B+D (packet and signaling on D)

You get voice or data on demand; this means your customer-provided equipment (CPE) requests one or the other through the D channel.

So that's it. What do about 95 percent plus of the ISDN subscribers take? Just exactly what you want: 2B+D (only signaling on D). The cost differences among the selections between one and two B channels are several dollars, but not so great as to make most users opt for only one B.

If you plan to do only D channel packet, you're in a different game and will save on B channel cost, but you may pay additional packet traffic costs.

If you want all the key telephone services that make so much of the ordering look complex, that can be handled on a case-by-case basis. Most feel the fancy phone features will be taken over by PBX equipment at the subscriber location. That equipment will appear as an NT-2 in the ISDN circuit.

Contentious SPIDs

I'm just about to talk about multiple devices contending for the B channel. What is this? It turns out the ISDN specification is designed to allow eight devices to use the same B channel. Since any two cannot use it at the same time, the devices are said to "contend" for the B channel. To make this work, the telco has to assign different SPIDs (remember service point identifiers) to each device.

What I'm pointing out here is the fact that a number of telcos have decided not to support contention on the B channel; therefore they don't provide multiple SPIDs. Why do you care? You're used to putting each extension phone on the same wire, aren't you? When you pick up one phone, you can hear the conversation on an extension. That doesn't work with ISDN. Each device has its own SPID; that SPID is associated with the telco's switch and a terminal identifier (TEI). The way ISDN works, you can't just wire in another phone and expect it to work. It must be associated with a SPID. If the telco issues only one SPID per B channel, you can't have an extension phone!

Your solution? Establish your own PBX. This will probably not be a big deal. Keep an eye on the merging of telephones and computers. Chances are the PBX will simply be some software and a card in one of your computers. Your PBX can then establish extension capability within your phone system. You may also use the electronic key telephone set (EKTS) features available as options with ISDN to establish a conference between the phones. The second-best solution is for all the telcos and switch makers to provide support for multiple SPIDs; up to eight SPIDs are allowed per B channel.

The best solution? Eliminate SPIDs. They're a product of overly-sophisticated design in North America. The rest of the world gets along quite nicely without them, thank you. And while you're at it, eliminate any need to enter the directory number when you configure ISDN customer equipment. Since these aren't needed for modems, why should they be needed for ISDN? (I am paraphrasing Dan Kegel, and I am in total agreement with him.)

Incidentally, just so you don't think eliminating SPIDs is totally "off the wall," check out none other than AT&T, 3Com, US Robotics, et al, for the ISDN Forum with the *numero uno* goal of eliminating SPIDs.

http://www.att.com/press/0196/960123.nsa.html

Multiple devices contending for a B channel are not supported; so that issue is also passed to a local PBX. What we have here is the phone company giving you the power and control of ISDN and saying, "Make all your decisions through intelligence at your location. We'll provide the carriage, you provide the brains."

N O T E Which is better: building blocks, ISDN ordering codes or limited options? Which is better: chocolate, vanilla or strawberry? At least to some degree, it's a matter of your own way of doing things. How your telephone company handles ISDN plays a big part. If you find yourself always making spreadsheets when faced with a decision, the building block approach is a natural. If you would rather someone else keep the books, try the ordering codes. And if you just want to cut to the chase and get on with it, go for limited options. It takes all kinds. ▨

Ordering and Provisioning with the Interexchange Carrier

All this discussion has dealt with issues surrounding your local exchange carrier. Doesn't that take care of it? At the most, it would seem you'd tell the person taking your order that you want to use X long distance carrier. Not so fast.

There are interexchange carriers and there are interexchange carriers. And some know about ISDN and some don't. And that's not the problem of your local exchange carrier; that's your problem. You've got two big problems:

- ▨ Function
- ▨ Cost

Part

III

Ch

7

Function means whether or not the interexchange carrier (telephone talk for long distance carrier) can take your 64 kbps data and transmit it across the country or around the world without smushing it into something that looks like last year's compost heap at the other end.

How could this happen? Easy. These long distance guys aren't going to take up a full 64 kbps for your data if they think it's voice, and therefore can be diced and sliced in a way that allows much more traffic to flow down the same pipe. So they dice and slice, and your data is...well, you get the picture.

If you're going to be sending data over long distance ISDN, you need "clear channel 64 kbps" transmission from your carrier. Guess what? Most don't have it, or might not have it where your local exchange switch passes the stuff the to "tandem switch" that passes it to the interexchange carrier.

Your solution: check out your long distance company. If it doesn't offer clear channel 64 kbps, you'll need to find someone else who does.

Aye, there's the rub. If someone offers more data capability, chances are they'll charge more; it stands to reason. So check out the price. Get sophisticated. You'll probably want to send data over your ISDN, but you'll probably also want to use it for voice or other analog (modem or fax) forms that don't need and can't use the full clear channel 64 kbps—so why pay for it? Your long distance carrier must have the following for you:

- Clear channel 64 kbps circuits
- Voice grade circuits
- The ability to sense which you want through D channel signaling
- The ability to switch on D channel demand
- A price break if you want voice grade

In the current market, some carriers are giving clear channel 64 kbps at voice rates. Others are seeing you are ISDN and charging more, forcing you to the higher service even when your D channel asks for voice. And some are perhaps even sensing the voice, giving you a voice-grade line, but still charging you clear channel 64 kbps because you're ISDN. Look out.

If you want to use packet-mode, you also need to find out the capabilities of your long distance carrier in that field. If your carrier cannot do packet, you must find another.

Whatever you do, be sure you know what your status is with your long distance carrier. If you don't, you could end up with an inability to transmit or receive data at a critical time, or a bigger bill than you anticipated.

CAUTION

Watch these interexchange carriers. Recently AT&T began to charge a flat $5 a month to ISDN customers regardless of whether or not they made calls. If you make no calls, you're charged $5. If you make a $3 call, you're charged $5. If you make a total of $10 of calls you're charged $10. In effect, you're paying for not having to dial a long-distance carrier access code (10288 for AT&T).

> Shortly after that I was "slammed" by Sprint. That means the long-distance service on my ISDN line was changed to Sprint without my knowledge or consent. Sprint doesn't even offer 64 kbps clear channel service out of the Southwestern Bell ISDN switch I use!
>
> You may simply tell your local exchange carrier to declare no interexchange carrier for your ISDN. Then you can select the carrier you want by dialing the long-distance carrier access code.

The Web-Based Answer to ISDN Order Simplification

You've seen the rest; let's look at the best. Well, maybe not the best, but a good step in the right direction of order simplification. This is, to a great extent, based on option reduction and ideas emanating from vendors like those in the ISDN Forum. I mean, of course, the Microsoft "Get ISDN Now" Web pages.

Emanating Penumbras

I never hear, or think of, the word "emanate" without recalling a complex legal opinion written by Justice William O. Douglas of the United States Supreme Court. Within a decision concerning human rights, Justice Douglas spoke of certain penumbras emanating from the U.S. Constitution, giving rise to rights not specifically enumerated.

Microsoft, along with a covey of other ISDN product makers, is hot to free ISDN from the grasp of the utility/government mindset in order to capture projected big bucks. For its part, Microsoft has used the "velvet hammer" of market strength to coax a number of the phone companies into coming clean with what they have for ISDN. These phone companies then allow Microsoft to put the information on a series of Web pages, complete with fill-in-the-blank forms launching your ISDN order to the telco (untouched by a voice call). All the questions are asked, and all the information, including the cost, is provided.

However, not all the telcos are involved. For example, when I tried to set up a hypothetical order for my area—Austin, Texas, served by Southwestern Bell—the Microsoft Web server told me "my" telco was not a participant in the program. This may have changed by the time you read this (hear that, SBC, the corporate identity of Southwestern Bell!). Since Southwestern Bell was not available, I chose to set up an ISDN order right in Microsoft's backyard, Redmond, Washington. It worked! Well, I didn't really submit it; that would have wasted some overworked telco person's time figuring out my bogus order. The jerks that set viruses loose are already wasting everybody's time; let's not heap abuse on this excellent step forward, even if it is by Microsoft, sometimes known as the arch enemy of the common man. Here's how it works.

Warm up your Web browser and hook up with Microsoft's Get ISDN page at **http://www.microsoft.com/windows/getisdn/home.htm**, where the first thing you'll see is shown in Figure 7.3.

Part

III

Ch

7

FIG. 7.3

Get ISDN Homepage on the Microsoft Web server. Notice the selections that guide you to an explanation of ISDN: why you need it and how to get it. The hand on the image map is pointing to "Get ISDN Now!" so we can get started.

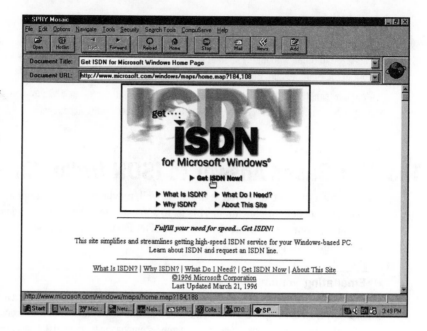

You see several options to answer the basic ISDN questions:

- What is ISDN?
- Why ISDN?
- What Do I Need?
- About This Site
- Get ISDN Now!

Select "Get ISDN Now!" with the usual hyperlink mouse click. This takes you to the next page, Figure 7.4. In most cases, Microsoft's Webmaster has, thoughtfully, kept page size to that size just fitting on the usual "landscape" monitor screen. Therefore, you don't have to page up and down to see what's going on.

 I use a monitor that rotates from landscape to portrait orientation. This is great, both for word processing and Web browsing. I find the natural environment of both should be portrait, while spreadsheets and presentation graphics fit landscape best, My monitor is a Portrait Display Labs Pivot 1700.

FIG. 7.4

Microsoft "Get ISDN Now!" entry screen explaining the details of ISDN ordering.

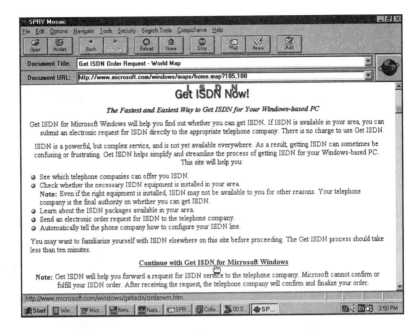

Figure 7.4 shows you the ins and outs of ordering ISDN, and it explains what the Microsoft pages will do for you. After you read this, click "Continue with Get ISDN for Microsoft Windows,"(the location of the hand). Next, you will arrive at Figure 7.5, a world map where you select your continent. Microsoft has a rather grand world view; perhaps this is similar to Napoleon's concepts before Waterloo?

FIG. 7.5

Select your continent for ISDN service. Early on, Microsoft's site supported only North America (read the United States and Canada). Now Miscrosoft's site is probably supporting most of the remaining sites having ISDN. Strange, I can't find Antarctica on this map—probably too little ozone and too much snow for those accustomed to the temperate climes of the Pacific Northwest and Japanese Current.

Part

III

Ch

7

Let's go for North America. With a click of mouse, we travel to the "far reaches" of the contiguous 48 United States (see Fig. 7.6). Next, we fearlessly push that button and hold the hand over the state named for the first President of the United States of America (George Washington, the guy with the hatchet standing next to the cherry tree).

FIG. 7.6

Here we are in North America selecting the state of Washington as our location for ISDN service.

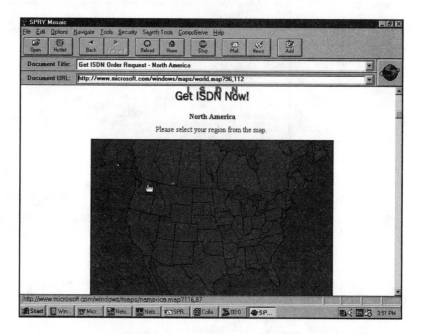

Bingo, it's time to fill out forms starting at Figure 7.7. There's a pop-down list of states in the highlighted region. If you click over Canada, the word "province" replaces state. Now, enter your phone number. That's right, the POTS phone number where you want the service. This determines the local exchange carrier. Decide if the line is for business use or residential use. Sometimes, like here in Austin, Texas, ISDN tariffs don't make such a distinction; but, frequently they do. The hyperlink "More info" goes into more detail. Now, the moment of truth.

Click the Next button. One of two things will happen: either you'll get a screen like Figure 7.8, which is good; or you'll get something to the effect of "The telephone company serving you doesn't participate in the "Get ISDN Now!" program," which is bad.

If your telco doesn't participate, you're probably stuck with the usual "use the voice phone to call up the local phone company" route. If the company supports the Web site, scroll down to Figure 7.9.

Since you're going to be a heavy user of ISDN, let's select the flat rate line. In reality, if your ISDN equipment is properly configured, as I'll suggest later in the chapters about configuring equipment, you'll probably find you don't need a flat rate line and can get along quite well with options such as the 25- or 50-hours-per-month selections. For now, pound down on "flat" to see Figure 7.10.

FIG. 7.7

Microsoft's "Get ISDN Now!" shows the first screen where you actually enter information including the state and phone number identifying where you want ISDN service, along with the designation of either residential or business.

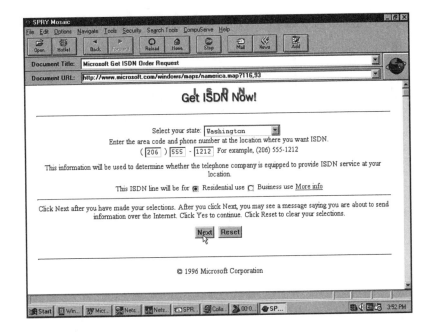

FIG. 7.8

So Far, So Good. When you get this screen, you know your telco is involved in the "Get ISDN Now" program, making your life simpler because you can order ISDN through the Microsoft Web site.

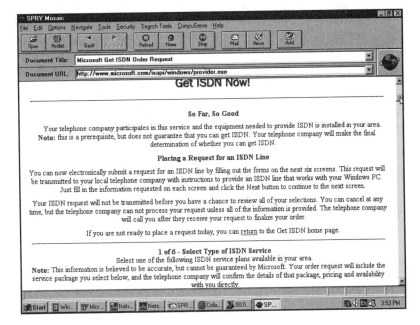

FIG. 7.9

Entry screen for a telco. Here GTE is supporting ISDN ordering through Microsoft's "Get ISDN Now!" Web site. Notice the three options for ISDN BRI service. Each is based on time-measured usage.

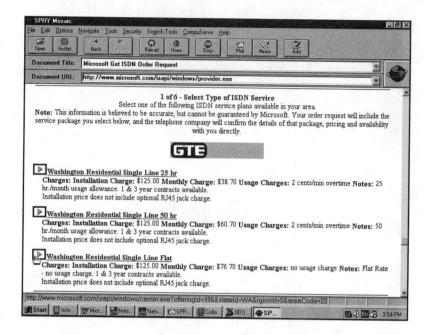

▶ **See** Chapter 9, "Selecting an External Terminal Adapter" (**p. 203**), Chapter 10, "Putting an Adapter Inside Your Computer" (**p. 257**), and Chapter 11, "Establishing ISDN for LANs" (**p. 307**), for more details on equipment configuration.

FIG. 7.10

Microsoft's "Get ISDN Now!" screen selection for a long distance carrier. This is a good place to start thinking about long distance options.

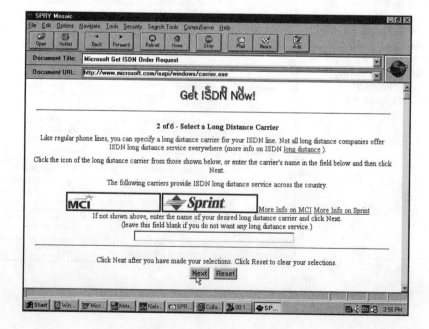

I'm impressed that Microsoft starts right off with a query on long distance. In my experience, most people overlook this and find they didn't get the carrier or deal they wanted. Take a look back at the previous section of this chapter, "Ordering and Provisioning with the Interexchange Carrier," to see some of the traps that can open up here. However, I've also noticed the details this Web site offers on the two carriers, MCI and Sprint, are rather sketchy and certainly don't address all the points I bulleted in my discussion. You'll have to dig more deeply for those answers.

An Appeal to Long-Distance Carriers

Lay out the full details of your ISDN offerings on both Microsoft's pages and on all your public contacts. Answer all the points in my bullets. Thanks, Jim.

After you click an interexchange carrier, click the Next button to begin the detailed selections needed to set up your ISDN line with the local telco shown in Figure 7.11. These options don't deal with the unique aspects of ISDN; but they do cover matters common to both POTS and ISDN, including telephone book listings, blocking 900 and 976 calls, blocking long distance calls, assignment of lines to hunt groups, and conversion of existing POTS service to ISDN. It is interesting to note that the form suggests replacing an existing line is "not recommended." Why not? The likely answer is that replacing an existing line costs the phone company money!

FIG. 7.11

This screen presents several non-ISDN-specific options. These options include phone book listings, call blocking, and hunt groups.

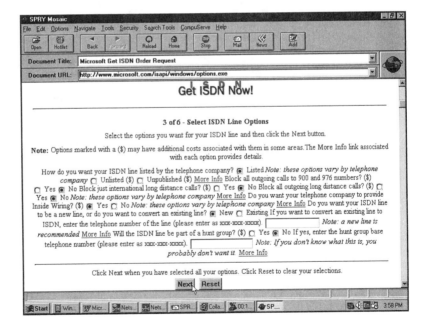

After you finish selecting the easy options, click "Next," getting into the real stuff of ISDN with Figure 7.12. Here you can opt to click the down arrow (pointed at by the arrow cursor in the figure). When you click the down arrow, you see a list of ISDN adapters for your computer.

This incredibly short list is by no means complete. I selected the U.S. Robotics Sportster ISDN 128K (formerly known as the ISC Securelink II until USR bought the company). I didn't show the list because it, undoubtedly, will change significantly by the time you read this. I want you to see that you can enter other products that are not on the list — entry boxes obscured by the pull-down pick list.

FIG. 7.12

Microsoft's "Get ISDN Now!" Web screen shows selections for ISDN adapter and the operating system to be used.

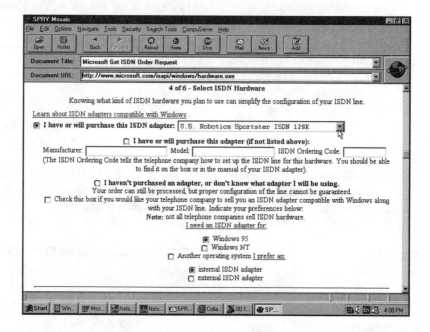

And now for an interesting question. "I need an ISDN adapter for: Windows 95, Windows NT or (Horrors!) Another Operating System." What's that got to do with ordering ISDN? Exactly nothing. But it's got a lot to do with Microsoft's market research. True, Microsoft offers ISDN support in both Windows 95 and NT, but information on the operating system of your computer is certainly not necessary for the phone company to set up your line.

▶ **See** Chapter 12, "Opening Windows 95 and NT to ISDN," for more information on specific ISDN components in these operating systems. **p. 381**

And look at what's missing. There aren't any questions on all the complex issues we covered about voice features and multiple call appearances, etc. If you want those, you'll have to call your local exchange carrier. The point, of course, is you probably don't want or need them to use ISDN to hook your computer to the Internet or your office; look how simple ordering ISDN really can be. Click on the Next button that's on the bottom of your screen when you scroll down and you'll see Figure 7.13, where you fill in your vital statistics.

Click on Next and you'll arrive at the last screen, Figure 7.14. Here you fill in your billing information. That's all there is to it.

FIG. 7.13

Here's where you fill in your name to tell the phone company who's buying the ISDN. If you've noticed the phone number shown is different from the 555 dummy number I've been using, you have sharp eyes. To really get through the form I had to use a real number; 555 bounced. So I put in Microsoft's main number (don't try to file an ISDN application for Microsoft; they and GTE already have that figured out).

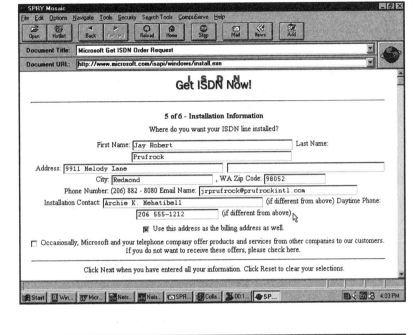

FIG. 7.14

"Get ISDN Now!" collects billing information you fill in on the last form to send to the telephone company for ISDN service.

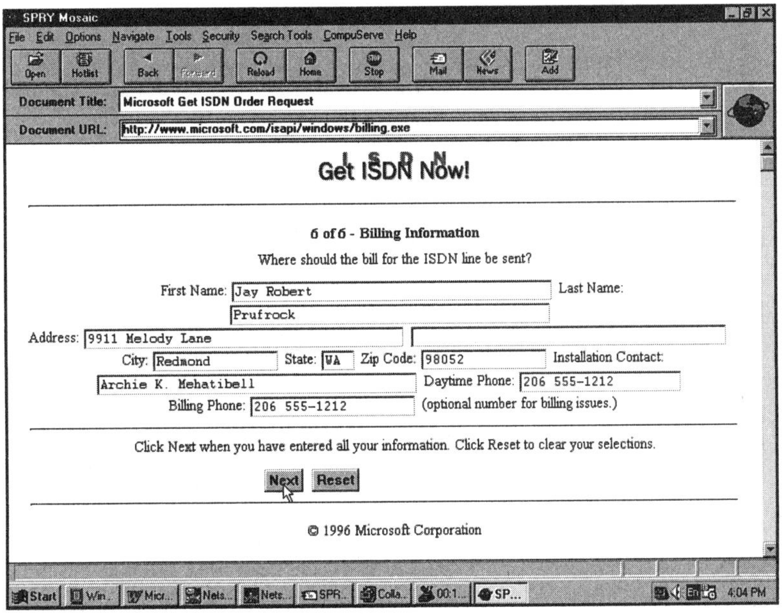

The following screens provide a review so you can be sure you put in the right things. At the end you click a button to submit the form to the telephone company. Don't worry, if your worst enemy—or your best friend with a poor sense for practical jokes—tries to sign you up, you'll have a chance to stop the process. The telco will call you up to confirm. And, I suspect, details of the Internet path traversed by the order could be resurrected to track down the perpetrator.

From Here...

We've taken a good look at what ordering and provisioning are and why they present a problem. Solutions include avoidance (that doesn't work); a massive (collection of) matrix (matrices) (this works, but may be unwieldy); limited options (this works too, but may not give you exactly what you want at a price you want to pay). Remember, the long distance carrier is also in this picture and must be able to work with ISDN. Now we'll move into really using this ISDN line you've just ordered.

- In Chapter 8, "Wiring and Powering Your ISDN System," we finally string it all together.

- Chapter 9, "Selecting an External Terminal Adapter," looks at boxes you can plug into ports on your computer and into ISDN.

- Chapter 10, "Putting An Adapter Inside Your Computer," reviews some of the boards that connect to ISDN.

- Chapter 11, "Establishing ISDN for LANs," considers bridges and routers for ISDN. Hint: you don't need a LAN to use many of these solutions; a single computer may benefit from LAN solutions.

- In later chapters we'll cover ISDN-specific software issues, use of multiple B channels, video, telephones, and so on.

Wiring & Powering Your ISDN System

Wiring? You mean to use ISDN I have to consider wiring? Unfortunately, yes. Because ISDN is designed to deal with much higher data rates than those of POTS, the wiring specifications for ISDN are more strict. This applies not only to wiring coming from the telephone company, but also to the wiring in your house or business.

▶ **See** "Noise," **p. 72**, and "Attenuation," **p. 73**

Remember our discussion of noise and attenuation? The farther a signal travels down a cable, the more it's weakened (attenuated) and the more non-signal interference (noise) increases to confuse or obscure our desired communications. This distorts the digital information, reducing the usable data rate and eventually making it impossible to operate within ISDN specifications. We'll look at some of the issues the phone company faces, then turn to some of your problems. ■

Restrictions on the phone company's cable system that affect ISDN

You'll learn how these limits aren't as limiting as you may have thought.

Where the phone companies leave off and you take over; or, Judge Greene creates the "demarcation" (demarc)

See how the demarc defines exactly where you start in your ISDN system design.

Cables and connectors to use with ISDN

You may think these things are too minor to consider, but, if they don't work, ISDN doesn't work.

Different ways you can string your wires ("topology" for math geeks)

You'll discover the bus and star topologies and figure out which is best for your needs.

The box you must have to hook up to ISDN (the secret code acronym "NT1")

The NT1 is essential to connecting to ISDN. Here you'll learn what it is and why you may or may not want an external NT1.

Wires and the Phone Company

Narrowband ISDN is designed to be carried over pairs of copper wire from the central office to the subscriber's location. At first, this design seems simple. The phone company has to install an ISDN-ready switch, ISDN software, and ISDN line cards at its central office. Then, when a subscriber wants ISDN, a pair of wires running from the central office to the subscriber is hooked to a line card.

N O T E Narrowband ISDN refers to the version of ISDN generally available for subscribers' connections and is the subject of the lion's share of this book. In Chapter 18 I discuss "broadband" ISDN that currently applies to some interconnections among telephone company systems. Some few years in the future, broadband ISDN may be available to large numbers of subscribers. If you have fiber optic cable delivering many megabits of data rate, you're a potential site for broadband ISDN. ■

▶ **See** "Broadband ISDN," **p. 526**

Great! But there are many questions confronting the phone company when it seeks to provide you with ISDN, including the following:

- Must there be an ISDN ready switch for each central office?
- How long can the twisted pair cable between the central office and the subscriber be?
- Are all twisted pair cables that fall within the length restrictions for ISDN usable?
- And many more…

N O T E Seeing what your phone company has to go through to bring you ISDN, your own wiring problems will seem more manageable. ■

Need for an ISDN Switch

Although it seems that the phone company would have to have an ISDN-ready switch in each central office to provide ISDN to the subscribers served by that office, this is not true. A single ISDN ready switch can be set up for an area.

Typically, we'd think of the area as being a city, but it could be much larger. For example, a subscriber at a rural location a hundred miles from the nearest city could receive ISDN service from a switch in that city. How? By connecting that switch to the subscriber's central office switch. This is a form of "foreign exchange" (FX) service.

> **CAUTION**
>
> Watch it if you're in a rural area. The cost for ISDN may be much higher. When anyone in the United States pays a phone bill, several dollars per line go to a federally mandated fund to make phone service available to places where it would not be economic without such a "spread the wealth" subsidy. Theoretically, this should make ISDN service available anywhere at rates comparable to those in cities. In practice, telephone

companies are resisting providing ISDN to outlying communities and want to charge rates based on long distance or mileage. These may be prohibitive to most users. The concept of ISDN as some kind of "special or premium service" is blocking a needed reform to support rural ISDN. In the meantime, the dollars collected just build up. If you're not in the United States, this may or may not be a problem; check to be sure.

▶ **See** "Regulations Affecting ISDN," **p. 56**

Within the city itself, the ISDN switch can be connected to other non-ISDN central offices by digital trunk lines capable of carrying the necessary ISDN signaling and traffic. The result is an "ISDN overlay" that makes ISDN widely available at a cost substantially below that of upgrading all central office switches to ISDN.

N O T E A *trunk line* is a telephone connection between switches. Here I'm talking about telephone company switches. But you could have a trunk coming to your office or residence and connecting to a PBX switch. ▨

▶ **See** "Using an ISDN PBX," **p. 473**

Additional Foreign Exchange Issues

Many of the telcos that offer no charge FX ISDN service to customers do so with an important limitation: if the customer's local office is converted to ISDN, the customer must either pay for the FX service or switch to service from the local CO.

Many telcos are still offering AT&T custom protocol for ISDN services supported by an AT&T 5ESS switch. If the customer's local CO is an NI1 standard Nortel DMS-100 or a Siemens EWSD, the ISDN terminals purchased for service under the custom protocol FX service will not work on the local switch. The customer needs to determine what type of local switch is being used and whether or not it will be converted to ISDN service.

The new National ISDN protocols (NI1, NI2, NI3 and subsequent ones to be numbered NI97 et seq.) should be used in any FX situation to reduce this type of problem. But this will not eliminate the problem, as some NI1 terminal equipment which works well on both the AT&T 5ESS and the Nortel DMS-100 will not work properly on a Siemens EWSD.

The level of service, in a voice application, varies greatly between a Nortel DMS-100 and an AT&T 5ESS using the custom protocol. Each switch offers services that are not supported on the other. The customer must ensure an application is designed to the lowest common denominator between the two switches so there is not a radical change when operation is on the local switch.

Finally, FX ISDN service (and really any ISDN service) probably will require a change of telephone number. Many individuals and many businesses have a great deal invested in a telephone number. The best solution here is probably to continue with one or two POTS lines under the old number for a transitional period of a few years.

The Long Wire

No matter how the phone company has brought ISDN to the central office that serves you, the next issue concerns wiring to your location. The basic rule is: a local loop copper connection for ISDN must be a twisted pair of wires less than or equal to 18 kilofeet from the central office to the subscriber's location (see Fig. 8.1).

 TIP The distance of 18 kilofeet is the length of the wire, not the distance a crow flies from the telco switch to your place.

FIG. 8.1
Eighteen kilofeet is the maximum length of twisted pair cable that may be used by the ISDN signal from the telco central office to your location.

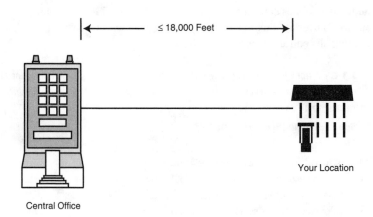

Central Office

Your Location

≤ 18,000 Feet

Lengths greater than 18 kilofeet lead to signal distortion and attenuation that fall outside ISDN specification and probably will result in errors or failure. A single repeater may be installed at mid-span to allow the distance to be increased to a maximum of 36 kilofeet in some circumstances.

Kilo-what?

How do you like this limit of 18 kilofeet? To save you the math, that's about 3.4 miles. I've never before seen the *kilo* prefix combined with a unit from the English system of measurement; it seems to be a creature created totally by the U.S. telephone industry.

You won't even see the English system of measurement anywhere other than the United States and a very few small countries; certainly you won't see it in the U.K. or England. This measurement system became obsolete long ago in most of the world outside the States. The U.S. is the only industrialized country that still uses pounds, feet, inches, slugs, gallons, and so on (although Canada was saddled with this absurdity until only a decade or so ago). How much longer can the U.S. pretend the metric system doesn't exist? Have you worked on a U.S. car lately? It takes two sets of wrenches, English and metric!

Remember, if you're from the U.S. and driving in Canada, the highway sign that says "Speed Limit 100" is talking about kilometers per hour; that translates to only about 62 miles per hour. Save yourself the ticket—the argument that you're from the States won't wash.

By the way, for everyone in the civilized world, 18 kilofeet is about 5.5 kilometers.

Part
III

Ch
8

The phone company has records reflecting the lengths of cable to certain locations. It also has instruments such as *time domain reflectometers* that can measure cable lengths by sending pulses down the wire and looking for the end, similar to how radar works.

Bridge Taps and Loading Coils

Once the phone company has determined that the wire between your location and the central office is less than 18 kilofeet long, the next issue is whether or not there are *bridge taps* on the wire. A bridge tap is a length of wire branching off of the original pair (Figure 8.2 shows how this might happen). You might have used analog phones on this run of cable for years and never had a problem. The worst thing a bridge tap usually does to POTS is reduce signal strength or introduce noise. The bridge tap probably was installed sometime in years gone by to deliver POTS service to a location different from yours. When your service was installed, the tap was disconnected at its far end but remained connected to the point where it and the run to your location join.

If you try this arrangement with ISDN, it often fails right away because the ISDN's complex digital waveforms are distorted by splitting off and going from the bridge tap to an end point that does not match what engineers call the "characteristic impedance of the circuit." When this happens, the waves become "standing waves" that are reflected back to interfere with the waves going to your location. So, the phone company has to check out all wires it proposes to use for your ISDN circuit and remove any bridge taps. If that can't be done, other wires must be selected.

 TIP In a few pages, I'll mention the need to have the correct "termination resistor or impedance" when you hook up your NT1. This is the same idea; the termination must be at the correct characteristic impedance.

FIG. 8.2
The bridge tap connects to the cable somewhere between your location and the telco central office.

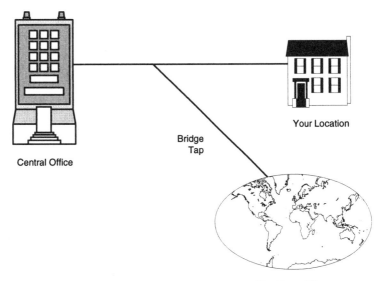

Central Office

Bridge Tap

Your Location

Who Knows Where

The bridge tap could wander for thousands of feet to someplace where the telco used to connect to a subscriber's phone. But now it's just cut off and can introduce serious problems into ISDN's digital signaling. Bridge taps must be removed by the telephone company when it installs your ISDN.

At the same time, the phone company must look for *loading coils*. These are small coils of wire inserted in the pair to overcome problems that result in long runs of wire that carry analog signals. The coils act as inductors to cancel capacitance that adds up over distance (see Fig. 8.3).

FIG. 8.3
Loading coils inserted in twisted pair cabling to overcome problems in long runs used for analog signals.

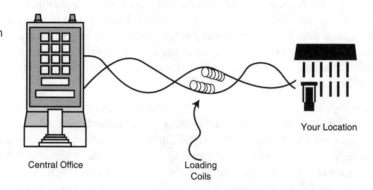

Central Office

Loading
Coils

Your Location

When digital signals use these cables, the coils seriously distort the digital waveforms. Loading coils must be removed by the telephone company when it installs your ISDN.

A Quick Tour of Some Important Concepts in Electrical Theory: Capacitance and Inductance

Two of the elements that make up electrical circuits are called *inductors* and *capacitors*. The longer the length of a twisted pair wire, the greater the *capacitance* that results in the overall circuit. This build-up of capacitance attenuates the strength of high frequencies much more than that of low frequencies, eventually resulting in voices that are all bass and impossible to understand. Insertion of inductance in the form of loading coils cancels the capacitance, returning the signal to normal.

Without getting into a whole course in electrical theory, you can think of capacitance as storing electrical energy. When two pieces of metal are close together and each is charged with electricity of opposite polarity (one positive, the other negative) the space between the pieces of metal stores a charge. When the source of electricity is turned off, the charge existing in the space remains.

This is why television sets have warning notices stating an electric charge exists in certain places even when the power is turned off and disconnected. The high voltage circuits associated with the picture tube have capacitors that store a charge; in fact the tube itself stores a charge. Never work on a device, such as a TV or monitor that could store such a charge until you have learned how to discharge the points of danger.

An inductor is a coil of wire. It has the property that it works in opposition to capacitance and "bucks" or eliminates capacitance. Lengths of telephone cable act like capacitors and store charge.

As an analog signal is alternating current constantly going back and forth from positive to negative, the charge is constantly building and collapsing. But the time to build and collapse is greater than the period (frequency) of the change of the alternating current signal. So it begins to distort the signal. The loading coils reverse this effect.

▶ **See** "Noise," **p. 72**, and "Attenuation," **p. 73**

When all bridge taps and loading coils have been removed from the wire, the phone company will connect it to the line card and begin testing to determine the *bit error rate (BER)* on the line. If the BER falls within the specification for ISDN, the line will be certified and your service connected. If it falls outside the specification, another line must be found or installed.

If the line is near 18 kilofeet—and certainly if it's longer than that—the phone company will install a *mid-span repeater* as close as possible to the midpoint between the central office and your location. This repeater's job is to take the bits it receives from the central office or from your equipment, determine which are 1s and which are 0s, and regenerate the same electrical signals to send further on.

> **CAUTION**
>
> The policies and tariffs regarding repeaters vary from telco to telco. Many such as PacBel and Southwestern Bell do not add any additional installation or monthly charge for repeaters. Others, such as Ameritech, may charge additional fees for installation or monthly service. As you probably have already guessed, I believe ISDN should be considered a basic service to be provided all subscribers, regardless of location, and provided to all at the same rate.

TROUBLESHOOTING

My NT1 and the telephone company switch don't seem to be able to make or maintain a connection through my loop that has a mid-span repeater. What's wrong? If your line has a mid-span repeater, you may have a problem with loop back tests between your NT1 and the telephone company's switch. Basically, the switch may misinterpret the repeater as an NT1, causing the switch to perform tests against the repeater rather than your NT1. As a result, you may be unable to establish or maintain a connection. The solution lies in software on the switch—this software must be designed to recognize the difference between a repeater and an NT1. I expect this problem to disappear within the next year. But, until telephone company staff members are fully experienced in ISDN, streets may be dug up in vain efforts to repair a defect in software on the telco switch.

In some cases, the hardware design of the switch itself leads to similar problems. For example, the National ISDN 1 Nortel DMS-100 is incapable of "seeing" any intermediate device, such as a repeater, for maintenance and testing purposes.

If you're more than 36 kilofeet from any switch, you might think the chances for ISDN in your area are nil—and you're probably wondering if you can return this book and get your money back. Wait! I can't let that happen and neither can your telephone company. They have at least one more trick up their sleeve.

It's true that you can't have more than 36 kilofeet of copper twisted pair cable between you and a switch: 18 kilofeet, a repeater, then another 18 kilofeet. However, that doesn't account for fiber-optic cable acting as a trunk extension from the switch. The phone company might already have brought fiber-optic cable within even a few feet of your location.

Look around for metal telephone boxes mounted on the ground; often they're light green. These are *subscriber line carrier circuit (SLCC) huts*. If you look inside (though you'd better not do this without the assistance of telephone company personnel), you'll find a fiber-optic cable from the switch connected to a small backplane holding line cards. Most of these cards convert the fiber-optic signal to an analog signal and send it on twisted pair cable to the locations of a number of subscribers. ISDN line cards can be plugged in at an SLCC hut (see Fig. 8.4).

FIG. 8.4

An SLCC can significantly extend the area of coverage from a central office switch.

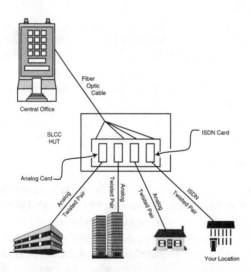

TROUBLESHOOTING

My NT1 says everything is normal, but I still can't connect with the switch. I know I'm connected through a SLCC. What's going on? Sometimes your own equipment will lead you astray. An NT1 connected to a SLCC may continue to indicate a normal operational state even if there is no connection beyond the SLCC to the switch.

Although by now you should have an appreciation for the complexities and expenses involved in providing ISDN to some locations, remember that the vast majority of subscribers in cities can be reached with existing twisted pair lines. I've merely described some of the measures that can be taken if you're in an outlying area. And, just because you're a difficult case, don't give up hope or endure exorbitant additional costs quietly. ISDN can, and should, be delivered to you—and at a reasonable price. It might just take a little time and "gentle" persuasion.

Where the Telco Line Stops and Your Wiring Begins (Demarc)

When Judge Greene issued the modified final judgment (commonly called "the MFJ") breaking up AT&T, a major problem remained: who owned all the wire in-place in people's houses and buildings?

N O T E A lot of the stuff in this section assumes the legal climate of the United States. I'm not so myopic as to believe things are the same in more advanced civilizations. So, if you're not in the U.S., consider this information solely for your amusement, and be sure to check on the practices, rules, and laws in your country.

The answer as far as the phone companies were concerned was, "We don't care; it's abandoned." So, all the wire became the property of whoever wanted it (this usually meant the owner of the real estate). However, a question lingered: "Where does the abandoned wire end and the wire that still belongs to the phone company begin?" This may seem trivial, but it's actually quite important.

CAUTION

We're starting to talk about the wiring at your house or business. If you intend to examine the wiring during this discussion, **PLEASE READ AND HEED THE FOLLOWING WARNINGS**:

DO NOT WORK ON TELEPHONE WIRING AT ALL IF YOU WEAR A PACEMAKER.

Telephone lines carry electrical current. To avoid contact with electrical current:

- Use caution when installing or modifying telephone lines.
- Never install telephone wiring during a lightning storm.
- Never install telephone jacks in wet locations unless the jack is specially designed for wet locations.
- Use a screwdriver and other tools with insulated handles.
- You and those around you should wear safety glasses or goggles.
- Be sure that your inside wire is not connected to the access line while you are working on your telephone wiring. If you cannot do this, take the handset of one of your telephones off the hook. This will keep the phone from ringing and reduce, but not eliminate, the possibility of you contacting electricity. (Ringer voltage is potentially much more lethal than the voltage used for talking.)
- Do not place telephone wiring or connections in any conduit, outlet, or junction box containing electrical wiring.

continues

continued

- Installation of inside wire may bring you close to electrical wire, conduit, terminals, and other electrical facilities. Extreme caution must be used to avoid contact with—thus, possible electric shock from—all such facilities.

- Telephone wire must be at least six feet from bare power wiring or lightning rods and associated wires, and at least six inches from other wire (antenna wires, doorbell wires, or wires from transformers to neon signs), steam or hot water pipes, and heating ducts.

- Before working with existing inside wiring, check all electrical outlets for a square telephone dial light transformer and unplug it from the electrical outlet. Failure to unplug all telephone transformers can cause electrical shock.

- Do not place a jack where it would allow a person to use the telephone while in a bathtub, shower, swimming pool, or similarly hazardous locations.

- Protectors and grounding wire placed by the service provider must not be connected to, removed, or modified by the customer.

This list of warnings is from the North American ISDN Users' Forum (NIUF) publication *ISDN Wiring and Powering Guidelines (Residence and Small Business).* Your local building codes, ordinances, and other laws govern over the suggestions made here and throughout this book. Please use common sense when working around electricity. This list and the book provide several suggestions to help you, but cannot cover all possibilities or dangers. If you don't have the necessary knowledge of electricity and proper methods for working around it, have a professional do the job for you.

We're about to enter the search for the demarc, the demarcation between the telephone company and you.

Let's see what happens when a phone line comes into your house or business.

The phone company always provides some form of lightning protection consisting of devices attached to each of the copper conductors. These devices appear as insulators to ordinary voice and ringer current on the wires, but if there's high voltage on the line, they shunt it to a ground. In many cases, the protection devices burn out and prevent passage of potentially dangerous or lethal electricity. Hopefully, this takes care of lightning and accidental contacts with power lines—but there's no guarantee. A large enough current at a high enough voltage could fry the protection devices and get inside.

The piece of gear performing the protective function helps you locate the point of demarcation.

CAUTION

Notice that I did not say the protection device (protection block) is the point of demarcation; it is not! Strictly speaking, you control everything more than twelve inches beyond the protection device. This is the infamous "12-inch rule." The Federal Communications Commission forbids you to even touch the protection block, and requires that your point of connection be at least 12 inches removed from the block (*Inside Wire FCC Docket 88-57*).

You'll probably find one of three situations:

- A *protection block* with your wiring directly connected to its terminals (see Fig. 8.5).
- A protection block with a length of wire attached to another screw terminal device where your wiring is attached (see Fig. 8.6).
- A *new type demarc* integrated device with the protection block behind a door, and an area with modular plugs and screw terminals for your wiring behind another door (see Fig. 8.7).

FIG. 8.5

The protection block guards against damages and personal injury that might result from high voltages that accidentally enter a telephone wire from lightning or contact with electrical lines.

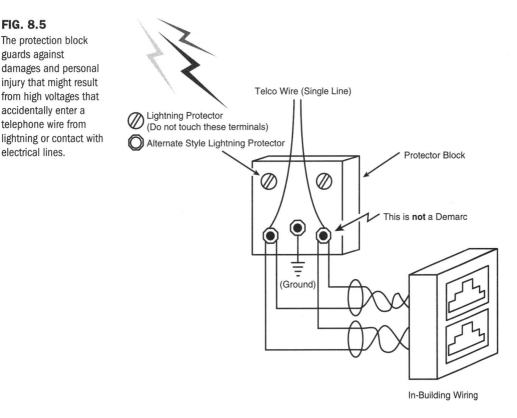

The protection block performs a function much like that of the "lightning arrester" on cable from a TV antenna. In both instances, the high voltage bleeds off to the ground. Such devices are a help but not total insurance against high voltage dangers.

The new type demarc allows a simple disconnection of the internal wiring by unplugging the modular plug. This provides safety for working on internal wiring. It also gives an easy test point. If your phones or ISDN equipment don't work, try unplugging the house wiring and connecting directly to the jack attached to the phone company's line. If the equipment works, the trouble is in your wiring. If it doesn't, the problem is with the phone company's lines.

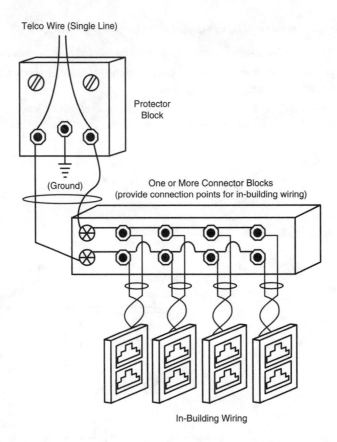

FIG. 8.6
A protection block with a separate terminal block gives a flexible and convenient way of connecting in building wiring.

Telco Wire (Single Line)

Protector Block

(Ground)

One or More Connector Blocks
(provide connection points for in-building wiring)

In-Building Wiring

Protection Block Only

If you have the first case where there is no connection point separate from the protection block, this is an illegal demarc. Before you can do anything, you'll have to clean up your act.

And you can't legally clean up your act, because you can't legally touch that protection block. Call your telephone company and request the installation of a legal demarc. Chances are they'll put in a *new type demarc*.

Protection Block with a Separate Terminal Block

If this is properly installed in accord with the 12-inch rule, you may attach any new wiring to the terminal block. If it is installed closer than 12 inches, you'll have to have the phone company modify it to meet the rule. Sometimes the separate terminal block provides modular plugs that can be disconnected while you work; sometimes it does not. Always disconnect the plugs if they're provided, and be sure a phone company representative installs a new type demarc if you have them come out.

FIG. 8.7

The new type demarc is the most convenient hardware for connecting to the phone company line.

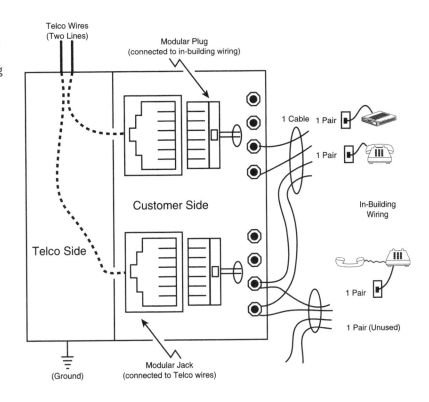

New Type Demarc

Today, most of us don't have to worry about this because recently installed telephone company equipment has the protector block integrated with modular plugs and screw terminal *entrance bridges* that make connection easy. You simply unplug the modular plug, screw your in-house wiring down to the terminals, and plug the modular plug back in.

We could spend a lot more time discussing possible wiring variations surrounding the demarc, but this information should be enough to get you going in most cases.

Cable and Connectors

Okay, you have the demarc worked out. Now, it's time to hook up the wire; you have some choices about the type of wire. In a house, you'll usually find *quad cable,* which consists of two twisted-pair wires which are color coded. Your first telephone line is carried on a red/green pair; if you have a second line, it's on a yellow/black pair. However, if you have phones with lighted dials, the yellow/black carries current for the lights, and is attached to a transformer plugged into a wall power receptacle. Table 8.1 shows the color coding and usages for quad cable. The pin numbers are the numbers used on a six-pin modular plug called an *RJ-11 connector* (see Fig. 8.8). The two extra pins are usually not used, but a pin out for their use is shown in Table 8.3.

CAUTION

Check whether or not a transformer is connected to some of your wiring. You might want to run ISDN over these wires; if there's a transformer connected, you'll fry some very expensive electronics because the transformer's alternating current voltage is deadly to your ISDN equipment. These transformers were installed to power lights on phones such as the "Princess." The power is usually carried on the yellow black pair. Remove the transformer and dial your phones in the dark! (Thereby casting darkness over "It's little. It's lovely. It lights."—the advertising slogan for the Princess phone. Wow! That's over 30 years ago, and I still remember it. The power of Madison Avenue. Where's my gray flannel suit?)

Table 8.1   Quad Cable with RJ-11 Cable Coding

Conductor	Color	Pin	Use
Pair 1	Red	3	Line 1
	Green	4	Line 1
Pair 2	Yellow	5	Line 2/Power
	Black	2	Line 2/Power

FIG. 8.8

6-pin modular plug (RJ-11). Usually only the four inner pins are used in this sort of connector. Refer to Table 8.1 for the pin out using four wires; see Table 8.3 for the pin out with six wires.

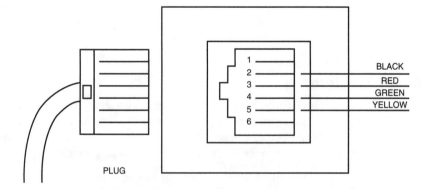

PLUG

JACK

ISDN connectors have eight pins, and usually are called *RJ-45 connectors* (see Fig. 8.9). Table 8.2 shows the color coding and pin assignments for four-pair wiring that fully populates these plugs. This table shows the standard coding to make a *T56A plug*. There is also a *T56B plug* shown that reverses Pairs 2 and 3; the end result is the same, so I suggest you use T56A if you're starting from scratch. Finally, the coding for three-pair wiring leading to a six-pin RJ-11 is shown in Table 8.3.

FIG. 8.9

8-pin modular plug (RJ-45). See Table 8.2 for the pin out using eight wires.

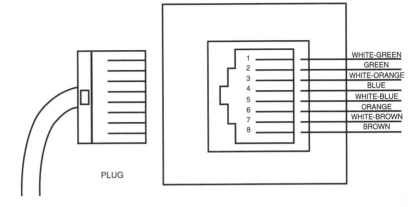

PLUG

JACK

Table 8.2   Four-Pair with RJ-45 Cable Coding

Conductor	Color	T56A Pin	T56B Pin	Use
Pair 1	White-Blue	5	5	Line 1
	Blue	4	4	Line 1
Pair 2	White-Orange	3	1	Line 2
	Orange	6	2	Line 2
Pair 3	White-Green	1	3	PS3 plus power
	Green	2	6	PS3 minus power
Pair 4	White-Brown	7	7	PS2 minus power
	Brown	8	8	PS2 plus power

Table 8.3   Three-Pair with RJ-11 Cable Coding

Conductor	Color	Pin	Use
Pair 1	White-Blue	4	Line 1
	Blue	3	Line 1
Pair 2	White-Orange	2	Line 2
	Orange	5	Line 2
Pair 3	White-Green	1	Line 3
	Green	6	Line 3

Notice how the pairs around a 6-pin RJ-11 are symmetrical. Pair 1 takes the pins on each side of the center, Pair 2 takes the next two pins out, and Pair 3 takes the next. The same is true for Pairs 1 and 2 in an RJ-45. And, an RJ-11 will plug into an RJ-45 female. So you can use an RJ-11 plug cable to carry Lines 1 and 2 from an RJ-45. Although you can use an RJ-11 connected to an RJ-45 in this limited manner, you should not make this a regular practice. And watch out! The next pair on the RJ-45 is *not* symmetrical around the center. So if you thought you could carry Pair 3, forget it.

The U interface should go to the center pins, Line 1. On the S/T side the ISDN data goes to the Line 1 and Line 2 locations; again, these are symmetrical around the center.

▶ **See** "Interfaces," **p. 79**

Table 8.2, showing the coding and connections for an RJ-45 with four-pair wiring, reveals one more fact. ISDN lines provide for some rather specialized powering options. If you're going to put in ISDN phones, or if you might sometime in the future decide to put in ISDN phones or some other piece of ISDN equipment that needs power, then pay attention. There are three ways that ISDN cabling provides power to devices:

■ *PS1 power*, also called *phantom power*, delivers power over the data lines, 4/5 and 3/6.

■ *PS2 power* uses 7/8 for power; pins 1/2 are not used. PS2 is often used by terminal equipment that needs external power.

■ *PS3 power* uses 1/2; pins 7/8 are not used. PS3 is only rarely used by terminal equipment at this time.

This power is usually supplied by the NT1, so you should take into account the powering needs of your terminal equipment when you select an NT1; some NT1 supply power, some don't.

CAUTION

In the event you're supplying power from your NT1, be sure you have the wires attached properly to the connectors. Notice that the data uses the inner four pins and the power uses two pins to the left and two to the right of these inner four data pins. Although I hope designers have built-in fault protection for the data circuits on your equipment, connecting power to those circuits through faulty wiring has the potential for equipment damage if the protection fails or is not there.

 T I P If all you're going to use ISDN for is connecting a computer to the Internet, these power options are irrelevant because your computer is already powered.

Now comes the final trick, the double-cross. Take a look at one of the POTS RJ-11 wires attached to your phone. If you examine it carefully, you'll see that the wire is rolled or crossed—the pairs are reversed. If it's a flat wire (most are now), stretch it out on a table or the floor until it's flat from one end to the other. Or, if you have one, look to see if there's a ridge molded into and standing out of the plastic insulation on the cable. This ridge will mark only one flat side. Now look at the RJ-11 on one end. Notice where the tab side of the connector is with respect to the ridge or whatever you use to mark one of the flat sides. Go to the other end; look at the RJ-11. The tab is on the same side of the cable. Think about this before you read the next paragraph.

Have you thought about it? Good. What happened to the order of the wires as demonstrated by their color and pin connections? They crossed-over, reversed at one RJ-11 relative to the other, and flipped! At one end red goes to 3, at the other end red goes to 4. At one end green goes to 4, at the other end green goes to 3. This *pair reversal* is exactly right for POTS. It's a disaster for ISDN. ISDN should be wired *straight-through* (see Fig. 8.10).

Part

III

Ch

8

FIG. 8.10

Straight-Through versus Crossed-Pairs cables. The crossed wiring is used for POTS equipment. The straight through is used for ISDN.

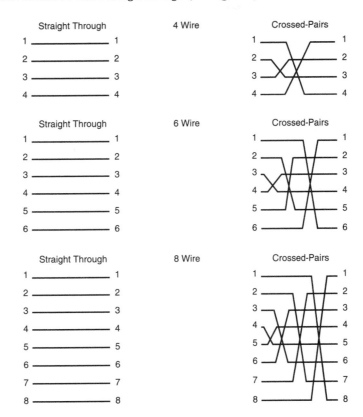

TROUBLESHOOTING

We're having problems getting ISDN to start working on our system. Check to be sure the cables you are using are wired straight-through, and do not have pair reversal. Pair reversal on the U (phone company) side will not cause a problem, but pair reversal on the S/T (your) side *could* have bad results. If you have more than one device on the S/T side, the chances of a problem are almost certain. The polarity of a single device is not critical, but when multiple devices are attached to the S/T interface, they all must have the same polarity. Use of crossed cables results in polarity-reversal and obviously violates this requirement, so good practice dictates that the cables on the S/T side of your NT1 be wired straight-through. Do this to eliminate one more possible source of problems either now or in the future when you expand your use of ISDN.

How long should your wires be? Equipment cables—those with RJ-11 and RJ-45 plugs that you connect to your equipment and then to the wall jack—should be no longer than 33 feet. These cables most often are flat, and can be stripped easily and have modular plugs applied. A modular plug tool for this purpose costs anywhere from about $5 for the plastic, grocery store variety, to about $100 for the top-of-the-line, commercial type... and you get what you pay for. If you're going to make a half-dozen cables, the cheap tool might be okay. If you're going to make more than that, however, I suggest you buy better equipment—it'll pay off sooner than you think.

The cable installed in your house or business should be individually twisted pair of 26-gauge copper wire specifically made for telephone use. The industry has adopted various "Category" designations. At a minimum, Category 3 ("Cat 3")should be used. Category 4 or 5 is certainly okay, but will cost more. However, there is a tendency to install Category 5 now, because it carries high data rates over significant distances for both telephone and local area network applications; I suggest you use Category 5, just in case your future needs could use it. The cable must *not* be *shielded* (covered with a continuous metallic braid or foil that is grounded). I suggest you use four-pair cable even though you may not use all the pairs now. Connect each wire to the appropriate pin using the color coding indicated in Table 8.2.

CAUTION

A *plenum* often exists between suspended ceiling tile and the next higher floor in modern office buildings; this space furnishes the return air duct for heating, ventilating, and air conditioning (HVAC) systems. If your cable goes through such an area, it must be rated as plenum cable. Basically, this means that the plastics used to make the cables are difficult to burn; therefore, they do not propagate a fire or give off toxic fumes in a fire. This is required by the National Electric Code, which has been adopted as part of the building code in most jurisdictions. In some cities, your cables must be placed in metal conduits if those cable are in plenums. In a few cities all cables must be in conduit regardless of whether or not the area crossed is a plenum. Check it out.

Since the specifications for ISDN cabling do not contemplate shielding such as would be supplied by a metal conduit, the lengths of cable in conduit may be less than possible outside conduit. If your cable runs are close to the maximum, it may be necessary to run tests to determine if the shielding effect of the conduit has introduced problems. Time domain and spectrum analysis along with bit error rate testing may be needed.

Topologies for Wiring Your Installation

What about the lengths of cables in the wall and ceiling of your house or business that are on the other side of the RJ-11 or RJ-45 jack? There are different geometric figures that may be used as patterns for how the wires are arranged. These patterns are called *topologies*. To some degree the uses you plan for your ISDN installation determine your selection of topology:

■ Will you use existing telephone wiring or install new wiring?

■ Are you going to wire more than one location?

■ Will you have more than one device connected to ISDN?

These questions work together. If you're going to have only a single device connected to ISDN, you'll go to only one location and will want to bring the U interface to the location of the device. This is the simplest technique, since the U interface uses only one twisted pair.

In a typical house, it's probably possible to find an unused twisted pair that's already installed to the location. Chances are, the house is wired with quad cable but only the red/green pair is used for a single analog phone line. This leaves the yellow/black pair for you to use to carry the U interface from the phone company. Check to be sure that no transformer is connected to the yellow/black pair. Also, check to see how the cable is distributed throughout the house. In most cases, you'll find that it *goes* from room to room; this is not a desirable circumstance for ISDN. If possible, the U interface pair should go directly from the demarc to your equipment location with no bridge taps to different locations. Figure 8.11 shows some of these issues.

FIG. 8.11

Hitting a home run with existing wiring.

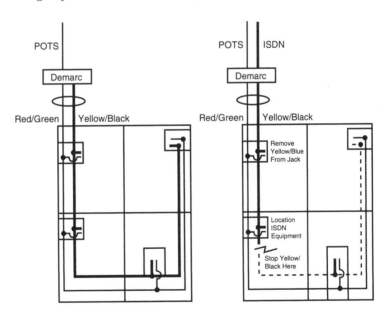

Home run wiring means running a single wire from one point to another and placing only one device on it. In the picture on the left, the yellow/black pair is not a home run because it connects to several locations. On the right, the yellow/black pair has been modified to run only to one location.

Your ISDN location is represented as the second room on the wiring in Figure 8.11. You'll probably find that the quad cable goes to each room, and that each conductor is cut, stripped, and wrapped around a terminal on a telephone jack. Follow the cable from jack to jack until you reach the desired location. Once you're there, remove the yellow/black pair that continues to the remaining rooms. Then, go back to each of the earlier rooms and remove each yellow/ black pair from its terminal. Use an *inline splice device* to join the wires without using the jack terminals. Congratulations. You've just made a *home run, a* connection between the demarc and your ISDN location with no other connections before or after.

N O T E   Inline splice devices are available from most electronic supply stores and other places that carry a simple line of telephone wiring supplies. I can buy them at the local supermarket. You may use electrical tape if you like, but the specialized splices are usually more reliable. If you do use tape, I suggest you firmly twist the wires together and cover them with 3M "Scotch #88" electrical tape. This tape (as opposed to #33) stands up to extremes of temperature and humidity for a long time. ▩

There is no guarantee that a home run of this type is the best connection, because quad cable comes in a multitude of forms and cannot be expected to meet the requirements of the Category 3 or better cable specification that's best for ISDN. You might be lucky, however, and if the distance is short, everything might work well.

If you don't have a free pair, don't trust the wiring that's in place (I never do); use new wiring. If you've tried to use the existing wiring but it hasn't worked, then you'll have to install new cable. In the long run, new cable installation is the best option, anyway.

T I P   When you install new cable, you should use Category 3 with four twisted pair cable, and be sure it's color coded as shown in Table 8.2.

The topology (geometrical layout) of your installation for ISDN is different from the typical residential single cable. With rare exceptions, the best wiring method for ISDN is the *star topology* (see Fig. 8.12).

Using star topology results in a means of testing and controlling each device from the central hub location. Right now, it may look like more work than it's worth. However, in the next few years this single location will be the place where you put items such as a PBX, specialized computer servers, and management electronics. If you put the wires in this way to start, it's all a lot easier and more flexible. This method is based on the Telecommunications Industry Association standard TIA/EIA-570.

The rules for a star topology require a home run from the distribution device to each of the service outlets where you connect your equipment. These runs are on the S/T interface. Two pair are needed to carry data, and an additional two pair are needed for powering equipment. While you may not have devices now that require powering, I suggest you install and connect all four pair to allow future use. There are a few other rules:

- Each of the legs of the star must be no more than 295 feet long, that is, .295 kilofeet! Or, if you're fortunate enough to live in the more advanced portions of the universe, 90 meters.

- The NT1 must provide a 50-ohm termination. Your NT1 documentation will describe how to set the termination impedance to 50 ohms.

- Your terminal equipment should be set for no termination.
- The NT1 should be set for fixed timing.
- The NT1 should be located within 10 feet, three meters, of the distribution device.
- Although you may provide as many legs off the star as you like, it is recommended that no more than four be active at one time. That is, no more than four devices should be on at a time. This recommendation is based on the additive effect of each device's load on the line and effect on the line impedance.

FIG. 8.12

Star topology provides a single cable to each device.

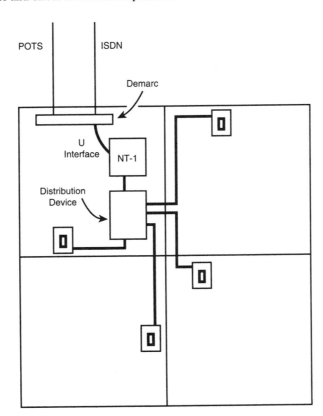

Termination Resistance and NT1 Timing

Hooking up ISDN devices on the S/T interface can be achieved in several different ways. I've suggested the two most frequently used: point-to-point connection to a single device and star topology wiring to multiple devices. There is some debate among experts on the best methods.

For example, the same star topology I just described may be accomplished by providing no termination at the NT1 and a 100-ohm termination at each of two ISDN terminal devices. In this case, those of you familiar with Ohm's law will recognize the two 100-ohm terminations are in parallel and result in 50 ohms. The real issue arrives when you add a third or fourth device. If you maintain the 100-ohm termination at each device you end up with 33.3 ohms overall with the third and 25 ohms overall with the fourth. This certainly will degrade and probably kill the circuit. Thus this method only works with two devices. (For those not familiar with Ohm's law, it says, in this case: Where there are *N* resistors each with the same resistance *R* connected in parallel, the resulting resistance is R/*N*.)

Timing is also a major issue and is the cause of most of the problems reported in new ISDN installations. Most of the NT1s on the market have timing as well as termination options. (The exception is the Tone Commander NT1 which automatically senses and sets the proper timing.) If the timing is not set properly for the chosen wiring scheme, the NT1 will begin to experience timing slip on the D-channel. This problem can take several months to show up but will eventually cause the NT1 to shut itself down. The user experiences a dead terminal and "solves" the problem by unplugging and replugging his ISDN terminal into the S/T bus. This action forces the NT1 to reinitialize the timing and the slipping process begins again and continues until the user is once again confronted with a dead terminal.

The timing options are "fixed," which is used for the short multipoint (the form I suggest where the NT1 is within 10 feet, three meters, of the distribution device) and "adaptive," which is used for extended multipoint (where the NT1 may be up to 285 feet, 90 meters, from the distribution device) and all point-to-point applications. These options may be set with DIP switches, pin jumpers, or software, depending on the NT1.

A significant amount of ISDN terminals in the home will be installed in the point-to-point mode (only one terminal connected to an NT1). This configuration requires adaptive timing and a 100-ohm termination set at the NT1 and at the ISDN terminal. Ohms law buffs will recognize this as resulting in 50 ohms.

If your terminal device has no termination resistance, select 50-ohms termination resistance in your NT1 and fixed timing.

N O T E *Impedance* is a critical measure of the electrical nature of a transmission line that carries alternating current (ISDN signals fall into this category). If a line is not properly terminated in its characteristic impedance, it won't work! ▪

 When you locate the NT1, remember that it requires AC power from somewhere. For most of us that somewhere is an electric utility company; this is usually called *mains power*. If your NT1 does not have a built-in battery backup, be sure to provide a separate backup battery supply. If you don't, a failure of mains power will shut down all your ISDN equipment, including telephones. This is a major difference between POTS and ISDN: POTS derives power over lines from the central office, but ISDN does not. (In Europe, there is an emergency method to bring ISDN power from the central office, but this is not a part of the U.S. specification or implementations.)

N O T E Since ISDN developed in the commercial context, much ISDN equipment, including NT1s and their power supplies, is rated under the Federal Communications Commission Class A designation for commercial use. This means that it may radiate more electromagnetic interference (EMI) than would be allowed for the Class B designation for home use. Don't let this hold you back. If

Class A tears up your TV, you're better off surfing the Internet anyway. A lot of the stuff I test is Class A or not even rated because it's alpha or beta design. I've never had a problem. I've worked with EMI most of my life, as I've been an amateur radio operator (W5HFS, Extra Class) for over 40 years. If my 1000-watt transmitters don't tear stuff up, none of these piddling computer toys will! ▪

The suggestions I've made here are based on providing the easiest connection for a single equipment location, or the most flexible connections for multiple equipment locations. The specification details more options. The termination impedances and cable lengths may vary under different conditions; however, I believe the options I've suggested will serve most installations, cause the least trouble, and provide the most flexibility for the future. Specific options in devices, especially in your NT1, might offer alternatives; be sure to consult the manufacturer's documentation.

NT1

As you've probably surmised by now, the NT1 is a vital part of your system, so let's take a quick look at it.

▶ **See** "Interfaces," **p. 79**

The telephone side of the NT1 provides the U interface, and carries information in both directions simultaneously over one pair of wires. The NT1 changes the signals to separate transmit components from receive components, and places each component on a pair of wires on the S/T interface side.

 TIP Remember, one pair is sufficient to get ISDN to your NT1 from the telephone company, but two pair are required to connect to your equipment using the S/T interface, and more pairs would be needed to power your equipment from the NT1.

Wait a minute! You say your terminal equipment doesn't need an NT1, because it has a U interface connection already? This means an NT1 is built into your device. Such a design is a mixed blessing: you avoid the added cost and complexity of a separate NT1, but you often give up the possibility of connecting other equipment to your ISDN line. Why? Because you may connect one and only one NT1 to a BRI line.

▶ **See** "Basic Rate Interface (BRI)," **p. 75**

So, if one piece of equipment already has an NT1 built in, you can't connect any other equipment, unless your device provides an S/T interface for that purpose. In addition, even if your device has an S/T interface, it may not provide power, which is needed by some products. When you purchase equipment, remember the mixed advantages and disadvantages. If all you'll ever want to do is connect the U interface to your computer—and you know you'll never need to use other devices—take the built-in NT1. But for greater future flexibility, use an external NT1.

NT1s come in many flavors. The simplest ones provide a U interface and S/T interface with a few option switches for termination impedance, and perhaps some signal lights to let you know what's going on (much like a modem).

Motorola NT1D NT1

The Motorola NT1D, shown in Figure 8.13, is a good example of this simple design. It provides an RJ-45 jack for the U interface, the place you connect to the line from the telephone company. The NT1D has two RJ-45 jacks for the S/T interface. The instruction book makes several suggestions for cabling and setting the terminating resistors built into the unit. It has power for terminal equipment available from its S/T RJ-45s on pins 7 and 8. This Motorola unit is a good, simple NT1. Similar devices are available from Tone Commander, Adtran, Alpha Telecom, and a number of other companies.

FIG. 8.13

Motorola NT1D.

 TIP Set your web browser URL location to **http://www.motorola.com/MIMS/ISG** to check it out.

TROUBLESHOOTING

I can't get my ISDN stuff to recognize connection to the telco switch, and the lights on my NT1 are flashing in funny ways. What do I do? Look at the indicator lights on the front panel of the NT1. Check the manual and find out exactly what each light means. In the case of the Motorola NT1D, the front has six LEDs labeled with rather cryptic acronyms.

- **SC:** This lights when the telco switch sends a test voltage down the line and finds proper termination in the NT1. The acronym comes from the sealing of the current loop.

- **ACT:** You have to count flickers to understand this light. In general, it monitors activity on your ISDN line. If it stays on, you're connected. If it blinks off and on rapidly, something is interfering with your connection to the telco switch—a fault in the U interface connection. If it goes off and on about once a second, the S/T connection has a problem. If it's off, your U interface and your S/T interface are both down.

- **LB:** This shows that the telco switch is sending a test signal to make sure the NT1 and intervening circuit are properly connected. The switch loops back a signal to see if it is properly transmitted.

- **LP:** When this light is on, your local power is OK.

- **RP:** This light checks the power at your terminal equipment, remote power. For example, you might have an ISDN card in your computer connected to the NT1D. When your computer is on and powering the card, the RP light should be on. When you turn your computer off, thereby removing power from the card; the RP light goes off.

- **RPR:** This also has to do with power at the remote device; If the light is on now, it indicates the polarity of the power is reversed; and, as far as the NT1 is concerned, remote power is reversed. This condition might occur if your cables are flipped somewhere along the line. See the earlier discussion in this chapter on cable wiring.

Once you've deciphered the lights, you've isolated the problem to a specific part of your installation. Now, concentrate on finding the defect in that part.

Other NT1s can be very complex. Commercial varieties are made to rack mount so panels containing the NT1s can be screwed into vertical rack standards and software can provide centralized management and troubleshooting of all the units. Some provide a number of optional features to enhance your use of ISDN.

Alpha Telecom UT620

Alpha Telecom has concentrated on making a wide range of NT1 devices. Alpha Telecom offers everything from the simplest unit, exemplified in the UT620, to elaborate rack mounted systems. The UT620, illustrated in Figure 8.14, is about as simple as an NT1 can be, with an RJ-45 for the U interface connection to the telco. There are two other RJ-45s to provide the S/T interface to your equipment.

 To determine the alpha and omega of Alpha Telecom head **for http://iquest.com/~ati_usa**.

One version of the Alpha Telecom UT620 comes with a simple power supply that powers only the NT1; a second version is provided with a power supply that also provides power over the S/T interface for those devices you might have that need such power. The difference in price for the second, S/T powered device is only a few dollars; I suggest you buy it for future flexibility, even if you don't have equipment that needs S/T power now.

FIG. 8.14
Alpha Telecom UT620.

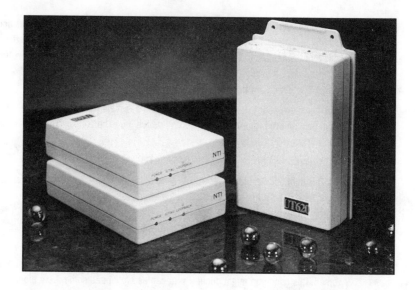

There are only three indicator lights, and they are clearly labeled: "POWER," "S/T&U," "U LOOP BACK." The Power light is on while the power is connected. The S/T&U light has four states:

- If the U interface isn't active, it blinks eight times a second.
- If the U interface is not activated, the LED lights.
- If the S/T interface is not active, the LED flashes once per second.
- If both the S/T and U interfaces are linked, the unit is operating in normal mode and the LED is off.

Granted, you still have to have documentation to understand these, but the information is all you need to monitor your NT1.

One other feature of the UT620 may be handy. The UT620 comes with a mounting plate that can be screwed on the wall. This plate has three tabs aligning with holes on the device, making it easy to remove and replace the UT620. Most equipment designed for wall mounting only comes with holes for hanging, forcing you to adjust screw depths to achieve a good bond. This only works well on a perfectly smooth wall.

IBM 7845 NT1

The IBM 7845 ISDN Network Terminator Extended provides a U interface and S/T interface, and also contains an internal battery and an R interface for connection to POTS devices. The internal battery, which makes up more than half of this NT1's weight, can carry the NT1 and attached ISDN devices for a few hours following a power failure.

N O T E The R interface is not defined as an analog telephone connection in the ISDN specifications; rather, it refers to any interface that is not a connection to ISDN equipment. However,
just as the phrase *terminal adapter* has come to mean an external, serial port device of the type we'll
cover in Chapter 9, the R interface has come to mean an interface that looks like an ordinary POTS
line. You can plug POTS phones into the R interface and use them exactly as you would expect, but
watch out for one frequent limitation: often, these connections do not pass ringer current. As a result,
you can make outgoing calls; but your phone won't ring, and your FAX machine won't respond to an
incoming call. This limitation appears frequently in cards that plug into your computer (see Chapter
10). All of the NT1s with R interfaces (more properly, R interfaces designed to mimic the POTS line)
discussed in this chapter provide ringer current. ▣

This IBM NT1 is much more elaborate that the ones I outlined previously. The 7845 can use
one B channel for ISDN equipment and the remaining B channel for standard POTS. While the
B channel for ISDN provides a vanilla S/T connection, the POTS side throws in a lot of features:

- Distinct number ringing to tell you which of as many as three different directory
  numbers is calling
- Special alert ringing to alert you to a call the device has reached through repetitive
  dialing you asked it to do when your first attempt hit a busy signal
- Call waiting, with additional call appearances activated on your telco's switch, you can
  have several calls waiting at one time
- Last number redial
- Speed dialing of up to 30 numbers
- Return last incoming call. You know from the frame format of ISDN that the calling
  party's number is contained within ISDN frames; so, as long as you have ISDN, maybe
  you don't have to pay for caller identification as an added feature. Please keep this a
  secret, and don't tell the phone company where you heard it! Of course, you'll have to
  have ISDN hardware or software to make it work; because your analog caller and
  number ID stuff won't do. The IBM 7845 does this for you.
- Call blocking
- Conference call with as many participants that are supported by the configuration you
  have with your telco switch

T I P Set your web browser URL location to **http://www.ibm.com**.

N O T E Although the IBM 7845 provides a great way to get a lot of the ISDN voice features without
buying ISDN phones, you must still have your telephone company provision the switch to
provide features, such as multiple call appearances and conference calling. If you're only going to use
the 7845 for data, this special provisioning is not required. ▣

The IBM 7845 gives you the benefits of ISDN supplementary services for voice without having to use special ISDN phones. This works as long as you're willing to use only one B channel for true ISDN equipment. Should you want to use the IBM 7845 without the POTS you can reconfigure it so both B channels are available at the S/T interface. It's kind of the best of all worlds.

▶ **See** "Supplementary Services," **p. 95**

▶ **See** Chapter 7, "Ordering ISDN Services," **p. 141**

Alpha Telecom Super NT1

The Alpha Telecom Super NT1 offers more than the standard NT1 features (see Fig. 8.15). These center around using one or both B channels with ordinary POTS equipment. The Super NT1 has:

- A U interface for connection to your BRI.

- Two S/T interfaces for connection to ISDN terminal equipment.

- Two POTS connections that each use an ISDN B channel and convert it for communication with ordinary POTS equipment such as telephones, modems, and FAX machines.

- An LCD panel that provides set-up and diagnostic information in alpha-numeric form.

- ISDN supplementary services integrated with the POTS connections include call waiting, hold, conference calls, and call transfer. This list is not as extensive as that available with the IBM 7845, but it is offered on two lines.

- Selection of speech or 3.1 kHz audio on each POTS connection. Using the 3.1 kHz audio setting for a fax machine usually results in better fax operation than using a speech setting.

- A built-in battery backup as an option.

FIG. 8.15
The Alpha Telecom
Super NT1.

Notice the LCD panel for programming and troubleshooting. The NT1 you thought was an unnecessary cost might turn out to provide you with more flexibility than you realized. In fact, an added-feature NT1 is a step toward bringing more and more intelligence into your control and away from the telephone company, so that the telco can devote its time and resources to providing better and faster carriage for all those bits you shape.

From Here...

Your ISDN service is ordered and installed. The cables and NT1 are up and running. Now, it's time to hook it up to something—but what?

- If you found a lot of the information in this chapter rough going because of the terminology, review Chapter 3, "Defining Narrowband ISDN" for the terms and theory.

- Chapter 9, "Selecting an External Terminal Adapter," explores the possibility of using an ISDN device that seems like a modem—it connects through the serial port on your computer and responds to modem AT commands.

- Chapter 10, "Putting an Adapter Inside Your Computer," considers plug-in cards: sometimes they look like modems, sometimes they look like network cards, and sometimes they look like bridges or routers.

- Chapter 11, "Establishing ISDN for LANs," reviews external boxes that connect to your local area network cable as bridges or routers. If you don't have a LAN, this solution might work for you—even if you have only one machine, don't skip this chapter.

- Part IV, "Software and Applications," finds ways to use all this ISDN stuff you've bought.

Selecting an External Terminal Adapter

The first category of ISDN hardware we're going to consider is the *external ISDN terminal adapter.* You'll also find terms like *ISDN modem* or simply *terminal adapter* or *TA* used for these boxes. The distinguishing characteristics are:

- A stand-alone box with its own power supply
- Connection to your computer through the serial port, parallel port, or Universal Serial Bus
- Use of the AT command set so that the device works with your existing modem programs

As we'll see, this equipment provides a straightforward solution to using ISDN. There are drawbacks, however, and we'll also take a look at those as we go along.

This chapter offers "hands-on" encounters with some representative external ISDN terminal adapters. Before deciding on particular equipment, though, you need to understand all the devices available to you, and examine some complicated issues. ■

Connecting through the serial port seems simple, but it's not. The port can be a real bottleneck

You'll learn about serial port problems and solutions.

The AT command set looks appealing, but it was designed for POTS. What's missing when you use this command set for ISDN?

Find out what you need to use AT commands and what you'll have to add.

3Com offers the Impact as one of the simplest external serial port devices

We'll see how you set up the Impact.

Motorola has captured a large market share with its BitSURFR

We'll see how ready the BitSURFR is on both the PC and the Mac.

Adtran has the Express XRT. This box can detect the type of ISDN switch you're connected to and automatically enter the SPIDs

You'll see how the Express XRT is configured and also look at the somewhat more commercial ISU Express.

> **N O T E**   In the language of the ISDN specification, a terminal adapter is any device used to connect ISDN with computers other than those of the telephone system. By that definition, the internal cards of Chapter 10 and LAN routers of Chapter 11 are also terminal adapters. However, usage over the last few years has tended to narrow application of the phrase *terminal adapter* to a device external to a computer that provides ISDN connection for the computer through the serial, parallel, or Universal Serial Bus.
>
> This evolution and ambiguity of terms reminds me of words from history's most famous maker of dictionaries:
>
> *I am not yet so lost in lexicography, as to forget that words are the daughters of earth, and that things are the sons of heaven. Language is only the instrument of science, and words are but the signs of ideas; I wish, however, that the instrument might be less apt to decay, and that signs might be permanent, like the things that they denote.*
>
> *Lexicographer: a writer of dictionaries, a harmless drudge.*
>
> *Dr. Samuel Johnson anticipating the language of technology and commenting on life's station.* ■

Serial Port Issues

The common denominator for all these devices is their use of the serial port on your computer. Some equipment has been designed for the parallel port and the Universal Serial Port is discussed as a possibility below, but the serial port is so ubiquitous that I'll just stick with it for now. Since I expect most readers of this book to use Microsoft Windows, the discussion is directed that way. (Where there are differences between Windows 3.x and Windows 95 that are germane to the discussion, I'll point them out.) If you're using another operating system, your concerns might differ. When I talk about the BitSURFR, we'll take a look at its Mac version, too.

▶ **See** Chapter 12, "Opening Windows 95 and NT to ISDN," **p. 381**

Windows 3.x Serial Port Operation

Windows 3.x is designed so communications applications do not speak directly to the serial (COM*x*) ports. Rather, Windows provides a device driver to handle serial port communications. In Windows 3.x ,once an application has called the Windows application program interface (API), the Windows 3.x communications driver, COMM.DRV, takes control and speaks to the serial port. The efficiency and configuration of the communications driver—COMM.DRV or whatever you might use as a replacement—determines the flexibility and speed of your serial communications.

Basically, COMM.DRV places characters in a queue and sends them onward through the machine using interrupts. Almost everyone has noticed how a machine running Windows 3.x and doing serial communications seems to slow down when a lot of communications activity occurs. This is primarily due to intense interrupt activity demanding CPU attention character-by-character. Most computers running Windows today are 386 or better machines that run Windows 3.x in enhanced mode. In this mode, Windows creates a virtual device that looks in software like a serial port. This somewhat improves operation by instituting buffering between the real serial port and the virtual serial port.

All this software, virtual device, and interrupt activity can seriously drag down serial port performance. Why does this matter to you? Well, if you're using an external ISDN terminal adapter connecting through a serial port, then the serial port becomes a bottleneck.

If you don't believe that the serial port is a bottleneck, take a look in Windows 3.x itself. Go to the Main program group and bring up Control Panel (see Fig. 9.1). Notice that this figure has a port icon as part of the Windows 3.x standard configuration programs. In addition, it shows the addition of TurboCom/2, a third party program that improves Windows 3.x performance. Go into the ports and look at the options you have for port speed. You'll find the maximum speed available is 19,200 bits per second (bps). See Figure 9.2. The settings shown are the ones you have in Windows 3.x as it comes from Microsoft. The fastest data rate is 19,200 bps.

FIG. 9.1

The Windows Control Panel gathers most of the configuration elements you need to work with Windows.

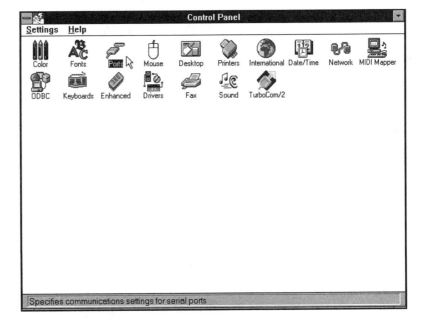

FIG. 9.2

You can make Windows port and data rate selections from a submenu within the port icon.

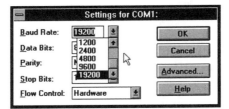

What do you think happens to that wonderful 64,000 bps you're paying for with telephone company bills and with the hardware you're buying? That's right—you'll lose most of the speed you're paying for. If you set Windows 3.x as high as it'll go in Control Panel, you're still at less than a third of the speed your hardware and line can handle. There must be a solution! There is, and it involves several things:

- Replacing serial port hardware if it's not up to the speed standard you need
- Replacing serial port driver software
- Configuring your system for higher speeds

We see more about these options in a minute.

Windows 95 and the Serial Port

Moving to Windows 95. As you can see in Figure 9.3, Windows 95 allows for much higher data speeds on the serial ports. As Figure 9.4 shows, you also have easy control over serial port buffering in Windows 95. These controls are accessed from System Properties. Click the Device Manager tab, then double-click a particular COM port line to open the Communications Port properties. Finally, click the Port Settings tab. Even though the list goes up to 921,600 bps, you must have hardware available that can actually realize such a data rate, most cannot.

 T I P In my opinion, the improvement in serial port operation is reason enough to move to Windows 95. Besides Windows 95 crashes much less often than Windows 3.x!

FIG. 9.3
Windows 95 allows data speeds of up to 921,600 bps—more than enough speed to handle an external ISDN terminal adapter.

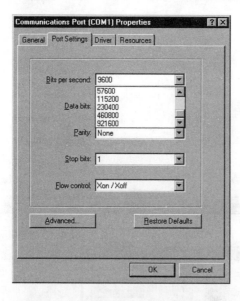

FIG 9.4

Windows 95 gives you easy access to controls for FIFO buffering with a 16550 UART.

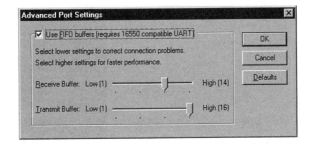

Windows 95 performs all this magic using VCOMM as its communications device driver for protected mode services. This software only loads drivers when they're needed by applications. VCOMM supports Plug-and-Play, which eases installation if your hardware follows that specification.

N O T E A new *universal serial bus (USB)* design pushing serial data rates to 12 megabits per second and supporting up to 63 devices with isochronous and asynchronous data is being developed by Intel, Compaq, DEC, IBM, Microsoft, NEC, and Northern Telecom. It will probably appear late in 1995. Hardware and software supporting this design will become available; in fact, Windows NT and Windows 95 are expected to incorporate drivers for this. With new hardware and software, the speed-related issues I've been discussing should go away. ■

 T I P Drive your bus to **http://www.teleport.com/~USB** for a look at the details of USB.

Serial Port Hardware

The *universal asynchronous receiver/transmitter (UART)* you have in your computer is a determining factor in whether or not you can realize any real benefit from ISDN. In fact, the UART also weighs on the effectiveness of faster modems such as the 14.4 and 28.8 kilobit per second (kbps) versions that are now extremely popular. In Windows 3.x go into the Microsoft Diagnostics program (at the DOS prompt, enter **MSD**). After an introductory screen, you'll reach the main menu (see Fig. 9.5). Our interest now is in the COM ports, but many other tests are available. Press **C** to select COM Ports. This gives you an analysis of the COM ports in your machine (see Fig. 9.6). As you can see, the machine in this figure has a 16550A UART for COM2, set at 57,600 bps. We'll soon see how the speed is set, but first let's examine what a 16550A UART is.

N O T E Curiously, Windows 95 does not report UART version along with the serial port information available through Device Manager. You can still find this out if you have a modem installed on the COM port Select "Modems" in the Control Panel and choose the COM port in question on the Diagnostics tab. Be sure a modem is attached. Then choose More Info and, after the program examines the port and modem, you'll be presented with details including the type of UART. ■

FIG. 9.5

In Windows 3.x Microsoft Diagnostics main menu shows the broad range of tests you can run.

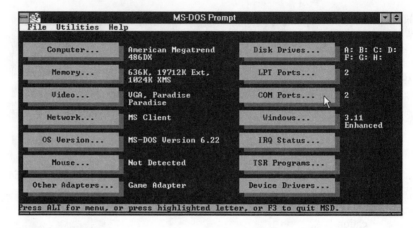

FIG. 9.6

COM port analysis in Microsoft Diagnostics for Windows 3.x shows the status of each port and the type of UART chip used.

COM Ports	COM1:	COM2:	COM3:	COM4:
Port Address	03F8H	02F8H	N/A	N/A
Baud Rate	1200	57600		
Parity	None	None		
Data Bits	7	8		
Stop Bits	1	1		
Carrier Detect (CD)	Yes	No		
Ring Indicator (RI)	Yes	No		
Data Set Ready (DSR)	No	Yes		
Clear To Send (CTS)	No	Yes		
UART Chip Used	8250	16550AF		

OK

Earlier versions of the UART used in PCs didn't have the ability to work effectively with data rates beyond about 9,600 bps because they had to handle each byte individually, and provided no buffering. The 16550A provides a first in, first out (FIFO) buffer that can store 16 bytes of receive or transmit information. The buffers can hold data while the CPU services any communications interrupts.

N O T E   The whole point of this discussion is to persuade you to have 16550A UARTs for any connection to ISDN, or for modems with data rates greater than 9,600 bps. 16550A serial boards, which cost between $25 and $75, are a very good investment. Faster serial boards with larger buffers and on-board processing are available from manufacturers such as Hayes, Digi International, and Boca. ■

Serial Port Software

Windows 3.x currently lacks the proper software to take full advantage of the 16550A or special cards such as those from Hayes. In some cases, replacement software is included with the hardware you purchase. In other cases, you might find freeware or shareware through the Internet or a bulletin board service (BBS). You can also buy commercial packages.

> **CAUTION**
>
> Windows 95 has provided much better serial drivers; this software is not needed with Win 95. In fact, the software might prove harmful. I expect the serial software companies will come up with some improvements over Microsoft's drivers eventually.

One of the most popular free products is CyberCom from CyberSoft Corporation in Australia; it's probably available on your favorite BBS. Installation is fairly straightforward, though you have to be comfortable editing INI files.

 If you want the details on Windows 3.x serial communications hitch your port to **http://www.microsoft.com/Support/KBSL/PEROPSYS/windows/Q92447.htm**.

TurboCom/2 is a commercial program from Pacific CommWare. It remedies a number of the deficiencies in Windows 3.x serial communications. Among other things, TurboCom/2 supports:

- Data rates up to 115.2 kpbs
- Background data transfer
- Concurrent serial communications and LAN operation
- DOS communications programs under Windows
- Extended and even shared interrupts in some circumstances
- Out-of-sequence access to serial ports
- Fine-tuning of communications
- Up to 9 COM ports in the TurboCom/2 Plus version

    ▶ **See** Appendix B, "ISDN Products: What To Ask and Who To Ask," for details on manufacturers, including their addresses, faxes, phones, and many Internet sites. **p. 577**

Installation of TurboCom/2 is quite straightforward if you have made no changes in the standard Windows comm drivers. If you *have* added special drivers, these must be removed manually within the SYSTEM.INI file.

> **CAUTION**
>
> Damage to the SYSTEM.INI file can bring strange results. Windows will even fail to start if certain things are wrong. Be sure to follow instructions in documentation when you make changes to SYSTEM.INI. It's best to use the special editor, SYSEDIT, provided with Windows to make changes in SYSTEM.INI. SYSEDIT protects against some problems—such as insertion of non-printing characters—that may cause problems with SYSTEM.INI. To use SYSEDIT, go to Program Manager; open the File menu and choose Run, then type **sysedit** and press Enter. You're presented with a series of windows including AUTOEXEC.BAT, CONFIG.SYS, WIN.INI, and SYSTEM.INI. Click the title bar of the SYSTEM.INI window to make it active, then begin your edit.

Once TurboCom/2 is installed, an icon is placed in the Control Panel (see Fig. 9.7).

FIG. 9.7

TurboCom/2 icon in
Control Panel.

To work with your communications ports now, use this icon rather than the Ports icon in Control Panel. Clicking the TurboCom/2 icon brings up a selection of ports (see Fig. 9.8).

FIG. 9.8

Port selection in
TurboCom/2 is simple.
Just click the port name.

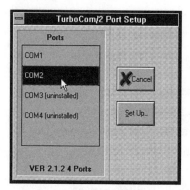

In Figure 9.9, you see a larger selection of serial port speeds (and much higher rates) than those available in the Windows 3.x software. Use of a communications utility such as TurboCom/2 provides more than an easy way to set speeds. You can set speeds directly by going into the WIN.INI file and entering speeds under the [ports] section as anything you want. But this doesn't mean your software or hardware will actually support the speeds you select. To be sure the speeds you desire are supported, you need a 16550A UART and a good communications utility.

FIG. 9.9

Here's where you do the
basic communications
port setup in Turbo
Com/2.

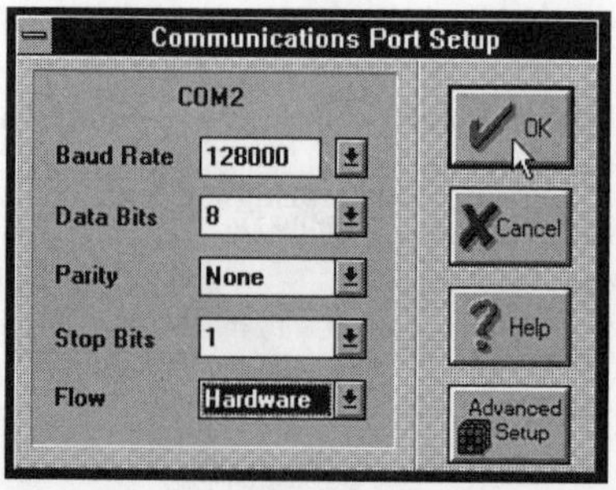

TurboCom/2 also provides an easy way to fine-tune a number of other settings; some of these are available in drivers supplied with Windows, but many are part of TurboCom/2 itself (see Fig. 9.10).

FIG. 9.10

A wide variety of advanced communications port settings is available in Turbo Com/2.

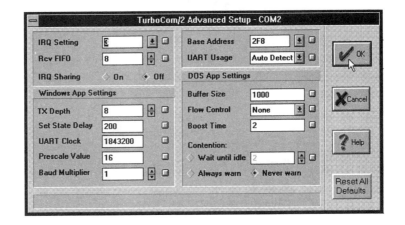

Finally, Pacific CommWare, which makes TurboCom/2, also has an ISA board that can support data rates up to 460.8 kbps.

All this discussion is directed toward making your communications ports function the best they can, so that any ISDN device or analog modem will give you maximum performance. But there's one more, frequently overlooked trick. Most people think the data rate in their software should be set for the data rate of the device being connected. In other words, you look at a 14.4 kbps modem and say, "I'll set this puppy for 14.4 kbps." Of course, the first thing you run into is that there's no selection available for the number you want. What do you do? It seems like you ought to be able to choose the next highest (in this case, probably 19.2 kbps), but you may actually lose a great deal of speed that way. Why? Because of compression.

Take a look at Figure 9.11, which shows the connection between your equipment (a modem or ISDN device), the phone line, and the same situation at the other end. Each computer is connected to a modem and the modems are connected together through the telephone network. Compression is built into each modem. For our example, the bit rate on the telephone network is set at 14.4 kbps. But each modem is compressing information at much greater data rates between itself and its computer; so the computer hardware and software must be set at the maximum rate that might occur using compression.

The raw, physical data rate between the two communications devices over the phone line is, let's say, 14.4 kpbs. That makes sense, because they're both 14.4 modems. But, let's say the information being transmitted over that link is plain English text. You know there's a lot of redundancy and space within ordinary text. This is a circumstance that cries out for compression to get rid of redundancy and wasted space. In effect, compression increases the data rate.

Most of us use compression through features built into our communications hardware (such as a modem). So, the data rate over the phone lines is 14.4, but once the information gets into the device, internal compression squeezes outgoing data and expands incoming data. The result? The data rate over the cable between your computer and the device could be anywhere from two to four times greater than that on the phone line. You should set your serial port to account for that. If you have a 14.4 kpbs modem and there is the possibility of a 4:1 compression ratio, set your port to 14.4 x 4 = 57.6 kpbs. There's even some possible added data rate from buffering and other tricks, so push for higher data rates with your software settings until it fails. Then back up one notch.

FIG. 9.11

Data rate to the phone lines/Date rate to your computer.

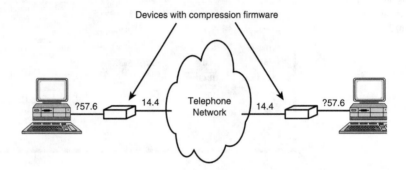

NOTE   Don't be misled. If the ISDN device combines a fax/modem, compression occurs with V.42 and MNP 4 and 5 compression methods. But this applies only to the analog, modem part. Compression on the ISDN side, which complies with a universal standard, can be negotiated on-the-fly. It uses a different method that should be set out in the specifications. ■

This seems to imply that if you use a single B channel with your ISDN device at 64 kpbs, you should set your port at $64 \times 4 = 256$ kpbs. That's even beyond what might be shown with some of the fanciest hardware and software for serial ports! Exactly—that's why we're all interested in the souped-up serial cards or the new design for the USBCompression techniques for ISDN were in limbo for a long time. Devices from the same company can do compression well when talking to each other, but interoperability among products from different vendors can be a problem. Thanks to intensive standards-setting work by the Internet Engineering Task force, agreements among many vendors and interoperability testing, through the California ISDN Users Group, most of these issues are behind us. We'll return to this briefly in Chapter 13, "Tying It Together: Two B or Not Two B."

NOTE   Yes, Virginia, there is no free lunch. The only time compression is going to arrive at such multiples as 2 or 4 is when your data is compressible! But a lot of the data we want to send are, including: images, spreadsheets, video, voice, and plain text. Compiled programs or files that are already compressed are examples of data that aren't very compressible (or aren't compressible at all). So, when vendors assert that their 14.4 modem sends data at 57.6, they're halfway correct but fully misleading. The bits, traveling between modems, still go at 14.4 kbps; the human information content might, or might not, be compressible as great as 4:1 or whatever the particular compression ratio is. Well, actually the electrical exchange goes at 2400 baud, the modulation technique delivers 14.4 kbps, and compression might, on occasion, deliver 57.6 kbps. And the marketers want you to buy the highest and least certain number! ■

AT Command Set

The *Hayes Standard AT command set*, commonly known as the *AT command set,* is used by all these devices. The set is a standard to the extent that the most common commands are used by all modems, by all external ISDN terminal adapters, and by some internal cards. The leading common commands are:

+++	Enters the command state
AT	Precedes any command
ATZ	Resets the device
ATH	Hangs up

TROUBLESHOOTING

This is a pop quiz. What very common AT command is *not on* the list I just presented? Tick-tock, tick-tock, tick-tock...give up?

ATDT	Tone dial a number

That's right. There are instances in which ATDT fails with these devices. The recommended dialing command is often ATD followed by the number!

Each of these devices has its own unique AT commands and uses for the S registers. Check the manuals carefully, and don't assume that everything you've used for modems carries over to terminal adapters.

Finally, and most importantly, software you use to dial, usually called a "dialer," might fail or give strange results when used with ISDN devices. This could result from AT command conflicts, incorrect setup strings, or timing errors. Try carefully dialing manually. If manual dialing works, but the dialer doesn't work, then the problem is in the dialer.

Based on my experience, the worst case is when something sending AT commands—for example, a dialer—really messes with the ISDN device's mind. In that case, you can't do anything; simply power down the device, then turn it back on and try again. If that doesn't work, try whatever reconfiguration and reset alternatives you have available.

One really easy thing to overlook is the use of ctrl+M (^M) for the suffix. What this means is every AT command must be ended with a ˜M or it won't work. So you might be adapting a modem setup to work with your ISDN device. You find sending the modem setup string destroys the configuration of the ISDN box. So, you remove the string. Then nothing happens. Simply insert ATZ˜M for a full reset and go merrily on. You owe me hours of overlooking the last ˜M.

Hayes or V.xx "compatible" means things don't catch on fire if connected even when not made by Hayes. Hayes or V.xx "compliant" means things work like they're supposed to, for instance, as if Hayes had made them.

Equipment for ISDN Connection through the Serial Port

Connection through the serial port is quick and has the great advantage of working with the AT command set so you can use your current programs. As a result, many manufacturers are making serial ISDN equipment. Let's look at three of the market leaders. Remember, these are examples, this is not a complete list or recommendation. Keep up with what's going on by following the trade press and checking out the tip.

 TIP Keep up with ISDN at **http://alumni.caltech.edu/~dank/isdn** and **http://www.bryce.com/~bryce**.

3Com Impact

The 3Com Impact, formerly the AccessWorks QuickAccess Remote, was the first terminal adapter device I tried when these products began to appear on the market. I had the opportunity to use this equipment while it was being beta tested, and it already worked well. Now, let's evaluate the production model (see Fig. 9.12). The box has a serial port to connect to your computer, and an RJ-11 connection you can use for analog (POTS) phone equipment. I usually plug a modem into such a port, but you might use a fax machine or ordinary phone.

FIG. 9.12
Notice the very simple front panel of the 3Com Impact has only a handful of indicator lights. This is the 3ComImpact IQ that comes with a graphical user interface for Windows that includes the SPID Wizard, a utility that detects switch type and SPIDS much like the Adtran discussed later in this chapter.

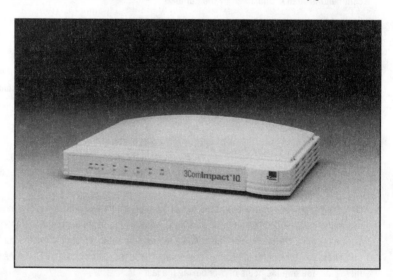

 TIP Make your computer communicate compatibly with **http://www.3com.com** for more information.

N O T E By the way, 3Com provides a version of this box to work with the Macintosh. The attractive part of its design apparently is simplicity, making many things easier on that device than they are on the IBM-compatible device. "Of course," I can hear the Mac folks asking, "what would you expect?" ∎

Here are the basic steps needed to make the Impact work:

- Plug the ISDN line into a modular jack on the box.
- Plug a line from your serial port into the D-shell connector on the box.
- Turn the box on.
- Load the software.
- Configure the box.
- Use your AT command-based communications software.

At least, that's the idea… let's see what really happens.

N O T E I'm assuming from here on that you've read and understood Chapter 4, "Choosing ISDN Services," Chapter 7, "Ordering ISDN Services," and Chapter 8, "Wiring and Powering Your ISDN System." Specific instructions regarding some of these issues usually are included with the devices I'm discussing in this and subsequent chapters. I'll point out unique issues and possible trouble spots. ■

Right away you may be confused by the supplied instructions and cables. You're told to plug the RJ-45 end of the furnished cable into the RJ-45 jack on the back. The label on the box makes it clear that you should plug this into the U interface from the phone company. This means an NT-1 is built into the 3Com Impact. The instructions then tell you to plug the other end into the ISDN telephone jack.

TROUBLESHOOTING

I installed my ISDN wiring according to strict specifications, so my wall jack is an RJ-45. The 3Com instructions say to connect the RJ-11 connector end of the cable to the RJ-11 telephone ISDN jack. What can I do? That certainly seems like a problem (recall that an RJ-11 has up to six pins; an RJ-45 has up to eight pins and is wider than an RJ-11), but it's easily solved. The Impact is wired so only the two center pins of the RJ-11 plug are used (because the U interface needs a single twisted pair). You can insert this RJ-11 plug into an RJ-45 jack and properly connect the center pins, so go ahead and do it. In fact, 3Com has preserved flexibility by supplying an RJ-11 for your wall connection; had they provided an RJ-45, everyone with an RJ-11 jack would be unable to connect. Unfortunately, the Impact's documentation doesn't make it clear that connecting the RJ-11 plug to an RJ-45 jack is okay. Don't worry—it is.

▶ **See** "Cable and Connectors," **p. 185**

Once you get through that connection unscathed, you connect the serial cable. 3Com supplies a male-to-female 9-pin cable that should work with most machines. If your equipment has a 25-pin connector, you'll find an adapter in the box. Most modem cables today are made with a female 9-pin for the computer end and a male 25-pin connector for the device end. If you have to use a cable different from that supplied, be sure it is a modem-style cable with the correct connectors and be sure it is *not* a "null modem" or "serial printer" cable with the transmit and receive lines crossed.

So far, so good; the connections are made. Now, let's load the software. 3Com supplies an Installation and Diagnostic Utilities disk with files for both DOS and Windows.

DOS Installation   Make a directory on your hard drive and copy the entire contents of this disk. Then execute QARCFG to start the configuration. The entry menu appears, (see Fig. 9.13), and asks you to provide the COM port number, speed, and interrupt (IRQ). Your selection of the port determines the interrupt as the standard default; don't change this unless you really know why you're making a change.

N O T E   Why are we starting with DOS, and why do 3Com and most other makers provide DOS setup and utilities? Because you should always be able to make these simple means of accessing a device work. Your Windows environment may be a total mess, you may want to use the box in a different environment with some off-the-wall operating system (Bill Gates would take that to mean anything Microsoft doesn't make). The DOS means of control preserves your options.

By the way, 3Com offers a version of the Impact with a built in POTS modem. I'll not go through that setup since it's explained well in the book. In my opinion, you are well advised to stick with the model without the modem, which gives you more flexibility as new modem designs and speeds come out.

3Com also provides a graphical user interface for Windows installation. This software can detect the switch type and SPID in much the same way as the Adtran XRT discussed later in this chapter. ■

FIG. 9.13

The 3Com Impact configuration entry menu shows selections for COM port and interrupt.

 The defaults are for COM1 and 19,200 bps. Set the COM port to the one you're connected to on your computer. Don't worry about the 19,200 bps; this only applies to the terminal mode connection you use to set things up. When you actually use the modem, the rate is set much higher elsewhere.

When you're finished, press F10 to connect to the device. The next screen, Figure 9.14, provides selections for telephone switch type, directory numbers, and SPID numbers. Here, you'll need the results of your earlier work with the phone company when you ordered your service, found out the switch type, and were assigned directory numbers and SPIDs. Three selections are included. The first two are National ISDN 1 (NI-1) compliant, and the third is custom (proprietary):

- AT&T 5ESS
- Northern Telecom DMS100 and Siemens
- AT&T 5ESS custom

FIG. 9.14
Here you see the 3Com Impact switch with number selections for directory numbers and SPIDs.

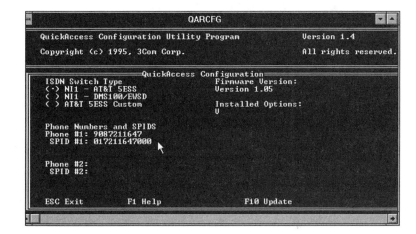

▶ **See** Chapter 7, "Ordering ISDN Services," **p. 141**

When you ordered your ISDN service, you were assigned two *directory numbers.* These are just the telephone numbers that are used to call you. You were also issued a *service profile identifier (SPID) number* for each directory number. The switch keeps track of your ISDN configuration through the SPIDs and through *terminal identifier (TEI) numbers* it assigns dynamically; you don't have to worry about the TEIs. But you must enter the SPIDs just right, or things won't work, so be sure to get the SPIDs from your phone company before you begin.

> **CAUTION**
>
> The form of the SPID varies from one switch to another—and perhaps one telephone company to another. Sometimes, the SPID contains 01, then your telephone number including area code, and then a 0; for example, 0151234567890. The switch I use here in Austin with Southwestern Bell is a Siemens, and the form of my SPID is simply a telephone number followed by 01; for example, 512345678901. Because there's no general rule, you'll have to ask the telephone company.
>
> One very important thing: notice that the SPID has no spaces or dashes. If you put any in, the SPID probably won't work.
>
> If your ISDN line has been configured as point-to-point, don't include SPID #1.
>
> Southwestern Bell is about to change from the Siemens to an AT&T switch. This will be a complex transition; SWB has to schedule the change over line-by-line with each ISDN subscriber.

When you've made the necessary changes, press F10 to save and be returned to the main menu; exit with escape. You then have to power down the unit. Give it about 15 seconds to settle down, then turn it on again.

Now, you can test it. Go into your favorite communications program that uses the AT command set. Configure it for a Hayes modem on the port you've connected to the 3Com Impact. Type **AT** and press Enter. If you receive an OK, you're probably all set. If you don't receive an OK, check all the connections and configuration, then try again.

When it works, dial an ISDN number, using ATD plus the number (do *not* use ATDT; it won't work). You should receive the expected response from the number you dialed. For instance, if you've dialed a typical Internet service provider, you'll see the name of the provider and login. Go ahead and give it a try. You should be able to operate from this point just as you would with a modem. When you're done, hang up. If you're directly using the AT commands, enter **ATH**. Otherwise, use the disconnection options available in your dialer.

> **N O T E**   Watch the B-1 and B-2 lights on the box. When you dial a data call, one lights up green. As long as the call is connected, the light remains green. When you hang up, the light goes out. I strongly suggest you form the habit of checking the light when you connect and disconnect. If it fails to go out when you think you've disconnected, then you still might be connected. In most places, the telephone company charges for each minute of ISDN used, so you don't want to leave a line up when you're finished. If you live where I do, Austin, Texas, there's no time charge. Even if the phone company doesn't charge by the minute, your Internet provider might. Finally, even if you aren't charged for time by your Internet provider, anytime your line is up, someone else might be getting a busy signal. So, to be a good guy, hang up whenever you're done using a connection. ■

We're not through testing yet. Plug a POTS phone into the RJ-11 Phone Out port on the back of the box. You should be able to make a call with this phone. You can try the same thing using a modem.

TROUBLESHOOTING

I seem to have poor performance with my ISDN device. What can I do to make it go faster? There are many possible configuration settings that you can make with most of the equipment used for computer communications. Take a careful look at the documentation you receive and check the homepages of the vendors. Sometimes the littlest details can make a big difference.

For example, the manual for the Impact is short and readable; I suggest you go through it as soon as you get the device. I found an interesting tidbit buried in Table B-3 of Appendix B. This concerns setting the S registers for V.120 frame size. (About as exciting as watching moss move north on a tree trunk, right?) In the middle of the fine print, it says to set the maximum frame size to 253 for Adtran compatibility. Since one of the Internet providers I use has Adtran equipment configured for V.120, I made the change. The speed of operation was noticeably faster. But the big benefit came in fixing a problem with one of my Web browsers. I've been using Spry's Internet in a Box and found intermittent operation when I used ISDN with the Air Mosaic browser included with the Spry package. Setting the S74 register to 253 fixed this.

To see how your registers are set, go into a terminal mode using your modem program or the terminal program in Windows. Enter AT%R and read them off. To change them, you need to enter, for example, AT S74=253; put whatever you need in the setup string when you configure your dialer. What *do* you need? That's the hard part. I happened to know, before I saw the reference in 3Com's documentation, that one of my Internet service providers receives my calls on Adtran equipment. This problem was pointed out and cured after testing by the Texas ISDN Users Group. 3Com has worked hard to make this machine sense what is needed, and their engineering staff tells me the device looks at the first signals it receives and adjusts to match. The Adtran anomaly happened to crop up long after design, and is one of very few special settings that need to be made.

Over time problems crop up and fixes are developed by vendors. New features are added. The Impact and most other devices can be upgraded by loading software into a built programmable ROM. A utility is provided for changes through software (see Fig. 9.15). You can get this new software from 3Com's Web site, **http://www.3com.com** after you have first checked the technical support information to be sure you should make the upgrade.

FIG. 9.15
3Com Impact firmware upgrades are made through software downloads using this screen for control.

Although there are many other possibilities, the real world of BRI ISDN use is boiling down to two types of connections:

- *Dialup Asynchronous* at 57.6 kpbs. When I connect to my Internet service provider with the Adtran mentioned above, I used this method for some of my tests.

- *Dialup Synchronous* at 64 kpbs. This is the type of connection you'll encounter if an Internet provider is using a router, or if you're dialing into a router at your office. I used this for other tests. It seems pretty clear now that this has become the dominant connection method.

In the beginning, most of these terminal adapters only supported dialup asynch 57.6. But most Internet providers and offices use routers, and therefore use synch 64. 3Com, Adtran, and Motorola—the ones we're looking at in this chapter—all support at least these two methods and perhaps others. In the case of the 3Com Impact, there doesn't seem to be a setup option to switch between synch and asynch; the equipment is smart enough to sense what it's talking to and adjust. This is good design; you shouldn't have to figure this out. It appears that 3Com (really, the company 3Com bought their device from) decided to try to make the device as simple as a modem. I hope they finally can, because I shouldn't have to know I'm connecting to an Adtran using V.120 with a specific frame size, for which I must manually adjust.

N O T E I've noticed a rather parochial tendency in many of these ISDN devices. It seems the default line speed is set to 56 kbps. You know, of course, that ISDN is supposed to provide B channels at 64 kbps but in some blighted parts of the universe, notably California, much of the phone system is limited to 56 kbps, as discussed in earlier chapters. So, since much of the design and manufacture of ISDN hardware takes place in California, and since those who live on the "left coast" considers themselves to be leading rather than following, you end up with 56 kbps as the default data rate. On the 3Com Impact, you cure this by changing the setting of register S60 to 64 kbps.

Issues surrounding the setting of S registers also crop up with Multilink PPP, which enables aggregation of B channels, as I describe in Chapter 13. 3Com's documentation lays out the details well so I'll just alert you to read that portion of the rather short manual to be sure you've covered all bases. On the whole most of the details that you have to set manually with other equipment are automatically set with the Impact.

(OK, for you Californians who have taken this all too seriously—circle with me now and share the experience of understanding. I suspect 56 kbps is the default because the boxes always work whether the switch handles 56 or 64 kbps. Were the default set to 64 kbps, service lines would be besieged with calls from those in 56 kbps areas.) ▪

Windows Installation   You'll probably be able to avoid the DOS installation method and the detailed S register "tune up" I've discussed. However, I wanted to be sure you're aware of these options and take the time to consider them so you derive optimum usage from the Impact or any other equipment you use.

If you're using Windows 95, it's hard to conceive of any easier set up than the plug-and-play, which is built into the Impact. Be sure your computer is turned off. Plug the Impact into the serial port; turn the Impact on and then turn the computer on. Windows 95 loads up and detects the new hardware, then asks if you want it to be automatically set up. Respond yes. You'll be stepped through the process. If you're using Windows 3.x or if you have Windows 95 and don't use plug-and-play, start the set up from the Run selection. Be sure the Impact diskette is in drive A: and execute setup; you find yourself in the Setup screen as shown in Figure 9.16.

Choose Continue and the software attempts to find your Impact. Be sure it's on; if it's not you could get an error message like the one in Figure 9.17. This may be caused by the device being off; there's also a possibility that the software can't find the right COM port.

FIG. 9.16

Installation of 3Com Impact Software.

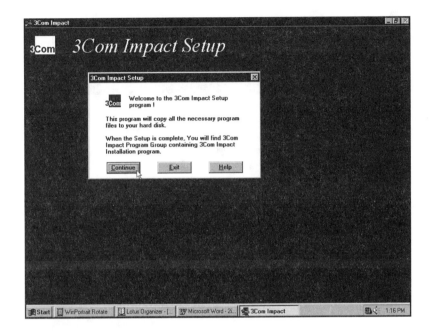

FIG. 9.17

An error message appears when Impact software can't find the Impact.

When you click OK in the error message you are taken to Figure 9.18 and given an opportunity to select a COM port. Now this is where it gets interesting. If your mouse stops working, it means the software, in attempting to find the COM port with your Impact, tested the port with your mouse and destroyed its connection. Don't worry; use your ALT and TAB keys to select the correct port on this screen.

FIG. 9.18

Selection of COM port in the event the Impact software fails.

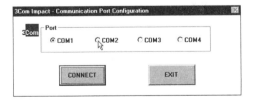

Then, using CTRL ALT DEL and the selection to shut down your computer, shut down and restart. Now the proper port is selected, and you are able to continue the installation without the COM port conflict problem. Figure 9.19 shows the screen you've been waiting for; fill in the requested information on your ISDN line. If your Impact has a built-in POTS modem you are asked to check off a couple of boxes regarding which number should be associated with internal POTS modem and which POTS port should be used for the attachment of an external device. If you have the option of using two B channels through multilink PPP, check that box. If you have only one SPID do not check the Enabled box for the second SPID.

FIG. 9.19

The main Windows set up screen for the 3Com Impact.

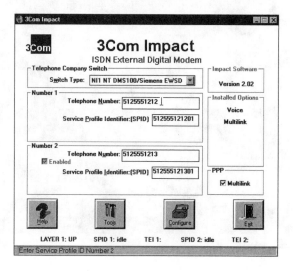

Enter your directory numbers and SPIDs. If you have a built-in POTS modem, there are boxes in which you select the B channel line to be used by the modem. Be sure to check the multilink PPP box if you can aggregate both B chanels.

When you've entered all the information, click Configure and then choose OK to load the new configuration into your Impact, (see Fig. 9.20). Then turn the Impact's power off, wait fifteen seconds, and turn it back on so it does a clean reboot with the new information.

FIG. 9.20

Load the new configuration into the Impact by selecting Configure and OK. Remember to turn the Impact off for fifteen seconds and then back on for a clean reboot with the new software.

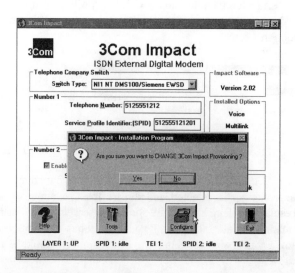

Select the Impact icon again and go back into the Set up screen. Choose Tools to pop up the menu shown in the upper-right corner of Figure 9.21.

FIG. 9.21
The "Tools" menu for the Impact.

We're going to run a quick test here. First, look at the bottom of the screen. You should see a line of text similar to that in Figure 9.22, which indicates that the ISDN line is up and properly communicating with the switch.

FIG. 9.22
Notice the text at the bottom of the screen shows that the line is "up."

Now choose Tests on the Tools menu, and you find yourself in the screen shown in Figure 9.23. Enter a telephone number and click Call. Text explaining what's happening appears rapidly; here it shows the call connected properly. When you've confirmed this, click Drop and the call disconnects, as shown in the last line of text. Incidentally, the 800 number shown here is an airline reservation number; since it's answered by an auto attendant and I was only on for a couple of seconds, it provides a quick test. You can use any phone number you like.

FIG. 9.23

In this test sequence for the Impact, notice the successful placing and completion of the call as shown in the text window.

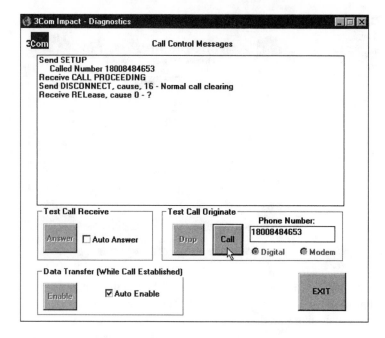

Dial-Up Networking   This is all pretty neat, but you haven't connected to anyone to really use your ISDN. We're about to go through the set up of dial-up networking in Windows 95. The same procedures apply to all devices that are addressed using the AT command set.

First, you select My Computer from the desktop by double-clicking the icon with the left mouse button. You get a listing of the resources available on your computer, similar to the one shown at the left top of Figure 9.24. On my computer this includes other network servers as well as dial-up networking. In this screen shot, I've combined three steps so you can follow the procedures in one picture. Double-click with the left button on Dial Up Networking and the small screen of the same name pops up as shown in the middle of Figure 9.24. Double-click the left button again, this time on top of Make New Connection. This gives you the panel you see at the right bottom of Figure 9.24. Here you name the connection and select the 3Com Impact as the modem to make the call.

FIG. 9.24

Setting up dial-up networking for the 3Com Impact using Windows 95 is easy. Double-click with the left button on the My Computer icon first, then the Dial Up Networking icon, and finally, the Make New Connection icon.

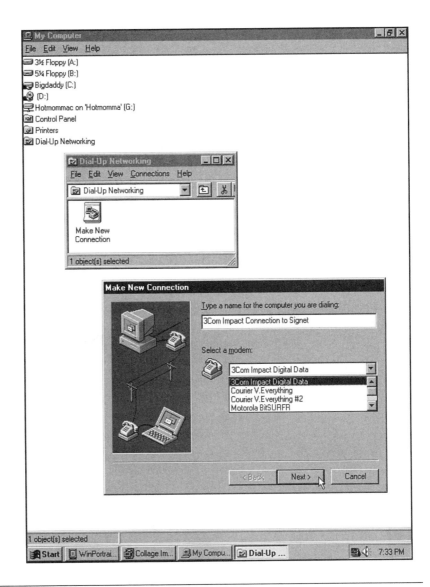

Consider Using a Vertical Monitor

The vertical screen shots in this book were made using a monitor that can be rotated between horizontal (landscape) and vertical (portrait) aspects. I find a vertical monitor much easier to use for writing. I've also noticed most Web pages work better with the vertical format. I don't need to scroll down nearly as much and can grasp the screen's context much better; in fact, I've noticed a large percentage of the Web pages fit totally on one vertical screen. For regular size paper (A4 or 8 1/2 x 11) an entire ordinary page appears lifesize on one screen. I think such monitors are a worthwhile

continues

continued

investment of your computing dollar. The monitor I use is a Portrait Display Labs Pivot 1700; I understand this monitor is jointly marketed under two or three different names. As far as I know, there may be only one or two other monitors that can be rotated. Funny how some of the best ideas just don't get the wide market play they deserve.

Choose Next and enter the telephone number and other information, as shown in Figure 9.25. Then select Finish and, if the dial-up networking software isn't already installed, you are asked to insert the Windows 95 CD or the appropriate diskettes.

FIG. 9.25

Installation of 3Com Impact Software.

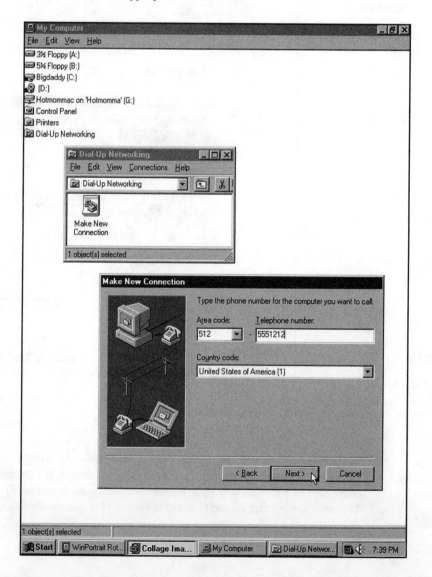

The result of all this effort is the creation of a new Dial-up Networking icon. If you plan to use this often, I suggest you make a "shortcut" copy of it and put it on your desktop. At any rate, in Figure 9.26, you see the icon and the panel that pops up when you click it. The number and user name are already there; you can change them if you like. Enter the password, then click Connect and you're hooked up.

FIG. 9.26

Here's dial-up networking installed and ready to use. Click the Dial-up icon, enter any information not already there, and click Connect.

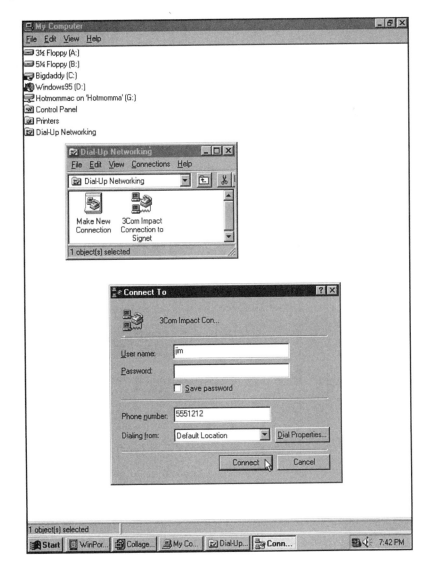

If you're dialing into an Internet service provider or your office, there's more to it. You have to set up TCP/IP in accordance with the instructions of the ISP or your office computer whiz. All of this is outside the issue of making the ISDN work; however, if you don't have the TCP/IP properly configured, the ISDN does connect, but you won't be able to reach the Internet.

Adtran Express Products

Adtran provides two smaller serial port terminal adapters that are appropriate for the small office and home market. The first is the ISU Express; it's built to commercial specifications. The newest is the Express XRT; it's designed to meet the competition in both price and ease of installation. Let's look at both of them.

ISU Express   Adtran knows what it's doing with its ISU Express offering in the terminal adapters market (see Fig. 9.27). If there's a repeater on your ISDN line, chances are it's an Adtran. Earlier I mentioned that many Internet providers use Adtran asynch devices for ISDN.

FIG. 9.27
The Adtran ISU Express.

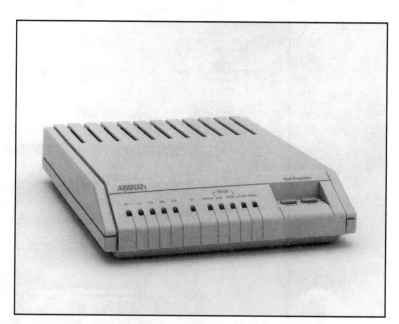

TIP   Express your browser to **http://www.adtran.com** for the company view.

The ISU Express has a U interface; an NT-1 is integrated inside. Options include a built-in modem, plus an RJ-11 for connecting POTS equipment. Moreover, it has an internal power supply. I'm sure I'm not the only one who's tired of trying to find some way to plug those brick supplies into wall or extension sockets (or who gets really confused by which of the half-dozen bricks plugged into the sockets connects to which box).

CAUTION

Polarities and voltages from these supplies can vary all over the map—there's no meaningful standard. Plug the wrong power supply into some expensive gear, and you could fry a fortune! MARK YOUR POWER SUPPLY CABLES and be careful—or, if you choose the Adtran ISU device, thank them for putting the supply inside.

Connection is much the same as with the 3Com Impact. Plug the U cable into the RJ-45 jack. Plug a DB-25 male serial cable into the back of the device, and connect the other end to your computer. Plug a regular phone into the RJ-11 jack so you can test the POTS function.

Now, it's time to configure. There is no special configuration program. You run a VT-100 terminal emulation program on your computer to set things up.

N O T E You don't think you have a VT-100 emulation program? Sure, you do. Within the Windows 3.x Accessories program group, find the icon labeled Terminal. Double-click this to start Windows Terminal, a program that can do everything you need right now. Open the Settings menu and choose Terminal Emulation, then choose DEC VT-100 and click OK. Next, open the Settings menu and choose Communications, then set Baud Rate to 9600 and Flow Control to Hardware; click OK.

If you're using Windows 95 select Accessories, then the icon labeled HyperTerminal. Now click File and choose Properties. Go to settings and choose VT-100. Close Properties menu and choose Connect from the ribbon. In the modem select list choose "Direct Com x" where "x" is the number of the Com port you're using to connect to the Adtran. Now choose Connect and you'll be talking with the box. ■

Type **AT!V** on the terminal and press Enter. This puts the ISU Express into configuration mode, and brings up the configuration menu shown in Figure 9.28. Notice number 14, "bit rate"; leave this at 9600 for your configuration work.

N O T E One of the selections on-screen is number 14: Bit Rate, which shows 9600. Leave this alone. Even though it's tempting to set it to something like 57,600 or 64,000, don't. If you do, you'll lose communication for your configuration and have to start over.

To get back to ground zero, unplug the box and wait 30 seconds. This should reset it so you can try again. The manual says you can press down the Select and Test buttons simultaneously to reset the device, but that's never worked for me. ■

You're up and talking now. All you probably need to enter are the following details:

Menu number	What You Enter
2	The type of switch the phone company is using. Adtran allows all the same switches 3Com does, plus NEC (see Fig. 9.29).

continues

continued

Menu number	What You Enter
3	The data rate. This should be 64 kpbs if you have full ISDN clear channel, or 56 kpbs if you have a bit-robbed system using transitional in-channel signaling while SS-7 is implemented (in certain parts of California, for example).
4 and 5	Your SPIDs. These are the same as I discussed for the 3Com device. Remember not to use dashes or spaces, and be sure the SPIDs are correct for your telephone company.
6 and 7	Your directory numbers; again, omit dashes and spaces.

FIG. 9.28

Adtran ISU Express configuration menu showing SPIDs, directory numbers and several other parameters.

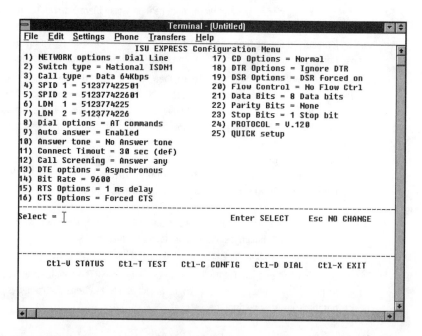

Okay, we've come to the moment of truth. There's a whole bunch of other bewildering stuff on-screen. Don't tear your hair out; I've done this too much, and now must wear a hat year-round to fend off sunburn in the summer and to stay warm in the winter. Adtran has tried to help by providing a number of standard configurations. Select menu option 25, QUICK Setup, for a list of choices (see Fig. 9.30).

Even this list has too many selections, so I'll narrow it down for you. You'll probably need one of the following three selections:

Selection	Description
1	Dial 56K synch. Use this if your telephone system uses the bit-robbing technique and you're connecting to a router.
2	Dial 64K synch. Use this if your telephone system supports a full 64 kpbs ISDN.
7	Dial 57.6 asynch. Use this if you are connecting to asynch equipment.

Part III

Ch 9

FIG. 9.29

Adtran Switch Types are shown at the bottom in response to menu item 2.

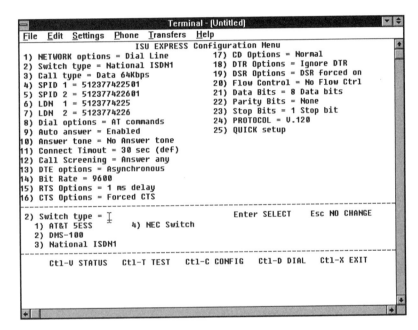

If you have particular needs such as a direct, no telephone switch connection, the manual can help get you through.

▶ See "BONDING," **p. 420**, and "PPP Multilink Protocol," **p. 424**

Also, if you're going after higher data rates using the device's BONDING features, the manual can be a great help.

 T I P The manual for the Adtran ISU Express is good, but in my copy—and presumably in many others—you need to add 4 to the page numbers given in the index to actually find a topic.

Adtran has several technical tests available through the test menu selection. Press Ctrl+T to reach the test menu. There are several rather technical tests that are briefly explained in the manual (see Fig. 9.31). However, I haven't found any way to get back to the configuration menu once I've entered the test menu.

FIG. 9.30

Choosing one of the QUICK setup options simplifies and speeds up configuration of the ISU Express.

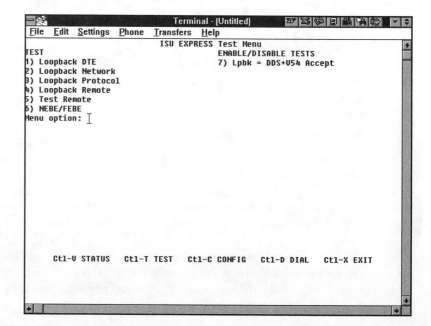

```
Terminal - [Untitled]

File   Edit   Settings   Phone   Transfers   Help
                    ISU EXPRESS Configuration Menu
1) NETWORK options = Dial Line      17) CD Options = Normal
2) Switch type = National ISDN1     18) DTR Options = Idle when Off
3) Call type = Data 64Kbps          19) DSR Options = DSR forced on
4) SPID 1 = 512212456701            20) Flow Control = No Flow Ctrl
5) SPID 2 = 512123456801            21) Data Bits = 8 Data bits
6) LDN  1 = 5121234567              22) Parity Bits = None
7) LDN  2 = 5121234568              23) Stop Bits = 1 Stop bit
8) Dial options = AT commands       24) PROTOCOL = V.120
9) Auto answer = Enabled            25) QUICK setup
10) Answer tone = No Answer tone
11) Connect Timout = 30 sec (def)
12) Call Screening = Answer any
13) DTE options = Asynchronous
14) Bit Rate = 9600
15) RTS Options = 1 ms delay
16) CTS Options = Forced CTS
-----------------------------------------------------------------
25) QUICK setup = |                  Enter SELECT   Esc NO CHANGE
   1) Dial 56K sync    4) Dial 128K sync    7) Dial 57.6 asyn   0) More
   2) Dial 64K sync    5) TBD               8) Dial 115.2 asy
   3) Dial 112K sync   6) V32 19.2 async    9) Fallback 57.6k
-----------------------------------------------------------------
      Ctl-V STATUS   Ctl-T TEST   Ctl-C CONFIG   Ctl-D DIAL   Ctl-X EXIT
```

Another key combination from the configuration menu, Ctrl+V, is supposed to display the status of the last 20 operations. All it really does is hang the machine; you'll have to unplug the power and start again. The product manual lists the status key combination as Ctrl+S, but that combination doesn't work, either.

FIG. 9.31

The Adtran test menu provides an extensive collection of tests adequate to maintain the equipment in a commercial environment.

```
Terminal - [Untitled]

File   Edit   Settings   Phone   Transfers   Help
                    ISU EXPRESS Test Menu
TEST                          ENABLE/DISABLE TESTS
1) Loopback DTE               7) Lpbk = DDS+V54 Accept
2) Loopback Network
3) Loopback Protocol
4) Loopback Remote
5) Test Remote
6) NEBE/FEBE
Menu option: |



      Ctl-V STATUS   Ctl-T TEST   Ctl-C CONFIG   Ctl-D DIAL   Ctl-X EXIT
```

Oh well, these things eventually get straightened out. The ISU Express has flash memory for upgrading, so keep in touch with Adtran to stay up-to-date. Actually, the same is true of 3Com and Motorola; each company has a planned means of upgrading the equipment.

Express XRT   The Express XRT, shown in Figure 9.32, is designed to be competitive with the 3Com Impact and the Motorola BitSURFR. The "T" indicates that it includes two POTS connections, one for each B channel. There is also a version, Express XR, without the POTS jacks.

The Express XR and XRT (I simply refer to it as the XRT from now on) make the ISDN set up automatic. Believe it or not, the Express XRT can detect the telco switch type and enter the SPIDs for you. All you need to do is enter the directory number.

FIG. 9.32

Adtran Express XRT.

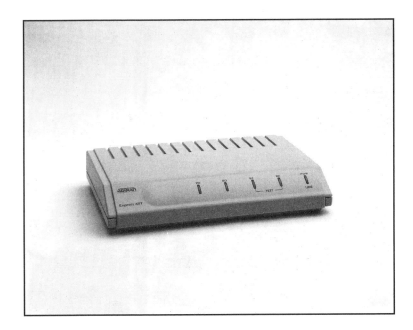

How does this amazing animal work? Basically, Adtran engineers figured out that each different switch has some unique responses to certain signals. The Express XRT sends those signals to the switch in question and waits to see the responses. When it finds one that fits, it determines the switch type. Next, it takes the directory number and adds each of the several suffixes or prefixes that are used in switch provisioning schemes. When it finds one the switch accepts, it enters it as the SPID. You see, all SPIDS are simply variations on the directory number.

- 512555121201 is one form of a SPID in which a number is suffixed to the directory number to make the SPID.
- 015125551212 is another form where a number is prefixed to the directory number.

There are a number of other forms. You don't have to worry about those, the Express XRT does it all for you. Let's see how it works.

We'll skip the physical connection of the cables; that's covered well in the manual and at the beginning of the chapter in the Impact discussion. Adtran supplies one disk for Windows 3.x and another for Windows 95; each of these is called the Express Configuration Wizard, an apt name. I use the Windows 95 software here. Installation could not be simpler. First, double-click the My Computer icon on the desktop, then double-click the Control Panel icon and finally double-click the Add/Remove Programs icon and choose Next with a final click (see Fig. 9.33).

FIG. 9.33

Use the Express Configuration Wizard software for Windows 95 when installing Adtran XRT.

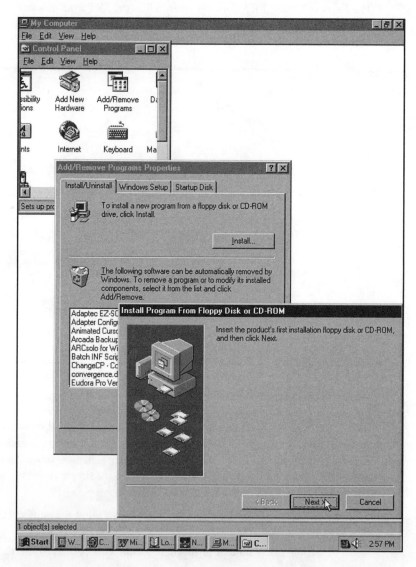

You are stepped through a few windows where you enter your name and decide whether or not to install the additional program HyperAccess Lite, an excellent communications software program. That's it for the install; here comes the configuration.

Go into your Start menu and choose the Adtran group created by the installation. Now, click Express Configuration Wizard and you get the window shown in Figure 9.34. This is really a simplified configuration. It gives you a selection of potential uses. This is much the same as the selections we covered above in the ISU Express, but it's more intuitive. I chose Factory: Internet 128k configuration, as the Adtran factory suggested, for a 128 kbps connection to an Internet provider. I clicked Preview to see the exact setup.

FIG. 9.34

Adtran's Express Configuration Wizard with a preview of the details set up when Factory: 128k is selected.

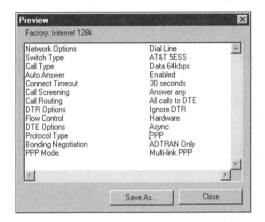

> **N O T E** You can configure both the ISU Express and the Express XR and XRT by using any of three methods: VT-100 terminal emulation, as shown in the discussion of the ISU, Express Configuration Wizard in Windows, which we're covering now, and AT commands.

When you're satisfied you have the right general conditions, (for example, I selected Factory: Internet 128k) click the Wizard button and the Start screen for the amazing Wizard appears, as seen in Figure 9.35.

The Wizard first determines the model of your Adtran device and the COM port it's using. I must note, I didn't have to reboot my computer or the Adtran unit. My mouse, attached to COM 1 continued to operate properly. In Figure 9.36 the Wizard finds the unit on COM 2 and determines it's an Express XRT. In the event the Wizard has made a mistake, highly unlikely, you can change the port or model here.

FIG. 9.35

The Adtran Wizard starts when you click Wizard at the top screen and select Next at the bottom.

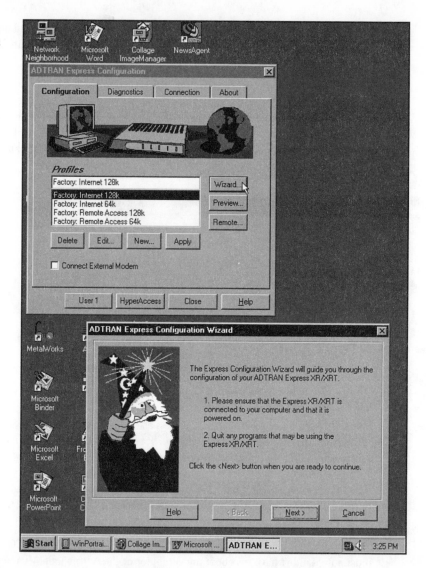

FIG. 9.36

The Adtran Wizard figures out the XRT is connected to COM 2 and is an XRT.

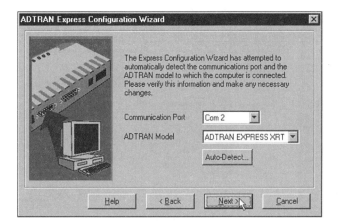

Now for the big time. Enter your ISDN telephone number(s) (see Fig. 9.37).

FIG. 9.37

The Wizard takes your ISDN telephone numbers.

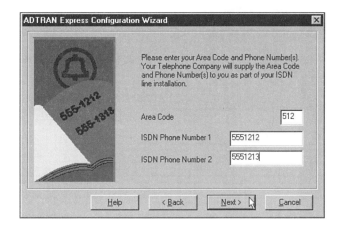

The next screen (see Fig. 9.38) asks you to enter your ISDN switch type and SPIDs—but you don't have to. Read the fine print; you can just click Next and let the XRT figure it out for you (see Fig. 9.39). Choose Auto Detect SPIDs/Switch Types, to let it work.

FIG. 9.38

You're given the opportunity to enter your switch type and SPIDs, if you know them. Otherwise you can click Next and have the XRT do this for you.

FIG. 9.39

Click the Auto Detect SPIDS/Switch Types to have the XRT determine your switch type and SPIDS.

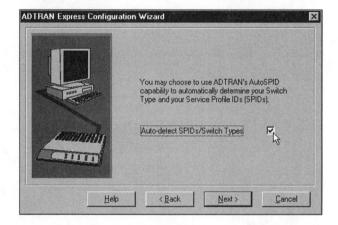

Just in case you didn't properly select your intended use at the very first, here's your opportunity to choose Internet or Remote, 64 or 128 kbps (see Fig. 9.40).

FIG. 9.40

Choose your type of use.

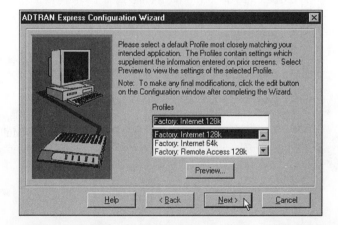

You're given a chance to name the new profile now being created. I decided to enter one that's fairly descriptive to me (see Fig. 9.41).

FIG. 9.41
Give the new profile a descriptive name.

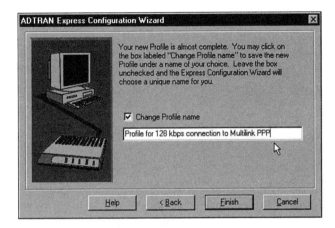

Part

III

Ch

9

When you click Next in the profile selection, the program grinds through a myriad of variations, probes the telephone switch for its identity, and discovers how it deals with SPIDs. (see Fig. 9.42).

FIG. 9.42
The Adtran XRT runs through an investigation of switch types and SPID forms.

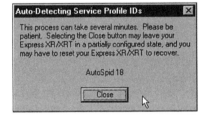

If everything works you are greeted with Congratulations and can begin using the terminal adapter with any program that sends AT command strings (see Fig. 9.43).

Motorola BitSURFR Pro

Motorola revised their popular TA210, one of the first serial port terminal adapters aimed at a broad market, into the BitSURFR in various guises:

- The BitSURFR supports V.120, PPP, and BONDING protocols. It comes with a U interface (the NT1 is internal). It has a single POTS R-J11 jack.

- The BitSURFR Pro supports everything the BitSURFR does plus Multilink PPP and Async inverse multiplexing (AIMux). It also adds a second POTS jack and is designed to pass many voice features, like call waiting and conference calling to the POTS ports with standard analog phones.

■ Both models support the Macintosh and PC worlds. In fact, since they're serial devices, any equipment that can talk the AT command set through a serial port can probably use a BitSURFR. The common denominator, then, is the use of a terminal emulation program that can act like a DEC VT-100. However, Motorola packages both a Macintosh and a PC version; the only difference is the software. We'll look at both.

FIG. 9.43

Congratulations! You made it to a successful Adtran XRT configuration.

Upgrading Your TA-210 to a BitSURFR

If you have a TA210 that you want to change to a BitSURFR, Motorola can supply the ROMs—but, you'll have to put them in. "That's no big deal for me," you say bravely, but you haven't tried to open the clamshell container that holds the device. I finally gave up and called Motorola's technical support. The very helpful support person said it was a big problem for him, too, but he *was* able to explain the less-than-elegant technique.

First, you flip the case onto its back. Since it's rounded on top, this is much like flipping a turtle. Push a screwdriver with a 1/4" to 3/8" blade inside each of the six slots on the bottom. What you're trying to do is to push over a molded plastic clip holding the two halves together. As you release each one, slip in a fingernail to keep it apart as you do the next. Even if you're not an octopus, you might eventually get it open. It's good strong plastic, but if your finesse is a bit too forceful, you can use a super-adhesive to fix the cracks.

Addition of the new ROMs to a TA-210 or actually using a BitSURFR provides proper operation with synchronous PPP connections to routers; as I've already mentioned, this is an important issue for Internet use and telecommuting. A POTS connection makes it easy to use the BitSURFR for regular phone or fax calls. Upgrading is an easy task in all currently built units since they use flash ROMs that can be programmed with a disk, a phone call or over the Internet.

I strongly recommend the BitSURFR Pro. The two POTS jacks, voice features, and, especially, the Multilink PPP prove invaluable. Figure 9.44 is a photograph of a BitSURFR Pro44.

FIG. 9.44

This picture of the Motorola BitSURFR Pro shows the box for the Macintosh version. Please remember there is no difference in the hardware between the Mac and PC versions; the only difference is in the software, documentation, and cables.

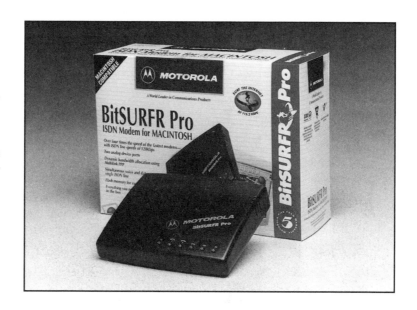

Part
III

Ch
9

 T I P   Flash to **http://www.motorola.com** for fast-breaking changes.

What's That Switch For?

The BitSURFR Pro has a 4-position switch on the back. All of the switches should be in the UP (OFF) position. This "factory reset switch" is used to test and to overcome certain unusual conditions. The only switch function, of importance to users, provides a way to overcome a loss of the ability to respond to AT commands.

For example, if the data terminal equipment (DTE)—that is, your computer emulating a VT-100—data rate is set higher than 57.6 kpbs, the AT AutoBaud function could become disabled. It's also possible to issue the AT command @P1 AT and disable AT response. Finally, if you enable V.25bis dialing, AT operation is disabled.

The solution is to move position 4 of the switches to the ON position, and turn the power off momentarily. After you turn the power back on, test to see if the AT commands work. When you confirm that they do, move that switch back to the OFF position, and once again cycle the power off and on. This is incorrectly documented as position 1 in the *User's Guide* I suggest you consult with Motorola technical support before making any other switch changes. Equipment for ISDN Connection through the Serial Port Equipment for ISDN Connection through the Serial Port.

You hook up the wires the same way I explained for the other two devices. Motorola uses a 25-pin, D-series connector just like the Adtran does. You can configure the BitSURFR Pro through AT commands listed in the manuals, or through a Windows program. I suggest using the Windows program, and that's the method I'll review here.

N O T E   If you use a Windows 3.x emulation of a VT-100, you must make the cursor movements flow
through Windows to the BitSURFR. In the Windows Terminal program, you do this by
opening the Settings menu and choosing Terminal Preferences, then deselect (remove the X from) the
option labeled Use Function, Arrow, and Ctrl Keys for Windows. This ensures that the arrow keys will
flow through to the program, which is what you want. ■

You can avoid all the technical terminal stuff and use one or both of the Windows programs
Motorola has provided to set up the BitSURFR.

■ SURFR Setup is the simplified procedure. It can be used with Windows 3.x and has
specific "INF" files for Windows 95. I cover SURFR Setup first.

■ Configuration Manager provides more detailed control in a graphical interface, but it
requires more technical knowledge to use. I cover it second using Windows 3.x.

CAUTION

Motorola also supplies TurboCom/2, the communications program I mentioned during discussion of the
serial port earlier in this chapter. This program should only be used if you're running Windows 3.x. If you're
using Windows 95, DO NOT USE TURBOCOM/2 because Windows 95 already has fixed everything
TurboCom/2 does and Windows 95 has optimum drivers built in.

SURFR Setup   Do the usual Windows 95 install. Let's just use Run from the Start Menu.
Enter a:\setup.exe (assuming you put disk Number 1 of SURFR Setup in drive A:) and click
OK. After a little grinding, you are asked to insert disk 2 and eventually you arrive at Figure
9.45.

FIG. 9.45
The initial installation
screen for SURFR Setup.

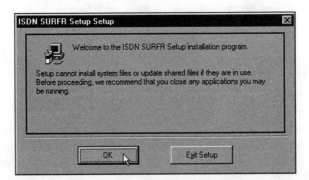

As you go through the install, you are asked where to install the program. The default is in
C:\SURFR. I suggest you hew to the Windows 95 convention of installing programs in the
Programs directory and change the directory to C:\Program Files\SURFR as shown in Figure
9.46.

FIG. 9.46

When you change the directory for the SURFR Setup installation, select Change Directory, choose the PROGRA~1 directory and make the new SURFR directory with it.

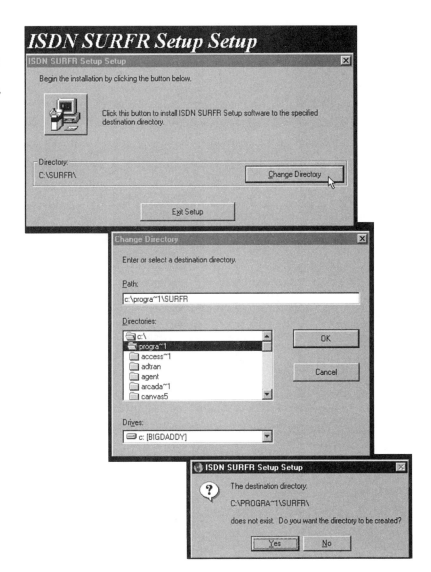

Now go to the SURFR group created during the install and double-click the only icon in the group. That brings up the SURFR Setup main screen and, if this is the first time you started the program, it hops into configuration, as seen in Figure 9.47.

When you go through the blanks on this screen, you notice something new. There are check boxes for your telephone company. Motorola has provided configuration information based on their knowledge of the telcos and area codes. This has the potential to really speed up your work. Notice, that as you enter the SPIDs, the directory numbers appear. This isn't the automatic action we saw in Adtran, but it's a recognition that if you know one SPID, you certainly know the other. (So ask yourself, "Why do we have SPIDS?" Many in the industry are trying to get rid of what has proven to be a bad idea.)

After I filled in everything, I hit Configure and Test but the test said something's wrong, so I clicked the Diagnose button and ended up with Figure 9.48, which shows an error in either switch selection or SPIDs. I just happen to know what is wrong. The numbers I entered were incorrect. I fixed that and passed (see Fig. 9.49).

FIG. 9.47

Start SURFR Setup: If this is the first time the program has run the configuration screen comes up automatically. If it has run before, you must click Configuration.

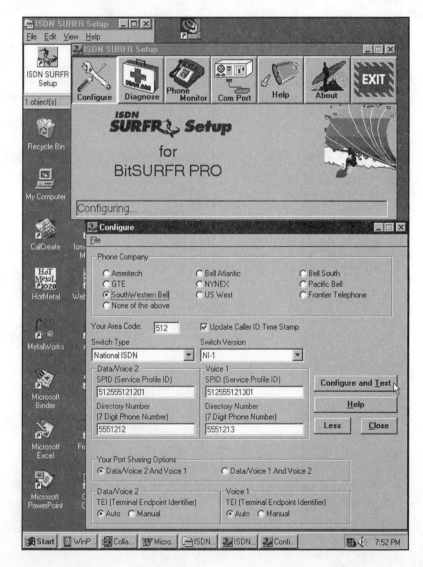

FIG. 9.48

These results of a diagnoses following an incorrect configuration show that I should look at my SPIDs and switch type. It's not shown here, but when I return to the configuration screen those two areas are highlighted in yellow.

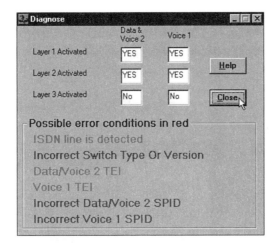

FIG. 9.49

Now I'm properly configured.

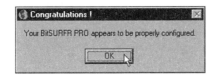

N O T E We won't delve into it here, but there are a number of configuration options for voice features. The BitSURFR Pro supports call waiting, three-way conferencing, and calling number ID. It can be configured so it uses both B channels for data, but, if you pick up the phone or a call comes in from outside, one of the B channels is dropped to make or receive the call. As soon as the voice call is complete, the second B channel resumes. ▨

Configuration Manager Now for a look at the Configuration Manager program. This gives you more control than the SURFR Setup. Install the program in the usual way through the Start Menu with Run or through Settings, Control Panel, and Install Software. From here on, I assume that you're familiar with Windows 95 installation procedures.

▶ **See** "New Communications Features of Windows 95," **p. 411**

From the main screen, open the Access menu and choose Define Adapter (see Fig. 9.50). In the Define Adapter dialog box click the Model drop-down arrow; in the drop-down list, click BitSURFR Pro, and then click OK.

Open the File menu and choose New. You'll see a screen resembling Figure 9.51, with four sheet tabs toward the bottom of the page.

On the ISDN sheet, you can fill in the details of your ISDN provisioning as established in your order with the telephone company. Fill in the SPID and directory numbers (don't use spaces or dashes). Click the Switch Type drop-down arrow, and click to select the appropriate type from the drop-down list. If you have no information to the contrary from your telephone company or other sources, leave both Terminal Endpoint Identifiers options set to Automatic.

▶ **See** Chapter 4, "Choosing Services," **p. 89**

▶ **See** Chapter 7, "Ordering ISDN Services," **p. 141**

FIG. 9.50

The BitSURFR Define Adapter selection in Motorola's Configuration Manager provides a way to choose among Motorola's ISDN devices. Here we're choosing the BitSURFR Pro.

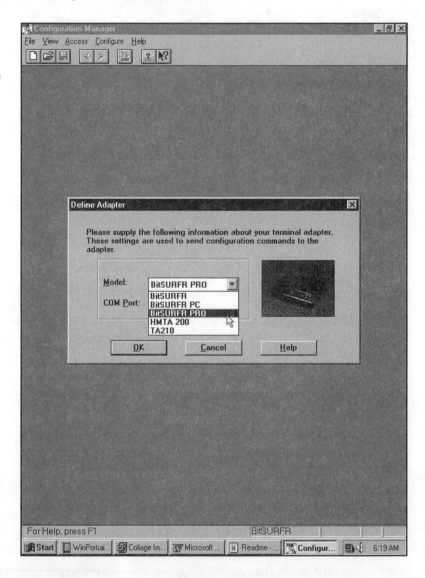

Click the Protocols tab. On this sheet, you should choose the V.120 option if you're connecting to a serial device (see Fig. 9.52). (If you're connecting to an Adtran, change both the transmit and receive frame sizes to 253.) If you're connecting to a router, choose PPP. For the moment, don't worry about BONDING; we'll discuss this later in Chapter 13.

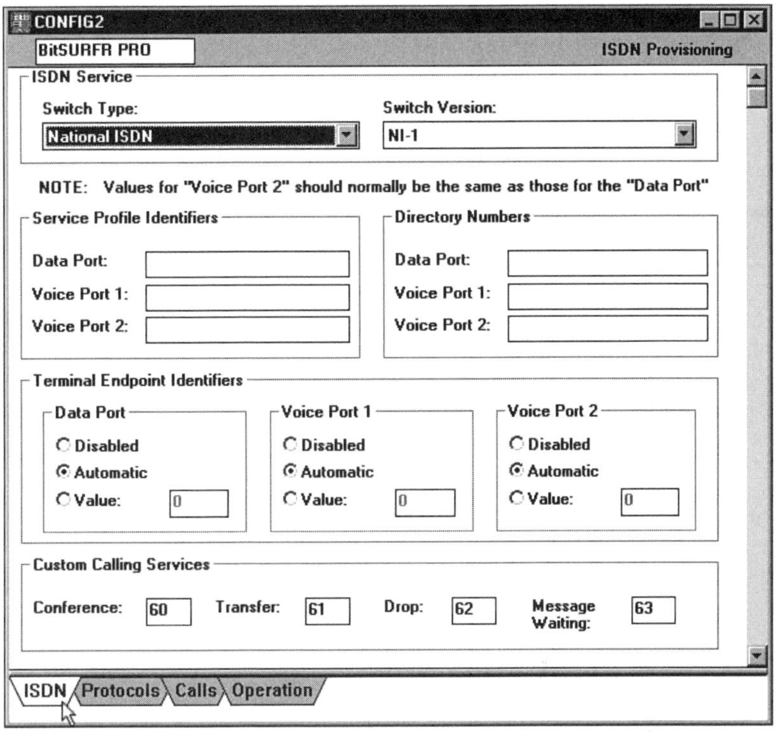

FIG. 9.51

BitSURFR Pro
Configuration Manager
ISDN Provisioning
selections are reflected
on the tab labeled
ISDN. Insert your SPIDs,
directory numbers and
switch type.

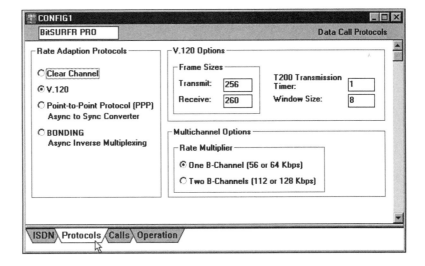

FIG. 9.52

The BitSURFR Pro
Configuration Manager
Protocols tab selection
allows you to select
from among V.120,
clear channel (64
kbps), PPP async to
sync and BONDING.

Click the Calls tab. On this sheet, set Channel Speed to 56 kbps or 64 kbps, depending on what's available from your switch (see Fig. 9.53). If you don't want Autoanswer (most people don't), click its Disabled option. Leave Speech for the Originate Voice Calls As setting, and Data for the Originate Data Calls As setting.

TIP   Don't overlook the fact that the default data rate is 56 kbps. I guess Motorola received so many calls from California they decided to sacrifice performance for the civilized world J in exchange for reduced phone traffic? Set this to 64 kbps if your switch supports it.

FIG. 9.53

The BitSURFR Pro Configuration Manager Calls tab has a large number of selections for establishing and terminating. Toward the bottom the tab provides a number of selections including caller identification and stored numbers.

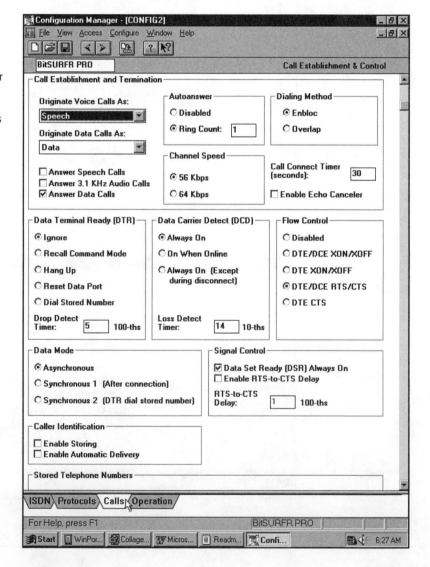

In the DTR area, start with Ignore. If your line doesn't hang up, you can later try Hang Up or Reset.

If you're calling another serial device, select Asynchronous for Data Mode; if you're calling a router, select Synchronous 1; if that doesn't work, try Synchronous 2.

Click the Operation tab. On this sheet, I suggest you select the Enable Extended Response Messages option in order to receive more extensive messages while the BitSURFR is placing calls or encountering errors; these will help to avoid or diagnose problems (see Fig. 9.54). Enabling local character echo puts the characters you type on your screen, escape sequence guard keeps brief glitches from bringing the device down and the dial response messages give you an indication of what's going on the same as the responses from a modem such as "CONNECT" and "BUSY."

Part

III

Ch

9

FIG. 9.54

The BitSURFR Pro Configuration Manager Operation tab sets up the AT command operations.

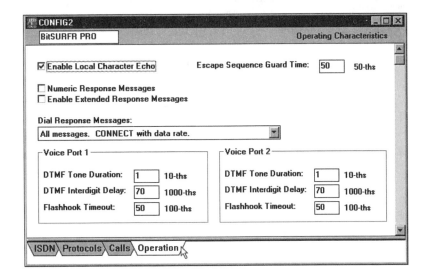

When you're done changing as many configuration options as you want, click the Update tool (it's third from the right on the toolbar). You get a window asking if you want to update the device's configuration with the new material. Choose Save and Restart. A percentage meter appears to display how much progress has been made updating the terminal adapter (see Fig. 9.55). Now, you still need to save your configuration to a file. Open the File menu and choose Save As; give this configuration a file name, then press Enter.

FIG. 9.55

The BitSURFR Pro Configuration Manager in the midst of an update to its configuration.

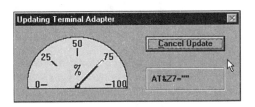

Motorola, just like Adtran, has provided several options to preconfigure, so you don't have to do anything but enter your switch type and numbers. Open the Configure menu and choose Quick Setup. The four available choices for asynch and synch operation will take care of the needs of 95% of all users (see Fig. 9.56). You still might want to do minor customization—such as disabling the Autoanswer feature—but for the most part, you'll find that choosing Quick Setup is easier than trying to figure out what the myriad configuration settings are, and what you should do with each one.

FIG. 9.56

The BitSURFR Pro Configuration Manager Quick Setup selection lets you set up all the parameters for a number of common ISDN configurations.

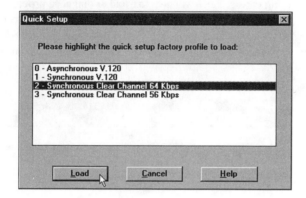

A new feature was added to the Configuration Manager program recently. The status screen provides a way to watch what's going on while the BitSURFR Pro is operating (see Fig. 9.57). This gives more detail than the panel lights.

FIG. 9.57

The BitSURFR Pro Configuration Manager Status display.

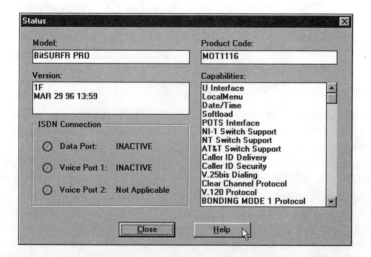

Motorola furnishes a version of the HyperAccess communications program with the BitSURFR PRO. This is a well-designed program that has specific features to work with the Motorola product. In particular, it provides a way to reset the adapter from within the communications program; I've found it very important to be able to reset. Whenever something seems wrong, or the line won't hang up, I reset the terminal adapter. This brings it back to a default state with the line on-hook (hung up), and does not alter the configuration. Figure 9.58 shows HyperAccess set up with four ISDN sites I frequently call.

FIG. 9.58

HyperAccess is furnished as the communications program in the BitSURFR Pro package.

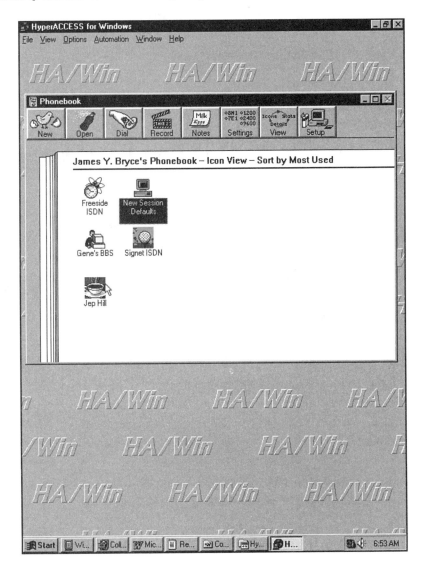

Macintosh and the BitSURFR Pro   Remember there is no hardware difference between the PC and Mac versions of the BitSURFR PRO; they're both designed to go through the parallel port. The only difference is in the cables, software, and documentation packaged with the unit.

Motorola provides a serial cable for connection to the serial port on the Mac. Hook this up, connect the ISDN U interface and the power supply. That's it for the hardware installation — it's the same for the PC.

Now for the software, first, install the Internet Valet software that comes with the package (see Fig. 9.59). This is a suite of Internet programs, browser, mail etc. You must either install it or already have a terminal program available to configure the BitSURFR Pro.

FIG. 9.59

Internet Valet entry screen for installation of suite on Macintosh.

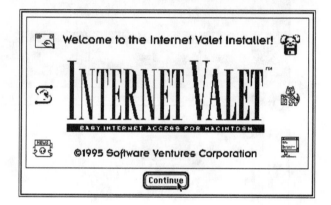

When the program installation finishes you pop into a terminal screen where you can enter AT commands to configure the BitSURFR, (see Fig. 9.60). You can use a character-based menu program Motorola supplies, called Local Menu. That is, you can use it if you can figure out how to get to it.

FIG. 9.60

The terminal screen of Internet Valet gives you AT command access to the BitSURFR Pro for configuration.

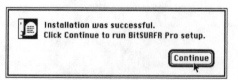

Surprise! PC Easy/Mac Not?

Does this surprise you? After all we just saw two different Windows programs used to set up and configure the BitSURFR, and, as I mentioned, you could also use the AT command route. Here we are with the Mac, a machine that is designed to ease the user interface and set up, but Motorola only supplies a most arcane set up and configuration method. What's going on?

I don't know? I scoured the documentation for references to graphical programs for set up and configuration but found none. I can only conclude that Motorola has taken the position that the Macintosh market is not large enough to justify the development of such software.

The *Getting Started Guide* tells you to click Scripts to start the Local Menu program so you can at least avoid the arcane AT commands to set up and configure your BitSURFR Pro. This only works if you're already in a terminal program. Of course, if you just loaded Internet Valet and said you wanted to set up the BitSURFR Pro, you should be there, if not you have to restart Internet Valet, select the BitSURFR Pro icon and find yourself back at the terminal screen. In any case, when you click Scripts in the menu bar at the top of your screen you should have at least one selection, Local Menu. Click this to arrive at Figure 9.61.

FIG. 9.61

You can set up and configure the BitSURFR Pro without typing in AT commands, if the Local Menu script is running on the terminal screen of the Internet Valet.

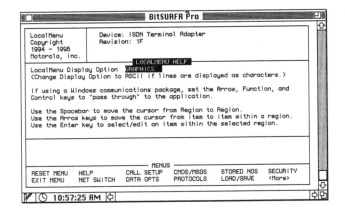

The first thing you need to know is your mouse doesn't work in this screen. You move around by:

- Depressing the spacebar to select between the Menu and Options sections
- Use the cursor (arrow) keys to go from item to item within the section. Welcome to the 1960's world of character-based, terminal to host computing. And you thought you had escaped by getting a Mac!

Press the space bar, if necessary, to move to the Menus section at the bottom of the screen, then move the cursor to Net Switch (see Fig. 9.62).

FIG. 9.62

Select Net Switch to begin configuration.

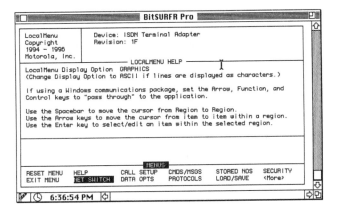

Press return and you are taken to a submenu with spaces; enter the details of your telco ISDN switch (see Fig. 9.63).

FIG. 9.63

Use this submenu to enter ISDN switch details for the configuration of BitSURFR using a Mac.

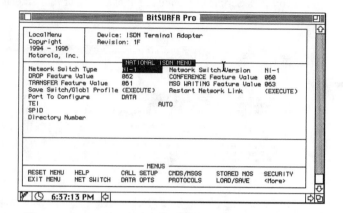

At this point, I believe I've gotten you over the big hump of figuring out how to set up and configure the BitSURFR with a Mac. The balance of the *Getting Started Guide* takes you through the details. They configure with exactly the same parameters we saw in earlier discussions. The only difference is the primitive method used. At least Motorola did supply a menu system to help. I'd hate to consign any Mac user, or really anyone, to setting things up with AT commands.

Comparisons Among the Impact, ISU Express, and BitSURFR

The intention of this book is to inform you about all major aspects of ISDN, particularly those aspects pertaining to its use with computers for Internet access and telecommuting. As part of this information, I've presented details on some representative hardware and software. There's so much coming into this exploding market, it's impossible to present a complete list.

I suggest you keep an eye on magazines which do extensive product reviews and tests to see the latest and greatest ISDN-related hardware and software. It's not my goal to do any rigorous testing of the equipment discussed in this book.

What I want you to see is where and how all the pieces fit together. The details in product reviews often skip the big picture, and specifications listed in reviews are sometimes incorrect due to misunderstandings, oversights, or product changes. Your best bet is to learn from this book how certain types of products fit into your overall use of ISDN; then, you should check with specific vendors to discover the most current information about their products.

TIP Keep an eye on Web pages, especially **http://alumni.caltech.edu/~dank/isdn** and **http://www.bryce.com/~bryce**.

All of the products in this chapter support Multilink PPP. It is still an open question as to whether or not they all support the most optimum compression methods possible. That is an issue that had not been fully settled and tested at the time of this writing. Check the Web pages, in the previous tip, for the latest information.

As a class, the external ISDN terminal adapters offer a seemingly simple way of connecting to your PC through the serial port; however, this is also their biggest downfall because of the slowness of COM port hardware and software. Development of a considerably faster serial port would go a long way toward making these devices indispensable. That's one of many developments in ISDN that we hope are just around the corner:

- Multilink PPP standards use both B channels in ways that allow everyone to talk with everyone. This gives a raw data rate of 128 kbps, already beyond that of even typical 16550A serial ports and better software drivers. Your only choice is to use more exotic hardware such as the Hayes ESP.

- About the same time your B channels are tied together in a universally accepted way, compression should come in to raise the effective data rate to the port by a factor of 2, 4, or even more. As a result, the port has to deal with upwards of half a megabit each second (2 ports × 64 kbps × 4 compression factor).

If your ISDN device can't keep up with this through upgrades, and if better serial communication doesn't arrive, you'll be left holding a dead box in a couple of years. Nobody knows. I predict that the companies making terminal adapters will continue to upgrade them, that the standards folks will work out compression and PPP, and that the serial hardware/software issues will be resolved. Of course, I'm an eternal optimist.

Differences among these devices and their predecessors have been almost completely erased by the push of competition and the pull of demand. All are flash upgradable, the most important consideration. All support more and more POTS, voice features, compression, and Multilink PPP. Manufacturers seem to be racing to beat each other in price cutting. Motorola has been successful in getting the first and biggest shelf space in retail, but that can change overnight. As I write, here are the features that are, unique to each:

- BitSURFR has the most sophisticated voice support.
- Impact has the simplest configuration.
- Express has the only automatic switch and SPID detection.

 TIP

Prices in this industry are very flexible, with software routinely selling for half (or less) of its list price. Hardware is not so deeply discounted, but you can expect prices of ISDN products to fall dramatically near the end of 1995 as standards solidify, competition heats up, and everyone discovers the unique values that ISDN offers.

From Here...

We've looked at three excellent representatives of the external terminal adapter class of hardware to hook you up to ISDN. You won't go wrong with any of these three, and chances are that you can find others of very similar design. Be sure to look over some that I haven't mentioned. My omission of a product is no comment on its quality or fitness for your needs; I'm just working with limited time and space, so I picked a few to get you started.

Remember to take care of the serial port hardware and software so you'll get full use from your new ISDN equipment. Watch for changes in serial communications technology that could radically alter how these terminal adapters work, and how fast they are.

Get ready to jump into other types of hardware, and explore more details of issues we've already broached:

- Chapter 10, "Putting an Adapter Inside Your Computer," covers ISDN cards and the advantages they may bring.
- Chapter 11, "Establishing ISDN for LANs," explores routers and bridges.
- Chapter 12, "Opening Windows 95 and NT for ISDN," delves into software issues surrounding ISDN use with Windows 95 and NT.

Putting an Adapter Inside Your Computer

If you're looking for ISDN-compatible adapters, prepare to encounter lots of variety. These products are computer cards designed to plug into the internal bus of your computer, and are made to suit the Industry Standard Architecture (ISA) bus, MicroChannel (MCA) bus, Enhanced ISA (EISA), PC Card (also called PCMCIA— and external bus extension), and a number of other buses. I expect newer buses such as the Peripheral Component Interconnect (PCI) bus to see rapid development of ISDN cards. For now, the ISA bus is dominant, so for simplicity we'll limit our discussion to that bus. Most issues presented in this chapter, however, carry over to other bus structures.

IBM WaveRunner

This is a card that can assume a number of personalities as we'll see, plus it can be an ordinary analog modem.

US Robotics Courier I-Modem

You'll find that this product is both an ISDN terminal adapter and a V.34 modem. It also has a jack for connection of a POTS phone.

US Robotics Sportster

This card provides support for a number of network operation systems, PPP and Multilink PPP, a POTS connection, and clear documentation.

ISDN*tek Commuter Card

This very card speaks WinISDN and is designed primarily for Internet provider connection.

Digi International DataFire

This is one of several products in the company's line that functions as a sort of bridge connected through ODI or NDIS.

Alpha Telecom CyberJet

This is a card designed for stand-alone PC use. It's available with or without POTS port.

N O T E While we view ISDN as fast compared to POTS, its speed is very slow compared to any of these buses. So you don't have to lose sleep over getting the fastest bus possible to support ISDN; any of the standard ones available will be just fine. If you're buying a new machine or motherboard, I suggest you be sure it has PCI, because that is the bus that clearly has the most potential for the future. ■

When we've finished looking at all these, we'll do a little comparing to see the relative strengths and weaknesses among the boards. ■

ISDN Boards in General

Out of the box, these boards offer a number of exciting possibilities. While Chapter 9, "Selecting an External Terminal Adapter," deals with modem-like devices connecting through a serial port, and Chapter 11, "Establishing ISDN for LANs," deals with bridges and routers, this chapter on internal boards must cover several bases. These boards may take on characteristics of:

- External terminal adapters operating just like serial devices, including on-board serial chips and control via the AT command set.

- Routers or bridges operating as purely network connection devices using internetworking protocols such as TCP/IP for control, and connecting through network interface card (NIC) protocols such as NDIS or ODI.

- Internal cards connected by drivers speaking with WinISDN, CAPI, or TAPI as the control language.

CAUTION

When you start handling these boards and the insides of your computer there is a risk that static electricity will build up on your body and discharge through the components that make up the computer or board. A static discharge could "fry" some of the sensitive components in use today. So, follow static prevention measures. Keep boards in their funny antistatic plastic envelopes until you need them. Don't run across the carpet in your leather shoes in the dead of winter in Aspen and then grab that CMOS chip on the new $1,000 board. Discharge any static build up by touching the bright silver power supply box or other clearly grounded metal. If you want to be extra sure, invest in an antistatic kit with a pad, wrist strap, and grounding line connected to a true ground point. If you do use a grounding wrist strap, use only one made for the task and containing a current limiting resistor; mine is made by 3M. The resistor could save your life in the event you stumble into a really live circuit with high voltage. The voltages on a computer motherboard are usually between 3.3 and 12 volts and should not be dangerous to you. But the voltages in the power supply can be in the hundreds of volts, very dangerous. In the monitor voltages can reach thousands of volts, worse. Safety pays.

And, of course, always have the power off when you insert or remove a board.

Oh, you're asking, "Shouldn't the machine be unplugged?" There is some debate about this. Some say leave it plugged in but with the power off. By being plugged into a properly wired outlet, the machine will be grounded through the ground prong of the power plug (the round one in circuits in North America). On the other hand, I'd suggest you just unplug the machine and provide for grounding by attaching a short length of wire to the chassis of another device that is properly grounded.

IBM WaveRunner

The WaveRunner is IBM's main entrant in the ISDN sweepstakes. It's an ingeniously designed device that takes advantage of the flexibility in digital signal processing (DSP) technology to provide all sorts of personalities for itself. The product is available in three forms:

- *ISA Card.* This is a full-length card with a speaker, full 16-bit connector, RJ-45 S/T interface for the ISDN line, and a plug for a telephone handset or headset.
- *MCA Card.* This is the MicroChannel version.
- *PCMCIA Card.* This card lacks the handset/headset connection, but comes with two special cables, one for analog modem use and one for ISDN. This card is also referred to as a *PC card*.

All the cards have S/T interfaces and therefore require a separate NT-1. I have used the IBM 7845 and the Motorola NT1D in testing, and found that both worked properly.

IBM's manuals are fairly straightforward and easy to read. I found a few rough spots in the manuals which I'll mention as we go along. Basically, the card originally provided a single B channel for computer communication; on-line upgrades of the internal download library now enable the card to support multiple B channels with Multilink PPP. All this upgradability is the result of Mwave technology, a trademark of IBM for a self-contained operating system that makes upgrades easy.

The WaveRunner provides several major features:

- Hayes AT command set.
- POTS analog modem communication.
- Bell 103J, Bell 212A, V.22bis, V.32, and V.32bis meaning modem operation up to 14.4 kbps.
- MNP4/MNP5 compression for analog modem operation.
- V.42 to V.42bis compression for analog modem operation.
- Group 3 FAX operation; the WaveRunner package includes Trio DataFAX software.
- COM port accelerator. The package I received included KingCom; TurboComm has also been supplied in the past. See the discussion of serial (COM) port issues in Chapter 9, "Selecting an External Terminal Adapter."
- V.120 encapsulation of asynchronous data.
- TCP/IP SLIP to TCP/IP synchronous translation; this feature requires a TCP/IP application on your computer, such as the NetManage Internet Chameleon I used for testing.

Part
III

Ch
10

- Interoperability with switched 56 kbps digital service.
- Network Driver Interface Standard (NDIS) network card interface standard support.
- WinISDN support with drivers downloaded from IBM's bulletin board or ftp server.

N O T E The inclusion of MNP4/MNP5 and v.42/v.42bis compression applies only to the analog modem operation at this time. As we'll consider in Chapter 13, "Tying It Together: Two B or Not Two B," standards surrounding compression use with ISDN are still unsettled. The Mwave design of the WaveRunner should help users upgrade quickly to any new compression standards that are established.

All of this is possible because the WaveRunner is a computer, a co-processor in its own right with downloadable software. Such devices have considerable ability to track new developments in software and retain their value. ■

WaveRunner Installation

The installation manual has an 11-point checklist for installation of the ISA card. It includes such things as checking the revision letter of the board you're using and ordering service from your telephone company. It explains how to use Microsoft Diagnostics (type **MSD** at the prompt) to find out interrupt and COM port information needed for installation. The software takes about 5 Mb of disk space, and specifies that you need RAM of 4 Mb; the machine I tested on had 8 Mb or RAM, which I think is the minimum amount necessary to run Windows effectively.

 Do the software installation with the board out of the machine so you can set switches on the board while you're looking at the screen.

▶ **See** "Windows 95 and ISDN," **p. 409**

You run the installation program from Windows Program Manager in the usual way, by opening the File menu and choosing Run, then typing **a:setup.exe** and pressing Enter (assuming your installation floppy is in drive A). Specify the directory in which you want the program installed, or simply accept the default; click OK. Now, you must tackle the first major question: are you using an ISA card Rev. A or Rev. B? The difference lies mainly in the number of COM ports supported. Rev. A supports only 1 and 2; Rev. B supports 1 through 4. Tell the program the revision letter by clicking on Revision A or Revision B as shown in Figure 10.1.

 There are some other differences between Rev. A and Rev. B that will matter more to us when we cover the video products from Vivo, "Vivo," **p. 450**, in Chapter 14, "Pictures and Video with ISDN."

FIG. 10.1

Selection of
WaveRunner revision.

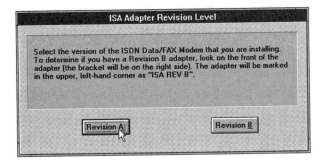

As you go through the installation program, it shows a picture of switches on the board (see Fig. 10.2). You must inspect the settings and determine if they conform to such things as available interrupts on your machine. Earlier, while running Microsoft Diagnostics, you noted possible conflicts and available interrupts in spaces provided within the manual. If the default is not correct for your selection, enter the proper parameters. The screen shows the switch settings, and you can arrange the switches on the board.

Part
III

Ch
10

FIG. 10.2

Switch selection
in WaveRunner
installation.

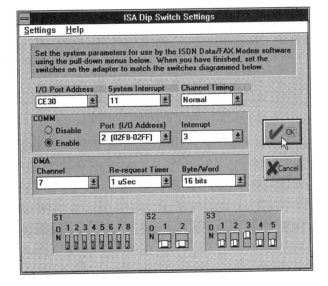

N O T E Remember that setting the parameters in the software does *not* set them on the card, even if the card's in the machine. If you're using a MicroChannel machine and card, follow the setting and reference disk procedures outlined in a different part of the product manual. ▪

Now, you're given the option of a full installation or custom installation (see Fig. 10.3). The custom installation saves space, and may be used if you know you won't need certain things (for instance, NDIS support).

FIG. 10.3

Full or custom
installation of
WaveRunner.

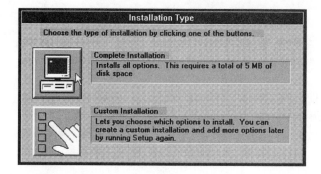

If you choose custom installation, you can select from among the options shown in Figure 10.4.

FIG. 10.4

Custom options for
WaveRunner.

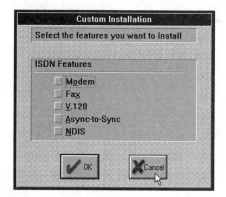

NDIS configuration uses the NDIS standard to create network drivers for the card. Explanation of this procedure is contained in README files within the NDIS subdirectory of the software. The installation screen calls your attention to procedures and the documentation (see Fig. 10.5).

FIG. 10.5

WaveRunner NDIS
explanation.

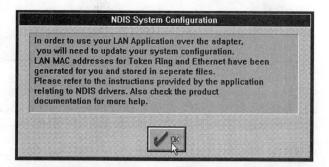

IBM provides a selection of different installations based on country. Figure 10.6 shows the North American selections, but there are also versions for various European nations, as well as Japan and a few other non-European countries. The major difference between versions really concerns the switch type selections.

FIG. 10.6
WaveRunner country selection.

The country selected determines which parameters you'll have to select for connection with your telephone company. Figure 10.7 shows the selections for the United States. The Canadian version dims a few selections to simplify configuration. In my case, I select National ISDN 1 because the switch is a Siemens that meets that specification. In general, the terminal identifier (TEI) is automatic; if not, your telephone company should advise you.

FIG. 10.7
WaveRunner telephone switch parameter selection.

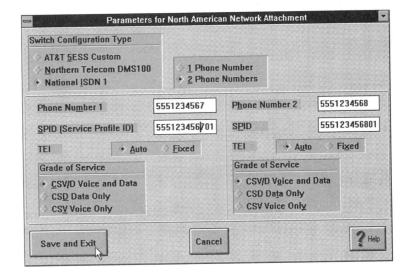

CAUTION

Notice that phone numbers and SPIDs are entered *without any dashes or spaces.* Inserting extra characters can blow the whole thing, and force you to spend hours trying to figure out what went wrong.

From here, it's a matter of waiting as the installation program copies files to disk; your only job is swapping floppies when requested. When the software installation is finished, exit Windows and turn off your computer. Set the card switches and install the card in an available 16-bit slot. Connect the card to your NT1 and turn the computer back on.

CAUTION

The manual goes a little out of order—it directs you to run diagnostics before instructing you to hook to the NT-1, yet the diagnostics won't work without line connection and without the configuration of switch parameters we're about to cover. If you're obsessively following the step checklist in the front of the manual, you'll do things in the right order, but if you simply go in page order, your diagnostics will fail.

When the machine has restarted, go into Windows and find the new WaveRunner Digital Modem program group created by WaveRunner (see Fig. 10.8).

FIG. 10.8

The WaveRunner Digital Modem program group contains eight icons showing the range of personalities the WaveRunner may assume.

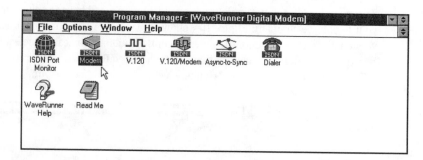

These icons show the various modes of operation the WaveRunner can assume. We'll consider these in the next section. For now, double-click the ISDN Port Monitor icon; it's at the far left of the top row of icons in Figure 10.8. You'll be met by status messages as the device checks the D and B channels (see Fig. 10.9).

FIG. 10.9

WaveRunner port monitor status.

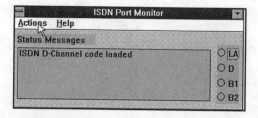

Open the Actions menu and choose Change ISDN Port Configuration.

N O T E This returns you to the parameter selections you saw in Figure 10.7 during installation. This can be handy if you ever want to go back and adjust the configuration parameters. ■

The WaveRunner comes packaged with a very flexible fax program, Trio DataFAX, that installs and integrates very well with the IBM product. The installation program for this fax program is simple and efficient (see Fig. 10.10). It includes KingCOM, a serial port driver replacement for the software that comes with Windows. This replacement driver improves performance, as I discussed in Chapter 9, "Selecting an External Terminal Adapter." From the options about KingCOM, you should select full driver replacement (see Fig. 10.11). Double-click on Install to begin the installation of Trio DataFAX. Unless you have good reasons, accept the default options.

FIG. 10.10

Trio DataFAX installation.

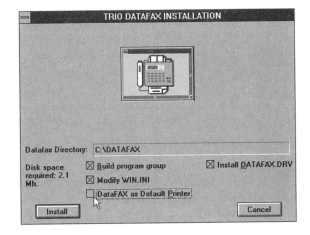

Part

III

Ch

10

FIG. 10.11

Trio DataFAX Comm Driver option.

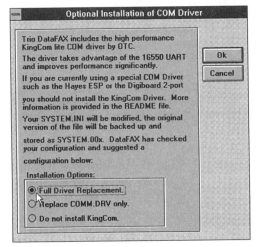

> **CAUTION**
>
> If you're using Windows 95 the drivers are already improved; in fact, Windows 95 handles serial communica-tion using far better techniques as I cover in Chapter 12, "Opening Windows 95 and NT for ISDN." As a result, you should not use the special driver supplied by IBM. Check IBM's Web site **http://www.raleigh.ibm.com**, for this product and the ftp site therein, **pub/standards/waverun**, for any revised software as they integrate the product with Windows 95 and the IETF Multilink PPP standards.

WaveRunner Use

Now that you have the WaveRunner installed, let's look at how it's actually used. There are five uses reflected by the icons in the WaveRunner Digital Modem group (refer to Fig. 10.8):

- Modem
- V.120
- V.120/Modem
- Asynch/Synch
- Dialer

Analog Modem   Modem provides an emulation of a V.32 14.4 Kbps analog modem that uses a single B channel. To use this function, double-click the icon. An electronic representation of the front of a modem appears (see Fig. 10.12).

FIG. 10.12
WaveRunner analog
modem selection.

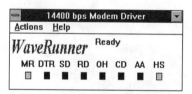

The small squares toward the bottom of the modem picture actually function like those on a physical modem. Each light, when it's on, indicates a certain activity:

Label	Full Name	Activity Indicated
MR	Modem Ready	The driver is loaded and operational. This light should be on at all times after the driver has been initialized.
DTR	Data Terminal Ready	The communications application is active.
SD	Send Data	The driver is transferring data from your com-puter to the remote system. When data is being transferred at fast data rates, this light may appear to be on steadily.

Label	Full Name	Activity Indicated
RD	Receive Data	The driver is transferring data from the remote system to your computer. When data is being transferred at fast data rates, this light may appear to be on steadily.
OH	Off Hook	The driver phone line is off-hook (in use).
CD	Carrier Detect	The driver has detected a remote modem's carrier signal.
AA	Auto Answer	The driver is set to automatically answer incoming calls.
HS	High Speed	The driver is set to connect at a line speed greater than 2400 bps.

Choose Actions, Configuration on the menu to set the modem speed (you get to choose from among the speeds shown in Figure 10.13). Choosing Change Phone Number Discrimination opens the dialog box shown in Figure 10.14, allowing you to discriminate among calls to make and answer. Since you have two B channels you can discriminate between them and make one answer only voice calls while the other doesn't answer any calls at all. Then you would attach voice telephone equipment to the WaveRunner's telephone port and be able to receive voice calls. You would use the other port only for placing outgoing calls, perhaps only for data calls to your Internet service provider.

FIG. 10.13
WaveRunner modem speed selection.

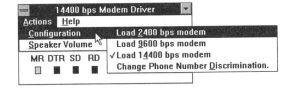

FIG. 10.14
WaveRunner modem call discrimination lets you set what each B channel can do.

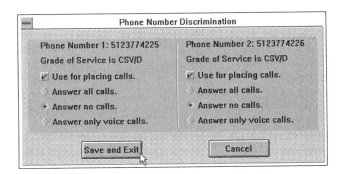

Part
III

Ch
10

With this driver running and emulating an ordinary modem, you can make calls using typical modem programs to other ordinary modems.

V.120   The next icon selection in the group is the V.120 driver. If you select this or any other drivers, and another driver is already using the COM port, an error message appears to remind you to close the other driver. To close an earlier driver, double-click the control menu icon in its upper-left corner.

After you clear the other driver and select V.120, the screen gives you an electronic representation of a modem. Open the Actions menu and choose V.120 Configuration; this displays your current settings for V.120 operation (see Fig. 10.15). V.120 provides higher data rates by enabling applications designed for asynchronous communications to use a synchronous 64 kbps ISDN line. V.120 is bit-oriented and therefore not as efficient or fast as truly synchronous protocols.

FIG. 10.15
WaveRunner V.120 configuration.

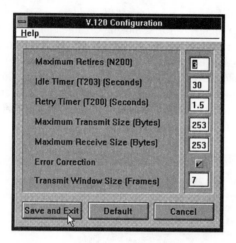

Calls normally are placed as 64 kbps data. Using choices on the Overrides menu, you can reduce the speed to 56 kbps, or change the type to voice (see Fig. 10.16). You'll need these changes if your calls might traverse 56 kbps lines or only need voice quality. You could save a lot by using voice if that's all you need in some cases; save, that is, if your long distance carrier charges more for clear channel 64 kbps than for voice transmission.

V.120/Modem   V.120/Modem is a very flexible feature. It allows the WaveRunner to receive both analog modem calls and V.120 ISDN calls. Therefore, you could have a single telephone number (your ISDN line) and people could call using either digital V.120 or analog signals. This could prove handy if you're running a bulletin board service and want to have only one number. Figure 10.17 shows the available modem and V.120 configuration options.

FIG. 10.16
WaveRunner Override.

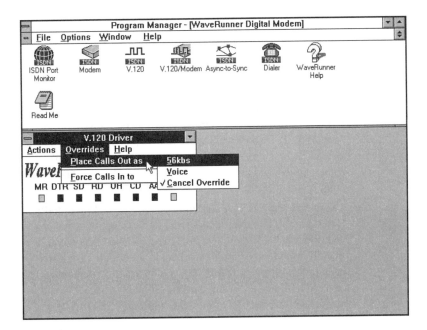

FIG. 10.17
This WaveRunner utility enables a single ISDN line to answer both analog and V.120 calls.

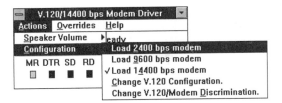

▶ **See** "Digital Subscriber Signaling System 1 (DSS1)," **p. 104**

N O T E You must have the telephone switch configured for circuit-switched voice and data (CSV/D). The telephone switch determines what type of call is being sent and provides signaling to the WaveRunner, telling it to set up for one or the other. ▨

Asynch-to-Synch Driver Double-click on the Async-to-Sync icon and you'll see this driver provides three options; I've described them in real English, and shown in quotation marks the way IBM describes them in the menus and documentation:

■ *Remote local area network access.* "HDLC/Asynch-to-Synch" This enables remote LAN access using LAN Distance (an IBM software package) or similar software. It provides remote access to all LAN services available locally on that network, allowing you, for instance, to work at home and dial into your company's LAN.

■ *Access to Internet and other TCP/IP systems with SLIP.* "TCP/IP SLIP-to-HDLC" This removes the serial line Internet protocol (SLIP) control characters and encapsulates the IP packets using HDLC, thereby allowing communication with ISDN routers that support TCP/IP. Your application program talks to the serial port while the device at the far end (for example, a router at an Internet provider) thinks it's talking to another router. Smoke and mirrors! Be aware that SLIP is gradually being replaced by point-to-point protocol (PPP).

■ *Connection using TCP/IP and frame relay.* "TCP/IP SLIP-to-RFC 1294" Even if you knew HDLC and SLIP, and understood the first two options, this one would probably throw you. RFC stands for "request for comment" and turns out to be the specifications for TCP/IP usage issued by the Internet Engineering Task Force (IETF); RFC1294 has been totally replaced by RFC1490; both speak to *frame relay,* a high data rate technique covered in Chapter 18, "Anticipating Broadband ISDN." So, this option provides communications fitting into the frame relay world.

Select one of the three options by clicking the appropriate check box (see Fig. 10.18).

FIG. 10.18

WaveRunner asynch-to-synch configuration.

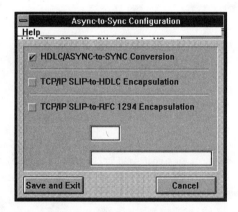

NDIS   Network Driver Interface Standard (NDIS) was developed by 3Com and Microsoft for network interface card (NIC) drivers. It offers a way of creating drivers from a combination of software supplied by the card manufacturer and by the network operating system manufacturer. Novell developed Open Datalink Interface (ODI) to perform the same task.

In the case of ISDN cards such as the WaveRunner, NDIS offers a very efficient way for you to talk directly to the card.

T I P It is far better in terms of speed of operation to use NDIS (or ODI) to speak with your card than to use the AT command set talking through the COM port.

Unfortunately, the WaveRunner documentation is unclear on this advantage and how to really make it work. So, let's take a look at installation and configuration of NDIS. You'll find some information on this subject within the WAVERUN subdirectory created by the WaveRunner software during installation. There's a subdirectory of WAVERUN named NDIS, and another subdirectory named EXAMPLES. You'll find a number of possible environments, including Windows for Workgroups and NetManage. I'll use NetManage for this discussion, since it's such a popular TCP/IP Windows package. IBM provides model files for AUTOEXEC.BAT, CONFIG.SYS, and PROTOCOL.INI. It takes a little figuring out, but ultimately what you do is add the following lines to each of the named files:

AUTOEXEC.BAT:

```
c:\waverun\ndis\netbind.com
```

CONFIG.SYS:

```
device=c:\waverun\ndis\protman.dos /i:c:\waverun\ndis
device=c:\waverun\ndis\wrndis.sys
device=c:\netmanag\netmanag.dos
```

PROTOCOL.INI:

```
[PROT_MAN]
     DriverName=PROTMAN$
[WRMAC1B]
     DRIVERNAME=WRNDIS$
     NETADDRESS=I0200EE4C82B3
[NETMANAGE]
     DRIVERNAME=NETMNG$
     BINDINGS=WRMAC1B1
```

Make those changes in your existing AUTOEXEC.BAT and CONFIG.SYS files. Create a new file named PROTOCOL.INI and make the entries listed above for NetManage or other programs as suggested in the examples or other literature. Then, put PROTOCOL.INI into the location shown in your CONFIG.SYS line:

> c:\waverun\ndis\PROTMAN.DOS /I:C:\waverun\ndis

Everything following the /I switch is the location of the PROTOCOL.INI file. Of course, you must substitute the appropriate directories if your directory structure differs from this example or other examples provided by IBM.

N O T E Not all NetManage products include NDIS support. The product I'm using in this example is NetManage Chameleon*NFS* version 4.5. This is a very robust version with numerous options. ▨

Part
III

Ch
10

When you've finished the NDIS configuration, reboot the computer and return to the WaveRunner group. Select the ISDN dialer (see Fig. 10.19). This dials a number through your card using NDIS.

FIG. 10.19
WaveRunner dialer
for NDIS.

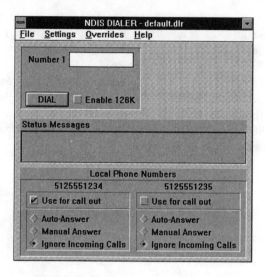

WinISDN   IBM provides WinISDN support for the WaveRunner. You can download the necessary files from IBM's bulletin board, ftp site, or CompuServe forum. The file you get is WINISDN.EXE, a self-extracting file that comes with an instruction file named README.NOW contained within the self-extracting file. The only application it mentions for support is NetManage. You take the file IBM.DLL (it comes out of the extraction) and place it in your NetManage subdirectory. Then, double-click the Custom icon contained within the Chameleon*NFS* group. When the Custom program appears, open the Interface menu and choose Add, then select ISDN from the list that appears. Open the Setup menu and choose Hardware to reach the Hardware dialog box (see Fig. 10.20), and fill in the fields as shown:

Vendor:	**Other**
Section Name:	**Wave0**
Vendor Name:	**IBM**
Driver File:	**IBM.DLL**

▶ See "WinISDN," **p. 119**

FIG. 10.20
WaveRunner
WinISDN/NetManage
configuration.

The Section Name in the figure does not read WAVE0 because the program had not yet run when the screen capture was taken; it shows the directory where the software is. When you're finished, restart Windows. Double-click the ISDN Port Monitor icon in the WaveRunner Digital Modem program group to make the card active; then, go into NetManage and select the connection option you just set up by choosing "Custom" and then the interface name you gave it.

Part
III

Ch
10

> **N O T E** IBM's BBS number is 919-517-0001; WaveRunner material is in File Access Area 32. You can find other information at **http://www.raleigh.ibm.com** and get files via ftp from the pub/standards/waverun directory at that address. ▤

U.S. Robotics ISDN Card Products

U.S. Robotics is the largest modem maker and has taken after ISDN in a big way. The company offers two card-level products. The Courier I-Modem is a true combination of an analog modem and an ISDN terminal adapter card. The Sportster ISDN 128K is strictly an ISDN terminal adapter card and is optimized for MultiLink PPP connections.

USR Courier I-Modem

U.S. Robotics makes six versions of the I-Modem:

- Internal with S/T interface
- Internal with U interface
- Internal with U interface and POTS port
- External with S/T interface
- External with U interface
- External with U interface and POTS port

Because this is a chapter on internal boards, we'll stick with them. I used the one with the U interface and POTS port, but the material we cover is the same as you'll need for the external models. The POTS port is available for connection to your regular phone, FAX, or modem. The internal board is shown in Figure 10.21 and the external version is displayed in Figure 10.22.

FIG. 10.21
USR Courier I-Modem internal card version.

FIG. 10.22
USR Courier I-Modem external version.

The nice thing about the Courier I-Modem is that it's an ISDN terminal adapter, a V.34 modem, and a FAX. If you dial up a number that has an analog modem, it connects with the analog modem. If you dial up a number with an ISDN device, it connects with the ISDN. You don't have to think about it; the equipment figures it out on its own.

When Is an Analog Modem Really an ISDN Device?

You might call what you think is an analog modem and find you're connected with ISDN. How could this happen? As you'll see in Chapter 17, "ISDN Access for Internet Providers and Corporations," there is equipment that can answer a call, determine if it's from an analog modem or an ISDN device, and respond accordingly. That way an ISP need only have ISDN lines and can handle both ISDN and POTS calls with the same lines and the same equipment.

Do you wish you could do that? You have that power with the USR I-Modem. You have even more! When it places a call it listens and responds as either a POTS modem, ISDN terminal adapter, or FAX. It does the same when it receives a call. You don't have to set it up for different numbers; it figures it all out.

Part
III

Ch
10

One of the most powerful features of the I-Modem is flash memory. This feature gives you a way to upgrade as standards change. Perhaps the most important changes center around Multilink PPP and related compression. These weren't built into the device I tested, but were anticipated to be available for flash upgrade when the standards settle. With flash memory, a call to USR's BBS, Web, or FTP site enables you to obtain the latest software to meet the new standards.

Let's take a look at configuring the I-Modem with the Configuration Manager supplied. Installation of the Configuration Manager uses standard procedures so I'll skip straight to the screen where you enter the relevant information (see Fig. 10.23). You can see the usual blanks for SPIDs and directory numbers. Notice the Call Type selection. The possible selections are:

- Automatic Service Choice
- V.120
- V.110
- Analog Modem

If you choose Automatic Service Choice, the I-Modem determines the type of connection being offered at the far end location you're calling and changes to make the connection. It starts by trying V.120, then V.110, and finally, analog modem. You can force it to select only one type of connection, but I suggest you leave it on automatic unless you have a very good reason not to.

Notice that the box at the top is labeled Data Channel and the box below is labeled Analog Device Channel. The I-Modem is furnished and supports only one digital data B channel. The remaining B channel is assigned to carry analog information: FAX, Voice, and analog modem. Flash upgrades, which will provide digital data for both B channels and support Multilink PPP, are anticipated by the time you read this. Check the Web site of USR.

Once you've completed filling in the blanks and connected your I-Modem to the ISDN line, click on the Test button. You see Switch Connectivity Test, which shows the results after checking both the Physical Layer and Data Link Layer of your ISDN connection (see Fig. 10.24). Expect to see the Physical Layer show Active in just a couple of seconds. It may take 30 or more seconds to confirm the Data Link Layer as shown at the bottom of Figure 10.24.

FIG. 10.23

With the U.S. Robotics Courier I-Modem Configuration Manager, everything you need to set up the I-Modem is on this one screen.

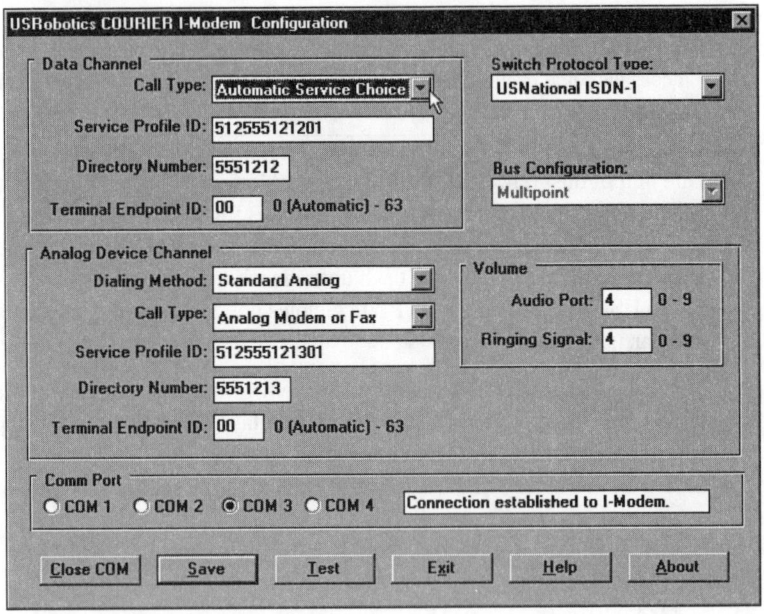

USRobotics COURIER I-Modem Configuration

Data Channel
Call Type: Automatic Service Choice
Service Profile ID: 512555121201
Directory Number: 5551212
Terminal Endpoint ID: 00   0 (Automatic) - 63

Switch Protocol Type:
USNational ISDN-1

Bus Configuration:
Multipoint

Analog Device Channel
Dialing Method: Standard Analog
Call Type: Analog Modem or Fax
Service Profile ID: 512555121301
Directory Number: 5551213
Terminal Endpoint ID: 00   0 (Automatic) - 63

Volume
Audio Port: 4   0 - 9
Ringing Signal: 4   0 - 9

Comm Port
○ COM 1   ○ COM 2   ◉ COM 3   ○ COM 4   Connection established to I-Modem.

Close COM   Save   Test   Exit   Help   About

FIG. 10.24

The U.S. Robotics Courier I-Modem Configuration Manager testing your ISDN configuration and connection.

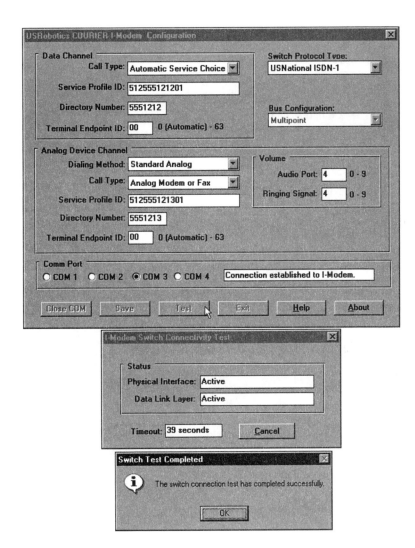

US Robotics Sportster ISDN 128K

US Robotics bought ISDN Systems Corporation in mid-1995. Prior to the purchase by USR, ISDN Systems Corporation and Intel had joined forces in the original development of the SecureLink card. The first cards were marketed by both companies. It's my understanding that ISC redesigned their card so the offerings of the two companies were no longer identical. US Robotics renamed the card the Sportster ISDN 128K; it's shown in Figure 10.25. It has a number of important features, including:

Part
III

Ch
10

T I P   Secure your understanding with a visit to **http://www.usr.com/home/spisdnds.html,** the USR site for the Sportster ISDN 128K.

- PPP and Multilink PPP support
- Compression between SecureLink adapters and with compression algorithms of other companies such as Ascend
- A version with a built-in NT-1
- Security
- NDIS, ODI, WinISDN, and TAPI interfaces
- TCP/IP, IPX, NetBIOS and DECNet support
- Analog phone port

FIG. 10.25
USR Sportster ISDN 128K internal card terminal adapter.

N O T E   V.120 asynch is *not* supported by the Sportster card.

The Sportster comes with two manuals, each 20 pages or so. One is for use with DOS and Windows; the other is for Windows NT. Both are clear and concise.

N O T E   Because the Sportster was originally made by ISDN Systems Corporation and named SecureLink II, you'll probably see several references to SecureLink II in the literature, software, and screens. This is certainly true in several of the following screen shots. Remember SecureLink II and Sportster ISDN 128K mean the same thing.

In the manuals, there are references to "the Reference Guide." Don't waste time looking for a book; this guide is an electronic file in Windows Help format, and is contained on the installation disks.; so you must wait until installation to read it from within Windows. In my case, I found it quite helpful to have the Reference Guide available prior to installation so I went through the procedures described in the note; I'm one of those strange people who actually reads the documentation—sometimes even before I do an installation.

N O T E To read a file in Windows Help format, start Help in the Windows Program Manager by double-clicking on Help in the ribbon at the top of program manager or executing Alt+H. Double-click on the File menu and choose Open, then specify the name of the file you want to read. In the case of the Sportster ISDN 128K, the file name is REFMAN.HLP, but you won't find that file on the disk—it's buried in a *zipped file* on the second disk. After installation, it will be available through an icon, but if you want to read it prior to installation, you can use the PKUNZIP program supplied on Disk One to extract the help file. Make a temporary directory on your hard drive and copy PKUNZIP.EXE from Disk One to the new directory. Then, copy DATA.ZIP from Disk Two to the same temporary directory. Execute `pkunzip data`, and you'll find REFMAN.HLP among the files exploded from the zipped file. When you're through with reading this you may erase the files in your temporary directory and remove the directory. ▪

Additional information is also contained on the first disk. Execute the `readme` command to start the Intel Documentation Viewer on the disk and review additional details for specific installation environments.

Sportster ISDN 128K Physical Installation   I'll bet you know how to open up your computer and install a board, so we'll skip that. But before we do, let's look at a few things on the card. There are two jumpers, JP1 and JP2. When installing for DOS, Windows 3.x, or Window 95, make sure these jumpers are *not connected*; that is, make sure each jumper covers only one prong. The I/O base address is made through software. If you're using Windows NT, you may use the jumpers to select the card's I/O base address as directed in the manual. Otherwise, the address is set by software.

While the card is out, notice the speaker in the upper-left corner and check the back. If you find two LEDs, then the card has an internal NT-1 and the top connector is a U interface. The round connector in the middle is for an external power supply (an optional accessory); you'll want this only if your telephone company switch detects loss of an NT-1 and goes into an alarm condition. The power supply does not make the POTS connection work when your computer is off; when your computer is off, the POTS port is dead.

If there's only one LED on the card, the card has no internal NT-1 and the top connector is an S/T interface.

N O T E Since there's no ringer current on the POTS port, if you decide to use a FAX or modem connected to the card, the device is not able to answer incoming calls (the usual circuit for those devices depends on detecting ringer current). Since this has become a major issue with many users, including me, USR provides a Ring Generator that connects to the analog port and creates ringer current.

Some of the documentation says the card's method of encoding analog information may not work well with modems, but I've been satisfied with such operation. In fact, if you have a V.34 modem, it is much more likely to work properly on the POTS port of an ISDN device than over an analog line, very many of which do not quite have the standard waveform or voltage required to achieve or sustain 28.8 kbps.

In fact, we've discovered that in Austin, subscribers connected by a SLCC hut to an AT&T 5ESS switch cannot, that's right, CANNOT get a full 28.8 kbps modem connection from an analog line. The only way to make such a modem work to its maximum speed is to use an ISDN line with a POTS interface device!

You may decide to opt for the S/T interface with a separate NT-1 to provide more flexibility for the future; this way, you can add more ISDN devices. The U interface model is the only ISDN device that can use your line. So to use an ISDN phone, you'd have to physically disconnect the card and connect to the phone, or, more likely, to an NT-1. ▓

Sportster Software Installation Using DOS You may do installation from the DOS prompt, without Windows running. Two options are provided:

- ▓ *Complete Installation.* This includes all features.

- ▓ *Internet Package.* This takes less space and asks less questions; it only provides for WinISDN support.

Which should you choose? That depends on your needs. At this time, many users will only want dial-in connections, so the Internet selection with WinISDN is just fine. In reality this is more than Internet support; you may call any location using telephone dialing. What you give up with this installation are the more elaborate Ethernet and token ring connection options.

▶ **See** "TAPI," **p. 131**

From here on, installation amounts to following very clear steps in a graphical flow diagram in the book, and swapping floppies twice when instructed. Both the Sportster ISDN 128K and TAPI software are installed, so you'll be ready for TAPI-enabled Windows applications or, if you're using Windows 95, you can use the TAPI apps already there. At the end of installation, a diagnostics program checks the card and ISDN connection.

T I P If you have an S/T card, the diagnostics program checks the connection from the card to the NT-1 only, not to the actual telephone company line.

During installation, you'll be asked for the directory number, SPID, and switch type. As part of the diagnostics at the end of installation, you'll test these by calling another phone number. If all of that works, you're finished setting up the board. The next thing you need to do is to select a connection protocol to be used. These are your choices:

■ *Proprietary.* Use this if you're calling a remote device that also uses a Sportster device or one designed by ISDN Systems Corporation. A number of optimized features such as compression are included.

■ *PPP.* Point-to-point protocol is what you'll probably use if you're connecting to an Internet provider or other networks that do not use ISC products. This uses one B channel. You may not want to have the card execute PPP if your application does.

■ *ML/PPP.* Multilink point-to-point protocol allows use of multiple B channels for increased data rate. As I discuss in Chapter 13, "Tying It Together: Two B or Not Two B," this protocol is just being standardized.

■ *Transparent Mode.* Use this if your application handles the handshake between your equipment and equipment at the other end. NetManage Chameleon*NFS* and Frontier Technologies SuperTCP Pro are examples of this sort of software.

You'll also need to select the type of LAN at the other end, Ethernet or token ring. Ethernet is usually a safe bet for an Internet connection. Next, you plunge into modification of your network files. The Reference Guide is mandatory here. If you've chosen the simplified Internet installation using WinISDN, you probably won't have to go through this. If you have a more involved installation, you probably have to make modifications to your AUTOEXEC.BAT, CONFIG.SYS, and PROTOCOL.INI files, and perhaps other files. We'll look at the NetManage Chameleon NFS version 4.5 issues.

It's best to install the card first and then NetManage. When you've got the card installed, go into NetManage and double-click the Custom icon in the ChameleonNFS program group created during installation (see Fig. 10.26).

Part
III

Ch
10

FIG. 10.26

NetManage
ChameleonNFS
group.

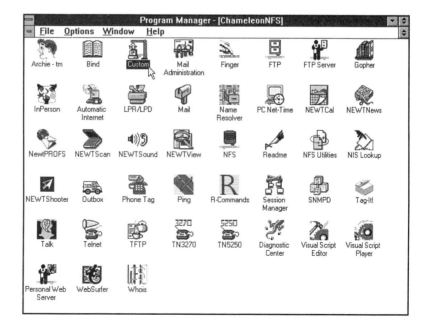

N O T E   The version of NetManage Chameleon shown here is not the version you usually find
included with books, including many books from Que. For information on ordering
NetManage Chameleon NFS version 4.5, call 408 973-7171; **http://www.netmanage.com**.
Frontier's SuperTCP Pro also incorporates WinISDN support; call 414 241-7084; **http://
www.frontiertech.com**. ■

Open the Interface menu and choose Add (see Fig. 10.27). This figure shows several interfaces
already existing; if you've just installed Chameleon, none of the items in the lower part of the
screen will show.

FIG. 10.27

NetManage
ChameleonNFS
custom selection.

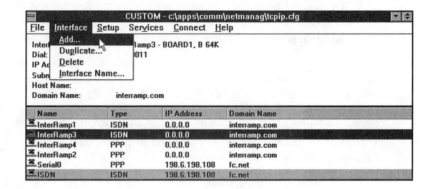

You'll find a selection of several types of interfaces. If you've used the more extensive installation method for the ISC card along with Chameleon, you'll also find Ethernet and token ring on
the list. We'll choose WinISDN for this simplified installation; that's indicated simply by "ISDN"
in the list (see Fig. 10.28).

FIG. 10.28

NetManage
ChameleonNFS
Add interface.

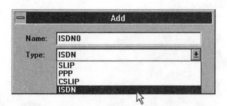

Open the Setup menu and choose Hardware; from the Vendor drop-down list, choose **Other**.

Then make the following entries for the USR card:

Section Name:	**isc00**
Vendor Name:	**isc**
Driver File:	**isc.dll**

Figure 10.29 illustrates these entries.

FIG. 10.29

NetManage
ChameleonNFS
USR Sportster
ISDN 128K card
entries.

 TIP There's a good chance that information for the USR Sportster card will be included within the selections in Chameleon.

Although the simplified installation and other installations are supposed to make modifications to your configuration files, it's a good idea to check things out for yourself. USR provides example files in the directory C:\RX\EXAMPLES. These files end in the extension XMP and show where the changes are to be made in your existing files. If you customized your directory structure, substitute your customization for RX.

> ### CAUTION
> Although this is all supposed to be created automatically during installation, I found a couple of glitches. If you use a directory structure that avoids having many directories off the root (in other words, with longer paths to most of your directories), you may find the paths incorrectly formed by the installation program. You would think that when you specified a directory to be created under, for example, your C:\APPS\COMM directory, that path would carry over to all aspects of the installation program. For me it did not, and I had to manually correct some directory calls placed in my configuration files by the installation program. It became even worse when I found the call to one program entered before the path statement in AUTOEXEC.BAT. The call had no path reference but needed to look in the NETMANAG directory. The path inclusion of NETMANAG came several lines later. This ride can feel a little bumpy if you haven't been down this road before, but if you're comfortable changing your configuration files, you'll have an okay trip.

USR Sportster ISDN 128K Use   We have the ISC SecureLink II installed and configured. How do we use it? This all depends on what you want to do. If you're doing Internet access, the tools within a program such as NetManage Internet Chameleon are a good start. Right now we'll look at the utilities supplied by USR.

Figure 10.30 shows the main group created by the Sportster installation. Notice the Release Notes for the most current information. The information regarding interoperability came from these notes.

FIG. 10.30

USR Sportster ISDN 128K utilities.

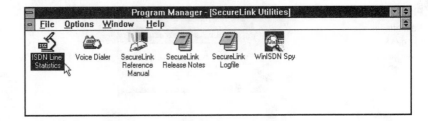

The utilities include the ability to log an extensive collection of statistics concerning activity on the ISDN line. This information includes usage of each channel, telephone numbers called, and numbers of packets and bytes transmitted and received (see Fig. 10.31).

FIG. 10.31

USR Sportster ISDN 128K line statistics.

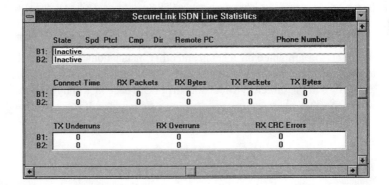

Double-clicking the Voice Dialer icon starts a dialer for a voice phone connected to the POTS port on the card. It's an elegant utility. Figure 10.32 shows the face of the dialer, and one of the options opened to show calling card numbers. Another option provides location identification and details. This dialer uses the Microsoft TAPI interface and illustrates a simple application. Much more elaborate applications using TAPI will plug right in.

Double-clicking the Sportster Logfile icon brings up a very helpful log of activities that have used the card (see Fig. 10.33). While I was trying to debug my installation, this file and the WinISDN Spy (see Fig. 10.34) were invaluable. I combined their indication of when and where things failed with an examination of paths in my configuration files (as described in the preceding caution) and was able to figure out all the errors in paths.

FIG. 10.32

USR Sportster ISDN
128K voice dialer.

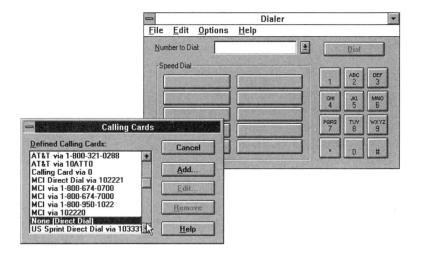

FIG. 10.33

USR Sportster ISDN
128K Logfile.

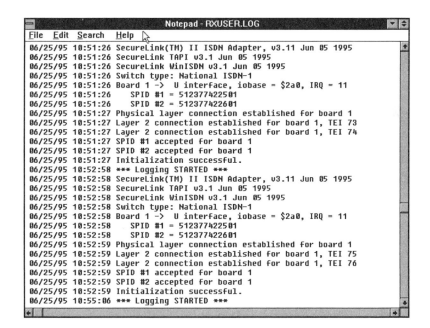

FIG. 10.34

USR Sportster ISDN 128K WinISDN Spy.

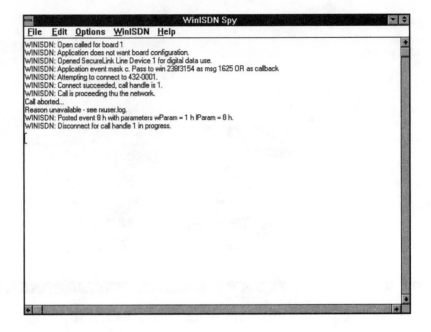

Using the Sportster ISDN 128K with Windows 95 The Sportster ISDN 128K has a new graphical user interface that takes advantage of many of the features available for the first time in Windows 95.

 TIP Remember USR bought ISC, so many of the references still speak of the card using its ISC name SecureLink.

USR has taken advantage of the Windows 95 utilities and GUI to make an outstanding ISDN interface. The Sportster ISDN 128K Manager main application window is shown in Figure 10.35. Notice the totally graphical presentation of an ISDN connection as the management screens unfold. In this first graphic, the D channel is shown connecting your computer to the ISDN network. The Tool buttons and Menu Selection Bar provide controls to set up connections.

 TROUBLESHOOTING

How do I know the connection is good? When the connection to ISDN is good, the line is black and you know your ISDN connection is ready for use. If the line is red the connection is bad. The graphic also presents a box with proposed solutions. You may need to troubleshoot items like cabling and problems at your telco switch.

FIG. 10.35

The USR Sportster ISDN 128K Main Application Window shows the initial connection ISDN has over the D channel in the graphical ISDN connection section. At the top, the Tool buttons and Menu Selection Bar provide controls.

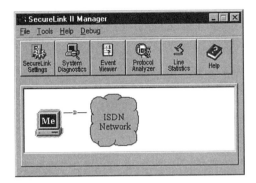

When an ISDN call is made and a connection completes, B channels appear in the graphic. If the connection is a single 64 kbps channel, one B channel appears; if two 64 kbps channels are connected, two B channel lines appear (see Fig. 10.36). The B channels are numbered B1 and B2 and have arrow heads showing the direction of the call. A data call is represented by a green line connected to a computer; a voice call is shown by a blue line to a telephone (see Fig. 10.37). The ISDN software is configured so a voice call takes over one B channel out of a previously existing pair using MP for data. The remaining B channel continues to carry data.

FIG. 10.36

An ISDN data connection shows B channels and indicates data transmission with a blue line connected to a computer picture.

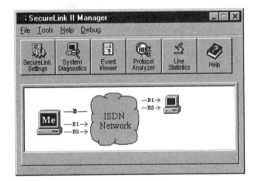

FIG. 10.37

An ISDN voice connection is shown by a green line for the B channel and a picture of a telephone.

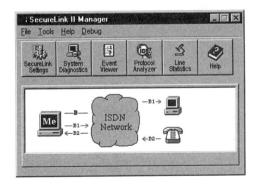

Figure 10.38 shows the tool bar buttons:

■ Sportster Settings enables you to change the Sportster configuration settings.

■ System Diagnostics tests the system, board, and line.

■ Event Viewer traces line and call activities.

■ Protocol Analyzer traces real-time ISDN protocol action.

■ Line Statistics gives real-time status of the ISDN connections.

■ Help puts you into the Reference Guide.

FIG. 10.38

Tool Bar Buttons in the Sportster ISDN 128K Manager provide configuration and diagnostic tools.

When you select the Sportster Settings button you're faced with the Settings page (see Fig. 10.39). This is the first of three options: General, Telephone Company, and Adapter Board.

FIG. 10.39

The Sportster Settings screen shows the General option on top with Telephone Company and Adapter Board tabs.

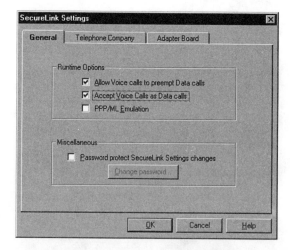

■ *Still Connected Reminder* sets a timer to remind you that you are still connected to ISDN. Since many telcos and Internet service providers charge by the minute, this is an important option. Your settings can range from 1 to 10 minutes. You can set the reminder to off.

■ *Allow Voice Calls to Preempt Data Calls* lets you have both incoming and outgoing voice calls preempt data calls. If you have one data call set up that is using two B channels, the voice call takes one of the B channels regardless of how this option is set.

■ *Password Protect Sportster Settings Change* applies a password to the settings you are making in this series of tabbed options, General, Telephone Company, and Adapter Board.

■ *Change Password* button enables you to change the password set if you elect to protect the settings.

Click on the Telephone Company tab to show the page in Figure 10.40. This provide all the options required for ISDN setup. Enter your telco switch type, SPIDs, and directory numbers. The Sportster ISDN 128K supports both North American and European switch types:

■ AT&T 5ESS Custom or G3 PBX

■ Euro-ISDN (European ISDN only)

■ INS-64 (European ISDN only)

■ National ISDN (NI-1)

■ Nortel DMS-100 Custom

Part
III

Ch
10

 Remember: Enter the numbers with no spaces or hyphens.

FIG. 10.40

The USR Sportster ISDN 128K Telephone Company options page provides switch selection, SPIDs and directory number entries.

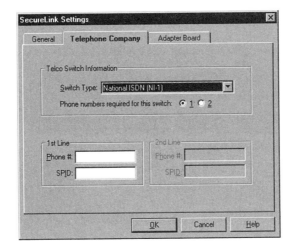

Click on the Adapter Board tab (see Fig. 10.41). This shows the options available for the Sportster board itself:

■ I/O addresses are used to communicate between your computer and the Sportster board. Working with Windows 95 the program presents a list of available I/O addresses. Select one from the pick list.

▶ **See** "Serial Port Hardware," **p. 207**

■ IRQ selects the interrupt for the board. Again the software gives you a list of available interrupts from which to pick.

N O T E The automatic IRQ and I/O testing within Windows 95 is a big advance over Windows 3.x, but it isn't perfect. If you have problems, check out possible conflicts using the Device Manager inside System within the Control Panel or use the Windows 95 version of Norton Utilities. Also, visually check device jumpers, switches, and software settings. ■

■ *Voice Ringing Pattern and Test* button provides eight distinctive rings for incoming voice calls. It only works with an attached analog phone. The *Test* button rings the phone. Choose External if you're using the external Ring Generator

■ *Beep on Data Calls* does what it says.

■ *Serial Number* helps you keep up with the number on your board for your records.

■ *MAC Address* helps keep up with the addresses for your records.

■ *On-board U Interface* tells you whether or not the board has a built in NT1, hence a U interface. USR make both U and S/T interface boards.

■ *Voice Capability* tells you if the board has an analog interface since you can buy the board with or without such an interface.

■ *External Ring Capability* tells you if the board can work with the external ring adapter. Earlier versions could not.

FIG. 10.41
USR Sportster ISDN
128K Adapter Board
page.

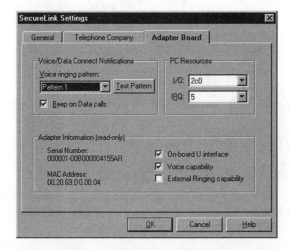

Once you've finished setting up all the pages in the Sportster Settings you can leave by clicking on Exit. Then click on the System Diagnostics button in the tool bar, bringing up the System Diagnostics page (see Fig. 10.42). In diagnostics you can check system integrity, the adapter, and the ISDN line. The Self-Call Test calls from one B channel to the other. If both lines are data the call goes through. If one is data and the other voice you receive a busy signal. Other failures are reported with details and often involve a switch provisioning problem.

FIG. 10.42

USR Sportster ISDN 128K System Diagnostics.

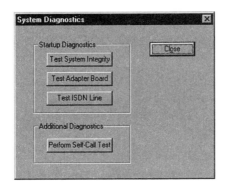

Additional buttons provide other diagnostic tools:

- *Viewer* shows real-time traces of line and call activities.
- *Protocol Analyzer* shows real-time traces of ISDN activity.
- *Line Statistics* shows real-time statistical summaries of the current B channel connections with the number of channels in use, the type of call (voice or data, incoming or outgoing), speed of the connection, connection protocol, and compression.

The Help button gives access to the Reference Guide and suggestions for Quick Start Up and Installation.

The Menu Selection Bar at the top provides access to the same tools as the Tool Bar buttons. The Menu Selection also provides configuration for the Sportster Manager itself through the File selection.

Interoperation with Other Devices   The Sportster ISDN 128K has well-documented interoperability with products from a number of other vendors. Tests by PacBell and the California ISDN Users Group have confirmed this. Such tests continue and will be reported in periodicals and on the Internet during. USR provided the following list of satisfactory interoperability in the version 3.11 release notes. I have been successful connecting to Ascend routers and the 3Com Impact.

N O T E   Interoperability is a moving target. The California ISDN Users Group is running most of the tests in North America. See their Web page at **http://www.ciug.org**. ▪

According to USR, the Sportster ISDN 128K interoperates using both PPP and PPP Multilink Protocol (MP) with products from at least the following vendors:

- 3Com
- Ascend
- Digi International
- Gandalf
- KNX

They add that the following vendors have products that interoperate using PPP, but not MP:

- Microsoft
- Motorola

ISDN*tek Internet Card

This is the simplest card we've tried, and perhaps the simplest card available. All it does is connect to ISDN using an NT-1. It gives you a single B channel of communication. The company is bringing out additional cards with analog ports and two B channels, but let's look at their initial product to see how simple and easy it can get.

V.120 asynch is not supported. The card is specifically designed to work with WinISDN and Internet Chameleon. The installation is simplified and directed toward selecting an Internet provider and plugging in. Providers such as PSI offer starter software based on Chameleon.

N O T E ISDN*tek provides a number of other cards supporting multiple B channels and X.25 over the D channel. The firm advises me that they are now directing their efforts toward providing ISDN hardware, software, and expertise to other manufacturers as an OEM. Check it all out at **http:// www.isdntek.com**, where you'll find information on all the products. ▪

Wait! Don't plug the card in yet. First, install the software and run the diagnostic program. Why? Because the program tells you how to set the switches on the card; why insert the card, then run the program and have to remove the card to set the switches?

Insert Disk 1 of the ISDN*tek software into your floppy drive and open File in the Windows Program Manager. Select Run and enter A:setup to start the program. (Use B: if your disk is in the B: drive.) An ISDNtek group will be created with a Test icon. Double-click this icon and bring up the screen shown in Figure 10.43.

The Board Settings area is where you select the IRQ and I/O options for the board. The switches for the IRQ and jumpers for the I/O are set exactly as shown on this screen. In the ISDN Line Info area, enter your SPIDs and an analog phone number to call for testing. Notice that Voice is checked on the ISDN Line Info section; this makes the call to your analog phone, the number you entered in Test #. The Test Board area tests the card itself. The Test ISDN Line area places a call to the number you entered in the ISDN Line Info area. If the phone rings, your setup is good.

FIG. 10.43

ISDN*tek setup screen.

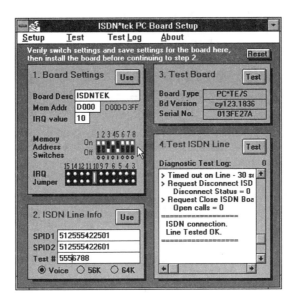

Part III

CAUTION

I'm again going to use NetManage Chameleon NFS as my application. I've used it with the two previous cards (and a bunch of stuff you don't want to hear about). Know what my directory structure, AUTOEXEC.BAT, CONFIG.SYS, WIN.INI, SYSTEM.INI, and certain other files look like? They're a total mess! A mess that'll make each succeeding installation and configuration even more of a nightmare that leads to days and days of lost time that would never happen if each installation had been done from scratch. It's terrible to find yourself saying, "Let's see, did that earlier setup change my CONFIG.SYS in a way that'll impact this new installation? Hmmm... what about the WIN.INI?"

You've got to clean up your act when you start fooling around with this much complexity. My solution? An uninstall program that keeps up with all of this. I've used Uninstaller, version 2 by MicroHelp for these tests; version 3 is more sophisticated and tracks all installations. Other companies offer similar products, but Uninstaller might have been the first; MicroHelp claims to keep on top of all the Windows program complexities to make sure little bits and pieces are swept up properly. It's worked for me.

continues

continued

Windows 95 has a registry to track installations of 32 bit programs and help in their removal. It does not keep up with 16 bit programs. MicroHelp provides a Windows 95 version of Uninstaller to add considerable functionality to installing, uninstalling, tracking and moving your applications around. A similar program, Clean Sweep, is available from QuarterDeck.

Your next step is loading the NetManage Chameleon software or any other software that supports the WinISDN interface. The procedure is much the same as I described with the USR Sportster ISDN 128K card, but ISDN*tek is already one of the options for hardware, so it's even easier. That's all there is to it. I know of no faster ISDN card to install and use. Granted, this card is more limited that a card like the IBM WaveRunner that has tons of options. But if all you plan to do is call an Internet provider, ISDN*tek is a great way to go. It works with synchronous PPP and certainly works with Ascend equipment, since that's what PSI uses (see the following sidebar).

Simpler Products Cost Less

This card lists for $395, but it usually sells for much less. In California PacBell, ISDN*tek and PSI (as an Internet provider) have offered it for $79 in a package. You'll have to buy an NT-1 for this one, but ISDN*tek is now integrating an NT-1 on other models for about $100 extra on the list price.

Digi International DataFire

DigiBoard recently changed its company name to Digi International. The company has a broad line of ISDN products, including the DataFire, pictured in Figure 10.44. In my earlier research, Digi International seemed directed toward LAN-to-LAN connection, expecting its products to be at both ends. There was virtually no mention of the Internet on the their Web site. There was a lack of information on interoperation with other vendors and standards. Fortunately, all that has changed. Digi International now highlights its interoperability with products of other vendors and touts its support of PPP standards.

 TIP Dash over to Digi's words on the DataFire:

http://www.digibd.com/prodprofiles/profiles-prices/digiprofiles/prodpages/datafire2.html

First go to the Microsoft Web site, **http://www.microsoft.com,** and retrieve the ISDN Accelerator Pack for Windows. Copy the contents of the pack to a directory on your hard drive; I put it in C:\ISDNACCL. Then select the Control Panel from the Settings sub-menu of the Start menu. Within the Control Panel select the Network icon, as shown in the upper left of Figure 10.42. Within the Network Menu click the Add button to pop up the Select Network Component Type menu, as shown toward the bottom right of Figure 10.42. Then click on Adapter to bring up the Select Network Adapters menu. Scan through this menu to see if Digi International is listed; the chances are it is not, so click on Have Disk as shown at the bottom right of Figure 10.45.

FIG. 10.44

Digi International DataFire ISDN internal card terminal adapter for ISDN.

FIG. 10.45

The sequence of installing the DataFire.

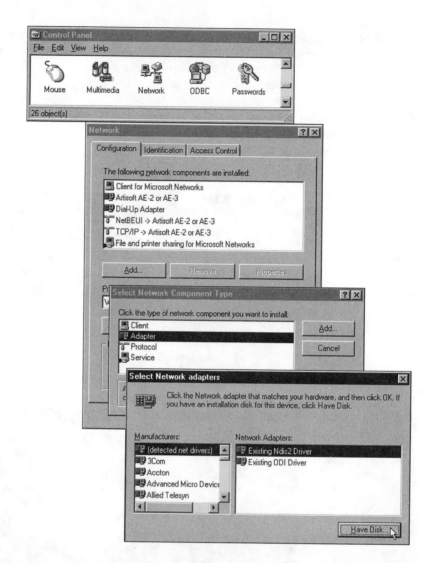

You are asked for the location of the disk with the information on the hardware. This is probably a disk in your floppy drive. Enter that appropriate location, click OK and review the Select Network Adapters menu, as shown in Figure 10.46. Here I've selected the Digi DataFire - ISA1U ISDN Adapter because I'm using the DataFire for an ISA bus and the adapter has a built in NT1, consequently, it has a U interface.

FIG. 10.46

Selection of the
DataFire from the
Select Network
Adapters menu.

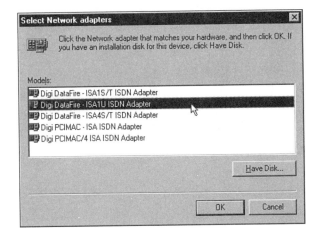

After you complete the questions, including the all important information on the I/O address, the software loads and you begin the process of configuration for ISDN use (see Fig. 10.47).

FIG. 10.47

Start of configuration
for the DataFire.

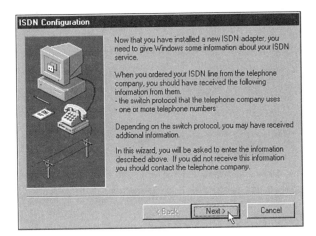

You must choose a switch type (see Fig. 10.48). Notice that most of the protocols available throughout the world are supported.

FIG. 10.48

Selection of switch type for the DataFire.

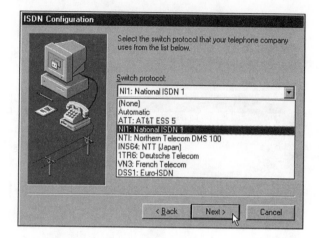

Then enter your directory numbers and SPIDs, as shown in Figure 10.49.

FIG. 10.49

Enter directory numbers and SPIDs as usual for the DataFire.

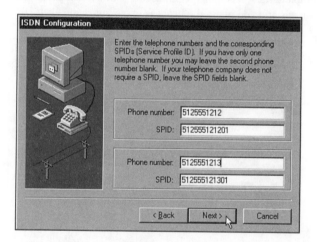

You are asked to insert the ISDN Accelerator Pack diskette (see Fig. 10.50). Since there may be several places that ask for these files, I suggest you put them on a diskette. Finally you're asked whether or not you want to restart the machine (see Fig. 10.51).

Get the ISDN Accelerator Pack from **http://www.microsoft.com/windows/getisdn**, where you'll find all sorts of other useful ISDN information.

FIG. 10.50

Here you're asked to insert the Microsoft ISDN Accelerator Pack diskette.

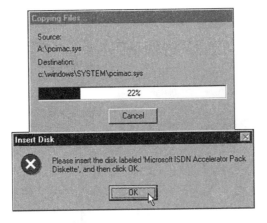

FIG. 10.51

Choose to restart your machine.

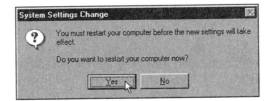

Once the machine has restarted, go to the My Computer icon on the desktop, double-click to bring up the My Computer screen at the top left of Figure 10.52. Double-click the Dial-Up Networking icon and once you're on the Dial Up Networking screen, shown in the middle of Figure 10.52, double-click the Make New Connection icon to start the process of setting up a real call.

 TIP If you need to change the switch type, directory number or SPID, click on Configure in the Make New Connection screen and you'll be presented with appropriate selections.

Click Next and proceed to the next screen, where you enter the phone number you want to call (see Fig. 10.53). After a final click on Next, another screen pops up, and you're through. You now have an icon for your new service (see Fig. 10.54).

FIG. 10.52

The process of setting up a dial-up networking connection.

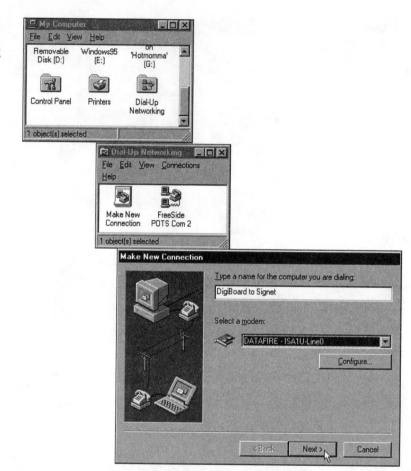

FIG. 10.53

Entry of phone number for the call.

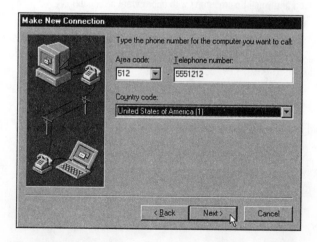

FIG.10.54

The new Dial-up Service icon.

Double-click the new icon and you're off and running. Or are you? Remember you must have set up the TCP/IP information for this to work in the typical Internet service provider situation. So, let's take one baby step back and click on the right mouse button of our new icon. This brings up a sub-menu with the Properties selection (see Fig. 10.55).

FIG. 10.55

Right-click the mouse and bring up the Properties sub-menu to begin set up of TCP/IP.

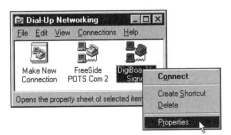

When you click here the general description of your connection appears, as shown in the upper left of Figure 10.56.

Click on Server Type and you see options regarding protocols in the lower right of the screen (see Fig. 10.56). Since all we're interested in is TCP/IP click NetBEUI and IPX/SPX off. You may now click on the TCP/IP Settings button and enter the appropriate IP addresses as shown in Figure 10.57.

At this point you're ready to connect and log on. Just return to the Dial Up Networking screen, double-click on the icon, enter any user name and password needed and hit Connect (see Fig. 10.58).

FIG. 10.56

General description of the dial-up connection followed by TCP/IP configuration settings button.

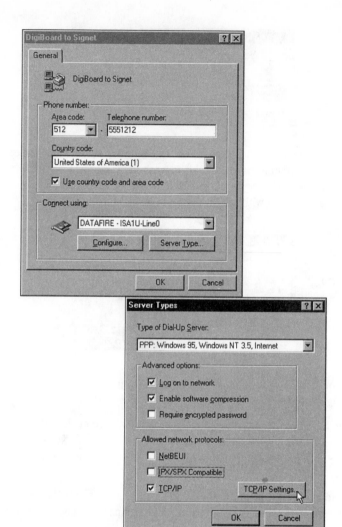

Alpha Telecom, whose NT1 products I mentioned in Chapter 8, makes the CyberJet internal ISDN card. It's available both with and without an analog port and in either S/T or U interfaces. Figure 10.59 shows the CyberJet.

FIG. 10.57

Here's where you put all the TCP/IP information. If you're unfamiliar with TCP/IP addressing, speak with your system administrator or Internet service provider.

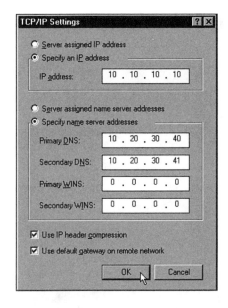

FIG. 10.58

Use the dial-up networking screen when you want to call a service using the DataFire or any other device configured for dial-up in Windows 95. © Alpha Telecom CyberJet.

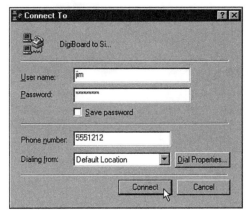

Part

III

Ch

10

TIP Jet to **http://iquest.com/~ati_usa** for information.

FIG. 10.59
Alpha Telecom CyberJet
internal ISDN terminal
adapter.

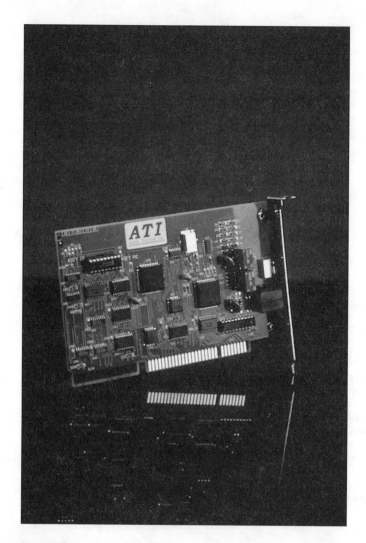

Lion DataPump

You can't even buy the Lion DataPump board in North America yet. It's offered in Europe and provides quite a bit, despite its low price (it starts at about $US300 list):

■ Two B channels

■ AT, CAPI, PPP command sets and protocols

■ Asynch ISDN-to-ISDN using V.110

- Synch ISDN-to-ISDN using PPP and V.120
- ISDN-to-POTS "modem" at 9600 bps and higher in some versions with MNP 2-5, V.42, V.42bis
- Fax capability using Group 3, Classes 1 and 2

To cut to the chase, the Lion DataPump offers essentially the same suite of features as the IBM WaveRunner in a smaller and less expensive package. So, where's the problem?

Well, this card's not available in North America. Its current version has no way to enter the SPIDs characteristic of our national ISDN specifications. Its documentation is difficult to understand, and its installation, configuration, controls, and user interface remind me of machine language programming.

 TIP Check out the head lion at **http://www.freebsd.org/˜jhs/lion/graphics.html**

Part
III

Ch
10

I've spoken at length with the company, though, and I've played with the card, and I see real potential here. The hardware and firmware is there; added ease-of-use could bring the DataPump tremendous success.

What Should You Get?

We're back to the main question. If you need asynch V.120, your choices in this group are the IBM WaveRunner and the USR Courier I-Modem (or the Lion Datapump, if it becomes a reality). It's my opinion, though, that the V.120 mode of operation will fade quickly and be replaced by synchronous PPP as part of TCP/IP. Probably the only other protocol of much interest is Novell's IPX, which is supported by the ISC SecureLink II and Digi International DataFire, but will also probably be taken over by TCP/IP. So, here's a summary of the choices to be made:

- If all you want is Internet access and a low price, consider the ISDN*tek card or other simple cards such as the ATI CyberJet.
- If you want lots of flexibility, with analog support and V.120 plus PPP, try the IBM WaveRunner or the USR Courier I-Modem.
- If you already have an external modem, don't need V.120, and might want to use ODI or NDIS along with WinISDN, take the ISC SecureLink II for a spin. This card and the Digi International DataFire support PPP and Multilink PPP, the most important protocols for the future.

All of these companies have proven their commitment to elements I deem important for successful vendors of ISDN products:

- Interoperability
- Clear user interface

- Well-written documentation
- Ease of installation if configuration
- Upgradability
- Excellent service and support

Other companies undoubtedly meet these criteria now, and many more will in the future. Finding ISDN products that make your life as productive as possible is a never-ending search; hopefully, the exciting innovations you encounter along the way will make the search enjoyable.

From Here...

In this chapter we've covered some good representatives of cards that can connect you to ISDN. Every day the selection gets greater, the price gets lower, and the field becomes more standardized.

In the following chapters, we'll continue to look at the nuts and bolts that make up your ISDN world:

- Chapter 11, "Establishing ISDN for LANs," gives you the third and final way to hook up to ISDN, through your local area network using an external bridge or router.
- Chapter 12, "Opening Windows 95 and NT for ISDN," a is totally devoted to issues of these two operating systems use of ISDN.
- Chapter 13, "Tying It Together: Two B or Not Two B," looks at joining B channels and compressing data.
- Chapter 14, "Pictures and Video with ISDN," examines the use of video with ISDN.
- You might want to look back at Chapter 6, "Unscrambling APIs," especially the WinISDN portion.

Establishing ISDN
for LANs

In Chapter 9, "Selecting an External Terminal Adapter,"
I discussed the use of an external terminal adapter for
connection to ISDN. These devices simply connect
through your serial port and use the AT command set; as
a result, your existing modem communications software
probably will work with them.

In Chapter 10, "Putting an Adapter Inside Your Computer,"
we looked at ISDN cards to plug into your PC bus. Things
grew more complicated because some of these devices
look like AT controlled modems, some like network cards,
and some like specialized devices. In short, they're a
mixed bag with a considerable amount of configuration
variations and possible combinations. ■

**Why a LAN may be the best
way to connect to ISDN even if
you have only one PC**

You'll learn about the data rate and,
yes, simple advantages a LAN can
bring.

**Routers and bridges are used
to connect a network to the
outside world**

You learn how they differ, see how
they are related, and understand
enough to distinguish one from the
other.

**Why network operating system
software requirements can be
simpler than you thought**

Find out that network operating
systems may even be contained
within you computer's operating
system.

**Cisco, the company with the
largest share of the commercial router market, is just now
providing routers for home and
small office networks—introducing the Cisco 1000 series
of routers**

You'll learn about this family of
routers based on Cisco's IOS router
operating system.

N O T E Consider this chapter a mystery story. As you read through all the commands and gyrations needed to set up routers, realize there is a resolution, a solution. If you just can't take it anymore, don't scream out the window, cheat like some mystery readers and jump to some of the descriptions of the newly developing graphical user interfaces. They are making setting up routers much like setting up a simple Windows computer. The year 1995 marked the end of command line dominance. ■

Now, we move on to connecting to ISDN through your LAN. At first blush you might think this would simplify things *if* you had a LAN. If you don't, though, I expect you're about to skip this chapter. Don't! I'll talk about why in the following section.

The products I'll mention are a sample of those in the marketplace. I've selected them because they illustrate a number of important issues. I've also selected these because they are in the range of prices I expect most readers to want. While routers can cost tens of thousands of dollars, these are priced between $U.S.500 and $U.S.1500, and the prices are dropping. Prices also are very slippery; the manufacturer's suggested retail price is only a starting point for discounting. As the market heats up and these hit the big computer store chains, they'll drop below $500. I'll only have time and space to address a few of the features of each product. The limitations we see will diminish over time as technology advances. Other companies do and will make similar products. In the end, you'll need to check out the current state of the products before you make your selection.

In my opinion, 1996 marked the "Year of the ISDN Router." Previously, routers were expensive and hard to set up. Most small-to-moderate-sized users avoided them as a result. In 1996, routers became much cheaper and developed graphical user interfaces, which make configuration and maintenance much easier. Now everyone interested in ISDN can seriously consider taking advantage of the router's universal nature. Routers support communication, independent of the hardware platform. So you can have a mixed network of Macs, PCs, UNIX workstations, etc., and use a single router to hook them all to various other sites including the Internet. All they need to share is a common protocol, usually TCP/IP and/or IPX/SPX. While you may need a particular computer or operating system to monitor and maintain a router easily, this is no limitation on its use with any other kind of computer for general routing functions.

T I P I'll post suggestions for your research on my Web page: **http://www.bryce.com/~bryce**. And keep an eye on **http://www.alumni.caltech.edu/~dank/isdn**.

Basic Ideas in LAN Connection to ISDN

Up to this chapter in the book, I've discussed connection of your single computer to ISDN. Now we're covering a way to do that through a LAN. The difference is fundamental. When using a single computer, our only concern is making sure that our computer and the ISDN hardware work together. When connecting through a LAN, we need to make sure the hardware and configuration work for everything we want to talk with on the LAN.

LAN Connection to Wide Area Networks

At first using a LAN as the connection method seems to make things harder. However, it actually makes things far easier than the single-computer methods I described earlier. Some of the disadvantages you'll notice in those methods include:

■ When you use the external terminal adapter (some people call these "ISDN modems" but that's an oxymoron) technique you run into all sorts of problems and limitations with the serial ports and often must buy and configure a better grade of port and driver software to realize the ISDN data rate.

■ When you use an internal ISDN card such as those discussed in Chapter 10, "Putting an Adapter Inside Your Computer," you run into a number of often difficult configuration and interface issues. Many of these are unique to the particular card.

On the other hand, when you connect through a LAN your operation is far cleaner. LAN interfaces for your computer have been developed and stabilized over the last decade and are well understood and standardized. All you need to do is insert a LAN card, install and configure its driver software, and connect a cable. This hookup is displayed in Figure 11.1.

FIG. 11.1
PC and Router on an Ethernet.

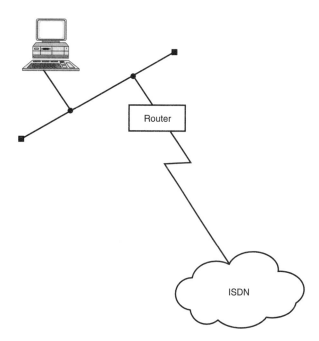

Part
III

Ch
11

Currently the technology for plugging in a LAN card is nearly "stick it in and turn it on." This removes all the PC hardware problems of the other two types, external terminal adapter and internal ISDN card. Plus you have a LAN interface with a data rate far in excess of your ISDN connection. If you use Ethernet, you have 10 megabits. If you use token ring, you have 4 or 16 megabits. In either case the rate is far more than your serial port, and the network card is easier to work with than today's ISDN card hardware.

Even though you may not now have a LAN, and even though you may have only a single machine, please consider using these LAN methods. All you need do is insert a LAN card (cost for an Ethernet card should be between $50 and $100) and attach some cable.

Once you've installed the network card, you simply cable to the ISDN router or bridge and configure that device. This is where the fun begins. Until late 1995 configuring a router was, invariably, a difficult task. As we go through a number of the routers in this chapter, you'll see just how difficult. Most of the problems come from a very user antagonistic interface. However, in 1996 a number of router makers introduced graphical user interfaces and the world of configuration changed dramatically.

LAN Connections Take Over

In the next two to three years you'll see a shift away from external terminal adapter (or "ISDN modems" in some corners of the techno world) devices and away from internal cards. The shift will be in favor of LAN-type connections. Why? Because most small offices and home offices will be using LANs even if they have only a few computers. Small LANs are inexpensive and easy to administer while giving a great deal of flexibility for use and expansion of the computing environment. And LANs furnish a standard base upon which to build ISDN connectivity.

Right now the easiest ISDN connection to make is through an external ISDN adapter, using the serial port on your computer. In large measure, this is due to the adapter makers' concentration on clear user interface designs and simple configuration plus the backwards compatibility offered by AT command control that can work with existing modem software.

Unfortunately this ease has not been the case with card, router, and bridge makers. The rapid price drops and introduction of easy-to-use graphical user interfaces is changing things radically. This will substantially erode the market share of external ISDN adapters. Internal cards continue to have a place, but they are confined to a limited role, due to their difficulty of configuration and their use only by one machine. In the end, routers will take over. In effect, routers will become the replacements for modems.

And for you Windows 95 people: Networking is so simple for a small system of two or three computers, you'll certainly have one set up. So go for the router to ISDN. You can connect from any of your computers, not just the one with the ISDN card or the external adapter. (Yes, yes, I know it may be possible to make those available to other machines on the network too, but a router will be easier and more flexible.)

This is totally opinion. But since it's mine, I'm sure it's right!

Routers and Bridges

I've used the terms *router* and *bridge* without strict definition. It's time to own up. What are they?

A bridge is a device that connects different networks and operates up through only ISO layer two (see Fig. 11.2), the data link layer. The bridges are each made up of the first two layers of the model. The lightning bolts in Figure 11.2 are from Captain Marvel (Shazam, to you younger fans); they represent connection to the WAN, in this case an ISDN cloud. This figure is a contemporary representation of comic proportions.

Because a bridge operates up through only ISO layer two, it can filter the addresses of devices on each network because those addresses are carried in layer two. It can't, however, filter the network addresses that identify different networks because those are carried in layer three. It also cannot make sophisticated decisions about optimum routing for packets.

FIG. 11.2

Bridges shown as parts of the ISO OSI Model.

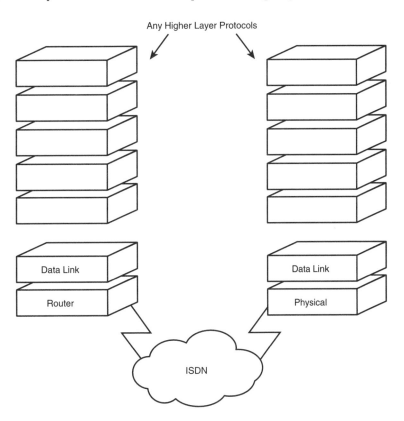

"So what?" you ask. When you use a bridge, it's unable to look at the information carried in the third layer (network) of the packet that might tell how the packet could be sent through the network. The bridge has to use simpler algorithms that may be far less efficient than those based on third-layer information. On the other hand, the bridge is simple and inexpensive to design and build when compared to a router. And, since a bridge does not look at the third layer, it's independent of any protocols at that layer and above it; you don't have to worry about configuring a bridge for TCP/IP, IPX, or some other protocol.

Routers do look at the third layer and must be configured for specific kinds of protocols (see Fig. 11.3). The routers are each made up of the first three layers of the model. In Figure 11.3 the lightning bolts are from Zeus (Jupiter, to you friendly Roman countrypersons); they represent connection to the WAN, in this case an ISDN cloud. This figure is a classical representation that presents thorny problems.

You may have a router configured for TCP/IP (often we just say "IP") and then have to buy additional software and do additional configuration when you want to carry IPX (Novell NetWare) packets as well. One way around this is to decide on one protocol and package or "encapsulate" all other protocols within it. So you might decide to use only TCP/IP and encapsulate IPX within the IP packets. This simplifies your networking at some cost to efficiency.

FIG. 11.3
Routers shown as parts of the ISO OSI Model.

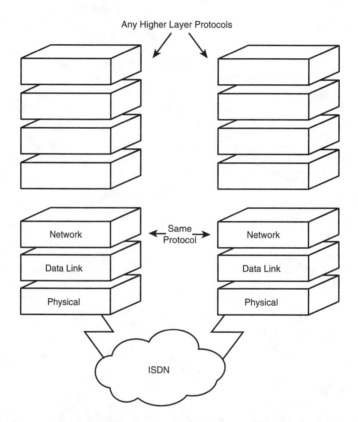

NOTE At this time, the move toward general use of TCP/IP is so strong that we see just the sort of suggestion I made (encapsulate IPX in IP) being done often. In fact, where there is an option, as there is with NetWare, many LANs are being converted from protocols such as IPX to TCP/IP so everything uses a common protocol.

There's some irony here, because a few years ago it was thought that TCP/IP would be replaced by a protocol suite developed by committees of the International Standards Organization under the OSI banner. The OSI proposals became complex and expensive to implement; at the same time TCP/IP was proven to be so effective and widely accepted that it became the hands-down choice for internetworking.

On the other hand, TCP/IP is difficult to administer due to the fixed IP addressing. So a number of hardware and software gateways have evolved to connect from TCP/IP to IPX/SPX. Then you use TCP/IP for wide-area communication and IPX/SPX for LAN communication. You never have to worry about assigning unique IP addresses to your LAN devices. Novix from FireFox and Internet Junction from Cisco are two examples of such gateway software.

Over the last year, a number of things have happened to solidify the movement to routers:

- Costs of router manufacturing have dropped greatly.
- Wide standardization on TCP/IP, at least in some measure due to Internet growth, has reduced the need for expensive multiple-protocol support.
- Competition in routers has heated up and prices have dropped.
- The user interface has evolved from command line to graphical.
- Demand for routers has accelerated.

All of these factors and more have reduced the price difference between routers and bridges so much that most firms are now selecting routers because of their greater flexibility and security. This has altered the directions of many companies and made for wholesale migration to routers. For example, Combinet, whose ISDN products I'll discuss soon, used to emphasize bridges; now, merged with Cisco, they are moving rapidly into primarily making routers.

Network Operating Systems

If you've had experience with networks, you may be asking, "Don't I have to have a network operating system like NetWare or Lantastic, and isn't that just more complexity and expense?"

No! This comes as a surprise to a lot of people, but you don't need a network operating system installed to use a router. You can have a network with no network operating system because all you're using the network for is connection to your router. To do this you must install a protocol stack on your machine (usually this is TCP/IP) that is identical to the one supported by your router. Then you configure the stack on your machine to fit with the router. Products such as the Chameleon line from NetManage, Inc., SuperTCP from Frontier Technologies Corporation, and TCP/IP software from FTP Software, Inc., are good representatives of commercial products containing the TCP/IP protocol stack and a good range of applications for its use. You also can simply use the TCP/IP that comes within Windows 95.

▶ **See** Appendix B, "ISDN Products: What To Ask and Who To Ask," **p. 577**

Of course you can have a network operating system. So if you're using NetWare, or Lantastic or Windows NT, you might select TCP/IP as the protocol for your LAN; then you have a common protocol for your router and your LAN. To make it more complex, in some instances you can run multiple protocols. For example, you might have NetWare with IPX. On each workstation you could load both IPX and TCP/IP. When you're using network resources such as file or print servers you communicate with IPX; when you go out the router you use TCP/IP. You would select this multiple protocol environment to gain the advantages of each protocol for your system. You must weigh what you gain by maintaining multiple protocols against what you lose by maintaining the added complexity.

As I mentioned in the earlier note, you may also elect to have a gateway on your network connecting TCP/IP—for example, IPX/SPX. On a NetWare network this could be software running as an NLM on a server. Then your LAN runs totally using IPX/SPX; the gateway connects to the TCP/IP of the outside world.

My purpose here is not to show you how to do all this, but to remind you that it can be done. We'll stick with the simple case of using TCP/IP over an Ethernet for the sole purpose of talking from a machine on the LAN to a router and then through ISDN to another router on a network either at your office or at an Internet access provider.

Of Baby Ducks and Threes

Scientists have done a great deal of research on imprinting during the first phases of an animal's life. For example, baby ducks that see some animal other than their mother first often imprint the animal as their mother and follow it around.

"What weird psychobabble is this guy throwing at us now?"

I'm glad you asked. With a new technology, the first instance you see, learn about, and use strongly shapes your perception of how and what that particular technology is. Then the next way of implementing the same type of technology seems wrong and out of step. When you become involved with a third implementation of the technology, you begin to see the general principles behind all implementations.

You've probably seen (and maybe you are) a fresh, young, bright person dive into something and absorb all its details, becoming an instant guru. The new guru thinks everyone else is a fool because they don't know the details. It's fun to watch when the guru must undertake another implementation. The result is confusion, criticism of how the designers did it, and so on. By the third implementation, the guru's now not quite so certain of the details of the first area, but has now grasped the general concepts of the field and learned that nit-picking details can be stored in documentation, thereby saving brain space for more mature understanding and judgment.

Just like the baby duck and the guru, we latch onto the first thing we encounter and often fight for the belief that it's the only way to go. Then, repeated exposures to other ways of accomplishing the same thing bring broadness of insight. It usually takes three different implementations to arrive at this stage. Let's call this the Baby Duck Syndrome crossed with the Rule of Three.

I'm presenting three chapters (9, 10, and 11) each covering different ways of implementing connections to ISDN from your computer. Within each chapter I've highlighted three different products (implementations). To repeat, my goal is not to become enmeshed in details of implementations, but to show there's more than one way to skin a cat, and each may be acceptable. I hope in the end you're conversant with the general principles; don't get hung up on the details.

My thanks to the J.J. Johnson, the Wizard of Industrial Cyberspace Designs, for this insight. I designed the chapters first. The Wizard then pointed out the brilliance of the design; great minds move in the finest circles (ahem).

 J.J. knows TCP/IP and routers the way a mare knows her foal (a little Texas for y'all) **http:// www.incyb.com/~incyb is his Web address; jjhnsn@incyb.com** is the e-mail address.

Cisco 1000 Series of Small Routers

Before you go one paragraph further, be sure and read the preceding sidebar, "Of Baby Ducks and Threes." Now you can tread into the murky depths of router design and configuration protected by those feathered numbers.

Cisco has the largest share of the commercial router market at this time. Their products are well-respected, very flexible, very reliable, and, until now, very expensive.

The Cisco 1000 series is designed for the remote office or home. It comes with an Ethernet 10BaseT (twisted pair) port, BRI ISDN connection, a terminal (console) port, and an internal PCMCIA flash memory card for configuration. Figure 11.4 shows the Cisco 1000 series router.

FIG. 11.4
Cisco 1000 series router.

You are now going to see how the user interface and configuration of a router can turn on a dime when a company makes a commitment to change. The 1003 that I reviewed for the first edition of this book was a beta unit just prior to final delivery. I think the only thing that made it beta was need for final FCC acceptance. The software reflected "experimental." In the first edition text, I pointed out some of the problems I encountered while using this product and expressed the hope that Cisco would remedy those that could cause you the most grief. In a word—Cisco has.

N O T E Companies usually send out a number of their devices or software packages for testing by potential users. These "beta" products are essential, because they provide real-world testing and lead to the discovery of bugs the developers didn't anticipate. Companies usually internally test the "alpha" versions; these are often fraught with a lot of problems. Beta (and alpha) testers are usually rewarded with free or reduced-cost products when the final "gold" (if the product is software) version ships to the general public. I participated in a number of beta, and some alpha, tests. They can be fun, but very demanding. The free products are never worth the amount of time you spend testing. So test if you like, but like what you test. ▪

This discussion of the Cisco 1000 routers is divided into two parts. The first is the very detailed description of my experiences with the 1003 supplied for the first edition. As you can tell from perusal of my observations, set up and configuration was a daunting task—so daunting that I provided Cisco with a "Bill of Particulars" describing the many problems that I ran into that I expected would be barriers to all but the most technically skilled and experienced users.

Cisco responded by totally redesigning its documentation and providing a graphical user interface to configure the routers. This interface, ClickStart, is usable with any of the Cisco router lines. In less than a year Cisco jumped from esoteric, command line driven, user antagonistic documentation and interface to one of the best in the industry. They're still not perfect, but they're doing much better.

The following is verbatim from the first edition. It includes the problems I encountered and the vital technical details about cables that you should know for the future. It also has all the IOS (Cisco's router operating system) commands to set up a Cisco router. If, and when, you need to know this stuff, it's here.

Cisco Configuration in the Dark Ages

> **CAUTION**
>
> Please, please don't get bogged down in this discussion of command line configuration and documentation issues. I suggest that you at least read the Notes and Tips along the way for ideas. You'll find useful information about Cisco, TCP/IP, and routers here, also. But, remember, the next major section, "Cisco Enters the Enlightenment," explains what Cisco has done to ease your life. Hopefully, you can avoid cabalistic incantations emanating from the darkness of the past.

I received what Cisco described as the final release documentation (a 36-page manual). I also looked over some documentation and release notes from Cisco's Web site: **http://www.cisco.com**. Cisco supplied a CD, "UniverCD," covering in-depth documentation and specifications for their whole line.

> **CAUTION**
>
> It's my understanding the UniverCD does not ship with the 1003. Since it contains a good deal of information you'll find useful in working with any Cisco router, and understanding "Cisco-speak," I strongly suggest you obtain it. When you use it, be aware the navigation is confusing. Going out on the directory tree branches is clear, but crawling back toward the root often offers you no way to review the intermediate steps you had traversed. Cisco, please consider redesigning the navigation to work more like Web browsers such as Mosaic. This CD is now called "Cisco Connection Documentation," a far more descriptive term.

Installing the Cisco Hardware   Let's hook this router up. I've installed Ethernets for over a decade and I like to keep little ones simple. So the one in my office uses the simplest cabling system possible for a handful of machines. Informally, the method is called "thin net" or "cheaper net," but when we're formal, it's called 10Base2. It's RG-58 A/U coaxial cable with BNC connectors. It works great. But, I've got a problem with the Cisco 1003. The only port it has is 10BaseT, twisted pair Ethernet. Ooops.

TROUBLESHOOTING

How do I hook up my thin coax Ethernet (10Base2) to the Cisco? You don't! In many cases, devices have an AUI (*attachment unit interface*) 15 pin Ethernet connection. This ties to an Ethernet transceiver. Transceivers are available for coax, twisted pair, and fiber optic cables. Cisco's assumption is that everyone is using twisted pair. This is not a valid assumption. Many smaller networks use coax. With coax you don't need to spend an extra few hundred dollars for a twisted pair hub. Besides, some of us find coax easier to work with in small networks. So, Cisco, please, provide a coax port and/or AUI, or even better, all three. Your competitors do; it doesn't cost much with today's Ethernets burned into hardware. I solved the problem by installing a hub that takes all three, but, at a cost of about $200 or more, why should you?

N O T E   Not that anything is wrong with twisted pair; I just don't like to see options left out for no good reason, especially when competitors include them. If you'd like to use a hub you'll find any number of simple ones that can handles four to eight devices priced in the few hundred dollar range. Hubs of this sort are commodity items. In a small system you don't need to pay for such bells and whistles as SNMP (simple network management protocol) in the hub. This feature could double or triple the cost. On the other hand, if you're in a large network that uses SNMP or you're connecting to a large network with SNMP, be sure the hub has the support.

Cable Follies—A Prelude to Disaster

When you cable up, pay careful attention to the back panel. The power supply connector is on the far right when you look at the box from the back. On the left are three *identical* RJ-45 jacks. This means you can get in real trouble, real fast.

The RJ-45 jack on the far left, at the outside of the box, is the ISDN BRI S/T interface connection. ISDN is stamped on the box, but it doesn't say S/T or U. It's an S/T interface; you'll need an NT1. Use a "straight through" cable for connection to this ISDN U interface.

The connector in the middle is for your twisted pair Ethernet cable. If you have a twisted pair hub (concentrator) the cable you use should be wired "straight through." That is, the same color wire should go to the same pin numbers at each end. I hope you have clear connectors. If you do, take each connector of the cable; hold them next to each other so their springy locking tabs are down and look at the order of the colored wires in each. If the order is the same, the cable is wired "straight through." If they are in reverse order the cable is "flipped," "rolled," "reversed," or "crossed-over" (the terms all mean the same thing). Chapter 8, especially Figure 8.10, shows this.

But there's even a third type of cable; a "null modem," or in our case, "null hub" cable. The intent of a "null..." is to connect transmit to receive; it's the same idea as a null modem cable that allows you to connect two serial ports together and then use modem programs as if you had a modem.

If you're connecting directly to an Ethernet card in the back of a computer, you must use a "null hub" cable to connect transmit to receive.

Cisco explains some, but not all of this in the manual. It also doesn't tell you how to tell the types of cable apart. Cisco supplies the cables, but doesn't explain that the two red cables are wired straight through and the single blue cable is a null hub. Don't rely on these cable colors; check your own.

The third connector from the left is the "Console." This goes to a VT-100 type terminal you use for setting up the router. In your case, it most likely goes to the serial port on your computer where you are running an emulation program that looks like a VT-100. If you actually have a VT-100, you certainly could use it. Among the cables I received from Cisco, the flat "silver satin" cable was flipped and used with an RJ-45 to female DB-25 connector to connect to a terminal or serial port.

Cisco's manual only directs you to use the "appropriate cable" in each instance. It provides nothing on how to select that cable or the colors they have supplied. This is absurd. I suggest to Cisco that they place durable labels on each cable explaining the type and use. The manual devotes three pages to telling you how to screw the box to the wall and the same number of pages to not telling you what you need to know about cabling!

If you use the wrong cable or connect the wrong device to the wrong port, you could damage or destroy the router and/or your other equipment. Be careful!

Finally, you insert the PCMCIA flash memory card into the back of the box and connect the power supply.

TROUBLESHOOTING

My Cisco 1003 doesn't seem to be able to talk to the NT1; what's wrong? The Cisco 1003 doesn't terminate the S/T bus. This means you must terminate the bus in your NT1. Check your NT1 documentation to confirm how to do this. Again, the Cisco manual does not tell you this.

Initial Configuration of Cisco 1003   Now it's time to move into configuring of the 1003. In this arena, the device is both blessed and cursed. Blessed because it's in the Cisco family and basically has most of the power and flexibility of the family, for example:

- Once you get the Cisco configured, it's able to switch easily among several telephone numbers.

- You can associate multiple subnets with multiple phone numbers. With this you can have the router configured so traffic for your Internet service provider rings up the ISP's router, traffic for your Chicago office rings that office and traffic for your network at home rings that number. You never have to think of who you're calling or what the number is. Each place is a subnet with a unique IP address. When the router sees that IP address on your network, it connects to the subnet using the phone number already configured. It's a miracle! Stick with me kid; when we reach the end of the Cisco section, you'll be a star.

- Complex filtering can protect you from hackers and limit excess network traffic.
- Multiple protocol supports gives you IP, IPX, Appletalk (perhaps at added cost).

And cursed because:

- The Cisco router configuration and syntax are obscure, obtuse, and the province of a cult of black magic wielding wizards. Unless you're one of these wizards, you'll have a rough time making it work. I'll step you through our model setup and hope to guide you past most of the deep ravines. This dangerous journey would have been impossible and disastrous without help from the Wizard of Industrial Cyberspace Designs.

 T I P Whiz to the Wizard at **http://www.incyb.com/~incyb**.

- Cisco basically assumes the router will be set up and maintained by these wizards and doesn't seem to understand the marketplace for the 1003 wants simple to understand and well tested documentation along with cookbook examples for typical uses such as Internet access and remote office connection.

Enough said. All said and done, the box works, but you may tear your hair out and lose sleep making it work for you; I did. Let's see if I can help. Go ahead; carefully hook those wires up and plug it in. Bring up your terminal emulation program, set it for 9600 bps, hardware flow control, 8 data bits, 1 stop bit and no parity. I used the terminal program that comes with Windows in the Accessory Group for my setup. Use what you like.

Part

III

Ch

11

 ### TROUBLESHOOTING

The screen of my terminal looks like Figure 11.5, displaying the `lost carrier, Transceiver problem?` **error message. What do I do?** This involves something else Cisco didn't tell you. If you have no active Ethernet nodes or hub on your network, you get this error message. In a big network you expect some active link. But you may be setting up one router with one PC and have no software loaded that can activate an Ethernet node. This is what you get.

By the way, you will get this error as well if you've not connected the Ethernet cable between your computer and the router. However, if you're connected to a hub, you don't get the problem because the hub creates the active state.

Solution: Some network interface cards you might use in your computer will transmit a link status signal and you won't have this problem. Other cards might not. If the one you have does not (your best indication is this Cisco error) you must load a program such as Chameleon and specify the Ethernet interface with your card parameters, thereby creating an active node.

Again, the Cisco's failure to understand the market results in your time wasted and another technical assistance call. This book's already paid for itself!

FIG. 11.5

The Cisco Lost Carrier/ Transceiver Problem is shown on this screen of continuous error codes. Check out the preceding Trouble-shooting box if you encounter this.

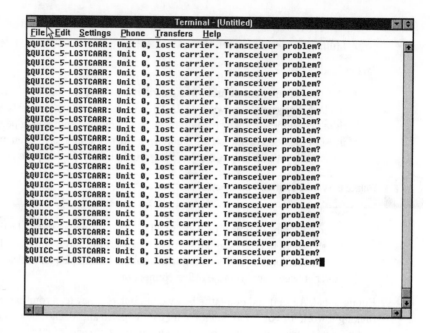

```
%QUICC-5-LOSTCARR: Unit 0, lost carrier. Transceiver problem?
%QUICC-5-LOSTCARR: Unit 0, lost carrier. Transceiver problem?
%QUICC-5-LOSTCARR: Unit 0, lost carrier. Transceiver problem?
%QUICC-5-LOSTCARR: Unit 0, lost carrier. Transceiver problem?
%QUICC-5-LOSTCARR: Unit 0, lost carrier. Transceiver problem?
%QUICC-5-LOSTCARR: Unit 0, lost carrier. Transceiver problem?
%QUICC-5-LOSTCARR: Unit 0, lost carrier. Transceiver problem?
%QUICC-5-LOSTCARR: Unit 0, lost carrier. Transceiver problem?
%QUICC-5-LOSTCARR: Unit 0, lost carrier. Transceiver problem?
%QUICC-5-LOSTCARR: Unit 0, lost carrier. Transceiver problem?
%QUICC-5-LOSTCARR: Unit 0, lost carrier. Transceiver problem?
%QUICC-5-LOSTCARR: Unit 0, lost carrier. Transceiver problem?
%QUICC-5-LOSTCARR: Unit 0, lost carrier. Transceiver problem?
%QUICC-5-LOSTCARR: Unit 0, lost carrier. Transceiver problem?
%QUICC-5-LOSTCARR: Unit 0, lost carrier. Transceiver problem?
%QUICC-5-LOSTCARR: Unit 0, lost carrier. Transceiver problem?
%QUICC-5-LOSTCARR: Unit 0, lost carrier. Transceiver problem?
%QUICC-5-LOSTCARR: Unit 0, lost carrier. Transceiver problem?
%QUICC-5-LOSTCARR: Unit 0, lost carrier. Transceiver problem?
%QUICC-5-LOSTCARR: Unit 0, lost carrier. Transceiver problem?
```

The 1003 that I received already had been configured. I proceeded to clear the non-volatile RAM that held that configuration so steps would look like those you would face with an unused machine. According to the manual, you may have a slightly different entry screen than that in Figure 11.6, but the remaining steps will be the same. The figure shows the non-volatile RAM (NVRAM) as corrupted. This is the message you receive when you have erased it. The device uncompresses the software. This can take more than a minute and in some cases may lead to problems because that's very near the time-out limits of some TCP/IP applications such as Telnet and FTP. This long time is characteristic of the entire line of Cisco routers.

You are next asked if you want to enter the Initial Configuration dialog box seen in Figure 11.7.

Respond **yes** to the question "Would you like to see the current interface summary?" and you'll receive the top part of the screen picture in Figure 11.7. This shows the initial configuration summary; you will definitely want to see it.

Now we're ready to begin configuration in earnest. In the default condition, Cisco has provided typical IP answers for most questions. The real question is which ones are typical for you, so let's see what we can figure out. As shown in Figure 11.8, I've entered cisco1003 as the name for the router. The next line asks for the enable secret; this is the password on the router; I've entered 1003.

Check out the screen sentence that follows your entry of the router name and its enable secret:
`The enable secret is a one-way cryptographic secret used instead of the enable`
`password when it exists.`

FIG. 11.6

The Cisco Startup Screen shows the erase of nonvolatile RAM.

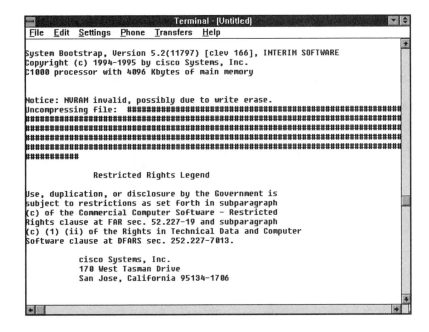

```
                        Terminal - (Untitled)
 File   Edit   Settings   Phone   Transfers   Help

System Bootstrap, Version 5.2(11797) [clev 166], INTERIM SOFTWARE
Copyright (c) 1994-1995 by cisco Systems, Inc.
C1000 processor with 4096 Kbytes of main memory


Notice: NURAM invalid, possibly due to write erase.
Uncompressing file:  #######################################################
###############################################################################
###############################################################################
###############################################################################
###############################################################################
###########

             Restricted Rights Legend

Use, duplication, or disclosure by the Government is
subject to restrictions as set forth in subparagraph
(c) of the Commercial Computer Software - Restricted
Rights clause at FAR sec. 52.227-19 and subparagraph
(c) (1) (ii) of the Rights in Technical Data and Computer
Software clause at DFARS sec. 252.227-7013.

             cisco Systems, Inc.
             170 West Tasman Drive
             San Jose, California 95134-1706
```

FIG. 11.7

Cisco Initial Configuration dialog.

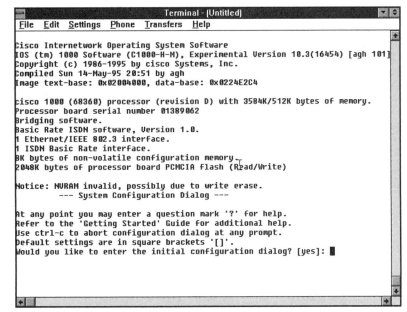

```
                        Terminal - (Untitled)
 File   Edit   Settings   Phone   Transfers   Help

Cisco Internetwork Operating System Software
IOS (tm) 1000 Software (C1000-H-M), Experimental Version 10.3(16454) [agh 101]
Copyright (c) 1986-1995 by cisco Systems, Inc.
Compiled Sun 14-May-95 20:51 by agh
Image text-base: 0x02004000, data-base: 0x0224E2C4

cisco 1000 (68360) processor (revision D) with 3584K/512K bytes of memory.
Processor board serial number 01389062
Bridging software.
Basic Rate ISDN software, Version 1.0.
1 Ethernet/IEEE 802.3 interface.
1 ISDN Basic Rate interface.
8K bytes of non-volatile configuration memory.
2048K bytes of processor board PCMCIA flash (Read/Write)

Notice: NURAM invalid, possibly due to write erase.
          --- System Configuration Dialog ---

At any point you may enter a question mark '?' for help.
Refer to the 'Getting Started' Guide for additional help.
Use ctrl-c to abort configuration dialog at any prompt.
Default settings are in square brackets '[]'.
Would you like to enter the initial configuration dialog? [yes]: █
```

Part

III

Ch

11

FIG. 11.8

Cisco Router Name and Passwords don't really mean names and passwords the way you probably think. Read the text carefully to see.

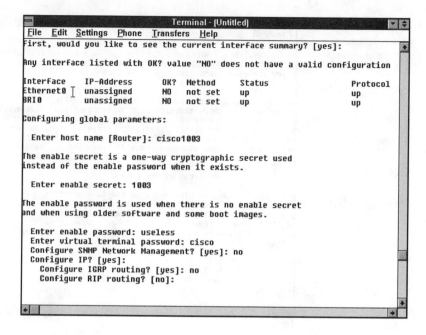

```
 ┌──────────────────────────── Terminal - (Untitled) ──────────────▼▲┐
 │ File  Edit  Settings  Phone  Transfers  Help                       │
 │First, would you like to see the current interface summary? [yes]:  │
 │                                                                    │
 │Any interface listed with OK? value "NO" does not have a valid configuration│
 │                                                                    │
 │Interface    IP-Address      OK?  Method    Status          Protocol│
 │Ethernet0 I  unassigned      NO   not set   up                  up  │
 │BRI0         unassigned      NO   not set   up                  up  │
 │                                                                    │
 │Configuring global parameters:                                      │
 │                                                                    │
 │  Enter host name [Router]: cisco1003                               │
 │                                                                    │
 │The enable secret is a one-way cryptographic secret used            │
 │instead of the enable password when it exists.                      │
 │                                                                    │
 │  Enter enable secret: 1003                                         │
 │                                                                    │
 │The enable password is used when there is no enable secret          │
 │and when using older software and some boot images.                 │
 │                                                                    │
 │  Enter enable password: useless                                    │
 │  Enter virtual terminal password: cisco                            │
 │  Configure SNMP Network Management? [yes]: no                      │
 │  Configure IP? [yes]:                                              │
 │    Configure IGRP routing? [yes]: no                               │
 │    Configure RIP routing? [no]:                                    │
 │                                                                    │
 └────────────────────────────────────────────────────────────────────┘
```

Now please tell me what the sentence means? Give up? So does everyone else. I'll translate for you. There are no users for a Cisco router. Rather there are privilege levels. There is an *enable password* and an *enable secret.* The enable secret is the "one-way cryptographic secret...." What makes the entire sentence I quoted above so hard to understand is its lack of a clear antecedent. The antecedent of "it" is "enable secret." So the enable secret overrides the enable password. "One-way cryptographic secret" translated from Cisco-speak means the secret (a password) is created in an encrypted form by the router but cannot be decrypted by the router (hence the "one-way"). The reason for going through all this is historical, and concerns routers using older software that has an "enable password." That's probably not your problem, unless you think about it too much.

The Use for Useless

If you're using this software to set up on a router previously configured with earlier software releases, then you must consider these issues. But this is a new, virgin router, and you're only going to be using this latest software. You'll only use the "enable secret," so this whole procedure is useless. Enter **useless** for the enable password as I have.

You're saying, perhaps, "Oh my heavens to Jehoshaphat, everyone who reads this book will enter 'useless' and everyone can break into everyone else's system. Help!"

Balderdash!!! The enable secret is an artifact of the past and "useless" to you. It only complicates your installation. If everyone in the world enters "useless" here, it won't jeopardize anyone's security one whit.

The virtual terminal password I entered is `cisco`. This is the password used to come in over the network and manage the router as if you were connecting through the console port as you are now.

N O T E Cisco routers have a privileged mode that is entered by executing the ENABLE command. When you do this you have total control over the configuration and status of the router. You can manage a router without a password on enable only through the physical console port on the router. You may then enter a password (as we just learned, Cisco-speak for this is "enable secret") for connection through that port. However, you cannot manage that router by logging in, for example through Telnet, from any other location until you attach an additional *virtual terminal password*. This protects against hackers getting into your most sensitive areas of router configuration.

TCP/IP Configuration of Cisco 1003   Now we'll go through a number of other questions assuming, as usual, you'll be using TCP/IP protocol in a small, new environment.

Configure SNMP (as shown in Figure 11.7) concerns your use of *Simple Network Management Protocol*. If you're involved with a large network, check with your network manager to see if you need this. If not, say **no**; be sure to say no, because the default is yes. Were you to enable SNMP on your router and your network manager to have it enabled on a larger network you're connected with, the manager could observe, and to some extent, control network activities on your equipment for fault diagnosis and security.

Configure IP should be answered "yes." That's the whole ball game in hooking to the Internet and the majority of other networks designed for broad connectivity. But the next line asking about IGRP defaults to "yes" when the chances are you'll want it to be "no." What on earth is *IGRP*, the International Goof-Off Recreational Phoxtrotters? Not quite. It means *Interior Gateway Routing Protocol,* Cisco's own way for routers to exchange routing information. You'll only be involved with this if you're connecting to another network and the system manager advises you of the need for its use. For a simple connection to an Internet provider this is irrelevant. By the way, were you to answer "yes," you'd know you're in trouble; the next question would be, "Your IGRP autonomous system number [ ]."

The next question concerns *RIP*. This is *Router Information Protocol*. It's an old IP protocol for routing. It's only useful for LANs now, because it floods a network with a lot of router "noise," router administration constantly has to update tables, and it causes disks to thrash continually. Unless an administrator tells you otherwise, answer **no**, the default.

The next series of questions asks about other possible protocols. My router had Appletalk and IPX. I think you could have a number of others such as XNS, Apollo, CLNS, and Vines; Cisco sells such additional protocol support as needed. Figure 11.9 shows some of these protocol options at the top.

Part

III

Ch

11

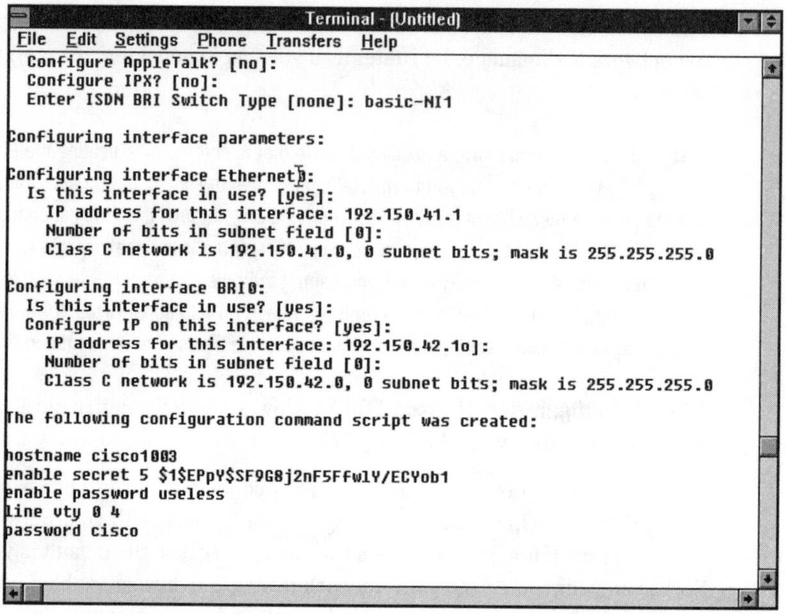

FIG. 11.9
Cisco Protocol Support
is shown at the top
within the selections
asking for configuration
of AppleTalk and IPX.

```
Terminal - [Untitled]
File  Edit  Settings  Phone  Transfers  Help
  Configure AppleTalk? [no]:
  Configure IPX? [no]:
  Enter ISDN BRI Switch Type [none]: basic-NI1

Configuring interface parameters:

Configuring interface Ethernet0:
  Is this interface in use? [yes]:
    IP address for this interface: 192.150.41.1
    Number of bits in subnet field [0]:
    Class C network is 192.150.41.0, 0 subnet bits; mask is 255.255.255.0

Configuring interface BRI0:
  Is this interface in use? [yes]:
  Configure IP on this interface? [yes]:
    IP address for this interface: 192.150.42.1o]:
    Number of bits in subnet field [0]:
    Class C network is 192.150.42.0, 0 subnet bits; mask is 255.255.255.0

The following configuration command script was created:

hostname cisco1003
enable secret 5 $1$EPpY$SF9G8j2nF5FFwlY/ECYob1
enable password useless
line vty 0 4
password cisco
```

OK. We made it to the ISDN stuff. This is the exciting part, folks. And here's the relevant question as it appears in Figure 11.8: `Enter ISDN BRI Switch Type [none]:`

Now you can see I entered `basic-NI1`. How did I know to use this since you'd expect from everything else we've read about that I'd enter NI1? I looked in the manual and found the possibilities:

■ basic-NI1

■ basic-5ess

■ basic-dms100

To be more precise, I looked at the manual, entered "?" at the prompt, and consulted the CD reference. The manual did not reflect the "basic-dms100" for the Northern Telecom switch. At this point the manual varies from what I saw on the screen. In the manual there are several questions on Ethernet configuration prior to the switch type. You learn to finesse around such matters, sometimes at great cost in time and money.

TIP Enter **?** at the Cisco prompt for help.

Here we go with setting up the Ethernet. Answer **yes** to `Is this interface in use?` This is an example of the fact that this is the same software used on the "big" Cisco routers which can have many different interfaces. The 1003 has only one. The next line asks if you want to configure it; answer **yes**. But now you may run into a problem with the next line, `IP address for this interface:`, because it fails to remove all the letters in the default response and you end up with some left-over characters as shown in Figure 11.8. In this case the characters are o]:. They didn't seem to affect our configuration.

At this point you're supposed to put in an IP address for this interface. But what IP address? Get that information from your office network or Internet provider. I selected a couple of Cisco's, 192.150.41.1 and 192.150.42.1, that are registered as test subnets. These are for demonstration only; if you actually used them and tried to communicate with the Cisco networks in question, things would bounce.

The next question is about the number of bits in the subnet mask. This really is obtuse. It comes up all the time in TCP/IP configurations. Let's take it a word at a time. A "subnet" is a defined a part of another network that's smaller than the whole network; for math freaks, a subnet is a proper subset of a larger network. In your case of using the Internet, the Internet is the largest network of concern.

Your Internet service provider (ISP) has established a network which is a subnet of the Internet. When you connect to your Internet service provider, your network becomes a subnet of the ISP's subnet of the Internet. Still with me?

Now, as you know, your Internet service provider either assigns you permanent IP addresses or dynamically assigns you addresses each time you connect. These addresses must be within the IP addresses available to the Internet service provider and defining the ISP's subnet (including customers' networks). Let's say your ISP has applied to the powers that be of the Internet (the InterNIC is such power that be) and received permission to use 192.150.41.xxx, where xxx is any number from 0 through 255.

Part
III

Ch
11

The ISP network administrator has the authority to parcel out the 256 available numbers in the last "octet" as needed; no one else can use these 256 numbers. Why do I use the word "octet?" Because the binary representation of the numbers 0 through 255 will take eight bits; 2 to the 8th power is 256. So your subnet can have addresses assigned by the ISP using any numbers in this range. For example, 192.150.41.78 and 192.150.41.193 would be numbers that could be assigned to devices on your subnet.

"OK, OK, so what's the subnet mask?" I'm glad you asked. Let's say you have a small network with 10 machines. Obviously you don't need 256 numbers to uniquely identify each machine. Since we're working in binary you need only 2 to the fourth power, 16 numbers, actually less. Using the subnet mask idea you have to work with binary places; you need more than 2 to the third power, 8. Once you've figured out the least power of two that will have enough numbers to identify all your devices, you apply the mask. The mask says to IP, "I only need to use up to the fourth power of two, so mask off four of the binary places and leave me with the remaining four. I'm reserving any numbers that fit outside that mask."

Now the logic gets tortured. In the example I've just used of four bits, filling in the subnet mask number of bits box is easy; enter 4. But what if you have six machines that need IP addresses and thus need only three bits, 2 to the third power, 8? Is that 3 subnet mask bits or 5? Does the number mean the places you use or the places covered up that you don't use?

Questions, questions, questions? Let's mask out some of this. That's it! The mask masks out 5 bits. There's the answer. The number of bits in the subnet mask is the number of bits masked out. Whatever is left over, 3 in this example, is the power of two that gives the number of addresses you have available, here, 8.

So entering 3 gives you the fifth power of 2, 8. Entering 7 gives you the first power of 2, 2. What does entering 0 do? Zero results in all 256 numbers being available; there is no subnet mask. If your ISP is assigning the addresses either dynamically or statically zero is fine. If you're building a more complex network with multiple nodes, each needing an address you assign, the subnet mask should be declared so you use up, "burn," the least possible number of IP addresses while allowing reasonable room for subnet growth.

N O T E The subnet mask is the key to what stays on your LAN subnet and what's sent outside. Any destination IP address that's in the IP address range defined by the mask and your source IP address is assumed to be addressed to devices on the same LAN subnet. Any other IP address is assumed to be for a device somewhere else. Packets with IP addresses outside the range are handed off to a router.

You have to have an official IP address or addresses to participate in the Internet. Official IP addresses are assigned by the InterNIC. You get your IP address assignments from your ISP or your company network administrator; these folks also assign your network mask to associate with these IP addresses. Never use IP addresses not assigned to you.

If you want to configure a test network or configure an internal network that won't access the Internet, you may use addresses that start with the number 10, for example 10.189.56.34. Any address that starts with 10 in the most significant, leftmost octet is not routed by the Internet backbone. Historically 10 addresses were assigned to the original ARPAnet, the predecessor of the Internet. When the final Internet design was in place, the addresses starting with 10 were retired for all time. It was like retiring the quarterback's number.

Obviously there are thousands of possible addresses of the form 10.xxx.yyy.zzz where xxx, yyy and zzz are each decimal numbers from 0 to 255. By using these numbers internally you don't have to worry about cluttering up the Internet or burning the limited and rapidly dwindling supply of IP addresses for nodes that will never participate in the Internet.

Assigning IP addresses from the 10 network to sensitive internal computers can be an effective part of an Internet security policy. You may also choose to use some IP addresses from the 10 network while waiting on assignment of your official IP addresses. That way you can begin configuration and test of your hardware and software for IP operation. However, you'll have to reconfigure the IP addresses and subnet masks later if these nodes are to participate in the Internet. ▩

The screen provides you a rundown of the entries you've made and creates a command script for you, as illustrated in Figure 11.10. If it's what you want, answer **yes**; if not, answer **no** and start over.

FIG. 11.10

Cisco Configuration
Command Script.

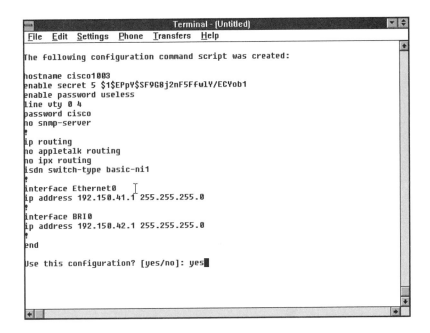

```
                        Terminal - (Untitled)
 File   Edit   Settings   Phone   Transfers   Help

The following configuration command script was created:

hostname cisco1003
enable secret 5 $1$EPpY$SF9G8j2nF5FfwlY/ECYob1
enable password useless
line vty 0 4
password cisco
no snmp-server
!
ip routing
no appletalk routing
no ipx routing
isdn switch-type basic-ni1
!
interface Ethernet0
ip address 192.150.41.1 255.255.255.0
!
interface BRI0
ip address 192.150.42.1 255.255.255.0
!
end

Use this configuration? [yes/no]: yes
```

Making Your Cisco 1003 Ready to Call Out   When you enter "yes" the router restarts with the new configuration as shown at the top of Figure 11.11. You now need to enter more configuration information. After the router restarts you'll see a > prompt. Type enable at this prompt and hit return. From enable mode you can enter additional configuration commands; you'll no longer be queried.

When enable runs you'll be asked for a password; enter the "enable secret." Now you're working directly in the privileged command mode as indicated by the # prompt. Y To continue router configuration you must first enter **configure terminal**, meaning configure from a terminal (as opposed to downloading a file).

Now you'll start entering the actual configuration commands that make your router work from day to day. First enter **no service config** to prevent the router from trying to load a configuration from across the network.

TROUBLESHOOTING

My router's gone into an endless series of loops trying to autoload configuration files that don't exist followed by multiple time outs that destroy my work. What happened? You've failed to enter "no service config." Of course, if you're on a network that has Cisco configuration files to download to routers, those files may be loaded and may not be what you want.

Part

III

Ch

11

FIG. 11.11

Cisco Configuration of ISDN SPIDs and PPP.

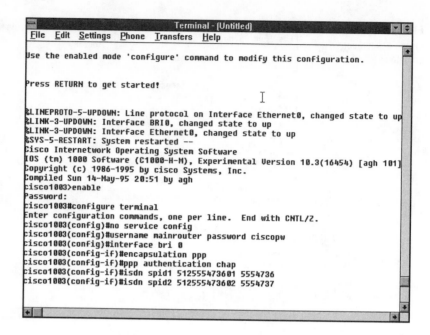

```
Terminal - [Untitled]
File   Edit   Settings   Phone   Transfers   Help

Use the enabled mode 'configure' command to modify this configuration.


Press RETURN to get started!


%LINEPROTO-5-UPDOWN: Line protocol on Interface Ethernet0, changed state to up
%LINK-3-UPDOWN: Interface BRI0, changed state to up
%LINK-3-UPDOWN: Interface Ethernet0, changed state to up
%SYS-5-RESTART: System restarted --
Cisco Internetwork Operating System Software
IOS (tm) 1000 Software (C1000-H-M), Experimental Version 10.3(16454) [agh 101]
Copyright (c) 1986-1995 by cisco Systems, Inc.
Compiled Sun 14-May-95 20:51 by agh
cisco1003>enable
Password:
cisco1003#configure terminal
Enter configuration commands, one per line.  End with CNTL/Z.
cisco1003(config)#no service config
cisco1003(config)#username mainrouter password ciscopw
cisco1003(config)#interface bri 0
cisco1003(config-if)#encapsulation ppp
cisco1003(config-if)#ppp authentication chap
cisco1003(config-if)#isdn spid1 512555473601 5554736
cisco1003(config-if)#isdn spid2 512555473602 5554737
```

Now we'll specify the name and password for the router we're going to be calling; get these from your network administrator or Internet service provider. At the # prompt enter: **username mainrouter password ciscopw**. For our example the router is named "mainrouter" with "ciscopw" as the password. In this example we're using CHAP for authentication; ciscopw is our example CHAP secret and mainrouter is our example name of the router we are calling.

> **CAUTION**
>
> Look out! The username and password are not the same as you have for your account with the ISP. Rather, they are specific to the router.

Let the box know you're configuring the BRI 0 interface by entering **interface bri 0** at the next # prompt.

Establish use of PPP by saying **encapsulation ppp** at the next #.

Set up CHAP authentication next with **ppp authentication chap** following that next #. This establishes the Challenge Handshake Authentication Protocol that is usually to authenticate PPP connections; check with your network administrator or Internet service provider to determine if you need this.

Finally, set up your SPIDs and directory numbers with:

    isdn spid1 512555473601 5554736
    isdn spid2 512555473701 5554737

or whatever SPID form your switch requires where the first number in the string is the SPID and the second is the directory number.

 T I P I've said it in other chapters, but I want to say it here again so you don't waste your time. Enter the SPIDs and directory numbers without any punctuation of any kind—no commas, no dashes, no spaces. Otherwise it will fail to work.

Now it's time to tell your Cisco 1003 how to call the other router, the one at your Internet service provider, office or wherever. Follow these steps in Figure 11.12.

FIG. 11.12

Cisco Dialer Setup and Partial Configuration Results.

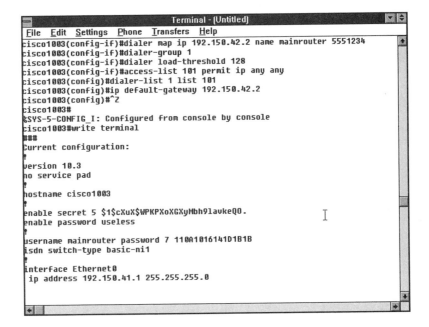

```
Terminal - [Untitled]
File  Edit  Settings  Phone  Transfers  Help
cisco1003(config-if)#dialer map ip 192.150.42.2 name mainrouter 5551234
cisco1003(config-if)#dialer-group 1
cisco1003(config-if)#dialer load-threshold 128
cisco1003(config-if)#access-list 101 permit ip any any
cisco1003(config)#dialer-list 1 list 101
cisco1003(config)#ip default-gateway 192.150.42.2
cisco1003(config)#^Z
cisco1003#
%SYS-5-CONFIG_I: Configured from console by console
cisco1003#write terminal
###
Current configuration:
!
version 10.3
no service pad
!
hostname cisco1003
!
enable secret 5 $1$cXuX$WPKPXoXGXyMbh9lavkeQ0.
enable password useless
!
username mainrouter password 7 110A1016141D1B1B
isdn switch-type basic-ni1
!
interface Ethernet0
 ip address 192.150.41.1 255.255.255.0
```

Part
III

Ch

11

1. Enter **dialer map ip 192.150.42.2 name mainrouter 5551234** using the IP address assigned to the router you're calling (mainrouter), the name of the router you're calling, and its telephone number.

2. Enter **dialer-group 1**. This works with the access list you'll create next. The "1" is an arbitrary number you assign.

3. Enter **dialer load-threshold 128** to say when the system is to use a second B channel to increase the data rate.

   Calls will start off using one 64 kbps channel. The parameter I've set at 128 says the second B channel is to be called when activity on that channel is sustained at 50% or more of that 64 kbps.

   How did I get 50% out of 128? Simple, if you think in binary. The parameter where 128 is can be any number from 255 to 1; 128 is 50% of 255 (about). If I wanted a higher percentage, I'd choose a higher number.

N O T E This load-threshold thing works so long as the routers on both ends agree on how to do it and both routers are configured to do it. If both routers are Ciscos you're in like Flynn. If the other one is so configured. But if the other router is from a different company, you're embroiled in the interoperation questions that are only now being settled among vendors. Stay tuned to breaking events by following the trade press, Internet newsgroups such as **comp.dcom.isdn** and Web pages such as mine, http://**www.bryce.com/~bryce**, that direct you to the latest scenes of battle. ■

4. Enter **access-list 101 permit ip any any** (the repeat of "any" is correct) to permit connection from any IP address to any other IP address. This defines the access list, and it is wide open to all IP addresses.

5. Enter **dialer-list 1 list 101** to create a list of access lists. Our list has only one element in it. The referenced list 1 points back to the access list (access is understood).

6. Enter **ip default-gateway 192.150.42.2** using the IP address of the router you're calling.

7. Press ctrl+Z. This terminates your configuration and returns you to the # prompt.

8. Enter **write terminal** to take the configuration you have done and write it to the screen so you can check it out. Figures 11.12 and 11.13 show this process.

9. When you're satisfied that you entered things correctly, enter **write memory** to store the configuration in the non-volatile memory of the router.

N O T E If you want to configure the router to communicate with more locations, you may repeat the numbered steps making new lists associated with different locations. Everything is keyed to IP addresses, not applications. ■

FIG. 11.13
Cisco Remaining
Configuration Results.

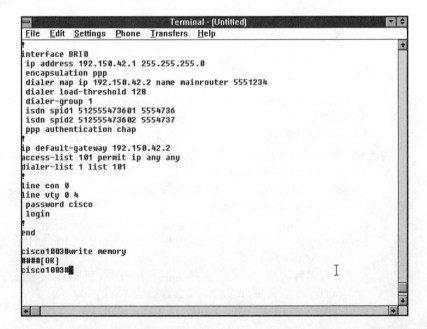

```
                          Terminal - [Untitled]
 File   Edit   Settings   Phone   Transfers   Help
!
interface BRI0
 ip address 192.150.42.1 255.255.255.0
 encapsulation ppp
 dialer map ip 192.150.42.2 name mainrouter 5551234
 dialer load-threshold 128
 dialer-group 1
 isdn spid1 51255547360l 5554736
 isdn spid2 51255547360l 5554737
 ppp authentication chap
!
ip default-gateway 192.150.42.2
access-list 101 permit ip any any
dialer-list 1 list 101
!
line con 0
line vty 0 4
 password cisco
 login
!
end

cisco1003#write memory
####[OK]
cisco1003#
```

That's it. That's it? Wait a minute. What about how I dial up the other router? How does my system know when to call out to send and receive packets? Good questions. In fact, they are the exact questions I asked my router wizard, JJ. Here's the trick. As long as the Cisco 1003 (or any other router) sees that a packet has an IP address that is within the subnet mask as you defined it during the configuration, the router assumes the packet is destined to travel only within your LAN. But when it sees a packet with an IP address outside your subnet mask, the router assumes that packet is destined outside, calls up the router at your Internet provider or main office and passes traffic. Is that slick or what!

Multiple Protocols   Of course, you have to make sure there are no broadcast packets or other overhead packets bouncing around and making the line go up all the time. One way to do this is to use one protocol for your LAN, for example IPX, and another for your WAN (wide area network), for example, IP. Then, when you want to send LAN traffic outside, encapsulate the LAN protocol in the WAN protocol with an outside address. The router senses the outside address and sends the packet out.

I've used TCP/IP for my examples, but many routers, including the Cisco 1003, can be configured for multiple protocols. If you like, you could have TCP/IP, IPX and AppleTalk all using the same router. Similar configuration procedures are involved with putting each on the router. In many instances you could have multiple protocols running on your users' computers. NetWare provides this option; Windows 95 can have a number of ISO layer 3 and layer 4 protocols (that's where SPX/IPX, TCP/IP and AppleTalk reside) running simultaneously. So you could be using Windows 95 to network with other computers on your LAN and have Frontier's SuperTCP TCP/IP stack loaded to communicate through your router with your Internet service provider. At the same time you could have IPX loaded so you could talk with NetWare nodes on your LAN and also talk with those at a remote location through your router that is configured for both IPX and TCP/IP.

You can also set time outs so connections don't stay up very long after information flow ceases. A router can be configured to receive calls from another device or LAN. So you could set up your router to answer calls from your ISP when Internet traffic with ftp, mail, or whatever arrives for you at your ISP.

The beauty of ISDN is obvious when you use routers: Not only does ISDN provide a higher data rate than POTS, it also gives a very rapid (often less than a second, sometimes less than half a second) setup and tear-down of calls so you only need to connect while actually exchanging packets. With analog equipment the 30 to 60 second setup/tear-down makes such use much less pleasant.

> **N O T E**   I really, really mean what I say here. It seems hard to take when you come from the idea of connecting and staying connected. But those days are over; connection when nothing is being exchanged wastes everyone's resources and does nothing for you even if you think it does. The less of this waste we have, the greater data rate each will have when it's really needed.
>
> The whole point of routers and ISDN is to use resources only when they're needed. If I'm reading a Web page already loaded into the memory of my computer, I don't need to be connected to my ISP. I only need to connect when I want another page that's not in my machine's memory. The speed of ISDN and

Part
III

Ch
11

a router makes the fact that I'm only physically connected when really necessary totally transparent. Believe it. It's true. Ah, yes, I saw a flash of understanding cross your eyes; or was that disbelief, boredom, or an urge to open another beer? ▉

Cisco Enters the Enlightenment

 Cisco discovered new tricks in 1996.

I doubt the marginal ditty will win any poetry prizes, but it's true. In fact, it's true for many other router companies, who suddenly realized they had to mend their ways and make routers understandable to "real" people.

In Cisco's case, response to enlightenment came in the form of a graphical user interface called ClickStart and total redesign of their CD based documentation that was renamed *Cisco Connection*. You can still do the same things with the 1000 series routers, but now it's much easier.

In this procedure, I assume you've already set up TCP/IP on your computer. ClickStart establishes an IP address for your router and configures it, using TCP/IP. If TCP/IP is not available on your computer, these procedures won't work. ▉

When I opened the box with the router Cisco sent me for the second edition I found a 1004 router. The 1003 and 1004 differ only in the ISDN interface; the 1003 has an S/T interface while the 1004 has a U interface.

The written manual I received still speaks of the command line configuration. Feel free to look it over, but your main reference is the CD. Pop it into your computer, select the Windows subdirectory (or Macintosh as the case may be) and run setup. You'll be greeted with the familiar Mosaic browser interface; you don't have to learn how to navigate a new menu or help system, just browse HTML/Web files. In fact, at certain points the hyperlinks are to outside resources. If your machine is already connected to the Internet, you'll be taken to the location. For example, if you need general information on ISDN, click on a link to find yourself on Dan Kegel's ISDN page.

 Here's yet another chance to visit Dan Kegel's page **http://www.alumni.caltech.edu/~dank/isdn**.

Much of what I found to be a problem in the earlier documentation is solved with the CD information. I was concerned about the confusing cable selection; the CD has a full explanation of all the types of cable—wonder where they got the idea that that was needed? Figure 11.14 is the page that explains this.

FIG. 11.14

Cisco CD help explains how to determine which cable to use to connect Ethernet to the router.

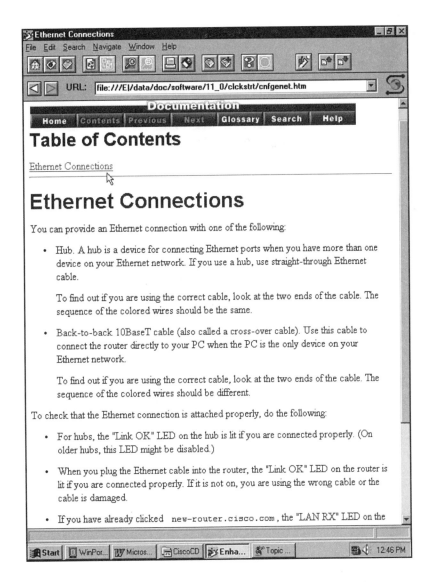

You get the idea. Let's actually look at some of the screens you encounter while setting up a 1003 or 1004 using the CD documentation and ClickStart. Figure 11.15 is your starting point. You get here by clicking on the icon that was created when you installed the CD, then searching for ClickStart.

FIG. 11.15

The ClickStart beginning page for configuration of the d1003 and 1004 Cisco routers.

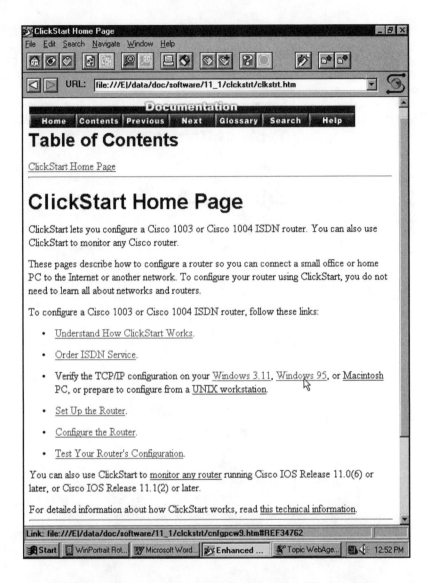

I'll assume you're using Windows 95 to set up the router. If you're using Windows 3.x or Macintosh, it's about the same. All you need to do is click on the Windows 95 Start button, select Run, and insert the CD drive letter (usually D:) in the drive field. Then put in the path to the ClickStart executable file \WINDOWS\CLICKHELP.EXE. When you run this, the screen illustrated in Figure 11.16 appears without the indicated IP address.

FIG. 11.16

ClickStart resolves an IP address for your router so you can communicate with the router over your LAN and continue configuration.

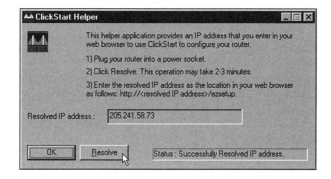

When you click on Resolve the software queries the LAN and devices for an appropriate IP address to assign to the router. During this time you encounter several Windows 95 error messages indicating conflicts with IP addresses; don't worry; click OK on each one. Finally an IP address appears. Now here's the trick. This IP address has been placed in your router. The browser then communications with the router using this IP address. So, do what it says: copy down the IP address and insert it, together with the EZSETUP reference as a URL, in the browser running on the CD (see Fig. 11.17).

FIG. 11.17

Insert the URL with the IP address just found into the browser, by using CLICKHELP.

Now all you have to do is fill out the form shown in Figures 11.18 and 11.19. Enter your switch type, information on the router names, and passwords, telephone numbers, SPIDs, and TCP/IP details. Remember that the program applied a heuristic method to determine the TCP/IP configuration; if this does not match your situation, be sure to change it here. Watch out for the line speed; it defaults to 56 kbps. If your ISDN line is 64 kbps, be sure to check that speed. When you're satisfied that everything's correct click on Submit.

FIG. 11.18

Notice the typical selections for router names, passwords, ISDN switch types, and phone numbers in the top half of the information form to configure the Cisco 1000 series router.

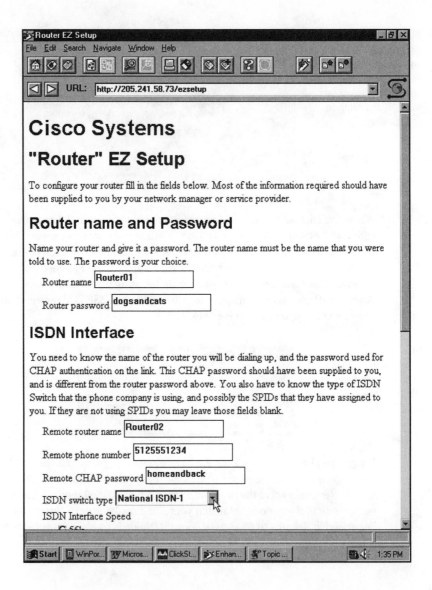

FIG. 11.19

In the bottom half of the information form (to configure the Cisco 1000 series router) you may want to change the IP address and other TCP/IP information to fit your network. In some cases the heuristic method Cisco applies doesn't get everything right. Be sure to set the line speed; it defaults to 56 kbps; if your ISDN connection is 64 kbps, be sure to click that selection.

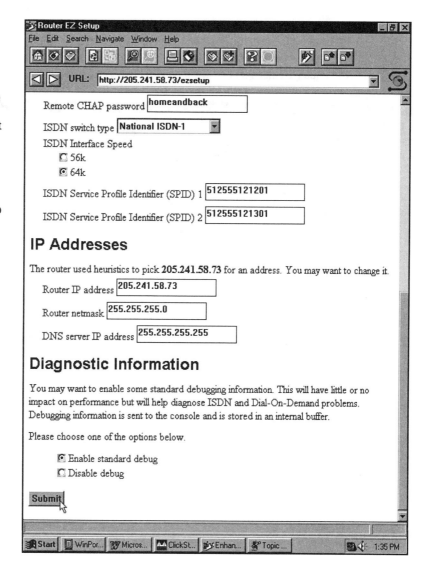

If you're successful, you'll be greeted with Congratulations, as in Figure 11.20. Now that the router has a recognized IP address you can use a TELNET program to communicate with it and enter the commands just as I illustrated in the earlier command line set up. You may also go to the Router Homepage, by clicking on that hyperlink (see Fig. 11.21).

FIG. 11.20

The Congratulations screen confirms that you've set your router up correctly. Notice the suggestion that you make a bookmark in your browser so you can visit your router at any time for configuration information.

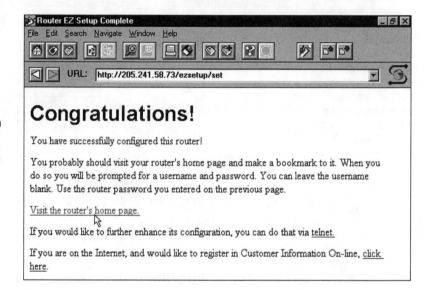

If you're sort of handy with hardware and software, you'll probably be able to get the 1003 or 1004 up in a couple of hours. This is a vast improvement over the tens of hours I found necessary when I tried to work my way through the command structure. Although there are still some rough spots that call on the intuitive feel of experienced users for a fast solution, set up and configuration is far better than a year ago. A hearty thanks to those at Cisco who made this possible.

FIG. 11.21

The router homepage with hyperlinks to various functions enables you to manage your router from any Web browser you have. You might have noticed the previous figures were in a Mosaic browser supplied by Cisco; this figure uses Netscape with the Cisco 1000.

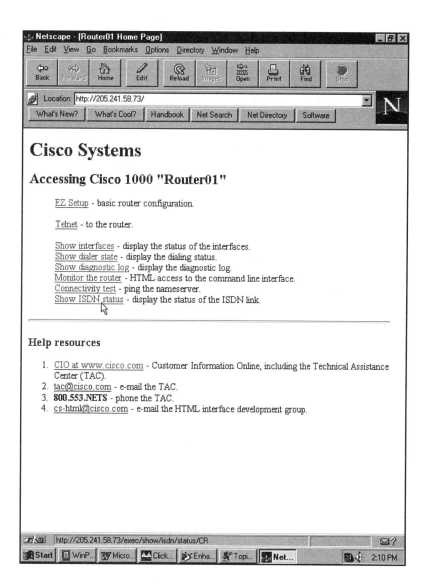

Ascend Pipelines

We started with the Cisco 1003 and noted that Cisco has the lion's share of the router marketplace. That's true for routers in general, but it's not true for ISDN routers in particular. That title goes to Ascend. Check out your local Internet provider that offers ISDN. The chances are very great that Ascend is the router used by your provider. Ascend has concentrated on ISDN router design while the bigger guys were buried in classic dedicated line and similar connections. Ascend has a good head start on them though in ISDN routers. In fact, Ascend is the box to connect with if you're selling to folks using the Internet through access providers.

NOTE   All is not sweetness and roses with Ascend and the makers that want to connect. Ascend joins B channels and uses compression in ways that are at odds with other vendors and with developing standards. This problem is rapidly disappearing as standards become more settled. See Chapter 13 for some discussion on compression and multiple B channel use. Ascend and the IETF committee involved are cooperating with the remainder of the industry to push this along. ∎

The Ascend Family

Ascend has two major families of ISDN routers. The MAX family consists of large routers for big organizations and Internet service providers. The Pipeline family has a number of members for the smaller office and home environment. I'll cover the MAX in Chapter 17, "ISDN Access for Internet Providers and Corporations." Now let's look at the Pipeline members for the SOHO world illustrated in Figure 11.22:

- Pipeline 25-Fx includes one ISDN BRI port, two analog ports, bridging, optional IP or IPX routing, optional data compression, ad four-user capacity.

- Pipeline 25-Px includes one ISDN BRI port, two analog ports, IP routing through ADIA IP addressing, optional data compression, and single user capacity.

- Pipeline 50 is available in ST and U interface. It includes one ISDN or Switched 56 port, IP and IPX routing, bridging of all other protocols, SNMP, Telnet, Syslog management, and unlimited user capacity.

- Pipeline 75 is now available in ST and U interface. It includes one ISDN port, two analog ports, IP and IPX routing, bridging of all other protocols, SNMP management, and unlimited user capacity.

- Pipeline 130 includes two ports support, one ISDN BRI or Switched 56 connection and one frame relay or leased line connection at speeds ranging from 56 Kbit/s up to T1, IP and IPX routing, bridging of all other protocols, SNMP management, and unlimited user capacity.

These routers have been the most popular workhorses for small office and home use. The various forms add or remove a few features such as the number of IP addresses that can be supported on your LAN. These differences are just the creation of Ascend's marketing mavens probing for the right mix to sell. The list prices vary from about $600, for the stripped version of the 25, to more than $1,500, for a loaded 130. I suggest that you'll want the IP routing and compression options with the 25-Fx. Other than that it boils down to POTS port support, and that's what distinguishes the 75 from the 50. In this section we'll look at the configuration of a 50 or 75 as the POTS ports are the only real difference.

 TIP Rise to **http://www.ascend.com**.

FIG. 11.22
Ascend Pipeline series
router.

▶ For the MAX, **see** "A Practical Example for ISDN Internet Service Providers," **p. 507**

Ascend's other products include the Pipeline 400 Series, which can support up to 24 analog/digital dial in users and the MAX that supports 96 such users over T1s or PRIs. These are the boxes your Internet provider is probably using. For example, the national provider PSI uses a MAX in Austin configured so you dial a single telephone number. The MAX determines if you're calling with a modem or ISDN and answers accordingly. Slick! So far as I know, all of our Austin, Texas Internet service providers that offer ISDN are using at least some Ascend equipment.

Setting Up the Ascend Hardware

The Pipeline 50 and 75 have both 10BaseT and AUI Ethernet connectors. So you can hook up any type of Ethernet cabling system though you may have to add a transceiver to connect through the AUI port. They have an RJ-45 jack for connection to your ISDN; different versions offer either an S/T interface, needing an external NT1, or a U interface with built in NT1. Terminal connection is through a nine-pin D series connector.

▶ **See** "Installing the Cisco Hardware," **p. 316**
▶ **See** "Cable and Connectors," **p. 185**

Part
III

Ch
11

CAUTION

The same rules regarding cables apply here as in the case of the caution about cables and connectors on the Cisco. At least the Ascend has only two identical connectors, an RJ-45 for 10BaseT and another for ISDN.

Be sure to use RJ-45 cables wired straight through. That is, be sure the same color wire goes to the same pin number on each end. The one exception to this is the case where you are connecting to an Ethernet card in a single computer and not using a hub. In this instance you'll need a cable that crosses receive and transmit pairs. The vendor for your router should be able to supply this cable.

Connect the Ethernet, ISDN, and terminal cables. Fire up your favorite VT-100 terminal program or use a real VT-100 and hook it up.

Hook up the Ascend and plug in the power supply. The 50/75 has no power switch. The little switch on the back is "reserved for future use." When you look at the terminal you will see a screen similar to the one in Figure 11.23.

FIG. 11.23

Ascend Power On Self Test.

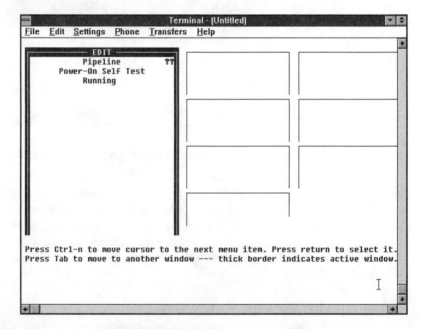

Configuring the Ascend Identity for ISDN

Now Press Ctrl+L to refresh the screen and a screen similar to Figure 11.24 appears. You traverse down the configuration list either selecting from items by toggling or entering strings of characters. The greater than (>) sign appears to the left of the item you're working with; in

Figure 11.24, > appears next to My Name=. On items such as the switch you toggle by pressing Enter until you get the right item, NI-1 in Figure 11.24. The next selection Chan Usage would usually be set as shown, Switch/Switch, unless you have some sort of dedicated line arrangement. My NumA and My NumB refer to the directory numbers of your ISDN line; the SPIDs are set on the following lines. When you enter a string, brackets ([ ]) appear and you insert the characters within them; when you finish and hit enter, the brackets disappear. Notice that you press Ctrl+n to move down the screen; in some terminal connections you're cursor (arrow) key will work, but don't count on it.

FIG. 11.24

Ascend Configuration starting with POST.

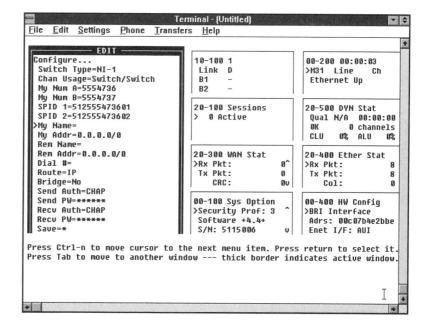

Press Ctrl-n to move cursor to the next menu item. Press return to select it.
Press Tab to move to another window --- thick border indicates active window.

T I P The form of the directory numbers and SPIDs is dependent on your local exchange carrier (the fancy way to say your local phone company whose ISDN switch you're using). All Ascend or any other ISDN device you have does is send the information to the switch. If that information is not in the correct form for the specific switch, it won't work. Check with your phone company. I've noticed the Pipeline requires you enter directory numbers *without* area codes but SPIDs *with* area codes.

As you continue down the screen to My Name, brackets appear and you enter the name of this router. This can be anything you like. In our example, shown in Figure 11.25, Ascend-p50 was used. Although it was used in the example, you don't have to use the maker's name.

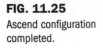
FIG. 11.25
Ascend configuration
completed.

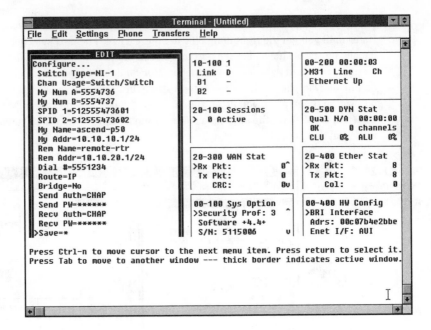

Configuring Ascend for TCP/IP

Continue on down the screen, selecting the address next. Your network administrator or Internet service provider will give this number to you.

Next, you enter the number you want the router to call when it sees IP addresses outside your network. Select No at the next field to avoid bridging. Below that, select CHAP and enter passwords for both transmit and receive. Now save the whole thing by pressing Enter when you reach Save at the bottom of the screen.

> **N O T E** Hats off to Ascend for a very clear manual on how to install the Pipeline 50. It's about 35 pages long and fairly easy to use. Of course you can still run into a brick wall if you don't have a network administrator to tell you what to put in for an IP address; Ascend presupposes that administrator. I'll do my best to fill in.
>
> The 75 came with two larger manuals in substantial detail. I found the "Users Guide" hardware setup and quick start chapter most helpful. ■

Press the Esc key until you arrive at the Main Edit Menu, as shown in Figure 11.26. Here cursor down and select System. This puts you into the System submenu where you can select Sys Diag as shown in Figure 11.27. We're about to test all of our setup so we have to burrow through the menu system to set things up. Get out your digging tools.

FIG 11.26
Ascend Main Edit
Menu.

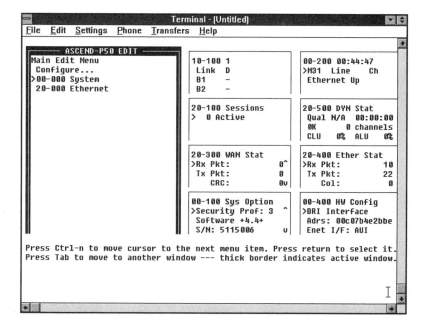

FIG. 11.27
Ascend System
Diagnostics Selection.

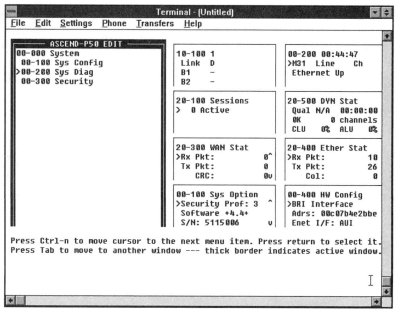

Within the diagnostics selection choose Terminal Service, as shown in Figure 11.28.

FIG. 11.28

Ascend Terminal Service.

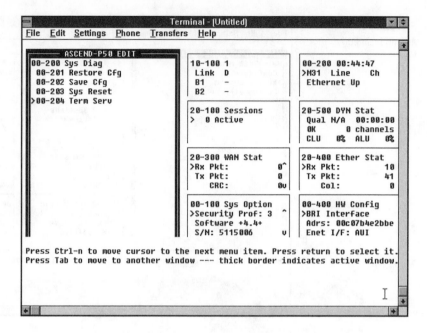

```
┌─────────────────────── Terminal - [Untitled] ─────────────────────────┐
│  File   Edit   Settings   Phone   Transfers   Help                     │
├────────────────────────────────────────────────────────────────────── │
│  ┌── ASCEND-P50 EDIT ──┐   ┌──────────────┐   ┌──────────────────┐     │
│  │ 00-200 Sys Diag     │   │ 10-100  1    │   │ 00-200 00:44:47  │     │
│  │  00-201 Restore Cfg │   │  Link  D     │   │ >M31  Line    Ch │     │
│  │  00-202 Save Cfg    │   │  B1    -     │   │  Ethernet Up     │     │
│  │  00-203 Sys Reset   │   │  B2    -     │   └──────────────────┘     │
│  │ >00-204 Term Serv   │   └──────────────┘                            │
│  │                     │   ┌──────────────┐   ┌──────────────────┐     │
│  │                     │   │ 20-100 Sessions  │ 20-500 DYN Stat  │     │
│  │                     │   │ >  0 Active  │   │  Qual N/A  00:00:00│   │
│  │                     │   │              │   │  OK      0 channels│   │
│  │                     │   │              │   │  CLU   0%  ALU   0%│   │
│  │                     │   └──────────────┘   └──────────────────┘     │
│  │                     │   ┌──────────────┐   ┌──────────────────┐     │
│  │                     │   │ 20-300 WAN Stat  │ 20-400 Ether Stat│     │
│  │                     │   │ >Rx Pkt:    0^   │ >Rx Pkt:      10 │     │
│  │                     │   │  Tx Pkt:    0    │  Tx Pkt:      41 │     │
│  │                     │   │    CRC:     0v   │    Col:        0 │     │
│  │                     │   └──────────────┘   └──────────────────┘     │
│  │                     │   ┌──────────────┐   ┌──────────────────┐     │
│  │                     │   │ 00-100 Sys Option│ 00-400 HW Config │     │
│  │                     │   │ >Security Prof: 3^│ >BRI Interface  │     │
│  │                     │   │  Software +4.4+  │  Adrs: 00c07b4e2bbe│   │
│  └─────────────────────┘   │  S/N: 5115006  v │  Enet I/F: AUI   │     │
│                            └──────────────┘   └──────────────────┘     │
│  Press Ctrl-n to move cursor to the next menu item. Press return to    │
│  select it.                                                            │
│  Press Tab to move to another window --- thick border indicates active │
│  window.                                                               │
│                                                                  I     │
└────────────────────────────────────────────────────────────────────── ┘
```

This brings up the internal terminal on the router. Figure 11.29 shows this terminal screen after we've requested help by entering help at the ascend% prompt. This gives you the types of help available here. Now at the ascend% prompt, type **test** to call the number 5554737.

FIG 11.29

Ascend Test of ISDN Configuration.

```
┌─────────────────────── Terminal - [Untitled] ─────────────────────────┐
│  File   Edit   Settings   Phone   Transfers   Help                     │
├────────────────────────────────────────────────────────────────────── │
│ ascend% help                                                           │
│ ?                       Display help information                       │
│ help                         "        "        "                       │
│ quit                    Closes terminal server session                 │
│ hangup                       "        "        "                       │
│ test                    test <phone-number> [ <frame-count> ] [ <optional fields>│
│ local                   Go to local mode                               │
│ set                     Set various items. Type 'set ?' for help       │
│ show                    Show various tables. Type 'show ?' for help     │
│ iproute                 Manage IP routes.  Type 'iproute ?' for help    │
│ telnet                  telnet [ -a| -b ] <host-name> [ <port-number> ] │
│ tcp                     tcp <host-name> <port-number>                   │
│ ascend% test 5554737                                                   │
│ calling...                                                             │
│ Error: call failed                                                     │
│                                                                        │
│ ascend% show isdn                                                      │
│ PH: ACTIVATED                                                          │
│ DL: TEI ASSIGNED  85                                                   │
│ DL: TEI ASSIGNED  86                                                   │
│ NL: CALL REQUEST: 56K, #5554737                                        │
│ NL: CALL CLEARED WITH CAUSE: 4  #5554737                               │
│                                                                        │
│ ascend% █                                                              │
│                                                                  I     │
└────────────────────────────────────────────────────────────────────── ┘
```

Oops, it failed. Let's ask it to show the status of ISDN by entering **show isdn** at the prompt. This tells us the phone line is activated, the terminal identifiers 85 and 86 have been delivered from the switch to the router through association with the SPIDs, and a call request has been made at 56 kbps to the number 5554737. But the sad news is we have an error, `call cleared with cause: 4 #5554737`. What happened?

Unfortunately the cause code 4 while documented, is still unclear; the documentation tells us Cause Code 4 means *send special information tone*. While I'm glad Ascend has this in their current manual (it wasn't in the manual I had for the first edition) it's unfortunate that the code is not more specific. But that's not Ascend's oversight; these are standard codes for ISDN. Fortunately, we figured out the problem: 5554737 is not a valid ISDN number.

While the external terminal adapters and computer cards frequently have tests using analog lines, routers almost never do. If you have a separate directory number for each B channel, try calling one B channel from the other. You'll probably run into a couple of errors before your configuration works. Persevere. A successful test would show something like the following:

```
ascend% test 5554747
calling......answering....testing....end
100 packets sent, 100 packets received
```

N O T E If the test fails, check out the parameters you've entered. Also check to see that you actually saved them. Then reset the router by using the Sys Reset function in the Sys Diag menu. Sometimes things don't really reset until you've rebooted. Use Quit to get it to terminate. ■

So, a couple of test questions:

- *Why do you suppose most illustrations use 555 as an exchange?* Because there are no standard subscriber numbers that use that exchange. I know 5551212 gives information and there are few other special numbers for the telephone company, but 555 assures us that people won't be calling our numbers if they follow the screens literally.

- *How did we end up with a 56 kbps data rate?* It seems the device defaults to 56 kbps. You see Ascend is in California. Unfortunately much of California's telephone system does not have Signaling System 7 (see Chapter 5). Consequently, they have to carry the ISDN D channel signals within a 64 kbps channel, thereby robbing 8 kbps of data rate and leaving 56 kbps. Ascend, thinking that if California has such an impediment, the remainder of the world, always more backward than California, couldn't possibly have any better, assumes everyone is using 56 kbps and defaults the box to it. I've even been told by Europeans that we in the States are blighted with 56 kbps everywhere. When I've traced the fount of their knowledge, it invariably leads only to California. We in Texas never have slowed down to wait for California; we go full bore with 64 kbps and "real" rather than "robbed" ISDN!

Escape back to the Main Menu, then select the Ethernet Menu and you'll see a screen similar to the one in Figure 11.30. Select Connections, as shown, and go on to review the current state of your configuration by drilling down through 20-100 Connections and selecting the remote-rtr. This takes you to the current configuration shown in Figure 11.31; these are the settings from the original configuration. Many are defaults you may want to change. From here you can drill down to any of the settings and make adjustments. To change the 56 kbps select Telco options and you'll find the line speeds. Notice the numbers are well organized. You started at 20-100 Connections and went to 20-101 remote-rtr, as sub-menu.

FIG. 11.30

Ascend Ethernet Configuration.

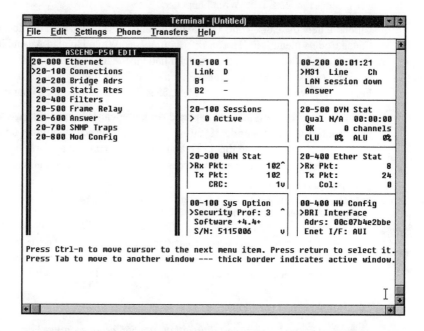

FIG. 11.31

Ascend Connection Profile.

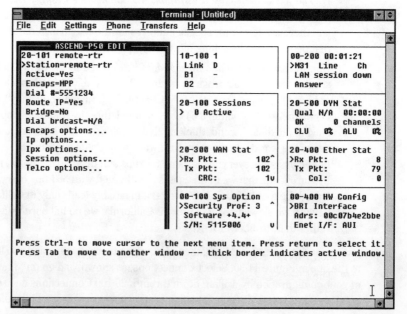

Once you catch on to the way you jump among the screens, the Ascend menu system is fairly easy to work with. It's a great improvement on working directly in commands. But it would be better yet if Ascend would design a graphical front end that would work under Windows (and perhaps other operating systems) making everything nearly intuitive. And they have. It's called the "Configurator" and was in the process of development as I wrote this book. Figure 11.32 shows the Configurator screen based on software for the MAX 200.

 TIP If you didn't receive the Configurator with your Pipeline, check out **http://www.ascend.com** for a free upgrade. You may find it in **ftp://ftp.ascend.com/pub/software-Releases/Configurator** also.

FIG. 11.32
Ascend Configurator graphical user interface for setup, configuration and management of the MAX 200 router. A similar interface is available for the Pipeline series.©Cisco 752 (otherwise known as Combinet 2060).

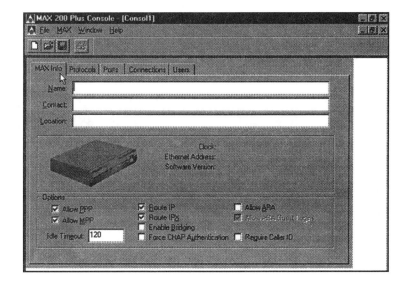

Part III

Ch 11

Cisco 750 Series Routers

Combinet was founded to be well-focused on ISDN products. It's been so well-focused that Cisco acquired Combinet in mid-1995.

We'll concentrate on the Combinet 2060 device in the 2000 series. This is now known as a Cisco 752, and I'll probably hop back and forth between the two designations as we go; most people in the industry still view the Cisco 1000 line and the Combinet 2000 line as very distinct. I'm sure over time there will be a melding. Here's a description of the various 750 routers:

- The Cisco 751 multiprotocol ISDN router connects small offices or home offices that have Ethernet LANs to WANs using an ISDN BRI port. The Cisco 751 is the solution of choice for international users or users who prefer to use an external Network Termination 1 (NT1) device for connecting to the ISDN network.

- The Cisco 752 router includes a built-in NT1 device for ISDN users in North America. In addition to the integrated NT1, the Cisco 752 provides an external S/T port to support additional ISDN devices, such as ISDN telephones.

■ The Cisco 753 includes both an external analog telephone interface and a built-in NT1. Using Cisco's call priority feature, the Cisco 753 can drop one data channel to accept or initiate a voice call if both B channels are being used for data. Initial configuration options for the Cisco 753 can be entered using a standard touch-tone telephone.

This is a conveniently designed unit with 10BaseT (twisted pair) and 10Base2 (thin coax) Ethernet ports. It has a built in NT1 so the ISDN uses a U interface. Another model, the 751, comes with an S/T interface and requires an external NT1. The 750s also have a nine pin D series connector for attachment to a VT-100 terminal or emulator and a power connector for an external power supply. Don't forget the power switch on the back. Some of the other boxes we've looked at don't have a switch, the 750s do. One more connector is on the back of the 752 and 753—an ISDN S/T interface for connection of additional ISDN equipment such as an ISDN phone or FAX. The installation manual explains that an external power supply may be needed for such equipment and describes how to use it. The 750 products route TCP/IP and SPX/IPX; they bridge everything else.

CAUTION

The back panels of the 752 and 753 have three RJ-45 modular jacks. The one on the far left as you look from behind is the ISDN U interface. The next one is the S/T interface for connection to other ISDN equipment, *not an alternative for connection to an external NT1*, then you'll find the BNC connector for coax and the last RJ-45 for twisted pair Ethernet.

As I said earlier in a caution within the Cisco discussion, please be careful in connecting to such RJ-45 jacks; an incorrect connection could be costly.

In the package I received, I found two gray cables with RJ-45 plugs wired straight through and one gray cable with RJ-11 plugs wired straight through. The *Installation and Hardware Guide* has clear instructions and diagrams on cabling. If you have a hub, connect an RJ-45 cable from the 10BaseT, or 10BT, port to the hub. But if you have only a computer with a 10BaseT card in it, you'll have to reverse transmit and receive.

In the Cisco 1000 case I described previously, you must carefully choose from among three possible types of cable. With the 750 series, you always use the same straight through cable and make the reversal by moving jumpers inside the unit as described on the last page of the installation guide. Also, unlike the Cisco 1000, should you be using a device without an internal NT1, such as the 751, you may set internal terminators as described in the installation manual.

The 750 series stands out from competitors by having truly useful and understandable indicator lights on the front. Take a look at this list of lights, their functions and the nomenclature used on the panel to see what I mean:

■ *Rdy.* Powered, and software loaded and ready

■ *NT1.* NT1 connected to switch: a steady light means fully synchronized with the switch; fast blink means it's attempting to synchronize with the switch; slow blink means it's attempting to synchronize with the ISDN terminal device

- *LAN.* A packet has been received from the LAN and the LAN connection is therefore active
- *RXD.* Blinks each time a LAN packet is received
- *TXD.* Blinks each time a LAN packet is transmitted
- *CH1.* Blinks when a call is being connected to ISDN channel 1; stays on when connected
- *RXD.* Blinks for each channel 1 packet received
- *TXD.* Blinks for each channel 1 packet transmitted
- *CH2.* Blinks when a call is being connected to ISDN channel 2; stays on when connected
- *RXD.* Blinks for each channel 2 packet received
- *TXD.* Blinks for each channel 2 packet transmitted

These indications are very easy to understand, reassuring, and helpful in running down problems. Cisco is expanding this line with the 760 series. Figure 11.33 illustrates the 760. Notice that the indicator lights are just as I described with the important addition of two more lights, PH1 and PH2, one for each B channel. This is a very important addition. It enables you to monitor your ISDN lines at a glance.

FIG. 11.33
Cisco 760 series router. Notice the addition of two indicator lights for B channel usage.

 TROUBLESHOOTING

My NT1 light is out or blinking quickly. You're not yet synched with the switch so there's no reason to check elsewhere until the light goes steady. If it continues to blink or doesn't come on, chances are you've got a bad connection. First check the wiring from the demarc to the device. If you find no problems there, call the phone company to ask for a loop back test from the switch to see if they can see your NT1. If they can't see the NT1 and you're sure the wiring is good, it implies there's a problem with the telco system prior to the demarc.

▶ **See** "Where the Telco Line Stops and Your Wiring Begins (Demarc)," **p. 181**, and "NT1," **p. 195**

The same goes for the LAN lights. If there's no activity there, but the NT1 light is steady, then chances are you have LAN problems. Again check the cabling first, then check over the configurations and IP addressing.

"Wow, is he trying to sell me the Cisco 750?" I hear you. So much for the flowers; here come the brick bats. The equipment comes with four manuals:

- *Setting Up Your ISDN BRI Service* is a pretty good run through of how to do it.
- *Cisco ConnectPro User Guide* takes you through the graphical user interface, as you'll see.
- *Installation and Hardware Guide* provides excellent information on how to set up the hardware as I suggested in the previous caution. But it falls down in explaining the software configuration in a single, coherent order.
- *Everyware Software Reference Guide* is a nearly 400-page book packed with all the 750 commands and several initial chapters on theory and practice. But it floods the user who simply wants to connect to the Internet or office with far too much scattered information. Cisco needs to lay out a quick installation and configuration procedure, anticipating connection to third party routers using PPP and Multilink PPP for remote office and Internet use. You can do it by bouncing around in this manual and parts of the installation manual, but this could take a lot of time—it sure took me much more time than I'd planned.

Loading New Release Software in the Cisco 750 Series

The first and biggest thing that led to trouble was the mystery of what to do with the disk of recent release software that came with the box. I received a disk labeled *Everyware™ 2000 RO ISDN BRI Router Release 3.1(2) Software NI-1, 5ESS, DMS-100*. Now this looked important. It would seem I should do something with it. But nowhere—in the installation manual, BRI setup manual, or even in the release notes that came with the disk—did I find what to do with the disk. The big reference guide didn't seem to have any helpful information, and its installation section simply directed me back to the installation manual.

 You must have Release 3.1(2) or later of the software to use the ConnectPro graphical user interface.

I played with the unit and seemed to run into problems. I surmised maybe the disk had software that would help; but how to load it? Bong! Let's try the reference manual index. Load, load, let's see—nothing. Revision, revision—nothing. Update, hmm—nothing. Software, Software Load Command 331—jackpot!

N O T E With the 750s, or any other devices, if you receive a new release of the software with the
unit, figure out how to load it. Then load it. Most of these "revisions" are bug fixes that will
often, though not always, make your installation easier. ▨

Loading any new software is a very important first step. Why it's so hard is beyond me. At the
very least, I suggest a sticker be put on the front of the installation manual and on the disk
advising buyers to load the revisions first and directing them to the "Software Load" part of the
reference guide. That said, let's see how to do it.

You have two ways to go. Just as in the case of the Cisco 1000 series, you can use the command
line route. We'll look at that first. I suggest you use the new ConnectPro graphical interface to
install and configure the 750 series router. You may still need to use the VT-100 method for
some things or to get started, but ConnectPro makes things so much easier.

Configuring the Cisco 750 Series by Command Line

Connect your VT-100 or use an emulation program in your PC to connect through the PC's
serial port to that on the 750 just as I've described earlier in this chapter. Almost the same
setup: 9600 bps, 8, 1, N, *no flow control* (this is different from the others that used hardware
flow control).

When you receive the > prompt enter **SWL** to begin the software load process, as shown in
Figure 11.34.

FIG. 11.34

Cisco 750 Series
Software Load.

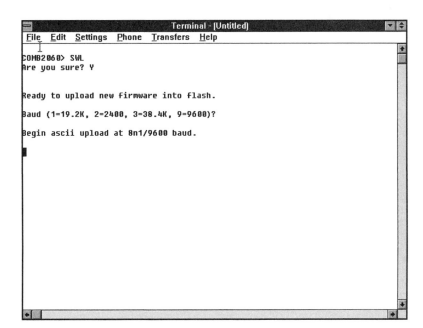

Now the trick is getting the software on the floppy into the 750. You'll use a text file transfer. If you're using the terminal program in the Accessory Group that came with Windows 3.x, take a look at Figure 11.35 so that you choose Transfers, Send Text File.

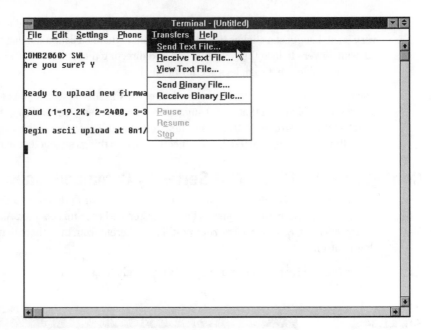

Now the terminal program will pop up the selection screen so you can choose the file you want to send (see Fig. 11.36). The file we want in this example is wbe301.us. How did I know that? It's the only file on the disk other than the readme; if there were any others I'd be in trouble. If that were the case, I'd hope Cisco would give instructions on what to use in the readme. Once the revision is loaded, continue with the installation.

FIG. 11.36

Windows Terminal File
Selection.

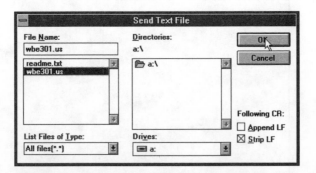

Setting Up the 750 for TCP/IP

From here on I'll describe how to set up the 750 for PPP communication with another router such as an Internet provider. The 750 documentation is much more detailed and spread throughout several hundred pages. I hope this singleness of purpose I'm following here will help you find your way to a working configuration quickly.

One very useful feature of the 750 software is the use of *user profiles*. A user profile is a collection of configurations set up for a particular remote user. In this case you can think of the remote user in question as the router at your office or Internet provider. So you can create one profile for the office and one for the Internet provider. Then you can just select the profile you want to speak with for a particular call. Enough theory; let's see if we can start a fire in this thing.

Set the name of your router with the command **set system....**. In the example shown in Figure 11.37, I've used comb2060 for the name. Look on down Figure 11.37 and see the method of setting the switch, directory numbers, and SPIDs. As I've said, the switch here in Austin is a Siemens provisioned for NI1. With the 750, any time you have an NI1 switch you use the DMS identifier just as you would for the Northern Telecom DMS-100 (by the way that company just changed its name to Nortel). The commands for the switch information are

```
set switch .......
set 1 directorynumber ..........
set 2 directorynumber ..........
set 1 spid .........
set 2 spid .........
```

Part

III

Ch

11

FIG. 11.37

Cisco 750 Set Switch IP Commands.

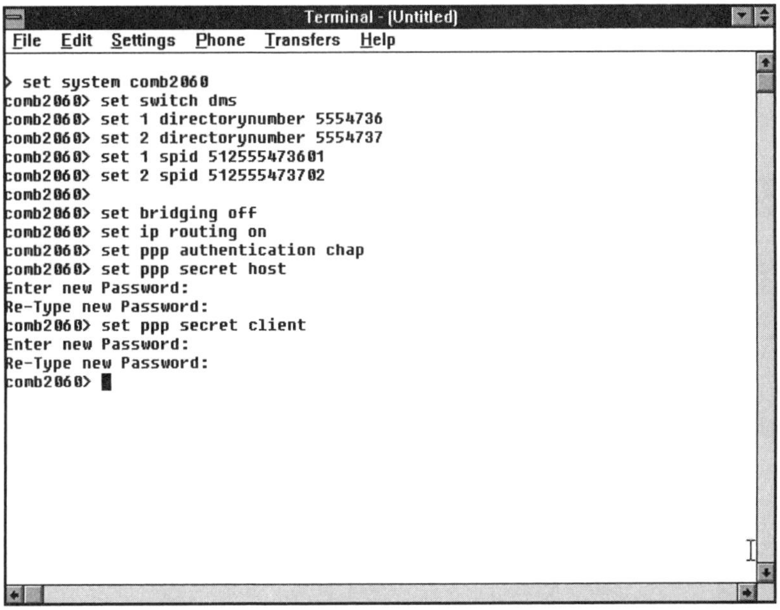

```
Terminal - [Untitled]
File   Edit   Settings   Phone   Transfers   Help

> set system comb2060
comb2060> set switch dms
comb2060> set 1 directorynumber 5554736
comb2060> set 2 directorynumber 5554737
comb2060> set 1 spid 512555473601
comb2060> set 2 spid 512555473702
comb2060>
comb2060> set bridging off
comb2060> set ip routing on
comb2060> set ppp authentication chap
comb2060> set ppp secret host
Enter new Password:
Re-Type new Password:
comb2060> set ppp secret client
Enter new Password:
Re-Type new Password:
comb2060> █
```

NOTE Remember SPIDs are generally needed only in Canada and the United States. The number of directory numbers, SPIDs, and their forms are dependent on the switch. Check your telephone company for details.

CAUTION

The local router name (system name) and some user profile names to be covered later are used in PPP authentication. The case of the letters in these names may be important when connecting to other PPP routers and must match exactly.

Figure 11.37 also shows the settings for IP and PPP. Right before them though, bridging is turned off, because I want only routing. Then Challenge Handshake Authentication Protocol (CHAP) is set up for security. The reference guide explains the nomenclature and procedures very well in the section entitled "Set PPP Password." Basically CHAP arranges an exchange of random numbers between the machines. The machine receiving a number from the first machine performs arithmetic on that number using a previously agreed upon secret; a secret is a string of up to 16 characters used as an encryption key. The sending machine does the same calculation. If they match, the call is allowed. The commands used to establish this originally are

```
set bridging off
set ip routing on
set ppp authentication chap
set ppp secret host
set ppp secret client
```

Let's set up the actual routing information now. Notice in Figure 11.38, I changed directories to LAN with the command cd lan. This is followed by these commands:

```
set bridging off
set ip routing on
set ip address 10.10.10.1
set ip netmask 255.255.255.0
```

NOTE Use an IP address starting with 10 because all IP addresses with the first octet set to 10 are retired and cannot travel through the Internet. You don't care since the IP is only for your LAN's internal use. ARPANET, the precursor of the Internet, used 10; when ARPANET was phased out as the final Internet design took hold, so were all its numbers. If you receive a real IP issued through the Internet system, use it.

I know this is getting involved, but stay with me; it's worth it to grasp some of this IP stuff. Look on down Figure 11.38 and you'll see a cd back to our router's root and then the creation of a new user profile for a user named remote-rtr to match the remote router to call:

```
set user remote-rtr
set bridging off
set ip routing on
set ip address 10.10.20.1
```

```
set ip netmask 255.255.255.0
set ip framing none
set encapsulation ppp
set number 5551234
```

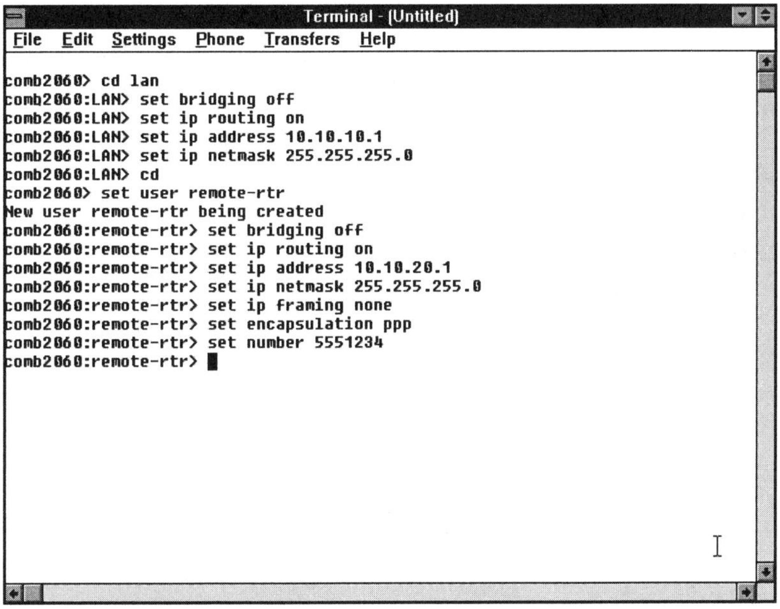

FIG. 11.38

Cisco 750 LAN IP
Configuration.

```
┌─────────────────────────────────────────────────────────────┐
│ ▭           Terminal - (Untitled)              ▼ ◆ │
│ File  Edit  Settings  Phone  Transfers  Help              │
├─────────────────────────────────────────────────────────────┤
│ comb2060> cd lan                                          │
│ comb2060:LAN> set bridging off                            │
│ comb2060:LAN> set ip routing on                           │
│ comb2060:LAN> set ip address 10.10.10.1                   │
│ comb2060:LAN> set ip netmask 255.255.255.0                │
│ comb2060:LAN> cd                                          │
│ comb2060> set user remote-rtr                             │
│ New user remote-rtr being created                         │
│ comb2060:remote-rtr> set bridging off                     │
│ comb2060:remote-rtr> set ip routing on                    │
│ comb2060:remote-rtr> set ip address 10.10.20.1            │
│ comb2060:remote-rtr> set ip netmask 255.255.255.0         │
│ comb2060:remote-rtr> set ip framing none                  │
│ comb2060:remote-rtr> set encapsulation ppp                │
│ comb2060:remote-rtr> set number 5551234                   │
│ comb2060:remote-rtr> █                                    │
└─────────────────────────────────────────────────────────────┘
```

Part
III

Ch
11

The IP address is the local IP address to be associated with the PPP/ISDN connection. It would usually be best to make a more limited IP netmask such as 255.255.255.248 that would use up only eight IP addresses for your network. The last lines set up normal IP encapsulation and provide the ISDN directory number to call for the remote router.

N O T E Frequently, manufacturers seem to think you'll only be connecting to their equipment, the simplest case. You won't, so often examples in documentation are no help. Here, to use standardized PPP when connecting to non-Cisco 750 series routers you must be sure to set ip framing to **none** and **encapsulation ppp**. These are not the defaults because the 750 seems to assume you'll be connecting to another 750 that doesn't require such settings. ▨

CAUTION

The manual says user profile names are not case sensitive. But the local router name (system name) and the user profile name are used in PPP authentication. PPP authentication is case sensitive when connecting with other PPP routers. So watch that case.

At this point it's a good idea to go through your configuration to see how things look. You do this using the SHOW command alone and with various parameters. In the case of the setup just covered, I suggest you look over the following:

- *show config all* shows the general configuration of your router. Figures 11.39 and 11.40 illustrate the two screens.

- *cd remote-rtr* followed by *show config* shows the remote router configuration (see Fig. 11.41).

- *show users*

- *show ip configurations*

- *show security*

- *cd remote-rtr* followed by *show security*

- *cd lan* followed by *show config*

FIG. 11.39

Cisco 750 General
Configuration Screen 1.

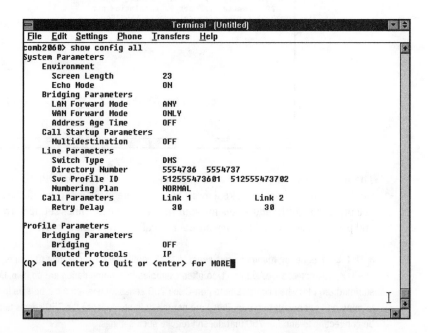

```
                          Terminal - (Untitled)
 File  Edit  Settings  Phone  Transfers  Help
comb2060> show config all
System Parameters
    Environment
       Screen Length         23
       Echo Mode             ON
    Bridging Parameters
       LAN Forward Mode      ANY
       WAN Forward Mode      ONLY
       Address Age Time      OFF
    Call Startup Parameters
       Multidestination      OFF
    Line Parameters
       Switch Type           DMS
       Directory Number      5554736   5554737
       Svc Profile ID        512555473601  512555473702
       Numbering Plan        NORMAL
    Call Parameters          Link 1            Link 2
       Retry Delay              30                30

Profile Parameters
    Bridging Parameters
       Bridging              OFF
       Routed Protocols      IP
<Q> and <enter> to Quit or <enter> for MORE
```

N O T E I only put in a few screen shots of the SHOW command, because they all begin to look the same; naturally yours will differ in details.

And, very important, some of the changes you make will not show up until a reboot.

FIG. 11.40
Combinet General
Configuration Screen 2.

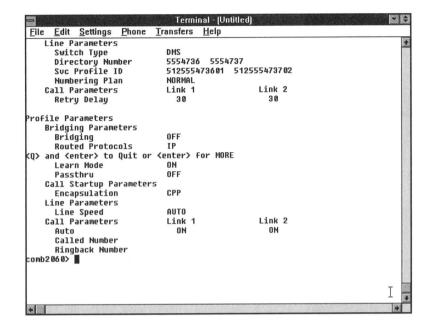

```
┌─────────────────────── Terminal - [Untitled] ─────────────────────┐
│ File  Edit  Settings  Phone  Transfers  Help                      │
│     Line Parameters                                               │
│       Switch Type            DMS                                  │
│       Directory Number       5554736   5554737                   │
│       Svc Profile ID         512555473601  512555473702          │
│       Numbering Plan         NORMAL                              │
│       Call Parameters        Link 1            Link 2            │
│         Retry Delay          30                30               │
│                                                                  │
│ Profile Parameters                                              │
│     Bridging Parameters                                         │
│       Bridging               OFF                                │
│       Routed Protocols       IP                                 │
│ <Q> and <enter> to Quit or <enter> for MORE                    │
│       Learn Mode             ON                                 │
│       Passthru               OFF                                │
│     Call Startup Parameters                                    │
│       Encapsulation          CPP                                │
│     Line Parameters                                            │
│       Line Speed             AUTO                               │
│     Call Parameters          Link 1            Link 2          │
│       Auto                   ON                ON             │
│       Called Number                                          │
│       Ringback Number                                        │
│ comb2060> █                                                   │
└──────────────────────────────────────────────────────────────┘
```

FIG. 11.41
Cisco 750 Remote
Router Configuration.

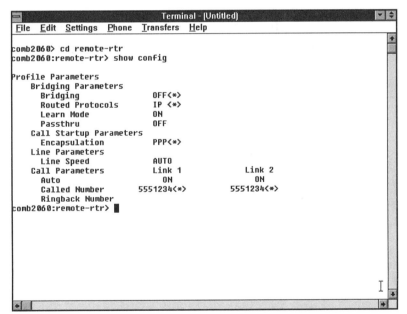

```
┌─────────────────────── Terminal - [Untitled] ─────────────────────┐
│ File  Edit  Settings  Phone  Transfers  Help                      │
│                                                                  │
│ comb2060> cd remote-rtr                                          │
│ comb2060:remote-rtr> show config                                │
│                                                                  │
│ Profile Parameters                                              │
│     Bridging Parameters                                         │
│       Bridging               OFF<*>                             │
│       Routed Protocols       IP <*>                             │
│       Learn Mode             ON                                 │
│       Passthru               OFF                                │
│     Call Startup Parameters                                    │
│       Encapsulation          PPP<*>                            │
│     Line Parameters                                           │
│       Line Speed             AUTO                              │
│     Call Parameters          Link 1            Link 2         │
│       Auto                   ON                ON            │
│       Called Number          5551234<*>       5551234<*>     │
│       Ringback Number                                        │
│ comb2060:remote-rtr> █                                        │
└──────────────────────────────────────────────────────────────┘
```

Part
III

Ch

11

Now reboot the router by issuing **reboot** at the > command. When the reboot is complete, issue a call to the remote router by entering the remote-rtr directory and issuing **ca 1** to call the number. Then use a *ping program* to bounce off the router you've called. Ping programs are generally available in TCP/IP packages such as NetManage Chameleon.

TROUBLESHOOTING

Why don't I get responses to my pings? If you receive responses to your pings the router is up. If not, try entering **show packets** at the > prompt on the Combinet router. Also take a look at the lights on the router to see if they show communication is actually taking place.

The Cisco 750 series is configured in profiles that make it easy for you to make calls on-demand to many different numbers. Think of these profiles like the phone book entries you probably use with your modem program. They're more complex because they can carry all the PPP, IPX, and other information that is not a part of the ordinary modem world.

Configuring the Cisco 750 Series with ConnectPro

Enough! Stop the insanity! Why should router setup be so complex and fraught with danger? It shouldn't, and Cisco (really the Combinet team) developed ConnectPro to overcome the difficulties. Be sure you have at least Release 3.1(2) of the ROM software loaded into your 750 before you start. Then load the ConnectPro software using the Windows Run procedures.

Now double-click on the ConnectPro Icon that the installation program created during install. You find an entry screen asking for one of three possible addresses for your router:

- Ethernet
- IP
- Serial number

Take your pick. You'll find the Ethernet address and serial number on a tag stuck to the bottom of the 750. If you've previously configured the router with an IP address, you can enter that. Since I had previously entered an IP address, I put it in here (see Fig. 11.42).

FIG. 11.42
The ConnectPro entry screen has a space for Ethernet, IP, or serial number identification of the Cisco 750 series router.

TROUBLESHOOTING

I can't seem to see the router no matter what numbers I put in; what can I do? I've had this happen too. Even though ConnectPro is supposed to work with the Ethernet address or serial number, I've found that sometimes, it does not. In those instances I go into the command line using VT-100 emulation as I described in the earlier section. Then I enter an IP address, as we discussed in that section. Then I go back and use that IP address for ConnectPro. This has always worked. Granted it takes you back to the command line for a minute, but it's far better than doing the whole thing from the command line.

When you've entered the address and clicked OK, the program goes looking for a router with that address; if it finds it, a transfer of packets is shown on the screen and you've made it, (see Fig. 11.43).

FIG. 11.43
ConnectPro has found the router and is exchanging packets to begin the configuration.

Then choose the Simple Configuration from the following screen to start the process (see Fig. 11.44). If you choose the other option, you'll go to the Advanced set up screens and be faced with a plethora of options, probably the equivalent of everything you could do with the command line. You might want to return to the Advanced area later; right now, let's keep it simple.

FIG. 11.44
Selection of simple configuration for the 750.

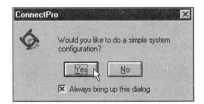

Does this next screen look familiar (see Fig. 11.45)? Of course, it's the switch, directory number, SPIDs, router name tango.

The router checks to see if your switch configuration is correct. This bounces if you're not connected to your ISDN line. When that passes, you'll have an opportunity to set up the profile using the phone number of the router to be called and specifying the protocol (see Fig. 11.46). PPP is the most likely choice. Use CPP only if your calling another router that supports Combinet Packet Protocol.

Part III
Ch 11

FIG. 11.45

Entry of the ISDN environment information.

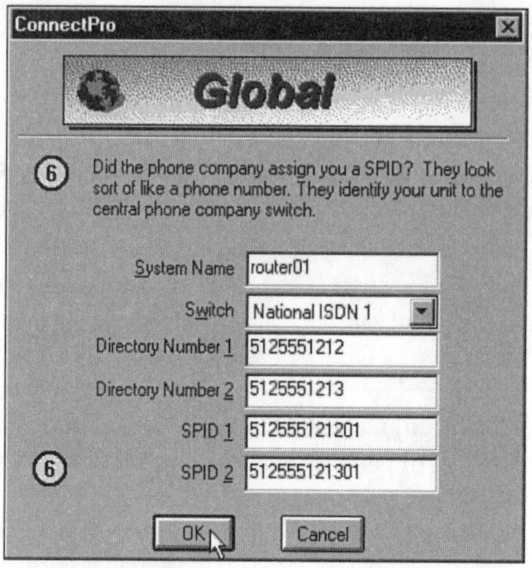

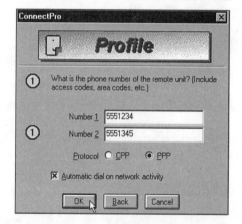

FIG. 11.46

Insert the number of the router to be called and the protocol you'll use. Notice the check box to make the call whenever there's network activity.

That's it for the simple set up. For more detail you can hit the Advanced selection offered as you back out of the set up. Figure 11.47 shows one of the many screens you can negotiate within Advanced. You'll need to enter these selections to set up security parameters, sophisticated time outs and such. Indeed, you can do everything in these graphical screens that you would have done with the command lines, and without much possibility of error or need to page back and forth in the manual. Thanks Combinet, er ah Cisco.

FIG. 11.47

A detailed screen using the advanced option in ConnectPro.

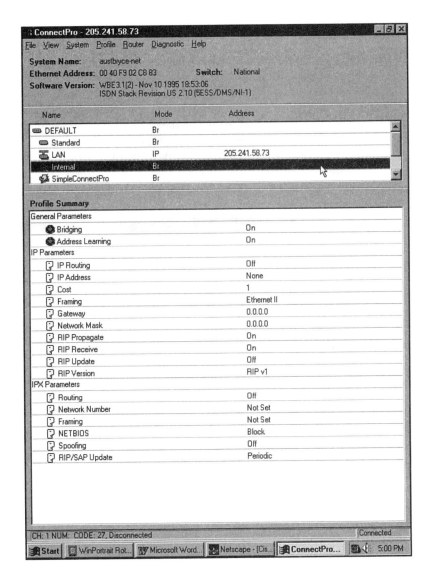

N O T E Those of you familiar with the first edition may remember I described the only graphical interface router I could find. It was from JRL Systems and still in beta testing. Well, unfortunately, that router never went into commercial production. It's a great design and interface; it works fine, but business decisions redirected the company. Hats off to the excellent effort; I'll bet some of the interfaces I've described borrowed something from JRL's work. ■

Trancell WebRamp

Now it's time. We're moving from the horrendous complexity of setting up a Cisco using the IOS command line to a little box, the Trancell WebRamp, that you don't even need written instructions to install. How do I know that? Because I lost the WebRamp manual. All I have is the box, power supply and a disk with the intriguing name, WebRamp Wiz 1.0. Here goes. I put the disk in my A: drive and go through the usual Windows two-step with Run and click on the setup program. It whirs, presents all sorts of pretty stuff implying it's loading software and ends up asking if I want to configure my WebRamp. Of course I say yes. I did hook it up—you know, the usual ISDN U interface here, Ethernet there, and power supply someplace else. The screen comes up, says it's looking for WebRamps and presents Figure 11.48.

FIG. 11.48

The Wizard of WebRamp appears inviting you to journey through the configuration. There's even a little soliloquy on the Internet at no extra charge.

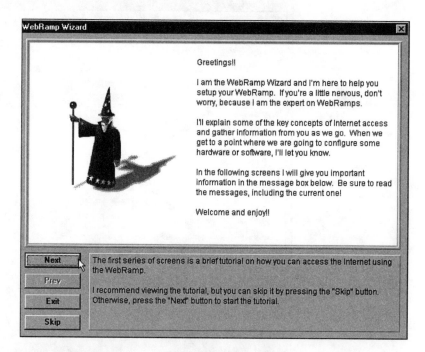

I won't take you on the whole trip about the Internet, but look at Figure 11.49 for the flavor. This shows how the WebRamp fits into the total picture. Notice anything unexpected? That's right; the WebRamp seems to have a lot of extra RJ-45s on the back. Why? Because it's a combination router and Ethernet hub, two in one. This model has eight 10BaseT ports plus an AUI connection you can use to install a transceiver. In my network I used a transceiver to connect to thin Ethernet, 10Base2. Trancell has at least three versions of the WebRamp:

- An eight-port hub supporting TCP/IP routing: this is the version I tested. It lists for about $825.

- A four-port hub with POTS ports and TCP/IP routing: this lists for about $595, and I'll bet you'll find it on the street for less than $500.

- An eight-port hub supporting gatewa functions between TCP/IP and IPX/SPX: this allows you to run only IPX/SPX on your LAN and use only one IP address for connection to the WAN. The gateway design greatly simplifies your LAN. This version lists for about $1,195.

The remainder of these introductory screens contains references to Internet service providers who offer ISDN and telephone company contact numbers with Web addresses. These folks know why you bought the WebRamp.

FIG. 11.49

Notice, in this overall picture of how the WebRamp fits into your network and the Internet, that it is both a router and an Ethernet hub.

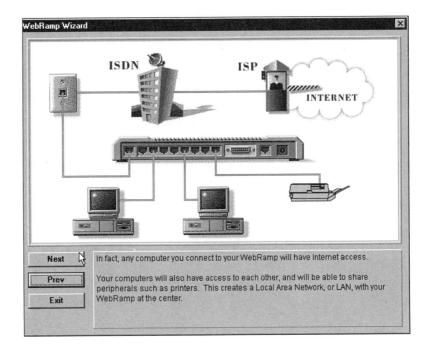

Once you've gone through additional screens explaining how to hook things up to the ISDN U interface ("use the gray cable," the instructions remind you) and to the Ethernet ("use the black cable," the instructions remind), you're given a list of things you'll need to complete the installation and popped to a request for TCP/IP information (see Fig. 11.50).

FIG. 11.50

The list of things you need and advice on TCP/IP shows you all you need to know.

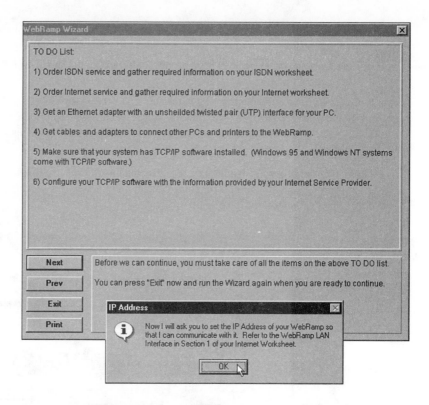

You enter your IP address information along with the subnet mask, as shown in Figure 11.51.

FIG. 11.51

WebRamb entry screen for TCP/IP information.

You'll go through a few more very informative screens and arrive at one to tell the WebRamp about the place you'll be calling and the Internet service provider (see Fig. 11.52). Notice the very clearly marked boxes in which to enter information. Now look at the sub-menu I popped up for Multilink PPP. You can choose whether or not to use two B channels all the time, never, or dynamically; I suggest dynamically, assuming your ISP supports this.

FIG. 11.52

WebRamp information page for your ISP and Multilink details.

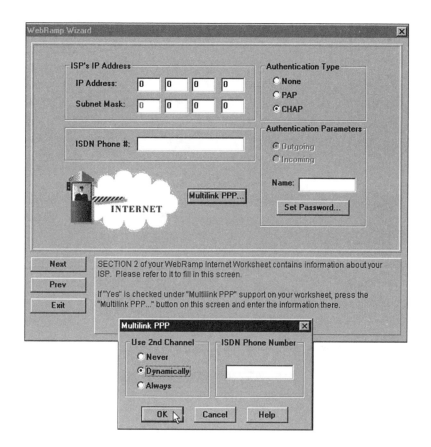

Then we finally arrive at what you've seen so many times before, the information about your switch (see Fig. 11.53).

 TIP Do not enter area codes for your directory numbers, but do enter area codes for your SPIDs. Otherwise your tests may bounce.

Finally the software configures the WebRamp and begins a series of tests. If these tests are passed, you see a screen like the one in Figure 11.54. If there's a problem, the software reports details of the problem and offers to return you to the configuration area where you may need to make changes. Excellent!

For additional details you can look at the WebRamp Manager Monitor as illustrated in Figure 11.55. This shows you, second-by-second, just what's going on with both your LAN and your connection to the Internet.

Part

III

Ch

11

FIG. 11.53
WebRamp telco switch information screen.

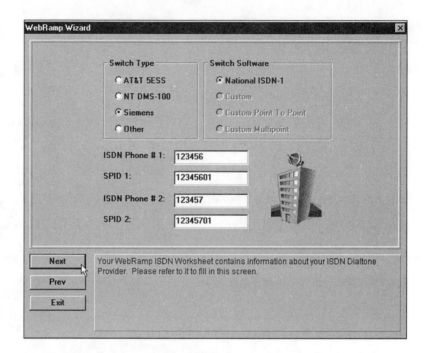

FIG. 11.54
Congratulations! You got it right and can hop on the Internet by simply clicking on a Web hyperlink or asking your mail program to check for new mail.

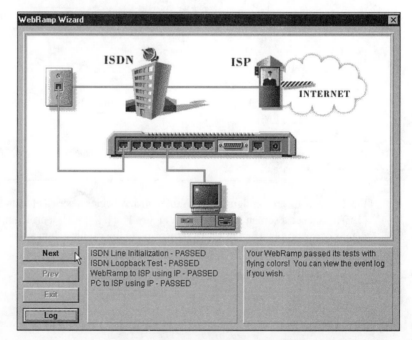

FIG. 11.55
The Monitor gives you real time information on the WebRamp's connection to the Internet.

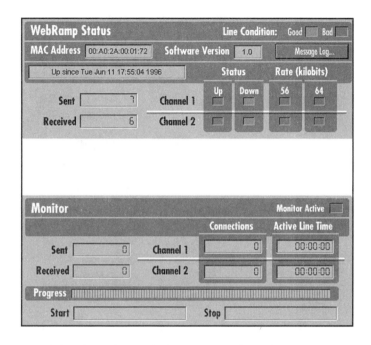

In case you're worried that the WebRamp looks simple and limited compared to the other routers, take a look at Figure 11.56, which shows just the start of the Filter section in the Advanced selections. You can use this to tune the configuration and establish wide area links, other than the initial one you made the first time through.

FIG. 11.56
A sample of the Advanced selections available with the WebRamp configuration software. Here you can set filters to control your network traffic.

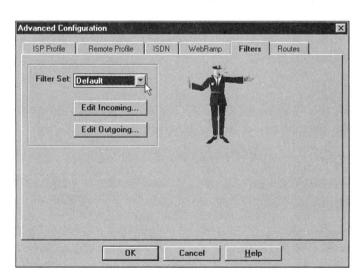

Part III
Ch 11

Okay. You're going to think I made all this up. But I really, really did set the WebRamp up without ever reading any of its documentation. In fact, I just now found the WebRamp book under another router I'm testing. And here's a picture of it (see Fig. 11.57).

FIG. 11.57
Trancell WebRam.

The Trancell folks did a bang-up job of making a quick and simple-to-use router for ISDN.

Other Routers

I'm excited about what's happening to the routers for ISDN. They're getting easier to use and much less expensive. But I've run way over the space allotted for this chapter and haven't even scratched the surface of what's out or coming out. So, knowing I'll be missing a load of other good routers, I'll just close with a few notes on some I've had the pleasure to work with.

Gandalf

Gandalf has a collection of routers and/or bridges aimed at the small office and telecommuting market. The LANLine 5250i (see Fig. 11.58) is an IP and IPX router that can accommodate up to T1/PRI connections. The LANLine 5242i (see Fig. 11.59) is an ISDN bridge with BRI that sets up using the DTMF (Touchtone™) signals from your analog phone! Both have support for Windows console configuration in software XpressView. Gandalf also provides XpressWay central site hardware for larger systems. Gandalf also OEMs (resells) the Trancell routers.

T I P Gandalf is one of those router makers that figured if you can't beat 'em join 'em. They incorporate software to talk with Ascends and emulate the Ascend MP+.

FIG. 11.58
Gandalf 5250I.

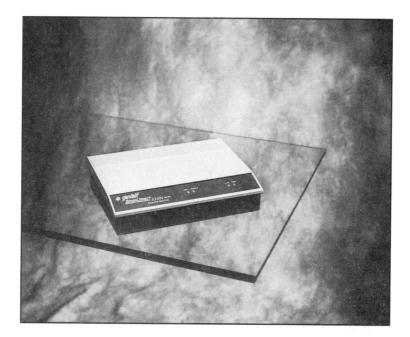

FIG. 11.59
Gandalf 5242i.

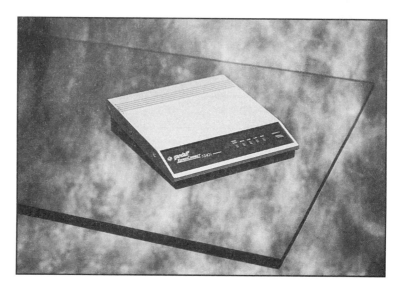

TIP Gallop to **http://www.gandalf.ca**.

3Com

3Com is acquiring companies that have designed and produce a wide range of ISDN products. A firm in the United Kingdom, Sonix, recently joined the 3Com fold with a line of routers and bridges named "Arpeggio." Figure 11.60 is the AccessBuilder Internet 400 that was developed out of the line.

FIG. 11.60
3Com AccessBuilder Internet and 400 3Com AccessBuilder Internet 400 are designed for the SOHO world. They list at $845. These are directly competitive to the routers I've covered earlier.

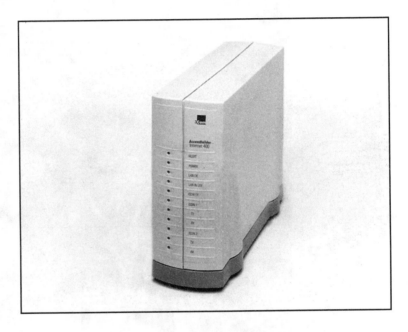

TIP Trip over to **http://www.3com.com**.

3Com also has two lines of stackable communications products:

- OfficeConnect Family is designed for the SOHO environment and priced accordingly.
- AccessBuilder Family is designed for the larger organization with higher performance and pricing.

Farallon

Farallon is famous for its development of the improved cabling method for Apple's LocalTalk; the Farallon product is called PhoneNet. Now they offer the Netopia ISDN router. It comes with step-by-step set up and configuration instructions. Farallon guaranties you'll get the router set up.

Fall for Farallon at **http://www.farallon.com**.

Because Farallon came from an Apple background, the hardware and software has excellent support for both the Mac and PC. The equipment has a PhoneNet connection; this means you can plug any Mac ever made in using the Mac's built in LocalTalk network. It also has both an Ethernet AUI connection and two twisted pair Ethernet jacks; these jacks support Farallon's daisy chain method of cabling called EtherWave. With this technique you don't need a hub; you use small EtherWave AAUI transceivers at each computer to daisy chain from computer to computer.

Farallon has a service called Up and Running, Guaranteed! It supplies a PCMCIA card analog modem to plug into the Netopia. With this, their technical staff can call in and configure the device for you. Figure 11.61 is a picture of the Netopia.

FIG. 11.61
The Farallon Netopia Internet router supports both Ethernet and LocalTalk.

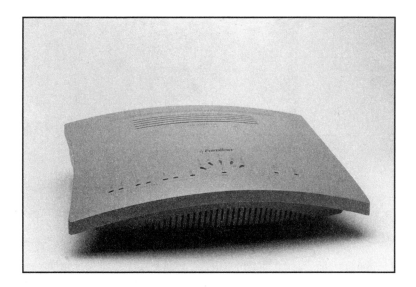

Part
III

Ch
11

ZyXEL

ZyXEL has designed the Prestige 2864I ISDN Modem for easy installation. It still uses the terminal emulation/command line interface configuration, though I'll bet on a graphical user interface soon. It provides U interface connection to your ISDN line, both AUI and 10BaseT Ethernet connectivity, and a POTS RJ-11. AppleTalk, TCP/IP, and IPX/SPX are all supported protocols.

The Prestige package includes Stampede Remote Office Gold and WanderLink remote control software.

 Zip to ZyXEL at **http://www.zyxel.com**.

Proteon

Proteon, a recognized leader in communications technology for 20 or more years, is a major developer of token ring, fiber, and router technology. The GlobeTrotter 70 and 72 (see Fig. 11.62) provide multi-protocol routing and bridging to an ISDN BRI. They support Multilink PPP and STAC compression. In line with the GUI trend I've emphasized, Proteon supplies the "GlobeTrotter Graphical Setup Utility." This graphical interface even pictures the GlobeTrotter connectors as an aid in setting up. The routers have a fairly elaborate selection of features including bandwidth reservation and IPX spoofing.

FIG. 11.62

Proteon GlobeTrotter 70 router.

TIP Check the pros at **http://www.proteon.com**.

You start configuration of the GlobeTrotter by loading the program and checking off some information about your router. Since this software is designed for a wide range of routers Proteon makes, it's very flexible in accommodating routers with a number of different kinds of ports. I'll just stick with the simple BRI/Ethernet single port unit. Figure 11.63 shows the screen where you enter the IP address; notice the picture of the back of the GlobeTrotter 70.

If you need to configure the details of PPP, compression, and a number of very technical parameters, Figure 11.64 provides an easy way to go about it. Notice the precise control of compression.

There are several screens I've not presented, but when you've finished the configuration, you're greeted with Figure 11.65 giving you the opportunity to export your work to the router. There are three possible avenues: file, console port on the router, or network connection.

FIG. 11.63

Proteon GlobeTrotter Setup Utility picturing the back of the router and providing an entry form for IP addressing.

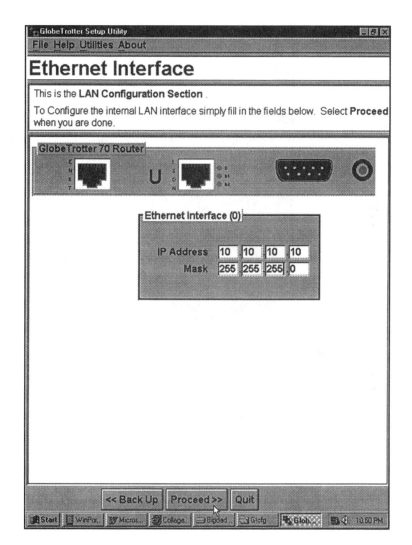

Part

III

Ch

11

You

That's right, *you*. If you want to try your hand at building a router, get a LAN interface card and an ISDN card, plug 'em in a computer and use the KA9Q TCP/IP software to roll your own. I'm not saying this is the way to go for everyone, but if you like to tinker, why not?

 TIP Connect with KA9Q at **http://www.fit.qut.edu.au/~lynda/readings/ka9q.htm**.

FIG. 11.64

Proteon GlobeTrotter
Setup Utility with
details for PPP.

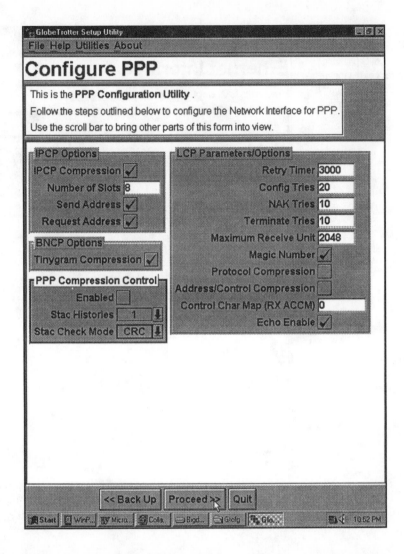

You might even try the same thing with commercial Novell software available to build routers
in NetWare servers. You don't even need to be using file and print services to make a router.
Again, you simply plug the appropriate cards into the server. Digi International provides a line
of cards known as the PC IMAC for this very task.

FIG. 11.65

Proteon GlobeTrotter Setup Utility with export options.

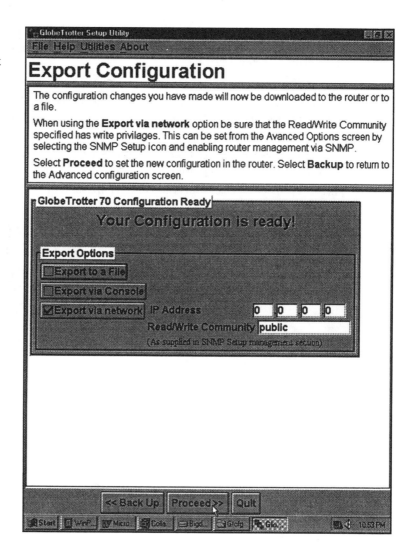

From Here...

In the last three chapters I've covered the major hardware groups you can select from to connect to ISDN. Now let's get into really using it.

- The next chapter, Chapter 12, "Opening Windows 95 and NT to ISDN," covers issues of software and ISDN. I'll talk about a couple of programs, but we'll spend a lot of time on Windows NT and Windows 95.

- I've set you up with PPP in this chapter about routers. Chapter 13, "Tying It Together: Two B or Not Two B," looks at using Multilink PPP to tie B channels together. It also covers compression and BONDING, Bandwidth on Demand.

- Chapter 14, "Pictures and Video with ISDN," shows the big picture with video over ISDN and the issues surrounding standardization. We'll also be looking at sharing applications and real time meetings over ISDN.

- Chapter 15, "Changing Telephones to ISDN," takes a brief look at ISDN phones.

- Chapter 16, "Putting ISDN to Work," takes a, sometimes surprising, look at social and other issues surrounding telecommuting and how to use ISDN to broaden your organization.

- Chapter 17, "ISDN Access for Internet Providers and Corporations," takes a peek into the ISDN world of Internet providers and larger organizations.

- Part V, "The Future," deals with issues on the horizon.

Software & Applications

CHAPTER 12

Opening Windows 95 & NT to ISDN

In the previous three chapters we looked at different types of hardware to hook you up to ISDN. In most cases my illustrations used Windows 95; in some cases I used Windows 3.1 or 3.11 and in a couple I used the Macintosh OS. Now it's time to look at the issues surrounding the operating system in more detail. New operating systems are replacing old. You have several choices:

- OS/2
- Macintosh O/S
- Various forms of UNIX
- NetWare
- LANtastic
- LANServer
- Windows 95
- Windows NT

Because virtually all of us will be using TCP/IP with ISDN in at least some of our computing, we'll take a look at the standard that makes Windows talk with TCP/IP and WinSock

Also, you'll see that this standard is being expanded to IPX/SPX, AppleTalk and other protocols, and—even better—it's being changed to include ATM and ISDN!

Microsoft gives you two choices for the Windows world: Windows 95 and Windows NT

Let's see if we can figure out the major differences between the two.

While all the ballyhoo about Windows 95 has been going on in the front room, Windows NT has been working away in the back room (does this sound like Microsoft's "Back Office" hype?)

Find out what's so great about NT? Watch out. That back room is about to expand a hundred fold or more.

"But many that are first will be last, and the last first." Matthew 19:30 (RSV)

We're stepping into the world of technological religion and politics with true believers on all sides. Each of these choices has excellent technical arguments in its favor and a proven track record with thousands of users doing good work day in and day out. But the steamroller driven by Microsoft has managed to outflank some and roll over others to such an extent that—at least for the next few years—Microsoft's system software will dominate the market, determine application development, and generally make life miserable for developers of competing operating systems. In the meantime, rapid growth of the Internet spawning new rivals, such as Netscape, will give Microsoft quite a run for the money. It's just possible the Internet will take the edge off the advantage of controlling the dominant operating system. Maybe the Internet will make it difficult to sustain any such grasp in the hands of one or a few companies. But Microsoft essentially made a U-turn when the Internet became so important. In effect Bill's gang is inserting Internet elements into everything the company makes.

To cut to the chase, as much as I like most of the other operating systems, and as much as I can argue day into night why one or another is better than Microsoft's offerings, I know—and you do too—which way this train is going. So we'll stick to just what it is Microsoft is doing with Windows 95 and Windows NT that will affect you as you use ISDN. If you're using other operating systems—wonderful; much of this information will apply or will help you integrate with the Microsoft environment. And, since the Internet is perceived to be changing everything, you may soon have many more choices and less worry over playing only in Microsoft's field. In a way the Internet is the standard to meet. Once an operating system can be made to work transparently over the Internet, run plug-ins, Java, and whatever else the flavor of the year, month, or day happens to be, the question of which operating system happens to be on your particular machine becomes much less important. For now we'll deal with Microsoft's approaches; even if control slips to a more general environment created by the Internet, Microsoft has set a number of *de facto* standards. ■

WinSock

WinSock, short for Windows Sockets, is an application program interface (API) developed in 1991 that continues to evolve. The most widely used release is Version 1.1. Version 2.0 adds considerably to WinSock and will overtake the earlier version soon. WinSock is the *de facto* standard for Windows-based, communications-capable applications.

As an open network, API standard WinSock was designed to provide a programming interface for all versions of the Windows operating system, including Windows 3.x, Windows for Workgroups 3.x, and Windows NT. Stardust Technologies, Inc., maintains the WinSock documentation.

> **T I P** To find the inside scoop on WinSock, feed your favorite Web browser **http://www.stardust.com**. Follow
> Microsoft at **http://www.microsoft.com/intdev/inttech/winsock.htm**.

Microsoft was a founding member of the WinSock Group of thirty companies, launched in 1991. As a result of the success of WinSock, hundreds of others are now signed on, and Microsoft has changed its communications API from NetBIOS to WinSock. Microsoft's Windows Open Systems Architecture (WOSA) includes WinSock.

Commercial vendors, including Novell, FTP Software, NetManage, and Wollongong, provide WinSock as a part of their TCP/IP offerings. The popular Trumpet WinSock, which furnishes the basis for thousands of Internet TCP/IP Windows installations, is a hugely successful shareware package based on WinSock. And WinSock is included as part of the TCP/IP support in Windows 95.

> **N O T E** The protocol, WinSock, is a general specification for use by all who write protocol stacks.
> One of the most popular such stacks is Trumpet WinSock. Trumpet WinSock is an instance of the use of the WinSock protocol. Often people seem to confuse the two and think Trumpet WinSock and WinSock are the same. Many other TCP/IP stacks use the WinSock specification; for example, Microsoft's.
>
> If you'd like to use Trumpet WinSock you can download it by anonymous ftp from **ftp.trumpet.com.au**. ■

WinSock, version 1.1, supports only TCP/IP. version 2 supports:

- TCP/IP
- IPX/SPX (NetWare)
- AppleTalk
- OSI

Part
IV

Ch
12

Isn't TCP/IP Now the Only Important Protocol?

Thanks for asking. Most of the time we tend to consider only TCP/IP when thinking about the Internet and WinSock. But there are big advantages to including other protocols in the middle layers of the seven layer model. Think about it. Probably the most widely used protocol for LANs using the Wintel platform ("IBM PC" type machines with Intel processors and Windows) is IPX/SPX developed for NetWare by Novell. If you're running Apple Macintoshes, AppleTalk occupies those layers.

Since WinSock has rapidly become the *de facto* standard for Windows program communication, wouldn't it be cleaner to use it for all communication to those middle layers? That's the aim of version 2. This allows developers to write to the WinSock standard and forget about the underlying software.

continues

continued

Wait a minute, why don't we just always use TCP/IP? Have you ever tried to manage a LAN using TCP/IP? Let's say you have a NetWare LAN. What you'd probably do is load IPX/SPX and TCP/IP on each workstation, thereby using a substantial amount of resources for essentially redundant protocol stacks. Then you'd have to manage all the IP addresses for the workstations. Why not stick with only IPX/SPX that was designed for the LAN and is free of such minutia as address management? You can with WinSock 2.

This idea of using Winsock with IPX/SPX, rather than TCP/IP, is at the heart of a number of LAN gateways to the Internet, such as NOV*IX and Internet Junction among several others. In this model, gateway software running on a server connects to your Internet provider using TCP/IP and repackages the information you're exchanging into IPX/SPX. The gateway then distributes, drops those into your LAN where they're distributed to the workstations that need only run IPX/SPX and the corresponding version of WinSock. All applications, such as browsers and electronic mail, designed for the WinSock interface work perfectly well. LAN management is simplified and performance is frequently better than the TCP/IP over the LAN route.

This gateway idea is covered at length by James E. Gaskin in *Netware to Internet Gateways*, described in the bibliography.

 Open the gate at **http://www.cisco.com and http://www.firefox.com**.

So with Version 2, all of these protocol suites have a common way of communicating with Windows operating systems. This simplifies matters and therefore reduces the cost of software and maintenance. Version 2 will provide backward compatibility with Version 1.1 by accepting all calls from applications designed with the earlier version as shown in Figure 12.1.

WinSock Version 2 also provides a generalized name and service resolution. This interface is independent of other name service designs and brings us several steps closer to interoperation among different naming systems.

I've saved the best for last. WinSock 2 supports additional physical media and media access methods directly, including:

- Wireless
- Asynchronous Transfer Mode (ATM)
- ISDN

So in WinSock 2, we have an API designed for Windows and ISDN. This substantially reduces the time and costs of configuration and programming, while increasing performance, as all vendors design their products to be WinSock compliant as a part of their overall Windows developments. The work done with Version 1 is backward compatible with Version 2.

▶ TAPI is covered in detail in Chapter 6, "Unscrambling APIs," **p. 117**

FIG. 12.1
WinSock 2 accepts requests from applications made for it and for those designed for WinSock 1.1. It provides connection to TCP/IP, IPX/SPX, AppleTalk and OSI in the middle layers of the opens systems model.

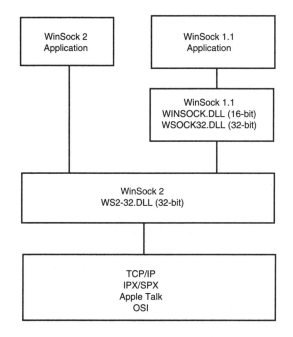

Finally, the WinSock API works in concert with the Telephony API (TAPI), which was designed by Microsoft to control telephone communications with Windows. Uniting the two means that applications, such as videoconferencing and workgroup application sharing, can be written to use TAPI and WinSock and never have to be concerned with detailed issues of telephony or protocols, such as TCP/IP.

Windows 95 and Windows NT

When Microsoft eased out of the OS/2 deal with IBM in 1989, it said Windows development was just to furnish a new software platform for smaller machines already in place—so called "legacy machines," such as the 286—while OS/2 was still the software for future equipment. So, for a time, two operating systems seemed to hold sway, Windows for legacy machines and OS/2 for the new machines. Then, somehow, OS/2 development began to disappear at Microsoft, and Windows grew from a platform for legacy machines to a basis for the desktop using newer hardware.

At the same time as the demise of Microsoft OS/2 development, a new Windows course heading for the most advanced machines began to surface. It was backed by operating system gurus, newly imported from Digital Equipment Corporation. The result was NT. Windows 3.x and Windows NT 3.x have been fairly distinct products. Windows 3.x clearly lacks the ability to handle complex multitasking environments; NT is designed for them. According to Microsoft, Windows 95 closes the gap. Does it? Why would Microsoft create two products that do the same thing? What's the difference?

Here's the big difference in purely pragmatic terms: Windows 95 is more prone to crash than Windows NT. Any other differences are simply bells and whistles by comparison. Microsoft made some market decisions that led to this. Windows 95 assumes a user who wants fast performance with lots of features on inexpensive hardware. Windows NT assumes a user who is willing to sacrifice performance—or at least to pay for more hardware to get performance—for rock solid stability.

Given these two alternatives, Microsoft came up with different underlying architectures for each operating system.

Windows 95 is built very much like Windows 3.1 in that it creates a virtual machine with DOS and the *kernel* (core code running on the central processor) in the lower 4 megabytes of memory. Then it provides space for running 32-bit applications, each with its own private address space. Keeping the 32-bit applications separate provides a measure of protection against any of those applications crashing the whole machine.

Even so, 16-bit applications must run in the same address space as the graphical user interface and Windows management; any application could conflict with these system processes and cause a total machine crash. 32-bit applications also call directly into the lower one megabyte of RAM—where the most critical operations of the virtual machine are running. When multitasking, Windows 95 makes calls through the memory space where 16-bit applications are running; this can also result in crashes.

Windows NT operates in quite a different way. NT creates a distinct virtual machine for each process, and each process has its own private address space. NT totally protects the kernel by isolating its space from any direct calls from applications. NT does this by providing a "local procedure call facility" that applications must use; an application cannot access the hardware directly. In computerspeak, the kernel runs at *ring 0* and the programs run at *ring 3*. By definition, ring 3 processes cannot talk to the hardware but must go through an intervening subsystem—the local procedure call.

Enough of the technical details; obviously there's much more than we can cover in this book on ISDN. But the question remains, Why on earth did Microsoft make Windows 95 prone to failure with this design? Because the design allows faster execution with less hardware than NT architecture.

You can run Windows 95 with as little as 4 megabytes of RAM. I've done it—once. Start the machine, get a cup of coffee, load an application, walk the dog, load a second application, go to lunch. You get the idea. The fact that Windows 95 *can* run in 4 megabytes doesn't mean you can do anything useful with it in that cramped space. Basically, it spends all of its time disk swapping. The practical minimum amount of memory is 8 megabytes. It works pretty well then. But truly effective work requires 16 megabytes; with this amount of memory, 95 really flies.

Since Windows 95 doesn't have to go through the "NT two step" of local procedure calls, it saves a lot of time in execution and uses less memory overall.

Windows NT needs 16 megabytes to run. It does a reasonable job with that much memory, but an additional 8 or more megabytes is well worth it. A fast processor also helps a lot.

Really, the decision between Windows 95 and Windows NT is pretty easy. Buy Windows 95, if you want fast execution at as minimal an investment in hardware as possible. But be sure to carefully test your routine application mix, and watch for frequent crashes; if you encounter any, change that mix. Also, make frequent saves and backups. Windows 95 is a good choice if you can provide such a stable environment and you're using it personally or in a small business.

The Backup Lecture

You've probably heard it, but I'm determined to say it here. Backup often, often, often—at least once a day. If you're reading this book, you're contemplating spending several hundred dollars, or more, on ISDN. With Windows 95 or NT, you're going to spend more money. If you don't have a backup system—STOP RIGHT NOW! Buy the best backup system you can afford. And while you're at it, be sure to get a *UPS* (uninterruptible power supply) for your machines. And install anti-virus software on your workstations and on your servers; incidences of viruses have multiplied since the Internet took off in 1995. If this means you don't get ISDN or a new Windows OS or the latest game, so what. Backup, power systems, and virus protection are far more important. If you don't think so, you've just never had a bad crash, power failure, or virus attack. Don't wait 'til the cow's out of the barn to close the gate!

Watch out for another backup caution in the Windows 95 section.

Part
IV

Ch
12

Windows NT is your clear choice if it's likely the cost of a crash will exceed the cost of the additional hardware needed to run NT effectively. This is a consideration for large organizations and for a number of small businesses and individual users. Big outfits simply cannot afford the support time and lost productivity that preventable crashes entail. An additional $500, or more, spent on each machine for more RAM and a faster processor is cheap—amortized over just a year or two—when compared with the cost of technical support and loss of productivity. And, please, I'm not saying it would take that much more money to make an effective NT machine compared with a 95 machine; you might do it for half as much or less. It depends on where you're starting from and what level of performance you require.

The other features Windows 95 brings include a much better graphical user interface than Windows 3.x and some added tricks. The same interface and most of the other features of Windows 95 are in Windows NT version 4. We'll see in a minute that portions of NT's design for communications are actually incorporated into 95. So for ISDN, there's much that is identical under the surface of the two operating systems.

Windows NT and ISDN

As shown in the following screen shots from Windows NT, 3.51 NT comes with a considerable amount of communications software built in. It overcame the Windows 3.x limitations of data rate. As shown in COM port speed selections in Figure 12.2, NT supports up to 115,200 bps.

FIG. 12.2
Windows NT COM port data rate selection shows up to 115,200 bps.

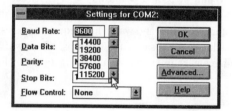

If you're not using an external serial port terminal port adapter, you may choose to insert a card. Windows NT provides a network card selection process that may include ISDN cards of the type that emulate network cards. Figure 12.3 shows the Control Panel screen with the pointer preparing to select the Network.

FIG. 12.3
Windows NT network option selection in the Control Panel.

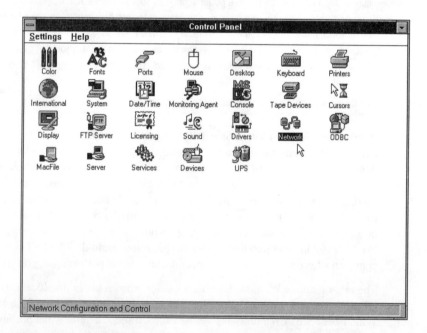

Once you've opened the Network Settings control panel, choose the Add Adapter button. This brings up a dialog box where you can access a pick list and choose your ISDN card. In the case shown in Figure 12.4, the card is a DigiBoard PCIMAC card for the ISA bus. This is a cousin of the DigiBoard DataFire I described in Chapter 10.

FIG. 12.4

The Windows NT pick list includes a DigiBoard PCIMAC card.

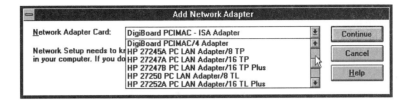

Now that you have picked the card, it becomes a part of your regular network configuration along with any other network cards you have. Figure 12.5 shows both the DigiBoard ISDN card and an Intel EtherNet card installed in the same computer. Since each has a different configuration, you can use your computer on the EtherNet while connecting to another site through the ISDN card. Both appear like network connections to Windows NT.

FIG. 12.5

Windows NT network card installed devices.

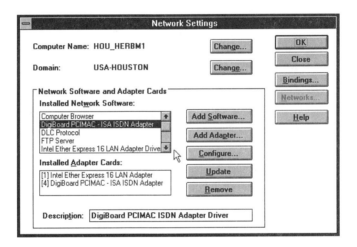

Part
IV

Ch
12

During the process of installation, you'll set the usual interrupts and memory addresses, but now you have to also set the ISDN specific matters, such as switch type, as shown in Figure 12.6.

FIG. 12.6

Windows NT ISDN card parameter and switch selection.

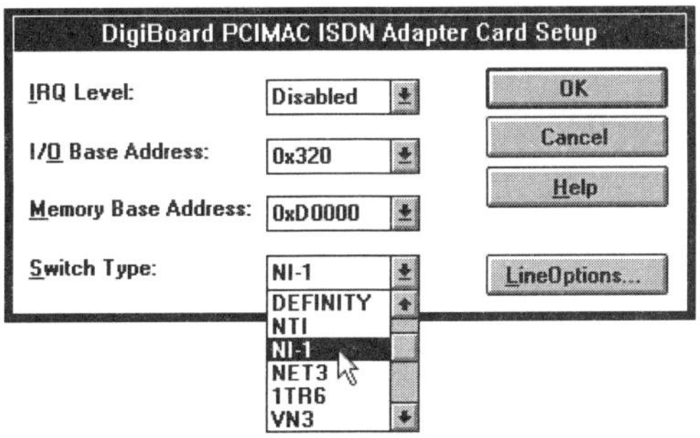

Instructions for the DigiBoard installation are included within the Windows NT help menus, as shown in Figure 12.7.

FIG. 12.7

Windows NT includes DigiBoard installation in Help.

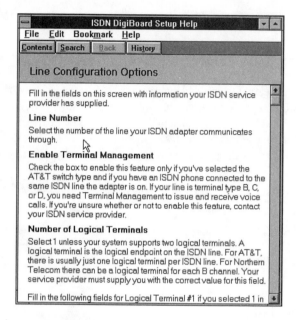

Once you've selected the switch type, you insert the usual information for ISDN; directory number, SPIDs, etc., as shown in Figure 12.8.

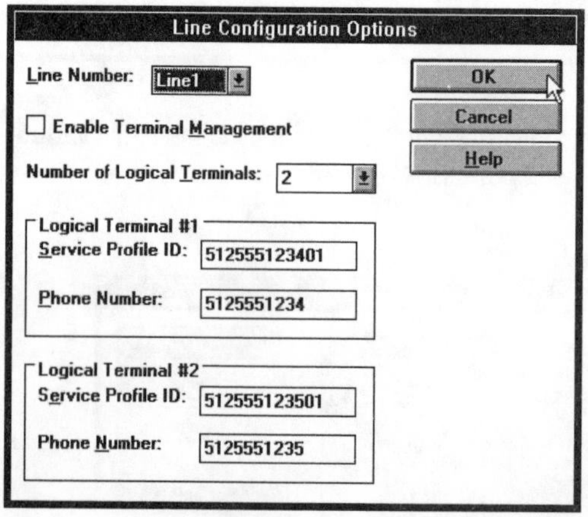

FIG. 12.8

Windows NT directory number and SPID configuration.

Windows NT includes *Remote Access Service* (RAS). A similar facility is provided in Windows 95. RAS is designed to connect your remote computer to your organization's network. In general, there are two ways to make this connection:

T I P Windows NT includes the RAS server software. Windows 95 needs a separate package, Microsoft Plus!, for the RAS server function.

■ *Remote control* is a method that turns your computer into a terminal connected over the telephone lines to a host computer that is physically attached to your firm's LAN. Everything you do executes locally on the physically attached machine. Your remote machine is simply a keyboard and monitor—in effect a dumb terminal to that host. This method has the advantage of reducing traffic over the phone line. If you're running all sorts of typical DOS or Windows applications that are essentially single user, this solution is a good choice. Symantec's PCAnywhere is an example of a program that implements remote control. A drawback of this method is that you must totally run the application at the LAN. This usually requires a CPU—or even an individual machine— at the LAN for each remote connection that is maintained at the same time.

■ *Remote access* is the method used by Microsoft's RAS. Your remote machine runs the application programs it needs; other programs are run on the RAS server on your organization's LAN. Since a good deal of the processing takes place on your remote machine, it takes less processing effort on the server to maintain your machine. So, in a RAS environment, one server CPU with adequate RAM can handle several remote sites at the same time. The optimum use of RAS contemplates distributed computing, client-server operation. Applications are designed so that portions of the application run on the remote machine and other portions run on the server. A database is the best example. The user interface, query language, and report generator run on the remote, while the sorting, indexing, and general database maintenance run on the server.

Microsoft's RAS uses our old friend PPP for multiprotocol routing. RAS service is able to use TCP/IP and Internet connection for operation. As you see in Figure 12.9, RAS support can be setup for ISDN.

FIG. 12.9
Windows NT Remote
Access Service and
ISDN.

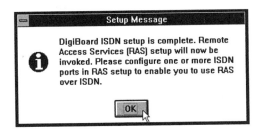

In Figure 12.10, you select the ISDN card and ISDN line number for RAS use.

Part
IV

Ch

12

FIG. 12.10
Windows NT RAS and
selection of ISDN line.

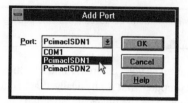

You can now configure the port on the ISDN card to only dial out, only receive, or both receive
and dial out. This selection is characteristic of NT, because NT can be the basis of a server.
Notice that your NT machine need not be set up as a server for you to exercise the receive
calls option. However, if you set up an NT workstation to receive calls, it can only receive one
call at a time, and the caller cannot go through the machine to reach other network resources.
If you set up an NT server to receive calls, it can receive as many calls as your communications
hardware can accommodate, and it can give callers access to other resources on the network.
Figure 12.11 shows these selections.

FIG. 12.11
Windows NT selections
for dialing and receiving
calls.

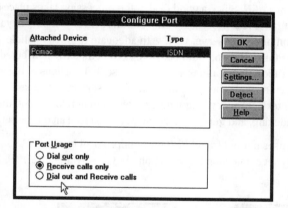

Once you have set up your ISDN card, you can configure it for TCP/IP using the utilities accessible through the Network Settings menu, as shown in Figure 12.12.

Windows NT includes a phone book system, which can be used with the four basic communications methods supported by RAS:

■ Modem

■ X.25

■ ISDN

■ Local Area Network

FIG. 12.12
Windows NT TCP/IP
entry configuration.

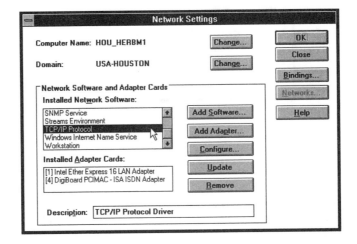

Figure 12.13 shows the Add Phone Book Entry selection with the pop-down menu for communications resources. Here I'm choosing the DigiBoard ISDN card. Notice the buttons at the
bottom for setting security and selecting among the communications methods.

FIG. 12.13
Windows NT phone
book with ISDN number
being added.

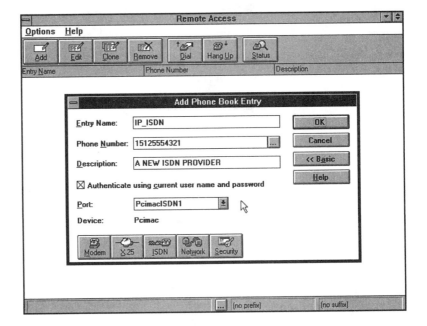

After entering the phone number, click the ISDN button to specify the ISDN configuration for
this number. As shown in Figure 12.14, I'm using 64 kbps and two channels. In other cases, I
might choose a single line.

Part
IV

Ch
12

FIG. 12.14

Windows NT phone book
ISDN configuration.

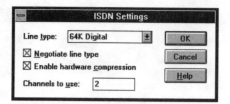

TIP I suggest you use someone else's TCP/IP software if you're doing more than RAS. NetManage, FTP, and Frontier make packages that are much more flexible.

Since most of our communication is based on TCP/IP, Windows NT provides the protocol stack. You set it through the PPP TCP/IP Settings menu illustrated in Figure 12.15. While this looks great, remember, it's aimed only at RAS. If you want to use Microsoft's NT TCP/IP stack for anything else, you're on your own. You'll have to write a script in a text editor, to take care of things such as dialing sequences and bringing up PPP or SLIP. The script language is rather limited; you can automate PPP, but SLIP requires user intervention to enter the IP address passed from the other machine.

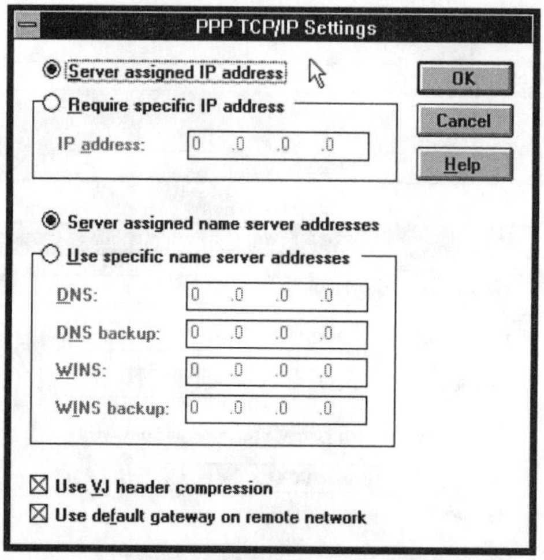

FIG. 12.15

Windows NT PPP TCP/IP
setup menu.

NT PPP TCP/IP

Can you really believe that I can string together 10 letters and a symbol, and you understand what they mean? Can you understand them spelled out: "New Technology Point-to-Point Protocol Transmission Control Protocol Internet Protocol"? Is this a protocol cubed?

While RAS is running, you can put an image on the screen that looks very much like the front of a modem with lights for transmit, receive, errors, and carrier, as shown in Figure 12.16.

FIG. 12.16
Windows NT graphic RAS monitor with lights for transmit (TX), receive (RX), error (ERR), and carrier detect (CD).

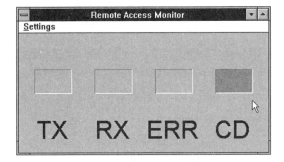

Windows NT also presents details on communications port activities. Figure 12.17 shows an ISDN session using 2 B channels for a data rate of 128,000 bps and information on the numbers of packets, compression, and other facts.

FIG. 12.17
Windows NT Port Status monitor.

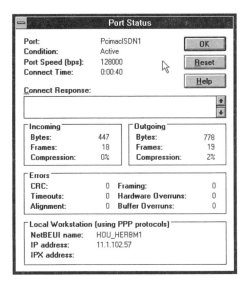

Part
IV

Ch

12

Windows NT provides a full range of ISDN and other communications support in a well-protected environment. It is designed to create a workstation, a server, or a combination of both.

Windows 4.0

As you look at the screen shots of Windows NT 4.0 compare them with those of Windows 95. There's virtually no difference, and that's the idea. We'll take a look at installation of the Motorola BitSURFR Pro and the Digi International DataFire. You might also like to compare the DataFire installation under 4.0 with that under 3.51.

Windows NT 4.0 Installation of Motorola BitSURFR Pro   Go into the Control Panel and select the Telephony icon by double-clicking. This will bring up the Dialing Properties screen as illustrated in Figure 12.18; click Telephony Drivers within the Dialing Properties screen.

FIG. 12.18

Select Telephony on the Control Panel to show Dialing Properties. Select the Telephony Drivers tab.

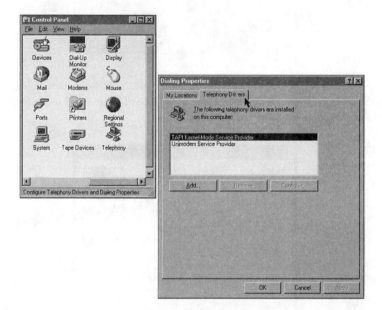

Now highlight the Unimodem Service Provider selection on Dialing Properties and click Configure to start the Install New Modem Wizard (see Fig. 12.19). Click Next to continue the Wizard process. Notice the check box Don't Detect My Modem… is NOT checked.

Oops! Figure 12.20 shows that the Wizard could find the new modem, but couldn't identify it. What happened? Even though the Motorola BitSURFR is plug-and-play and even though it is detected by Windows 95, Windows NT 4.0 does not have the same plug-and-play capacity as Windows 95 and was unable to figure out the device was a BitSURFR. So you'll have to tell Windows NT 4.0 what's attached to COM1. Click OK.

FIG. 12.19

Unimodem Service Provider selection starts the Install New Modem Wizard.

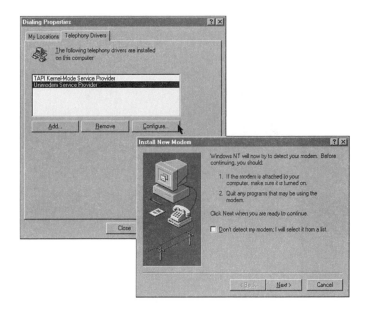

FIG. 12.20

Windows NT 4.0 can find the modem on COM1 but is unable to determine what it is.

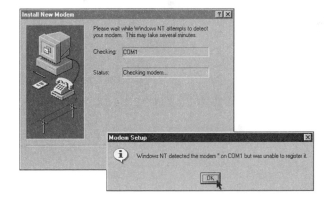

Part

IV

Ch

12

When you click OK the Wizard asks you to pick the modem from a list; click Next (see Fig. 12.21)

Windows NT 4.0 provides an extensive array of modem and modem-like devices. In this case I've gone down to Motorola and selected the BitSURFR; there is no separate selection for the BitSURFR Pro (see Fig. 12.22).

FIG. 12.21
Begin manual selection
of your modem.

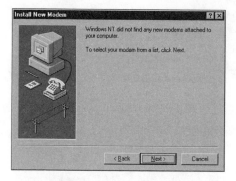

FIG. 12.22
Selection of BitSURFR
in the Windows NT 4.0
pick list.

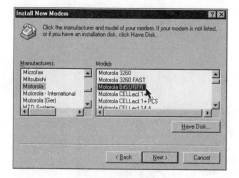

Now simply choose COM1 as the port for the BitSURFR (see Fig. 12.23) and click Next. Then
click Finish to close out the Wizard (see Fig. 12.24).

FIG. 12.23
Selection of COM1 for
the BitSURFR.

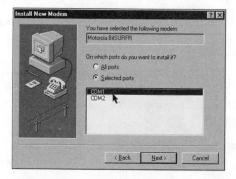

FIG. 12.24
Finishing the Install
New Modem Wizard.

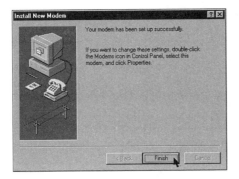

When you click Finish in the Install New Modem Wizard you're sent back to the control panel with the Modems icon highlighted. Double-click the icon and you'll see the Modems Properties screen with BitSURFR illustrated (see Fig. 12.25).

FIG. 12.25
The Modems Properties
screen with BitSURFR
shown.

Click Properties in the Modems Properties screen and choose a Maximum Speed of 115200 (see Fig. 12.26).

N O T E Take a look at the discussion of compression in Chapter 9, "Selecting an External Terminal Adapter," in the section on "Serial Port Software." You'll notice that the line speed is not the maximum speed because compression can increase the data rate between your serial port and the external (modem) device considerably. This means the maximum setting of 115200 kbps in Windows NT could limit effective use of a device with efficient compression that might push the data rate to upwards of half a megabit. If you have a serial card that can handle such a rate, you must go into the configuration files for NT and set the higher rate with a text editor. ▓

FIG. 12.26

Choose the Maximum Speed on the Motorola BitSURFR Properties screen.

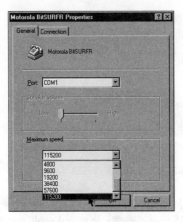

After you've finished configuring the BitSURFR Properties screen, click OK and return to the Control Panel. Double-click Network to show the Network screen (see Fig. 12.27).

FIG. 12.27

Begin setting up the details of using the ISDN BitSURFR connection with the Network screen.

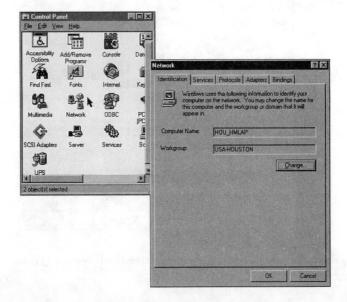

Choose the Services tab on the Network screen and select Remote Access Service to enable dial-in and/or dial-out to other systems. Then click Add on the Remote Access Setup screen. Select Motorola BitSURFR on the Add RAS Device screen to add the unit to your options (see Fig. 12.28).

FIG. 12.28

Addition of BitSURFR as a Remote Access device.

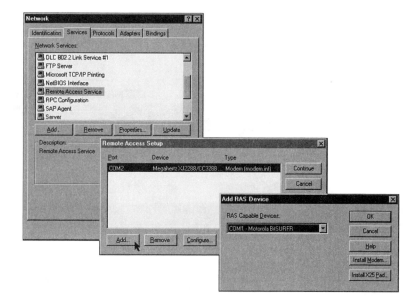

Click the Configure button of the Remote Access Setup screen and choose whether or not this connection will be Dial Out Only, Receive Calls Only, or Dial Out and Receive Calls (see Fig. 12.29). Click OK.

FIG. 12.29

Configuring Remote Access Setup.

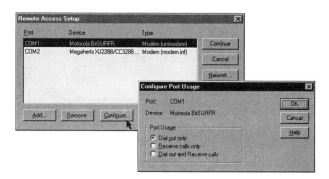

Part
IV
Ch
12

Now choose Network on the Remote Access Setup screen and select the network protocol(s) to use from the Network Configuration screen (see Fig. 12.30).

It's time to set this up for use. Double-click the My Computer icon on you desktop and double-click the Dial-Up Networking icon in the My Computer screen. Click New in the Dial-Up Networking screen and you'll see a New Phonebook Entry Wizard where you enter the new phonebook entry (see Fig. 12.31).

FIG. 12.30
Selection of protocols on the Network Configuration screen.

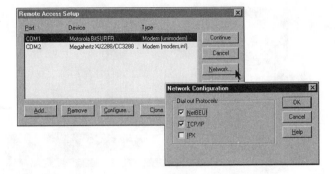

FIG. 12.31
Creation of a new phonebook in Windows NT.

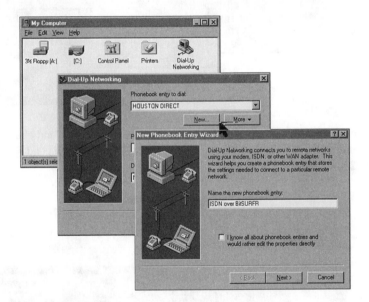

Click Next to set up User Preferences.

CAUTION

When you use the New Phonebook Entry Wizard there's a check box labeled I Know All About Phonebook Entries and Would Rather Edit the Properties Directly. If you check this box, the Wizard skips all the remaining steps to let you set up this phonebook. But it also sets a parameter for the future; every time you want to set up a new dial-up network configuration, you'll be kicked out to manual editing of the properties. To recover from this you must go into the Dial-Up Networking screen, click More and recheck the box Use Wizard To Create New Phonebook Entries (see Fig. 12.32).

FIG. 12.32

Recovery of Wizard setup for phonebook entries.

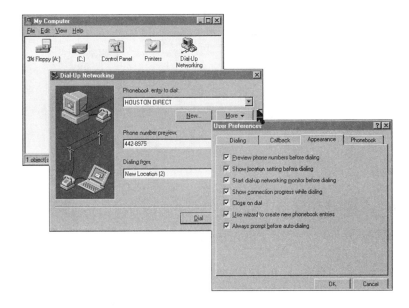

Assuming you didn't fall into the trap I described in the Caution, the Wizard will take you to the selections for a server that include the Internet, plain text password and non-NT servers (see Fig. 12.33).

FIG. 12.33

Selection of server for connection.

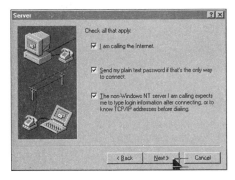

Part

IV

Ch

12

You're asked for the device to be used. In this case we'll select the BitSURFR (see Fig. 12.34).

FIG. 12.34
Selection of the device
for connection.

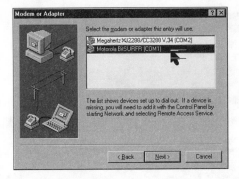

The next Wizard screen takes the number to be dialed (see Fig. 12.35).

FIG. 12.35
Enter the telephone
number to call.

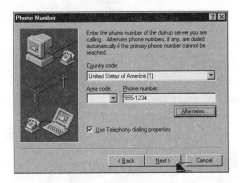

If you click on alternates in the Phone Number screen, you can enter alternative numbers to dial-in the event the first number is unavailable due to a busy or a bad connection (see Fig. 12.36).

FIG. 12.36
Selection of alternative
phone numbers.

When you're finished with Phone Numbers, click on Next and the Wizard moves you to Serial Line Protocol, where you choose between PPP and SLIP. As it says on the screen (see Fig. 12.37), choose PPP if you're not sure.

FIG. 12.37
Selection of Serial Line
Protocol: PPP or SLIP.

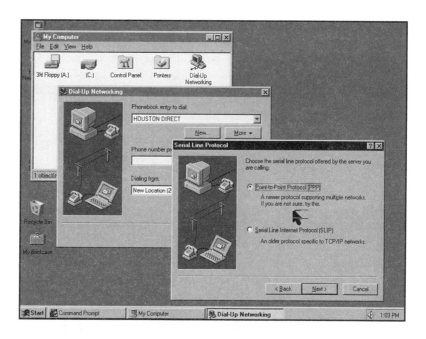

The next Wizard selection gives you the opportunity to select among login responses (see Fig. 12.38). You also can write a login script by clicking the Edit Script button.

FIG. 12.38
Login script options.

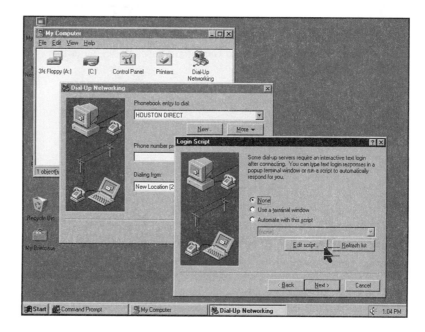

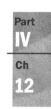

It's finally time to enter the IP addresses. The Wizard first asks you for your IP address. If you've been assigned one, enter it here. On the other hand, if the server is going to assign an IP to you each time you login, enter 0.0.0.0 as shown in Figure 12.39.

FIG. 12.39

Enter your IP address.

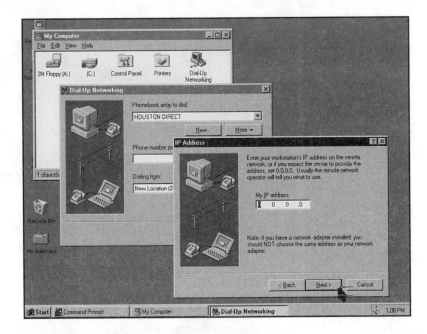

The Wizard moves to entry of Name Server Addresses (see Fig. 12.40). Enter the name server IP address in the DNS field. If your system uses WINS, enter that IP.

FIG. 12.40

Entry of name server IP addresses.

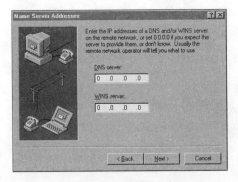

N O T E   *DNS* stands for Domain Name Service. This service provides the database that relates IP addresses to domain names. *WINS* is Windows Internet Naming Service. WINS in combination with *DHCP*, Dynamic Host Control Protocol, provides a unique IP address to each station as it logs in. The IP addresses are maintained in a pool. This technique eliminates the need to assign fixed IP addresses to every machine in your network. As a result, you don't have to keep up with IP addresses for potentially hundreds of machines. This method also reduces the load on the overall pool of IP addresses. ▓

You've made it. Click Finish in the last Wizard screen to save your selections and begin using the new device (see Fig. 12.41).

FIG. 12.41
Finish the new phonebook entry and begin using your new device.

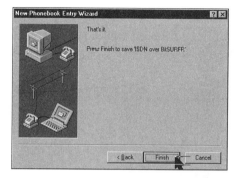

Windows NT 4.0 Installation of Digi International DataFire   We went through installation of a DataFire under Windows NT 3.51. Now let's see how Windows NT 4.0 handles the same device. Double-click the Networks icon in the Control Panel, bring up the Network screen and select the Adapters tab. Then click Add and select your adapter; here we'll choose DataFire (see Fig. 12.42).

FIG. 12.42
Start installation of adapter card from the Network screen by clicking Add and selecting your adapter.

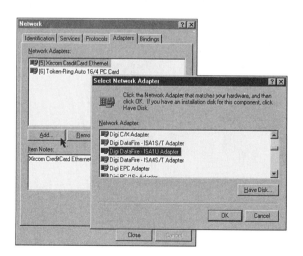

The card we're installing is an ISA bus card. The machine I'm using for this demonstration has three possible buses: ISA, PCI, and PC Card (PCMCIA). With such multiple bus machines, you'll get a selection like that shown in Figure 12.43. If your machine only has one type of bus, this screen will not appear.

FIG. 12.43
Bus selection for the
new adapter card.

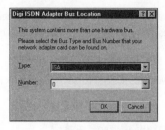

NT will copy the appropriate files from its files or disks you supply. Then you're asked for the initial setup information, including I/O Base Address and ISDN Switch Type as shown in Figure 12.44.

FIG. 12.44
Digi DataFire ISDN
Adapter Card Setup
selection.

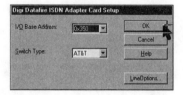

When you've inserted the I/O and switch information, click Line Options to provide more detail, including the SPID(s) and directory number(s) (see Fig. 12.45)

FIG. 12.45
Line configuration for
the DataFire.

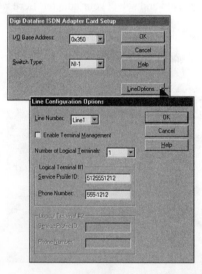

After you've entered the line configuration, click OK and the Remote Access Services selections appear (see Fig. 12.46). From here on the setup is similar to that we covered for the BitSURFR.

FIG. 12.46

The Remote Access
Services selections.

Windows 95 and ISDN

Now for Windows 95. I started with Windows NT because it contains all the communications elements from Microsoft. There has been some delay in providing these tools to Windows 95. ISDN support delivered some months after Windows 95 originally shipped to the general market.

The Promised Second Backup Lecture

As amazing as it seems, Windows 95 shipped without any significant Microsoft or third party support for backup using high capacity, high speed tape drives. In all the hoopla, no one seemed to think backup was very important. True, Windows 95 does contain some software to use DAT drives on NetWare servers. This is great if you have a NetWare server and back up to a drive on the server. But what if you have a small network and want to use the built in Windows 95 networking? What if you have a stand-alone machine? There was some support for QIC type tapes, but the higher speed and capacity tape drives such as SCSI DAT drives went begging.

Well, why not use the Win 3.x/DOS backup program you already have for such drives? Watch out! Those programs won't back up long file names. Even if you don't make long file names yourself, Windows 95 does and uses a lot of them internally. Such Win 3.x/DOS backup programs also won't backup the registry, a fundamental component of Windows 95.

Shortly after the introduction of Windows 95, one software company delivered a program supporting all the new elements of Windows 95. Arcada Software supplied Arcada Backup for Windows 95 Desktop Edition. A few months later Cheyenne produced ARCSolo for Windows 95. Now several more backup programs are available. Arcada is part of Seagate, **http://www.seagate.com**. You may reach Cheyenne at **http://www.cheyenne.com**.

There's a really novel product call "Tapedisk" that makes your tape drive work just like a disk drive. You issue the usual commands for disk resources such as entering the name of a program to run or asking a file to be copied. Tapedisk looks just like a disk drive in the command. I don't recommend you use it to run programs of any size, because the speed is considerably lower than that of a disk, but it's a very flexible way to backup, archive, and make "near line" storage easily available. Check it out at **http://www.tapedisk.com** where you'll find the homepage of Tapedisk Corporation.

Part
IV

Ch
12

Installation of Windows 95

Since this isn't a book on Windows 95, I'm just going to give you a few pointers on installation and how it might relate to ISDN. Windows 95 has some handy features that are used during installation. It scans the machine for attached devices determining how best to install them. This means it's usually good practice to have everything attached to and installed in your machine when you install Windows 95. If you have devices that meet the Plug-and-Play specification supported by Windows 95, all or nearly all of their configuration will be done for you.

TIP If you don't already have a CD drive on your machine, please install one before you install Windows 95, so you can use the CD version of 95. Things will be much easier.

But there is a drawback to this automatic installation system. Windows 95 may not be able to handle some hardware. When this happens, the installation will hang and you'll have to start all over. That's the reason I suggest in the tip that you use a CD. You may have to stop and restart the installation a number of times before it completes; you don't want to do that with floppies.

What if I Run Into Trouble?

If installation hangs during the time Windows 95 is checking out your hardware, be sure to note what hardware was just being checked. If you let the installation go by the fully automatic "Typical" setup option, you may not be able to figure this out. So here's stuff that's not in the book that comes with the product.

The trick to figuring out where things went wrong is to go through the installation step-by-step. There are two ways to do this.

When it hangs, the installer has recorded some information it can use to try to skip over the offending hardware. So when you restart, it's all set. But let's help it out. Rather than going back to "Typical," select "Custom" for the type of setup. This gives you much more control. When you come to the hardware checking phase, you'll be given an opportunity to step through each piece of hardware the installer thinks it detected. Look at each one. If you know you don't have it, reject it on the selection screen. This may be enough to get you through. If it doesn't, then you'll find that the machine hangs at the point you say OK to a particular item. Now you've isolated the problem. Try install again. If it still hangs on that item, don't select it, but put it in later manually.

Another way to approach this is to start the installation from the command line. If you've been pitched out midway through an install, you'll find that when you turn the machine off and back on again as instructed, it will skip the command line and go straight to the graphical interface. You don't want this. So, as the machine starts, and just after it runs through its memory check, start pressing F-8. It may take a few tries to get this right (you're supposed to do it just as the "Starting Windows 95" message appears). This will result in the machine presenting you with a menu of startup options. Choose 6, Command Prompt Only.

Now you're where you want to be. From here you can enter command line switches that will give you more control of the installation. Type setup /? to see some of the switches. The one I suggest is /p b. This will skip the hardware detection modules. You won't find this among the options when you type /?. You won't even find it in Microsoft's "Windows 95 Resource Kit," a 1300-page book. It's in this hint as a gift for you. Don't let anyone know I spilled the beans on one of the big Windows 95 secrets.

I don't mean to imply that the automated installation is a problem. Look at Figure 12.47, which shows Windows 95 detected the Motorola BitSURFR ISDN terminal adapter, I had turned on and connected to COM port 2 during installation. I shot this screen after installation because it was impossible to have my screen shooter, an excellent program called Collage, installed during installation of Windows 95. This device uses the Plug-and-Play specification, and all of its COM settings were done by the Windows 95 installer.

FIG. 12.47
Windows 95 installation of Motorola BitSURFR by Plug-and-Play. This screen was shot after installation because installation should not be attempted with any other programs running.

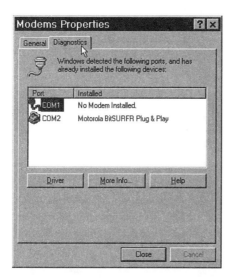

New Communications Features of Windows 95

When it comes to serial and parallel communications, Windows 95 brings a whole new way of doing things. You'll remember from Chapter 9, "Selecting an External Terminal Adapter," that Win 3.x is limited to 19,200 bps with its native drivers. As a result, you need to install a third-party driver to take advantage of ISDN data rates if you're using a serial port device. Windows 95 does away with this need for third-party software and dramatically improves communications at the same time. Figure 12.48 illustrates data rate selections up thorough 921,600 bps!

You've already seen several instances of the Windows 95 installation automation in Chapters 9, 10, and 11, when I covered a number of specific items of ISDN hardware.

So let's go through the manual installation of your most common communications device under Windows 95. I've chosen a 14.4 kbps modem.

To install this new device, choose Start, then choose Settings, and then Control Panel. This opens the control panel Window.

Part
IV
Ch
12

FIG. 12.48

Windows 95 supports serial port data rates up to 921,600 bps.

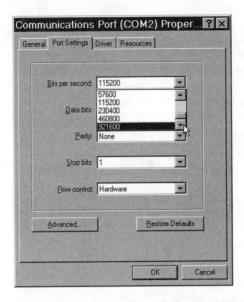

At this point, double-click the Modems icon, as shown in Figure 12.49, and the Modem Properties sheet, as shown in Figure 12.50. What you see here is the General page. (In Figure 12.47 showing the BitSURFR, you saw the other page, Diagnostics.) Click Add.

FIG. 12.49

Windows 95 Control Panel with Modems icon.

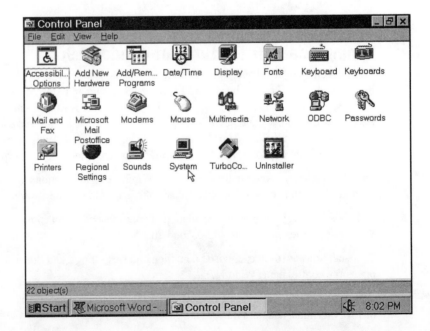

FIG. 12.50
Windows 95 selection
to Add modem.

The next screen gives you the opportunity to do the installation either manually or automatically. Let's see if Windows 95 can detect the modem I've connected to COM 2. It did; it found my Practical Peripherals 14400 FXMT, as shown in Figure 12.51.

FIG. 12.51
Windows 95 COM port
device detection.

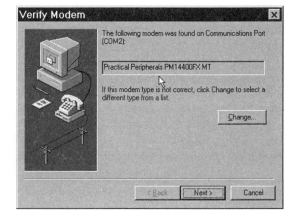

Part
IV

Ch
12

What we've seen is a combination of the Plug-and-Play specifications and UNIMODEM, which provides a single universal modem driver. This means that you will no longer be selecting a modem type within your applications—Windows 95 takes care of that for you. It's much the same as the move from needing applications to contain drivers for every printer under DOS to being able to write solely to the Windows printer software. Now, applications that use modems, or ISDN terminal adapters that are addressed as modems, need only write to UNIMODEM. It's easier for the writers, and it's easier for the users.

▶ **See** "TAPI," **p. 131**

Windows 95 also provides Windows Telephony API (TAPI) as a part of the Windows Open Services Architecture (WOSA). Figure 12.52 shows the telephone dialer built into Windows 95 that uses the underlying TAPI structure.

FIG. 12.52

Windows 95 Phone Dialer.

ISDN Add-Ons to Windows 95

As long as you're using the serial/parallel/USB type of device I described in Chapter 9, "Selecting an External Terminal Adapter," you'll use the same procedures to set up such an ISDN device as you would an ordinary modem; I've covered these for particular products in Chapter 9 and in the section just above.

If you use a router, as I described in Chapter 11, "Establishing ISDN for LANs," your concern is selection and configuration of the TCP/IP stack and/or gateway (as I described in Chapter 11 and earlier in this chapter on the subject of WinSock.)

But, if you have an internal card for ISDN, the picture changes. I covered these cards in Chapter 10, "Putting an Adapter Inside Your Computer." These cards sometimes can be addressed like a modem. In that case you will set them up with the modem procedures of Windows 95 that we just stepped through. In other cases they are designed to look like a network interface card, and you use network interface card steps, usually addressing the card using either NDIS or ODI.

Microsoft and a number of card makers have designed special software to ease your installation and use of many of these cards. From mid-1996 forward, Windows 95 issue disks have come with drivers specially designed for some cards.

FIG. 12.53

Microsoft's ISDN Accelerator Pack Web site. The hand is selecting download of the pack. Notice that a list of card makers begins at the bottom of the screen.

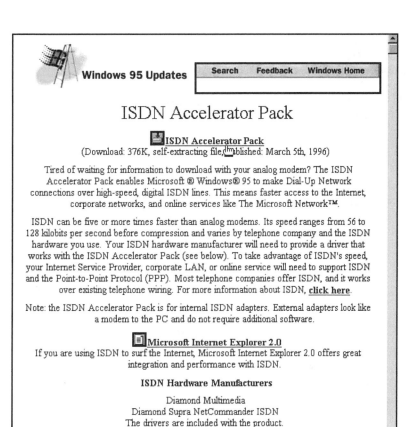

Even if you bought your copy of Windows 95 the first day it was available, you can download the ISDN support software you need from the Microsoft Web site area called the "ISDN Accelerator Pack." Go to **http://www.microsoft.com/windows/software/isdn.htm**, as shown in Figure 12.53. Here the cursor hand is on the link to download the Accelerator Pack software.

But this is only half the required software. The remainder is specific to the card. Sometimes this is included with the card when you buy it. In other cases, you download it from the Microsoft or, perhaps, the maker's site. Figure 12.54 shows the cursor hand selecting Digi International software.

Part

IV

Ch

12

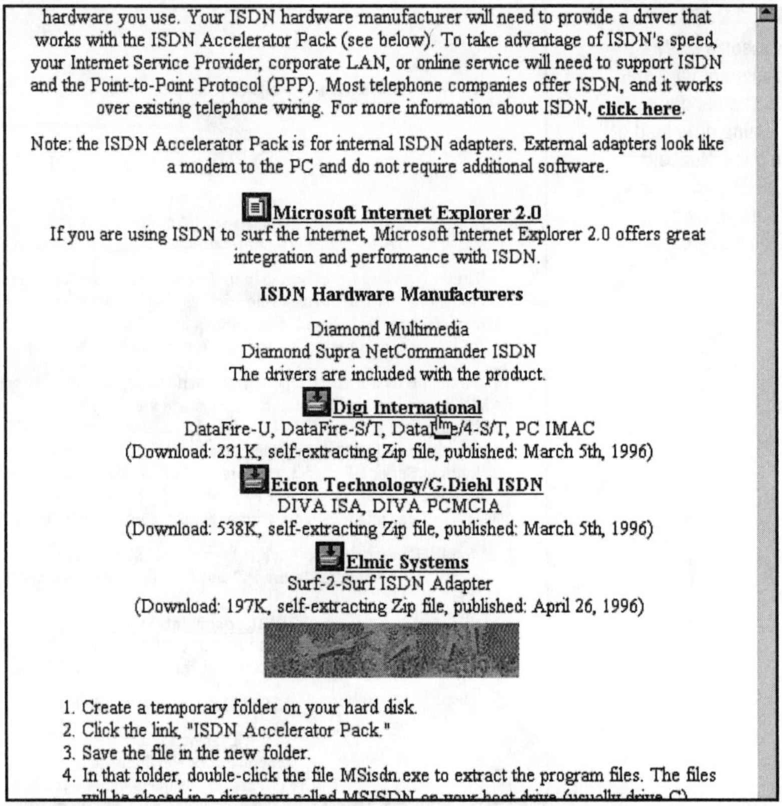

FIG 12.54

Selection of hyperlink to Digi International site where the maker's half of software supporting cards is located.

hardware you use. Your ISDN hardware manufacturer will need to provide a driver that works with the ISDN Accelerator Pack (see below). To take advantage of ISDN's speed, your Internet Service Provider, corporate LAN, or online service will need to support ISDN and the Point-to-Point Protocol (PPP). Most telephone companies offer ISDN, and it works over existing telephone wiring. For more information about ISDN, <u>**click here**</u>.

Note: the ISDN Accelerator Pack is for internal ISDN adapters. External adapters look like a modem to the PC and do not require additional software.

Microsoft Internet Explorer 2.0

If you are using ISDN to surf the Internet, Microsoft Internet Explorer 2.0 offers great integration and performance with ISDN.

ISDN Hardware Manufacturers

Diamond Multimedia
Diamond Supra NetCommander ISDN
The drivers are included with the product.

 **Digi International**

DataFire-U, DataFire-S/T, DataFire/4-S/T, PC IMAC
(Download: 231K, self-extracting Zip file, published: March 5th, 1996)

Eicon Technology/G.Diehl ISDN

DIVA ISA, DIVA PCMCIA
(Download: 538K, self-extracting Zip file, published: March 5th, 1996)

Elmic Systems

Surf-2-Surf ISDN Adapter
(Download: 197K, self-extracting Zip file, published: April 26, 1996)

1. Create a temporary folder on your hard disk.
2. Click the link, "ISDN Accelerator Pack."
3. Save the file in the new folder.
4. In that folder, double-click the file MSisdn.exe to extract the program files. The files will be placed in a directory called MSISDN on your boot drive (usually drive C)

Once you have these two pieces in hand, create temporary directories for each file. Then first execute the Microsoft Accelerator Pack file MSISDN.EXE file. You may do this by going to the DOS prompt and entering the file name or by double clicking it within the Windows Explorer, as shown in Figure 12.55.

The program asks if you want to install the Accelerator Pack, as shown in Figure 12.56. Since it will be creating a new directory and, perhaps, make other changes, Microsoft wants you to be sure you really, really mean it. Check "Yes."

Figure 12.57 reflects what has become the standard legal notice that even though you got the program from the Internet for free, you still recognize that Microsoft owns it as part of Windows 95.

FIG. 12.55

Double click the MSISDN.EXE file, while in Windows Explorer. This will cause the file to self extract creating the MSISDN directory from the root of your boot drive.

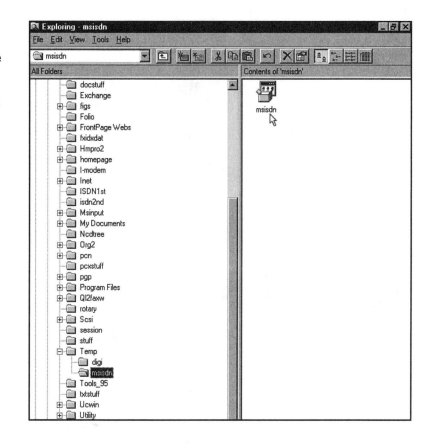

FIG. 12.56

Installation confirmation for ISDN Windows Accelerator Pack.

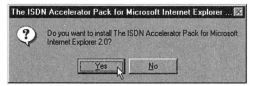

Finally, you'll arrive at Figure 12.58, which tells you to download the software for your particular card and follow the instructions it contains. In Chapter 10 we stepped through this procedure for the Digi International DataFire card.

FIG. 12.57

Microsoft's notice that Windows ISDN Accelerator Pack is part of Windows 95.

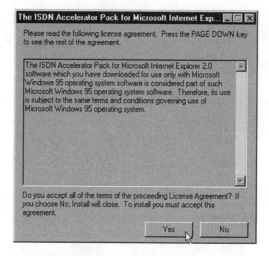

FIG. 12.58

The instructions for use of the ISDN Windows Accelerator Pack with your card's software.

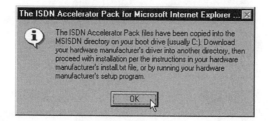

Microsoft will continue to update this software to ease use of the ISDN products that can benefit from specialized recognition during installation. This requires close coordination with the card makers. All of this makes your job easier.

From Here...

We've just discovered the exciting possibilities of Windows NT and Windows 95. Now let's take a look at more ways we can make ISDN work with them.

- In Chapter 13, "Tying It Together: Two B or Not Two B," I'll talk about how you can join B channels and use other techniques to realize higher data rates.

- Chapter 14, "Pictures and Video with ISDN," takes us into video over ISDN.

- In the remaining chapters of Part IV, we'll take brief looks at how ISDN can help your telephones, how it can be used at work, and how it functions for BBS and Internet providers.

- Part V introduces you to the future of ISDN.

CHAPTER 13

Tying It Together:
Two B or Not Two B

Up to this point, we've concentrated on getting you hooked up to ISDN, figuring out how to use it, and selecting appropriate hardware and software. Now we're going for more. Let's take a look at how B channels can be combined, *aggregated*, to provide higher data rates.

Combining B channels is not the only way to increase data rate. As I mentioned in Chapter 9, "Selecting an External Terminal Adapter," and illustrated in Figure 9.11, compression offers an additional means of increasing the effective data rate on many types of information.

All of this is tied up with issues of standards. There are a number of schemes for channel aggregation and for compression that are proprietary and used by only one or a few manufacturers. These are of no use unless the equipment at both ends is the same, and many vendors have naively assumed that would be the case.

- **BONDING (Bandwidth on Demand Interoperability Group) provides a method by the same name that puts B channels together**

    You'll see how that works and look into the future of this technology.

- **Multilink PPP is the TCP/IP approach to channel aggregation. As TCP/IP is now the most widely accepted protocol for multi-vendor environments and is the basis of the Internet, Multilink PPP is becoming the method of choice for aggregation**

    Find out how this is by the far the most important issue surrounding interoperability.

- **Compression is a part of proposed PPP and MP standards now under consideration. The TCP/IP community essentially agrees on how to do compression, but legal issues have slowed down final approval**

    Don't make the error many make. Just because a product supports Multilink PPP does not imply it supports a universal compression standard.

N O T E This chapter is concerned with combining B channels using hardware and software at your location and that of the party you're connected to. Your local exchange carrier or inter-exchange carrier may offer some form of aggregation such as *multirate ISDN* now or in the future. These options are subject to the technology and tariffs available to the carriers. In my opinion, point-to-point connections using your own equipment for aggregation are probably going to be more flexible and less expensive than if you use the carrier's. For occasional multi-point connections using aggregation, I expect the carrier-provided solutions to be worth investigating. ■

Now users are demanding interoperability among all vendors' products. Any vendor foolish enough to haul out the old saw that its proprietary way of doing channel aggregation or compression is the best, and should be used at the expense of interoperability standards, is playing the same old song that users rejected with mainframe and mini systems. The fate of such vendors will be the same as that of many in the mainframe/mini world—a slow, bleeding death or marginalization into the zombie world of the living dead. ■

BONDING

BONDING is a trademark of the BONDING Consortium—Bandwidth ON Demand INteroperability Group. It's a great acronym; one of the few that really describes what it is. Hats off to the Consortium. The folks that worked it out are primarily engaged in making *inverse multiplexers*.

T I P Bond your browser to **http://www.hep.net/ftp/networks/bonding/aaareadme-bonding** to learn more about BONDING.

Inverse Whatsits?

A multiplexer is a device that takes two or more signals (or channels) and places them in one communications circuit. So your telephone call is combined with many others into one massive communications circuit for transmission across the nation or world. At the other end, your call is *demultiplexed* from the others and sent on its way to the party you're calling.

An inverse multiplexer takes a single signal from your equipment, for example a flow of data at 128 kbps, and divides it into a number of channels for carriage over the communications circuit. If you're using BRI ISDN, the 128 kbps is chopped into two streams of 64 kbps, and each is directed to a different B channel. At the other end, an *inverse demultiplexer* reassembles the streams into the original 128 kbps data stream.

In the real world, the code and components that do the (inverse) multiplexing and (inverse) demultiplexing are usually contained in the same hardware or software.

Figure 13.1 provides a graphical view of multiplexing.

FIG. 13.1
Multiplexing and
demultiplexing.

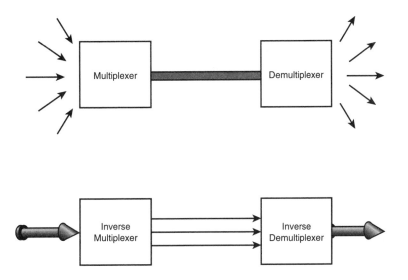

Let's take a look at the general problems facing those of us (really all of us) who want higher and higher data rates when using channelized communications technologies such as ISDN. We need ways to:

- Synchronize and align several information carrying channels that assure us the information can be reassembled in the same order and relationship originally sent by the transmitting application
- Exchange and agree on phone numbers, data rates of the channels, and other issues
- Find out when and how things fail during a session
- Change the data rate during the course of the session without destroying the session

These are the purposes that any technique devised to join channels to reach higher data rates must have, and these are the basic goals of BONDING as described in "Interoperability Requirements for Nx56/64 kbit/s Calls" published by the Consortium and available by ftp from the National HEPnet Management Network Information Center (**ftp.hep.net/afs/ hepafs1.hep.net/public/anon_ftp/networks/bonding**).

The trick to making all this work involves breaking up the data streaming from your computer into individual frames and sending each frame down the different channels. It's a gross over-simplification according to the "technosperts," but let's think about a big box of fruit you want to send to your Aunt Matilda.

The box you've collected weighs a hundred pounds, and Aunt Matilda's giant fruit basket—the one you gave her last Christmas—is just the right size to hold the load. In fact, the basket is identical to the one she admired in your house yesterday; it was filled with alternating layers of apples and oranges just like the ones you're about to send her. She commented on it as you took her to her private jet in your '72 Chevy.

However, Confederate Express won't take any box that weighs more than 50 pounds. So, just before the boys in blue and gray get to your house for the pickup, you split the fruit into two 50-pound boxes. One guy comes up and takes only one box; it seems there's not enough room left in his truck for any more. In a couple of minutes, another guy picks up the second box and puts it in another truck.

Now it just so happens that ConfX uses both trains and planes for transportation. The first pickup goes on a plane; the second on a train. The first arrives at Aunt Matilda's two hours before the second. Unfortunately, Aunt Matilda can't do anything with the fruit she received first because it's almost all apples, and there aren't enough oranges to make the alternating layers. So Matilda must wait for the second box. When it arrives, she scurries around constructing the beautiful arrangement. When it's all done, she phones you and, using ISDN with video (as we'll see in Chapter 14), gives you a panoramic tour of her *objet d'art*. She's thrilled.

You took one collection of fruit and divided it into two so it could be carried by ConfX. They could use alternate channels for transportation. At the other end, the problem became waiting for the slowest item before things could be put back together in order. A classic case of inverse multiplexing in action.

With BONDING, the same problems exist and the same solutions are applied. Your data is broken up into a stream of frames; each stream holds a percentage of the overall data rate to be transmitted. If you have two B channels with 64 kbps capacity, your equipment can pump almost (remember there's always overhead) 128 kbps by splitting the data—half to one stream and half to the other. For 384 kbps you'll need six B channels.

But now the problem is each B channel can, because of the way the telephone system is designed, take a different route resulting in a different *latency* (the delay among deliveries from each B channel at the receiving end). BONDING and the other techniques described below, must compensate for this latency. In effect, the slowest frame in a given set determines the overall wait for the information. Figure 13.2 shows the idea; the clock starts at zero when a 64 kbps frame leaves the inverse multiplexing device. After one time unit, the frames traveling the fastest route have arrived at the destination, but the slowest—having five times as much delay—are only 20% through the system. All other frames must wait until these slowest ones arrive so the information may be assembled in proper order.

BONDING provides four different modes of operation:

■ *Mode 0* provides for initial parameter negotiation and directory number exchange using the master channel. The master channel is the first to be established and is responsible for signaling and control.

■ *Mode 1* allows user data rates that are multiples of the bearer channel rate. For ISDN, the bearer channel rate is 64 kbps (except for those of you who are subject to bit robbing, then it's 56 kbps). So the Mode 1 BONDING will allow for any even multiple of 64 (or 56) up to the design maximum of 63 channels. Mode 1 does not provide "in-band" monitoring of errors; problems have to be resolved by external processes. Bandwidth cannot be added once a session is established.

FIG. 13.2

Transit delay over
different channels.

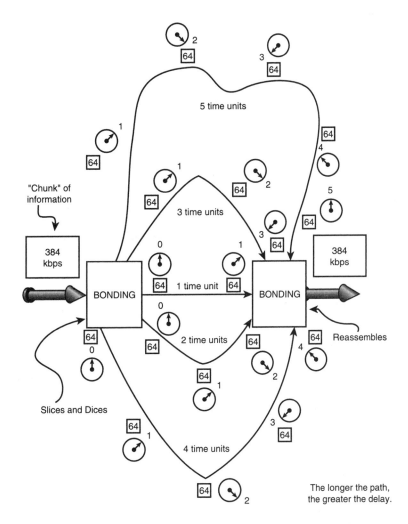

- *Mode 2* provides *in-band* monitoring to make sure delays are equalized, and it continually tests the bit error rate. However, it takes some overhead to do this monitoring; consequently, the data rate available on Mode 2 is 63/64 of the full bearer rate. Bandwidth may be added in channel size increments at any time during a session.

- *Mode 3* is the most sophisticated mode. It provides data rates that are an integral multiple of 8 kbps. Mode 3 usually adds an additional bearer channel to provide sufficient bandwidth to carry the monitor overhead without decreasing the user bandwidth. Bandwidth may be added, in increments smaller than a channel, at any time during a session.

Timing constraints within the frame structure of BONDING limit the maximum relative delay between channels to 1.024 seconds. This is a substantial delay in electronic terms, but there may be circumstances in which it would occur. Were that to happen, synchronization would be lost, and any slower channel would have to be dropped.

BONDING has been adopted by a number of manufacturers and often provides a higher data rate gain than the TCP/IP PPP Multilink described below. But the push of TCP/IP adoption will probably force BONDING into the background within a few years.

PPP Multilink Protocol

 I'm about to throw a bunch of stuff from the IETF at you. If you really want to see the details, link your Web browser to **http://www.ietf.org**.

We're now entering the domain of the *Internet Engineering Task Force*—known as the IETF for short. This world-wide group has responsibility for developing the technical aspects of new protocols in the context of the Internet. But the Internet has become so pervasive, along with its TCP/IP protocol suite, that IETF actions effectively define protocols for much of our computer communications—even those never touching the Internet proper.

IETF's working groups often produce *Requests for Comment,* RFC. In many, but not all, cases they become standards for the Internet and other systems. Often, drafts are prepared that are not yet RFCs but that seek to extend or alter existing RFCs.

Of Rules and the Future

If you've heard that the Internet has no one in charge, you've been seriously misled. Rules for most of the formal activities that keep the Internet going are promulgated by the Internet Architecture Board and the Internet Engineering Steering Group. These rules define relationships that may be involved with activities of the IETF, for example. Of interest to us now is a rule that says an RFC cannot be adopted if it incorporates intellectual property of others unless the holder of the property rights, such as a patent owner, has given permission for the use, and the details of the interest are publicly posted on the Internet—no clear definition of license requirements, no RFC status for a draft proposal. This is expressed in RFC 1602, section 5. Stay tuned to see why this is important.

We need to recognize the vital, though generally invisible, efforts contributed by the thousands of people involved in these Internet governing groups. These individuals not only give thousands of hours of their personal time and their combined organizations, but they also spend millions of dollars each year to coordinate, meet, and hash out the way the Internet works. Our discussion below is limited to issues of the PPP protocol, but there's a lot more to their efforts. Perhaps the most pressing concern in the long run (if "pressing" and "long run" may be made to fit together) is how to manage the nearly exponential growth of the Internet. The IP Next Generation (IPng) Area studies this problem.

The folks on the IPng not only see the near future creating a number of problems, but they are determined to avoid the mistakes of the past. Most of you who've worked with computers for a few years are aware of the dreaded turn-of-the-century problem—no one knows how much equipment and software was designed to assume that all years start with 19...; what will happen on January 1, 2000? Much of this equipment and software responds in ways that are unpredictable, but certain to cause havoc.

The IPng Area views the Internet in the same way. IP addresses are based on the so-called *IPv4 address space.* This means an address has the form www.xxx.yyy.zzz, where each letter group has a value between 0 and 256. Estimates are that we will exhaust such addresses by the year 2008, plus or minus tnree years. Therefore, not only does the *big Internet* of the future need a larger address space, but everything currently in place must be modified to accommodate that larger address space. Since work has started and everyone involved is aware of the problem, we can expect a smooth transition to a larger, more flexible addressing scheme. Thanks to those valiant knights of the IETF for their vigilance and hard work.

Point-to-Point Protocol

Point-to-Point Protocol is a method for exchanging packets between two computers; not a method designed for multipoint communication. PPP can carry different network layer protocols over the same link. PPP is implemented totally in software.

Each computer communicates its capabilities to the other. In this way, each computer can self-configure, starting with a default configuration, and build a more robust environment without operator intervention.

My goal here is not to take us into the *bits* and *octets* details of PPP. Rather, I want you to see that the protocol is designed to work on about anything. As a result, it is rapidly becoming the way to communicate. ISDN is the subject of RFC 1618, "PPP over ISDN."

TIP Request these comments (RFC) from **http://ds.internic.net/ds/dspg1intdoc.html** by entering the RFC number in the box and hitting return.

PPP Multilink Protocol

Given that PPP, a part of the TCP/IP suite of standards, has become the fundamental protocol for communication with your Internet access provider and probably your office, how does that help with channel aggregation?

TIP RFC 1618, "PPP over ISDN," recommends that PPP Multilink, as described in RFC 1717, be used for channel aggregation and that BONDING not be selected.

PPP Multilink Protocol (PPP-MP) is the next logical step. Since we've settled on PPP, let's use it as the basis for combining channels. RFC 1717 and a draft dated to expire December 15, 1995 that will probably modify or replace RFC 1717 provide the details.

NOTE What do we call this animal? MPPP, MPP, Multilink? There is considerable confusion on this point. The "official acronym" for *PPP Multilink Protocol* (the official full name) is *PPP-MP*; however, it appears by various other acronyms in discussions among the various experts. So much for standard nomenclature. The correct acronym is certainly not MPP, because this acronym is the property of a company in the field that extends the PPP standard in a proprietary fashion. There's considerable debate among the well-washed authorities about whether or not the proprietary extensions seriously corrupt PPP. We'll steer clear of that quagmire. ■

PPP-MP splits and recombines packets. When a machine running PPP-MP connects with another, they negotiate and determine whether either or both can support PPP-MP. If they both answer "yes," then they are saying that they can combine multiple physical links into a bundle. During this negotiation, a machine says it can:

- Combine several physical links into one bundle or logical link
- Receive higher layer protocol data units broken up or fragmented into pieces with a multilink header describing the fragmenting
- Reassemble fragments into the original protocol form so that the form can be passed to the processing on the machine based on that higher level protocol

 N O T E Whew! This is my attempt to paraphrase part of RFC 1717. It still looks complex, but I hope you get the idea. ▨

Anyway, once this deal is done, the machines can send their information using PPP-MP.

 T I P Documents from the IETF also suggest that ISDN users authenticate a connection using CHAP, and not PAP, because the IETF is phasing out PAP.

There's a lot of motion going on with respect to getting things trimmed up for ISDN. For example, there's a proposal from US Robotics that various "modes" of PPP-MP be defined for use over ISDN:

- Mode 0 is designed for multiple B channels running synchronous PPP. This is what most of us expect will be the general case soon.
- Mode 1 covers ISDN over multiple B channels using asynchronous to synchronous PPP conversion.
- Mode 2 provides for multiple B channels running V.120 rate adaptation.

The IETF has defined the PPP Bandwidth Allocation Protocol (BAP) and the PPP Bandwidth Allocation Control Protocol (BACP) to handle the actual aggregation of the B channels. These protocols can add and remove B channels dynamically as needs change.

T I P Formal definition of BAP and BAPC were still in process as this was written. See **ftp://ftp.shiva.com/ ietf-drafts/bacp-02_5.txt** or subsequent documents for details.

Interoperability, PPP, and PPP-MP

What makes PPP and PPP-MP really important is their near universal adoption by the user community. But since PPP-MP is such a newly developed protocol, and much of its contents are subject to different interpretations by those who would make implementations (that's a fancy way of saying the vendors), problems of interoperablity crop up.

In March 1995, the California ISDN Users' Group held a "bake off" among 25 bridge, router, software, and test equipment companies to see who could talk to whom. The tests used PPP MP with two B channels between devices. In a moment the results of that trial, but first a word from its participants:

- 3Com Access Products Group, Holmdel, NJ
- 3Com Personal Office Division, San Jose, CA
- ACC, Santa Barbara, CA
- Ascend Communications, Alameda, CA
- CO Systems, Inc., Sunnyvale, CA
- Digiboard, Eden Prarie, MN
- Flowpoint, San Jose, CA
- Gandalf Technologies, Inc., South Nepean, ON, Canada
- IBM, Research Triangle Park, NC
- ISDN Systems Corporation, Vienna, VA
- ISDN*tek, San Gregorio, CA
- KNX Corporation, San Francisco, CA
- Microsoft Corporation, Redmond, WA
- MPX Data Systems, Inc., San Jose, CA
- NetCS Informationstechnick GmbH, Berlin, Germany
- NetManage, Cupertino, CA
- Network Communications Corporation, Bloomington, MN
- Network Express, Ann Arbor, MI
- Rockwell Network Systems, Santa Barbara, CA
- Shiva Corporation, Burlington, MA
- Silicon Graphics, Inc., Mountain View, CA
- Stagecoach Communications, Inc., San Jose, CA
- Xyplex, Inc., Littleton, MA

 T I P Check out **http://www.ciug.org** (the California ISDN Users Group) for the results of these interoperability trials.

I hope that little commercial break didn't lose your interest. The verdict for the March 1995 round is reflected in Table 13.1. You'll notice there's no clear winner—no case in which someone could talk to everyone else.

Part
IV

Ch
13

Table 13.1 MP Test Results, California ISDN Users' Group, March 22, 1995

Product	3ComQ	3ComA	Asce	Comb	Digi	Flow	Gand	ISDNS	ISDNT	KNX	Micr	MPX	NetM	Netw	Shiv	Sili	Xypl
3Com APG Quick Access Remote	-	-	✓	✓		✓	-	✓	✓	✓	✓	✓	✓	-	✓	-	-
3Com POD	-	-						-		-	-	-					
Access-Builder 4000	-	-						✓	-	✓	✓	✓	-	-	-	-	-
Ascend Pipeline 50	-	-	-	-	-	✓	-	✓	✓	✓	-	✓	✓	-	-	-	-
Combinet EVERY-WARE 2000	✓	✓	✓	✓	✓	✓	✓	✓	✓	-	-	✓	✓	✓	✓	✓	✓
Digiboard DataFire	-	-	✓	-	✓	-	✓	-	✓	-	✓	-	✓	✓	-	-	-
Flowpoint 200	✓	✓	✓	-	✓	✓	✓	✓	-	-	-	✓	✓	✓	-	-	-
Gandalf Xpressway	-	-	✓	-	✓	✓	-	-	-	✓	-	✓	✓	✓	-	-	-
ISDN Systems Secure Link Ada	✓	✓	-	✓	-	✓	-	✓	✓	✓	✓	✓	✓	✓	✓	-	-
ISDN.tek	✓	✓	✓	✓	✓	✓	-	✓	✓	✓	✓	✓	-	-	-	-	✓

Commuter Card

KNX Remote LAN Workstation

Microsoft Windows NT RAS

MPX Remote Access 5.0

Net-Manage Chameleon

Network Express NEISDN Inter

Shiva LanRover

Silicon Graphics Indy Workst

Xyplex Network 3000

While you review Table 13.1, keep in mind the following points footnoted by the California ISDN Users' Group:

- A "✔" means both companies agree they interoperated. A "-" may mean the company just did not have time to make this test, or it may mean the test was not 100% successful.

- No tests were made of each product to itself; all these results are blank.

- This matrix is a snapshot of a rapidly changing situation. It gives the status as of the end of the workshop. These companies are continuing to test their products and resolve any problems identified. It is very likely that the current situation is much better than shown.

- The California ISDN Users' Group plans to publish information on the interoperability of products as they are announced and become available.

- NCC brought their 7300 Network Probe analyzer. It was used to analyze ISDN connections as well as MP on the B channel. It was used to decode MP on the following: 3Com APG, Combinet, Flowpoint, ISDN*tek, Microsoft, MPX NetCS, NetManage, and Shiva.

As the results of the 1995 trial were mixed, and as new standards, agreements, and products have appeared; the CIUG has conducted subsequent trials. At the time of this writing, none of the results have been published. CIUG and the participants agreed more engineering and firming of standards was needed before any test results are again published. I hope CIUG runs additional tests and publishes the results. This information is vital to us all. Keep an eye on **http://www.ciug.org** for results.

Compression

Combining B channels is a great idea, but it has one big drawback. The more B channels you use, the more you have to pay for. You may say, "I only have one BRI with two B channels. That's the least I can get; I might as well use them both through PPP-MP." That makes a lot of sense—especially if you're telecommuting to your office. In that case, your office might have a BRI for you, and the use of both B channels would be great. But what if you're calling an Internet access provider? Chances are, the provider is pricing ISDN access on a per-B-channel basis. Then the addition of a B channel will add to your costs. Of course, your use of a sophisticated router that only kicks in the second channel when you really need it will help. But something else might well give you a much higher effective data rate for no more bucks: compression.

Remember compression from our earlier discussion in Chapter 9? If the data you're sending is filled with empty spaces or repetitive information, compression can give you two, four, or maybe more times the effective data rate over a physical channel with a real rate that never changes. Compression algorithms remove the empty spaces, encode the repetitions, and do all sorts of other fancy stuff to save space and get more real data to you faster.

Modems use MNP 4 and 5 or V.42 bis to make this happen. ISDN vendors have proprietary protocols for compression. But the general solution lies with providing compression as an extension to PPP and PPP-MP.

Working groups within the IETF have put forth a number of proposals to do just that. There are suggestions for:

- PPP Stacker LZS Compression Protocol
- PPP Compression Control Protocol (CCP)
- PPP Gandalf FZA Protocol
- PPP Hewlett-Packard Packet-by-Packet Compression
- PPP Predictor Compression Protocol
- PPP BSD Compression Protocol

Of these, the second—CCP, *Compression Control Protocol*— is of most general interest for conversion into an RFC. It speaks to negotiating data compression over PPP links. Once this negotiation has taken place, the other protocols may be selected for use. So CCP is a necessary prerequisite to a flexible compression environment in which many methods to actually compress are used. And therein lies the rub.

Motorola has a patent on the very negotiation method proposed in CCP. The IETF and Motorola were in limbo for many months over this issue. Remember my mention of RFC 1602, section 5, in the note as we began discussing PPP? You know, the one that says the IETF can't use a piece of intellectual property in an RFC until the owner publicly posts information on the Internet about its rights, etc. Well, guess what? That's exactly where the whole question of CCP, the control mechanism for ISDN PPP compression, ended up.

Eventually, Motorola provided a letter from its attorneys stating that it was acceptable for the IETF to include Motorola's negotiation method in the standard; but Motorola has never put the letter in electronic form and posted it on the Internet as required by RFC 1602, section 5. I know the following is hard to believe, but insiders tell me it's true. Motorola provides a physical, signed letter from its lawyers saying, "Go ahead and use it;" yet we have the IETF saying, "That's not enough, Motorola. You've got to put it on the Internet." It begins to look like the engineer types are more obsessive about the strict wording of the rules than the lawyers. This absurd state of affairs ground on for a while; finally, the IETF decided it really was acceptable to use the Motorola lawyers' paper letter. Today, because of these events; it is acceptable for everyone to use the Motorola method of negotiating for compression.

Part

IV

Ch

13

N O T E Look into **http://www.ietf.org** for general information on the Internet Engineering Task Force. RFC 1915 details what happened with the Motorola issue. You may obtain any RFC by going to **http://ds.internic.net/ds/dspg1intdoc.html** and entering the RFC number in the search box. At the time of this writing, compression is still the subject of drafts such as draft-i3tf-pppext-compression-04.txt available through **http://www.ietf.org/ids.by.wg/pppext.html** which provides a listing of all drafts currently available related to PPP. Be sure to remember that drafts are only for IETF discussion; they are not standards. Requests for Comment (RFC) establish the standards. If you really want to delve into the details of how all this works, see RFC 1920. ∎

With all this worked out on compression, the IETF is close to providing a standard; but the specifics of implementation still have several potential options. As a result, the industry is moving toward adopting one or more existing proprietary standards to fill in the blanks. In the ISDN world using the Internet, the market dominance of Ascend in the Internet service providers' systems favors adoption of the methods used by Ascend. Ascend has offered to license its methods to other manufacturers for a relatively nominal cost. Adoption of Ascend's standards makes any adopting maker 100% compatible with the Ascend routers at many ISPs, not only resulting in performance gains to users of that maker's equipment, but also resulting in benefits for the whole market. There is some industry opposition to accepting Ascend as a standard-setter. However, this opposition seems to have the flavor of similar opposition to much larger companies, such as Microsoft and Intel, when they effectively dictate how things will be done. Ascend is not in such a position of total control. Therefore, by licensing, Ascend is actually ceding future market share to assure industry development. In my opinion, this is a win-win situation for Ascend, its competitors and their customers: you.

N O T E　A number of vendors are engineering their equipment to detect the channel aggregation and compression methods running on a foreign router. With that information, these new, flexible routers change to the most efficient protocols possible for the connection. This is an excellent way to deal with hold-over proprietary protocols. The final IETF standards will always be designed in. ■

From Here...

That's it for a compressed discussion, going from point to point in a way that I hope bonds you to greater understanding of how to most effectively multiply your links to use ISDN. We're moving on to:

- Getting you into pictures with ISDN and video is covered in Chapter 14, "Pictures and Video with ISDN."

- From there I'll talk to you about telephone with ISDN in Chapter 15, "Changing Telephones to ISDN."

- Since you're able to see and hear from anywhere, Chapter 16, "Putting ISDN to Work," puts you to work from home.

- Just in case you want to get in really deep, walk in the shoes of Internet providers and big corporations as they plunge into ISDN in Chapter 17, "ISDN Access for Internet Providers and Corporations."

- Then get out your crystal ball for the future in Part V.

Pictures & Video with ISDN

Up to this point, we've concerned ourselves with the rather pedestrian issues of gathering information and getting it through the ISDN pipe. Now we're moving into the real excitement that ISDN can bring. Its higher data rates, more flexible control, and rapid setup/teardown influence the kinds of applications we'll use.

Video transmission and cooperative, simultaneous work with applications are among the most interesting possible uses for ISDN. They furnish the basis for a really distributed, virtual office environment where everyone is working together regardless of each person's physical location. ISDN makes this possible because it furnishes the underlying vehicle to carry any information, anywhere, at as high a data rate as deemed necessary by the users consistent with the costs of transmission. ISDN allows this data rate, and corresponding costs, to be adjusted dynamically as need arises.

In order for all this to work, we need standards to furnish the basis for a cooperative environment, and we need products that use those standards. In this chapter we'll examine both. ■

_T.120_ encompasses the standards for conferencing in general

You'll see these standards don't require video, but video may be included.

_H.320_ establishes the standards for videoconferencing

Find out what these fundamental videoconferencing standards mean to you.

Vtel is one of the companies that provides products based on international standards

We'll look at setting up their system and touch on the wide range of products for desktop, small conference and auditorium use they offer.

Intel markets ProShare aggressively in the desktop videoconferencing world. Intel initially opposed H.320 and offered its own _de facto_ standard proposal

You'll see how Intel supports both to work in concert or, at least, to provide a basis for interoperation.

PictureTel is the market leader in large videoconference systems

You'll be interested to see that now it's entering the desktop conferencing arena.

Standards for Conferencing and Video

Whenever you plunge into discussions of videoconferencing you run headlong into two standards from the ITU-T: T.120 describes the multimedia basis for a number of different communication methods, including video; H.320 deals specifically with issues of video.

T.120—The General Multimedia Conferencing Standard

T.120 is designed to enable users to share information among different platforms and with multimedia features. In particular, T.120 seeks to provide interoperability among different applications to

- Send graphic images;
- Provide for real-time annotation;
- Do file transfers;
- Share applications;
- Exchange faxes.

A number of specific standards are encompassed within the purview of T.120. I'll give the number followed by the formal name in parenthesis.

T.123 (protocol stacks for videographic and audiovisual teleconference applications) provides a basis for using different types of networks for carriage; these include POTS, X.25, and ISDN. Unfortunately, LAN environments are not included; however, groups are working on adding TCP/IP and IPX.

T.122 (multipoint communications service—service description) and *T.125* (multipoint communications service—protocol description) define use of the *Multipoint Communications Services* (MCS) to give user options for setting up one-to-one, one-to-many, and many-to-many conferences. All of this is controlled by what is called the Multipoint Communications Service (MCS).

T.124 (generic conference control) provides for *Generic Conference Control* (GCC). This provides a standard way to establish conferences, maintain security, determine capabilities among different types of equipment at users' sites, and make different applications work together.

T.126 (still image transfer and annotation) is really important; it lays the groundwork for users in a multipoint conference to view and make notes on images, faxes, and various computer applications. It's designed to work with totally heterogeneous environments of different applications and different operating systems.

T.127 (multipoint binary file transfer) establishes a way for users to effect simultaneous multipoint file transfers.

T.128 (high level audio and video control) specifies the use of real-time audio or video along with a conferencing application that uses audio or video.

Some of the features of T.120 are mandatory for a vendor to claim T.120 compliance. Others are conditioned on whether or not the vendor is using a certain feature. Figure 14.1 illustrates the relations. Notice that Generic Conference Control, Multipoint Communications Service and Network Specific Transport Protocols are mandatory. Outside of the conditional and mandatory categories, vendors may supply different sorts of standard and non-standard applications.

FIG. 14.1

T.120 conferencing standard. Graphic courtesy Vtel and Bruce Kravitz.

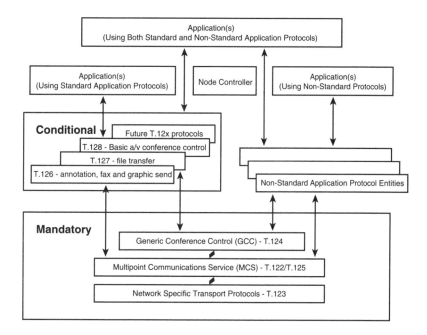

In Figure 14.1, the box labeled "mandatory" contains the portions of the T.120 standards a vendor has to comply with. Those labeled "conditional" depend on the need for optional functions.

H.320—The General Videoconferencing Standard

N O T E Should you want to tread more deeply into T.120, H.320, or any other ITU-T standards or issues, dog paddle on over to **http://www.itu.ch**. Direct access to the specifications through the ITU is only available by subscriptions measured in U.S. $1000s. If that's out of your budget range, and even if you've already subscribed, take a look at **http://www.csn.net/imtc/** for the International Multimedia Teleconferencing Consortium; this is where you'll find information on such important issues as interoperability among various products and many up-to-date details on multimedia teleconferencing issues. I also suggest you take a look at the whitepaper by DataBeam available at **http://www.databeam.com/Products/CCTS/t120primer.html** detailing T.120. ▪

T.120 deals in general with multimedia conferencing. The ITU-T has also developed H.320 to govern specific issues within video for conferencing.

H.320 provides three classes of vendor support for its standards:

■ Class 1: The vendor provides a minimum level of support.

■ Class 2: The vendor provides support as in Class 1 plus some optional features.

■ Class 3: The vendor provides support for Class 1 and all optional features.

The primary H.320 issue of interest to users concerns the quality of the components that make up H.320. These determine the quality of the received images and sounds:

■ Picture resolutions are available in two standards: *Quarter Common Intermediate Format* (QCIF) supports a resolution of 176 × 144; *Common Intermediate Format* (CIF or FCIF, the F is for Full) provides a resolution of 352 × 288. Class 1 only requires QCIF.

■ *Frame rates* of 7.5, 10, 15, and 30 frames per second are supported by H.320. Class 1 only requires 7.5.

■ *Pre-* and *postprocessing* refers to techniques that reduce the amount of repetitive re-coding and retransmission of unchanging background information. The less processing, the more the picture degrades because the system is wasting its time on information that doesn't change and need not be resent. With this waste, other quality enhancements are degraded, because processing power and bandwidth are reduced for needless repetition of the same picture elements. Only changes—that is motion—in the picture should be subject to encoding and transmission. Postprocessing also compensates for issues surrounding motion. Class 1 systems need no pre- or postprocessing.

■ *Motion compensation* estimates motion and compensates for it. This determines the direction of motion, and moves information being presented in anticipation of motion. This helps at lower data rates, such one or two B channels, as it encodes the motion only where it happens and not the whole picture. Class 1 systems are required to have motion compensation, but more complex forms of motion encoding are not required.

■ Audio options available in H.320 break down into three categories. *G.711* provides 48-64 kbps of narrowband audio; this is 3 kHz voice grade telephone quality. *G.722* provides 48-64 kbps of wideband audio; this is much higher quality that is equivalent to a 7 kHz telephone circuit. *G.728* provides 16 kbps of narrowband audio. G.728 is very important for lower data rate transmission (a single BRI), because it uses only 16 kbps to transmit audio of essentially 3 kHz telephone quality. Class 1 systems need only supply G.711. But this means that a full B channel would be used to transmit audio, which leaves only the second BRI B channel for video. A system that offers G.728 provides essentially the same audio quality while using only 16 kbps of a B channel. This leaves 48 kbps to add to another B channel, which results in 112 kbps for video transmission with a substantial increase in video quality (due to the added data rate).

While H.320 provides a basis for interoperation of different vendors' systems, the lowest class system will reduce the overall quality of the video and audio of any higher class system to which it attaches. Although we cannot go into all the details of each standard, Figure 14.2 shows the primary H.320 related standards and how they are related. These are the various standards and groups of standards that work together for videoconferencing.

FIG. 14.2

H.320 and related protocols for videoconferencing. Graphic courtesy Vtel and Bruce Kravitz.

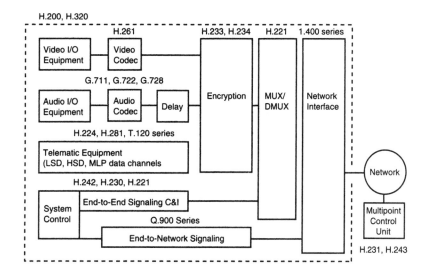

N O T E   To find why the DoD bought the COS document, drive your tank over to **http:// www.cos.com** where I hope you'll find the information. Unfortunately, I believe the Corporation for Open Systems, COS, may be closing shop and the whereabouts of the document are in limbo—the drawbacks to a Web reference. While you're at it, check out the sounds and sights at **http:// www.csn.net/imtc** to see how the International Multimedia Teleconferencing Consortium works with H.320 and T.120.

All of these standards and more are incorporated into the Industry *Video Teleconferencing Profile,* issued by the Corporation for Open Systems International. This is the document the United States Department of Defense has declared to be the standard for its video-conferencing.

Vtel

Vtel and other companies providing videoconferencing equipment often have three broadly defined lines:

- Large group conference systems, which are suitable for groups of 10, 20, or hundreds.

Part
IV

Ch
14

- Small-group-conference systems, which are suitable for a group of a few people. Basically, these systems consist of a PC with one or more 21- to 32-inch monitors.

- Individual, desktop videoconferencing for an individual and maybe one or two onlookers.

 TIP Don't tell, but you'll find Vtel at **http://www.vtel.com** with a substantial amount of product and standards information.

The standards and fundamental ideas are the same in all three approaches. Larger groups may entail more expensive equipment to satisfy the larger volume of coverage needed and the potential involvement of many people at one site. As I said before, in this chapter I'll be using the small group or desktop videoconferencing products as examples, as those are the ones most directly applicable to personal, small business, and telecommuting uses. I expect you'll certainly jump for such systems soon. If you also have larger systems, it's a fair bet you'll have several of the smaller ones too.

Vtel recently brought out the *Personal Collaborator* as a single-board upgrade to a Windows 95 PC. The board is both the video code and ISDN card (see Fig. 14.3). I applaud Vtel for providing this product that you can use on your current PC, so long as it's running Windows 95, is a 486/33 or better, and has at least 8 MBs of RAM. This is a move toward reality on the part of Vtel. In the past, the firm had insisted on selling the computer with the video products. They weren't alone; all the initial big players in video teleconferencing made you buy the computers and monitors to get their goodies.

FIG. 14.3
The Vtel Personal Collaborator single board upgrade to a Windows 95 PC takes advantage of the hardware investment you've already made.

Our Product Is So Great, You Have To Buy Everything From Us

How many times have you looked at some product that contained a large percentage of components you already had (or could buy at a good price)? The true worth of the product package offered was only a fraction of its price. In other words, you were being forced to accept components that you didn't want or need at an inflated price. To make matters worse, companies required you to buy other parts exclusively from them.

For example, the DEC Rainbow (no longer on the market), wouldn't run software or take hardware cards designed for the IBM PC. DEC pointed out that the machine was a much better design with better video, the ability to run all of the then dominant operating systems, CP/M programs, and a whiz-bang modular design that you could assemble and disassemble using only a U.S. 25 cent piece.

The Rainbow was going to be the machine that competed with and beat Apple and IBM. It was light years ahead in design, being both modular and state of the art. DEC needed to protect the machine, and you, from any possibility of problems. So, among other things, you had to buy the floppies pre-formatted from DEC. The software they provided had no program to format floppies. Interestingly, the price on those floppies was several times that of the more common, physically identical but unformatted, ones you could buy for Apple and IBM machines; yet the Apple and IBM machines came with a formatting utility. As I recall, it took about three months for someone to write and distribute a formatting program for Rainbow floppies.

Then there was IBM with the PC warranty. If you so much as dared to put someone else's card in the machine, or even a non-blue chip, you were alleged to have violated the warranty. And, of course, Radio Shack put out a version of MS-DOS that expired in a year or two to "protect you from an obsolete operating system"—and extract some shekels quickly when your whole business shut down on January 1.

The mainframe bandits tried to tie you to them. As you know, all this collapsed in the wake of fierce competition and more than a few lawsuits. That's what's happening to the video teleconferencing world—get the picture? A vast amount of their profit in the past came from selling (the fancy word is OEMing) you something you either already had or could have bought much cheaper elsewhere. But, if you wanted video teleconferencing, you had to take the whole enchilada; after all, it's so complicated and expensive, you couldn't possibly put it together yourself.

TIP The Rainbow was a DEC disaster. The opposite is true of Digital's Alpha chip and AltaVista, the fastest processor and search engine in the known universe at **http://www.altavista.dec.com**, where you'd better have on your fireproof gloves to enter screamingly fast total searches of the Internet.

The Vtel TC1000 is a system for small groups. It has a 27-inch (diagonal) monitor (see Fig. 14.4). It's based on a Pentium PC running Microsoft Windows 95. Let's step through the installation of Vtel's software to understand some of the major features available and standards involved. Figure 14.5 shows the original installation configuration with selection of a number of options available in the standards. Here you can choose to have one or two channels of communication. Since we're using ISDN, we want two: A and B. You may choose QCIF or FCIF for the quality of resolution. Vtel supports all three possible audio standards. The audio delay, in this case 310 milliseconds, is to compensate for the time it takes to process the video compared to the time it takes for the audio to get through. Since video takes a longer time, you need to introduce a delay to get the video and audio in sync.

FIG. 14.4

Vtel TC1000 small group videoconferencing system.

FIG. 14.5

Vtel configuration for
resolution, audio, and
channels.

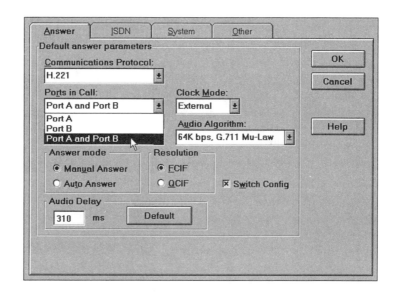

Figure 14.6 shows a selection of ISDN from among a number of other possible physical methods of connecting to another conference system.

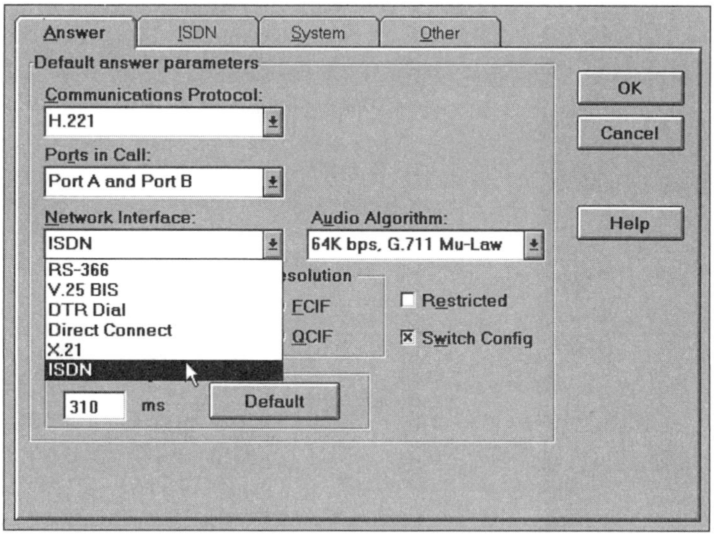

FIG. 14.6

Vtel configuration
selection of ISDN.

You can choose from the full range of audio options available under H.320, as shown in Figure 14.7. I'm choosing G.728 so we'll only use 16 kbps and not waste data rate that can be better spent on video.

FIG. 14.7
Vtel configuration selection of audio specification.

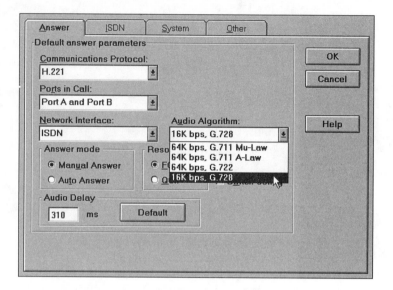

The ISDN specific configuration is shown in Figure 14.8, where you select the switch from among all the major types in the world, and enter the directory numbers and SPIDs in Figure 14.9. Of course, if you're using a switch that doesn't have SPIDs, the screen would appear differently.

FIG. 14.8
Vtel configuration for ISDN Switch Type.

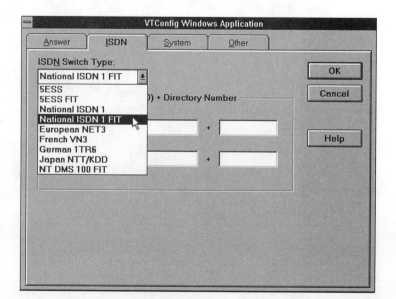

FIG. 14.9

Vtel configuration of
ISDN directory numbers
and SPIDs.

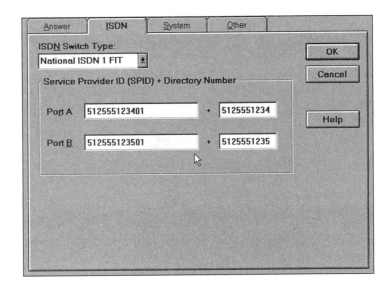

Vtel's products include hardware components. As a general rule, Vtel sells the entire computer with the components included. In Figure 14.10, you see the configuration screen for the videoconferencing hardware that Vtel supplies.

FIG. 14.10

Vtel configuration of
conferencing hardware.

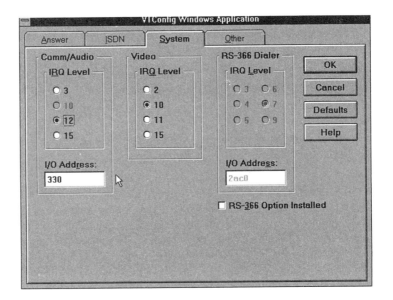

Now we'll get into some more interesting, video type configuration. Figure 14.11 shows selection of the Chroma Key color. This color keys the location where Vtel is to put the image received from a camera. It's exactly the same technology used by regular television. If you were in the television studio when the person presenting the weather report was talking, you'd notice that there's nothing behind that person's animated actions over the weather map. There's no map—just a light blue wall. But when you looked on monitors in the studio, you'd see the map.

FIG. 14.11
Vtel configuration of
Chroma Key.

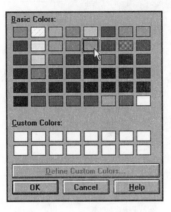

The trick is the chroma key. A color is chosen to be the key; it's almost always light blue. Then when some other video image is to be superimposed on the screen, it is "keyed" to that color. Anything on the original image that's the same color will pick up the superimposed image. If the announcer had on clothing with that light blue color, part of the map would take over the clothing. Since the same thing happens on your videoconference screen when an image is superimposed, you have the option to change the key color, should it present a problem.

A very flexible way to use Vtel is to combine it with Intel's ProShare. I'll be talking about ProShare below as a complete conferencing product including video. But ProShare is available in versions that supply the conferencing tools without the video features. The Vtel and Intel products can be used together to furnish the higher quality video of Vtel with the easy to use conference features of ProShare.

Intel ProShare

As I just implied above, Intel's ProShare name covers both videoconferencing products and group conferencing needs, such as whiteboard and application sharing.

N O T E   Get a look at what Intel pictures for videoconferencing using ISDN and LANs. Hook up your
Web and peer into **http://www.intel.com/comm-net/support/selfhelp/8159.htm** for
the full story. ■

In this discussion, I'll concentrate on the ISDN installation and configuration issues within ProShare.

While ProShare and Vtel can work together as I just discussed, Vtel has higher quality video because Vtel supports the 16 kbps audio standard G.728. This means Vtel can use 112 kbps for video on a BRI. ProShare is also able to restrict audio to 16 kbps, but has a maximum of 90 kbps available for video.

Intel designed ProShare with a *de facto* standard and originally did not support H.320. The Personal Conferencing Work Group, made up of Intel and many other companies, supported the Intel standard in opposition to H.320 until it became apparent that buyers would not commit to systems that were not H.320 compliant. In the first quarter of 1995, the Group modified its position and now requires its membership to provide H.320 compatibility. When, for example, two ProShare systems are talking, they are using the de facto standard developed by Intel, including a compression algorithm called Indeo. However, as the call started, the machines first automatically inquired of each other if such options were available. Since they were both ProShare systems, the call proceeded using the Intel developed standard. Had they determined that the Intel standard was not available, they would have proceeded using H.320. H.320 automatically becomes the least common denominator for videoconferencing, ensuring interoperation among vendors.

Figure 14.12 shows one of the initial setup screens concerning ISDN use with ProShare. The question is whether or not you're using an ISDN phone with your ProShare video.

As you go down the path of ISDN configuration for ProShare, you're asked about your ISDN switch, as in Figure 14.13, and for the directory numbers and SPIDs, as in Figure 14.14.

FIG. 14.12
ProShare setup for
ISDN phone.

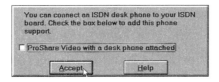

FIG. 14.13
ProShare ISDN switch
selection.

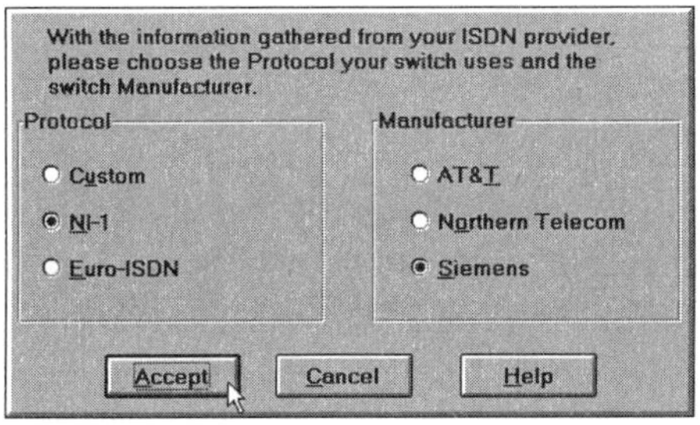

FIG. 14.14
ProShare directory
number and SPID
selection.

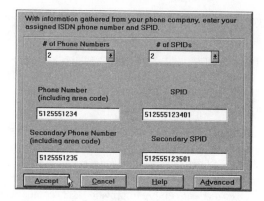

The ProShare "handset" window is illustrated in Figure 14.15. The two screens on the right may each be split from the dial and control panel on the left; you may move them around and place them anywhere you want on the screen.

FIG. 14.15
ProShare handset with
dial, control panel, and
video images.

TROUBLESHOOTING

To check things out and be sure your equipment is working correctly, perform a loopback test. To do this, you call a number for the test. The vendor or telephone company will supply this number. In Figure 14.16, I'm looping back from an AT&T test point in New Mexico. Notice the reversal of "handedness" in the pictures. I went out right handed and came back left handed. Those of you into mathematics and relativity physics might surmise that I traversed a four dimensional *Möbius* strip and was turned into a mirror image of myself! This came in very handy later in the day when my mirror self faced a right-handed pitcher. That night, I rounded up all my single gloves and shoes that had lost their mates. I sent them through the loopback thereby substantially increasing my wardrobe.

FIG. 14.16
Notice the reversal of
the image as a result of
the loopback test.

The real power of these systems comes when you combine everything. Figure 14.17 shows an application with the faces of the two persons working on it. At the same time, they're talking over the audio connection. By the way, ProShare allows you to almost double the size of the video images, but you cannot fill the screen with one.

FIG. 14.17
ProShare users sharing
an application.

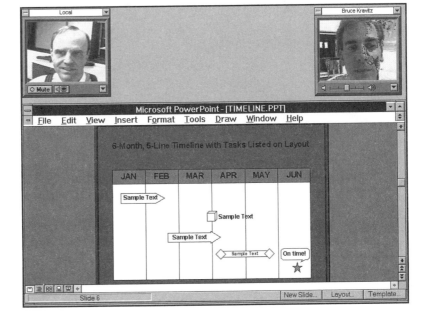

Intel's ProShare is an excellent product that is becoming very popular. The move to support H.320 for interoperability is adding growth to the videoconferencing marketplace. Recent pricing has dropped the cost below $1,000 in many instances. Intel has recently upgraded the product to the Intel ProShare Conferencing Video System 200. The screens are slicker and multipoint conferences are now supported. This means you can have a video conference with more than one site at a time. Take a look at Figure 14.18, which shows the start of a video conference among four people in different places.

FIG. 14.18

Intel ProShare Conferencing Video System 200 illustrates a conference among four people at different locations.

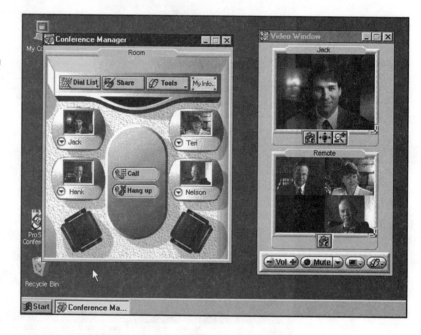

During the course of a conference you may decide to work with an application and present the results to the others. In Figure 14.19, a participant selects an application for group review.

When the sharing becomes effective, the document in question appears on everyone's screen (see Fig. 14.20). This assumes everyone has the same application installed on their local machines.

FIG. 14.19
Intel ProShare System 200 conference participant selects sharing an application.

FIG. 14.20
Intel ProShare System 200 enables several participants in a conference to share a document.

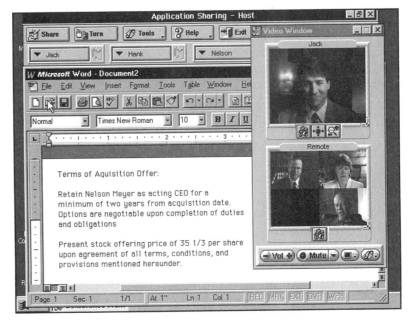

PictureTel, Vistium, and Corel

PictureTel has the lion's share of expensive videoconferencing now. Much of this consists of larger group and room systems. Desktop systems are just now reaching prices that make them reasonable. PictureTel offers the Live200 Series (Live200p and Live200i), made to run with Windows 95 PCs for the desktop videoconferencing market. This is a single board product with a supporting camera and uses the resources you probably received with your PC. As with the other products, ISDN is the communications basis for these systems. At the higher end of group and rooms size systems, much of the speed and quality of PictureTel relies on custom hardware designs. But their products are capable of communication with other H.320 compliant systems.

 T I P Picture yourself at **http://www.picturetel.com** looking over their wares.

N O T E   AT&T used to provide the Vistium line of videoconferencing hardware and software along with application sharing software. Now AT&T has dropped Vistium in favor of referrals to Intel and PictureTel. ■

Corel Video is a well thought out video system for use on the office LAN and, through ISDN connections to remote sites. Within the LAN it is transmitted over an extra twisted pair of cables that, hopefully, are available with your regular LAN cabling. The system produces top quality video and audio. It supports H.320.

 T I P Corral Corel at **http://www.corel.com**.

Everything we've looked at so far is directed toward selling you a particular company's hardware. But it's possible to put together a package with generic video and audio hardware and sell, or even give away the software.

Vivo

N O T E   If you use your own WaveRunner with Vivo, be sure the WaveRunner you use is a version B or later. Although IBM says the WaveRunner A and B differ only in the support for more serial ports on the B version, Vivo advises that their software only works with the B version because IBM included appropriate support for them in B. ■

Vivo offers a software package, with standard third-party hardware, that turns your desktop computer into a videoconferencing workstation. The Vivo Personal Videoconferencing 320 package includes:

■ IBM WaveRunner ISDN card

■ Logitech MovieMan video capture card

■ Camera

■ Microphone, earphone, and speaker

■ Vivo320 and DataBeam FarSite software to support videoconferencing with shared whiteboard and file transfer

■ Vivo TeleWork Center toolbar system for creating a work environment

■ WaveRunner application drivers

■ Trio DataFax

▶ **See** "IBM WaveRunner," **p. 259**

N O T E Vivo advised me that these are the very minimum requirements. They strongly recommend at least the following: Pentium 90 MHz, 16 MB RAM, 16 bit (64K) color video. ■

As you might guess from its name, Vivo320, the product is H.320 compliant. So, since Intel and others have agreed to support H.320, you can be sure you have at least basic interoperation with all other major videoconferencing systems. Since Vivo does everything in software, it has some stringent hardware requirements for your computer:

■ Intel 486DX2 66 MHz or Pentium 60 MHz

■ 8 MB RAM

■ SVGA video

■ Accelerated VESA local bus or PCI video card with 8-bit (256) color

Since Vivo runs in software, you have options to balance the load among functions. Figure 14.21 shows your options for speeding up document sharing or file transfer by slowing down video.

FIG. 14.21
Vivo data preference options.

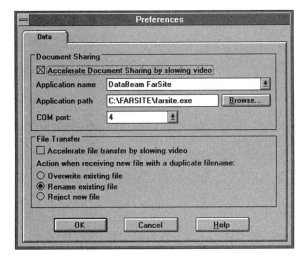

Part
IV

Ch
14

Of course, Vivo's software provides a means of setting up the ISDN parameters. Figure 14.22 shows the switch selection, and Figure 14.23 provides for directory number and SPID entry.

FIG. 14.22
Vivo ISDN switch selection.

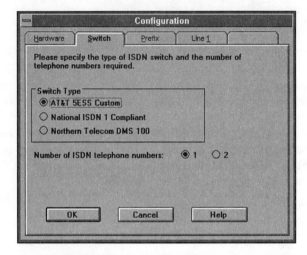

FIG. 14.23
Vivo ISDN line selection.

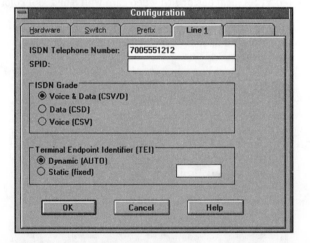

Vivo is tying this product into a collection of products called TeleWork-5 with five elements:

- Personal videoconferencing
- Screen sharing and file transfer for collaborative work
- Internet access using ISDN

- Remote LAN access using ISDN
- Fax/Modem Emulation

Once your Vivo is set up, you'll be able to have videoconferences with screens like the one shown in Figure 14.24.

FIG. 14.24
Vivo videoconferencing in progress.

They've taken the software they have, third party software, and third party hardware, and made a shot at the telecommuting marketplace. I doubt they'll be in this alone.

CU-SeeMe

CU-SeeMe is free software for conferencing using video, audio and text over the Internet or other TCP/IP environments. It was originally developed at Cornell University for the Macintosh and has recently been released in a Windows form. You can be only a receiver or both a transmitter and receiver.

> **T I P** The formal name of the software has a hyphen, CU-SeeME, but general use leaves it out, CUSeeMe.

> **N O T E** First take a look at **ftp://gated.cornell.edu/pub/video/README.First.1-16-95.txt** for the latest information and files on CU-SeeMe. Then aim at **http://bio444.beaumont.plattsburgh.edu:80/CUSeeMe.html** to start Web surfing. To find the latest scoops on all sorts of information (much like Dan Kegel's ISDN page, **http://alumni.caltech.edu/~dank/isdn**) see Michael Sattler's CU-SeeMe home page at **http://www.jungle.com/msattler/sci-tech/comp/CU-SeeMe**. ▪

CU-SeeMe can provide multiparty conferences on the Internet through the use of reflectors, UNIX computers running a program that reflects the images among several parties. If you're not connected to a reflector on the Internet, only point-to-point, two-party, communication is possible. Don't despair. There are public reflectors you may use for this. Development of the **M**ulticast **B**ackbone **on** the Internet (MBONE) is also contributing to multicast possibilities.

Chew on the MBONE at **http://www.best.com/~prince/techinfo/**.

When you're using CU-SeeMe, or any other program that needs a lot of bandwidth, pay close attention to the load you're putting on the Internet. There are a number of technical methods that may be used to reduce this load described within the documentation.

CU-SeeMe has become so popular it's now being licensed for commercial development. This prospect could have a very strong effect on the future of videoconferencing. Consider what's happened to the Web and Web browsers with commercial development.

Look at a licensee at **http://goliath.wpine.com/cu-seeme.html**.

Connectix

I want to use CU-SeeME. The software's free, but I have to buy all that expensive hardware, sort of like what's in the Vivo offering. I've got a sound card, mike, and speakers. My monitor's top flight. I'm big on ISDN and have a network so I've already got a fast router. Well that leaves the camera and its card. Those sure are expensive, but Connectix makes a digital camera that doesn't need a card; it uses the parallel port. It originally was only black and white, but now it comes in color, all for less than $200. Wow!

That's right; less than $200 gets you all you really need to utilize video. The little camera is the size and shape of a billiard ball and sits on its own rubbery stand (see Fig.14.25). Since it's round, you can point and swivel it any way you like—no need for an expensive tripod or mount. The market planners at Connectix looked at video and saw what all of us have seen: it costs too much. In the end the only special item is the camera; so they made a cheap, but quite accept-able, camera, figuring that most computer users in their target market would have the rest. Along the way they threw in the video and collaborative software. You can use what they supply with the camera, CU-SeeME, or whatever else you can find.

FIG. 14.25

The Connectix billiard ball all-digital camera and stand along with supporting software documentation.

I'm going to go through the installation and use of the Connectix camera and the Connectix VideoPhone collaborative software furnished with it. Take a look at Figure 14.26, which shows the initial setup screen after you've entered the setup program. Choose Quick Setup to install everything. If you're planning on using other software, you will probably want to choose Custom Setup.

Part
IV

Ch
14

FIG. 14.26
Connectix initial setup selection. In the typical case, choose Quick Setup to install all of the Connectix software. Should you want to use other software or exercise more control, choose Custom Setup.

The default directory selection is to put the program in the root of your C: drive. I suggest you use the program subdirectory as is typical in Windows 95 (see Fig. 14.27).

FIG. 14.27
Install the Connectix software in a subdirectory under Programs.

Now you can choose a LAN connection, standard telephone (POTS), ISDN, or serial port for your physical connection (see Fig. 14.28). Since this is a book on ISDN, only two of these are relevant to you. If you have a router on your LAN or your ISDN card is addressed as though it were a network card, choose LAN. If you're using a terminal adapter connected through the serial/parallel/USP port, choose ISDN; the same is true if you have an internal card addressed with the AT command set.

FIG. 14.28
Connectix options for
physical connection.

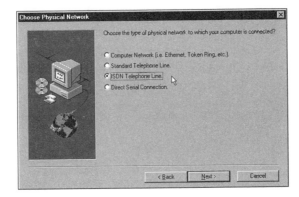

Figure 14.29 gives you the option of a direct dial to another computer; use this if you're simply calling up someone else using Connectix. If you're using a network or are dialing to a network such as an Internet service provider, choose either PPP/SLIP or IPX depending on which protocol is used on the network.

FIG. 14.29
Choose the protocol
you'll use during your
video session.

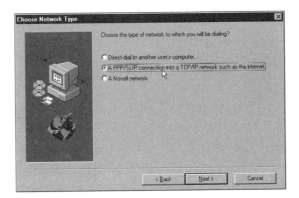

▶ **See** the discussion on protocol conversion gateways in the Chapter 12 sidebar, "Isn't TCP/IP Now the Only Important Protocol?" **p. 383**

Let's take the other path and choose a local area network. Remember to use this for a router or an internal card that configures like a network interface card (see Fig. 14.30).

In Figure 14.31 you again choose your protocol; in this case, you're limited to either TCP/IP or IPX. Be sure to check the cross reference above regarding IPX gateways to TCP/IP; if you have such a gateway, the proper selection is IPX. Even though you're ultimately speaking to an external TCP/IP network, your internal network is running on IPX. The gateway makes the conversion between the two.

Part
IV

Ch

14

FIG. 14.30
Select the local area network option for a router or internal card that configures like a network interface card.

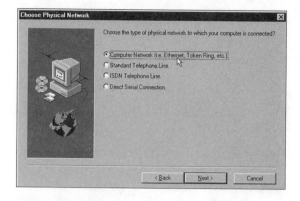

FIG. 14.31
Choose the protocol you use on your network.

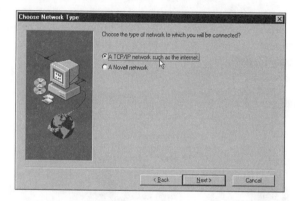

No matter what path you choose, you end up entering the name you want to use in the video conference (see Fig. 14.32).

FIG. 14.32
Enter your name for the conference. This will appear at the top of the picture you transmit.

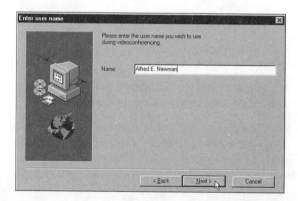

In Figure 14.33 you're given the option of having the Connectix VideoPhone software automatically run when an incoming call is sensed as a video call. I suggest you choose not to have this option turned on until you've become comfortable with the software.

FIG. 14.33
Choose automatic or
manual execution of
the Connectix
VideoPhone software.

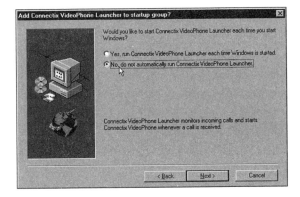

That's about it for the install and setup. You plug your camera into the keyboard and parallel ports. Don't worry, the keyboard connection has an additional connector; you can type and use the camera at the same time! On the other hand, you have to give up a parallel port for the camera. Connectix sells a switch that allows you to select between the camera and whatever else you might have connected to the parallel port, usually a printer.

NOTE If you obtain a switch for your parallel port from some source other than Connectix, be sure it switches all 25 lines.

If you want to add a parallel extension cable, it must have all 25 lines. Don't expect to be able to reach more than 10 or 20 feet with such a cable; beyond that you'll probably experience noticeable degradation of the video; (I have a 10 foot cable on my camera). I suggest you buy a top grade cable for this use; such cables usually have better connectors and shielding and give you longer distances and higher quality images. If you want to go a greater distance than I suggest, give it a try, but get an agreement to return the cable if the picture's bad.

Let's move to actually using the camera. Figure 14.34 is a good example of the kind of pictures you can take. Of course, this is a still picture in the book. But you have the option of capturing several seconds of a movie. Who needs a camera or VCR anymore? You can take the images and print them or you can embed them into your Web pages.

FIG. 14.34
A picture from the
Connectix camera can
be printed, transmitted
over the Internet,
embedded in your Web
page, and even used as
a movie. And, if I keep
this camera angle right,
you can't even tell I'm
not wearing pants!
Jamey is the producer.

Part
IV
Ch
14

For Connectix's next trick, see Figure 14.35, which shows the image magnified to fill your monitor. This slows down the frame rate and results in a rough image, but you might like to use it. You can select various sizes up to and including the full size of your monitor screen (see Fig. 14.36).

FIG. 14.35
Selection of picture size and characteristics within the Connectix VideoPhone screen.

FIG. 14.36
The picture magnified to fill an entire monitor screen.

To enable you to set up a connection easily, Connectix has all connection options available from pull-down menus (see Fig. 14.37).

FIG. 14.37
Selection of connection type.

You can adjust audio and image characteristics with pull down screens (see Fig. 14.38). The screen, at the right, sets timing for the voice activated (VOX) audio. The audio is only on when you speak into the microphone; these establish the timings to start and stop delivery of audio across your telephone or network connection. The video settings, on the right, set the amount of detail available in the picture. The more detail, like a greater gray scale or greater number of lines, the higher the image quality, but the less frame per second transmitted over the same data rate connection.

FIG. 14.38
Here I am looking at settings for voice activated audio and quality of picture. This shot shows gray scale because the camera I used is the black and white version. Similar controls are on the color camera.

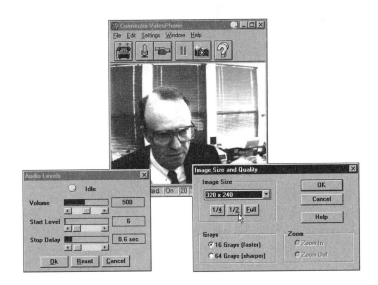

Connectix also provides VideoMail (see Fig. 14.39). This enables you to create a video/sound clip and send it to someone by electronic mail. In the mail, it's carried as a MIME message attachment. MIME software must be used to play the clip.

FIG. 14.39

I'm looking at the e-mail information needed to set up Connectix VideoMail.

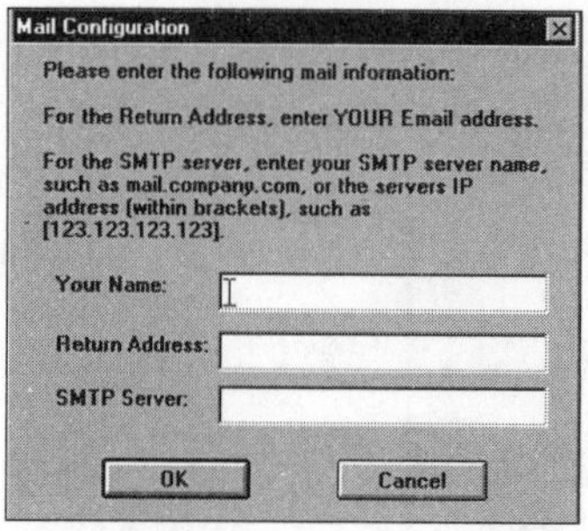

Mail Configuration

Please enter the following mail information:

For the Return Address, enter YOUR Email address.

For the SMTP server, enter your SMTP server name, such as mail.company.com, or the servers IP address (within brackets), such as [123.123.123.123].

Your Name:

Return Address:

SMTP Server:

OK   Cancel

Now let's look at an actual video conference (see Fig. 14.40). I've set up this one over the Internet. The bottom right-hand corner shows Network On and Modem Off. Had it been the reverse, I would have been using an ISDN, or even POTS, connection for the conference. Here I'm connecting through an ISDN router to my Internet service provider. The Internet takes me to California where Mike is on the phone. We've established the call using the whiteboard application, TALKShow, that's packaged with the Connectix product.

FIG. 14.40

This videoconference, in progress between Texas and California, is using ISDN from the office locations to the Internet and the Internet across the country. The whiteboard application, TALKShow, is being used to present a PowerPoint presentation that can be marked up by each party.

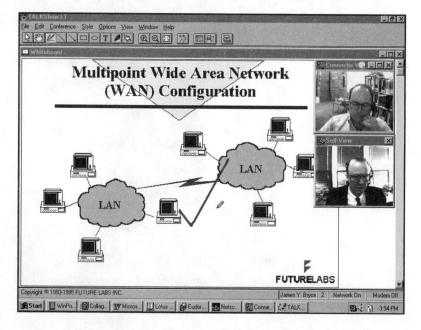

Look closely at the top of the TALKShow screen. You'll find the program is actually TALKShow LT. The LT means light. This version of the program does not allow real-time application sharing. That means Mike and I cannot work directly on the same application, changing its contents, and so on. Figure 14.41 reflects the fact the program can be upgraded to fully share applications.

FIG. 14.41

The light version of TALKShow can be upgraded to full application sharing for an additional cost.

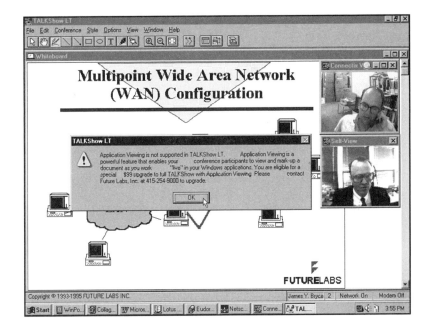

TIP You can use the ProShare collaborative computing software with Connectix hardware. Intel sells it without the video and audio hardware.

When it's all said and done, it's the lack of full application sharing that most limits the Connectix package in comparison to products such as ProShare from Intel. But with Connectix the price is right—under $200 compared to $1,000 is a big difference. And with another $99, TALKShow can be upgraded, giving you videoconferencing and collaborative computing at one-third the price.

NOTE Connectix has not complied with T.120, the collaborative computing standard, or H.320, the videoconferencing standard. But it has such a large market share due to its price, people argue it's the standard itself. Intel tried this with ProShare, as I said earlier, but at $2,000 a pop then, they had little chance of really grabbing a big market. Connectix took the plunge and apparently has won the gold ring. However, this means you can't call up ProShare, Vtel, PictureTel, or the other systems that offer T.120 and H.320 options, because you have no way to talk with them. I suspect Connectix will cave in and give such options too. ▓

From Here...

I hope you've gotten the big picture from this chapter. Remember, we covered more than just sending pictures around; a lot of the hoopla here concerns working on applications and whiteboards at the same time from scattered locations.

Part

IV

Ch

14

In the next chapters, we'll take up some other areas where ISDN is changing the way we do things:

- Telephones seem about as boring as anything, but the application of ISDN to telephones brings several new ideas in Chapter 15, "Changing Telephones to ISDN."

- Really making ISDN do something productive in the work environment is the subject of Chapter 16, "Putting ISDN to Work."

- Chapter 17, "ISDN Access for Internet Providers and Corporations," takes a quick look at how the Internet service providers and BBS people do and—perhaps more important— might use ISDN.

CHAPTER 15

Changing Telephones to ISDN

Almost all of this book is devoted to how you can use ISDN for your computer needs—that is, all except this chapter. Let's face it, ISDN is a telephone service. As much as we sometimes might like to avoid phones, we do need them, use them, and usually like them. In this chapter, we look at what it means to use ISDN for telephone service.

I pointed out in the first few chapters that ISDN was originally designed as the next logical step in telephone service. Connection to computers was an afterthought based on the idea that computers meant terminal-to-host connections to mainframes and minicomputers. This line of reasoning resulted in expensive options to connect computers with ISDN at approximately the same time that local area networks began delivering data rates tens and hundreds of times faster than ISDN. Thus, we saw the first death of ISDN.

Now, ISDN has risen from the ashes and become the preferred way to do wide area networking, Internet connection, computer video, and telecommuting. Amid all these computer applications, however, let's not forget the telephone capabilities of ISDN. ■

Telephone voice features potentially available in ISDN

You'll see that ISDN offers far more options than POTS.

Connecting analog telephones to ISDN

You'll find out how to use your existing POTS phones, modems, and FAX machines with ISDN.

Connecting ISDN telephones to an NT1 for a true ISDN voice system

You can really take advantage of what ISDN can do for voice communications with multiple phones connected to your NT1.

Using a console with the telephone company switch for your ISDN telephones provides a way to control incoming calls

The console gives you control as if you had your own in house PBX.

Using an ISDN PBX with your telephones gives you great flexibility and can increase economy, especially in larger environments

Design your voice phone system around ISDN for more flexible applications and future expansions.

ISDN Telephone Features

Chapter 4, "Choosing Services," talks about supplementary services, such as call forwarding, call deflection, private numbering plan, plus many more. Chapter 7, "Ordering ISDN Services," reviews issues encountered when ordering ISDN services. As long as you want to use ISDN for computer data carriage and an occasional analog modem or fax through a POTS port on your equipment, ordering service is fairly simple: get 2B+D with dynamic voice/data, either with or without packet bearer service on the D channel, and you're finished. Ordering becomes tricky when you need to choose from the plethora of ISDN voice features.

At that point, you're buried in all the nuances of voice service included in the supplementary services and the complexity of *electronic key telephone systems (EKTS)*. Finally, tariffs of the telephone company help determine what you can get and what it costs. Much of this is not a question of whether or not ISDN technology can do something; it's more a question of whether or not there's a tariff defining and allowing the technology to be used.

Let's not get too enmeshed in discussing regulations. My goal is to inform you of technological possibilities so that you can make informed judgments about what you want. Then, if you can't get what you want due to regulations, you can make your own decisions to work for changes in the regulations, the law, the competitive environment, or maybe all three.

▶ **See** "Supplementary Services," **p. 95**

To refresh your memory, here's a short list of the supplementary services:

- **Number Identification.** Direct dialing in, multiple subscriber number, calling line identification presentation, calling line identification restriction, connected line identification presentation, connected line identification presentation restriction, malicious calls identification, subaddressing.
- **Call Offering.** Call transfer, call forwarding busy, call forwarding no reply, call forwarding unconditional, call deflection, line hunting.
- **Call Completion.** Call waiting, call hold, completion of calls to busy subscribers, completion of calls on no reply.
- **Multiparty Services.** Conference calling, three-party service.
- **Community of Interest.** Closed user group, private numbering plan, multiline business group or city-wide centrex, multiline key telephone service, multilevel precedence and preemption, priority service, outgoing call barring.
- **Charging Service.** Credit card call, advice of charges, reverse charging.
- **Additional Information Transfer.** User-to-user signaling, in-call modification.

If you're going to use ISDN telephones with the ability to take advantage of these features, you'll need buttons on the phones and maybe even a console connected to the local exchange switch. You have to select the features you want and pay the appropriate tariff. If you're going to use your own true PBX, some of these features might be included in the PBX, but you still might need other features from the telephone company. Later, I'll explain how to tie supplemental service features together with features that reside in your equipment.

Using POTS Phones with ISDN

Figure 15.1 shows connection of POTS phones to ISDN by using an ISDN device that converts the ISDN signal back into an analog signal.

FIG. 15.1
An ISDN line can be converted to POTS by using an NT1 or terminal adapter with an R interface designed to handle POTS phones. This illustration shows an NT1 with the S/T interface connection going to other equipment. In the event you're using a terminal adapter or router, there probably won't be an S/T interface, but there will be some sort of connection to your serial/parallel/USB port, internal bus, or local area network.

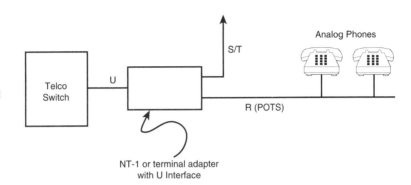

Several different types of equipment you can use with your computer might have this option:

- If you have an ISDN adapter card inside your computer, POTS could be supplied as an option. The US Robotics I-Modem covered in Chapter 10 provides a POTS port.

- If you have an external terminal adapter that connects through the serial port, there may be a POTS option available. The devices we reviewed in that category—including the Motorola BitSURFR, ADTRAN Express XRT, and 3Com Impact—all have such an option.

- Your NT1 could have a POTS option. The IBM Network Terminator Extended, for example, has such an option. A more elaborate variation is available from Alpha Telecom in their ISDN Super NT1. This device has a U interface for the telephone company's ISDN line. It has two S/T interfaces for your ISDN equipment and two R interfaces for your POTS equipment, including telephones.

- With the explosion of interest in ISDN routers, more and more are being made with POTS ports. Some of the ones we looked at in Chapter 11 include the Ascend Pipeline 75, Cisco 752, and ZyXEL Prestige 2864.

▶ **See** "3Com Impact," **p. 214** "Adtran Express Products," **p. 228** and "Motorola BitSURFR Pro," **p. 239**

▶ **See** "IBM 7845 NT1," **p. 198** and "Alpha Telecom Super NT1," **p. 200**

The Move to Combined POTS and ISDN

As you know, I've advocated the advantages of a separate NT1 and S/T port ISDN equipment based on flexibility. I still believe this is an excellent path. But the advent of more and more elaborate POTS support on U interface ISDN equipment is really providing most of that flexibility for many users' needs and at a lower overall cost. This shows what a truly competitive market can do. Now keep in mind some details.

Just because a device has an analog connection doesn't mean it will provide what you need from a telephone. Some pieces of equipment—for instance, the IBM WaveRunner and ISDN*tek cards—have a connection for a telephone headset, but this is far less useful than a full phone.

Some devices allow you to connect a telephone, but you cannot dial through the phone—your computer must do this. Some devices allow you to dial, but the phone cannot ring because the device won't pass ringer current; the US Robotics Sportster has this limitation, but an added device provides ringer current if you need it. Some devices can dial and ring, but won't handle features like call waiting and three-way calling. Some handle both basic and tricky features, but work for only one B channel. Finally, some work with both B channels and do all sorts of fancy voice things.

More and more designers are following the lead of companies such as Motorola in the BitSURFR Pro line. The equipment offers two POTS ports with sophisticated configuration options, which add or drop data and voice as desired and provide elaborate voice functions, such as caller identification and conference calling.

I strongly recommend that the ISDN product you buy have support for at least one POTS connection. It would be better to have support for two POTS connections; then you can take advantage of both B channels, using the ordinary analog devices, modems, phones, and faxes you already have.

This idea of having voice support is not as simple as it looks. What happens if someone tries to call you while you're making a data connection to a single location with PPP MP aggregating both B channels? The most logical decision for most users is to drop the second B channel and accept the voice call. Since the D channel can signal the "call appearance" on the second B channel, this can tell your ISDN device to do just that. Here are a few of the things to think about and possible modes of operation available in some devices with POTS ports:

- The arrangements you will need to make with your telephone company to support the voice features should be spelled out in the documentation. Voice services can be complex.

- If you want to make or receive two voice calls at the same time, you'll need two directory numbers. In the event your telco switch is an AT&T Custom Point-to-Point, only one number is supported. If your telco switch supports NIx (National ISDN number x), this is not a problem.

- If your device has two POTS ports and neither B channel is being used for data, you can make two voice calls at the same time, one on each B channel. This could be subject to limitations on certain switches if only one directory number can be assigned.

- If both B channels are being used for data, you can make a voice call by picking up a phone and dialing. This causes one B channel to be dropped for data transmission and given over to voice transmission. The fancy term for this is *outgoing call preemption.*

- If both B channels are being used for data and an incoming voice call appearance is signaled on the D channel, one of the B channels is dropped for data and given over to voice. This is *incoming call* preemption.

- As a general rule, if both B channels are used for voice calls, or one for data and one for voice, or one for data to location X and the other for data to location Y, dropping of connections does not apply.

- What if someone attempts to call you on a B channel number that is already being used for a data call? Several devices switch the call to the other B channel, if it's not in use.

- Call waiting is often supported with the same tone method you're used to with an analog phone. Since simple POTS phones don't have indicator lights and panels, the ISDN unit has to convert the ISDN signaling on the D channel to a tone and send it to the POTS phone.

- Distinctive ringing may be supported just like a POTS phone. The same is true of conferencing.

- One of the most interesting features becoming available is Data Over Voice Bearer Service (DOVBS). This allows data to be carried by a usually less expensive voice connection (this is often an issue in long distance connection). The device is advised that although the bearer service looks like voice, it's actually data and should be handled as such and passed to the LAN rather than the POTS port.

- Designers are attempting to adapt many of the supplementary services available with ISDN to simple POTS phones connected to a unit's analog port. In many cases adaptation will probably require some involvement with your computer. In network systems, the use of computer-telephony methods may provide these enhancements to otherwise inexpensive POTS phones.

Why on earth is there all this effort going into making POTS phones, and for that matter analog FAX machines, work over ISDN? Why not just use ISDN phones and FAXs? In one word—money. Group 4 FAX machines are very expensive and not widely used. ISDN phones have been designed for the high-end commercial market (those who can see their way to paying $400 or more for a fancy phone). This is unfortunate; ISDN phones have so much to offer, but unless the prices come down a lot, and quickly, developments of the sort I've talked about in this section will relegate them to a niche market. Let's see what true ISDN phones can offer.

Using ISDN Phones Stand-Alone

Figure 15.2 shows ISDN phones connected to an S/T interface coming from an NT1. Bear in mind that true ISDN phones are available that have a U interface, and therefore do not need an NT1. The problem, then, is how to connect additional equipment. The following tip sums up my opinion.

TIP In spite of the added cost of an external NT1, I recommend that you consider purchasing terminal adapters with S/T interfaces and an external NT1 with POTS connection capability. This setup gives you maximum flexibility now and for the future. But rapid developments with POTS ports on U interface equipment may end up with similar flexibility.

CAUTION

The descriptions of an ISDN phone often claim you can do anything with the phone, even connect it to your computer. Don't buy this! Remember that these were born and bred in the mainframe-and-mini mentality of smart hosts and dumb terminals also known as telephone switches. What these phones actually offer is usually a serial port connection limited to 19.2 kbps or less. This stuff has been useless since distributed computer networks became dominant several years ago.

FIG. 15.2

ISDN phones connected through an NT1. It's also possible to buy ISDN phones that have a U interface and connect directly to the ISDN line from the phone company.

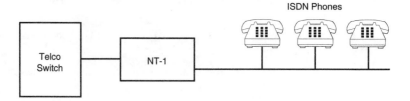

Now, things become complicated. ISDN phones don't work like POTS phones do. When you have several POTS phones on one telephone line, you can be talking on one of the phones and someone else can pick up an *extension phone* and join the conversation. This is not possible with ISDN. The B-channel communication is specific to the telephone instrument you're using. For a second person in your house or office to join the conversation you must create a conference. This is done through signaling the telephone switch on the D channel, which usually means pressing a button. Take a look at a typical ISDN phone in Figure 15.3; notice all the buttons and, on this one, the display panel that tells you what's going on.

Use of all these buttons requires the following steps:

- Buying phones with buttons so you can control the electronic key telephone system (EKTS) for ISDN. All the phones I've seen for sale in the United States and Canada have buttons. Some phones in countries that are almost totally ISDN might lack button features, but that trend hasn't hit North America.

- Ordering the features you want the buttons to control from the telephone company; refer to the list earlier in this chapter.

■ Programming the features into the phone's buttons. This takes cooperation between you and the telephone company setting up your service. It also requires that you understand the configuration steps for your phone; check the documentation before you buy.

CAUTION

While the ISDN specification says you may have as many as eight devices on a single BRI, some telephone switches support only two SPIDs per BRI. This can limit your ability to establish conferences within your office or house. Check with your phone company for details on such limitations.

FIG. 15.3
This is the Siemens-ROLM Optiset, a fully-featured ISDN phone with buttons and a display panel. It is available in models using either an S/T or U interface. Additional modules provide POTS equipment connection and even a serial terminal adapter; these modules plug in underneath the phone. There's even a module for the U interface phone that provides an S/T interface for other equipment; if you get the U Optiset with this module, you have an NT1 and phone in one.

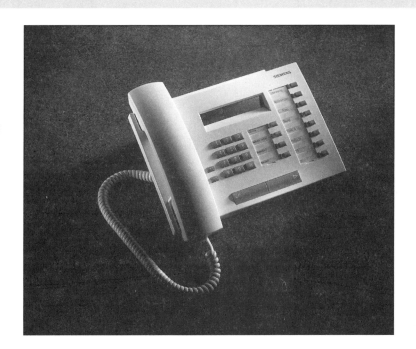

Using a Console to the Telephone Company Switch

You might already have guessed that when we start sending signals over the D channel to set up conferences, hold calls, or transfer calls with our key sets, we're using the central office switch like a PBX. The difference is that we don't own this switch, and therefore must pay the telephone company for the service. This type of use of a telephone company switch used to be called *centrex*; it has gone under other names, such as *plexar*. The idea is clear: the telephone company's switch does all the tricks, and you just send the requests. With signaling over the D channel on ISDN, this system works very well.

A good way to gain the most flexibility is to connect a console to the telephone company switch so that someone at your office can manage telephone traffic to suit your business needs. Figure 15.4 shows various phones connected to the telephone company's switch and an attendant console handling the calls.

FIG. 15.4

An ISDN attendant console controls a number of telephones through a telephone company switch. Notice that the telephones are connected to the switch and not to the console.

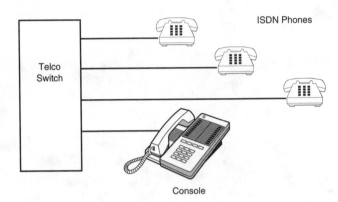

An example of this approach is the Tone Commander Model 40d120 ISDN attendant console, illustrated in Figure 15.5. This equipment is available with modular expansion features that can support up to 480 stations. It provides control to the telephone company switch using D-channel signaling. Notice that the telephones in the figure are not connected to the console; they're connected to the telephone company switch. This means that stations can be anywhere within range of the switch. If appropriate tariffs are in place, the stations might be in separate cities.

 Command your browser to **www.halcyon.com/tcs** and see what Tone Commander is all about.

The clear advantage of this solution is the flexibility you have in location and wiring. You don't have to fill telephone rooms with expensive equipment, or haul cable back and forth to a PBX and its console. The clear disadvantage is that you spend more money with the telephone company.

FIG. 15.5
This ISDN attendant console is the Tone Commander Model 40d120.

Using an ISDN PBX

The ISDN *Private Branch Exchange (PBX)* moves the switching of your internal business calls and creation of many features onto your premises, using your equipment. Figure 15.6 shows the idea.

FIG. 15.6
The NT2 described in the ISDN specifications takes the form of a PBX. A PBX may also have an attendant console attached, if the needs of the office dictate.

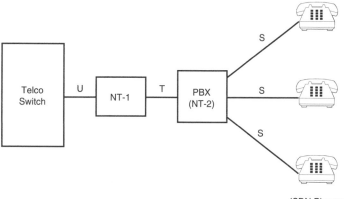

ISDN Phones

When you install your own analog PBX, the telephone company changes the way it delivers service to you. You receive each line as a *trunk* which is conditioned for use with a PBX. By definition, a trunk is a connection between two switches, so you never connect a telephone directly to a trunk. You connect a switch to the trunk, then connect a phone to the switch. A trunk can be either of the following:

- A *combination trunk* that handles incoming or outgoing calls from the attendant, and that can be used for outgoing calls from other users. Notice that all incoming calls must go through the attendant, a person who answers and controls incoming calls.

- A *direct inward dialing (DID) trunk* that carries calls from the outside directly to users in your firm, thereby bypassing the attendant. Notice that DID trunks do not carry outgoing calls.

It seems the telephone companies are trying to force connection to an ISDN PBX into a similar mold as that of the analog PBX, despite the fact that ISDN—by virtue of signaling over the D channel—already has all the characteristics needed to handle signaling between the telephone company switch and the PBX. The ISDN specification includes the *network termination type 2 (NT2)*, defined as an intelligent switching and concentration device.

N O T E   Strictly speaking, the definition of NT2 can include functions that cover the Network layer of the OSI model. This definition might even include devices such as LANs and routers connected to ISDN. Our discussion, however, is limited to switching functions only.

ISDN really has altered the landscape of telephone charges. With analog trunks, you needed to figure out the proper balance between combination trunks and DID trunks. There still might be times when several lines of one type were available while all lines of the other type were tied up. Also, the prices for the two types of trunks were different. With ISDN, you no longer have a distinction between the two in price or in function, since the D channel can handle signaling to indicate a direct inward call on any channel.

N O T E   In the analog world you must try to balance DID trunks against combination trunks for the optimum cost and usage; you can never get it just right. With ISDN you have greater potential use of all lines that often reduces the overall number of lines needed in contrast to the needs of an analog system. Sometimes, you can justify ISDN on this basis of less lines overall alone.

We're not going to dig into the big switches. I think the real excitement in ISDN will be the development of small switches and computer-based switches. Siemens ROLM provides the OfficePoint Communications System shown in Figure 15.7. While it doesn't satisfy all my criteria, and won't use just anybody's ISDN phone, it's a step in the right direction.

It's billed as the only ISDN BRI system on the US market. That claim can't last long! This potential market is huge, and includes everything from your dentist, to your lawyer, to your doctor, to your own house. Currently, the system sells in the $2,000 range, but competition could cause that to drop overnight. The system can handle up to three BRI lines and 16 of ROLM's digital phones specially designed for the OfficePoint. It has four analog interfaces and can connect up to four ISDN devices. It has built-in PC and TAPI support. I predict this little box is just the first of many that will blast ISDN voice capability into your office or residence.

FIG. 15.7
Siemens ROLM OfficePoint BRI small office PBX is a replacement for the classic "key service unit" (KSU) and provides features those clicking relays never could.

T I P   Roam to Siemens-ROLM at **http://www.siemensROLM.com**.

Regulatory Strictures

In many regions, ISDN PBX connection can be made only through a PRI, and PRIs cannot have EKTS functions. With such conditions, local exchange carriers are seeking to prevent the use of switching equipment that bypasses their long distance tariff structures.

For example, one possible feature is *call transfer disconnect*. This means that a call is made to one party, and then that party calls another party. All three parties are tied together, creating a conference. With call transfer disconnect, the middle party that set up the conference can disconnect, leaving the other two parties still connected.

Let's see why that's significant. You've probably done three-way calling on a POTS phone. You call up Kevin; once he's on the line, you call Wanda. Through a click or two of the switch hook, all three of you are talking together. When you decide to hang up, however, the connection is broken for all the parties. It seems reasonable that the call should be able to continue for the other two, if they want. After all, if you're still involved in the call and Kevin or Wanda hangs up, you can continue to talk with the other one. There's no technical reason that your hanging up should disconnect the other two.

There is, however, an economic fear on the part of the telephone company. The company is worried that you might become a telephone exchange to the public. You might arrange to be strategically located so you could take calls from two metropolitan areas for no—or reduced—toll rates as opposed to the costs of one area calling the other directly. Calls could be placed through you so that standard tolls were circumvented. This would be a neat business if you automated the process. The telephone company makes sure that it won't work, by requiring you or your equipment to remain on the line to conduct three-way calls, therefore setting the overall economics against you.

"Wait a minute," you're saying. "What's this got to do with my ISDN PBX?"

Everything. The phone company's attempt to prevent the *long distance toll circumvention* I just described involves denial of a number of otherwise reasonable operations by your switch. In general, the telephone companies are attempting to prevent use of elaborate *customer premises equipment (CPE)* that would take full advantage of many features and controls in ISDN to allow you to establish a *virtual office*. The rationalization for avoiding this is such things as long distance toll circumvention, but that circumvention could be stopped by using the D channel to detect conditions where a toll should be charged.

The real telephone company reasoning behind slowing down full CPE utilization of ISDN is the potential loss of revenue from charges for central office switch features. The telephone companies want to cash in on the soon-to-emerge virtual office, where your firm is spread all over the globe, and its telephone management and switching have to be handled somewhere. That handling could take place with your own equipment and programs, which would turn the telephone companies into dumb bit-shippers that would have to charge commodity prices. They prefer to provide *added value services* and charge a premium price. Since anyone with the right technology can do the same thing, the telephone companies seek to restrict development of the virtual office outside their own switches.

This means that any ideas you might have about how you can use ISDN technology with computers will have to be tested in the legal, regulatory, and legislative fires before they can really take off.

Technical Hope

My opinion and hope is that these restrictive rules will begin to peel away in the next few years as more and more users become informed and push for reform and competition. Let's look, therefore, at some of the technology that can emerge, and at how to pick PBX equipment.

When you're looking at PBX equipment, vendors will tell you it's all standard and that they offer ISDN directly to the desktop. What most of them don't understand is that often all they're offering is a slow-speed serial hookup. In some instances they do offer a B channel, but a B channel is not ISDN. You need 2B+D to do much of what I've discussed in this book. If the PBX vendor has no convenient way to supply a BRI directly to your desk, how can the equipment be called ISDN?

Well, often it's not called ISDN; instead, the term "digital" is used. This is a dead giveaway, and always means that the equipment is *proprietary*. These days, you don't want proprietary equipment; you want it as generic as possible. Even if the telephones are legitimate ISDN phones that plug into a true BRI S/T interface, you might find disagreement on functioning and programming of the buttons on the sets. It will take a while, but these standards will appear.

Part
IV

Ch
15

N O T E The real test of an ISDN PBX is to see which other vendors' standard ISDN phones you can plug into the switch and use. Then, see what it takes to program and use the buttons on those other phones. Telephone switch makers are just facing the same reality of necessary interoperability that revolutionized the computer world during the last two decades. ▄

From Here...

We've covered some ground outside of computers. I hope you've gotten the idea that an ISDN line you're using can be a real phone line, not just something to which you tie your computer. Keep your eyes open for POTS port NT1s, ISDN phones, and ISDN PBX systems. Much innovation will occur in the next couple of years.

■ Chapter 16, "Putting ISDN to Work," looks at how you can take all this ISDN equipment and do something with it. Keep in mind that your telephones can go onto ISDN and work even better with your computers.

■ Chapter 17, "ISDN Access for Internet Providers and Corporations," takes a quick look at what certain entrepreneurs surrounded by computers and phone lines are doing with ISDN.

■ Chapter 19, "Forecasting Changes Due to ISDN," includes a discussion of the rise of telephony servers that replace the stand-alone PBX and bring the power and economics of computers to telephony.

■ Chapter 20, "Alternatives to ISDN," boils the caldron of more emerging technology, xDSL, cable modems, and others.

CHAPTER 16

Putting ISDN to Work

A this point, it's clear that ISDN offers substantial technical benefits. But in what types of places and situations can you use it? The earliest uses most of us find relate to work, but ISDN eventually can impact your personal life. This chapter explores the following ways that ISDN will take over and improve our lives. ■

Personal and family life will be affected by ISDN

Learn how ISDN will help you at home.

Educational opportunities will be spread more evenly and effectively through the use of ISDN

Find out that ISDN can offer major savings and possibilities for education.

Telecommuting will become an increasingly frequent alternative to the usual central office commute

See how ISDN will reduce pollution, stop over-building and save the world. Analyze your personality type with Dr. C. G. Jung. And you thought this was a techno-geek book.

ISDN helps large organizations

You'll see how ISDN can provide more capacity and flexibility for your computing and telephones.

Specific industries with a vertical market structure will benefit greatly from ISDN

If you're in broadcasting, medicine, retailing, or are concerned with ways of helping those with disabilities, ISDN can offer new solutions.

Enjoying Life with ISDN

This seems like a strange place to start. Most of the talk about ISDN centers around its use in business, government, and large organizations. But it can mean quite a lot to you right in your home, when you think about it:

- *A fast way to use the Internet.* Do research for all sorts of personal reasons: genealogy, school projects, trip planning, or whatever you want. With ISDN, the World Wide Web opens up and dances for you.

  ▶ **See** "Internet Service Providers," **p. 498**

  ▶ **See** Chapter 14, "Pictures and Video with ISDN," **p. 433**

- *Video calls to friends and family.* These are finally affordable using ISDN technology.

- *Daily or weekly e-mail to friends and family.* This allows you to keep in touch with an ease unimaginable until a few years ago.

- *Participation in online discussion groups.* With ISDN, you can exchange much more than just text; feel free to include graphics, video, and audio.

- *Banking and financial market monitoring.* ISDN provides vastly better access times than you get over analog lines.

- *Low-cost voice communication with children at college and people throughout the world.* Use of developing Internet phone technology might make this a reality.

  ▶ **See** Chapter 15, "Changing Telephones to ISDN," **p. 465**

  ▶ **See** "Circuit-mode Bearer Services," **p. 92**

This list could go on for a very long time. I'll talk about just a few items to give you a taste of the possibilities.

The large online services including Compuserve, America Online, and Prodigy not only offer ISDN service in selected markets, but they plan to expand that access to most markets soon. All online services have faced problems of clumsy interfaces and slow analog lines. ISDN flashes analog lines on the screen and enables development of newer environments based on World Wide Web browsers that are more fun to use.

Internet access shines with ISDN. My 17-year-old son and I recently swept around cyberspace looking at prospective liberal arts colleges. Many of the ones he has been considering turned out to be on the Web. When the addresses weren't obvious, we found them using Web search engines. Because the Internet is growing exponentially now, it takes some time—and an effective data rate—to be productive with these engines. I'm convinced that our work time was at least cut in half, thanks to ISDN. That left space for playing with my newborn child and celebrating my wife's birthday. Whenever ISDN rewards you with extra time for other activities, that's significant personal gain.

You've probably spent time in online forums. Think how different these will be with ISDN to deliver detailed graphics and even video. I'm on a listserver list concerning alternative transportation systems. Experts from all over the world are constantly posting the most exciting ways to overcome the congestion and environmental problems of automobiles and expensive mass transit. Discussion is limited to pure text, but most of the concepts beg for graphic expression. Many participants are tethered by POTS, and are choking on data rates too slow to convey pictures and motion that would show how their complex ideas would work. Think what would happen if we all had ISDN pipes to transmit the models of how transportation can be improved.

Every day, my wife sends e-mail to her mother. We set up a machine with scripts that make it easy for her mother to use e-mail. Since her mother lives in a rural area of Texas, her POTS connection is through an 800 number that charges according to the amount of time used. We'd like to switch to ISDN, dramatically reducing the connection time and cost, while offering the visual and audio potential already discussed.

A local bank asked me to test a customer banking access system over POTS. I couldn't believe it. The front end was pure VT-100 and virtually impossible for me to navigate without recalling headaches from years gone by. I advised them not to release the product for fear of driving business away. They told me I was the first to be so direct in my appraisal.

Corporate Survival

When the Emperor has no clothes, say so. The road to corporate bankruptcy, and unemployment, is filled with people who didn't point out that what the company was doing was just plain stupid. They saved the stress of not appearing to be a team player; six months later the team got downsized when the project failed. The worse that can happen is you'll be fired; then you can start a more effective business.

A number of larger banking systems are starting to adopt home banking by computer with GUIs. Those ready to stay at the front will provide ISDN options and Internet connections. With ISDN connected either directly to your bank or to the Internet, you'll be able to push a button and see the status of your accounts in graphics, sliced and diced any way you like. At the same time, you'll be able to track your investments in real-time with moving graphics and immediately make or cancel trade orders. Such real-time information is expensive now, and usually comes after a 15- or 30-minute delay. This stranglehold characteristic of brokerage, securities, real estate, and so on, will be destroyed in the very near future through new laws that are catching up with technology. Those brokers who depended on controlling information for profit will be on the street, while the ones who provide truly meaningful value-added services will do better than ever.

TIP Invest a little time in the Wall Street Journal Online **http://www.wsj.com**.

Now, here's the sleeper that's going to catch the telephone companies with their proverbial pants down: packet-based phone calls. That these are a real possibility is illustrated by nascent telephone services currently operating over the Internet. With ISDN to your Internet provider, these calls will get closer and closer to the timing and fidelity you expect from "the other telephone system." You'll keep in touch with your kids, friends, and business associates around the world through this unexpected benefit. Believe it!

Running Naked

"Internet-based voice applications will never significantly impact circuit-switched calls. It's not even a question! The number of people who are at the PC when they need information is very small compared with the number who have access to a phone. Voice is also the way people think...GUIs and mice are not intuitive. People were speaking before they wrote, and they will be speaking after they stop writing."

This is a recent quote from an official of a very large telecommunications corporation. Aside from the fact that the quote argues against itself by implicitly supporting the proposition that voice is an important means of communication—and that therefore any technology that fosters voice transmissions might be reasonably expected to grow—the quote also shows a failure to appreciate the historical demise of railroads, or of computer companies who staked their futures on mainframes.

"If men could learn from history, what lessons it might teach us! But passion and party blind our eyes, and the light which experience gives is a lantern on the stern, which shines only on the waves behind us!" (Samuel Taylor Coleridge, "Aids to Reflection: Moral and Religious Aphorisms, XXV" 18 December 1831)

▶ **See** "Using POTS Phones with ISDN," **p. 467**

▶ **See** Chapter 6, "Unscrambling APIs," **p. 117**

Education and ISDN

Our schools at whatever level can benefit tremendously from installation and use of ISDN. ISDN brings high data rates at low costs and with great flexibility.

Right now, a battle is raging for the billions of dollars educators want to invest to improve the quality of education in the United States. A similar situation exists throughout the world. Every indicator shows that education is the most important step toward improving everyone's lot. Yet how do educators determine which technology to buy, and which to avoid?

Educators are being asked what they want by vendors of products and services. The vendors see dollar signs and often show off the most elaborate, expensive solutions. Frequently, educators see only the fancy, full-motion, high-definition video offerings because the most potential profit lies in sales of one or two systems at a time. Representatives of all but the most wealthy school districts leave technology shows discouraged because they can't afford that type of equipment or services while still paying faculty. Some opt for cutting faculty, thinking technology will solve all their problems. Others approach school boards or legislatures, asking for support. When the technology arrives, it doesn't necessarily solve the school's needs. What goes wrong?

Most of the time, the problem is the blind acceptance of the whole concept that technology fixes anything. Technology can only provide access to more information and to resources not available at every school. Specialized teachers, elaborate laboratories, and faraway places can be brought to the fingertips of students and faculty. Everyone needs to know what the technology is and how to use it, so communications technology becomes a subject to teach and learn for itself.

Knowledge is Multiplying Like Rabbits—NOT!

Allow me to "debunk" the following statement: "Knowledge is multiplying manyfold every few years." Get real! What's multiplying is the amount of detailed records from business and technology; 99.99999% of this stuff has little, if any, enduring value. It's not knowledge; it's dead file storage! I just carted several hundred pounds of computer software and manuals to a landfill. Lots of this was less than five years old. Was that knowledge? No way. Knowledge is the enduring understanding of what life, the world, and others are about. You find knowledge in the world's great literature, philosophy, religion, and science recorded over thousands of years. Although some of the pointers to real knowledge can be stored in the form of texts in computer and communications systems, in the final analysis, conveyance of knowledge is a person-to-person experience.

Part

IV

Ch

16

Gadgets don't replace the relationship between teacher and pupil. Gadgets are only a means to enrich the surroundings of both. Gadgets can bring more relationships into any class, and expose everyone to different ways of perceiving and understanding ideas. The machines remain tools, however, and teachers are the real means of conveying knowledge to students. The bulk of a school's budget should remain spent on faculty. Grandiose schemes for *video theater classrooms* and *distance learning* should take a backseat.

"This guy's a Luddite; he's against technology," I hear you muttering. Not at all! I'm simply against wasting money on expensive toys today when I know three things about those toys:

- They're not needed.
- They'll be far cheaper before long.
- They soak up funds better spent on real people.

Ned Ludd

In England during 1811 and 1812, newly built textile mills were destroyed by bands of hand weavers. They were said to be led by a Ned Ludd. Though Ludd never surfaced, his name graces anyone who opposes technological progress.

The real Luddites of our times are the vested technological interests that seek to keep us tethered to products and services they control through market manipulation and illusory regulatory franchise.

In rides ISDN to rescue us. (You knew ISDN was on its way, didn't you?) I see a lot of vendors pushing for broadband hookups to schools before broadband is stable, pushing for cutting-edge video technology in a classroom where students have little (if any) access to the Internet. ISDN cuts through this waste by providing the best of all possible worlds, at a cheaper price than the hucksters want you to know about.

▶ See "Vtel," p. 437

We learned earlier in this book that a single BRI provides usable video with white board and other application support over two B channels at 128 kbps. Remember that a move to 3 BRI gives us 384 kbps and video that's quite satisfactory—even with motion—for use in a classroom setting. Of course, it's possible to have better definition, motion, and contrast...but is it necessary?

N O T E When someone tells you they have to have high-end video equipment, ask them what kind of car they'd like to have. Chances are they'll mention a Mercedes or some other car that costs around $50,000. Then, ask what car they actually own. Chances are it's a $10,000–20,000 car. Probe why they don't have the more expensive car. "I can't afford it," is a typical response. The cheaper car takes care of transportation needs as well as the more expensive car does; they realize this. Politely hide your smile, and point out that the cheaper ISDN takes care of educational needs as well as the more expensive technologies do. ■

There is absolutely no reason for our educational system to pay development costs for "bleeding edge" technology. But education is in the limelight, and some folks are convinced that technology is the panacea to fix it. What will more likely happen is a wholesale waste of money on rapidly obsolete, often proprietary equipment, along with a broad-scale financing of service providers' capital infrastructure. Very few students will benefit from these gold-plated demonstration systems.

 T I P See my presentation on techno-waste with gold-plated technology in education at **http:// www.bryce.com/~bryce/bangbuck.htm** and download the presentation with the FTP button.

What should you do now? Wait. For now, put BRI lines into schools and provide for Internet distribution to all your classrooms. Provide simple video systems using 1 to 3 BRI. Provide more workstations for your students and teachers to experience not only the video but also connection to the Internet, and through that to other schools. Then, with the money that's saved, when students are blowing out the tops of tests, and teachers are getting awards, you can give those teachers a raise.

Let's look in detail at some possibilities for education using ISDN:

- All schools have a staff and administration. ISDN can economically tie all these people together throughout a city, state, or country using the LAN methods for connection through ISDN to other LANs we discussed in Chapter 11.

- Take a good look at the use of packet mode over either or both the B or D channel. In some instances, you'll find you can exchange a lot of school information economically.

CAUTION

When you look at packet mode, look carefully at the tariff. Here in Austin, Texas it turns out it costs five or 10 dollars a month additional to use packet mode, plus a charge for the information sent. On the other hand, there is no time or quantity of information change on circuit mode—it's a flat rate. So here packet mode always drives costs up while circuit mode costs are a constant.

- Distance learning is a buzzword meaning that a teacher is at one location, and students are at a different location (or several locations). Video conferencing and desktop techniques bring them together. Often, however, you don't need the added cost and complexity of video to achieve distance learning. Sharing applications such as spreadsheets and white board, along with an audio link, might be sufficient.

■ Students and faculty can research and write from home or other location, and deliver work to each other over links optimized by ISDN. The Internet can play a major role in enriching the experiences of students and faculty in this environment.

Telecommuting Changes the Workplace

Telecommuting is a big buzzword now. Companies are going to save billions by switching to telecommuting. Workers are going to have better home lives because of the switch. But there are problems.

Part
IV
Ch
16

Possibilities for Telecommuting

Telecommuting covers several possible alternatives, depending on your needs and those of your organization. When you use this technology, you're transformed into one of the following:

■ *Cottage Worker.* This means you're linked to your office from your house, so you don't have to drive or ride public transportation. Essentially, you never go to the office at all. In fact, your office can be in some other city or country, where you rarely actually travel.

■ *Road Warrior.* In this role, you keep in touch with your office while you travel around, doing what you do best: selling, researching, vacationing, or whatever.

■ *Dilettante.* This type of arrangement has you hanging out at your house one or two days a week, but making the trip to the office the rest of the week.

■ *Time Shifter.* Here, you get to adjust the timing of your workday. You might log into your office network at 7 a.m., work until 10 a.m., then drive to work at 11 a.m. and return home at 3 p.m. for another two hours of work. You've shifted your travel time away from the rush hours but have maintained about the same amount of working time.

■ *World Surfer.* Here, you're jumping around the world, according to the clocks of the people you're contacting. When it's time to get up in Chicago, it's already lunchtime in Europe. This can flip things around. You might get up at 3 a.m. in Chicago to conduct your business at 10 a.m. in Denmark.

■ *Workaholic.* You get to extend the workday. You arrive home at 6 p.m., eat, then login at 7:30 p.m. to work until midnight. Then, you get up at 5:30 a.m. and login to work until you leave for the office at 8 a.m.

In every one of these roles, ISDN provides a superior environment for your work. All have social, personal, and business benefits, along with a few disadvantages. From the business viewpoint, having options for employees' working locations helps with the following:

■ Meeting environmental, pollution, and traffic congestion regulations that are rapidly appearing in urban areas.

■ Attracting employees that prefer the flexibility of such arrangements.

■ Increasing productivity. This is reflected in almost every test conducted on telecommuting.

■ Saving on office rental and other costs associated with maintaining a large staff at a certain location eight hours a day. People can share space if they work different times (or rarely come in). Some estimates project a reduction in space needs of between 20 and 50 percent.

From the viewpoint of the employee, telecommuting provides the following:

■ A more relaxed work atmosphere.

■ Relief from the stress of commuting and arriving at the office or home worn out from the trip.

■ A way to stay closer to family members while still getting work done. Children and aging relatives can be cared for by a working-aged family member, rather than by outside caregivers.

■ Comfort and flexibility of dress, eating, and exercising that are available at home and not in most formal offices.

■ Opportunities for people whose mobility is impaired.

Telecommuting and Personality Type

The primary drawbacks to telecommuting don't come from technology; they come from the emotions and psychology of management and workers. Some managers think they can't effectively manage people they can't see. Some workers suffer from isolation when placed at home away from coworkers. Almost all tests show that the managers' concern is unfounded—workers usually perform better telecommuting than at offices. However, the telecommuter's concern about isolation might have some foundation.

The Electronic Messaging Association recently produced a report titled *The Telecommuting Handbook* (cited in the bibliography) that explores telecommuting in depth. The isolation issue is singled out. The report provides an extensive analysis of personalities that are expected to be comfortable in the isolation of telecommuting, and those that are likely to be uncomfortable. The analysis is based on Carl Jung's personality types as tested in the Myers-Briggs Type Indicator.

The Myers-Briggs Type Indicator has been used for decades. It differentiates personalities into 16 types, based on four disjunctive criteria:

■ Extravert/Introvert

■ Sensor/Intuitive

■ Thinker/Feeler

■ Judger/Perceiver

People fall into one or the other of each pair. A personality type is described by concatenating the capital letters from each criterion met. For example, an ISTJ would be an Introvert, Sensor, Thinker, Judger, and would be expected to exhibit particular characteristics in particular situations.

We don't have time or space to dig deeply into this. The report does an excellent job, and there are a number of books on Jung or the Myers-Briggs test. Some books have short forms of the test so you can find out your typing. The report concludes that the following personality types are the strongest candidates for telecommuting:

- ISTJ
- ISFJ
- INTJ
- INFJ

It also suggests the following are potential candidates for telecommuting:

- ESTJ
- ISTP
- ESFJ
- ISFP
- ENTJ
- INTP
- ENFJ
- INFP

Here are the ones left out, who presumably aren't inclined toward telecommuting:

- ENTP
- ENFP
- ESTP
- ESFP

N O T E Guess where I'm writing this book? If you said at home, you're correct. Now, guess my personality type. Right, it's in the excluded group! I test ENTP with some tendency to go to ENFP. It looks like if you're both an extravert and a perceiver, you're in trouble with isolation. No wonder I'm on the phone and e-mail constantly!

I'd like to submit to you that ISDN can make things better, if not perfect, for us black sheep of the telecommuting psychological profile. How? Through intensive multimedia encounters with people over the wire. I think that the conclusions of the report are certainly valid when the telecommuter is sitting in front of a screen watching letters and charts stream by. When e-mail is introduced, things improve. But the big step—the one that brings my group of fast, fuzzy thinkers who perceive lots of ideas at once, and related types, into the fold—is the addition of video and audio. That, however, takes increased data rates, which takes ISDN.

Telecommuting won't work for everyone until the maximum possible sensory involvement can be delivered. ISDN enables that delivery.

Part

IV

Ch

16

Many companies think multimedia is hype for playing games. They think video is unnecessary for business, and that synchronized sound and applications are gimmicks. They are wrong! Using such reasoning, these organizations continue to pay for large, expensive offices that they could eliminate with telecommuting. They wear out their employees with driving. They spend millions on travel to more and more meetings.

Telecommuting and Expenses

Right now, a major church denomination is considering building a multimillion dollar building for administration. Nowhere in the plans have they considered telecommuting. Nor have they considered the virtual elimination of paper file storage by computer technology. They and most of us are still wedded to the idea of a fixed and expensive workplace, yet the answer is staring us in the face.

Some experiments in telecommuting have failed due to this lack of commitment. People are given the last generation of computers from the "real office" when it's replaced with new stuff. In reality, the opposite ought to be done. The best multimedia equipment must go out with the telecommuter. If he balances his checkbook and lets his kids play a couple of games on it, so what? While we're on that subject, just who does use telecommuting? According to *Making Work-At-Home Work* by David Goodtree of Forrester Research, Inc., 89 percent of tele-commuters are "casual, after-hours workers." This covers everything in my initial categories except the cottage worker. The whole industry has pictured telecommuting as clerical folks tending kids at home from 9 to 5, but that's really only 11 percent of the whole (see Fig. 16.1).

FIG. 16.1

Counting Telecommuters. This information was gathered by Forrester Research. It demonstrates the current preponderance of emphasis on after-hours telecommuting.

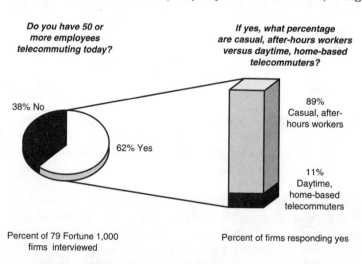

Do you have 50 or more employees telecommuting today?

38% No

62% Yes

Percent of 79 Fortune 1,000 firms interviewed

If yes, what percentage are casual, after-hours workers versus daytime, home-based telecommuters?

89% Casual, after-hours workers

11% Daytime, home-based telecommuters

Percent of firms responding yes

Source: Forrester Research, Inc.

The Forrester report concludes that all telecommuters must have top-notch equipment, and estimates an initial cost of about $4,000 to $5,000 for that. Annual expenses, including telephone connections with toll charges and service fees, range between about $1,000 and $2,000.

Now, here's the big one. Figure 16.2 shows the preferred telecommunications access method for today's telecommuter. It's obvious that if you're doing any more than terminal emulation or are telecommuting more than an hour a day, ISDN is the way to go.

FIG. 16.2

Telecommuter access methods by application. This graph, prepared by Forrester Research, shows the most desirable way of connecting, depending on function to be performed. Notice that ISDN becomes the most desirable method, as more than an hour or two of work of any sort is being done every day.

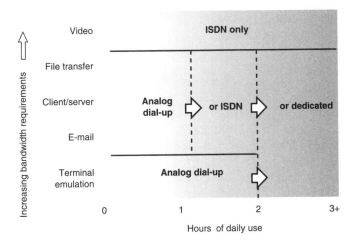

▶ **See** "Windows NT and ISDN," **p. 388**
▶ **See** "PPP Multilink Protocol," **p. 424**

The report anticipated that Windows 95 would embed remote access services, taking care of file synchronization, modem and ISDN setups, and PPP. The report was right.

Basically, an ISDN telecommuting system consists of equipment used by the telecommuter and equipment used at the office. The fundamental elements are illustrated in Figure 16.3. You're already familiar with ISDN devices such as an NT-1 and a terminal adapter. The new component is a *remote access server.* This is a computer running software that's specially configured to accept calls from outside, connect them to the office LAN, and provide remote users with the same resources they would have at the office. Speed of the telephone link is generally the weakest aspect of this, and ISDN boosts this speed dramatically. Ideally, the telephone connection becomes transparent to the user due to fast response. The remote access server can provide substantial security features to guard against damaging intrusion.

In some cases, a specialized remote access server might not be required. The best example of this is use of the Internet for connection. If everything your users need can be carried over the Internet, design scripts to make that use similar to LAN usage. This method presumes Internet security issues are either solved or not major to your business. In the event you do have major security issues, investigate use of firewalls and encryption techniques. A number of commercial programs are appearing that claim to solve these problems. Time will tell.

Part
IV

Ch
16

FIG. 16.3
ISDN Telecommuting System. The LAN at the office is illustrated at the top. It's connected to a router and then to ISDN. Telecommuters can dial in through ISDN from anywhere.

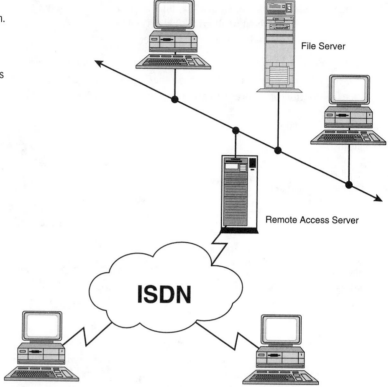

File Server

Remote Access Server

ISDN

Additional Uses for ISDN in the Organization

ISDN offers a clear advantage for telecommuting, but this is just one reason for ISDN to become a major part of your organization's communications planning. Use ISDN for all of the following:

- Telecommuting
- Telephones
- Backup connection in case dedicated lines fail
- Additional capacity when dedicated lines are congested
- Flexible bandwidth management
- Remote management and system fault diagnosis
- Multimedia meetings
- Training and teleconferencing with high-quality video and audio

Telecommuting and Telephones

We've talked about telecommuting, but don't forget your company's telephones. Sooner or later, you'll replace your current phones and PBX. Do not pass go...go straight to ISDN. Flexibility and expansion for the future is all built into ISDN. Smaller, cheaper, more flexible PBX devices are being built, based on ISDN. The integration of telephones and computers will use ISDN, as the PBX becomes hardware and software installed on a server. Plan for this now by blowing the whistle on continued expenditures for proprietary or analog telephone systems equipment. Then you'll be ready for expansion into video-conferencing and direct data transfer.

▶ **See** "Using an ISDN PBX," **p. 473**

▶ **See** Chapter 6, "Unscrambling APIs," **p. 117**

▶ **See** "Moving Control from the Telephone Company," **p. 540**

ISDN as Backup to a Dedicated Line

If you have a dedicated line between two major sites, provide each site with ISDN equipment. A number of combination hardware/software packages are available that can sense a loss of connection on the dedicated line, then automatically dial and connect using ISDN until the dedicated connection is restored (see Fig. 16.4).

FIG. 16.4

Failed Line Bypass with ISDN. Here two LANs are connected with a leased line. The routers at each end have a port for the leased line and another port connected to ISDN. When the leased line fails, the router directs traffic through ISDN. Remember the term "terminal adapter" is generic; it applies to more than the serial port devices of Chapter 9. In many instances, the router illustrated has one connection for the leased line, and another connection for an ISDN BRI or PRI integrated in modules.

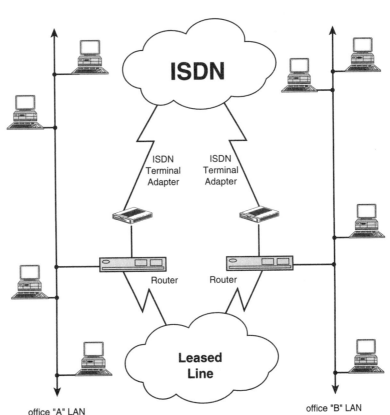

ISDN

ISDN Terminal Adapter

ISDN Terminal Adapter

Router

Router

Leased Line

office "A" LAN

office "B" LAN

ISDN for Added Capacity and Flexibility

In a similar manner, many packages can sense loading on a dedicated line. As the line approaches saturation, an ISDN connection is made to increase capacity. As activity drops, the ISDN connection also drops, controlling costs.

These techniques take advantage of ISDN's ability to set up and tear down connections in a second or less, carry information in digital form, and dynamically add B channels as loading increases. In effect, you can establish a system that ratchets up and down in 64 kbps increments.

ISDN for Remote Management and Fault Diagnosis

Technical staffs are expensive to maintain. When they travel, expenses mount whether or not effective work takes place. Use ISDN to establish links to smaller sites where fault diagnosis and repair can be performed while expensive technicians stay at a central site, guiding local staff through potential problem areas.

ISDN for Multimedia and Meetings

If your business requires intensive communications with clients, vendors, or other firms, establish ISDN for all parties to speed information exchange. If you're involved with graphics such as engineering drawings, the time involved to deliver these graphics to another location can be cut from days (for physical delivery) to minutes (for ISDN delivery). Even if you've been using modems, the time can be reduced from tens of minutes to just a few minutes. This is valuable when engineering staff members are working frantically to design or repair complex products. Use the same facilities for video and multimedia meetings.

ISDN and Training

The most important benefit, however, is one that's not often mentioned. Develop a training program based on the multimedia tools becoming available because of ISDN. Video, shared applications, white boards, high-quality audio, and so on, contribute to enrich training and ensure retention of material. Savings in travel for training can more than pay for the technology and ISDN costs within a few months.

Vertical Markets

Vertical markets involve businesses in specific industries. One of the primary characteristics of these markets is development of special hardware and software for their needs. Since such products are of very limited appeal, they usually are several times more expensive than general market products. Often the tendency is to say, "Let's just buy a standard database program and adapt it to our needs." Watch out! By the time you work it all out, your competitors are three generations ahead of you, and you've spent far more that the special products would have cost. Let's look at how a few particular vertical markets can use ISDN.

Broadcasting and Entertainment

A number of remarkable things are going on in broadcasting using ISDN. Musicians in different cities can perform together over high quality audio links established with ISDN's services. In Chapter 4, we discussed 7.5 KHz service, which provides pretty good audio over a B channel. If you bond two B channels, though, you can achieve 20 KHz of stereo. Think of the travel expenses and time that can be saved on big-name entertainers. If a singer is stuck in New York doing a Broadway show every night, and her accompanist has night club gigs in San Francisco, neither has to fly back and forth, sleep in hotels, or adapt to weather and time changes. ISDN makes afternoon sessions possible that otherwise would have been impossible because of the performers' bi-coastal commitments. Live shows can be conducted with people spread throughout the world.

▶ **See** Chapter 13, "Tying It Together: Two B or Not Two B," **p. 419**

Broadcasters soon can establish high-quality stereo connections between most major cities in the world through ISDN. Digital Courier International in Vancouver, BC has a computer system using ISDN that accepts audio feeds, compresses them, and sends them out to one or many locations. There's no longer a need to send tapes or CDs to tens or hundreds of places by overnight courier.

▶ **See** "H.320—The General Videoconferencing Standard," **p. 435**
▶ **See** "T.120—The General Multimedia Conferencing Standard," **p. 434**

Telemedicine

Exchange of detailed graphics such as x-rays has been restricted to expensive, high-speed dedicated links. In medicine, this limited the number and variety of sites. What happens if a rural site needs an immediate second opinion from a specialist in the city? As ISDN becomes widespread, adequate bandwidth can be assembled on-the-fly, permitting connections at any time for reasonable cost, even to remote locations. Video consultations with specialists anywhere can be arranged so that a patient and her doctors feel higher confidence about her diagnosis. This can be bolstered by transfers of patient records, color video files, ultrasound scans, EKG, EEG and countless other tests and measures. At this time, I've found many physicians, especially radiologists, installing ISDN BRI connections among all their hospital and office sites, and even to their houses. This way, a doctor can review x-rays and other radiographic information wherever he or she is, at any time of the day or night.

Services for the Deaf

Deaf persons have been communicating by teletype for years. But this fails to convey much of the inflection provided by signing. ISDN can fill this gap. Here in Texas, people are experimenting with video desktop conferencing systems using ISDN as a means of providing signing. This gives the full effect of inflection. Plans include establishing conferencing systems with interpreters available full-time to assist anywhere in the state. For example, a deaf person might be the victim of a crime. Communicating the details to police would be a difficult task, but the police could call up an interpreter, using ISDN and video, and conduct the interview in a quick and natural way for the victim.

Retailing

Point-of-sale information for inventory and charge approval can be carried over D channel packets. This reduces approval times to just a couple of seconds, making checkout lines move considerably faster despite the fact that more customers will start using credit cards. In Texas, the food stamp program has eliminated paper coupons and replaced them with a magnetic card that works like a credit card. Stores that sell food items run this card through point-of-sale machines; one swipe ensures that the items are authorized products, verifies that the card's user has money left in the account, and then transfers payment, substantially reducing the possibility of fraud. When ISDN D channel packet is used for this, delays in waiting at the supermarket line are substantially reduced.

Small retail establishments should consider installing only one telephone line, ISDN. The store can use each of the B channels for voice calls. It can use one or both B channels for data, such as the Internet as needed, and it can set up D channel packet for credit card exchanges. This is certainly faster and it may often be cheaper than three analog business lines.

From Here...

As ISDN develops and becomes available everywhere, applications that were once prohibitively expensive are becoming dirt cheap. Applications never dreamed of before are now saving lives and improving the quality of others. We've only touched on a few areas of personal, educational, and business uses. Maybe you'll come up with a stunning application that takes off and makes you millions because you can use ISDN. When that happens, remember where you first learned about ISDN—you can send my cut to the address you'll find on my e-mail and Web site, thanks ;-).

We're nearing the end of our ISDN adventure.

- Chapter 17, "ISDN Access for Internet Providers and Corporations," discusses the issues of connection for these larger users.
- Chapter 15, "Changing Telephones to ISDN," gives you a number of ideas on using ISDN with voice communications.
- Chapter 4, "Choosing Services," outlines the types of services available and breaks down the various audio services.
- Chapter 6, "Unscrambling APIs," shows how the Application Program Interfaces can help you make ISDN and telephony in general work together.
- Chapter 14, "Pictures and Video with ISDN," focuses on how video works, especially in the desktop video-conferencing environment.
- Chapter 12, "Opening Windows 95 and NT to ISDN," shows how these new operating systems will help you with ISDN.
- Chapter 13, "Tying It Together: Two B or Not Two B," explains how multiple B channels work.
- Chapter 18, "Anticipating Broadband ISDN," looks toward much greater bandwidth.
- Chapter 19, "Forecasting Changes Due to ISDN," moves you into future developments.
- Chapter 20, "Alternatives to ISDN," examines other flavors of communications to see how ISDN stands up.

ISDN Access for Internet Providers and Corporations

Earlier chapters have looked at ISDN as a means for telecommuting, joining LANs, and connecting to the Internet. Now, let's turn things around and see what ISDN can mean to Internet service providers and larger organizations. In reality the needs of those two are the same: connections from subscribers come in from one side, and connections to resources go out the other. There are opportunities for ISDN on both sides.

I'll start with a history of the model that predated the electronic bulletin board. Then we'll go in-depth on several issues for larger Internet service providers and organizations. ■

Basics of a bulletin board system (BBS)

You'll learn the history of the somewhat chaotic BBS world and how it forecast much of how we'd use Internet and organizational access.

Basics of an Internet service provider system

All of us are concerned with Internet access. Most of us need to connect through a provider that is directly attached to the Internet. Let's see how we can use ISDN.

Use of ISDN to connect with subscribers and with resources

The larger organization needs to connect its various offices and staff together. Here's how ISDN can help.

Bulletin Board Systems

A *bulletin board system (BBS)* is a combination of a computer communications program with a database. The bulletin board contains information of all sorts; this might be information on computers, cooking, travel, or any other topic. Some boards specialize in certain areas of interest, and some don't. The addition of communications equipment makes the contents of the database available to any authorized caller. Once the caller has *logged in* to the board, she may wander through the collection of information, download files, and, if permitted, even upload files for the use of others.

> **N O T E** Check out the lists of ISDN BBSs at **http://www.alumni.caltech.edu/~dank/isdn/ bbs.txt#TELCO**. ▨

A BBS is an excellent way for a firm to distribute news to its employees and support to its customers. Tests have shown that the majority of calls for technical support can be grouped into a limited range of categories and answered with responses stored in a database. Many customer support operations have evolved into telephone call centers with people sitting around answering the phone, punching buttons to find routine answers, and reading those answers over the phone to callers. Offering users a BBS relieves much of the load on personnel. Fax response systems provide a similar alternative by sending users answers to routine questions they find on a standard list. Finally, Internet support through World Wide Web, gopher, and ftp tools gives users a third alternative.

A single database can be designed so that it's accessible by fax, BBS, or Internet. The advantage of the BBS is its simplicity for users, and the low cost of setup and maintenance. You don't have to put in a fancy fax system, or maintain an online Internet connection. All you need is an inexpensive BBS program, a computer with a few modems and telephone lines, and some way of putting information you already know into the computer. Most often, users pay their own telephone toll charges to reach your BBS.

Over the last ten years, privately run BBSs have also evolved. Thousands of boards are maintained by individuals just for fun. It's reminiscent of amateur radio, where some individuals spend thousands of hours (and dollars) building and running a radio system that the law forbids be used for commercial business. BBSs, however, don't suffer from non-commercial restrictions, and many BBS operations that started as hobbies have evolved into thriving businesses.

The original BBS design was the product of Randy Suess and Ward Christensen in 1978. Improvements and additions by countless others have resulted in several designs; some are available as commercial products, while others are available for free use within the BBS community. Figure 17.1 shows a typical screen produced by the commercial BBS program Major BBS from Galecticomm. This BBS is typical in that the opening menu gives the user a chance to search a particular library, download files, and do a variety of other tasks. Here, I've listed the libraries of information maintained on this BBS.

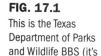

FIG. 17.1

This is the Texas Department of Parks and Wildlife BBS (it's open to the public at 512-389-4430).

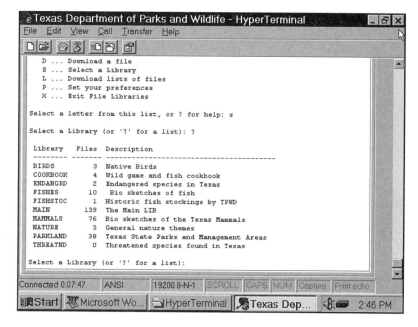

Long before the Internet became generally accessible to everyone, the BBS community devised a structure for interconnection of BBSs. In 1984, Tom Jennings wrote BBS software named Fido. Jennings lived in San Francisco, and his colleague, John Mandrill, lived in Boston; they used Fido to exchange BBS contents at night when long distance telephone rates were low, and developed scripts to automate the process.

Over time, FidoNet grew and developed a routing system for the entire world. Now, BBSers throughout the world routinely dial each other and exchange international traffic. The world is divided into *zones* as follows:

Zone 1	North America
Zone 2	Europe
Zone 3	Oceania (a combination of the south and central Pacific islands, Australia, and New Zealand)
Zone 4	South America

Each zone is divided into *regions* with a two-digit number for each; the regions are divided into *networks*. Finally, major users within a network are referred to as *points*. A typical FidoNet address looks like this:

1:343/21.1

The format is *zone:region/network.point*.

Part

IV

Ch

17

Currently, an exciting and money-saving technique involves the use of satellite links connecting all of North America with geosynchronous satellites. Each day, participating BBSs call an earth station in Tennessee, upload their messages, and sign off. The earth station transmits all the messages to the satellite, which rebroadcasts all its messages and newsfeeds over the continent simultaneously. Since there's a very small amount for each BBS to upload, but a huge amount available to download, this method has resulted in significant phone cost reductions for BBS operators.

▶ **See** how this asymmetrical need for quantity of information carries over into the design of the most sophisticated transmission systems in Chapter 20, "Alternatives to ISDN," **p. 555**

Many BBS Sysops (system operators) are offering Internet connection through their board to subscribers that dial in. As a by-product, often subscribers can telnet from the Internet. This is moving BBS operations from front-end providers connected to the dial-in phone system to back-end providers servicing through the Internet. In the process, many using BBS have adopted ISDN.

Internet Service Providers

As the Internet became more generally available and open for commercial use, BBSs began to offer access to the Internet through their existing BBS hardware. Initially, this access simply used the BBS computer as a *host* on the Internet while the users logged in as *terminal users*. This sort of shell account usually was based on a version of UNIX running on the BBS computer.

Users had to be educated in the arcane command structures of UNIX, TCP/IP, and C to do much with these connections. BBS operators, now becoming Internet access providers, worked hard to simplify the interface to the Internet. A real breakthrough came when providers began to offer—and users began to demand—*Serial Line Internet Protocol* (*SLIP*) accounts.

SLIP allowed the computer user, connected by a modem over a serial line, to become a full-fledged host in the Internet world. This meant that the user's computer gained an Internet *IP address* and was recognized as a peer with all other computers on the Internet. With this identity, the tools available to individual users jumped light years ahead of the terminal-to-host shell connection. Most importantly, the user could run a *graphical browser* for the World Wide Web (Mosaic and Netscape are examples of such browsers). While SLIP did a good job, it was quickly replaced by point-to-point protocol (PPP). Recall that PPP is the basis for much of our use of ISDN.

N O T E In order for things to work with a SLIP or PPP connection, your machine has to have an IP address that is unique throughout the Internet during the time of the connection. Since the supply of IP addresses is dwindling, many Internet access providers dynamically assign IP addresses to their dial-up accounts each time an account makes a connection. This means that the provider maintains a list of IP numbers which no one else can use. Then, whenever you dial up, the software on your machine and the software on the provider's machine work together to assign an IP address for your use during the current connection session. When you log out, that number is returned to the pool and can be used by another dial-in user. These methods of dynamic IP assignment work independently of whether the user dials in with POTS or with ISDN. ■

A Brief Excursion into Virtual Cyberspace Intended to Blow Your Mind

ISDN provides control signals over the D channel, and the D channel is always up. If you don't believe this, look at Figure 10.32 in Chapter 10, "Putting an Adapter Inside Your Computer"; this is a graphic showing the D channel up when you plug into ISDN regardless of whether or not you've made any B channel connections.

A system could be set up so users are always logged in, but B channels are not connected until requested by the D channel. In effect, this creates a full-time "virtual connection" but the resource that may have a metered charge, B channels, is used only as needed. Security and authentication take place when the system is installed and the D channel is up, not on each B channel connection.

Now for the *coup de grâce*; the D channel can maintain 255 virtual sessions simultaneously. So you could have your system virtually connected to 255 sites at the same time, popping among them and merrily delivering information from and to everywhere all at once. Yet, you'll only be paying for the actual B channel when it really is passing traffic because the D channel pops B channels on and off to wherever needed at will within a fraction of a second. Think of it as a giant combination call holding, call waiting, and conference call with your equipment hopping all over and all the lines staying up so it's real fast.

Can you get this ready to go today? Not as far as I know. Can it be built with existing technology. Yes. Will it be? Yes. When? Soon. What economic effect will it have? Big.

Part
IV

Ch
17

▶ **See** "LAN Connection to Wide Area Networks," **p. 309**

▶ **See** "PPP Multilink Protocol," **p. 424**

I don't mean to imply that BBS folks were the only ones to get into the business of providing Internet access. Many people who were never involved with BBS activities have set up successful Internet provider operations. Now, of course, a number of larger firms such as IBM, PSI, AT&T, and Microsoft are entering the field. Time will determine how well the large approach works out versus the small approach.

My bet is that big operations will take over the commodity business of connecting users to the Internet. Little guys who survive will offer services that the big ones can't or won't offer: domain name service for smaller enterprises, customized mail service, specialized Web service, and a host of other services off the back end of the Internet (as opposed to the front end through which users dial up).

Providers frequently started in the first half of the 1990s with a single 56-kbps connection to a larger seller of Internet access. As demand grew, the useful minimum for a provider in a metropolitan setting became a T1 line (1.544 Mbps). Today's growth in demand and in users' access data rates (especially through ISDN) are pushing many providers toward 10 Mbps access to their Internet connections.

Using ISDN to Connect Subscribers

A look at BBS operators reveals they generally use a machine with serial ports and a modem pool for subscriber dial-in. When they go to ISDN service, the most direct technique simply replaces some of the modems with ISDN equipment such as serial line terminal adapters. The same is true of Internet service providers. Using this method, the BBS operator or ISP and subscribers can continue to use scripts developed in the modem world using the Hayes AT command set. This usually means that asynch V.120 is the protocol.

▶ **See** Chapter 9, "Selecting an External Terminal Adapter," **p. 203**

N O T E   Some BBS software is limited to 19.2 kbps or 28.8 kbps. But this data rate has been increasing to meet the demand for ISDN. For example, one of the most popular BBS software packages is Wildcat!; it now supports 115.2 kbps (Mustang Software, Inc. 800 807-2874; get on your wild thoroughbred, quarter horse if you're from Texas, and ride on to **http://www.mustang.com** to find out more. Windows 95 has built-in support for communications, thereby removing a lot of the headaches from BBS developers that migrate. ▨

N O T E   As noted earlier, I expect asynch V.120 to fade out over the next year or two in favor of PPP. Under those circumstances, BBS operators will go to PPP using multiple hosts on Ethernets with routers to ISDN lines. ▨

Internet providers began their ISDN connection strategy with this method: Multiple hosts on an Ethernet connected through a router to ISDN lines. That model is quite different from private point-to-point use of ISDN to connect two LANs or to connect an occasional telecommuter to an office. The Internet provider's optimal system must be able to do the following:

- Accept dial-in ISDN from any subscriber
- Respond to a number of subscribers at once
- Expand and contract bandwidth (in, at most, B-channel increments) as a subscriber's needs vary during the course of a connection
- Call the subscriber's router upon receipt of data traffic for the subscriber
- Compress data as much as possible to effect the highest possible information transfer
- Rapidly set up and tear down connections
- Sense a caller's type of equipment as POTS or ISDN, and accept the connection accordingly, so that callers need to call only one telephone number for either POTS or ISDN service and the ISP need have only ISDN lines
- Offer options of PRI or multiple BRI so that the provider can take advantage of markets where tariffs make several BRIs cheaper than a PRI
- Interoperate with all vendors products that meet industry standards for PPP, Multilink PPP, and compression methods

You Mean This Turkey Can Go Up and Down All the Time and Still Work?

You may be asking: "If these calls are constantly being set up and torn down, I would think that the caller (customer) would have problems with Internet apps. If the ISP uses dynamic addressing, that would cause a lot of problems for applications if the IP is constantly changing. Even with permanently assigned IP addresses, I don't know of any mainstream Internet software products that would answer the call if the ISP's equipment tried to call the subscriber as described in the fourth bulleted point. This could be a real issue. You can get fairly long delays between packets of data on a Web site. You may get the text in one packet, part of a graphic in the next, wait 30 seconds or a minute for the next graphic, etc. You can't have the ISDN hardware tearing down the connection and setting it back up every time the ISP senses a break in the data, can you?"

Indeed you can. That's the whole point. ISPs can configure dynamic or static addressing and manage dynamic addressing by session, node, or port. If they are aggregating BRI/PRI with routers like the Ascend 25/50s, 400s and Maxes, a dynamic reassignment would not occur unless there were a security-breach-type really big timeout instigated by the router. If the user were working with an ISDN terminal adapter through an NDIS or ODI driver, the make/break would be quite transparent.

You're thinking of using a terminal adapter the same way as a modem when you are lead to the conclusion this can't be done. In modem-like operation you don't make/break circuits save at login and logout. In bridge or router operation through a network interface card (NIC) "spoofing" is used to make fake session management packets even while the circuit is shut down. The user and ISP both have to be doing modem-like or NIC-like stuff; should one use one method and the other the opposite, nothing will work. If there's mid-session making and breaking of circuits, it will be mediated on both sides by the security regime. Efficiency will tolerate long breaks with lots of spoofing. Security will look for irregular breaks and spoofing by a hacker trying to steal something, not a collaborating ISDN device trying to save money.

That's quite a list. Since most routers were designed for point-to-point single connections, it's been hard to fill. The leading router manufacturers concentrated on hooking one division of a giant enterprise to another. In the meantime, Ascend Communications must have decided that the Internet provider market was going to be big enough to justify development of a router line answering most of the wants I just listed. Its MAX series of routers is just what Internet providers need (see Fig. 17.2).

Ascend doesn't have all the answers; it just asked the right questions and beat everyone to market. Now, the trick is interoperability. With Ascend holding up to 80% (some estimate even more) of the Internet service provider market, especially for ISDN access, they're the company to beat and the routers to connect with. Unfortunately, Ascend has done some things in proprietary ways—for example, compression and channel aggregation—but they're coming around, as I discussed in Chapter 13, "Tying It Together: Two B or Not Two B."

The other leading router makers have smelled real money here, so consumers can expect to see features increase and prices drop. U.S. Robotics provides the Total Control line illustrated in Figure 17.3 to meet Ascend's challenge. 3Com is doing the same thing with its Access-Builder 7000 shown in Figure 17.4. Bay Networks and Cisco provide similar equipment.

FIG. 17.2

Ascend MAX 4000, a router for Internet service providers can be used for remote LAN access and tele-commuting. Modules include "digital modems" to ISDN lines that sense calls are ISDN or POTS and respond accordingly.

FIG. 17.3

The U.S. Robotics Total Control line is designed for rack installation using modules to build systems for specific needs. The modular form includes hot swap options so repairs, expansions, and replacements may be made without shutting down.

FIG. 17.4

The 3Com Access-Builder 7000 is a modular system providing a concentration of multiple BRI, PRI, and POTS lines with routers and bridges.

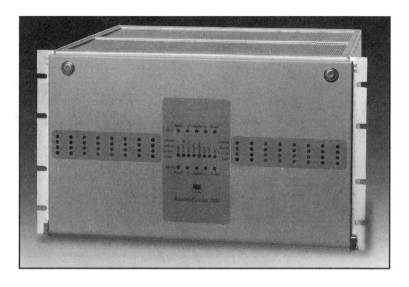

With modular designs offering flexible expansion, these products are all designed to address several markets:

- Internet service providers
- Corporate intranet
- LAN to LAN
- Telecommuter

N O T E Check these URLs for more information:

Ascend: **http://www.ascend.com**

3Com:**http://www.3com.com**

Cisco: **http://www.cisco.com**

Bay: **http://www.baynetworks.com** ▨

Here's the next debate: Once a provider has made an investment in ISDN hardware and lines, two types of service could be sold:

- Service designed for users that dial in as needed to use an Internet connection.
- Service designed for users that dial in and never hang up (in effect, "dedicated" ISDN).

N O T E I've put the word "dedicated" in quotes because its use in this context is not technically accurate. From the telephone company's perspective, the line is still dial-up, but from the user's perspective, the line is dedicated because it's dialed up once and never disconnected. ▨

The first type of service anticipates users who will be connected only for short periods of time. Ideally, each user would have software and hardware to take advantage of the rapid setup and teardown of ISDN. Ascend equipment does this, as do many other vendors' routers. With everything properly configured, a user is sitting at a computer on a network with a router connected to an ISDN line. When the user clicks a hyperlink to the Web, the computer requests a response from the IP address associated with that link (initially, the name server at the user's Internet access provider). Since that IP address is not on the user's LAN, the router dials up the provider to pass the request. The name server looks at the address, converts it to another IP address, and sends the user's request across the Internet to the target machine. The response comes back, fills in the user's browser screen through a series of packets and stops. A time-out runs on the user's router and perhaps the provider's router; since no data traffic occurs during that time, the ISDN call is disconnected. The user clicks another link...

This model has the advantage of using the ISDN connection only during the time of actual exchange of information, plus a few seconds of buffers to determine if anything else is on its way soon. If the telephone company bills based on time usage, this can cut telephone costs and give the Internet service provider a line and router port to spread costs to others, so the end user doesn't get charged as much by the provider, either. This model, however, has two disadvantages:

- There's some time required to connect and disconnect. This usually takes a second or less for each access with all equipment and the telephone company switch properly functioning.

- In areas where ISDN connection is billed on usage, there's often a higher rate for the first minute of use as opposed to subsequent minutes during the same connection. Often, the difference is considerable, with the first minute costing 3 to 4 times what additional minutes cost. Users therefore have to evaluate their usage to make sure they get the advantage of not being connected too long, but also make sure they're not setting themselves up for drastically increased costs because they're connected in the high cost first minute most of the time.

Get Rid of Call SetUp Charges

In my opinion it is very short-sighted for the phone companies to charge more for the first minute. This discourages the most effective use of ISDN. This setup charge is clearly a leftover from a time when human intervention and/or substantial machine activity were required to set up a call. Current technology really bears no such added costs for call setup. The fact these absurd charges continue is additional proof the tariff system is antiquated. Users should petition the appropriate legal bodies to remove such inefficient tariffs.

If, for example, your telephone company charges you three cents for the first minute, and one cent a minute after that, you'd probably want to stay hooked up for four or five minutes at a time if you or a program were actively using the connection every couple of minutes. What would it cost if you just dialed up and stayed connected? Well, if the telephone company only charged you from 9 a.m. to 5 p.m., Monday through Friday, your weekly cost would be $24.00. On the average there are 4.3 weeks in a month, so your monthly metered usage charge would be $103.20. Add this to a typical base rate of $25, and you end up with a "dedicated" ISDN connection payment to the telephone company of $128.20 a month or $1538.40 a year. It looks like "dedicated" is not the way to go, so see if you can work out a way to minimize your usage during those business hours.

I did this rough calculation from the user's end. The same thing applies from the provider's direction. These economics play into your decision of whether or not to establish "dedicated" ISDN connections when there's a telephone company meter running. The same consideration affects the provider who has to have a designated port on a router for every such connection.

Now, let's consider the other possibility. There are regions where the use of ISDN is not metered by the telephone company. Here in Austin, for example, usage of ISDN for an unlimited time costs $70 a month, including taxes, title, and insurance! That's a lot more than the base rate of about $25 a month in California, but California has metered charges similar to those used in the preceding example. In Austin, providers set up many "dedicated" ISDN connections as a result. In fact, the economics are such that the providers seem to favor establishing "dedicated" ISDN customers rather than occasional dial-in customers. With "dedicated" customers, a provider knows exactly how many ISDN ports and lines are needed. The provider doesn't need to worry about peak times when subscribers fight for a limited number of lines.

"Dedicated" ISDN certainly makes sense for a business that's very active on the Internet, if the telephone company's rate structure is similar to the one in Austin. It makes sense for the Internet providers because it gives them a secure, predictable cash flow without as many statistical issues of dial-up demand. Is it, however, fair to the phone company? I'll resist the impulse to begin questioning who's being fair to whom. Rather, let's look at the underlying technology. A wire from the provider to the switch is tied up all the time; the same is true of a wire from the user to the provider. Nobody else could use that wire anyway, so there's no loss.

The switch has set up the connection, so is the path through the switch displacing some other users? That would be true in the world of old step-by-step switches that actually established a physical path. With modern protocols and modern switches, however, we're just throwing packets in when needed; when there's no traffic being sent, the space and time not used by our "dedicated" ISDN line can be used by someone else. "Wait a minute," you say. "Surely something maintains the connection." Yes, the software in the switch maintains the connection, and a minimal number of CPU cycles is needed to keep the virtual path alive, but this consumes very few resources. And don't forget, the D channel is always up in an ISDN system.

In Condemnation of "Dedicated" *ISDN*

I am very concerned that widespread use of "dedicated" *ISDN*, with flat-rate tariffs, will result in the blow that killed the goose that laid the golden egg. By that I mean the telco will observe the substantial number of users that maintain continuous off-hook conditions on ISDN, a switched service. Then the telco will move to change the rate structure. US West filed for a flat rate of about $185 in some of its areas citing the "dedicated" *ISDN* issue. One might expect a similar move by other telephone companies. Such companies might also be tempted to go to a time charge. These moves should be actively opposed.

continues

continued

> But, in opposition, it would be best for users to go in with clean hands by showing they are using the resource in an efficient and responsible way. ISDN is especially well-designed for efficient use. The rapid set up and tear down of an ISDN connection fosters careful adjustment of connection time. I suggest all ISDN users explore this more efficient use and move away from the dedicated ISDN idea. In that way, we may prevent a move by the carriers to raise flat rates or go to metered rates, and we will be in a good position to oppose any such moves by a showing of our responsible efforts to limit usage to only that really useful for exchanging information.

Using ISDN to Connect with Resources

The flip side where the connection is from the Internet service provider to the Internet itself is different. In the BBS world, the exchange of information over FidoNet and to a central transmission site for satellite rebroadcast clearly can benefit from ISDN. When a BBS has to call many sites a night, or receive calls from many others, the speed to set up and tear down connections becomes tremendously important. This is especially true for a central satellite broadcast site. Long connection times could result in a need for more lines and equipment; therefore, ISDN can result in significant savings.

In the Internet world, connection to the Internet backbone or to a larger Internet provider usually has been through switched or dedicated 56 kbps or T1 methods. ISDN is dramatically cheaper than either dedicated or switched 56, so for providers that have such a need, moving to ISDN can upgrade their service to 128 kbps and reduce their costs simultaneously.

"Dedicated" T1 service is a different matter. Now, we have to compare PRI, with its 23 channels that are nearly the same carrying capacity as the 24 of a T1, to multiple BRIs using some sort of channel aggregation. Tariffs and equipment costs will determine which way a provider should go.

There is certainly a good argument, however, for an Internet provider to use some dialable ISDN lines for connection out the back to the Internet. What happens when the primary Internet connection used by the Internet provider goes down? The provider's users can't get to the Internet. In the competitive world of Internet services, and with increasing business dependence on the Internet, downtime costs big money.

The solution for a provider: have at least one ISDN PRI that can be dialed rapidly to different resources in case of a failure in the primary connection or Internet site. When this line is not directed to an alternative resource, it can be used for additional bandwidth elsewhere in the system.

A Practical Example for ISDN Internet Service Providers

Let's say you're thinking about directing your ISP operation toward ISDN and want to know how best to do it. Look over the list of Internet provider's optimal system items discussed in this chapter under "Using ISDN to Connect Subscribers."

> **CAUTION**
>
> This look is just that, a look. While I'll talk about some technical details and give you a peek at some configuration screens, there's a lot more to setting up this device and a major ISDN Internet service operation than I can cover between the covers of this book. In Chapter 9, "Selecting an External Terminal Adapter," Chapter 10, "Putting an Adapter Inside Your Computer," and Chapter 11, "Establishing ISDN for LANs," I really got into the details in hopes of giving you all you'd need besides the documentation that came with your equipment. In this chapter, I can only give you a good taste of the issues and problems you'll face. But I hope you'll find a number of good ideas here and in the balance of the book that you can profitably integrate into your business.

Part
IV
Ch
17

Equipment and Configuration

As I suggested earlier, Ascend routers satisfy the criteria for Internet service providers, and Ascend has the biggest chunk of the ISP market for ISDN. So let's take a close look at its popular big router, the MAX 4000.

> **N O T E** Much of the information in this chapter and especially this section was provided through the very active help of Freeside Communications and Signet Partners, both Internet service providers for Austin and other cities. Free your browser toward **http://www.fc.net** to learn more about Freeside Communications. Partner up with **http://www.sig.net** for the big picture on Signet Partners.

The Max 4000 can be configured with multiple BRI, PRI, or T1 interfaces. It has an Ethernet port. It has six module slots to add devices such as the "digital modems" Ascend provides to enable access from both digital and analog callers. Now let's see how all this fits together for your ISP business. Take a look at Figure 17.5. This is a drawing of the Max used in conjunction with a Cisco 2501 router and a smaller Ascend Pipeline 400 router.

FIG. 17.5

Schematic Diagram of an Internet service provider with extensive ISDN services. Courtesy Signet Partners.

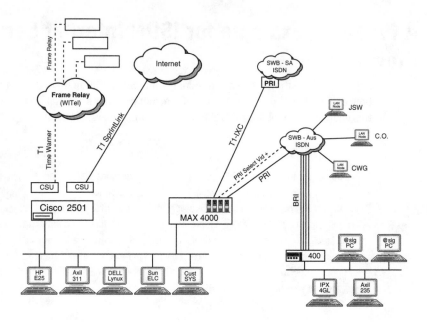

As you examine Figure 17.2, notice the wide variety of telephone services used. Frame relay comes in from a number of cities at the top left using WilTel as the interexchange carrier. WilTel passes the frame relay to Time Warner that connects over a T1 to a CSU (channel service unit) at the provider. This connects to the Cisco 2501 router. Right away you can see that this provider supplies not only Internet service, but also frame relay.

Now look at the Internet cloud in the middle. It's hooked up through a T1 carried by SprintLink to another CSU on the Cisco 2501. This is the ISP's connection to the Internet. This link provides Internet service to all the clients.

The Cisco 2501 attaches to an Ethernet within the ISP's facility. Several different computers are hooked to this Ethernet and are used for system control and maintenance, domain name service (DNS), UNIX accounts, and e-mail post offices.

The Ascend MAX is also connected to the Ethernet. The MAX then connects over a T1 using an interexchange carrier to a PRI port on an ISDN switch at Southwestern Bell in San Antonio. This connection provides clients in San Antonio with access to the ISP's facilities.

Another port on the MAX connects over a PRI to an ISDN switch at Southwestern Bell in Austin. There is no interexchange carrier here because the ISP's equipment is located in Austin. An additional link uses a Southwestern Bell trademarked service, "Select Video Plus." Ins and outs of a complex tariff determine just how the ISP will use these connections; in summary this particular tariff allows callers throughout the Austin LATA (Local Access and Transport Area, an area substantially larger than Austin itself) to call in using ISDN or POTS and receive an Internet connection.

Now get the rest of the picture. A number of BRIs go from the Austin telco switch to an Ascend Pipeline 400 router connected to another Ethernet connected to several computers.

And additional single BRIs go to three separate PCs at the far right. What's going on? Redundant systems are available. Should the MAX fail, the Pipeline 400 could carry some load. Should the Cisco fail, a port on the Max could be used to dial up an Internet connection.

Then get the really to slick part of this and realize the T1 from San Antonio and the PRI from Austin that connect to the MAX provide the way for clients to get into the system and then through the Ethernet to the Cisco and then the Internet. Obviously ISDN clients can use this link. But the MAX has Ascend's "digital modems" installed. These can detect analog calls and accept them too.

▶ **See** "Transmission," **p. 23**

▶ **See** "Digital and Analog," **p. 70**

"What? Wait a minute?" I can hear you saying. "You mean the analog calls come down the PRI?" Yes. Let's face it. Except for the local link, all calls are carried as digital information anyway. So when a client with an analog modem places a call through any switch, it's converted to digital information when it reaches the switch. All we're doing here is eliminating reconversion to analog. The signal comes over the PRI to the MAX. The digital modems detect the analog modem signature, the handshake, etc. squalls you hear when modems hook up. The MAX's digital modem knows it now must talk to the analog modem in a language it will understand, so the digital modem fakes an analog modem handshake to satisfy the analog modem. Once that's done, the connection's established and information transfers. The client can call one number using either an ISDN device or a POTS modem. The MAX figures out which. Simplicity for the client. Efficient use of resources for the ISP.

▶ **See** "Ascend Pipelines," **p. 340**

Let's take a look at some of the MAX screens. They look a lot like the one's we saw on the Ascend Pipeline in Chapter 11, but there's more going on. Figure 17.6 shows a typical screen with a lot of useful information. The instructions on the bottom show you how to navigate among the presentations by pressing Ctrl-n to move the cursor to the next menu item and hitting return to select it. Tab moves to another window and a thick border indicates the active window. The thick border is around the screen you can change. In this case it shows the Main Edit Menu.

Look at the details in the Main Edit Menu on the left. The numbers designate locations in the MAX. To the right of each number there's a description:

- 00-000 System is the MAX system itself
- 10-000 Net/T1 is one of the T1 or PRI connections
- 20-000 Net/T1 is a second T1 or PRI connection
- 60-000 V.34 Modem is one digital modem card
- 70-000 V.34 Modem is another digital modem card
- 90-000 Ethernet is the Ethernet port
- A0-000 Ether Data is a logical port for Ethernet
- B0-000 Serial WAN is another WAN connection

Part
IV

Ch
17

FIG. 17.6

Ascend Max Main Edit
Menu.

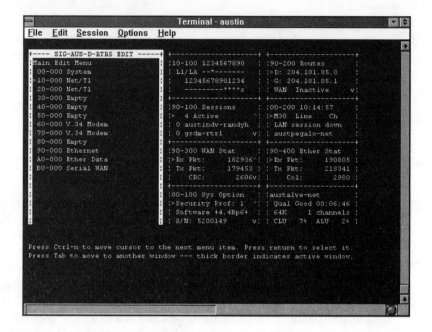

You may track the operation of any of these by highlighting the item, pressing return and reviewing statistics about the device's operation.

The right side of the screen stays the same. There are eight boxes:

- The upper left box shows the lines connected and in use.
- The second box on the left records active sessions by the name of the client as known by the system.
- The third box on the left reflects activity statistics on the wide area network showing packets transmitted and received.
- The fourth box on the left tracks software version numbers and security options.
- The upper box on the right shows routes being used with IP addresses.
- The second box on the right reflects the status of pending calls.
- The third box on the right shows Ethernet statistics.
- The fourth box on the right tracks line quality and utilization. A parameter can be set so additional B channels are allotted to a client as that client's utilization increases. In this system when utilization on a B channel exceeds 70%, an additional B channel is added. Then, when utilization reduces below 70%, the additional B channel is dropped.

Figure 17.7 shows the Modify Configuration window in the highlighted left portion. Notice the right side boxes remain the same. This configuration window is a part of the configuration process that allows you to:

- Assign a name to the router

- Set up the Ethernet

- Set up the wide area network

- Manage SMTP (simple mail transfer protocol)

- Set up a number of security matters including protection against telnet entry

- Insert the domain name

- Insert the domain name server IP addresses

- Establish the authorization method

FIG. 17.7
Ascend MAX Modify
Configuration Screen

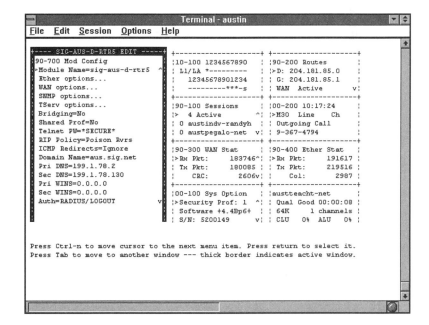

NOTE If you set up your MAX to call out, it will start with the lowest available number in your line hunt group and make the call. If the telco switch is set to pass incoming calls to the lowest available hunt group number too, there are possible problems. So, ask your telco to start the hunt group for incoming calls at the highest available number and count down. This means your outgoing and incoming calls converge on the middle rather than step on each other. ■

There are countless other screens. But you get the idea. The MAX can be configured in just about any way to satisfy the list of criteria I mentioned at first.

Troubleshooting in an ISDN Internet Provider System

Once you have the system up and running, your concerns turn to keeping it going and keeping your clients happy. Figure 17.8 is a flow diagram for handling problems at an ISDN Internet service provider.

FIG. 17.8

Flow Diagram for
Troubleshooting an ISDN
System at an Internet
service provider.
Courtesy John Darden
and Signet Partners.

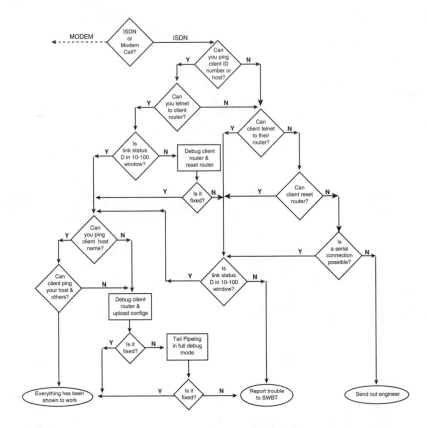

Let's flow down this diagram and see what's going on. I'll assume you're familiar with such
TCP/IP terms as ping and telnet and drop down to "Is link status D in 10-100 window?" This
refers to the 10-100 "Telephone Line Status" window shown in the top middle of Figure 17.7.
Here each channel of the T1 or PRI shown as 10-100 at the left of figure ("Net/T1") is tracked
and its activity is reflected. The numbers "1234..." show the channel numbers. Notice that the
numbers continue with the first digit 1 or 2 assumed in the second row in the middle of the
box. So, in all there are numbers from 1 through 24 shown representing the 23, for a PRI,
or 24, for a T1, channels available.

Under each channel a dash (-) means the channel is not in use (idle), a star (*) means it's in
use, and a "d" means it's dialing. The flow diagram asks if there's a "D" for the link representing the channel. The upper case "D" is used in the Pipeline series to show a connection to a
multi-point location with two SPIDs. This is the sort of location you would expect for a properly
operating ISDN connection. The figures here don't show that but look back at Figure 11.14 in
Chapter 11; this shows a Pipeline. Notice the 10-100 presentation and general screen is much
like the MAX; so management is consistent from the smallest (Pipeline) to the largest (MAX)
in the Ascend line. In Figure 11.14 "Link D" is the indication mentioned in the flow diagram.
The other phrase that's a mystery on the diagram is "Tail Pipelog in full debug mode." You
UNIX hackers may get this, but real humans feel like they fell through a looking glass and

down a rabbit hole simultaneously. Tail means use the monitor to show the log of system activity being maintained by the "Pipe"line; get it? The chart is prepared for the Ascend Pipeline family of routers, and its log was named Pipelog at the time the installer configured the equipment. This log is to be printed to the screen so you can see what's going on. You'll see a great deal of detail about exactly what is happening during the connection in question.

Table 17.1 shows some of the most interesting information the log records. The table is a list of the "ISDN Cause Codes" sent back by the telco switch. That's right, you can receive the codes from the switch. As you gain familiarity with the switch and your system, you'll build a list of the most common problems shown by the log and the most likely defects so you can fix things quickly.

Table 17.1   ISDN Cause Codes Returned by the Switch

Code	Cause
1	Unallocated (unassigned) number
2	No route to specified transit network (WAN)
6	Channel unacceptable
16	Normal clearing
17	User busy
18	No user responding
21	Call rejected
22	Number changed
28	Invalid number format (Incomplete number)
29	Facility rejected
30	Response to STATUS INQUIRY
31	Normal, unspecified
34	No circuit/channel available
38	Network (WAN) out of order
41	Temporary failure
42	Switching equipment congestion
43	Access information discarded
44	Requested circuit channel not available
45	Preempted
50	Requested facility not subscribed

Part
IV

Ch
17

continues

Table 17.1 Continued

Code	Cause
52	Outgoing calls barred
54	Incoming calls barred
58	Bearer capability not presently available
63	Service or option not available, unspecified
65	Bearer service not implemented
66	Channel type not implemented
69	Requested facility not implemented
81	Invalid call reference value
82	Identified channel does not exist
88	Incompatible destination
96	Mandatory information element is missing
97	Message type nonexistent or not implemented
98	Message not compatible with call state or message type nonexistent or not implemented
100	Invalid information element contents
102	Recovery on timer expiry
127	Internetworking, unspecified

If you still can't fix the problem, the log with its cause codes will prove valuable to the telephone company (Southwestern Bell in this example) in working with you.

Remote Office and Roaming Using ISDN

So far I've covered issues for Internet service providers and, by implication, for large organizations that may want a large number of users to dial in and participate in what is rapidly becoming the corporate intranet. But what about the small to medium size organization or the remote office and what about its roving staff?

You certainly can select among the ISDN devices mentioned in earlier chapters and arrive at an excellent solution. An alternative is to select equipment specifically designed for the remote office/roaming situation. Shiva has made a business out of that market; the company provides a line of LanRovers specifically designed to support organizational remote access. Figures 17.9 and 17.10 show the LanRover/2E Plus.

FIG. 17.9

The Shiva LanRover/2E Plus front panel view.

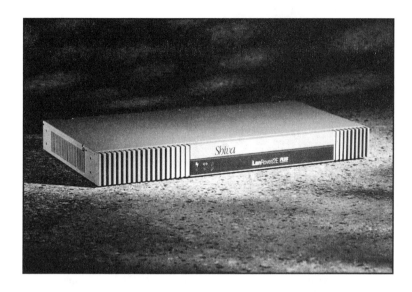

FIG. 17.10

This back view of the Shiva LanRover/2E Plus shows the ports; notice the locations for additional BRI or analog modules on the left. Typically, router devices are displayed with the back view so you can see the port design.

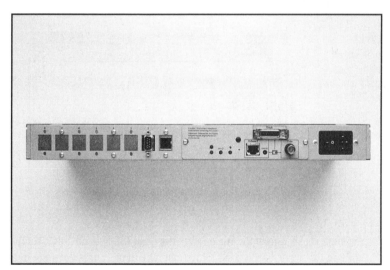

Recently Shiva began offering WebRover software to support users who dial into a LanRover supported LAN and then hop onto the Internet through that connection.

T I P   Roam over to **http://www.shiva.com** to see how its remote access works.

The advantage of Shiva's product line is its clear focus on supporting remote access needs. Figure 17.11 shows the configuration information for Port 3 of a LanRover/2E Plus equipped with BRI modules. The 2E Plus can handle up to eight ports of either ISDN, POTS, or both types. Notice that this does not mean eight BRIs. Each BRI counts as two ports, because each has two B channels. So you can have a maximum of four BRIs connected to the LanRover/2E Plus.

FIG. 17.11

Notice the typical entries for switch type and SPID on the ISDN configuration screen for the Shiva LanRover/2E Plus.

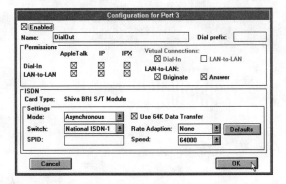

Once you've configured the LanRover for ISDN and POTS lines you can get an overall view of the lines, as illustrated in Figure 17.12.

FIG. 17.12

Information screen shows all the lines established to a Shiva LanRover/2E Plus.

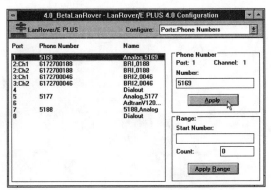

As you'll recall, one of the major advantages of ISDN is its quick setup and teardown time—both on the order of a second. Shiva can take maximum advantage of this by creating *virtual connections* between remote LANs and computers. Since Shiva has optimized protocol and authentication exchange, little time is lost in reestablishing a dropped connection. Figure 17.13 shows the configuration of a virtual connection between LANs. The timeout interval here is set for 300 seconds (five minutes).

CAUTION

Be careful with the minimum timeout interval. If you set it too low, you could end up spending more money than if it's too high. Why? In many instances you're charged a minimum increment, like five minutes, for a call. If you set the increment to thirty seconds and make three calls to the same number in the space of five minutes, you would be charged as if you had made three five-minute calls. The same caveat holds for the high call setup fees I mentioned earlier.

As a general rule of thumb, never set the timeout interval to less than the minimum billing increment, and never set it to cut off before you've used the full period of the setup charge. In fact you'll probably want to add a few minutes past the setup time to take advantage of the existing connection and not be charged for setup again just as you drop the line. I really don't like penalties like the setup charge because they mitigate against effective use of the system.

FIG. 17.13
On this virtual connection screen for the configuration of the Shiva LanRover/2E Plus, timeout is set for 300 seconds (five minutes).

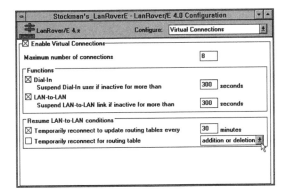

Shiva uses the technique known as spoofing to make the various communications protocols think the connection is still really up. For example, if you're using Novell NetWare's IPX/SPX there is a frequent transmission of *keep alive* information from devices on the network. Such transmissions are filtered out so they don't bring up the physical connection and a spoofing packet is sent, if needed, to reassure an inquiring machine that the machine it's looking for really still is alive. If this were not done, the real connection would probably be coming up often just to pass unneeded overhead.

From Here...

There's a lot to be gained by seeing the world from the perspective of the Internet service provider. It's a very complex business that's changing by the hour. If you're in it, be sure you analyze all your costs and income in detail. You'll need this knowledge to survive and may eventually need it to sell out to a bigger operation so you can move on to another venture.

If you're in charge of an organization that must stay in communication with its many locations and traveling staff, the technology I've described is well-worth considering.

We've spent a lot of time looking at the current state of ISDN. In the last part, Part V, of this book I'll cover the future.

- First, in Chapter 18, "Anticipating Broadband ISDN," we'll take a look at the future with broadband ISDN.
- Then, in Chapter 19, "Forecasting Changes Due to ISDN," we'll look at the major changes in technology and everything else that will result as the world's telecommunications structure changes for the next century.
- Finally, Chapter 20, "Alternatives to ISDN," looks at various options that will be developing in the next few years; we'll try to figure out if they'll replace or supplement ISDN.

The Future

CHAPTER 18

Anticipating Broadband ISDN

It's time to prepare for what's ahead and take a look at the technical future of ISDN and closely related technologies. A great deal of the work that went into ISDN in the last twenty or so years has contributed to two very important methods of shipping information around: *frame relay* and *asynchronous transfer mode* (ATM). Along the way, we'll run into a couple of other terms that are helpful to understand: *switched multimegabit data services* (SMDS) and *synchronous optical network* (SONET). ■

What switched multimegabit data services (SMDS) are, and how they fit into ISDN

You'll find this is a fast way to communicate, but it's not widespread.

Where frame relay came from (hint: ISDN), and why it's important

See why frame relay is rapidly growing.

Why broadband ISDN and ATM are related

You'll understand that ISDN is really the big picture.

How asynchronous transfer mode (ATM) is related to another technology (hint: ISDN), and why it's being used in both LANs and as the basis of broadband ISDN

You'll learn how ATM might fit into both the wide-area and local area world, but maybe not.

What synchronous optical network (SONET) is

See the fastest thing on greased glass. SONET is the ultimate carrier for the telecom network.

How all this stuff fits together

You and most others have thought all these acronyms were unrelated. Here they all come together in one picture.

Switched Multimegabit Data Service (SMDS)

Switched multimegabit data service (SMDS) was devised by BellCore as a connectionless packet-mode data service. It's a step beyond X.25 and incorporates parts of the design that went into ATM. It offers 56 kbps through 34 Mbps data rates dependent on interexchange carrier offerings. The payload size of an SMDS packet is 48 octets, the same as ATM. SMDS has been growing in use since its introduction. Currently, there are a few hundred firms using the service. Often it is not available in a region; for example, Southwestern Bell covers several states, including Texas; SMDS is not among its offerings. Projections of SMDS future are varied, but it seems frame relay and then ATM will become dominant, and SMDS will fade. ATM can carry SMDS and frame relay.

TIP Switch to **http://www.cerf.net/smds.html** for multimegabits of data on SMDS.

Frame Relay

We hear a lot about "spin off" from various programs, especially those paid for with our tax money. Remember how much you still hear about new technology from the space program? There is even an excellent journal, and it's free, devoted to getting out the word: *NASA Tech Briefs*.

TIP Get out your navigational gear and plot your shuttle course to **http://www.nasa.gov** and see what's up.

The same thing's happened without much fanfare and with considerably less tax money in the ISDN world. Frame relay is based on a good deal of the work that went into ISDN. Yet frame relay is expanding wildly outside the auspices of ISDN development proper.

Reports not only show that frame relay was about U.S.$1.5 billion (billion = 10 to the 9th power) in the United States during 1996, but also that growth of frame relay was speeding up in Europe. This shows the value of frame relay in providing a way to take existing communications needs and merge them into a more economical form.

Structure of Frame Relay

So what's frame relay? In a few words, it's a major improvement in the way packet switching has been done under X.25. The difference becomes clear when you realize frame relay is packet switching with most of the overhead removed.

TIP Frame your questions and set up a relay to **http://frame-relay.indiana.edu** to find out about the Frame Relay Forum.

First off, frame relay eliminates a whole layer of the ISO OSI model. That'll save you tons of cost and time sending your packets around. Take a look at Figure 18.1. This shows the three layers required by X.25.

FIG. 18.1
X.25 Layers.

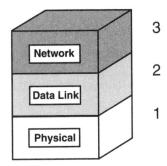

3

2

1

X.25

Now look at Figure 18.2. There are only two layers used in the frame relay structure. This means considerably less processing is used along the way from frame handler to frame handler throughout the network. Translate that as reduced time and reduced cost.

Part
V

Ch
18

FIG. 18.2
Frame Relay Layers.

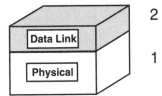

2

1

Frame Relay

How Frame Relay Works

How can frame relay throw away a whole layer and still take care of the job? First let's look at what goes on with X.25. In layer three, the protocol handles a number of questions:

- Is this a data packet?
- Is the connection active?
- Have I received a valid layer three acknowledgment?
- What is the next expected sequence number, and does the packet I just received have that number?

If all of these questions are answered yes, an acknowledgment is sent back. If any are answered no, error recovery is undertaken. Now that's just at layer three. Here's what happens at layer two:

- Is this a valid frame?
- Is this an information frame?
- Have I received a valid acknowledgment?
- Move window to accommodate information.
- Are all frames acknowledged? If no, restart timer and see if window fits. If yes, request retransmission. If no, recover from error.
- Send acknowledgment of layer two.

If the answer to any of these is no, another error is created at layer two.

TIP Don't spend your day trying to figure out all of what is going on here. Just notice that there are acknowledgments, connections, and sequence numbers passing through the process.

Here's what goes on in frame relay. Since there is no layer three, "all" of this is at layer two:

- Is this a valid frame?
- Does it use a known data link connection identifier?

That's it. While X.25 requires at least ten frame processing steps across two separate layers, frame relay does the job in two steps within a single layer. Moreover, it's done without acknowledgments or sequence numbers. Frame relay recognizes that its transport will most likely be through a reliable digital network and risks problems that were expected to be remedied by acknowledgments and sequence numbers in X.25.

Frame Relay Format

The frame relay protocol is *link access procedure for frame-mode* (LAPF) bearer services. You may remember from our discussion in Chapter 3 that frames in most of the other ISDN protocols have a control field. LAPF is even simpler as the space used for that field is available for addressing. Figure 18.3 shows the contents.

FIG. 18.3
LAPF Frame Format.

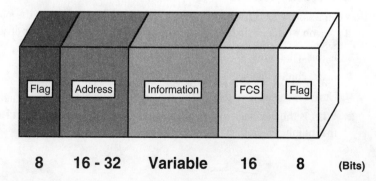

| Flag | Address | Information | FCS | Flag |
| 8 | 16 - 32 | Variable | 16 | 8 | (Bits) |

If you look at X.25, you find it has call control packets using in-band signaling to set up and tear down virtual circuits. Frame relay uses the out-of-band common channel signaling technique characteristic of ISDN.

X.25 multiplexes using layer three. Frame relay makes virtual calls or circuits to multiple destinations. X.25 uses layers two and three to provide error handling and flow control including sequencing. Frame relay preserves sequencing in transmission, checks for simple errors in frames, and relies on higher protocols to catch the occasional sequence or other error.

As a result of using higher layer protocols for these functions, frame relay dispenses with the X.25 method of providing flow and error control between each device in the connected network. X.25 requires the originating device and the first packet switch to exercise such control. Then that switch and the next do the same, and on and on until the destination node is reached. With frame relay, the higher layer protocols do flow control and error detection from end to end.

Frame relay is designed to carry multiple protocols transparently. The data link connection identifier (DLCI) is the key to connecting different conversations and thereby multiplexing. Each conversation is uniquely identified by a DLCI. But, unfortunately it's not quite that simple.

You see your machine here contacting another on the other side of the world for packet-mode operation is not really talking with the other machine. It's talking with the frame handler, the frame relay device. The DLCI is assigned for the conversation between your machine and the first frame relay machine. Then that machine maps that conversation to another DLCI it uses for its conversation with the next frame relay machine and so on until the end machine is reached.

Congestion Issues

One problem still remains. What happens when traffic gets heavy in a frame relay system? The short answer is: "Things slow down." If you're familiar with Ethernet, you're aware that at some point the amount of traffic and the number of collisions begin to mount in such a way that things get slower and slower. Fortunately for both Ethernet and frame relay, most data traffic is *bursty*. That is, it comes in brief spurts of a second of two. As more and more nodes use a system and greater traffic appears, the system becomes congested. As a rule of thumb, congestion becomes a problem when the sustained load approaches about 80 percent of the maximum design capacity.

The standards created by ITU-T offer several possible approaches to preventing collapse as frame relay congestion increases:

■ **Discard:** A part of the LAPF protocol includes a bit that may be set to allow discard of the frame under conditions of congestion. Basically, the frame handler establishes a maximum data rate with a station sending packets to it. If that station exceeds the rate, each of the frames sent during such excess is tagged with a "discard eligible" bit. If congestion occurs downline, those frames may be discarded to reduce congestion.

- ■ **Implicit congestion control:** Higher layers in end systems will notice frames have been discarded. This is evidence that congestion is a problem, and the higher layers can initiate flow control.

- ■ **Explicit congestion notification:** The address field for the frames can be used to notify end stations that congestion is building up. Higher layer protocols at the ends can then exercise flow control.

N O T E Is there a risk in using frame relay since it seems to do away with all the protections built into X.25? Not really. Any higher layer protocol you might be using with frame relay will catch what frame relay misses. The real problem might be a substantially diminished performance contrasted with X.25 in the case of truly poor or noisy conditions. But then our assumptions are that you'll be using frame relay over clean digital circuits and not over a wet string stretched between two cardboard oatmeal containers. ■

Originally, frame relay ran at data rates from 56/64 kbps up to 512 kbps, that is it ran at rates less than T1/E1 line speeds, 1.5/2.0 megabits. Frame relay is capable of running at much higher data rates, however; and rates up to 52 megabits are now supported in standards. The data field size is dependent on vendor; the maximum is 4096 bytes. Because frame relay has a variable data field contrasted with the fixed field of 48 bytes in ATM as I'll describe below, it has a low overhead compared to ATM.

Ironically, as telephone companies install ATM to carry more and more traffic, frame relay will be carried over ATM. The two methods do not conflict; they are complementary.

Broadband ISDN

Broadband ISDN deals with data rates in excess of those delivered by the primary rate interface. Rates in the hundreds of megabits a second are standardized. The ITU-T is working to make this broadband network a reality. Alongside ITU-T stands the ATM Forum establishing the groundwork for ATM as not only a major part of ISDN, but as a significant part of general computer networking in the local and campus wide environment.

 T I P Go into transfer mode and synch up with **http://www.atmforum.com/home.html** for ideas on ATM.

N O T E In Chapter 2, I provided a few words from the ITU-T laying out the broad outlines of narrowband ISDN. Those were from Recommendation I.120. The next, Recommendation I.121, deals with broadband ISDN:

1. Asynchronous transfer mode (ATM) is the transfer mode for implementing B-ISDN and is independent of the means of transport at the physical layer.

2. B-ISDN supports switched, semipermanent, and permanent point-to-point and point-to-multipoint connections, and provides on demand reserved and permanent services. Connections in B-ISDN support both circuit-mode and packet-mode services of a

mono- and/or multimedia type and connectionless or connection-oriented nature and in a bidirectional or unidirectional configuration.

3. The B-ISDN architecture is detailed in functional terms and is, therefore, technology– and implementation–independent.

4. A B-ISDN will contain intelligent capabilities for the purpose of providing advanced service characteristics and supporting powerful operation and maintenance tools, network control, and management. Further inclusion of additional intelligent features has to be considered in an overall context and may be allocated to different network/ terminal elements.

5. Since the B-ISDN is based on overall ISDN concepts, the ISDN access reference configuration is also the basis for the B-ISDN access reference configuration.

6. A layered structure approach, as used in established ISDN protocols, is also appro-priate for similar studies in B-ISDN. This approach should be used for studies on other overall aspects of B-ISDN, including information transfer, control, intelligence, and management.

7. Any expression of network capabilities or change in network performance parameters will not degrade the quality of service of existing services.

8. The evolution of B-ISDN should ensure the continued support of existing interfaces and services.

9. New network capabilities will be incorporated into B-ISDN in evolutionary steps to meet new user requirements and accommodate advances in network developments and progress in technology.

10. It is recognized that B-ISDN may be implemented in a variety of ways according to specific situations. ▨

T I P Unite with the International Telecommunications Union at **http://www.itu.ch**. You'll find all sorts of interesting information including the full text of ITU Recommendations; however, there is a substantial subscription fee for these.

Part
V

Ch
18

Broadband Data Rates

Broadband ISDN offers a dramatic increase in data rates. As the expense of carriage at these rates is expected to be considerable, the divisions are more sophisticated than those in narrowband.

- **155.52 Mbps full duplex:** This is expected to be the initial standard service.
- **155.52 Mbps from the subscriber to the network and 622.08 Mbps from the network to the subscriber:** The idea here is the network is going to be delivering the bulk of the information, so why saddle the subscriber with the cost of a data rate that won't be used from the subscriber's direction?
- **622.08 Mbps full duplex:** This is the fastest currently available data rate.

Broadband Services

You'll recall that, historically, telephone companies and their regulators consider service as the commodity supplied the consumer. What are the services in broadband ISDN?

Two kinds of services are provided. Interactive services are designed for two way communication between subscribers or subscribers and service providers. Distribution services are basically broadcasts from a service provider to a subscriber, one way.

Interactive Services   These services provide two way interactions for research and exchange of information.

- **Conversational Services:** Two way communications taking place in real time. These include video, sound, and data exchange such as between LANs, and document transfer and review. Several of these may be combined to give a group document review and conferencing environment.

- **Messaging Services:** The primary character of this service is that it is not real time, rather messages are handled in a store and forward mode. This covers not only classic electronic mail for text, but also video and audio mail.

- **Retrieval Services:** This is the same idea as access to databases of information downloadable files. These can be text, pictures, sounds, or any other media. Of course similar information is available over narrowband now, but broadband affords more flexibility and the promise of significant lengths and details within multimedia materials.

Distribution Services   Here the emphasis is on wide distribution of information to many users. It's sort of like radio or TV broadcasting.

- **Distribution Services without User Presentation Control:** These are broadcasts. The situation is much like a television or radio broadcast; a station transmits to a virtually unlimited number of receivers. The receivers cannot control the flow of information. The only control the receiver has is to either select the broadcast or not select it.

- **Distribution Services with User Presentation Control:** It takes a little thinking to figure out what this is. It still is a broadcast. But the distinguishing feature is the fact that the broadcast is repeated frequently. So the receiver can be set up to select a portion of the repeats. For example, in your hotel room you are shown a menu on the TV screen. When you select one of the menu options, perhaps you've noticed it may be several seconds before the response appears. This does not result from the equipment searching a disk for your information. It comes from a wait while the proper part of a continually repeated series of messages returns. In the hotel, at low data rates comparable to narrowband, the acceptable longest wait is a few seconds. This limits the total text transmitted to perhaps a few thousand words. With broadband transmitting at much higher data rates, the same wait could, in effect, select from hundreds of thousands of words.

Asynchronous Transfer Mode (ATM)

In I.121, the ITU-T declares asynchronous transfer mode the means of implementing broadband ISDN. Creation of ATM has had influence beyond ISDN since ATM is quickly emerging as the basis for:

- Local area network backbones that tie traditional LANs together.

- Replacement of traditional media access methods, such as Ethernet or token ring throughout a local area network.

- Replacement for the originally perceived contender for such applications, fiber distributed data interface (FDDI).

ATM Drives Convergence of Computers and Telephones

The fact that ATM, a technology originally developed for the telephone system, has now essentially taken over the computer local area network arena is the clearest proof yet that telephone and computer technology are converging at a rate far greater than most predicted. Prices for ATM adapter cards to use in PCs have dropped to less than $900 list; this is for a card that operates at 155 Mbps! When I installed some of the first Ethernets for PCs a little over a dozen years ago, the price for each card was $1,000 and the data rate was 10 Mbps. Today, with much cheaper dollars, I can buy 15 times the raw data rate for less money. Slower versions of the ATM cards operating at about 25 Mbps are selling for $350 list. ATM vendors are clearly trying to demolish development of 100 Mbps Ethernet and token ring technologies. But 100 Mbps Ethernet cards are selling for less than $200, so this may not work. They're also delivering ATM devices to attach to existing Ethernets and token rings as an aid in transition. If your local area network is using ATM, connection through ATM related protocols within ISDN is the most logical step. ATM is rapidly becoming the technology for all seasons. As we'll soon see, ATM is bandwidth efficient, scaleable, and protocol transparent. But 100 Mbps Ethernet is an updating of well-understood, proven technology. We may continue to use Ethernet on local area networks leaving ATM for larger area interconnections.

Part
V

Ch
18

It's difficult to pick up a computer communications journal without seeing an article on ATM. The same is true of a telephony journal. What is ATM?

Let's boil it all down: ATM is a way of transmitting information in *cells* that are a fixed length of 53 octets (bytes). These cells are handled in a way that creates a hybrid of circuit-mode and packet-mode. ATM is so fast that it can emulate both modes! Speed is the key.

ATM does more than use fast small cells. It negotiates a path with the network. Once this path is established, ATM is smart enough to use it not only for the traffic that was the subject of the original negotiation but also for other traffic that needs to transit between the same points.

Switching is the basis of ATM. In the terminology we have used in this book, ATM is a packet-mode technology. As a result, ATM provides:

- Each connection with a dedicated bandwidth
- Flexible speeds

- High overall bandwidth
- Connection procedures that are well-defined

This last element, "well-defined," contributes to ATM's flexibility. Because cells are a fixed length and procedures are well-defined for these uniform units, operation of ATM is very predictable. Contrast this with other methods such as frame relay that use variable length frames. It is more difficult to control and predict issues of network loading. So ATM sacrifices flexible information size for uniformity and control. If the data rates were a few thousand or million bits per second, problems of synchronization and jerky delivery, especially of voice, would become apparent. But ATM works at tens and hundreds of megabits effectively masking such problems.

The ATM Cell

I've just said the ATM cell is 53 octets long. Why? Let's look at what we want to send over the system. Voice is subject to problems when there is much delay. Think of those times you've been talking over a satellite link or watching television when the speakers were using such a link. Remember the disturbing delay following one person's asking a question and the other person's answering? They're the result of the half-second it takes for a signal to travel from Earth to the orbiting satellite and back. The delay increases by at least a half-second with each satellite link that's added to the end-to-end circuit. With packet transmission of voice, a similar problem crops up within the words themselves.

We've got to make a trade off. Say we put ten words in a packet and then send it out. In the context of transmitting a hundred words, we'd make ten packets. Before we send out each packet it has to be filled. So there will be at least the time it takes to say ten words between each packet. At the receiving end, this means the receiver would have to wait at least the time it takes ten words to be spoken, inserted in a packet, and propagated before they could be heard. This results in the same delay phenomenon as the satellite situation.

Now, what happens if the contents of the packets are not full words, but are whatever sounds we seek to transmit broken up in units to fit the packet boundaries? This means, for words, that a word can be broken in the middle. Now any slight difference in transmission time becomes apparent to the listener as distortion in the sound received. These problems become apparent even if the differences are a few thousandths of a second.

In regular telephony, the problem is solved by effectively using a packet the size of the total phone call; we call this a *circuit*. It's maintained from beginning to end and there is no possibility of timing differences in the manner I mentioned. So, circuit mode has been our selection for voice transmission. However, it suffers from poor resource use. We maintain the circuit even though we know approximately half the time nothing is being transmitted over it.

The flip side is bulk data transmission. Data is bursty; it tends to be sent in large chunks followed by significant periods of no transmission. Such bursty data can withstand variations in timing of receipt and adapts well to packet mode. Because packet mode is efficient in resource use, it's the logical selection for such transmissions.

Now the question is: How do you achieve the efficiencies of packet mode while preserving the timing qualities of circuit mode? The answer lies in design of the packet itself. Of course, it's not that simple. The greater the distance of travel, the greater the propagation delay and the more desirable a longer packet. In Europe, researchers arrived at a design for packets, now called cells for this technology, that carried 32 octets of user information. In the United States and Australia, much larger countries where propagation delays are more noticeable, 64 octets looked best.

We have a two to one ratio of sizes for the cell. What to do under these circumstances? It's not science or engineering; it's politics. Let's do a little political math:

$64 - 32 = 32$

$32/2 = 16$

$32 + 16 = 48$

$64 - 16 = 48$

The compromise on cell size arrived at 48 octets for the payload field. An ATM cell has an additional 5 octets for its header containing all the overhead information. Figure 18.4 shows the ATM cell.

FIG. 18.4

This ATM cell is far simpler and smaller than frame relay. This simplicity coupled with very high data rates is what makes ATM work.

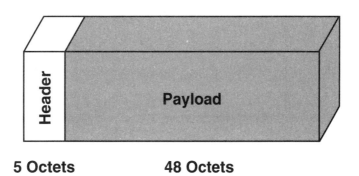

5 Octets   **48 Octets**

Header, Virtual Paths, Virtual Circuits

To understand how ATM works, we'll have to dig a little deeper. The header has considerably more detail than our first figure (18.4) shows. Figure 18.5 shows more detail.

The first portion, *generic flow control,* is used only within user to network communication. It does not exist in network to network communication and its four bits are given over to the virtual path identifier. The use of flow control is currently optional with designers.

> **N O T E**   Your feeling now is probably expressed: "Ugh, it's getting deep. What's this all about?" I
> agree. There's so much to ATM it's impossible to lay it out simply in a few pages. Just get
> some of the ideas. You won't have to design this stuff. Remember, ATM is the protocol for all things. It
> carries all kinds of information well. Its creation of cells is *isochronous,* or regular. Whether or not there

continues

continued

is information in a cell, the cell is created. This means your computer can put things in at any time, *asynchronously*, even though ATM keeps everything orderly by its isochronous, regular, cell creation. This maintains timing and assures that time critical information, audio and video, come through undistorted. ■

FIG. 18.5

Interior of the ATM Cell.

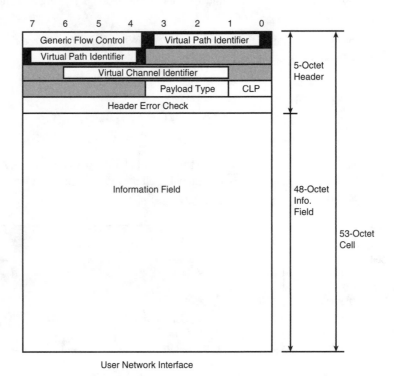

CLP=Cell Loss Priority

We'll skip over the virtual stuff for now; being "virtual," it's not really there. The payload type actually can carry quite a bit of information. It tells whether or not the cell is a user cell. A lot of cells may just be idling along. A fundamental principle in ATM is that cell flow continues whether or not there is any real user payload information. This field may also carry congestion alerts and other control. The header error check is based on the usual concept of the sending station doing some arithmetic on the cell contents and putting the results in the field. The receiving device does the same arithmetic on the contents and compares the results with the field. If the results are the same, it is assumed that the cell contents are valid. If the results are different, the assumption is that there has been an error. This usually results in a request to retransmit the contents.

Now we get to the interesting part. Have you ever noticed that computing is all virtual? This is a way of saying that computing is all smoke and mirrors. Nothing is what it seems and may change in an instant. ATM provides virtual elements carried within virtual elements:

- **Virtual Channel:** A stream of information being fed between two nodes.
- **Virtual Path:** A collection of virtual channels.

Figure 18.6 tries to make some sense out of this by showing the channels as wires sheathed into small cables (the paths), all going through a larger cable (physical reality). Whew. Does this really do anything for us?

FIG. 18.6
Virtual Channels and
Virtual Paths.

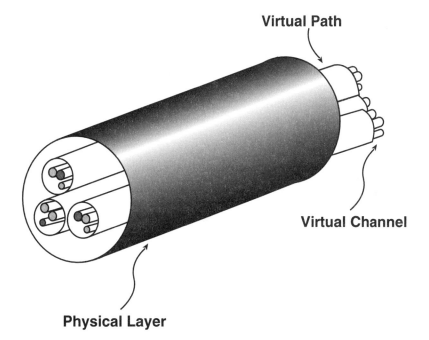

Virtual Path

Virtual Channel

Physical Layer

Part
V

Ch
18

The answer is yes. ATM is concerned with speed. When a channel is established, it defines a way to connect two nodes. It is very often the case that those two nodes will have a need for many channels. Each channel is associated with related processes running on each node. As other processes need channels, those channels may be established by using the virtual paths already set up.

ATM details involve the identification and switching of these virtual channels and paths. For our understanding at this point, the most important relation that can be made to narrowband ISDN is that of the D channel. There is no D channel in ATM or broadband ISDN. Instead of a D channel providing control, ATM provides various methods creating "semipermanent virtual channels" and "metasignaling channels" among others. These creatures of the moment take over the tasks narrowband ISDN assigns to its D channel.

ATM Adaptation Layer (AAL)

ATM is designed to carry all kinds of data forms. I've already mentioned carrying frame relay and SMDS over ATM. Since many of these forms were designed for different environments of connection or connectionless, constant, or variable bit rate, ATM provides AAL to adapt to these differences. Table 18.1 shows the classifications the ITU-T has given to AAL.

Table 18.1   ATM Adaptation Layer Classifications

	Class A	Class B	Class C	Class D
End to end timing	Required	Required	Not required	Not required
Bit rate	Constant	Variable	Variable	Variable
Connection	Connection oriented	Connection oriented	Connection oriented	Connectionless
Type	Type 1	Type 2	Type 3/4, Type 5	Type 3/4

Because protocols such as frame relay have much larger frames than ATM, segmentation and reassembly are essential AAL services. Problems of errors, flow control, and misaligned or lost cells are also handled by AAL.

Each lettered class is associated with a protocol type. Each protocol type is associated with various services. For example, type 1 includes 64 kbps voice. This is logical because voice requires timing and a constant bit rate; a connection is the usual condition of voice use. ATM adapts to this by handling type 1 frames to establish end to end timing, constant bit rate, and what appears to be connection oriented exchange. Due to the speed of ATM, the low layer fact that this is really a packet-mode environment never affects the use.

Type 2 could be video using a sophisticated variable bit rate system. AAL still provides end-to-end timing, but now the bit rate is variable. The connection mode continues to be connection oriented.

Type 3/4 is the result of a recent decision by ITU-T to join types 3 and 4. It can be used to carry such data services as frame relay or SMDS, among others.

Type 5 is a new specification to provide very fast transport in cases where connection-oriented higher layer protocols take care of much of the overhead used by other AAL types.

The ATM adaptation layer has answered the original design direction of ATM by creating a way for one size (ATM) to fit all (AAL types). Accelerating adoption by the computer world in local area networks proves the wisdom of this design. As ATM comes into its own in telephony, we'll see faster and cheaper carriage for any kind of data.

SONET

Synchronous Optical NETwork (SONET) is the recommended standard fiber optic transmission method for ATM. However, ATM is being adapted to many other media through the work of the ATM Forum in conjunction with ITU-T. Specifications are available so ATM can operate over coax, shielded twisted pair, unshielded twisted pair, and both single mode and multimode fiber. Data rates and cable lengths vary greatly among the different media as you would expect.

SONET has a frame of 810 octets that is designed in a matrix form with 9 rows of 90 octets each. Perhaps the most amazing thing in SONET is the capability to drop and insert portions of this frame without need to reproduce the entire frame. This facility uses pointers to each information unit within the SONET frame. Removal or insertion of information simply requires readjustment of pointers in a manner similar to a data base. The design of SONET contemplates data rates approaching 2 1/2 gigabits/second. Figure 18.7 shows the frame.

FIG. 18.7
SONET Frame.

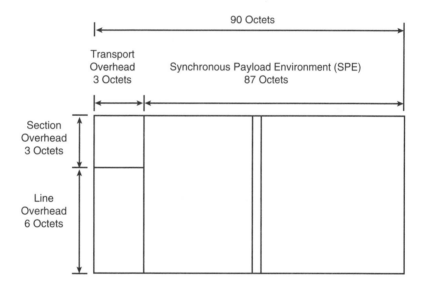

Part
V

Ch
18

How All This Stuff Fits Together

Obviously, the amount of technical detail presented on each of the broadband technologies simply scratches the surface. Probing more into the contents of frames, timing issues, and other minutia would quickly lose us all. Unless you're actively engaged in the standards setting process you can't change any of these details. You're given the standards to use. So what you need is some understanding about fitting them together.

You already know about narrowband ISDN. You're using it or soon will. In that case, what difference do these other protocols make to you? ATM and SONET will probably soon form the backbone that carries information from one telco switch to another. Your narrowband ISDN data will be repackaged in ATM cells and then be passed into SONET frames and flashed across the country and around the world. When those SONET frames arrive at the other end, after transit through a number of other switching systems, they'll be unpacked into ATM cells. Then those cells will be delivered to the local switch at the receiving end and repackaged into narrowband ISDN frames sent to your destination.

The same will be true should you use frame relay or SMDS. The frames of each are repackaged into ATM, and then into the larger SONET frames; the reverse occurs at the other end.

When the happy day arrives that you connect by broadband ISDN directly, your frames will leave the house or office already in ATM frames. If you're using a local area network with ATM, passing LAN frames to the telephone system will be quick and simple.

These possibilities are illustrated in Figure 18.8. This emphasizes the variety and carrying capacity of ATM. SONET is simply the way ATM can most effectively use fiber. It all works by the magic of *time division multiplexing*. The transmission system can send huge amounts of information in a very short time. The ratio of the amount of information it can send to the amount of information any process being sent needs, for example a phone call, is on the order of thousands or millions to one. This means many other individual processes can be sandwiched and never even know they are all sharing time in transmission. Speed, more speed.

N O T E Please catch the double meaning of speed. The transit, propagation, and time of any given bit down the system is the same; it's some large percentage of the speed of light, on the order of 70 to 80 percent. So, strictly speaking, there is no way to speed up propagation. If you find a way, you'll have a heck of a time around all the work Albert Einstein did based on a constant speed of light. Good luck. By the way, light travels about 300,000 kilometers/second (186,000 miles/second)—fast, but, in electronic terms, a major factor in engineering design.

The other meaning of speed for us is quantity of information measured in bits per second. As we move from narrowband ISDN to ATM to ATM over SONET, the data rate type of speed goes up by orders of magnitude (powers of ten). It is these very high data rates, in comparison to the data rates each individual process needs to operate, that make it possible to carry so many different things on one transmission path. ▪

Narrowband ISDN, SMDS, frame relay, and even ATM from your local area network all will be sent to an ATM switch. There, ATM will travel among various switching sites until the larger capacity of SONET is used to repackage it for transmission over great distances at very high data rates. The process is reversed at the other end.

FIG. 18.8

The Big Picture of everything packed into ATM and then into SONET.

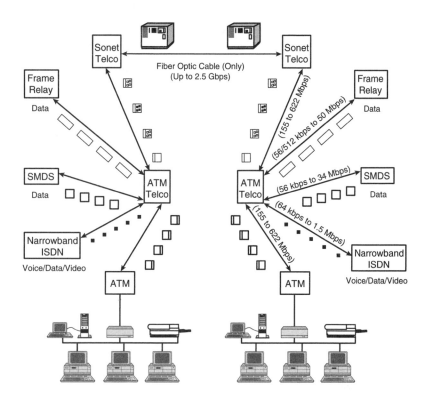

From Here...

We've seen that switched multimegabit data service (SMDS) and frame relay built on ideas developed within ISDN. Frame relay simplifies and speeds information exchange. Broadband ISDN encompasses data rates beyond the 1.544 Mbps of PRI and sanctions ATM as the transmission method. Asynchronous transfer mode (ATM), through its short 53 octet cell, creation of virtual channels of virtual paths, and adaptation layer provides hundreds of megabits/second data rates while adapting to all the various types of traffic that might be carried in local, metropolitan, and wide area networks. SONET takes ATM and provides carriage at the highest data rates over fiber optics. With these technologies, our telephones and computers come together in the start of what has come to be know as "computer telephony." In the final chapter we'll examine this idea:

- Much of this discussion of broadband ISDN presupposes an understanding of the issues covered in Chapter 3, "Defining Narrowband ISDN." You might review that chapter to check on items of interest.

Part
V

Ch

18

■ Chapter 19, "Forecasting Changes Due to ISDN," will look at how ATM leads into the union of computers and telephones. Chapter 19 also considers what business and social changes will result from the general introduction of digital telephone technology.

■ Chapter 20, "Alternatives to ISDN," raises the question of technologies often deemed competitive with ISDN. But are they really?

Forecasting Changes Due to ISDN

You're nearly home; this is the next-to-last chapter . To quote the last frames of a movie I saw at a young age: "This is the end of the beginning" (*Destination Moon*). The really last chapter takes up that beginning. Let's reflect on what's happened up to now.

We saw the telephone system develop from the telegraph. Regulations and standards played a major part in defining and using telephony. ISDN grew out of the logical move to digital techniques following digitization of long distance and interoffice links. Since ISDN offers considerably more flexibility than POTS, complexity developed in service selection and ordering. A signaling language (Q 931 and SS#7) supports ISDN. Application program interfaces are developing so computers can take advantage of all this variety.

When you order ISDN you'll probably have to upgrade your phone wiring and select new hardware designed specifically for ISDN. Then you configure your software, perhaps using some of the newly emerging APIs. You may join two or more B channels to increase data capacity. Soon, you'll use ISDN for video conferencing. Since I expect you're more inclined to install ISDN for your computers than for your voice phones, it may be some time until you actually adopt true ISDN phones.

Moving control from the telephone company

You'll find the monolithic telephone company is going the way of the dinosaur.

The rise of total telecommunications competition

You've already learned the U.S. telecommunications law was just revised to foster competition; now that competition is percolating throughout the world.

An accelerating rate of adoption

See the telephone industry enter the rapidly changing world of the technology, kicking and screaming.

Economic changes follow technological changes

Competition, control, and fast adoption lead to radical restructuring of the economic values away from centrally controlled telecommunications companies and agencies.

Social changes lag but make a big difference

You've already followed the arguments over free speech on the Internet. This is just the beginning.

In any case you'll start using ISDN more and more in your work and personal life. Bulletin board and Internet providers will provide ISDN access. Sooner than we might now think, broadband ISDN will bring multimegabit data rates to our offices and houses.

What's this all mean for the future? I suggest the movement into ISDN will have a much greater effect than most currently realize. ISDN is fundamentally a different technology from POTS. ISDN moves the intelligence from the central telephone system to each business, house, and person. This will result in a number of shifts in emphasis and a few major, revolutionary changes. We'll look at some prognostications in this chapter: ■

Moving Control from the Telephone Company

Technology is filled with unintended results. Railroads (through the dangers and destruction they brought) created legal theories of negligence that later evolved into concepts of strict liability for dangerous products. Air travel created a need for reservations systems that drove the development of transaction processing. The desire to build more and cheaper pistols resulted in standardized parts and assembly line production of all goods.

In each case, the initial technology I cited resulted in effects that restrained what had been dominant social and economic forces. A hundred years ago, the railroads basically ran the country. But their high-handed acts of destruction and monopolistic tendencies gave birth to a legal system designed to restrain total power in any corporate entity. Now we see antitrust laws from that era used against IBM, AT&T, and Microsoft to prevent their domination of social and economic strength.

When they set up reservations systems, the airlines worked in an atmosphere of regulated competition. The systems helped sell tickets at government-fixed prices. With the advent of deregulation and open competition, the same systems gave consumers an instantaneous way to shop fares and force lower and lower fare bidding wars.

When Colt started mass-producing pistols with interchangeable parts, it grabbed a lot of market share. But when all manufacturers started using the same techniques, the quality of manufactured goods went up, and the profit on each piece dropped drastically.

Each of these changes was beneficial to the consumer, the user, you. The same thing is about to happen with the telephone system.

For a hundred years, local telephone service has been the province of only one carrier in a given area. It had to be this way. Early attempts at stringing countless parallel systems bankrupted multiple entrants. Telephone regulation is based on that world.

NOTE   In the first Edition where "province" is in the preceding paragraph "providence" was printed.
On reflection I wonder if that was a Freudian slip reflecting a more profound insight. My dictionary defines "providence" as "The care, guardianship, and control exercised by a deity; divine direction." [*American Heritage Dictionary Second College Edition* (Houghton Mifflin Company, Boston 1985)] ■

But ISDN changes the world. Remember, basically ISDN provides two things:

- Digital transmission for all forms of communication
- Flexible and sophisticated signaling

In the last 40 years, our technology has made digital techniques so cheap they are literally used to control and run inexpensive appliances like dishwashers and electric mixers. Digital transmission allows much greater data rates to travel down the same cables we've used for slower analog transmissions. And with digital technology the fundamental rule is:

BITS IS BITS

What does this guy mean? Remember the old joke. You go to the fried chicken place to get a bucket of chicken. They hand you a bucket. You ask, "What's in here? I want drumsticks and breasts." The response:

"Parts is parts."

Groan. That's a bad joke. I must have left something out. But it gets the point across. Once something is processed in a certain way—chicken deep fried in grease and covered in batter—it loses its original character and may be handled and processed the same, regardless of what it was. We perform the same operations on it.

So it is with information. Once it is converted from speech, or music, or numbers, or pictures or whatever to bits, it is processed for carriage and control in exactly the same fashion. This vastly reduces our costs and increases our control over information—or chickens?

This is "the chicken approach" to final divestiture of control over the local loop in the hands of one company. Since bits is bits, and anyone can cheaply manipulate those bits, there is no longer any reason for the local telco to perform all the processing on your telephone data stream.

Think about all those "services" we covered in chapters 4 and 7. Variations in bearer services, and differences among supplementary services, teleservices. Why on earth would we need the phone company to use their central switch to blink a light on our phone telling us another call is coming in? The information on that call already exists in the SS#7 and Q.931 D channel signaling. Where is the most efficient place to use that signaling? At a central point that senses it, charges for it and then sends it on again to our equipment? The only benefit here is to the telco: they get paid for it. Our own equipment has the intelligence to detect the conditions and perform whatever we want. All we need from the telco is B channels provisioned to carry anything and D channels to tell what to do. Fancy bearer services beyond carriage and certainly supplementary and teleservices can be performed more flexibly, quickly, and cheaply with our own equipment.

Think about it. The elaborate telephone switch is a mainframe computer by a different name. How much does it cost to do word processing on a mainframe (and how good is it) compared to a PC? You know the answer because you're using a PC (not a mainframe) to do word processing and virtually everything else mainframes used to do a decade ago. The advent of client/server, distributed logic, peer-to-peer computing on local area networks has taken over all but the most massive database problems from mainframes and that final move is just a few years away.

Telephone technology is lagging computing by more than a decade. Time sharing is a dead, dead business in computing, but it is the rule in telephone systems. Can its elimination be far behind as soon as the word is out? Up until ISDN, you couldn't exercise peer control over the telephone network from your house or office. But no longer. ISDN ushers in a new way of using telephones.

Think about those ISDN interfaces. You remember the NT-1 with a U interface connected to the phone company, and an S/T interface connected to your equipment. Now what's the difference between the S and the T? They are both electrically the same: two twisted pair, one for transmit, one for receive. But should you have an ISDN PBX, it is connected to the T interface. Now ISDN PBX is called an NT-2 and it provides the S interface to connect to your other equipment.

So what, you say. That PBX, that NT-2, can have all the intelligence to take over virtually all of the functions that have been centralized at the telco switch. Sure, you say, but I can't afford a PBX for my house or small business.

You already have one, or two, or three or more. Look at that PC. What is it? A device that manipulates bits. BITS IS BITS. All you need is a card to connect to the NT-1, some software (remember those APIs) and maybe some other cards for specific applications. Zoom, there's your PBX. And it's a lot cheaper, faster, more flexible, and upgradable than any PBX—or central office switch—you could buy.

We've ended up with what may be called a telephony server on your LAN, as illustrated in Figure 19.1. This is the convergence of telephone and computer technology: *computer telephony.*

It goes on. Look at the central office switch again. Now we've reduced it to switching calls as directed by our equipment over the D channel. We have all the remaining intelligence in our equipment. But how does the telco switch work? Well, right now it does, indeed, switch calls. This is its reason for being. Think back to our comparison of circuit mode (switched) versus packet mode (switched). The circuit mode information followed a "circuit" established by a series of telephone switches. Once that circuit was set up, it continued until the call was terminated. In the case of packet mode, a circuit was never established. Rather, each packet contained sufficient "intelligence" to find its way through the telephone network using very simple packet switches.

This is somewhat like the rule I learned in computer science:

Algorithms + Data Structures = Programs

N O T E The phrase is from the title and theme of the excellent book—a classic of computer science—*Algorithms + Data Structures = Programs* by Niklaus Wirth (Prentice Hall, 1976). This work is part of the series *Prentice Hall Series in Automatic Computation.* ■

FIG. 19.1

Telephony Server connecting your local area network of computers and your telephones to the worldwide network of everything (what we used to call the telephone network).

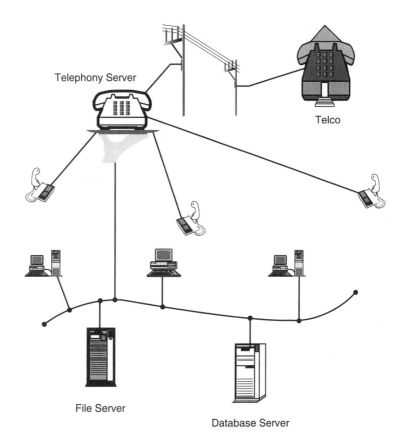

Telephony Server

Telco

File Server

Database Server

You've got a choice. You can have simple data structures and complex algorithms, or you can have complex data structures and simple algorithms. Either can give you a program that does what you want to do. When we make a packet, we're making a data structure. The more complex that data structure, the simpler the accompanying algorithm can be. Guess what the accompanying algorithm for a packet is? You got it: the network it traverses, especially the active parts, the switches.

Now stay with me. We put a lot more in our packets (data structures) with our own computers, that is, computer telephony servers; then we pass the packets to a relatively simple transmission system. All of a sudden we don't have to spend much on transmission because the packets take care of most of one of the major costs of our telephone carriers, switches. That leaves their major costs in the transmission lines, cables themselves.

Well, that's fine in theory, but of course it couldn't really work in practice. It would take a whole 'nother system for carriage of information. One that can deal with the complicated packets and thereby reduce the costs of switching. Certainly there's nobody who's built that sort of thing on any scale that could be useful.

Think again! Can you say…

Internet?

Right. I've just described how the Internet works. Well, some of my Internet guru friends would say I left out a few details, but the main idea is there. The Internet is designed to pass complex packets based on a well-defined protocol (TCP/IP) through a simple and even unreliable network that may experience frequent problems, reroutings and even delays. Real-time voice and even video is carried over the Internet. Granted, carriage of such real-time-intensive information is in its infancy, but it works, and thousands are using it right now.

My point is that the telephone network, not may, not should, not might, but *will*, I said *will*, evolve into an Internet sort of system for all traffic. The complex switching now used cannot be justified economically when complex data structures, packets, created by your equipment can be carried so much more cheaply. It's not a case of you deciding to beat the phone company out of a few bucks by using the Internet. It's a case of all of us realizing we're wasting money on telephone switches when we could do so much more with a better technology. The local exchange carrier has been receiving something like 40 percent of the long distance revenue for hooking its switch to the long distance carriers. If the need for such a complex switch is eliminated, the justification for much of this charge evaporates.

Continuing to use the complicated, expensive model when the simple, cheap switch Internet system is proven is just as foolish as continuing to use manual switchboards when automated exchanges are perfected. Statistics now say there would not be enough people to handle all our current calling using manual switchboards. In a very short time, the same thing will happen to our complicated telephone switches; we will not be able to afford to make enough switching capacity to handle the traffic to be switched. We will be driven to the Internet model, like it or not. ATM is a big move in the direction of a simpler switch, dealing with the lowest protocols and leaving most of the decisions to the higher layers running on end systems, such as yours.

Some, whose entire economic base has rested on the switching technology, will resist and resist and resist. They are the same ones who say there is no significant demand for ISDN, or that ISDN should be tariffed as a premium or discretionary service, or that ISDN need not be made available to areas of low population density. These will fall by the wayside, while their more farsighted cousins will reap the benefits of a revolutionary change in the way information is transmitted through common carrier systems.

However, those who resist will affect not only themselves. If some organization chooses to commit corporate suicide by failing to heed the handwriting on the wall, that's its option. But if its failure retards the economic and social advancement of a city, state, province or region required by the regulated monopoly model to be dependent on it for communication, we all have a problem. In that case, legislators and regulators must step in, remove all barriers to entry of competitors, and disenfranchise the reticent before the reticent destroy us all.

Boy, that was fun. Now to move from revolutionary mode and point out that ATM and frame relay are both methods that, to a large degree, incorporate the technology I have outlined. We can see telephone companies adopting compatible technologies that will speed the changes we need.

The Rise of Total Communications Competition

The U.S. Congress, various federal agencies, and many state legislatures have grappled with major changes in telecommunications law. Competition is at the heart of all these changes. ISDN is involved in much of this, as I mentioned in Chapter 2, "Understanding Standards and Regulations."

ISDN enables competition due to its two major elements: digital transmission and sophisticated control. Throughout this discussion, I'll support the proposition that ISDN is the technology that should be delivered to the subscriber *now*, in replacement of POTS.

We currently have competition in long distance service. The big issue is competition in the local loop. Stated simply, there are several ways this competition could provide service to existing subscribers of the heretofore single local exchange carrier. A competitor could:

- String new cables to subscribers
- Bulk-buy use of existing connections to subscribers from the current local exchange carrier
- If a television cable company, use its existing distribution system
- Buy existing access from television cable providers
- Distribute by wireless methods

Currently the telephone, cable television, and electric utility companies have the necessary rights of way and established physical structures to carry information to houses and businesses. Pipeline carriers such as water, sewer, and gas also may offer alternatives. You think this last one is far-fetched. Check out the background of Wiltel, one of the largest long distance carriers in the U.S. It was originally an oil and gas pipeline company. Given the right of way, and pipes to string cables through, why not? Other entities hold valuable rights of way: railroads, canal companies, irrigation co-ops, etc.

Let's take up the most ready and obvious potential competitor in the local loop market, cable television systems. Right now most of these systems still are focused on delivering hundreds of megabits downstream from their central facility, the "headend" location of all the transmission equipment. Most systems have negligible, if any, ability to accept information from the subscriber direction.

▶ **See** Chapter 20, "Alternatives to ISDN," for more information on cable systems, **p. 555**

This is ironic, as the FCC and many local franchise-granting governments attempted to require two-way technology years ago. It seems this change was resisted by the industry. Now they find themselves less able to step into providing local loop access as a result. In any case, if a cable company is ready because it has a two-way system or is prepared to make the investment and changes necessary, it should be possible for it to enter quite quickly.

So what should be provided? I suggest ISDN technology. Look at the advantages to the provider and to us. ISDN is the proven digital telephony method. Hundreds, thousands of hardware and software products are being developed for ISDN. If the cable company takes ISDN

Part

V

Ch

19

from the telco switch, modulates its radio frequency plant to carry the bits, and converts it back into ISDN at the subscriber's location, everybody maintains the greatest flexibility. The cable company and the existing local exchange carrier don't need any more special equipment to deal with ISDN.

The cable company must carry telephone information by some method. Were it to use analog telephony, cable would be buying into a dying technology. The subscriber should want ISDN from any local loop vendor. If the subscriber can be assured of an ISDN signal, the subscriber can make the investment in equipment and not be married to the cable company due to special equipment needed for the cable or some other special technology. ISDN is here. It works. It will continue into the future at higher data rates. I question spending one dime on a special piece of hardware from the cable company unless that piece of equipment, at a very reasonable price, enables me to use what is becoming a universal ISDN technology. This may mean simply adopting the D channel signaling method over the cable, while using hardware designed specifically for cable. There are many ways to work this out.

The same argument goes in spades for any other organization that has current right-of-way for wires or pipes. Anything they do should be designed to deliver ISDN or, at least, the most defining characteristic of ISDN, D channel signaling, to the subscriber. Of course, if they want to provide fiber media all the way, that's great. But to be competitive, they must be prepared to provide the simplest single BRI with 2B+D voice or data on demand at a low price. The fact that they use fiber may not pay off for them today, but it will tomorrow when broadband ISDN becomes reasonably priced. All they'll have to do is change out the electronics.

Anyone else that wants to try to acquire right-of-way and authority to string cables is welcome. ISDN should be adopted as the base technology, especially for signaling.

That leaves us with those who buy local access service in bulk to resell at retail. This is starting to happen now. Rochester, New York is probably the leading example of a local access carrier allowing its competitors to resell its access. The Federal Telecommunications Act of 1996 and various state laws seek to require this resale (see Chapter 2, "Understanding Standards and Regulations"). In this environment, ISDN will again be the winner. If the current local loop carrier is the source, ISDN should be an offering. If the cable television system is the source, the earlier arguments still apply.

In every one of these cases, ISDN, through its signaling on the D channel, enables the sophisticated control and accounting methods needed for multiple local loop providers, using the same or different cables. In addition, this opportunity for keeping up with the accounting may well be the determining factor.

The final possibility for local loop delivery is free space, radio, wireless. In this case, I still suggest the technology adhere to the ISDN model for simplicity of use and programming. The hardware for cable/ISDN would be expected to be very similar to that for wireless/ISDN since both must be designed to work with a radio frequency signal.

Wireless has the greatest long-range possibilities for competition. Look at its advantages:

- No right-of-way costs
- No complex installation costs
- Quick delivery to a subscriber

Under the "there is no free lunch" theory, there must be some disadvantage to wireless. Sure:

- Government licensing
- Limited spectrum space
- Limited data rate
- Security
- Interference

Spectrum space limitation is the primary reason for government licensing. Some systems proposed to work using satellites and directional antennae in the multi-gigahertz range have the advantage of transmitting over a very small area. As a result, widely separated devices could share frequency allocations without interference.

Advanced modulation methods, especially spread spectrum, will use radio frequencies very efficiently. So the density of use could be high.

N O T E   *Spread spectrum* is a technology that may be visualized as transmitting information in very brief bursts. Each burst is transmitted at a different frequency within a range that may be several kilohertz or megahertz wide. A formula called the *spreading algorithm* provides a key to the way the transmissions hop around. This algorithm is in both the transmitting and receiving equipment. In a practical system, the signal level is maintained near the noise level so all the spreading does is appear to slightly raise that noise. This is effective for spectrum conservation and security. By using only as much power as is needed for communication, we avoid interfering with others any more than necessary. By keeping the signal low, we prevent others at greater distances from even knowing a signal is present. Of course, it is nearly impossible to find out a spread spectrum signal is present if you don't have the spreading algorithm. This method has been used for 50 years in high-security military communications. It is also the basis of most wireless local area networks. As such a well-developed and spectrum-saving technique, it may work its way into telephony and low or medium data rates in competition with wireline carriers. ■

But there will always be a limit on how much information can flow through a wireless system, given the spectrum and interference constraints. Although wireless is an excellent choice for voice and data in the several hundred kbps range, when we step into many megabits delivered to densely populated areas, wireless is probably going to face limitations because of spectrum limits.

Certainly putting in new cables would establish service. But the costs are great and construction would take months and years, entailing not only dollars but also community disruption. Yet this alternative will be used in many areas. The existing copper local loops will be deemed inadequate by historic local exchange carriers.

As a competitive tactic, alternative carriers will install and provide broadband ISDN over fiber early on. There is no way to justify new entrants providing copper twisted pair. What reason would you or I have to switch? Perhaps there will be some price incentive. But as soon as that incentive is offered by the new entrant, the historic carrier will match it. So new entrants must offer fiber connection and broadband service to keep one jump ahead and garner our business.

All of a sudden the historic carrier's insistence that it cannot lower prices to us or increase data rates will go out the window. Accounting methods that have caused switches to be depreciated over decades will be scaled to a handful of years. As a result, investment in switchgear will drop while transmission cable quality increases to meet the competitive fiber. Concurrently, sub-scribers will have to invest more in intelligence at their sites to take up the slack from declining intelligence in centralized network switching. Does this sound like the argument about loss of control in switching at the local exchange carrier and a move to telephony servers at the users? It is. Competition pushes transmission investment at the expense of switching investment. I'd like to say that one more time, for emphasis:

Competition pushes transmission investment at the expense of switching investment.

This means you must make up for the removal of intelligence from the carriers' networks. You must supply that intelligence at your end, and the parties with whom you communicate must do likewise. This is achievable as long as there is some way to tie everything together with signaling. Consequently, we're back to the D channel and its cousins at the higher data rates (see Chapter 18).

This is a win-win situation for buyers and sellers of telephone services. The only losers will be telephone service providers who refuse to join in the change early on and rest on their past strength to assure profits through active lobbying efforts and regulatory gambits. Success from those techniques is gone in many jurisdictions and will be gone from all within two or three years. Time spent trying to live in the past will be very costly when it takes away from development for the future.

Switch manufacturers who have depended on high profits from switches sold to companies in a regulated environment also will be in trouble. In the past, the price of such switches and, more importantly, their software could be almost anything, as those costs entered into calculations of cost and rate of return in tariff debates. In the future, as switches move toward great speed and capacity with limited intelligence and as competition gets stronger, costs will determine suc-cess or failure in the real marketplace, as opposed to the looking-glass world of telephone company accounting, inflated switch costs and underfinanced regulatory oversight.

You'll get much more for much less.

Accelerating Rate of Adoption

Bound by regulation and dominating any given market, telephone companies have had little incentive to move into new technologies. That's not to say they don't develop them. Remember that much of the original semiconductor research was done in Bell Labs, while AT&T *et al* were all tied together. But adoption of new technologies was primarily to provide greater return to the company, not greater function for the subscriber. There was little impetus to provide that function if no one else competed with alternatives.

We Can't Block That Switch

Way back when there was only one telephone company, and I was a student in college, I maintained language laboratory recording equipment for the school. We had a number of continuously playing tape machines with language exercises. Students would come to the lab and listen to exercises. I hit on the idea to set up a dial-in service so they could listen to tapes over the phone. It seemed like a good idea. You could practice your Spanish just prior to going to bed and repeat it again in the morning. I think educators call that "distributed practice."

Anyway, in those pre-Carterfone days (see Chapter 2) it was illegal to connect anything to the telephone network without telco consent. I went to the headquarters of AT&T in New York to discuss my proposal. I remember a long meeting, an even longer noontime with several having the famous three-Martini lunch, and absolutely nothing happening. "You see," I was told, "We think yours is a fine idea, but its use would block our network. We can't have someone using the telephone for something it wasn't designed for." Remember, I simply wanted to put 10 minute exercises on the phone.

I later found the real reason my project wasn't approved. It wasn't fear of network overload. About a year later, a demonstration project went in at a university in another state. The sponsor was "the telephone company" and the project was virtually identical to mine. I've never known if my proposal triggered that project or if my proposal was killed so it wouldn't compete with a marketing plan. This instance of telephone regulatory and monopoly power blocking innovation is becoming rapidly less likely. The rule now is, if you can conceive of doing it with the phone system, go for it.

With digital standards in ISDN, competition opening up and innovations from every direction aimed at the telephone system, new technologies are being adopted at an increasing rate. This is changing the business the phone companies are in. Soon they'll become systems integrators, offering products to increase network usage. Most of the classic "Baby Bells" are already in this market. Most of the company people I meet are thinking of how we can expand the system, not restrain use. But it takes time to change old methods. Time is running out.

Economic Changes

A lot of what I've mentioned so far implies economic change, especially more function for fewer dollars. But other changes are on the horizon.

Strategic alliance has been the buzzword for several years in high-tech industries. A strategic alliance is a collection of companies that find they have some common interest in a certain niche. They agree to join together for development of that niche. In most other areas they may be major competitors, but in the alliance they push forward—sort of an honor among thieves, if you're cynical about this sort of thing.

The regional Bell operating companies, creatures of divestiture, have maintained some standardization and other support through BellCore. That may soon go away as more competition is opened up and the terms of the modified final judgment are altered. When I penned (actually word processed) the first edition, Judge Harold Greene of Modified Final Judgment fame (see Chapter 2) had just granted limited authority to some RBOCs' entry into long distance services. At the time, Judge Greene implied that the MFJ should not continue to rule on such issues indefinitely. Now, as I word process the section edition, the Federal Telecommunications Act of 1996 is rapidly bringing that statement to fruition. The RBOCs are beginning to coalesce into something similar to the AT&T of old, albeit with competition unimagined in those earlier days. In addition, the RBOCs are running headlong for the long distance market, while trying to block entry to their local loops by the big IXCs, such as MCI, AT&T and Sprint. It seems the RBOC motto is "Competition is fine; just don't compete against **us**!"

Over the past decade, a number of consortia have been formed to provide research and development for companies beyond the limited agreements exemplified by strategic alliances. One of the first formed was Microelectronics and Computer Technology Corp. (MCC). MCC applied for and received U.S. Justice Department approval to bring together a number of major computer competitors in the United States to work on research and development. Ordinarily, an agreement such as that forming MCC would have violated the antitrust laws; the Justice Department approval avoided that issue. Similar organizations were formed subsequently. In many cases at least one expressed purpose has been to make the United States more competitive in the global marketplace.

It looks like that global marketplace is developing its own similar approach for telecommunications. Within the last year and a half, the Telecommunications Information Networking Architecture Consortium formed. TINA-C is a consortium of more than 40 of the largest computer and telephone companies/agencies in the world. Its mission reads like a casebook for the future of broadband ISDN:

TINA-C MISSION

The TINA-C provides a consistent reference architecture for open telecommunications architecture, encompassing services, operations/management, and technology management.

The TINA-C makes use of the most recent advances in distributed computing/ODP and in object-oriented design to achieve interoperability, reuse of software and specifications, flexible placement of software on computing platforms, and consistency in the design of services and their management.

The TINA-C architecture would lead to a multisupplier environment for telecommunications.

It should make it possible to introduce new services and supporting technologies rapidly, maintain and extend them quickly, customize them, and make them accessible to customers regardless of the access technology that serves the customer. (Some capabilities of a service may be lost when interfacing to some customers, however.)

TINA-C was formed to gather the efforts many companies and agencies are making for the Intelligent Network (IN) and the Telecommunications Management Network (TMN). The Intelligent Network contemplates the introduction of new capabilities and services; many of these will be under the customer's control. The Telecommunications Management Network is to do just as it says, manage networks. TINA-C is establishing an international headquarters and provided a demonstration at Telecom 95 in Geneva, Switzerland during October 1995. Much of the organizational work was done at Bellcore.

Current telecom provider members of TINA-C are:

- Alcatel
- AT&T
- Bellcore
- British Telecom
- Cable & Wireless
- CSELT
- CSELT (2)
- DEC
- Deutsche Telekom AG
- Dutch Telecom
- Ellemtel
- ERICSSON
- Korea Telecom
- EURESCOM
- France Telecom
- FUJITSU
- GPT
- Hewlett-Packard
- HITACHI
- IBM
- KDD
- KPN
- MCI
- NEC
- NOKIA
- Norwegian Telecom Research
- NTT
- OKI
- Portugal Telecom
- Samsung
- Siemens
- Sprint
- Stratus Computer
- Stentor
- SUN
- Swiss Telecom PTT
- Tele Danmark
- Telenor
- TELIA Research
- TELSTRA
- Unisys

TINAC Member Company Subsidiaries:

- Bell Atlantic
- Ameritech
- Pac Bell
- Nynex
- U S West
- Bell South
- Southwestern Bell

Other Interesting Industry-Related Companies:

- EUnet Network Information Services
- INESC

Part
V

Ch
19

When I assembled this information for the first Edition, a quick analysis showed this list heavy with the following: European telecom providers, telecom equipment manufacturers, and United States computer equipment manufacturers. Now the list is longer, and the United States is well-represented in all categories. Things shift rapidly.

I have taken the time and space to present TINA-C to you so you will be aware of this organization. Keep an eye on its activities and watch who else joins. TINA-C has a number of plans in the works contemplating growth of both narrowband and broadband ISDN and the intelligent network.

 TIP Tiptoe to TINA-C's web site at **http://www.tinac.com**.

TINA-C is perhaps the best example of what I expect will be the most serious economic development in telephony and probably most of the world's technology and economy: the emergence of cross-national or international consortia that step beyond standards-setting, beyond strategic alliances and into serious projects that will determine the future of telecommunications or other technologies in the next decades.

As governments become less able to regulate entities of this size and scope, what these conglomerations of power plan to do and actually *do* do becomes more important. I suggest that, within the next decade, effective regulation of telecommunications will pass from the world's nation states to these unelected organizations.

The Politician as a Worn-Out, Overstuffed Couch

This movement of power from governments to consortia and transnational entities will blunt the transparent attempts of politicians, best characterized as "furniture" [a term of derision applied to essentially useless members of the Texas legislature by the magazine "*Texas Monthly*"].

These characters avoid serious issues of state, such as medical systems in shambles and budgets so awry that the government runs out of money every few weeks. Instead, they trump up things they think they can sell to their constituents as "God, Mother, and Apple Pie" matters, purportedly of great concern.

For a real example in the United States, witness the great furor over protecting our apparently-naive and impressionable youth from the terrible smut of the Internet. The protection, veiled within enacting sections of the Federal Telecommunications Act of 1996, alleges to stop such dangerous Internet contents at the borders of the country when smuggled in innocent-looking packets dressed as tourists returning from a visit to France.

"Mon Dieu, our children are being corrupted!" Riding to the rescue is a law already found unconstitutional by a three-judge court; the appeal to the U.S. Supreme will waste even more time and money. Of course, it's such a grand way for these politicians to avoid the real issues while still garnering votes. These fools deserve the condemnation of their vastly more intelligent and perceptive constituents: throw them out on the street and elect someone with the intestinal fortitude to deal with the real, though intractable, issues.

Although the U.S. is always good for a laugh on such matters, you other nations shouldn't be quite so smug. Attention, those of you in the UK, for example! You know "Yes, Minister" only thinly veils as fiction the real inner workings of your exalted system. Lighten up!

Social and Personal Issues

The challenge in this removal of telecommunications control from elected official oversight in governments to unelected bodies in economic organizations may be considered more of the same by many who consider our regulators to have been under the thumbs of the "regulated" from the start. I believe much of our regulation in the past has helped grow our society and economy. Now the technology has outstripped classic regulation and something new is needed.

It's a hard call. I don't expect the movement of this power to be perceived soon enough for significant government resistance to develop. What are the possible social and personal ramifications?

- Freedom of speech is constitutionally guaranteed in the United States, but this is not true universally. Congress' attempt to censor Internet traffic for port is probably proof that the movement cannot be stopped. So whatnography (as mentioned in the previous sidebar). I doubt there will be much value to an effectively-governing economic body if it cuts off free speech. However, it bears watching.
- Spying is a possibility. In the U.S., the Clipper chip idea of placing a special chip in all communications equipment to encrypt in a way that could be read by the government under court order has been met with total opposition. Could that technology resurface?

There are probably other negative possibilities. But on the whole, I expect a coordinated effort of capable business and technical leaders will result in a worldwide telecommunications system that will serve to expand, rather than contract, human rights and protections. The genie of universal communication is out of the bottle. Internet has demonstrated that. Neither persons nor organizations can put it back.

We're well into the world of the "global village" forecast by Marshal McLuhan a generation ago. In case you're not familiar with McLuhan, I suggest you read his best known book, *Understanding Media* (1964). He coined the phrase "the medium is the message." His analysis of media such as television included a classification into "hot" and "cold" media. After you read his stuff, decide whether ISDN and Internet are hot or cold.

Part
V

Ch
19

"People and Their Governments in the Information Age: A National Electronic Open Meeting" was organized in May, 1995 by the United States Office of Management and Budget. It ran for two weeks as a serious, organized attempt to involve people directly in governing. Discussion proceeded over the Internet. Public places offering Internet access were set up. The topics covered were:

- **Services**: From emergency help and health care to business licenses
- **Benefits**: From social security and food stamps to small business grants
- **Information**: From declassified secrets and travel aids to satellite weather maps
- **Participatory Democracy**: Ensuring everyone's chance to be heard in a democracy
- **Technology**: How the technical portion of electronic government will work

We're looking at a new way of governing, a new way of doing business, and a new way of communicating. We have arrived at this through our technology. ISDN will make these new ways available to all, ushering in a new century of universal dialog among all, and providing our children with the benefits of an internationally nurturing global village.

From Here...

This chapter forecasts a number of changes that will come about, partly due to the movement to ISDN. These changes include a reorganization in communications control, the rise of total telecommunications competition, and an accelerated rate of adoption in the use of ISDN in governmental, economic and social changes. Refer to the following chapters for background information, and look to the last chapter for confluence of technologies.

- Chapter 2, "Understanding Standards and Regulations," provides information on the standards and regulations discussed in this chapter.
- Chapter 4, "Choosing Services," and Chapter 7, "Ordering ISDN Services," describe the services offered now and also gives you a framework for understanding this chapter's discussion of communications control.
- Chapter 16, "Putting ISDN to Work," describes how ISDN works in the social and economic context.
- Chapter 18, "Anticipating Broadband ISDN," discusses changes to broadband ISDN technology that will affect the types of services that can be delivered.
- Chapter 20, "Alternatives to ISDN," stirs all this hodgepodge together in ever-greater variety with speed, more speed.

Alternatives to ISDN

If you follow the computer trade press you've seen articles on technologies that compete with ISDN. You've heard that ISDN is a transitional technology. You're afraid that ISDN is too little, too late. What's going on?

Every statement above is both false and true! If you've studied logic you know that can't be. Welcome to the real world of "maybe." Let's take a look at a number of the technologies in question:

These are the exciting areas of future development. It may be a while before you can get your hands on this stuff, but it'll be worth the wait. ■

Most of the communications we use don't have an even balance between the amounts we receive and the amounts we transmit

Find out why this unbalanced (the buzz word is asymmetrical) situation exists and how you can take advantage of it.

Cable Modems is a term applied to the idea of carrying information for our computers over the cable system now in place for cable TV

You'll learn how cable TV systems work and can be adapted to carry computer information.

xDSL: ADSL, HSDL, SDSL, and VDSL are all acronyms regarding various forms of Digital Subscriber Loop carrier transmission methods

You'll find out how xDSL technology works and what the different forms are all about.

Wireless: You already know what wireless is: radio

Get a more detailed idea of how wireless technologies can apply to computer communications.

Check out The High Bandwidth Web Page
http://plainfield.bypass.com/~gzaret/hlband.html

An Unbalanced Look at Communications

Here's a list of the several things we'd like do with communications in the small office/home (SOHO) environment:

- Receive television broadcasts at several megabits/second
- Receive Web page information at several hundred megabits/second
- Receive and transmit electronic mail at several kilobits/second
- Receive and transmit voice at several kilobits/second

Granted this is a short list, and it's over simplified, but the point is made; the small office and the home need vastly greater data rates delivered downstream, FROM a central source than upstream, TO the central site.

"So what," you say. "I may want to send megabits of data every second too." Of course you may, but the cost of that high data rate uplink may dissuade you from its purchase. It happens that continuing to maintain the lopsided nature of most data communications, with much higher data rates FROM a central location than TO that location, makes a terrific difference in your costs. This asymmetry is an element in the methods discussed in this chapter.

ISDN is symmetric; the B channels each deliver 64 kilobits/second in both directions simultaneously. For most of us, one or two B channels deliver our upstream information quite rapidly. How much information do you have to send to a Web server to request another page—just a few bytes giving the page address. Contrast this with the amount of information you expect from that page—several tens, hundreds, or even millions of bytes. The same is true of video— a few bytes request a video feed, millions return that feed. While ISDN is great for our general upstream needs, and we like it much better than POTS even for downstream, there's this nagging feeling that more speed on the downstream side would be better.

The technologies in this chapter give that higher downstream data rate and take advantage of the economics of asymmetry. Each has its own reason for preserving this unbalanced condition.

- Cable television systems were designed from the beginning to be asymmetric to the extreme; they delivered only one way communication. Conversion of these systems to two way is a very expensive proposition. Conversion to two way with symmetric data rate delivery is prohibitively expensive.
- Twisted pair copper loops suffer from a phenomenon known as "far end crosstalk." Remember the discussion of noise and attenuation in Chapter 1; the two together became the limiting factors on how we could transmit a signal at a given data rate. It turns out our attempts to transmit in one direction adversely affect the signal we're trying to receive from the opposite direction. The signal we're trying to receive has been

attenuated and distorted over the distance it traveled. We're trying to transmit with a strong signal; our signal is very loud noise (cross talk at our location, the "far end" with respect to the received signal) to the one we're trying to receive. The higher the data rate we try to transmit, the more our attempt distorts and destroys the one we're trying to receive. The solution is to transmit vastly lower data rates than we're receiving.

■ Wireless broadcasts require antennas and transmitters. Transmission of high data rates requires more and more complex, expensive, and powerful equipment. There is limited spectrum space available. All this means it is more economic to have a central site transmitting to many other sites at a higher data rate than the dispersed sites transmit back.

■ Satellites face a situation very similar to wireless, in fact they are also wireless. It takes an expensive and powerful satellite transmitter to put down a "footprint" covering a large area of the Earth's surface. The transponder within the satellite that receives, converts in frequency, and retransmits the signals from a central surface station, cannot economically deal with receiving and retransmitting signals from many, many smaller surface stations. The cost of adequate surface stations at each of these smaller sites is prohibitive in the extreme.

In every instance the economics weigh very heavily in favor of large data rates TO us in comparison to the rates FROM us. If we have a need to transmit large amounts back, the optimum solution is to lease services from a supplier that is "closer" to the system than we are, for example the Internet. So, if you want to have a large and powerful Web presence, you don't put in powerful Web servers at your location and attempt to run them over the lower data rate transmission path available, and you don't pay for a high data rate transmission channel. Rather you pay a Web service provider, connected by expensive high data rate lines TO the Internet. That provider distributes the cost of such an expensive connection TO the Internet among a number of other clients thereby substantially reducing the costs to each client.

Keep this asymmetry in mind as you read about the different methods available.

Cable Modems

Part
V

Ch
20

Cable modems is shorthand for use of the existing cable television system to deliver data. In order to understand this technology it's necessary to understand cable TV.

Broadband and Baseboard

I'm about to use a term in a totally different way and with a totally different meaning from what that term has meant elsewhere in this book. Don't despair, just remember: "Whenever I use a word, it means exactly what I want it to mean, nothing more and nothing less." (Humpty Dumpty)

The word in question is *broadband*. If you look in other chapters of this book, especially Chapter 18, "Anticipating Broadband ISDN," you'll find the word defined as: a means of transmitting high data rates. What is defined as a high data rate varies with the year in which you're using the term. Broadband used to mean data rates greater than those necessary to carry one verbal conversation, perhaps a few thousand bits per second. Now, at least in the ISDN world, broadband appears to mean transmission at rates greater than a PRI, that is, a few megabits per second.

In order to understand broadband in the sense of our current discussion, you'll first have to understand the meaning of *baseband*. So here goes.

Baseband signaling is an electrical method of putting digital information directly on a piece of cable. The signal placed on the cable occupies a frequency spectrum starting at zero Hertz and extending upwards to the maximum bandwidth required for the signal. Figure 20.1 illustrates this idea with the x-y axes representing the amount of spectrum occupied and a metaphorical picture of a packet traveling down a piece of cable.

Figure 20.1 contains the keys to baseband:

- Baseband signals begin at zero Hertz, DC, the base of the electromagnetic spectrum, and expand up in frequency using as much spectrum as necessary to transmit the signal (just how much depends on the specification for modulation of the signal). As a general rule, the higher the data rate, the more spectrum space needed. Ethernet uses baseband signaling and requires about 20 MHz of spectrum space for a 10 megabit/second data rate.

- Baseband can accommodate only one frame of information passing a given point on the cable at any one time. Notice that the stylized cable is totally filled in its diameter by the frame. No other frames can be placed next to it so they could pass the same location at the same time.

FIG. 20.1

Baseband signaling. The x axis is the bandwidth occupied by the signal; the y axis is the amplitude of the signal. The fanciful cylinder is a cable with a data frame traveling inside; fields within the frame are shaded differently. Notice that only one frame may pass a given point on the cable at any time. This is because the frame takes up all the spectrum space available starting with 0 Hz or DC.

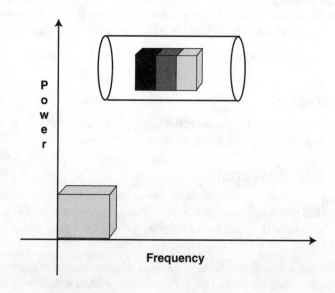

"OK," you say, "I've got the idea that baseband starts at DC and takes up some of the spectrum, and nothing else can be sent on the cable, but if a frame takes up the whole baseband transmission capacity of the cable at a given time, how can I have a multitude of data exchanges sharing a cable?"

Since you asked, I'm reminded of television here in Austin, Texas, during the 1950s and the early 60s. During those times there was only one television station in the city. In fact, Austin was the largest metropolitan area in the United States with only one television station.

One Station?

How could it be that Austin had only one station? It seems the allocation of channels throughout Texas was done in such a manner that there would have been interference to other stations had an additional VHF station operated from Austin. True, channel 9 was available for public broadcasting, but no commercial VHF channels could be allocated. An interesting engineering conundrum. Determination of the station's ownership is left as an exercise. You may wish to consider leisurely bounding jackrabbits darting over the hill where the station's tower sprouted as a starting point.

During that time there were three commercial TV networks, CBS, ABC, and NBC. Each had prime time shows. Let's take a spot in prime time and consider your question. On Wednesdays at 8 PM CBS fed *I Love Lucy*, NBC fed *Gomer Pyle*, and ABC fed *Get Smart*. (I don't really know if I have the times, programs, or networks right, but you get the idea.) The Austin station had deals with all three networks and received all three shows at 8 PM. But it could only transmit one at a time. Its viewers, well really, its advertisers, wanted all three shows. What to do? Pregnant pause—

Answer: Transmit *Get Smart* at 8 PM Wednesdays while recording the other two shows on videotape recorders. Then at some other time transmit *I Love Lucy* and at a third time transmit *Gomer Pyle*.

This is exactly what happens on a baseband system. You can't have more than one frame passing a point on the cable at a given time, but you can have frames of such a short length in time, that you can pick off those addressed to you from the ones addressed to others. Since the time between the frames is very short compared to the much longer time you (really your computer) need to get the pieces of the full message, made up of many frames, assembled; you'll never notice the holes used by communications of frames among other systems. Ethernet uses this method, so does ISDN, so does ATM. The fancy word for this is *time division multiplexing* (TDM); we're multiplexing (creating distinct information channels) by dividing up the times of use on our medium, cable. That takes care of baseband. Notice it's the technique for many of the technologies we use everyday.

Broadband signaling is considerably more complex than baseband. Consider a person speaking into the microphone of a radio transmitter. The sound of the speaker's voice is changed to electrical impulses within the audio range of 20 to 20,000 Hertz. The audio signal is a baseband signal; its frequencies are changed to electrical phenomena with exactly the same frequencies,

Part
V

Ch
20

all measured against the starting point, zero Hertz, and continuing up to the maximum required to carry the information; the frequency of each sound is exactly the same whether in air pressure or electrical form.

But when it gets to the radio transmitter something radically different happens. The radio equipment converts the audio signal into a radio signal. Technically you say the audio modulates the radio station's carrier frequency. This means the audio frequency signal is "mixed" with the radio frequency signal. Any physicist will tell you that when you mix two different frequencies together you get the sum and the difference of those two frequencies. Here's a fancy word for you; mixing two frequencies together makes them "beat" one against the other; the resulting beat is called a "heterodyne." You can hear these beats, heterodynes, when you vibrate two tuning forks of slightly different pitch near one another.

Then There Are Superheterodynes

In radio heterodyning two frequencies are fundamental to modulation of the radio signal, the concept we're discussing. This principle is also fundamental to the "superheterodyne" receiving technique, which is the basis for most of our radio, television, and other radio frequency communications equipment. In this system the radio signal received on the antenna is heterodyned with one created by the receiving device; the internally generated signal is selected so the resultant will always be the same, the so-called "intermediate frequency," or IF. Then this frequency is manipulated by precision circuits to remove interference and, ultimately, turned into information the end user wants, for example, sound.

Beating or heterodyning only occurs in "non-linear" devices, such as special electronic equipment.

In Figure 20.2, I represent the broadband ideas using the same sorts of symbols I did with baseband. Look at the differences. In broadband the signal on the cable does not start at zero Hertz. Rather, since it was mixed with a radio signal of much higher frequency, the carrier, it may occupy any portion of the spectrum of radio frequencies that can be carried by the cable. Typical coaxial cable can probably carry a spectrum up to 500 MHz or even more. To transmit a signal 6 MHz wide, take that signal in baseband form and mix it with, say a 100 MHz signal; you'll get two signals—94 MHz and 106 MHz. Well, actually, you'll get two sidebands, one on each side of 100 MHz. The lower sideband extends down to 94 MHz and the upper sideband extends up to 106 MHz. Then filter one sideband out, say the lower, and you're left with a 6 MHz wide channel extending from 100 MHz to 106 Mhz.

This is what radio and TV stations do. When you tune your receiver, you're choosing a carrier frequency. Then the receiver strips off the carrier frequency and *detects* the original signal by reducing it to baseband again.

Since you can move the signal anywhere within the spectrum available on the cable, and since the signals occupy far less than even half the available spectrum, more than one signal at a time can pass the same point on the cable without interfering with other signals transmitted on different frequencies. This is the same idea as ordinary radio and TV. This is how cable TV works. It's called frequency division multiplexing (FDM). For more complexity each channel created by FDM can use the time division multiplexing method I described earlier to carry many different exchanges among many different sources and destinations.

FIG. 20.2

Broadband signaling. The x axis represents the frequency range occupied by the signals; the y axis is the amplitude of the signals. The fanciful cylinder is a cable with data frames traveling inside; fields within the frames are shaded differently. Notice that several frames may be passing a given point on the cable at any time. This is because the frames are placed into channels of different frequency— frequency division multiplexing, FDM.

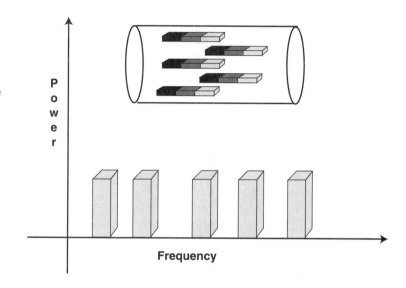

Figure 20.3 shows a broadband system of the type I just described. The central location houses the *headend* equipment, consisting of *translators* that perform heterodyning functions to translate the signals to frequencies desired for the channel design of the system. At each of the users' devices a radio frequency *cable modem* tunes in the appropriate channel and converts the radio frequency signal, which by its very nature is an analog signal, into a baseband digital signal fed to each user's equipment.

Part
V

Ch
20

Broadband Failed the First Time Out

In the 1980s there was a big push to design and install broadband local and campus area networks. These systems turned out to be incredibly expensive, usually tied to one vendor or a few proprietary technologies, and prone to massive failures. By the end of the 1980s those that had spent their millions for such RF broadband systems had generally abandoned them in favor of baseband. Baseband methods won because of their reliability and economics. Now we're returning to consider using broadband on a metropolitan area network scale by building on to the existing cable TV network. Will the technology make it this time? Stay tuned to this channel.

FIG. 20.3

A broadband system based on cable TV technology. The headend location houses the translators that perform frequency division multiplexing; this is also the point where communications connections to television, the Internet, and other sources are made. Each of the computers throughout the system has an RF cable modem to detect the information and put into digital form.

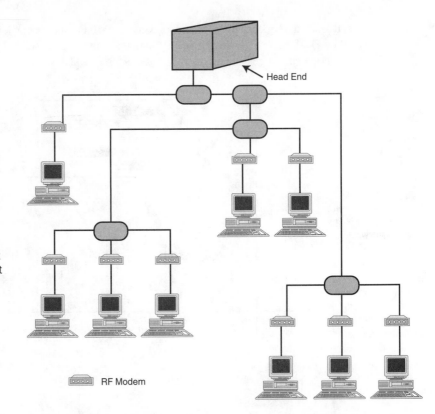

Head End

RF Modem

Fiber Fiber Everywhere, but When?

There's general agreement in the industry that the final solution for cable communication is fiber to the curb or even to and in the house. The real question is when and at what cost. Most pundits feels it'll be one to two decades before fiber become ubiquitous. What should we do in the meantime? The existing cable TV plant offers a middle ground. The cable industry has been gradually evolving to provide a *hybrid coax-fiber* answer to this transition question. Figure 20.4 shows how this works. Fiber is laid from the headend location to various neighborhood locations throughout a metropolitan area. Then the existing coax distributes to each house. The number of houses and offices in this coax distribution varies from one design to another; some envision a few hundred, others a few thousand.

Cable TV systems can be adapted to carry computer communications. But two problems arise:

■ The cable industry has a poor record for service and reliability. Do you want to trust your vital communications to the people who, in some areas, have left users with blank screens five to ten percent of the time? Contrast this with the telephone industry where loss of dialtone is measured in a small fraction of a percent.

FIG. 20.4
In the Hybrid fiber-coax system fiber runs from the headend to a neighborhood. Then distribution throughout the neighborhood uses existing coax. After Ham Mathews, Digi International.

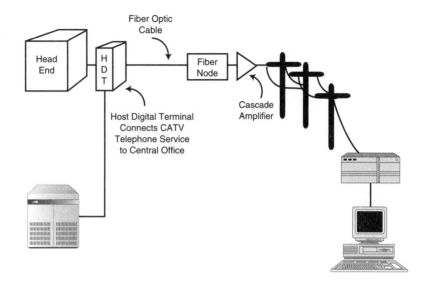

- Only about five percent of the cable systems in the United States offers two-way communication to the extent needed by computer. A massive upgrade of most systems will be expensive and time consuming.

N O T E The Web is starting to boom with continually updated resources on cable. The ones that follow will get you started. They have links to many, many more.

Sam's Interactive Cable Guide **http://www.teleport.com/~samc/cable1.html**

Cable Datacom News **http://CableDatacomNews.com/**

Cable Resources on the Web **http://rpcp.mit.edu/~gingold/cable/** ■

The first problem of cable involves service, quality control, and customer relations issues. These are totally in the hands of the cable companies; unfortunately, many companies have a lot of making up to do.

The second issue regarding the lack of two way systems can play into the hands of the existing telephone system, especially ISDN. Production lines are stamping out cable modems designed to combine the one way cable system with the phone system. For most of the small office/home office market, the need for data communications is asymmetric. SOHO users need far more data coming TO them than going FROM them. Chances are, if you're in the SOHO world, you want big downloads from the Internet TO you. All you'll be loading up is requests for Web links, electronic mail, and a few files. If you have a Web or FTP site, you probably lease space on servers from firms already connected by multi-megabit links to the Internet and other communications systems. You don't need a high data rate up-link.

Part
V

Ch
20

Your cable company can provide data channels TO you without rebuilding its system. All the company has to do is allocate channels on its headend to Internet service and offer that service to you. You'll either buy or lease the cable modem to strip the signal off the cable. You'll probably want to use ISDN rather than POTS for signals FROM you because ISDN give you much faster setup and data rates.

In spite of quality control and one-way drawbacks, cable modem technology is taking off. A number of companies are committing millions of dollars to research, development, and now full-scale manufacturing of the necessary equipment. This is driven by the prospect of both voice and data service in competition with the telcos.

xDSL Technologies

Faced with competition from cable's entrance into telephone service and cable's apparent technological advantages in carrying higher data rates than twisted pair, telco executives have been losing sleep and taking early retirement in droves. If coaxial cable systems already in place can pass vastly higher data rates than the telcos' twisted pair, the phone companies are cooked. What to do? Find a way to compete with high data rates on existing twisted pair. ISDN is a start, but it won't ramp up to multi-megabit delivery to the SOHO market, the economic numbers don't work. What's needed is a new technology.

The xDSL family is that new technology. These Digital Subscriber Line (DSL) technologies are rapidly emerging as the salvation for telephone companies. DSL can deliver high data rates in a number of different forms.

- Asymmetric Digital Subscriber Line (ADSL)
- Symmetric Digital Subscriber Line (SDSL)
- High Bit Rate Digital Subscriber Line (HDSL)
- Very High Bit Rate Digital Subscriber Line (VSDL)

Each of these has a different proposed use and economics.

ADSL

ADSL is the one you hear all about. It's been tested in a number of different places. There are a few technical differences to iron out concerning modulation techniques and standards, but the general technology is ready, reasonably priced, and in production. A very nice feature of ADSL is the incorporation of POTS telephone service using the same twisted pair that carries the higher data rate. A slight variation on this allows the addition or substitution of ISDN for POTS. ADSL offers a range of megabit data rates depending on the length and gage of the twisted pair available:

- 1.5 Mbps downstream and 160 kbps upstream over distances of 18 kilofeet
- 6.2 Mbps downstream and 640 kbps upstream over distances of 12 kilofeet

Other variations are available within these broad ranges. But the idea is clear: ADSL provides megabits of downstream data with kilobits for the upstream. Figure 20.5 shows the spectrum used by ADSL.

FIG. 20.5

ADSL spectrum usage. The exact nature of the signal is dependent on the technology chosen and the twisted pair lengths encountered. ISDN could be inserted in the area shown for the upstream signal. After Robert Olshansky, GTE Laboratories.

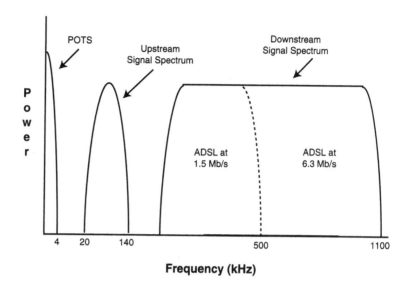

ADSL is ideal for the SOHO world. It uses existing twisted pair, supplies POTS and/or ISDN, gives adequate upstream data rates, and provides the megabits needed for effective Web and video use. Prognosticators of its cost estimate hardware for the phone company and for your location at $250/each. What a deal.

 TIP See Dan Kegel's ADSL Page **http://www.alumni.caltech.edu/~dank/isdn/adsl.html** for a vast amount of information.

But, remember, ADSL and all the other DSL technologies are transmission methods only. They are not complete communications systems. ISDN is a specification for the total telephone network. DSL can fit into that network.

One thing clearly lacking from ADSL, as it's currently being used, is switching. The typical ADSL system uses a twisted pair from the subscriber's location to the telco central office, but that twisted pair does not connect to the telephone switch. It goes to an ADSL modem. There the signal is split; the POTS or ISDN component goes to the public switched network; the remainder goes to a router that's connected to a LAN, usually an Ethernet. The LAN then communicates with whatever resources you've arranged to have available. Typically these resources will be an Internet connection and/or a video system.

Obviously the telcos can choose to provide whatever service they want to provide you. The really interesting question is what the competition might do. Here's a roadmap for competitive use of ADSL:

- Lease use of an existing telco twisted pair local loop. This should be a pair that is not terminated in the telco switch. It appears regulations will require the phone company to do this, but there may be some problems with the price.
- Co-locate electronics including ADSL modems, LANs, and routers at the central office. Again regulations probably require the telco to let you do this, but price is in question.
- Arrange connections to the Internet, video sources, etc. and drop them to routers on the LANs.

I anticipate quite a battle from potential competitors wanting to lease pairs and co-locate equipment. This is all to the good for users. The technology is here. The price is right. The only thing holding it back is the telcos and others taking the first step and actually offering service.

From the telephone company's perspective ADSL is a win-win proposition. It requires no special build-out. They don't have to totally revamp their systems and hope people will buy into the idea. The technology can be installed on a user-by-user basis, and each installation can return a profit in a reasonable period of time. Contrast this with providing fiber to the neighborhood, the curb, or the door of subscribers. ADSL buys a lot of time to place that fiber as needed; the companies don't have fall back on "build it and they will come."

SDSL

Symmetric digital subscriber line is a little different. It requires one twisted pair and is designed as a means of delivering T1 and fractional T1 service more economically than previous methods. Since it's symmetric the data rates are the same in both directions. It can even be used to extend ISDN BRI service. SDSL design, using 24 gage twisted pair and no repeaters allows:

- E1 or T1 data rates (up to 2.048 Mbps) over distances of up to 8 kilofeet with POTS included or 9 kilofeet without POTS.
- 400 Mbps over a distance of 21 kilofeet with POTS.
- 160 kbps over a distance of 23 kilofeet with POTS; this can provide an ISDN BRI.

HDSL

High bit rate digital subscriber line uses two twisted pairs and is designed as a repeaterless T1/E1 extender. HDSL can deliver E1 data rates (2.048 Mbps) over 24 gage twisted pair up to 13 kilofeet long without repeaters and without the need to remove bridge taps. This reduces the telco's equipment and labor costs substantially.

VDSL

Very high data rate digital subscriber line technology is the wave of the future. It provides, what now appear to be, huge data rates over existing twisted pair, while also providing POTS:

- 52 Mbps over 1 kilofoot
- 26 Mbps over 3 kilofeet
- 13 Mbps over 4 to 5 kilofeet
- 1.5 to 3 Mbps for the upstream channel

Current plans contemplate using VDSL to service groups, from a dozen or so homes or small businesses to several hundred. Figure 20.6 shows spectrum usage.

FIG. 20.6

Very high data rate subscriber line spectrum usage. Notice how ISDN can fit into this scheme. After Robert Olshansky, GTE Laboratories.

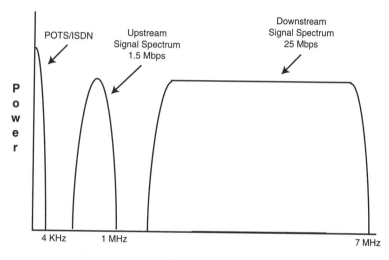

Wireless

When I use wireless in this context I'm concerned with any non-cable method other than satellite. One of the most interesting is usually called wireless cable. This was developed as a substitute for cable TV. It works using microwave radio in place of the cable (see Fig. 20.7).

 TIP Wire up to **http://www.cais.net/wca** at the Wireless Cable Association for more information.

FIG. 20.7

Wireless cable. Information collected from sources such as TV programs and Internet may come in by wired or satellite sources. It's retransmitted on the assigned microwave frequency to receivers throughout its line-of-sight distribution area.

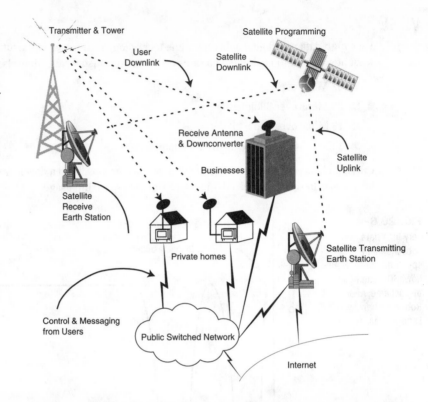

The big thing to notice here—the wireless cable system is absolutely asymmetric. You can't transmit microwave signals back. Then how do you control what you receive and send out your own stuff? Simple. You use ISDN or POTS if you must. Again, most of the data rate is needed TO you. There's real potential for putting Internet and other data services on this technology.

Other wireless methods include cellular and the newly emerging digital replacements for analog cellular. Personal communications services (PCS) provide wireless phone service more cheaply than cellular systems and might be adapted to carry moderate data rates.

Satellite

As you're already aware, the Earth is surrounded by a number of communications satellites in geosynchronous orbits; each stays over a fixed spot of the surface. Within the footprint area of signal coverage under the satellite any authorized user can receive, and perhaps transmit, using the satellite's transponders.

Since this is a book on ISDN, you'll be glad to know you can talk ISDN through a satellite link. Data TeleMark makes the electronics to take your existing ISDN into a satellite link.

TIP Beam up to **http://www.datatelemark.com/datatelemark/satellit.html** and find out how Data TeleMark does it.

Our quest in this chapter is to see what else besides ISDN can be used to satisfy our needs for more and more data. Satellites are really an extension of the microwave idea mentioned in the preceding section. But every point within the satellite's footprint is visible to the satellite, so much more ground can be covered. What a great way to deliver downlink information, such as the Internet.

Although you can buy uplink capacity, the costs of transmission equipment, and the requisite government licensing, probably aren't worth it when you again consider the asymmetric nature of the communication. The solution for satellite use and the SOHO world is the same as for microwave; use the satellite for the downstream link with multi-megabits of Internet and video; use ISDN, or POTS if you must, for the upstream link to control what you get and respond.

TIP For general coverage of satellites **http://www.teleport.com/~samc/cable10.html**.

But there's one catch with satellites. Since they're in geosynchronous orbits, some 22,000 miles above the earth, the round-trip delay up, through, and down is noticeable. It's generally on the order of a quarter of a second. You've already seen this on TV when a commentator in New York is connected by satellite to someone in Tokyo. There's just the slightest little pause within conversation that makes it appear something other than natural; that's the propagation delay over the long-haul through the satellite. This will probably not make any difference to you, but it's worth remembering in case timing is ever an issue.

Lest you think satellites are some sort of expensive stuff with astronomical prices consider the direct broadcast satellite industry that got off the ground in 1996. Already the hardware including a dish and the necessary electronics has been seen selling for under $300. Microsoft and others are planning to offer data over this already commercially viable network.

Part

V

Ch

20

ISDN and Transitional Technologies

Ever since the user community became aware of the possibility of cable modems, ADSL, and perhaps some of the other technologies I've mentioned, there's been a deluge of discussion on newsgroups, listservs, forums, seminars, and in the press implying that ISDN is just a transitional technology. This has had the effect of inducing some potential ISDN users to shelve ISDN plans in favor of waiting for the other stuff.

This is a very short-sighted decision. Every technology, every one, is transitional. The underlying driving force of technology is increasing function and decreasing price thereby increasing the overall value. Walking was following by riding animals. Riding animals was followed by railroads, railroads by airplanes, etc.

This book is designed for readers with moderate to advanced computer experience. Since you're reading it, the chances are you've bought a number of computers within the last several years. Did you at any time expect to be using the same machine, as your primary machine, four or five years after you bought it? Of course not. Did you expect the machine to retain any significant monetary value after that time? Of course not. You've been around the block. You know computer technology moves quickly. The issues in buying this technology are:

- Will it do what I want to do today?
- Will it do the job for a price I can afford to pay?
- Is it based on standards that are widely accepted in the industry?
- Will it earn back what I paid within the next couple of years, when I expect replacements to be far less expensive or totally new technologies to be available?

If you answer "Yes" to all these questions, you buy it. Otherwise, you don't buy it. This is not rocket science.

I would never contend that ISDN BRI at today's prices will look good in 2000, probably not even in 1999. But today, it looks great and is great. You can get it now. It's far better than POTS and far cheaper than the other alternatives you probably have available.

At some time in the future, one or more of the methods I've talked about in this chapter will be available to you. At that time you'll have to test the newly available option against your investment in ISDN. By then ISDN will have more than paid for itself while you used it. ISDN may just fit in with the new technology:

- The probably asymmetric nature of your communications needs could dictate that you continue ISDN as the return TO your connection with the Internet, video, or whatever.
- The other methods I've described are all transmission methods only. They do not incorporate methods of switching. ISDN is by definition a switched technology. You'll probably need it to deal with the switched public network. Your new technology will carry ISDN for your switched service and use packet mode for higher data rates.

From Here...

That's it. You've made it to the end of the book and the beginning of the telecommunications revolution of the 21st Century. I hope I've convinced you to use ISDN. I'm sure you'll be more than happy that you do. As time passes, you'll integrate more and faster technologies with ISDN. With each step up, more possibilities for human interaction and understanding open up. It's looking good moving down this road much traveled.

Appendixes

World Wide Web References for Standards & Organizations

This appendix is designed to be your first reference in finding details on many of the standards discussed in this book. Many of these standards are available in paper form, but they usually are expensive and it's often difficult to determine which you need. I suggest you first consult these addresses to see what's available. Often, you'll find more than you want in just a few minutes. Frequently, you'll be able to download the exact text of the standards you want, and you'll be sure it's the most recent version. Should you need additional information, the Web sites usually will tell how to address e-mail, make phone or fax calls, or use snail mail in the most effective manner. ■

ISDN Home Pages

Dan Kegel's ISDN Page

http://alumni.caltech.edu/~dank/isdn. This is the single most important place to start your search for information on the changing world of ISDN (aside from this book, of course). Kegel has done the ISDN world a great service by establishing and maintaining this page. Now it has grown to a large number of pages with hyperlinks to hundreds of sites throughout the world.

My Home Page

http://www.bryce.com/~bryce. I hope to furnish information of help to you here. I'm always receptive to your suggestions. I'll post additions and corrections to this book, advise you of later editions, include hyperlinks to other sites, and include new ideas I discover and you send in. If you send e-mail to me, please use a descriptive "Re:" and start it with "ISDN Book" so I'll know right away that it goes to the file for this book. Please be brief in your comments to help me handle the rather heavy e-mail load. There's a form on my Web site for you to fill in and register your book; there's also space to give me your ideas about the book. My e-mail address for this book is **ISDN2@bryce.com**.

Some General Standards Sources

ANSI Gateway to Standards Organizations

http://www.nssn.org/stds.html. A good list of standards organizations' resources available on the Web.

Rosetta Stone of Standards Bodies

http://www.isoc.org/images/univers.gif. This is a graphic showing the relations among many of the standards bodies. It's a real eye-opener.

Telecom Information Resources

http://spp.umich.edu/telecom/standards.html. A broad selection of starting points for your research.

Standards Organizations

Standards are available in published form from any of the following organizations. I've given the Web sites here because they are all so informative. In some cases, you can download the standards over the Internet. Unfortunately, some are now charging for this service. For example, in mid-1995 the ITU began requiring a subscription of several thousand dollars a year for use of its standards database. I hope this trend can be halted so the information that in many cases was created with our tax dollars is allowed to flow freely. The United States Court of Appeals for the Seventh Circuit specifically rejected the notion that it should charge a dollar a minute for connection to its BBS system and, by specific order, made the service free. The

Court reasoned that the savings in time and effort for its staff and the service to the public more than justified the small costs involved. I hope more organizations follow this reasoning.

App

A

American National Standards Institute (ANSI)

> **http://www.ansi.org**. ANSI is the member organization representing the United States in several international groups.

Bandwidth ON Demand INteroperability Group

> **http://www.hep.com/ftp/networks/bonding**. This group works out the methods of bonding multiple B channels. Although PPP Multilink Protocol is expected to displace bonding, bonding is still an important technique.

BellCore

> **http://www.bellcore.com/ISDN/ISDN.html**. This has specific information of ISDN standards and listings of telephone company contacts for ISDN.

Corporation for Open Systems International (COS)

> **http://www.cos.com**. COS established the demonstration project to interest the computing community in ISDN.

TIP It's currently unclear where COS is in cyberspace. I've retained this address for future reference.

Federal Information Processing Standards (FIPS PUBS)

> **http://www.cenus.gov/~blaplant/fips_idx**. This provides information on U.S. government standards including those that relate to ISDN. This site has recently become restricted.

International Multimedia Teleconferencing Consortium

> **http://www.csn.net/imtc**. Look here for details on using video and audio with ISDN.

International Telecommunications Union (ITU)

> **http://www.itu.ch**. The ITU is the primary source of ISDN standards.

Internet Engineering Task Force (IETF)

> **http://www.ietf.org**. The IETF sets the technical standards for the Internet and protocols, such as PPP and MP, which have become the de facto standards for ISDN connection for computers.

North American ISDN Users' Forum

> **http://www.ocn.com/ocn/niuf/niuf_top.html**. I've placed the NIUF within the standards organizations because of its close association with the National Institute of Standards and Technology and the active participation of many of its members in other standards organizations. Most importantly, NIUF drafts and promulgates standards in a very formal fashion. All of us owe a great deal of thanks to this volunteer organization.

Organization for International Standards (ISO)

> **http://www.iso.ch**. ISO sets many of the computing standards, including the seven layer ISO OSI model, local, metropolitan, and wide area networks.

Special Interest Organizations

ATM Forum

> **http://www.atmforum.com/home.html**. This group helps establish interest and standards in ATM.

California ISDN Users Group

> **http://www.ciug.org/ciug**. Remember, this is the place to keep your eye on for interoperability testing.

Frame Relay Forum

> **http://frame-relay.indiana.edu**. Standards and interest in frame relay are promoted by the Forum.

New York ISDN Users Group

> **http://www.isdn.org**. This users group promises to have a great deal of information on its Web site.

Texas ISDN Users Group

> **http://www.crimson.com/isdn/**. My personal thanks to the many members of this group that provided their experiences and help in making this book happen.

SMDS Interest Group Incorporated

> **http://www.cerf.net/smds.html**. This group promotes SMDS interest and standards.

ISDN Products: What To Ask and Who To Ask

This appendix is designed as your starting place for research into ISDN products. The market is moving so fast that it's not reasonable to print a list of products and specifications in a book and then expect them to stand still. Therefore, I encourage you to:

- At least page carefully through Chapters 9, 10, and 11 on different types of hardware to use in connecting to ISDN

- Check out the most recent periodicals for product reviews on ISDN

- Check the Internet sites I've suggested

- Ask the questions below as you do your research

- Keep an open mind; limitations listed in even a recent article may be eliminated by the next upgrade. ■

Questions To Ask

This is a short list. I've not included such questions as, "Does it connect by Ethernet, serial, or other method," because I expect those will be obvious to you. My intent here is to tickle your thought with some important, and sometimes, overlooked ideas.

 TIP   Ask your own questions and follow those of others on the newsgroup **comp.dcom.isdn**.

1. *Does the product support more than one B channel?* A number of products only have single B channel support. Often, the second B channel is available only for POTS connection. The future favors multiple B channel use, so anything you buy should have the option to use both B channels in a BRI for data. It should also have support for the IETF Multilink PPP method of aggregating B channels. As this standard is still slightly in flux, the manufacturer should provide some method, such as a programmable ROM, that can easily be updated as standards change. Notice that some manufacturers have their own, proprietary method of channel aggregation; for example, Ascend has MP+. While advocates for a vendor may argue their product is superior because of a proprietary method, don't be misled. In the long, or even medium term, standards everyone uses are the best path to follow.

2. *Does the product support compression?* You'll often see specifications stating ISDN products support V.42 bis and MNP 4 and 5 compression. On closer examination, you'll find these refer to an analog modem included within the device. The compression standards to be used with PPP and Multilink PPP are based on STAC designs adopted by the IETF. The manufacturer should provide an upgrade path that will be easy to follow as standards become final. Again, you'll hear all sorts of arguments about why a proprietary method is superior; hold fast for universally adopted standards.

   N O T E   I scream all this about standards. Now I'm going to contradict myself. Because of Ascend's dominance in the ISP marketplace, a number of manufacturers are providing Ascend compatible options for channel aggregation and compression. This overcomes the argument that the only device that will properly speak with an Ascend is an Ascend; but be sure the product also supports the IETF standards and can, in any case, be upgraded as things change. ■

3. *What analog telephone support is offered?* Many devices have some sort of connection for analog phone equipment, but there are a number of issues that surround the usefulness of such connections. The best provide connection for POTS type phones, FAX machines, and modems; such connections require creation of ringer current and DTMF tone signaling. However, a number of products require that your computer have software that detects calls and creates the DTMF tones. In these cases, you could not use ordinary FAX machines or modems on the ports; connection is restricted to telephone handsets and headsets. You also must consider what provisions are made for voice calls that

arrive, or that you want to make during data transfers. I suggest the best devices are designed to drop one B channel, if two are being used for data to the same location, thereby allowing you to use the voice phone. By the way, more and more you'll see two, not just one, POTS port available so both B channels can be used for analog.

CAUTION

On some of the equipment, the telephone handsets and headsets must be the old "carbon" type. If you plug in an electronic headset, the circuit will destroy your headset. Check before you connect.

---

4. *What application program interfaces (API) does the device support?* Check over Chapter 6 for details on relevant APIs. Generally, the AT command set preserves compatibility with your modem programs. In my opinion, this is helpful with today's limited selection of software, but rapid adoption of the more sophisticated APIs will eliminate the importance of the AT command set for ISDN equipment. It's more important to look for support of TAPI and, perhaps, WinISDN. If you're using a router, this becomes a non-issue since the only issue is TCP/IP communication.

5. *What kind of ISDN connection is provided?* The device can have either a U interface, which includes an NT-1, or an S/T interface, which requires an external NT-1. While your initial cost might be lower for a device with an internal NT-1, your prospects for future expansion are limited. Most products with an internal NT-1 provide no way of connecting to other ISDN equipment; one of the few exceptions to this is the Cisco 752/3 (aka Combinet 2060). So you're left with no way to connect those other computers, telephones, or FAX machines you'll buy for ISDN; you'll have to discard your first box with the U interface, buy one with an S/T, and buy an NT-1. My general recommendation is buy S/T products and use an external NT-1 so you can take full advantage of your ISDN line(s). Several makers provide NT-1s with POTS connections, so you can also eliminate the need for a POTS port on the ISDN devices you connect to the NT-1. However, there are some products that include an internal NT-1, true POTS port with ringer current and DTMF, and an S/T interface for other ISDN equipment. These certainly are a possible alternative to an external NT-1. The primary drawback to such devices, if they are internal computer cards, is the need to keep your computer on at all times to support the added equipment.

N O T E　In spite of my brilliant argument for the S/T interface, a very strong thrust in the North American market favors the U interface. With prices dropping fast, this may not be so bad.　■

6. *Does the equipment support IP and PPP?* It must support IP to be usable for connection to the Internet, and PPP is the best protocol for that connection. Because IP has become the *de facto* standard for heterogeneous computing, in my opinion, IP is mandatory for

any equipment. The second protocol, of importance, is IPX for NetWare. All other things being equal, if one device supports only IP and another supports both IP and IPX, I'd go for the one with both protocols. Support of additional protocols can be important to you, depending on your particular environment. In well designed equipment, the maker should be able to provide additional protocol support, as needed, through software or firmware upgrades. Third party support may also be available.

7. *Does the device provide network management support using SNMP?* Simple Network Management Protocol (SNMP) is the *de facto* standard for managing large and diverse networks. It is a part of the TCP/IP protocol suite and is used by virtually all network management hardware and software. If your system will be connected to a larger environment, which is being managed, SNMP is invaluable for configuration, trouble-shooting, and load analysis.

8. *Can the device sense B channel traffic and optimize usage?* In this case, the equipment measures the traffic on a B channel during communication. If there's a substantial increase in traffic, the equipment can connect another B channel and increase through-put. As traffic drops, the additional B channel (or channels) are dropped.

Manufacturers

This list of manufacturers of ISDN equipment and software is a starting point. It is by no means complete in this rapidly growing market; that would be impossible.

N O T E Dan Kegel maintains a list of manufacturers of hardware and software on his ISDN Web page: **http://www.alumni.caltech.edu/~Adaxnk/isdn**. I'll have some information on mine, but I don't try to dupliate the fine work of Kegel: **http://www.bryce.com/~Abryce**. ∎

I've inserted a few notes about some of the vendors. Please consider them as added help for you. They are not intended to emphasize one maker over another.

To Slash or To Backslash, That Is The Question

I have a number of "URLs" in this and other portions of the book. Please note that Uniform Resource Locators (URL) use only forward slashes "/" and never backslashes "\". This convention flows from development of most Internet tools (the URL is an Internet tool) with Unix machines. Unix does not use the backslash. The backslash is a creature of MS-DOS, which is sometimes bemoaned by its author, Paul Allen—he was Bill Gate's partner from the start and actually wrote the code; well he added to code done by another when IBM called looking for an operating system. In MS-DOS the backslash (\) indicates a directory and the forward slash (/) indicates a parameter. Don't feel bad if you get this confused. Everyone messes it up. I remember the total mess that used to exist in NetWare when some places in directory trees you had to use \ and others /, and you'd get such help as "Fatal syntax error B3458QR" which was never explained. Then NetWare always has been strange. Finally, Novell fixed it to take either kind of slash. See Mary Ann Pike et al, *Special Edition Using The Internet with Windows 95, Third Edition*, (Que 1996): 463-465, for a discussion of the form of the URL.

Manufacturer	Contact Info	Notes
ADAX	614 Bancroft Way Berkley, CA 94710 510 548-7047 FAX 510 548-5526 **matthis@adax.com** Henry Matthis, Marketing	
ADTRAN	901 Explorer Blvd. Huntsville, AL 35806 800 827-0807 FAX 205 971-8699 **infor@adtran.com** **http://www.adtran.com**	Adtran is presented in Chapter 9.
ADVANCED COMPUTER COMMUNICATIONS	340 Storke Rd. Santa Barbara, CA 93117 805 685-4455 FAX 805 685-4465 **acc.com**	
ALPHA TELECOM INC.	7501 South Memorial, Ste 212 Huntsville, AL 35802 205 881-8743 FAX 205 880-9720 **ati_usa@iquest.com** **http://iquest.com/~ati_usa**	Alpha Telecom makes a line of rack-mounted NT-1s. In addition, they have stand-alone NT-1s and a newly introduced NT-1 with POTS ports. They are mentioned in the NT-1 discussion of Chapter 8.
ANDERSON JACOBSON/CXR	2040 Fortune Dr., Ste. 102 San Jose, CA 95131 800 433-1425 408 435-8520 FAX 408 435-1276	
ASCEND COMMUNICATIONS	1275 Harbor Bay Pkwy. Alameda, CA 94502 800 621-9578 510 769-6001 FAX 510 814-2300 **http://www.ascend.com**	Ascend's equipment is presented in Chapters 11 and 17.

continues

continued

Manufacturer	Contact Info	Notes
ASCOM TIMEPLEX	400 Chestnut Ridge Rd. Woodcliff Lake, NJ 07675 800 669-2298 201 391-1111 FAX 201 573-6470 800 237-6667 Technical Support **http://www.timeplex.com**	
AVM COMPUTERSYSTEME VERTRIEBS GMBH	Voltastraße 5, D-13355 Berlin, Germany +49(0)30/46707-0 FAX +49(0)30/46707-299	
AVM OF AMERICA, INC.	80 E. Sir Francis Drake Blvd. Larkspur, CA 94939 415 464-4710 FAX 415 464-4701	AVM has a very broad line of ISDN products including ISA terminal adapters and PCMCIA terminal adapters and NetWare ISDN router software.
BRIGADOON.COM	3633 136th Pl. S.E. Ste. 100/P.O. Box 53168 Bellevue, WA 98006/98015-3168 800 835-9462 206 641-8779 FAX 206 641-8909 **http://www.brigadoon.com**	
CHASE RESEARCH, INC.	545 Marriott Drive, Suite 100 Nashville, TN 37214 615 872-0770 FAX 615 872-0771 **http://www.chase.com**	
CISCO SYSTEMS	170 West Tasman Dr. San Jose, CA 95134-1706 800 553-6387 408 526-4000 FAX 408 526-4100 **http://www.cisco.com**	Cisco's 1000 and 750 series are covered in Chapter 11.

Manufacturer	Contact Info	Notes
COMPATIBLE SYSTEMS CORPORATION	4730 Walnut St., Ste. 102 Boulder, CO 80301 800 356-0283 303 444-9532 FAX/Modem FAX 303 444-9595	
CONNECTIX	2655 Campus Drive San Mateo, CA 94403 800 950-5880 415 571-5100 FAX 515 571-5195 **http://www.connectix.com** **info@compatible.com**	The Connectix video equipment is covered in Chapter 14.
COSYSTEMS	1263 Oakmead Pkwy. Sunnyvale, CA 94086-4032 408 522-0500 FAX 408 720-9144 **INFO@COSYSTEMS.COM** Sales Info: **support@cosystems.com** (Tech Support)	
CR SYSTEMS CORPORATION	100 Hartsfield Ctr. Pkwy., Ste. 410 Atlanta, GA 30354 800 732-3664 404 767-8230 FAX 404 767-1372	
CRAY COMMUNICATIONS	9020 Junction Dr. Annapolis Junction, MD 21012 800 367-2729 301 317-7527 FAX 301 317-7697 Sales FAX 301 317-7535 Advertising & Marketing **http://www.cray.com**	
DEVELCON ELECTRONICS	856 51st St. East Saskatoon, Sakatchewan Canada S7K-5C7 800 667-9333 306 933-3300 FAX 306 931-1370 **http://www.develcom.com**	

App
B

continues

continued

Manufacturer	Contact Info	Notes
DGM&S	1025 Briggs Rd., Ste. 100 Mt. Laurel, NJ 08054 609 866-1212 FAX 609 866-8850	
DIGI INTERNATIONAL	6400 Flying Cloud Dr. Eden Prarie, MN 55344 800 344-4273 612 943-9020 **http://www.digibd.com**	Digiboard products are discussed in Chapters 10 and 12.
E-TECH RESEARCH	1800 Wyatt Dr., #2 Santa Clara, CA 95054 800 328-5538 408 988-8108 FAX 408 988-8109 **74774.301@CompuServe.com**	
EICON TECHNOLOGY CORPORATION	2196 32nd Ave. (Lachine) Quebec, Canada H8T-3H7 (Corporate Headquarters) 514 631-2592 800 803-4266 214 239-3270 Texas Sales Office FAX 214 239-3304 **http://www.eicon.com**	
ENGAGE COMMUNICATION	9053 Soquel Dr. Aptos, CA 95003 408 688-1021 FAX 408 688-1421	
FARALLON COMPUTING, INC.	2470 Mariner Square Loop Alameda, CA 94501 510 814-5100 FAX 510 814-5028 **http://www.farallon.com**	The Netopia is mentioned in Chapter 11.

Manufacturer	Contact Info	Notes
FRONTIER TECHNOLOGIES CORPORATION	10201 N. Port Washington Rd. Mequon, WI 53092 414 241-4555 FAX 414 241-7084 **tcp@frontiertech.com** **http://www.frontiertech.com**	Frontier makes an excellent TCP/IP stack for Internet and other use, SuperTCP Pro. They just introduced a CD research tool, "Cybersearch," that combines an extensive listing of Web sites with a search tool that allows you to check the Internet without connecting. Once you've done your search using the CD, you can connect and your browser goes automatically to the sites. They have added WinISDN support to their product.
FTP SOFTWARE, INC.	100 Brickstone Square North Andover, MA 01845 508 685-4000 FAX 508 659-6557 **http://www.ftp.com**	FTP makes TCP/IP software and is planning to integrate ISDN features, such as WinISDN. FTP has merged with FireFox, maker of Novix.
FUJITSU NETWORK SWITCHING OF AMERICA	4403 Bland Rd. Somerset Park Raleigh, NC 27609 919 790-2211 FAX 919 790-8376 **http://www.fujitsu.com**	

continues

App

B

continued

Manufacturer	Contact Info	Notes
GANDALF TECHNOLOGIES	130 Colonnade Rd. South Nepean, Ontario Canada K2E-7M4 800 426-3253 613 723-6500 FAX 613 226-1717 **http://www.gandalf.ca**	Gandalf is mentioned in Chapter 11.
GENERAL DATACOMM	1579 Straits Turnpike Middlebury, CT 06762-1299 203 574-1118 FAX 203 758-9129	
HAYES MICROCOMPUTER PRODUCTS	5835 Peachtree Corners East Northcross, GA 30092-3405 404 840-9200 FAX 404 441-1213 800 429-3734 BBS 800-429-3739 **http://www.hayes.com**	
HEWLETT-PACKARD COMPANY	8000 Foothills Blvd. Roseville, CA 95747 916 786-8000 800 533-1333 Customer Service **http://www.hp.com**	
HYPERCOM NETWORK SYSTEMS	2851 W. Kathleen Rd. Phoenix, AZ 85023 800 577-5501 FAX 602-548-2166	
IBM CORPORATION	One Old Orchard Rd. Armonk, NY 10504 800 426-2255 800 426-3395 IBM Info 800 426-3333 914 765-1900 FAX 914-765-7640 **http://www.ibm.com**	IBM's WaveRunner is in Chapter 9.
INFORMATION RESOURCE ENGINEERING	8029 Corporate Dr. Baltimore, MD 21236 410 931-7500 FAX 410-931-7524	

Manufacturer	Contact Info	Notes
INTEGRATED NETWORK CORPORATION	757 Route 202/206 Bridgewater, NJ 08807 800 241-3279 908 218-1600 FAX 908 218-0804	
INTEL CORP.	2200 Mission College Blvd. Santa Clara, CA 95052 408 765-8080 800 548-4725 FAX 408 765-9904 **http://www.intel.com**	Intel's ProShare video conferencing is covered in Chapter 14.
INTERNATIONAL TRANSWARE	1503 Grant Rd., Ste. 155 Mountain View, CA 94040 800 999-6387 415 903-2300 FAX 415 903-9544	
IDSN*TEK	P.O. Box 3000 San Gregorio, CA 94074 415 712-3000 FAX 415 712-3003 **http://www.isdntek.com**	ISDN*tek's Internet Card is in Chapter 10.
LINK TECHNOLOGY	69 Heron Rd., Ste. #1 Holland, PA 18966 215 357-3354 FAX 215 357-1670	
LION COMMUNICATIONS INDUSTRIES	117 Isabella Drive Farnborough, Orpington, Kent BR6 7UF, UK 44 1689 861208 **http://www.freebsd.org/ ~jhs/lion/graphics.html**	The Lion Datapump is mentioned in Chapter 10.
MICOM COMMUNICATIONS CORPORATION	4100 Los Angeles Ave. Simi Valley, CA 93063-3397 800 642-6687 805 583-8600 FAX 805 583-1997 **info@micom.com** **http://www.micom.com** **ftp.micom.com**	

App
B

continues

continued

Manufacturer	Contact Info	Notes
MICROSOFT CORP.	One Microsoft Way Redmond, WA 98052-6399 206 882-8080 800 426-9400 Sales 206 936-7329 FAX 206 936-6735 BBS **ftp.microsoft.com** **http://www.microsoft.com**	Microsoft's TAPI is covered in Chapter 6. Windows NT and Windows 95 are discussed in Chapter 12.
MICROTRONIX DATACOM	200 Aberdeen Dr. London, Ontario, Canada N5V-4N2 519 659-9500 FAX 519 659-8500	
MITEL CORPORATION	350 Legget Dr., /P.O. Box 13089 Kanata, Ontario, Canada K2K-1X3 800 267-6244 613 592-2122 FAX 613 592-4784 **http://www.mitel.com**	
MOTOROLA ISG	5000 Bradford Dr., S.E. Huntsville, AL 35805 800 451-2369 205 430-8000 FAX 205 830-5657 **http://www.motorola.com**	Motorola's BitSurfr is discussed in Chapter 9.
MULTIACCESS COMPUTING CORPORATION	5350 Hollister Ave., Ste. C Santa Barbara, CA 93111 805 964-2332 FAX 805 681-7469 **multiacc@silcom.com**	
NETMANAGE, INC.	10725 N. De Anza Boulevard Cupertino, CA 95014 408 973-7171 FAX 408 257-6405 **http://www.netmanage.com:80**	Their Chameleon line of TCP/IP software is delivered with WinISDN, which they co-wrote. NetManage is used in many of the configurations in Chapters 9, 10, and 11.

Manufacturer	Contact Info	Notes
NETWORK EXPRESS	4251 Plymouth Rd. Ann Arbor, MI 48105 800 553-4333 313 761-5005 FAX 313 995-1114	
NOVELL	122 East 1700 South Provo, UT 84606 800 638-9273 408 434-2300 FAX 408 577-5447 801 429-3030 BBS **ftp.novell.com** **http://www.novell.com** Netwire - forum on CompuServe	Novell's TSAPI is discussed in Chapter 6.
OST	14225 Sullyfield Circle Chantilly, VA 22021 703 817-0400 FAX 703 817-0402	
PENRIL DATABILITY NETWORKS	1300 Quince Orchard Blvd. Gaithersburg, MD 20878 800 473-6745, ext. 8653 **http://www.penril.com**	
PICTURETEL	222 Rosewood Drive Danvers, MA 01923 508 762-5000 **http://www.picturetel.com**	Picturetel's video products are mentioned in Chapter 14.
PROTEON, INC.	9 Technology Drive Westboro, MA 01581-1799 800 545-7464 508 898-2800 FAX 508 366-8910 **http://www.proteon.com**	Proteon's router for ISDN is in Chapter 11.
PROMPTUS COMMUNICATIONS	207 High Point Ave. Portsmouth, RI 02871 800 777-5276 401 683-6100 FAX 401 683-6105	

continues

continued

Manufacturer	Contact Info	Notes
RACAL-DATACOM	1601 N. Harrison Pkwy. Sunrise, FL 33323 800 722-2555 305 846-1601 FAX 305 846-4942 **http://www.racal.com**	
RETIX	2401 Colorado Ave. Santa Monica, CA 90404 800 255-2333 310 828-3400 FAX 310 828-2255 **http://www.retix.com**	
ROCKWELL NETWORK SYSTEMS	7402 Hollister Ave. Santa Barbara, CA 93117 800 262-8023 805 968-4262 FAX 805 968-6478 **http://www.rockwell.com**	
SHIVA CORPORATION	63 Third Ave., Northwest Park Burlington, MA 01803 800 977-4482 617 270-8300 FAX 617 270-8599 **http://www.shiva.com**	Shiva's LANRover/E Plus is discussed in Chapter 17.
SIEMENS ROLM COMMUNICATIONS INC	P.O. Box 58075/ 4900 Old Ironsides Dr. Santa Clara, CA 95052 800 765-6123 **htt://www.siemensrolm.com**	The OfficePoint PBX for three BRIs is discussed in in Chapter 15.
SPRY INCORPORATED	316 Occidental Avenue South, 2nd Floor, Suite 200 Seattle, WA 98104 206 447-0300 **http://www.spry.com**	Now a part of Compuserve, Spry makes Internet in a Box. WinISDN is being integrated into the package.

Manufacturer	Contact Info	Notes
SYMANTEC CORP.	10201 Torre Ave. Cupertino, CA 95014-2132 408 253-9600 FAX 408 255-9341 Inside Sales FAX 408 253-3968 Pub.Rel. **http://www.symantec.com**	Symantec's "Norton pcAnywhere" is being adapted to Windows 95 and ISDN. The "ACT!" contact manager integrates with the TAPI API, as mentioned in Chapter 6.
TELCO SYSTEMS	4305 Cushing Parkway Fremont, CA 94538 510 490-3111 FAX 510 656-3031 **http://www.telco.com**	
TELEBIT CORPORATION	One Executive Dr. Chelmsford, MA 01824 800 989-8888 508 441-2181 FAX 508 441-9060 **http://www.telebit.com**	
TELEPOWER	6451 Independence Ave. Woodland Hills, CA 91367 818 587-5540 FAX 818 587-5546	
TELIS	GmbH Dovestraße 2-4 D-10587 Berlin, Germany +49(0) 30/39928-00 FAX +49(0)30/39928-01 Telis Corp. 1818 Gilbreth Road # 211 Burlingame, CA 94010 415 652-9191	Telis makes a broad line of ISDN products including adapter boards and all-in-one software packages for PCs, video telephones and teleconferencing

App
B

continues

continued

Manufacturer	Contact Info	Notes
	FAX 415 652-9192	systems, PBX boards, and software.
TONE COMMANDER SYSTEMS, INC.	11609 49th Place West Mukilteo, WA 98275 800 524-0024 FAX 206 349-1010 **tcs@halcyon.com.**	Tone commander makes a broad line of stand alone and rack mounted NT-1s, plus ISDN attendant consoles.
3COM CORPORATION	5400 Bayfront Plaza Santa Clara, CA 95052 800 638-3266, Product Info 408 764-5000 FAX 408 764-5001	Some of 3Com's products are presented in Chapters 9 and 11.
	Accessworks 670 North Beers St., Bldg. One Holmdel, NJ 07733 908 721-1337 FAX 908 888-4456 **http://www.3com.com**	
TRANCELL SYSTEMS	3180 De La Cruz Blvd. Suite 200 Santa Clara, CA 95054 408 988-5353 **http://www.trancell.com**	
UB NETWORKS	3900 Freedom Circle Santa Clara, CA 95054 800 777-4526 408 496-0111 FAX 408 970-7300 **http://www.ub.com**	
US ROBOTICS	7770 N. Frontage Rd. Skokie, IL 60077 800 342-5877 FAX 708 676-7314 Cust. Serv., Personal Services Division	US Robotics products are covered in Chapters 10 and 17.

Manufacturer	Contact Info	Notes
	708 982-5092 BBS	
	http://www.usr.com	
	support@usr.com	
	9100 N. McCormick Blvd.	
	Skokie, IL 60076	
	708 982-5010	
	708 982-5151	
	Corporate Office	
	708 982-5092 BBS	
	http://www.usr.com	
	support@usr.com	
VIVO SOFTWARE, INC.	411 Waverly Oaks Road Waltham, MA 02154 617 899-8900 FAX 617 899-1400 **http://www.vivo.com**	Vivo's software video products are covered in Chapter 14.
VTEL CORPORATION	108 Wild Basin Road Austin, TX 78746 512 314-2700 FAX 512 314-2792 **http://www.vtel.com**	VTEL's video products are covered in Chapter 14.
WESTERN DATACOM COMPANY,	959 Bassett Rd., Ste. B Westlake, OH 44145 800 262-3311 216 835-1510 FAX 216 835-9146	
XYLOGICS	53rd Ave. Burlington, MA 01803 800 892-6639 617 272-8140 FAX 617 273-5392 617 273-1499 BBS	
XYPLEX	295 Foster St. Littleton, MA 01460 800 338-5316 508 952-4700 FAX 508 952-4702 **http://www.xyplex.com**	
ZYXEL	4920 E. La Palma Ave. Anaheim, CA 92807 800 255-4101 714 693-0808 FAX 714 693-0705 **http://www.zyxel.com**	Routers are covered in Chapter 11.

App
B

Internet Service Providers Offering ISDN

Internet service providers have been springing up throughout the world. Most offer connection through analog telephone lines. Some offer ISDN. The number grows every day. The original intent of this appendix was to present a list of those providers. But the remarkable growth of information available over the Internet offers a more up-to-date way. I suggest you take a close look at the following World Wide Web references as a starting point.

Please note that neither I, nor the keepers of these Web sites, can vouch for the accuracy of the information. In most cases, the Internet service providers give the details to the maintainers of the Web pages.

I've mentioned Dan Kegel's Web pages on ISDN several times before. He asks the providers to include the following information in their listings:

- Protocols used—V.110, V.120, TIA, SLIP, X.25, and others
- Interoperability testing results
- Login method—Unix shell, TCP/IP

Kegel has met with fairly good success in having the providers give this information. To his list, I would add:

- Clear statement of charges
- Multilink PPP support details
- Compression details
- If the ISP is using any "proprietary" protocols that you must have to take full advantage of the service, obtain information on the exact nature of such protocols (e.g. Ascend MP+). If the ISP advises you that you must use such protocols or must have hardware of only a certain maker to take full advantage of the services, please send me an e-mail with full details, including the names of the ISP, the hardware maker, model numbers, plus a description of what it is you will be giving up if you use the products of someone else. I am very interested in tracking these issues. Please address information on this to **isplimits@bryce.com**.
- "Dedicated" vs. "non-dedicated" options as discussed in Chapter 17

Kegel's page for Internet service providers is:

http://www.alumni.caltech.edu/~dank/isdn/isdn_ip.html

Cybertoday has another, more general, source for Internet service provider information. It's arranged by geographic region and services such as ISDN. It even includes a list of other ISDN provider lists!

http://www.cybertoday.com/cybertoday/ISPs/Products.html#ISDN

CAUTION

As I've examined these lists, I've noticed they all lack some providers that I know offer ISDN. I've also seen some providers on the lists who claim ISDN, when I know they really don't have it. As far as I can tell, they're testing the waters by claiming ISDN and then counting the number of calls they get and can string along for "just a few more weeks."

Rather than waiting for these guys that are trolling, I suggest you get with your favorite provider and help make ISDN a reality in that provider's business. It's a win/win situation for you and the provider.

Finally, please remember that I'll be posting some information about providers on my Web page:

http://www.bryce.com/~bryce

Bibliography

This is a selected and annotated bibliography. As a result, it does not claim to be all-inclusive. My intent is to guide you to resources related to ISDN that I have found helpful or current in the marketplace. Some of these are well-recognized authorities in communications that have been evolving for several years. ■

N O T E A number of these authors, including Jeff Fritz, Fred Goldstein, and Gerald Hopkins, have been sighted on the newsgroup **comp.dcom.isdn**. I might even show up there. ■

Books

Angell, David, *ISDN for Dummies*. IDG, 1995. Angell's book is designed as a quick-to-read introduction for computer users considering ISDN. It's sprinkled with samples of products and uses for ISDN.

Corporation for Open Systems, *ISDN Solutions*. Corporation for Open Systems International, Fairfax, VA, 1994. This book was prepared during 1994 tests and exhibitions of ISDN. It presents articles in magazine format that are authored primarily by representatives of vendors. This book is of great value in reflecting the interests and opinions of vendor members in COS that are involved with ISDN.

Flanagan, William A., *ISDN: A Practical, Simple, Easy-to-Use Guide to Getting Up and Running on ISDN*. Flatiron Publishing, 1995. Just what the subtitle says. This is an 8 1/2 x 11 inch format book with introductory material on ISDN.

Forrester Research, Forrester Research, Inc., 1033 Massachusetts Avenue, Cambridge, MA 02138; 617-497-7090. This research firm has concentrated on much of the communications market for several years. I cited their report on telecommuting in Chapter 16. They provide a subscription service for reports in the following titles: *Computing Strategy Service, Network Strategy Service, Software Strategy Service,* and *People and Technology Strategies*.

Fritz, Jeff, *Sensible ISDN Data Applications*. West Virginia University Press, Morgantown, WV, 1992. Mr. Fritz covers the ins and outs of installing computer and telephone systems involving ISDN on the campus of his university. He is a dedicated member of the North American ISDN Users' Forum and active in standards.

Goldstein, Fred R., *ISDN in Perspective*. Addison-Wesley Publishing Company, 1992. This book is an excellent technical introduction to ISDN. It explains a great deal of telephony and terminology. It goes into much more advanced methods and details than needed for an introduction but, certainly, is a good book to read after you've had an introduction.

Griffiths, John, *ISDN Explained, Second Edition*. John Wiley, 1992. This a very technical book that goes into the details of protocols and engineering terminology. Given that, it's an outstanding resource for a thorough understanding of ISDN.

Hardwick, Steve, *ISDN Design: A Practical Approach*. Academic Press, New York, NY, 1989. Mr. Hardwick's book is a classic for engineering design of ISDN electronics. It's certainly not for everyone, but if circuit design is your cup of tea, take a look.

Hopkins, Gerald L., *The ISDN Literacy Book*. Addison-Wesley Publishing Company, 1995. I've had the opportunity to discuss ISDN with Mr. Hopkins. He's very active in the North American ISDN Users' Forum and on standards committees. This book reviews the history and development of ISDN and standards together with social and economic implications.

Information Gatekeepers, *1995 International ISDN Yellow Pages, Third Edition.* Information Gatekeepers Inc., 214 Harvard Avenue, Boston, MA 02134; 800-323-1088. This is just what its name implies; a reference to vendors and products for ISDN. It has brief discussions of ISDN theory and practice. At the end, it presents detailed listings of ISDN standards. Information Gatekeepers is a re-publisher of standards materials.

Kessler, Gary, *ISDN: Concepts, Facilities and Services, Second Edition.* McGraw-Hill, 1993. Kessler's book is one of the first to address the needs of day-to-day users of ISDN.

Krol, Ed, *The Whole Internet: User's Guide & Catalog.* O'Reilly & Associates Inc., Sebastopol, CA, 1992. Subsequent revisions have been made, some for specialized environments. The most recent I have was published in 1995 in conjunction with Spry as a part of its Internet in a Box product. Mr. Krol's work is the standard Internet reference. The standard edition has been aimed at the UNIX and academic world. The later, specialized editions deal more with Windows.

Minoli, Daniel, *Video Dialtone Technology.* McGraw-Hill, 1995. The title is deceptive. I recommend this book because of its extensive coverage of "alternatives" to ISDN such as xDSL, cable, satellite, and wireless technologies. It's written on a level similar to that of the books by William Stallings. Minoli's work is a good secondary source because it pulls many complex and scattered standards together and explains them as a whole. However, be warned: it's written for a technical audience undeterred by complicated mathematical expressions and engineering jargon.

Motorola University Press, *The Basics Book of ISDN, Second Edition.* Addison-Wesley Publishing Company, Reading, MA, 1992. This very short book (about 50 pages) is fun to read and provides a lot of good ISDN detail. It's part of a series of such books in computer communications from Motorola.

Newton, Harry, *Newton's Telecom Dictionary, Ninth Edition.* Flatiron Publishing, Inc., New York, 1995. Harry Newton, the charismatic personality of telephony, is the publisher of the journals *Teleconnect* and *Computer Telephony*, and his firm conducts the Computer Telephony Conference and Exposition each year. He lays claim to fathering the term "computer telephony." Look it up in this dictionary for his own words. The dictionary is an invaluable reference of the minutia of this industry. Sometimes you won't find what you're looking for; most often you will. Sometimes you'll disagree with his definitions. It's sort of like *Dr. Johnson's Dictionary*—same personality? In any case, you'll be entertained.

Pacific Bell, *ISDN: A User's Guide to Services, Applications & Resources in California.* Pacific Bell, San Ramon, CA, 1994. Although this book is directed to PacBell's clients, it's quite a useful handbook for understanding ISDN. The company is making a full-court press into bringing ISDN to everyone in their service area. This book shows they're serious.

Pike, Mary Ann, et al., *Special Edition Using the Internet with Windows 95, Third Edition.* Que Corporation, Indianapolis, IN, 1995. This massive book is a great resource for getting on and using the Internet. It comes with a CD including all the software you need to get started. I wrote a number of chapters on high speed communications and ISDN. It will teach you to understand how to use the Internet while you're making ISDN work.

Sherman, Ken, *Data Communications: A User's Guide, Fourth Edition*. Prentice Hall, Englewood Cliffs, NJ, 1995. I've known the author for a decade. This is the authoritative text on "classical data communications." I find I'm constantly referring to it for concepts and practice.

Stallings, William, *ISDN and Broadband ISDN with Frame Relay and ATM, Third Edition*. Prentice Hall, Englewood Cliffs, NJ, 1995. This is *the* standard standards reference on what ISDN is all about. Stallings takes the complex language of the hundreds of standards that feed into making ISDN and converts it into an understandable whole. Still, this is a very technical work. It's a secondary reference to the standards. It's secondary only in the sense that the standards themselves are the primary reference. I strongly recommend you read this book if you want to gain an in-depth understanding of the technical aspects of ISDN. It's one of a series of books Stallings has done in the *Handbooks of Computer Communications* series. The others I have read and recommend highly include *The Open Systems Interconnection (OSI) Model and OSI-Related Standards,* which is about the ISO OSI model; *Local Area Network Standards,* which is about such things as Ethernet and token ring; and *Department of Defense (DOD) Protocol Standards,* which is about TCP/IP.

Tittel, Ed, and James, Steve, *ISDN Networking Essentials*. Academic Press, 1995. Ed and Steve both live in Austin, Texas, so I know 'em and say they've done a good job. Their book provides a lot of very useful information on ISDN and the hardware you'll need to make it work.

Zimmer, David A., *The Telecommuting Handbook*. Electronic Messaging Association, 1655 North Fort Myer Drive, Suite 850, Arlington, VA 22209; 703-524-5550. In Chapter 16, I discussed some of the findings and suggestions in this book. Because almost all businesses will be investigating telecommuting soon, Mr. Zimmer's work will prove invaluable.

Periodicals

The well-known general microcomputing journals such as *PC Magazine, Byte, InfoWorld, PC Week,* and others have provided some reports on ISDN and may be expected to increase those reports in the future. The journals listed are more specialized and have been carrying an increasing amount of ISDN information.

Communications Week. 600 Community Drive, Manhasset, NY 11030; 708-647-6834. This weekly tabloid covers the entire industry. Its scope is beginning to include ISDN.

Computer Telephony. 12 West 21st Street, New York, NY 10010; 212-691-8215. This and *Teleconnect* are published by Harry Newton. It tracks the growth of computer telephony integration. ISDN is a major component of its coverage.

Data Communications. 1221 Avenue of the Americas, New York, NY 10020; 212-512-2699. *Data Communications* has been the standard slick magazine in its field for many years. It used to be devoted to mainframes and terminals. In the last few years, it's moved to local area networks. Now the move to computer telephony integration is starting to appear among its pages.

Internetwork. 1300 Virginia Drive, Ft. Washington, PA 19034; 708-564-1385. This journal concentrates on communications standards and interoperability.

ISDN News. 1201 Seven Locks Road, P.O. Box 61130, Potomac, MD 20854; 301-424-3338. *ISDN News* is a newsletter concentrating on ISDN issues. It covers business, political, and technical details of the technology.

LAN. 121 Fairfield Way, Bloomingdale, IL 60108; 708-529-4888. *LAN* is a general interest local area network magazine. ISDN is being more frequently covered.

Network Computing. 600 Community Drive, Manhasset, NY 11030; 708-647-6834. *Networking Computing* ran two or three detailed reviews of ISDN hardware during 1995 and probably will continue to increase its coverage.

Network World. 161 Worchester Road, Framingham, MA 01701; 508-875-6400. I always scan this weekly tabloid the day it arrives. It's become the record for much of what's going on.

Telecommunications. 685 Canton Street, Norwood, MA 02062. A monthly journal directed at corporate users of telecom. It's had a number of good articles on ISDN.

Teleconnect. 12 West 21st Street, New York, NY 10010; 212-691-8215. *Teleconnect* is devoted to the details of the telephone industry. This and *Computer Telephony* are published by Harry Newton.

Trade Shows

I'm not sure this is exactly the right heading for inclusion in a bibliography, but trade shows are a great place to learn about technology and gather literature.

COMDEX. 300 First Avenue, Needham, MA 02194; fax 617-449-2674; **http:// www.comdex.com**. If you've never been to COMDEX, be warned: it's an ordeal. But it's well worth it for the overall perspective it gives you on the computer industry. The invasion of telephony is becoming more and more evident. In the Fall 1994 show, a substantial area was devoted to ISDN. The Corporation for Open Systems book mentioned above was designed primarily for the 1994 Fall COMDEX. The show takes place in November in Las Vegas; in the spring, a smaller version is held in Atlanta or Chicago.

Computer Telephony Conference and Exposition. 12 West 21st Street, New York, NY 10010; 212-691-8215. If this looks like a familiar address, it is—Harry Newton, at it again. This show had been held in Dallas in March for several years, but in 1996 it was in Los Angeles and Orlando is also scheduled. Check out the pig that flies at **http:// www.flatironpublishing.com**, for the address for the conference.

Networld+Interop. P.O. Box 5855, San Mateo, CA 94402; 800-488-2883; **http:// www.interop.com**. This giant show is held in Las Vegas in March. It had been two shows: Networld, devoted to local area networking having started as a Novell owned production, and Interop, a very technical computer communications show. The two were joined in 1995. Other cities have also been Networld+Interop sites within the same year: Berlin, Tokyo, Atlanta, and Paris.

TELECOM. TELECOM Secretariat, International Telecommunications Union, Place des Nations, CH-1211 Geneva 20, Switzerland; 41 22 730 6161; **http://www3.itu.ch/TELECOM**. This is the really big one. The next one will be in Geneva, October 10-17, 1999. During the intervening years, various smaller Telecoms will be held in different regions of the world.

Index

W

X-Y-Z

Check out Que® Books on the World Wide Web
http://www.mcp.com/que

As the biggest software release in computer history, Windows 95 continues to redefine the computer industry. Click here for the latest info on our Windows 95 books

Make computing quick and easy with these products designed exclusively for new and casual users

Examine the latest releases in word processing, spreadsheets, operating systems, and suites

The Internet, The World Wide Web, CompuServe®, America Online®, Prodigy®—it's a world of ever-changing information. Don't get left behind!

Find out about new additions to our site, new bestsellers and hot topics

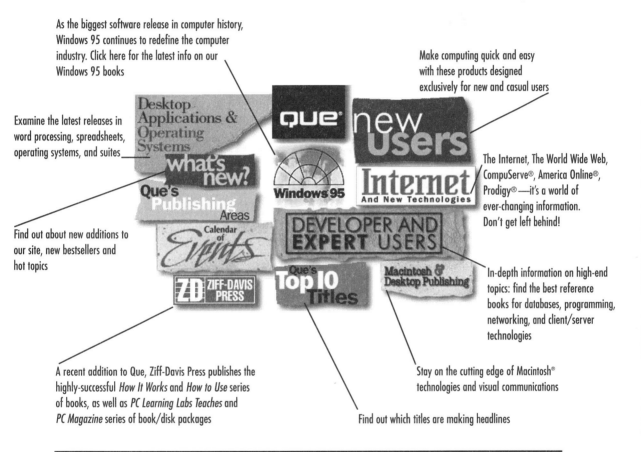

In-depth information on high-end topics: find the best reference books for databases, programming, networking, and client/server technologies

A recent addition to Que, Ziff-Davis Press publishes the highly-successful *How It Works* and *How to Use* series of books, as well as *PC Learning Labs Teaches* and *PC Magazine* series of book/disk packages

Stay on the cutting edge of Macintosh® technologies and visual communications

Find out which titles are making headlines

With 6 separate publishing groups, Que develops products for many specific market segments and areas of computer technology. Explore our Web Site and you'll find information on best-selling titles, newly published titles, upcoming products, authors, and much more.

- Stay informed on the latest industry trends and products available
- Visit our online bookstore for the latest information and editions
- Download software from Que's library of the best shareware and freeware

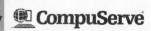

Complete and Return this Card
for a *FREE* Computer Book Catalog

Thank you for purchasing this book! You have purchased a superior computer book written expressly for your needs. To continue to provide the kind of up-to-date, pertinent coverage you've come to expect from us, we need to hear from you. Please take a minute to complete and return this self-addressed, postage-paid form. In return, we'll send you a free catalog of all our computer books on topics ranging from word processing to programming and the internet.

Mr. ☐   Mrs. ☐   Ms. ☐   Dr. ☐

Name (first) ☐☐☐☐☐☐☐☐☐☐☐☐   (M.I.) ☐   (last) ☐☐☐☐☐☐☐☐☐☐☐☐☐☐☐☐

Address ☐☐☐☐☐☐☐☐☐☐☐☐☐☐☐☐☐☐☐☐☐☐☐☐☐☐☐☐☐☐

☐☐☐☐☐☐☐☐☐☐☐☐☐☐☐☐☐☐☐☐☐☐☐☐☐☐☐☐☐☐

City ☐☐☐☐☐☐☐☐☐☐☐☐☐☐   State ☐☐   Zip ☐☐☐☐☐ ☐☐☐☐

Phone ☐☐☐ ☐☐☐☐   Fax ☐☐☐ ☐☐☐ ☐☐☐☐

Company Name ☐☐☐☐☐☐☐☐☐☐☐☐☐☐☐☐☐☐☐☐☐☐☐☐☐☐☐☐

E-mail address ☐☐☐☐☐☐☐☐☐☐☐☐☐☐☐☐☐☐☐☐☐☐☐☐☐☐☐☐

1. Please check at least (3) influencing factors for purchasing this book.

Front or back cover information on book .... ☐
Special approach to the content .... ☐
Completeness of content .... ☐
Author's reputation .... ☐
Publisher's reputation .... ☐
Book cover design or layout .... ☐
Index or table of contents of book .... ☐
Price of book .... ☐
Special effects, graphics, illustrations .... ☐
Other (Please specify): _____ ☐

2. How did you first learn about this book?

Saw in Macmillan Computer Publishing catalog .... ☐
Recommended by store personnel .... ☐
Saw the book on bookshelf at store .... ☐
Recommended by a friend .... ☐
Received advertisement in the mail .... ☐
Saw an advertisement in: _____ ☐
Read book review in: _____ ☐
Other (Please specify): _____ ☐

3. How many computer books have you purchased in the last six months?

This book only .... ☐   3 to 5 books .... ☐
books .... ☐   More than 5 .... ☐

4. Where did you purchase this book?

Bookstore .... ☐
Computer Store .... ☐
Consumer Electronics Store .... ☐
Department Store .... ☐
Office Club .... ☐
Warehouse Club .... ☐
Mail Order .... ☐
Direct from Publisher .... ☐
Internet site .... ☐
Other (Please specify): _____ ☐

5. How long have you been using a computer?

☐ Less than 6 months   ☐ 6 months to a year
☐ 1 to 3 years   ☐ More than 3 years

6. What is your level of experience with personal computers and with the subject of this book?

	With PCs	With subject of book
New	☐	☐
Casual	☐	☐
Accomplished	☐	☐
Expert	☐	☐

Source Code ISBN: 0-7897-0843-4

7. Which of the following best describes your job title?

Administrative Assistant .... ☐
Coordinator .... ☐
Manager/Supervisor .... ☐
Director .... ☐
Vice President .... ☐
President/CEO/COO .... ☐
Lawyer/Doctor/Medical Professional ...... ☐
Teacher/Educator/Trainer .... ☐
Engineer/Technician .... ☐
Consultant .... ☐
Not employed/Student/Retired .... ☐
Other (Please specify): _____ ☐

8. Which of the following best describes the area of the company your job title falls under?

Accounting .... ☐
Engineering .... ☐
Manufacturing .... ☐
Operations .... ☐
Marketing .... ☐
Sales .... ☐
Other (Please specify): _____ ☐

9. What is your age?

Under 20 .... ☐
21-29 .... ☐
30-39 .... ☐
40-49 .... ☐
50-59 .... ☐
60-over .... ☐

10. Are you:

Male .... ☐
Female .... ☐

11. Which computer publications do you read regularly? (Please list)

_____
_____
_____
_____
_____
_____
_____
_____
_____
_____

Comments: _____
_____
_____

Fold here and scotch-tape to mail.